THE EVANGELICAL FAITH

Other Books by Helmut Thielicke:

THE EVANGELICAL FAITH

by Helmut Thielicke

**Translated
and edited by
Geoffrey W. Bromiley**

Volume Three: *Theology of the Spirit*
The Third Article of the Creed
The Manifestations of the Holy Spirit
in the Word, the Church, the Religions,
and the Last Things

**William B. Eerdmans
Publishing Company   Grand Rapids, Michigan**

Translated from the German edition *Der Evangelische Glaube*
© Helmut Thielicke, J. C. B. Mohr (Paul Siebeck) Tübingen 1978

Library of Congress Cataloging in Publication Data

Thielicke, Helmut, 1908–
The evangelical faith.

Translation of Der evangelische Glaube.
Includes bibliographical references.
CONTENTS: v. 1. Prolegomena: the relation of
theology to modern thought-forms—v. 2. The
doctrine of God and of Christ—v. 3. Theology of the Spirit.
1. Theology, Doctrinal. I. Title.
BT75.2.T4513   230′.044   74-7010
ISBN 0-8028-2342-4 (v. 1)
ISBN 0-8028-2343-2 (v. 2)
ISBN 0-8028-2344-0 (v. 3)

In Grateful Memory of My Friends
John Doberstein
Eduard Thurneysen
Paul Tillich

Contents

Author's Preface

At the end of this third and last volume of dogmatics I have the feeling that I have completed the core of my life's work: a comprehensive survey of ethics and dogmatics in seven volumes plus an anthropology. If the grace of an active life is still granted to me, I should like to realize some pet literary projects which I have had to postpone for the sake of this giant task.

I set aside the last page of the manuscript with gratitude for the many stages of research and composition through which I have lived, yet also not without some uneasiness. I ask myself whether the totality of this work has not been perhaps too bold a venture, in which a single person has dared to look out over the vast panorama of systematic theology, or at least made some attempt to do so. At a time when new questions are escalating and new materials increasing, will it not draw down upon itself the charge of being arrogant or (even worse) anachronistic? In an epoch of unavoidable specialization are we not compelled to use the form of the monograph and corresponding collections? This would mean that in every section of the present volume (pneumatology, ecclesiology, eschatology, and the theology of religions) an expert would be needed, or that at the very least the great spheres of dogmatics and ethics would have to be treated apart, as has long been the case in Roman Catholic faculties and as is beginning to be so in Protestant faculties as well.

I am very conscious of the risk and the imperfection of the total survey that has been attempted and yet I cannot break free from the conviction that a comprehensive perspective is still needed and indeed that a failure to provide it would entail an impoverishment of theology. All these spheres intersect in the concrete man whom we address in our proclamation. They also intersect in ourselves as we proclaim and teach. In fashioning a theological system the methodological difficulty of breaking up the indissoluble whole into a discursive sequence shows how closely interwoven all the problem areas are. Hence the author continually finds that he has to look ahead and look back. I cannot deal with creation without Christology and the consummation being involved, and vice versa. I cannot conceive of a doctrine of the Word of God without addressing the dialectic of law and gospel which is also the central problem of ethics (and was also dealt with in that context). I have to speak about everything at once like the preacher who cannot talk about Christmas without touching on the theme of Good Friday and pointing out that the crib and the cross are hewn out of the same wood. There may be seen here the coherence and complementarity of all the theological "particles" and the indissolubility of the whole which must come to expression in a systematic survey. For this reason the present volume, although in itself it is rounded off as a theology of the Spirit, is full of references to what has been said or at least touched upon elsewhere.

In contrast, do not many of the fashionable modern monographs, whether as causes or symptoms, have a great deal to do with the growing one-sidedness of our theological thinking, which at one time focuses on social and political problems (many theologies of revolution in the last years have already swum downstream, not to speak of the death-of-God theology of the sixties), and then on another occasion turns back again to special themes in dogmatics and dogmatic history? There are, of course, honorable exceptions to this rule.

The salutary urge to consider the full structure of Christian thought should work as an antidote to protect us against disproportion and against the elephantiasis of individual doctrinal articles. In addition, it teaches budding theologians the patience to bore through the hard wood of a greater work instead of simply taking sporadic nips at themes that are in fashion.

We have today many examples of the one-sidedness to which mere specialization leads. In theology we find sociopathy and more recently techniques of communication which are very dubious—dubious in their exclusiveness! The recommendations against this which Plato gives especially to doctors in his *Charmenides* apply also to theology:

> As one should not seek, says Zamolxis, the God-King of the Thracians, to heal the eyes without the head or the head without the body or the body without the soul, it is also a fault that doctors among the Hellenes cannot master many ailments because they do not know the whole that has to be cared for, for if this whole is not well the part cannot possibly be so. For, he continues, the fault among men today is that some try to be doctors for one of the two apart from the other.

If in spite of my earlier criticism of the theology of genitives (the theology of hope . . . , of society . . . , of revolution) and the limitation that this implies, I myself use a genitive in the title of this volume (the theology of the Spirit), there are special reasons for this. In combination with the question of God and Christology (EF, II), this genitive is so surely and unequivocally that of *one* chapter of theology that the fear of one-sidedness which I have expressed elsewhere is pointless here. To be sure, the formulation in the genitive does not cover the whole range of themes in the third article of the creed. Nevertheless the statement of faith in the Holy Spirit is the dominant feature even in the confession of the resurrection of the dead and the life everlasting. The Holy Spirit makes present the "past" event of salvation as also the "future" one. He is at one and the same time the Spirit of both recollection *and* hope. To this extent pneumatology forms the background of all the statements of this article, and constitutes them a unity. It also provides the key to a theological understanding of the religions which it is one of our special exertions to achieve in this volume.

In this light it is understandable that the doctrine of the Pneuma stands at the heart of the event of Christian proclamation and is receiving increasing attention today along these lines. The efforts of proclamation and theological reflection have always been directed toward the goal of presenting the Christian message across the ages and bringing to light its contemporary relevance. One might say with Kierkegaard that it has always been a matter of displaying our contemporaneity with the message, of confessing that the Kyrios is among us. One of the axioms of the Christian understanding of grace as this is especially expressed in the Reformation slogan "by faith alone" is that this "making present" is not the fruit of methodological works, whether in the form of rhetoric, the practice of meditation, or other exercises, but that it takes place in the witness of the Spirit and is thus imparted as a gift.

When someone has spent a whole lifetime of theological activity, from the early efforts of youth to the present, wrestling with this problem of contemporaneity in both teaching and preaching, as the author may confess that he has done, then at some point an explicit doctrine of the Holy Spirit has to emerge. This would have happened even if the present dogmatic enterprise had not for systematic reasons led ineluctably to this goal and end. Understandably, in the course of asking about contemporaneity I could not help making some practical proposals for reform, especially in ecclesiology. In so doing I could not suppress some strong personal opinions and criticisms.

As concerns reverberations thus far of the German edition of this work, I have learned most from Roman Catholic reactions because they have been so profound and friendly even though critical. Sometimes they have ignored—rightly perhaps—the polemical debates on the doctrines of God and Christology. In this respect they will have much more to deal with in the present volume. For from chapter to chapter it becomes increasingly clear to what extent the understanding of the Holy Spirit is normative for many doctrinal differences between the confessions, especially in the sphere of church, Scripture, and tradition. It *also* be clear, however, that the prayer "Come, Creator Spirit" embraces the whole communion of saints beyond every frontier and relativizes the dividing lines.

The desire to stretch out a hand across the boundaries is not motivated by the banal irenic saying: "Be pleasant to one another," but by a clear establishment of what divides *and also* of what unites, a fraternal questioning and a readiness to speak and reply, and not last or least a seeing of many signs of hope that the fronts are moving and that we are getting much closer the closer we draw to the biblical substance of our faith.[1]

Hence the present volume contains an almost continuous dialogue with Roman Catholic theology on almost every theme, and often enough, as the reader will see, it contains a revision of the antitheses as they not only had to look but to a large extent did actually exist in the epoch of the Reformation. Since then the partners in debate, not least on the basis of their mutual encounters and questionings, have changed in not a few things and are to be found occupying very different positions. Thus the previous aim of many of the polemical shots is largely irrelevant now.

---

[1] Ulrich Wilckens in his great commentary has expressed the same hope in relation to common work on the Epistle to the Romans.

This applies with some certainty to changes in position (or the attainment of greater precision) in the sphere of the doctrine of justification and consequently to a theme of high confessional rank. But how about the understanding of tradition, the church, the papal teaching office, and some areas of eschatology? To what extent are confessional differences affected by the traditionally different schemes of thought in Roman Catholic and Reformation theology, e.g., the ontological schema of Thomas and the personalistic schema of the Reformers (as one might put it in brief)? May it be that the analogy of being, which is so vehemently attacked by Karl Barth, may be traced back "merely" to a different style of thinking? And if so, might it be relativized as a mere formality of speech and thus pushed back to what is perhaps an ultimately identical core?

We have to face these questions. We cannot do so by just quoting Denzinger (although he will be quoted often) and viewing Roman Catholic theology as a homogeneous block. Our concern will rather be to watch the movement of the waves over one and the same sea and to consider the various winds which fill the sails of the ship of the church (not least after Vatican II). Often enough we shall have to ask not merely what course this ship has *followed* but also what will be its *future* course and therefore whether the paths of Roman Catholic and Reformation theology might intersect or increasingly come to parallel one another.

In the forms of a systematic project of this kind the theme continually expands. One is reminded of the child who wanted to empty out the ocean with a cup. The older I get and the more decades I devote to contemplating the mystery of the faith, the more unfathomable it becomes. I thus see how much I have left undone and how much we need forgiveness for the theological work that we do. Humanly speaking, the fascination of theological reflection also finds expression in the fact that inwardly it is inexhaustible (how could it be anything else when it draws from the springs of living water?) and only outwardly from the perspective of the viewer does it sound like the same old story. "No one can understand the pastoral poetry of Virgil unless he has been a shepherd or a peasant for five years. No one can grasp Cicero (in his political writings) unless he has been in the service of the state for twenty years. And no one should presume to understand the Holy Scriptures unless with the prophets he has led the church for a hundred years." This is what Luther wrote on a piece of paper two days before his death.

If I were to reduce to the shortest formula the sum of what has come to me by way of theological insight, I should perhaps reverse dialectically the saying that Anselm originally envisaged as the title of his *Proslogion*. It reads: Faith Seeking Understanding, and it might be appropriately translated in this way: Faith Demanding Insight or Theological Reflection. Without, of course, contesting this statement, I might describe the opposite movement as the goal of the theological work done with this motive, namely: Understanding Seeking Faith, or Theological Reflection Moving Back Toward the Faith from Which It Comes. This reversal may also be found in Anselm and is not, then, directed against him.

The reason why there is this movement back to faith is to be found in the nexus of Christian truth. This is *proclaimed* truth and as such it triggers unending reflection, not vice versa. It precedes our thoughts about it. We can only think and limp "after" it. But we already *are* in this truth as we hear and accept it. The Spirit of God has already planted us in Christ before we examine the ground in which we are sown and study the botany that goes with the laws of our planting. Theology investigates the basis of this proclamation when it has already been *heard*. Thus the message always precedes theology as a text precedes its interpretation. For the same reason theology will never be healthy except when it goes back to its origin and finds its norm in it. It draws a map which must be constantly checked by the actual terrain.

Since Paul occasionally uses military metaphors, I might illustrate what I have just said by quoting the words of a Norwegian colonel in his illuminating report on some maneuvers. He ended it with these words: "If, which God forbid, Norway should become involved in a war, and if then, may the Lord of hosts grant it, we should stand on enemy territory, and if, gentlemen, we should then find that the terrain does not agree with the map, you may proceed on the assumption that the *terrain* is right." The terrain is always right.

Readers who are familiar with the first two volumes are advised to skip the introductory discussions, since these offer a brief summary of what has gone before. They may begin with chapter I (p. 8).

In conclusion I should like to express my thanks to the firm of J. C. B. Mohr for a relationship that has extended over many decades and a couple of generations. It has remained unbroken through good days and bad.

Abbreviations

AAS	Acta Apostolicae Sedis (1909ff.)
Anthrop	H. Thielicke, *Mensch sein—Mensch werden* . . . (1976)
BK	*Bekenntnisschriften und Kirchenordnungen der nach Gottes Wort reformierten Kirche,* ed. W. Niesel, 3rd ed. (1939)
CA	Confession of Augsburg
CAApol	Apology for the Confession of Augsburg
CD	Karl Barth, *Church Dogmatics*
CR	*Corpus Reformatorum*
DAS	*Deutsches Allgemeines Sonntagsblatt*
Denz.	Denzinger, *Enchiridion Symbolorum,* Editio XXXIII (1965)
DZ	*Deutsche Zeitung*
EA	Erlangen Edition of *Luther's Works*
EK	*Evangelische Kommentare*
Ep	Epitome (of the Augsburg Confession)
EF	H. Thielicke, *The Evangelical Faith* (1974ff.)
EG	H. Thielicke, *Der evangelische Glaube* (1968ff.)
EvTh	*Evangelische Theologie*
FAZ	*Frankfurter Allgemeine Zeitung*
FormConc	Formula of Concord
Hampe	J. C. Hampe, ed., *Die Autorität der Freiheit. Gegenwart des Konzils und Zukunft der Kirche im ökumenischen Disput,* I–III (1967)
HK	*Herder-Korrespondenz*
HThG	*Handbuch theologischer Grundbegriffe,* ed. H. Fries (1970ff.)
Inst.	J. Calvin, *Institutes* (1559), quoted from the Library of Christian Classics edition, XX–XXI (Westminster, 1960)

KKK · K. Rahner, H. Vorgrimler, *Kleines Konzilskompendium* (Vatican II), 10th ed. (1975)

LBK · *Die Bekenntnisschriften der evangelisch-lutherischen Kirche*

LC · Luther's Larger Catechism

LMH · *Lutherische Monatshefte*

LR · *Lutherischer Rundblick*

LW · *Luther's Works*

MD · *Materialdienst des Konfessionskundlichen Instituts Bensheim*

MS · *Mysterium Salutis*

Mu · M. Luther, *Ausgewählte Werke*, ed. H. H. Borcherdt and G. Merz, 2nd ed. (Munich, 1938ff.)

NDH · *Neue deutsche Hefte*, ed. J. Günther

NT · New Testament

Op. sel. · J. Calvini, *Opera selecta*, ed. P. Barth and W. Niesel (1926ff.)

OT · Old Testament

Rahner · *Schriften zur Theologie;* E.T. *Theological Investigations*

RE · *Realencyklopädie für protestantische Theologie und Kirche*, 3rd ed.

RGG · *Religion in Geschichte und Gegenwart*, 3rd ed.

SC · Luther's Small Catechism

SmalkArt · Articles of Smalkald

Sol · Solida Declaratio (of the Augsburg Confession)

Tappert · T. G. Tappert, ed., *The Book of Concord: Confessions of the Evangelical Lutheran Church* (1959)

TDNT · *Theological Dictionary of the New Testament*

ThBl · *Theologische Blätter*, ed. K. L. Schmidt, later H. Strathmann

ThE · H. Thielicke, *Theologische Ethik* I–III (1951ff.); E.T. (altered and abridged) *Theological Ethics* (1966ff.)

ThEx · *Theologische Existenz heute*

ThLZ · *Theologische Literaturzeitung*

TWNT · *Theologisches Wörterbuch zum Neuen Testament*, ed. G. Kittel and G. Friedrich

WA · Weimar Edition of *Luther's Works*

Weber · O. Weber, *Grundlagen der Dogmatik*, I–II (1955 and 1962)

ZAW · *Zeitschrift für alttestamentliche Wissenschaft*

ZEE · *Zeitschrift für evangelische Ethik*

ZsysTh · *Zeitschrift für systematische Theologie*

ZThK · *Zeitschrift für Theologie und Kirche*

Scripture sustains the church and the church guards Scripture. If the church is sick, Scripture is covered with dust. Thus the state of the church corresponds to its handling of Scripture.
JOHANN ALBRECHT BENGEL

When the Spirit of God departs, then even the truth itself becomes an iceberg.
CHARLES HADDON SPURGEON

Heaven and earth await a theodicy at the hand of him who has made heaven and earth. How can the soul into which the love of God has been shed abroad by the Holy Spirit take any rest before it sees God glorified in his creation and God's creation blessed in God?
GOTTFRIED MENKEN

The human comedy does not adequately enthral me. I am not wholly of this world. I am not from here but from somewhere else. And this somewhere else outside the walls must be found again.
EUGÈNE IONESCO

Was the Word really made flesh in order that it might be made words again by theologians?
LUDOLF HERRMANN

Orientation: Hope for a Theology of the Holy Spirit

In his epilogue to a little edition of Schleiermacher K. Barth expressed the hope that our generation might see the attempt at "a theology of the third article, and therefore predominantly and decisively of the Holy Spirit."[1] Now the present author does not presume to think that he can supply this awaited theology of the Spirit. He certainly does not flatter himself that the lines suggested here would have evoked sounds of pleasure from the grand old man. I may confess, however, that for some time I have been looking for a path that would lead to a pneumatological conception. The first volume of the present work made ample preparation for entry into this field.[2]

The hope expressed by Barth and others is certainly not to be understood along the lines of Joachim of Fiore, who, as is well known, constructed a trinitarian sequence of the world-epochs and after the epochs of the Father and the Son expected an eschatological consummation in the age of the Spirit.[3] The dissolution of the triad of Father, Son, and Holy Spirit in historical periods leads, as many examples show, to an emancipation of the Spirit from the Word and then logically to a secularizing identification of the Pneuma with the human consciousness.[4] Thus Lessing's age of the "everlasting pure gospel" is this eschatological time of emancipation in which the pupil of the *Education of the Human Race* has come of age and no longer needs the authoritative Word of revelation but has found his way to the freely roaming spirit of his reason.[5] Without having known Joachim, Schelling also arrived at the idea of a self-actualization of God in history according to a

---

[1] *Schleiermacher-Auswahl,* Siebenstern-Taschenbuch, CXIII/CXIV (1968), pp. 320ff. Cf. Barth's *Letters, 1961–1968,* No. 298 (Grand Rapids, 1981).

[2] Cf. chapters VII–XI.

[3] Cf. E. Benz, "Die Kategorien der religions-geschichtsdeutung Joachims," *Zeitschrift für Kirchengeschichte* (1931), pp. 24ff.; K. Löwith, *Weltgeschichte und Heilsgeschehen* (1953), pp. 136ff.; E.T. *Meaning in History* (Chicago, 1949), pp. 145ff.

[4] The historical influence of the Johannine sayings about the Pneuma is typical here; see G. Bornkamm, Part I, Bibliography.

[5] Thielicke, *Vernunft und Existenz . . . ,* 5th ed. (1967).

trinitarian structure. On the foundation laid in Christ a building is constructed which gradually encompasses all things human. This house will be a temple in which will flourish knowledge of a different nature from that imparted to the apostles by revelation, by a special relationship. It will be a knowledge that is possible and accessible to man in all circumstances, times, and places, in short, one that is universally human and therefore free and scientific.[6] The testimony of the Spirit has here become the argument of reason that each may call upon at any time.

Schelling's younger contemporary Richard Rothe put this idealistic conception into theological terms. The Holy Spirit as "inspired natural organism" guides the necessary evolution of the world-process as this is found in God. God's being is "the absolute process as the absolute process of the generation of life and the self" (*Theologische Ethik,* 2nd ed. [1867ff.], §28). Christ does not bring anything absolutely new. The second creation permeates the world increasingly with the Christian spirit, so that the church which first carries the process gradually makes itself superfluous and finally merges into the state. Hence two processes coincide: a world that becomes spiritual and a Christianity that becomes secular. We have here—for the first time to my knowledge—the idea of an "anonymous" or "unconscious" Christianity as men of the secularized age live according to echoes of the concepts that first came to them as revelation. Here, too, the Pneuma that is first met transcendentally has become an immanent consciousness which as adult knowledge no longer needs the faith once generated by the Word, though the knowledge posited in this faith is preserved in it.

It need hardly be explained to what extent this eschatology of the Spirit which is fulfilled in the human consciousness may also be found in Hegel and then in materialized form in Marx and Engels.

Expectation of a theology of the Spirit obviously cannot have in view this emancipation from the Word, which may be dispensed with by those come of age. It denotes instead a concept which is able, or, better, to which it is given, to grasp the Word not as a total letter[7] but as "God in action," not as the purely verbal repetition of something past but as the presentation of it, as its creative transposition into something new, not just as a Word that teaches but as one that fulfils.

Statements about the Spirit have, of course, different nuances in the OT and NT, and we cannot just read the NT statements into those of the OT. In P the Spirit is first the *ruach* of Yahweh, the rushing of God over the face of the water (M. Buber) which does not yet dispel chaos. Creation comes only by the Word. As *dynamis,* the movement of the Spirit belongs to God—so expressly that in what it does and will do it can no more be defined than Yahweh can. (On the name Yahweh, which is "open" in this sense, cf. EG, II, pp. 132ff.; EF, II, pp. 109ff.) The only definition here is the self-declaration that Yahweh will be true to himself as the one he is and will be. He can bless and judge by his Spirit, being tied neither to the one nor to the other (Isaiah 30:27f.; Jeremiah 4:4; Joel 3:1ff.). He works by his Spirit on nature and history as well as man and can either give or withdraw his creative Spirit (Psalm 104:29f.; Job 13:14f.).

---

[6] *Die Philosophie der Offenbarung, Gesamtausgabe,* XIV, p. 296.
[7] EG, I, pp. 234ff.; EF, I, pp. 175ff.

Wherever we find statements about the Spirit in the Bible, whether in P, John, or Paul, for all their breadth they all have one thing in common: They see in the Pneuma God's own presence. As God has disclosed himself and will meet us as Immanuel, God with us, the Spirit is bound to the Word by which the self-disclosure takes place. To that extent every theology of the Spirit has to do with the sole efficacy of the Word, the "spiritual" Word. The Pneuma does not say more than the Word. The Word is always the vehicle of the Spirit. The Spirit meets us as the power by which the Word reveals itself and comes to us.

Hence the Spirit is always that which comes upon us or he who opens himself to us. This implies from the outset that we do not open ourselves to the Word nor do our eyes see or our ears make hearing and understanding possible (Matthew 13:13–15). Without the Spirit as the divinely working power of disclosure we are left standing in the wings or before closed doors. The Spirit is he who must enlighten, unlock, and make the event of salvation present to those who of their own reason and strength cannot believe in the incarnate Word or come to him.[8] Only the Spirit can help our weakness (Romans 8:26).

If we are waiting today for a theology of the Spirit, for a new declaration of the sole efficacy of the Word, and if we venture some first steps—no more—in this direction, it is because of some experiences of the last generation or two. We then stood under the threat of losing sight of the monopoly of the Word as the one vehicle of the Spirit controlling the power of self-disclosure.

The decisive concern of any theology, whether orthodox or rational, "positive" or "liberal," is that of hermeneutical reflection. This reflection focuses on the question how the biblical records that meet us as the Word can be understood, how they can be appropriated, and how there can be an intelligible relation between them and us. We have already shown how a Christian pneumatology answers this question: The Word creates its own hearer by disclosing itself to me and making me ready by the Spirit for this disclosure.

Those who do not put the principle of the sole efficacy of the Word among the premises of their theological thinking, and who therefore have no theology of the Spirit or put it on the periphery, have to resort to special hermeneutical constructions if they are to bridge the abyss between the eternal (or supposedly eternal) Word and us temporal men. As an example we have only to think of the very typical case of Bultmann's existential theology.[9] Here the answer to the question how the kerygmatic Word comes to me lies in the statement that it links up with a certain pre-understanding, that it takes up my own existential themes (anxiety, guilt, hope, etc.), and that I may thus understand it because of its analogous relation to factors in my consciousness.[10] This consciousness, then, has at its disposal the ability to make the Word of the kerygma present. It can cooperate with it. The testimony of the Spirit is as it were delegated to it. Perhaps that is putting things too one-sidedly. A process in the opposite direction is also conceivable. Resort may not be had to the hermeneutical relation between kerygma and pre-

---

[8]SC, Article 1; Tappert, pp. 344f.
[9]In spite of some affinity to the Cartesian starting point, Tillich's principle of correlation lies on another plane; cf. EG, I, pp. 39f.; EF, I, pp. 48f.
[10]EG, I, pp. 57ff.; EF, I, pp. 59ff.

understanding because there is no doctrine of the Spirit. It could be that preoccupation with the existential questions of anthropology is what has increasingly minimized the role of the Spirit and pushed it out to the margin, the final result being what we have called the anthropological constriction of that theological school.

Yet existential hermeneutics (with its Enlightenment procedures) is not the only one to give the Pneuma a subsidiary role and see it as at most the result of faith rather than its condition. (As Bultmann says, "Paul does not describe pistis as inspired or trace it to the pneuma. On the contrary, the pneuma is the gift that faith receives [Gal. 3:2, 5, 14]"—as though these were alternatives [*Theologie des NT* (1953), p. 326; E.T. *Theology of the NT,* p. 330].) A certain scientific ideology can lead a theologian to the thesis that historical revelation is open to anyone with eyes to see, so that the claim of a theology of history can rest on its universal rational validity (cf. W. Pannenberg, *Offenbarung als Geschichte* [1961], p. 98; E.T. *Revelation as History,* p. 135; *Wissenschaftstheorie und Theologie* [1973], p. 402, n. 741; E.T. *Theology and the Philosophy of Science,* p. 407, n. 741). Hence the Holy Spirit cannot be the condition without which the Christ event cannot be known as revelation (*Offenbarung als Geschichte,* p. 100; E.T. *Revelation as History,* p. 136). Cf. the criticisms of P. Althaus in ThLZ, LXXXVII (1962), pp. 321ff. and Pannenberg's reply in ThLZ, LXXXVIII (1963), pp. 82ff. It is logical, then, for Pannenberg to go on to say that we do not have to bring faith to find God's revelation in the history of Israel and Jesus Christ, but the "unconstrained acceptance of these events is what first awakens true faith" (*Offenbarung,* pp. 100f.; E.T. *Revelation as History,* p. 137).

We naturally have to concede to Pannenberg that faith arises by way of these events and their proclamation and does not have to be already present at the start. That, however, is not the decisive problem. The real problem lies in the concept of the "unconstrained acceptance" that causes me to see the events. By this Pannenberg obviously means an objective ability to see which opens up the event of revelation even to the natural man and thus gives him faith. Now quite apart from the fact that when revelation may be seen in this way it is hard to conceive why it has to awaken *faith* (I understand in order that I may believe?), the deeper problem in this thesis is that the "lack of constraint" mentioned does not exist. A basic conviction of biblical anthropology is that man is a prisoner of his defection from God, that he is a sinner, and that the bondage of his will brings him under extreme constraint. The sayings of Jesus (already quoted) about blocked ears and blinded eyes and hardened hearts make this very clear. Their point is simply that there is no accessibility of the event of revelation unless it makes itself accessible. "The natural man does not perceive the things of the Spirit of God" (1 Corinthians 2:14), nor, therefore, the things of the Word and event that this Spirit alone discloses.

Here we can see vividly that the Pneuma has and *can* have no place in this conception. The point is even clearer in the broadly developed systematics of Pannenberg's *Theology and the Philosophy of Science* when with his own logic he integrates theology into the sensory experience of all the sciences (even though he does give it the special task of drawing attention to this experience and accepting its dialogical function in this setting).

How far this way of doing theology, for all its intellectual rank, falls short pneumatologically, is clearer still when Pannenberg deals expressly with the theology of the Spirit in his monograph "Der Geist des Lebens," *Glaube und Wirklichkeit* (Munich, 1975), pp. 31–56; E.T. *Faith and Reality* (Philadelphia, 1977), pp. 20–38. For although the Pneuma has no place in his system, he cannot simply ignore something which plays such an important part in the Bible and theological tradition.

What will be the shape of a pneumatology which has proved to be a failure at the decisive point where the issue is the self-disclosure of the salvation event by the testimony of the Holy Spirit?

Here too Pannenberg, faithful to his first principle, stresses that he wants to get away from a one-sided focus on the soteriological function of the Spirit and to get behind what he thinks is the whole subjectivist development of pneumatology. Instead he speaks of a kind of *cosmological* significance of the Spirit, or, somewhat epigrammatically, of the spiritual nature of the universe. Very typically—in reading the work we wonder when this name will crop up—he takes up Teilhard de Chardin's idea of a spiritual energy at work in the universe and the possible orthogenetic direction of evolution by it (cf. the chapter on Teilhard in my Anthrop [1976], pp. 473ff.). This Spirit achieves a special presence in man by way of the human capacity for self-transcendence. Man himself is a spermatic logos of spiritual cosmic energy. Subject and object are no longer distinct. In the world and history the I knows the working of the Spirit of which he is a part. In this sense world events are salvation events for Teilhard. The Spirit no longer blows where he wills (John 3:8) and no special revelations are needed. The world and man are alike incarnations of the Spirit, so that God is open to sight and perception.

Along these lines the dualism of God's Spirit and man's ceases. The Pneuma is not imparted (or denied) as a gift of grace. In Teilhard's sense he is "spirit in the world."

The intellectual line that Pannenberg is following here is unmistakable. He is adopting the Stoic analogy between the ontic logos (invested in the world) and the noetic logos (active in our ability to know). We also catch an echo of the idealistic view of Hegel that all cosmic forms are forms of the world spirit that is at work in the finite consciousness.

Pannenberg's pneumatology does not refute our thesis that with him the theology of the Holy Spirit is inevitably secondary. For his putting of God's Spirit and man's on the same plane means no less than that the biblical understanding of the Spirit loses its point—the point that the Pneuma is the power of him who discloses himself and that man cannot control this power but can only wait for it: "Come, Creator Spirit." This way can lead only to something that was already at work at the beginning, namely, a radical and rich regeneration of "natural theology."

Warned by this reduction and its failure to achieve a biblical pneumatology, we shall make it our own task to understand the Spirit as the uncontrollable power of presentation or making present.

That presentation in this sense cannot have the meaning of bringing out the "timeless validity" of what is said in the Word may be seen from our introductory discussion. Timeless validity might well be ascribed to an idea made out of the Word and satisfying to human reason. It would be identical with the constant accessibility enjoyed by the eschatological man of Lessing, who in supposed possession of adulthood has taken over as his own truth of reason that which originally came to him from outside as the educational Word of revelation. Timelessness would thus be contrary to the point of what has come to us in salvation history, namely, God's acting on us historically, his always being to us the wholly other in this action, yet his coming near to us in self-disclosure, his taking us up into his history.

His coming to us over the ages, which is what we mean by the presentation effected by the Spirit, is not, then, a timeless "any time" such as corresponds to the truth of reason or to a truth of revelation dissolved in rational truth. It is coming near in the sense of Kierkegaard's idea of contemporaneity. We relate to the past as something conditioned. It is relative to the reasons for its happening, just as we who see it are subject to the same relativity. But Christ, seeing that God is in him, is the unconditioned before whom the ages that separate us from him roll up. We are called into a relation of directness to him. We are his contemporaries and as such are either alienated by his servant-form or opened to faith in him. Since this openness arises only as the gift of faith, we do not control it but are called to it. To that extent the emerging of contemporaneity is the miracle of the Spirit.[11]

That we are dealing with a "historical" presentation made to me through the miracle of the Spirit explains why the Bible does not strictly have any doctrine of the Holy Spirit but offers accounts of events and experiences in which the Spirit was mighty and from which he also comes into *my* history, awakens *my* faith, kindles *my* love, and gives direction and goal to *my* hope. The miracle of presentation is that I *recognize* myself in the forms of the salvation event—from believing Abraham to doubting Thomas, from afflicted Job to comforted Stephen—and that from what happened to *them* I learn to understand what comes upon *me* too.

---

[11]Cf. S. Kierkegaard, *Philosophical Fragments* (Princeton, 1944), cc. 4f.; *Training in Christianity* (Princeton, 1947), pp. 66ff.

Part One

THE HOLY SPIRIT
AS THE POWER
OF PRESENTATION

Bibliography

H. Berkhof, *Theologie des heiligen Geistes* (1968); E.T. *The Doctrine of the Holy Spirit* (Richmond, Va., 1964, 1976); also "Der Vorschuss des Geistes," EK, XI (1975), p. 658; R. Bohren, *Dass Gott schön werde* (1975); G. Bornkamm, "Die Zeit des Geistes. Ein johannische Wort und seine Geschichte," *Heidelberger Jahrbücher* (1966); F. Büchsel, *Der Geist Gottes im NT* (1926); H. von Campenhausen, *Kirchliches Amt und geistliche Vollmacht in den ersten drei Jahrhunderten* (1953); E.T. *Ecclesiastical Authority . . .* (Stanford, 1969); W. Dantine, *Der heilige und der unheilige Geist* (1973); O. Dilschneider, *Ich glaube an den heiligen Geist* (1969); O. Dilschneider, H. Mynarek, H. Mühlen, and S. von Kortzfleisch, *Im Horizont des Geistes. Antwort auf eine Krise* (1971); H. Dörries, *De Spiritu Sancto* (1956); G. Ebeling, "Ortsbestimmung der Lehre vom Heiligen Geist," *Wort und Glaube,* III (1975), p. 316; also "Die Beunruhigung der Theologie durch die Frage nach den Früchten des Geistes," *ibid.,* p. 388; E. Fuchs, *Christus und der Geist bei Paulus* (1932); R. H. Grützmacher, *Wort und Geist. Eine historische und dogmatische Untersuchung zur Gnadenmittel des Wortes* (1902); H. Gunkel, *Wirkungen des heiligen Geistes* (1909); F. Hahn, "Das biblische Verständnis des heiligen Geistes . . . ," MD, V (1972), p. 90; W.-D. Hauschild, *Gottes Geist und der Mensch* (1972); I. Hermann, *Kyrios und Pneuma* (1961); also with O. Semmelroth, art. in *Handbücher theologischer Grundbegriffe,* II (1970); E. Hultsch, "Unser aller Gottes-Geist," LMH, II (1976), p. 89; E. Käsemann, M. A. Schmid, and R. Prenter, art. in RGG³, II (1958); G. Kretschmar, *Studien zur frühchristlichen Trinitätstheologie* (1956); W. Krusche, *Das Wirken des heiligen Geistes bei Calvin* (1957); H. Leisegang, *Der heilige Geist. Das Wesen und Werden der mystisch-intuitiven Erkenntnis in der Philosophie und Religion der Griechen* (1919); H. Meyer, W. J. Hollenweger, K. McDonnell, V. Vajta, and A. M. Aagaard, *Die Wiederentdeckung des heiligen Geistes* (1974); J. Moltmann, *Kirche in der Kraft des Geistes* (1975); E.T. *The Church in the Power of the Spirit* (New York, 1977); H. Mühlen, *Der heilige Geist als Person* (1963); W. Pannenberg, "Der Geist des Lebens," *Glaube und Wirklichkeit* (1975), p. 31; R. Prenter, *Spiritus creator* (1965); E.T. Philadelphia, 1953; O. Rodenberg, *Wort und Geist* (1969); E. Schweizer, art. in TDNT, VI, pp. 396–451; TWNT, VI, pp. 394–453; P. Tillich, *Systematic Theology,* III (Chicago, 1963); R. A. Torrey, *The Person and Work of the Holy Spirit* (New York, 1910); V. Warnach, "Ratio und Pneuma," *Wahrheit und Verkündigung* (Schmaus Festschrift, 1967), p. 429; S. Wittschier, *P. Tillich. Seine Pneuma-Theologie* (1975); on the Second Vatican Council: K. Rahner and H. Vorgrimler, ed., *Kleines Konzilskompendium* (1966ff.); J. C. Hampe, ed., *Die Autorität der Freiheit,* I-III (1967).

3

Introduction:
Link with Previous Discussions of Pneumatology

In EF, I especially the doctrine of the Holy Spirit has already been introduced in fairly lengthy chapters.[1] It arose there from a particular standpoint as the antithesis to modern forms of thought, and especially to what we described as the Cartesian starting point of these forms.

In analyzing them we recalled the methodological doubt of Descartes which logically led him at last to the unquestionably solid ground of the existence of the one who thinks and doubts (*cogito ergo sum*). The influence of this basis in self-certainty is most important, and we illustrated it by several examples. From that time on, the I took on normative rank as the *subject* of both knowledge and faith. We studied it philosophically in the transcendentalism of Kant and theologically in the doctrines of faith of the 19th century—with man as the subject of faith!—from Schleiermacher right on to the existentialist theology of our own time.

The question how theological knowledge, the knowledge of God, is possible is usually answered as follows in theologies which regard themselves as relevant, progressive, and modern. They find the conditions of this possibility in the I. The I discovers in itself some basic realities which themselves raise the religious question. These basic realities may vary from the feeling of absolute dependence (Schleiermacher) to openness to what affects us unconditionally (Tillich) and existential factors like anxiety, the sense of alienation, and hope (Bultmann). Negatively—so that with the help of the I-reference religion is "unmasked" and shown to be mere anthropology in the sense of projection—we find the same Cartesian starting point in Feuerbach and Freud.[2]

The conditions in the I for the possibility of faith and religious understanding always develop surreptitiously, as we have seen, into *normative* factors exercising dictatorial control. Every religious statement which claims to be true, including the kerygma itself, must justify itself before this forum. Anything that cannot integrate itself into existential concerns, or into what seems to be significant to them, forfeits its kerygmatic claim.

In a theology with this orientation the structure of the consciousness of the I threatens to become the real dominating factor. It has a monopoly when the acceptability or unacceptability of a message or revelation has to be decided. It is the measure of all the things that have to do with truth and the claim of truth—and this in spite of the fact that its initial intention is the positive one of showing that the biblical message is something which we can appropriate and which can become our truth. In this way, then, theology can surreptitiously be changed into an attribute of anthropology.

Because of their anthropological core theologies of this kind, and the anti-theologies which are their step-brothers, necessarily come up against the ques-

---

[1]VIII–XI.
[2]For a more detailed discussion cf. Anthrop.

tion: Who am I?[3] Am I the I which in this position, and understanding itself in the light of it, finds its self-understanding merely confirmed, transcended, or corrected by Christian truth and its mythical ciphers? Or does the encounter with Christian truth lead to a radical reorientation of this self-understanding, i.e., to a change of my identity, to a "new creature" (2 Corinthians 5:17; Galatians 6:15)? If the latter, then the question who I am must find a very *different* answer.

This is where the question of pneumatology is relevant.

The spiritual Word, as we have shown, is not just an imparting and instructing Word which builds on our epistemological presuppositions, which is limited by them, which makes contact with them, and which fits into their framework. Instead it is an active and creative Word. It ploughs up the old and fashions the new creature.

This raises the question of the relation between the old or former identity and the new. In this connection we discussed the continuity and discontinuity[4] expressed in Galatians 2:20: "I live—yet not I; Christ lives in me."

The question of this new identity that is forged by the Pneuma occupied us especially from four standpoints.

1. We considered first the relation between Spirit and letter.[5] The mere letter of the command and promise leaves the message outside, so that it cannot be appropriated by me. It thus has the character of the law with which I am in conflict (Romans 7:8, 15) and which unleashes opposition in me. The ministry of the law leads, then, to the tearing apart of the "old" man (7:23) either in the sense that I want to submit to him but cannot or in the sense that my will is opposed to God's law and resists it from the outset as self-will. Only as the Pneuma makes God present to me and overcomes the "outsideness" (both of the mere letter and of myself) does the new I arise which wills what God wills because it can now *love* God and thus stands in conformity to him.[6] From the old division there thus arises a new unity. But there is also posed the problem of continuity and discontinuity between the old I and the new. Luther expresses the dialectic of this relation in his statement that we are at the same time both righteous and sinners.[7]

2. We then defined the relation between Spirit and flesh.[8] The Spirit is not an elevating of the flesh, a new patch on an old coat (Matthew 9:16 par.), but the altering of a relation of dominion.[9] Though coming from outside, the Spirit takes us up into himself. But when he works on us, how can there be appropriation so that something new arises that is ours, something that we ourselves are, something that constitutes our identity?

The new being, as we saw, is not a quality of the old I that has been newly given us. It is something outside, a new relation to God that is opened to me (indicative)

---

[3]EG, I, p. 256; EF, I, p. 189.

[4]EG, I, pp. 244–49; EF, I, pp. 181–84.

[5]EG, I, p. 234; EF, I, p. 175.

[6]EG, I, p. 237; EF, I, p. 177.

[7]EG, II, pp. 386, 389; EF, II, pp. 313, 316. Cf. R. Hermann, *Luthers These "Gerecht und Sünder zugleich"* (1930); W. Joest, *Gesetz und Freiheit* (1956), p. 82 and *Ontologie der Person bei Luther* (1967), p. 265; G. Dehn, "Der alte und der neue Mensch," *Theologia viatorum* (1939), p. 67.

[8]EG, I, p. 249; EF, I, p. 184.

[9]EG, I, p. 252; EF, I, p. 186.

and that I have to claim as such (imperative).[10] The Spirit effects a new analogy between God and man. The servant-relation caused by the fall has been changed into a filial relation (Galatians 4:1–7).

3. The new analogy that thus arises leads to what we called the hermeneutics of the Holy Spirit.[11] The basic epistemological problem of theology is that God is not one object among others, that he thus escapes objectification, and lies outside the radius of human reason, which is limited by the horizon of experience. God is, of course, the basis of every possibility of knowledge, even of knowledge within this immanent horizon. (For it is he who as Creator confronts us with created being, presents it to us to know, and lends us the organs with which to know it. It is he who causes the ontic logos of being and the cognitive logos of our ability to know to correspond to one another. It is he who embraces subject and object.) Yet even though he makes knowledge possible, he himself is not knowable as the basis of knowledge. He upholds the world nexus but is not himself to be found in it.

This epistemological problem, however, is only a frontal one. The incompetence and inadequacy of reason to know God is no more than the symptom of a deeper ontic disturbance behind it, namely, the fall, which is always there in the background in any awakening to knowledge. From the moment of the disruption of creation and man's fall into alienation it has always been in man's interest that God should not exist, or at least that he should not exist as he has disclosed himself to us in the Bible as Lord and Judge, so that we are forced to understand ourselves in our dependence, in our being referred to him, and in our need of redemption. From this moment on we live in a state of permanently *suppressing* the truth, of *holding it down* by force (*katechein,* Romans 1:19ff.). We are no longer free to be opened to the truth. We have put ourselves in a position of bondage, of darkening (Romans 1:21), of being "given up" (1:24, 26). To that extent we are in bondage.

Since knowledge always presupposes an analogy between knower and known, we can express (and have developed) the state described along these lines. Man has fallen out of the original analogy between Creator and creature. He is no longer adequate in relation to God. He has moved away from God. He is alienated. Epistemologically sin is the basis and form of the lack of analogy. The only one analogous to God is God himself. Hence the only adequate knowledge of God is that which God has of himself, his self-knowledge (1 Corinthians 2:11).

This is where the hermeneutics of the Holy Spirit comes in. "The Spirit of God knows what is in God" (1 Corinthians 2:11b). He "searches the depths of God" (2:10). God's self-knowledge takes place in this Spirit. But not his alone, for he imparts himself and overcomes the natural man, who "receives nothing from him" (2:14), and creates the "spiritual man," for whom God will prepare, and to whom he reveals, what "no eye has seen or ear heard nor has it entered the heart of any man" (2:9; Isaiah 64:3). Revelation, we said, means being made to share in God's self-knowledge, in the analogy of the new creature, by the witness of the Spirit. God says who he is[12] and opens the men he addresses to receive this idea of himself.

---

[10]Cf. ThE, I, §§213–689; E.T. pp. 51–146.
[11]EF, I, chapter XI.
[12]Exodus 3:6, 14; 20:1. Cf. Genesis 32:30; Judges 13:18.

4. We then tried to link pneumatology to the doctrine of God in our chapters on the Trinity.[13] These led to an identification: God, and also Jesus Christ,[14] *is* the Spirit. The Spirit "is" God fulfilling what he intimates in word and "mighty acts" (Acts 2:11): the God of Abraham, Isaac, and Jacob disclosing himself in a history with his people and finally with man in general.[15] As it is contained in the doctrine of the Trinity, pneumatology points to "God in action."

In what follows we shall build on the basic theses of a theology of a third article as we have just summarized them.

---

[13]EF, II, chapters IX–XIII.

[14]Cf. the discussion of the "filioque" (EG, II, p. 217; EF, II, pp. 181ff.).

[15]The latter is plain in the Gentile mission (e.g., Acts 18:6; Romans 11:11ff.) but may be seen already in the promise to Noah (Genesis 9:9ff.).

I

The Holy Spirit as the Basis of Faith

1. THE SPIRITUAL WORD AIMED AT US

The power of presentation that is proper to the Spirit works by bringing and appropriating the Word to us. It moves toward us and we accept it. The saving address *to* us becomes an event of reception *in* us. As we are empowered to accept salvation we are drawn into it. We are taken up into salvation history.

The work of the Spirit is not an element that is added to God's words and deeds in salvation history. It is no more an additive of this kind than the doctrine of the Trinity, as we have seen,[1] extends the reality of God by adding the Son and Spirit to it. Instead this doctrine views the author of the salvation event in his triunity. So here the salvation event cannot be understood as a history that takes place outside us and is then directed and appropriated to us by an additional act. No, salvation history is itself already the sequence of God's communications, of his addressed words. Address means the inclusion of the person who is addressed in the words. It means that the point of the words is that they are directed to him, that they cause him to be present in them, that they call him by name (Isaiah 43:1; 45:4), that they expect him to hear and express sorrow when he does *not* (Luke 13:34b; 19:42). Salvation does not consist only in the doing of saving deeds and the speaking of saving words. It consists also in the fulfilling of salvation as it was intended, namely, as salvation in which I come to share. Being caught up in the salvation event belongs essentially to salvation as well.

Where salvation is refused and not accepted it undergoes a radical *mutation*. As the Woes of Jesus show, despised salvation becomes judgment and refused invitation becomes accusation. The greater the offer of salvation—and a greater than Solomon or Jonah is here (Luke 11:31f.)—the more incisive is the sentence, and the queen of the south and the people of Nineveh will come to accuse those who shared greater graces than they but still rejected them (cf. Matthew 23:28–36).

This is how the partaking of the unworthy is to be understood in Luther's doctrine of the Lord's Supper. Those who receive the gift of the supper with

---

[1]EG, II, §9, p. 154; EF, II, p. 129.

indifference, rejection, or pride do not receive nothing but receive judgment. The key text for Luther in this context is the promise in Isaiah (55:11) that the Word will not return empty. The Word does not vanish into thin air if people do not want to hear it. It always comes back laden, either bringing souls that have been won (Spurgeon) or those that are judged. It always brings back "something."

A doctrine of the relation between Word and Spirit is implied in these statements. If the Word were mere letter and sound, or contained only instruction and meaning, it might be no more than a passing sound, like Kant's *Critique of Pure Reason* read to a child at a special school. But it is a Word that contains the Spirit, i.e., a Word in which God himself is present. To refuse this Word is to do something. Nonhearing is not just a defect; it is hardening, *non*salvation. This is precisely the mutation of which we spoke (Matthew 13:15; Romans 11:7; Revelation 22:18, etc.).

Since participation in the salvation event is part of salvation, we can treat of the Holy Spirit and the power of his appropriating only in such a way that we thereby describe God's history with us. We would mistake the theme of the Holy Spirit if we were interested only in the intertrinitarian relationship of Father, Son, and Spirit. In this case we would also mistake the theme of the Trinity itself, for the triunity of God seeks to express God's self-unfolding, his condescension to a history with us.[2] Along these lines Melanchthon's famous christological saying in the 1521 *Loci* may be applied to the doctrine of the Spirit too: To know the Holy Spirit can only mean to know his benefits, his workings, the power of his appropriating.[3]

That participation in the salvation event is part of salvation means that if the Bible is to be passed on as "the Word of God" it cannot just be *quoted* but has also to be *proclaimed*. Mere quotation would leave the biblical Word in its own hour and time and destroy my contemporaneity with it. In contrast proclamation means that a witness seized by the Word causes it to grasp after those who seek it here and now. That he is a witness implies that he speaks as one who has been reached and affected, that the Word has made itself present to him by the Spirit, and that he for his part now calls those who are assembled into this presence. He does this in the name of him who as the "unique bearer of the Spirit"[4] has promised his presence to those who are gathered in his name (Matthew 18:20). This means, however, that proclamation aims at the hearer, that it has very concretely in view his situation, his cares and hopes, his guilt and need of redemption. Proclamation is actual proclamation or it is not proclamation at all. It makes present or it does not take place.

It should not be overlooked, of course, that there is an actualization that resists pneumatic presentation because it becomes human artistry, modish rhetoric, or even wordy nonsense, because, instead of accommodating itself, it conforms to the age and says whatever tickles the ears of the hearers.[5] Here, then, we have an arbitrary cooperation with the Word because the Word's own spiritual power of

---

[2]This is why in EF, II we chose for the doctrine of the Trinity the title "Revelation as a Word That Posits History" (p. 124) and dealt with it in constant connection with the addressee and his destiny.
[3]*Hoc est Spiritum Sanctum cognoscere: beneficia ejus cognoscere.*
[4]F. Hahn, in MD, V, p. 91.
[5]EG, I, pp. 9ff.; EF, I, pp. 27ff.

presentation is not trusted and a supposed pioneering initiative of man is therefore placed at its disposal. Naturally the power of presentation which is the Holy Spirit will always be modern and actual. The biblical Word of salvation will unite in unique and venturesome ways with what is read in the newspaper and seen on television. More important than the fact itself, however, is the way in which this actuality is achieved and the name in which it is achieved. The witness to whom the Word has actualized itself by the power of presentation can do no other than pass on in relevant form what has happened to him. If he has a concern to find examples and illustrations and concrete applications, this can no more be a concern that is additional to, or alongside, the Word, than the Holy Spirit is an added power working with it. The only point at issue is that like a good steward he faithfully passes on his own experience.

2. THE FAITH EFFECTED BY THE WORD AND SPIRIT

a. The State of Receiving. The Problem of Our "Passivity"

We begin with two theses which we shall develop in what follows.

First, the event in which salvation draws me into itself is faith. This discloses and determines the being of the new creature and it arises through proclamation in the power of the Spirit (Galatians 3:2). The Spirit's power of presentation expresses itself in making us contemporary with the Christ event. In faith we participate in Christ's death and resurrection by dying and rising again with him (Romans 6:4ff.; Galatians 2:19; Colossians 2:12; 3:1). We are drawn into salvation by it as we receive salvation and acquire access to it (Romans 5:2). By it God's Spirit finds an entry into us (Romans 8:9, 11), so that we are set in the new analogy.

Second, faith takes "form" in knowledge, love, and hope, in the assurance of faith, in the ability to pray, and in the gifts of the Spirit and the discernment of spirits.[6]

Both points (like our summary of Volumes I and II) indicate, without having to be developed further, the passivity of man in this dimension, or, better, the character of the Spirit as experience and the fact that man has not produced or even reproduced this of himself.

In saying this we note that we have some difficulty with the word "passivity" and use it only with reservations. At all events we cannot introduce it without some explanatory safeguards. For the alternative of active/passive is just as dubious as that of subject/object.[7] The terms are in order when dealing with objects like the hammer and the anvil but not in personal relations or even in the relation between man and animal, horse and rider. The inappropriateness of the alternative has come out most clearly thus far in the relation between indicative and imperative.[8]

On the one side it is clear that good fruits are not the product of our pious

---

[6]I use the word "form" with hesitation because it derives from the distinction between unformed faith and faith formed by love. Naturally the idea of faith as a mere disposition for justification does not underlie the present concept of faith taking form. I merely have in mind faith's implications. I certainly could not choose the even more heavily freighted terms "implicit" and "explicit" faith.

[7]On the latter cf. EG, II, pp. 530ff.; EF, II, pp. 429ff.; cf. also EG, I, pp. 206, 381; EF, I, pp. 157, 266.

[8]EG, II, pp. 252ff.; EF, II, pp. 209ff.; cf. ThE, I, §§314ff.; E.T. I, pp. 74ff.

subjectivity but modes of the working of the Holy Spirit.[9] Yet we are no mere objects of this event exposed to its activity only as passive recipients. We are caught up into it and must take up an attitude or respond to it. We reach at this point the limit of botanical or physical analogies, e.g., that of the tree producing fruit of itself or the stone getting warm "of itself" in the rays of the sun. To be sure, we are awakened from the dead—in the real sense of a miracle done on us—but we are also to give ourselves to God as those who are alive from the dead (Romans 6:13b). If we are risen with Christ, we are to seek the things that are in heaven and not on earth (Colossians 2:6f.; 3:1f.). Those who will not respond in this way, who will not let themselves be taken up into the experience of the Spirit but maintain an abstract passivity, put up barriers (*prohibitiva*) which block contact with the Spirit and therefore eliminate even passive experience.[10]

In spite of its dubiousness and limited competence, however, we cannot entirely dispense with the term "passivity." We have only to limit its applicability very precisely. Passivity qualifies the state of man to the extent that he regards his ability to be active, his motivations, his autonomy, even his "willing and doing," as a loaned possibility (Philippians 2:13; 1 Thessalonians 2:13). When Peter confesses Christ, this may well be an active decision, but his ability to reach it is not grounded in "flesh and blood" but is given to him by his "Father in heaven" (Matthew 16:17). Schleiermacher made this problem of passivity validly fruitful anthropologically when he put all human existence under the sign of "absolute dependence" and saw that not just all partial dependencies but also all activities are included in this. All our capacities and possibilities are first opened to us. We are made the ones we are. We are given to ourselves and then given over to what is given.

In a special way this prior passivity of receiving applies to our capacity to understand and appropriate the message of salvation. By nature we meet this with blinded eyes, deaf ears, and closed hearts (Matthew 3:13; 1 Corinthians 2:9; cf. Isaiah 64:3). For *us* to be able to be "active" an act of disclosure has to be performed on us.

Even this limited concept of activity is questionable (and we use it with tongue in cheek because we have to use whatever vocabulary we have and for good reasons do not have at our disposal a special set of spiritual terms).[11] We are not to understand the processes in view as if there belonged to God only the initiative of disclosure which gives us the necessary disposition, and after that he made possible for us our own initiative[12] and a kind of independent operation started. Instead, what we do in the status of the new creature is the fruit of the Spirit which he brings forth on the soil of our hearts.[13]

---

[9]ThE, I, §317; E.T. I, p. 83.

[10]Paul makes this clear by showing that the *adikoi* want experience of salvation but still give themselves to idolatry and fornication and therefore do not enter into the renewed power of the Spirit (1 Corinthians 6:9ff.; Ephesians 5:5). On the *prohibitiva* cf. ThE, I, §§334ff.; E.T. I, pp. 87ff.

[11]Cf. the discussion of the use of the Stoic concept of the logos in John 1:1 (EG, I, p. 161; EF, I, pp. 125f.).

[12]Cf. Trent, Sess. VI, c. 5; Denz., 1525; ThE, I, §1085; E.T. I, p. 222.

[13]Galatians 5:22; Ephesians 5:9; Matthew 13:8. Cf. John 5:2, 4, where the fruit of the vine is ascribed to the vine itself and not the branches; also 15:5, 8: We bring forth fruit only as we abide "in him" so that he can work through us.

Again we cannot wholly avoid the term "activity," for we are not called to play the role of a thing, e.g., a block of wood, but to be open, to receive, to enter. Being thus called as persons before God, we cannot get by without the auxiliary concept of an engaged activity. The creation story shows already that in distinction from plants and animals man is summoned to this responsible encounter with God, or, as it were, to working with God as his partner.[14]

That we need the opening and disclosing activity of the Pneuma and can hear and see nothing without it is because God cannot be located in the sphere described by man's self-produced postulates, world-views, and ideologies. Naturally, as one might say with Vico, man can grasp what he himself has produced and what is thus spirit of his spirit. Here, however, we have to do with the Wholly Other who made man and from whom man is separated not only by the diastasis of Creator and creature but also by the alienation of the fall. This is the reason why the Word that seeks and calls to us across the abyss needs the testimony of the Spirit to open up this Word to us. This is the state which—only within these limits—we have characterized by the ambivalent concept of the passivity of "reception."

b. Essential Marks of This State

That the Pneuma is a power that works on us and is not produced by us or summoned up by our cooperation may be shown on a broad scale of biblical and traditional statements.

(1) Faith Not Our Work

If, without trying to develop an explicit theology of faith, we consider faith from the special standpoint of this scale, our first thesis must be that theology is a reflection by faith on its basis and it presupposes faith. Yet faith does not begin with itself but with a prior history,[15] with the death and resurrection of the Kyrios into which it lets itself be drawn and by which the new creature is generated.

This preliminary statement does not contradict the standard Reformation definition of faith as "trust" in basic distinction from a mere "acceptance as true" or a historical faith. For trust is always intentionally directed and related to someone or something that one trusts. We do not produce trust on our own. It is won from us by something outside, by something other than ourselves. This is stated by our initial thesis that faith does not begin with itself but with a prior history. Trust is evoked by what is said and what takes place in this history.

As Calvin very strongly emphasized, this is connected with the fact that faith is in "a permanent relationship" to the Word and can as little be separated from it as "rays from the sun."[16] Faith detached from the Word and trust robbed of its intentionality degenerate into an attitude of soul which man regards as produced by his own power and for which we have the unmasking term "credulity." Since this

---

[14]We have in mind the addressing of man alone in the second person and the summons to him to grasp his destiny (Genesis 1:28; 2:16f.). The concept of the image of God is to be developed on this basis (ThE, II, 1, §§1246ff.; E.T. II, p. 305).

[15]G. Bornkamm, *Jesus* (1956), p. 20; E.T. p. 23.

[16]Inst., III, 2, 6.

attitude stems from our psyche, it is also tied to—optimistic or pessimistic—moods and is thus vacillating and unreliable. It is an attitude with no fixed point, a happy confidence with no basis.[17]

That the prior history wins from us the trust of faith means that it comes to us and becomes God's history with us. This takes place in such way that it makes us certain of our sonship through the witness of the Spirit (Romans 8:13–16; Galatians 4:6), or, negatively, that it frees us from the bondage which is the opposite of this intimacy. What bondage is Pauline theology makes clear by speaking of the dictatorship of the law. To stand in a relation of law toward God is to be subject to enforced obedience and to be put in the antithesis of affirmation and opposition in relation to the author of the law (Romans 7:17–20). In contrast the spirit of sonship implies that we are brought into the unequivocal relation of love, that the Spirit of God imparted to us frees us for conformity with him, and that the antithesis of consciousness and will caused by the law is removed. As children we can trust and say: "Abba, Father" (Romans 8:15; cf. Mark 14:16).

For this reason faith lives by the promise (which is always to be firmly *grasped*) that God wants to be this Father of ours in Christ. Faith lives, then, by proclamation. This can be so only because the witness of the Spirit is given with the Word of proclamation, so that the promise really applies to *us,* reaching across the ages to *me.* The very fact that I receive the Word in this sense grants the certainty that the Spirit does his work in me and opens me to this Word.

We believe because "the power of his might worked in us" (Ephesians 1:19). We have a kind of counter-proof of this example of the efficacy of the Spirit when we read in John that unbelief is caused by bondage to an alien power and can thus be overcome only by the Spirit of God who defies that power (John 8:43f.; 10:26).[18]

Being freed from bondage and legalism means release from authoritarian faith which certainly does not give me a spontaneous share in what I believe. We can find awareness of this outside Christianity, e.g., in Buddhism: "Do not believe with blind faith, do not believe on the basis of holy scriptures, do not believe merely in tradition. Do not believe me because I say it. When you have seen and investigated and experienced for yourself, then believe" (cf. Princess Pismai Diskul in *The Relevance of Religion in the Modern World* [The Hague, 1970], p. 34).

We do not autonomously resolve on faith, then, but are freed for this decision and loosed from the chains which cannot be broken by nature. We have here the battle of the Spirit of truth against the spirit of falsehood (1 John 4:6). We can as little fight this battle in our own name and on our own initiative as we can withstand secular forces as heroes of faith. Here again we are only instruments in the service of the Spirit of our Father who confronts the opposing spirit. Because it is he who takes us into service we can be told: "Do not be anxious how you are to speak or what you are to say . . . for it is not you who speak," you are not the real spokesmen; someone else, the Spirit of the Father, takes the responsibility

---

[17]Calvin describes it as "uncertain credulity" (*loc. cit.*).

[18]G. Dehn, "Der neue Mensch," *Theologia viatorum* (1939), pp. 67ff., 79f.

(Matthew 10:19f.; Luke 12:11; 21:14). In Qumran this confrontation between the spirit of falsehood and the Spirit of truth is radicalized into a strict dualism.[19]

That faith arises in this way as the victory of the Word, as its disclosure by the witness of the Spirit—as the victory over enslavement and the banishing of an alien spirit—confirms yet again the fact that faith does not begin with itself but with a prior history into which we are called. Faith is, epigrammatically, a secondary phenomenon. At any rate, as Hans Iwand rightly says,[20] it is not an absolute. It arises in relations, especially the relation to the salvation event that is proclaimed in the Bible and that takes us up into itself. Calvin expressed this relation most precisely with his ironical imperative: "Therefore, take away the word and no faith will then remain."[21]

In opposition to this the Cartesian line of thinking of our own (and an earlier) age threatens to make the existential reference of theology so dominant that the act of faith moves up from its secondary position and makes the Word a dependent function: "Take away faith and no word will then remain."[22] In this way faith necessarily becomes a work, or, better, an existential attitude, or the habit of credulity of which Calvin spoke. In reality my faith as acceptance of God's judgment is not contemporaneous with the decision of God in Jesus Christ but subsequent to it.[23] This is stood on its head by the total psychologizing of religion of which modern anthropocentric tendencies make use. This may be seen in the statement of Henri Poincaré at the grave of Pierre Curie: "Fundamentally it does not matter in which God one believes. It is faith, not God, that works miracles."[24]

It is perhaps understandable that Luther's Reformation slogan "by faith alone" should repeatedly have led to the idea that he, too, absolutized faith. Often adduced also in this connection is the thesis he took from Augustine, and frequently used, that not the sacrament, but the faith of the sacrament, justifies. Here, however, faith is not played off against the sacrament but only the automatic efficacy of the sacrament is questioned. The sacrament has a saving effect only as an appropriated promise and faith is the mode of appropriation. Hence everything depends on the fact that faith is not seen as the decisive or even as a cooperative event but as a readiness to let something be done to one. The sacrament does not justify because we perform it but because or when we receive it, knowing and receiving God's address to us (W. Joest, *Ontologie der Person* [1967], p. 405; cf. also pp. 399ff.; G. Wingren, *Die Predigt* [1955], pp. 143ff.; E.T. *The Living Word* [1960], pp. 111ff.).

To sum up, faith is to be understood only in terms of its relation to the Word and

---

[19]Cf. also John 14:17; 15:26; 16:13.
[20]"Glauben und Wissen," *Nachgelassene Werke,* I (1962), pp. 203ff.
[21]Inst., III, 2, 6.
[22]Cf. Iwand, *Nachgelassene Werke,* I, p. 207. Without accusing G. Ebeling I suspect that he ascribes to faith a dominant role; cf. *Das Wesen des christlichen Glaubens* (1959); E.T. *The Nature of Faith* (Philadelphia, 1961), esp. the Index of Subjects.
[23]Iwand, *Nachgelassene Werke,* I, p. 241. Naturally the term "contemporaneous" does not have a Kierkegaardian sense here.
[24]Eve Curie, *Madame Curie. Leben und Wirken* (Vienna, 1938), p. 300.

to the witness of the Spirit. It relates to these as creature to Creator. This relation is irreversible. I can say that if there is no Word and no witness of the Spirit, there can be no faith. But I cannot say the opposite, that if there is no faith the Word is invalid and it does not have the power of the Spirit. We have seen from the sayings of Jesus about hardening (as also from prophetic sayings that find no faith) that when the Word is not accepted it is not an empty sound, or nothing, but becomes judgment and retains its full power. God does not need our faith in order to be God (as though he could not live a moment without us). It is our faith that needs God in order to become possible.[25]

The most impressive formulation of the fact that faith is not grounded in itself or in the psyche which experiences or even produces it may be found in Luther's repeatedly used image of the mathematical point. As we let ourselves be appropriated in faith to God's righteousness, the subject of faith—the I—is like an unextended mathematical point. Faith has no place of its own on which to alight or to spread itself as experience. It is exclusively characterized by its object and not by the one who experiences it. To this extent the subject of faith is self-forgotten. It is no longer troubled by the introverted question whether it believes at all. It is freed from this kind of introspection and introverted self-control.

Luther uses the image of the mathematical point in his exposition of Psalm 45 (WA, 40/II, 527, 9; LW, 12, 239). Along these lines one might perhaps say that faith is ec-centric; it has its basis outside itself (*extra se*). For this reason it is not open to psychological self-observation. Curving in on the self is an inappropriate perspective. We know ourselves and our faith only when we see it with the eyes of God on whom it is directed. From this standpoint our whole life rolls up into an unextended mathematical point. Hence in his exposition of Psalm 90 (WA, 40/III, 572, 23; LW, 13, 128) Luther says that the Holy Spirit will so teach us to number our days that we know what we are and reckon a hundred years of life as a mathematical point and a brief moment.

It is logical, then, that Luther should also understand conscience as a mathematical point. This is ec-centric to the extent that the issue is not a good or bad conscience but a comforted or disquieted conscience. Which of these it is depends on its relation to God: whether it lives in alienation from him and therefore hates and fears him or whether from outside itself (*extra se*) it hears and accepts the pronouncement of justification. (Cf. G. Jacob, *Der Gewissensbegriff in der Theologie Luthers* [1929].) Conscience is thus described as an indivisible point in WA, 40/I, 21, 12; LW, 27, 35–39. Like faith, then, it is not characterized by its bearer, the moral I, but solely by its relation to God. Luther attacks the idea that conscience is to be regarded as the core of being in the sense of the metaphysics of the soul in Scholasticism or the Enlightenment. Instead, it is a point of contact for external operations (E. Wolf, "Vom Problem des Gewissens in reformatorischer

---

[25]Even the pagan Plato was essentially aware of this. While piety honors the gods (*Eutyphro*, 13a–d), this does not mean that they need it or are made better by it. Similarly Philo referred to the fact that the gods have no needs (in the same context of cultic veneration). Cf. M. Dibelius, "Paulus auf dem Areopag," *Sitzungsberichte der Heidelberger Akademie der Wissenschaften, Philosophisch-historische Klasse* (1939), p. 20.

Sicht," *Peregrinatio*, I [1954], p. 89; cf. also W. Elert, *Morphologie des Luther-tums*, I [1931], pp. 68ff.; E.T. *The Structure of Lutheranism* [St. Louis, 1962], pp. 77ff.).

Perhaps it is not wholly mistaken to see in the discovery of this ec-centric character of faith the true impulse behind Luther's turn to reform. It is well known how much—even in the cloister—he was tormented by unease of conscience and guilty fear in spite of his concern for sanctification and the sacramental round. Many psychological and historical insights have been and are continually brought in to explain this. It is too bad, however, if an obvious theological consideration is not taken into account as well. The sacramental understanding of grace that Luther encountered in his day was essentially marked by the concept—and even more so the popular idea—of infused grace, i.e., by a form of grace that automatically produced a specific habit and brought about its corresponding actualization.[26] The analogy to a medicine that is physically effective, being designed to establish and develop a standard of healing in the organism, suggests the need for self-control as a mental effect. The patient asks what symptoms of healing and improvement may be seen in him. The true crisis of Luther in the monastery is to be sought in this autistic implication. The empirical test of self-observation always indicated depressing failure.

In Luther's own terms, taken from Pauline theology, the schema of grace that was codetermined by the idea of infused grace resulted in a situation familiar to the legalist, or, more precisely, it did not free him from such a situation. It, too, is characterized by the fact that those in it must continually measure themselves by the normative imperative of the law's requirement and are thus reduced to despair. Infused grace can bring no emancipation from this bondage but can only intensify it to the degree that it enhances the expectation of possible fulfilment, of satisfying the law, and then is only the more bitterly disappointed. Luther himself attributed his ultimate liberation to the pastoral care of Staupitz, who pointed him to the crucified Lord and therefore to a reality that worked as an outside event *on* him and not *in* him. This prior history works independently of achievements, of despair or pride, of all subjectivity. Our note of indebtedness is torn up and nailed to the cross (Colossians 2:14). We are justified and pardoned—with no conditions, not even that of an achievement whose possibility is opened up to us by grace.

Faith, then, is the attitude of trust in which I let this happen to me. It cannot be seen as an achievement nor measured by its strength, which would force me back to introversion. No, faith is not to be characterized or qualified as an act of the subject. It presents the subject as a mathematical point, for it is determined by its object. I am thus delivered from the paradoxical need of having to believe in my own faith or to spend a good deal of time on my "credulity." The imperative is in force: "Do not rest on yourself or your faith but creep into Christ."[27]

The real break between the medieval mother-church and the Reformation was not caused, then, by Luther's insistence on the exclusiveness of grace. That grace holds the sole initiative in the saving of man, and that man cannot release this

---

[26]On infused grace cf. ThE, I, §§877ff.; 1141ff.; E.T. I, pp. 179ff.; 238ff.; cf. also EG, I, pp. 238f.; EF, I, p. 178.

[27]WA, 10/I, 126, 14. (Not all of Luther's *Works* have been made available in English translation.)

initiative by any cooperation, was said not only by the Reformers but already by the Council of Orange in 529 and then later by Trent in 1547.[28] The true difference arose exclusively over the question what grace is. Is it a work that is distinct from the one who does it, as a medicine is different from the doctor who prescribes it? The impression that this is so is inevitably given by the concept of infused grace—with all the interest that this entails in anthropological processes (habit and act, disposition, works, and merits).[29] Or does grace simply mean the gracious God and his attitude toward us expressed in the Christ event? Can grace be anything other than God's favor toward us? Only then, it seems, can faith cease to understand itself as man's own act (even if this is an act made possible by grace). Only then can it break free from self and creep into Christ, so that its subject becomes a mathematical point.[30]

That this difference arose in the understanding of grace may be due not least to an ontological schema of thought (derived from Aristotle) on the Roman Catholic side and the personalistic character of theological thinking on the Reformation side. If this is so, the observation must surely stimulate thought, and may even be a shattering one, that the autonomy of a certain style of thinking can have such results and cause divergences so great. Yet the opposite question might be asked whether a certain pre-understanding of grace—based on an earlier naivety not yet burdened with reflection—actually *selected* what seemed to be an adequate style of thinking, so that the thought-schema is not the cause of the theological divergence but the effect of a basic decision taken long before. What answer must be given here, and in what direction the movement went, we cannot know in this aeon. But the fact that we have at this point an open question rules out any final division, any one-sided and self-certain judgment on what goes on in and outside the church, any acceptance of supposedly definitive and hardened fronts. It is promising, then, that especially after Vatican II we not only have an atmosphere of ecumenical friendliness (a mere ''be nice to one another'' carries no great commitment!) but we also find real efforts to break through the barrier of thought-schemas and to deal with new questions of theological substance on the basis of the original rock of Scripture.

Fairness also requires us to say that in more recent Roman Catholic theology—not least under the influence of existentialism and historicism—tendencies are plainly visible which would relativize the ontological schema even in venerable texts of the fathers and express the ancient truths in different concepts. With the increasing closeness to the Bible which has contributed to this relativizing the understanding of grace is also dematerialized, or, if one will, ''personalized.'' If I am right, in more recent Roman Catholic literature the ideas of infused grace and automatic sacramental efficacy have been pushed into the background. The result is to give faith a new position as personal commitment. This reorientation does not

---

[28]Denz., 373ff. and 1525; E.T. 176 and 797. For the historical materials cf. ThE, I, §§1084–1174 on ''The Ontology of Grace''; E.T. I, pp. 222ff.

[29]Cf. Thomas, *Summa Theologiae*, Ia, II, q. 110, art. II; cf. also the materials in W. Joest, ''Die katholische Lehre von der Rechtfertigung und von der Gnade,'' *Quellen zur Konfessionskunde*, Heft 2 (1954), pp. 84ff.

[30]ThE, I, §§1148ff.; E.T. I, pp. 242ff.

have to mean a break with tradition but can appeal to tradition and bring to light factors hidden by that schema of thought. Thus the statement of Thomas that the sacrament does not work by being spoken but by being believed (*Summa Theologiae*, III, 60, 7 ad 1) could take on programmatic significance for sacramental teaching and its astonishing parallelism to Luther's understanding could be brought to light (cf. especially Luther's statements in the lectures on Hebrews). Cf. O. H. Pesch, "Besinnung auf die Sakramente," *Freiburger Zeitschrift für Philosophie und Theologie*, I-II (1971). Hans Küng in his early work on *Justification* (New York, 1964) points to analogies on the central issue which are well worth considering.

The battle about the significance of the thought-schemas fluctuates. On the one hand we have the thesis of H. de Lubac, J. Daniélou, and H. Boillard that the ontological terminology of Scholasticism is a hindrance to theological actualization and because of its time-bound nature should be abandoned for modern (existential) expressions. On the other we have the thesis of Pius XII in his encyclical "Humani generis" (1950) that we do not have in Scholasticism a short-lived, time-bound, philosophical system (to which the church should not be tied). We have rather a perennial theology. Some of the terms were used and solemnly confirmed by ecumenical councils. It is wrong, therefore, to deviate from them and move into dogmatic relativism (A. Hartmann, *Bindung und Freiheit des katholischen Denkens* [1952]). On the debate about the schemata cf. W. von Loewenich, *Der moderne Katholizismus vor und nach dem Konzil* (1970), pp. 278ff.; on the Roman Catholic understanding of faith cf. U. Gerber, *Katholischer Glaubensbegriff . . .* (1966); on faith in Tridentine theology cf. W. Joest, *Kerygma und Dogma*, IX (1963), pp. 64f.; W. G. Kümmel, "Der Glaube im NT, seine katholische und reformatorische Deutung," ThBl, X (1937); A. Peters, "Reformatorische Rechtfertigungs-botschaft zwischen tridentischer Rechtfertigungslehre und gegenwärtigem evangelischem Verständnis der Rechtfertigung," *Luther-Jahrbuch* [1964], pp. 77ff., esp. pp. 88ff.).

Nevertheless, especially since Vatican II, a greater freedom in relation to the scholastic tradition is noticeable. The scholastics, including Aquinas, are not just to be recited but to be interpreted. This can be done only with the words of the present age. If we said above that it is uncertain what was the causal direction between thought-schema and material statement, it is palpable that today we can say much more firmly that new material reflection on basic Christian truths is trying to put the schemata of thought in its service instead of being directed by them. To the extent that the sure thread of traditionally established terminology is set aside the danger will undoubtedly arise that Pius XII was already diagnosing as a present disaster—that of assimilation to the age and therefore of real relativism. But this is only a threatened possibility which must be overcome. At any rate there can be no doubt that this reorientation offers significant chances of bringing to light what was hidden and reaching new shores in theological dialogue, e.g., in the understanding of faith and grace.

(2) Faith "Also" Our Work?

Though faith is not to be understood in terms of the habit of him who believes, but relates by origin and intention to the spiritual Word, it can hardly be overlooked that even Luther, in apparent contradiction with his idea of the mathematical point, still sees faith sometimes from the standpoint of a work too. Does this mean that the human subject is smuggled in again by the back door and the significance of the Pneuma as the effective force is reduced? We must pay brief attention to this problem.

The significance of faith as a work occurs in Luther especially when he describes it as a psychological event—we would perhaps say today an experience or an act of decision. In this sphere faith is a work that must be done by man.[31] Luther can even stress the character of faith as a work in opposition to the papists who have made it into a habit. "They have not let faith remain a work but made of it a habit, as they say, though the whole of Scripture gives to nothing but faith the name of a divinely good work."[32] That faith is a fulfilment of the command stamps it as a work, indeed, as the chief work, which is not separate from all other works of virtue.[33]

In such formulations one should remember that Luther is describing faith only from a very restricted angle, though one that is legitimate in this context. He is seeing it as a process which takes place in us, even as a psychological process.[34] Faith naturally has also an emotional and a volitional aspect. It takes place in us.

When we understand faith for a moment as a psychological procedure, we do not come up against its real point, namely, that it is an event caused by the Spirit from outside. On this approach I act like a modern religious psychologist who registers psychological processes and is indifferent to the question whether they are to be explained psychologically or whether they have come into the psyche, and if so, where from? The truth claim of a psychological experience lies outside his sphere of competence.

If we see how partial this work-aspect is, then we shall also understand why Luther, when he calls faith the most excellent and difficult work, adds at once in the same context that it is God's work and not man's. This makes it a special work and sets it apart from other works. For while God does other works with and through us, he does this one work of faith alone in us and without us.[35] If faith is called a work, then, it is so only as something that takes place in us. It is like a trace that does not tell who or what has left it. In particular the psychological act of faith, its character as a work, does not justify and save us (as though it could be a meritorious work). No, it does not justify on its own but only because it accepts the promised mercy. The decisive deliverance takes place from outside, on us and not through us. Not our spirit but the Pneuma does the work.[36]

For this reason we cannot appeal to our faith. Insofar as we view it as a psychological process we cannot trust it. "I do not know *whether* I believe, but I

---

[31]WA, 23, 29.

[32]WA, 6, 206; LW, 44, 25f.

[33]*Loc. cit.* Cf. E. Schott, *Fleisch und Geist* (1928), pp. 44ff.

[34]Schott points out in this connection that living before God always means in fact living before self and others (*Fleisch und Geist,* p. 78).

[35]Cf. *The Babylonian Captivity;* E.T. *Three Treatises* (Philadelphia, 1973), p. 184.

[36]CAApol, IV, 56, 86; Tappert, p. 114. On this whole problem cf. also O. Hof, "Luthers Unterscheidung zwischen dem Glauben und der Reflexion auf den Glauben," *Kerygma und Dogma,* IV (1972).

know in *whom* I believe, and only thus do I know *that* I believe" (P. Althaus). Assurance can come only at the point where in faith we are not alone but creep into Christ and let the Word attested by the Spirit be mighty toward us. Those who believe in their own belief or their own unbelief often think they can see a psychological vacuum and therefore experience sharp "fever-curves" and can find no stable point of certainty. Dostoevski in his *Demons* illustrates this through his unholy and devilish Stavrogin, of whom it is said: "When he believes he does not believe that he believes. And when he does not believe he does not believe that he does not believe."[37] This uncertainty applies even to the faith that comes from grace (in the sense of infused grace). For it is at the mercy of a need for controls in relation to what is imparted by grace. I am freed from this need, however, the moment I no longer have to do with a gift imparted by grace but with the gracious God. For those whom God receives in grace he receives in their totality, since he does not share grace as he shares a gift. Wrath and grace affect the *person*.[38] They affect the whole person, whereas gifts are shared and given to individual members for specific purposes.[39] Certainty is grounded only in the relation of person to person, not of recipient to gift.

This is one of the essential reasons why the Holy Spirit is understood as the third person in the Holy Trinity and not as a mere force (*dynamis*) which enters me and becomes, e.g., the gift of enthusiasm. Even this form of spiritual emotionalism would give rise to the fateful introversion of viewpoint and the demand for controls. (It would lead to a curving in upon myself.) In contrast the personal understanding of the Spirit tells us that faith is thrown back on a Thou that guarantees the promise and does not leave faith resting on what *my* eyes tell it.[40] This is why the Augsburg Confession puts the decisive stress on the resultant negative statement that the Holy Spirit is not a created movement in creatures and is not, therefore, part of *our* spirit or an infused gift.[41]

In conclusion we have to ask why Luther spoke of faith as a work at the risk of obscuring his central thesis as this is expressed in the idea of faith as a mathematical point.

There seem to have been two chief reasons why he felt he had to view faith from these two angles.

First, even though God creates and gives, he does so only in such a way that we are not just passive objects and recipients but are called to be partners in a history with him. We either accept or refuse, and have to make our own decision. From this angle there takes place in the I an event for which we are responsible. In this sense and within these limits faith is a work of entry. This has to be maintained, and it shows how dubious is the use of the subject-object schema in this connection. We are neither mere objects on which God acts—how can objects be held responsible?—nor are we mere subjects of our faith—how could we generate our

---

[37]Cf. W. Rehm, *Experimentum medietatis* (1947), pp. 56ff.

[38]WA, 8, 107, 1; LW, 32, 228.

[39]W. Matthias, "Imputative und sanative Rechtfertigung," *Libertas christiana* (1957), p. 140.

[40]On the personal understanding of the Spirit cf. EG, I, pp. 243, 245; II, p. 198; EF, I, pp. 181f.; II, p. 165.

[41]CA, I, 6; Tappert, p. 28.

own faith? (Cf. G. Wingren, *Die Predigt* [1955], pp. 34f., 142; E.T. *The Living Word*, pp. 27ff., 110f.) Without this glance at the soil of the I, grace and the imparting of the Spirit would simply be the stuffing of an abstract docetic vacuum. The humanity of man would be lost to view.

Second, the two aspects of faith are simply variants on the two ways in which Luther sees man before God in other respects, e.g., as both righteous and sinner at the same time. We cannot develop here the latter formula with its many implications. (On it cf. R. Hermann, *Luthers These "Gerecht und Sünder zugleich"* [1930]; W. Joest, *Gesetz und Freiheit* [1956], pp. 55ff.; H. Iwand, *Rechtfertigungslehre und Christusglaube* [1930], pp. 15ff.) We may simply ask why Luther was not satisfied to affirm that man is extrinsically justified in his relation to God but amplified it and added to it by looking at the empirical I and saying that in fact and intrinsically he is still a sinner (WA, 56, 268; LW, 25, 258). Two approaches may be seen here. They derive from the law and the gospel, neither of which can be abandoned (cf. EG, II, p. 219, esp. pp. 229ff.; EF, II, p. 185, esp. pp. 192ff.). Only as I see myself as I am in the mirror of the law can I measure what happens to me through the justifying acceptance of the sinner. Once the dialectic of law and gospel ceases, it can no longer be made clear that I am taken up into a history of God with us. A static state of qualitative rightness replaces the justified sinner. (Cf. the discussion of Calvin and Barth in ThE, I, §§619, 596; E.T. I, pp. 123ff., 106ff.) Precisely because I know who I am, I can seek the meaning and unity of the new life imparted in justification, not in myself, but solely in God's promise that "just as I am" I am accepted by him. My life as it is has no "positive definition; it merely knows what it is not" (Iwand, *Nachgelassene Werke*, p. 53). But to know this it must see itself in its empirical condition. From that twofold angle we learn to see ourselves before God in perspective, as it were. This is no less true of statements about faith than about justification.

c. The Holy Spirit and the Human Spirit

We recall that in dealing with the relation between the Spirit and faith what kept us in suspense was that from different sides we continually came up against the fact that faith—even though it is an act that takes place in us—is awakened by an event that comes to us from outside us. It is kindled by the Pneuma that opens us to the Word of our liberation, or, conversely, that opens the Word to us. What causes our failure to hear and see is our bondage to an alien spirit (John 14:17; 15:26; esp. 1 John 4:6)—a bondage from which our nature cannot break free, not even by enlightenment.[42] Only the Pneuma of God can defy this alien spirit.

Nevertheless, as we have seen, terms like outside and inside are no more appropriate than passive and active or objective and subjective. In opening us to the Word the Pneuma does not act only from without but appropriates himself to us and in the new creation fashions for us a new identity.

---

[42]With great profundity, G. Wingren discusses this bondage in relation to Christ's resurrection (*Die Predigt*, pp. 34f., esp. p. 159). He adduces 1 Corinthians 15:17: Preaching as Spirit-mediated proclamation is an attack on the prison in which man is shut up. If the living Christ (disclosed in the Spirit) did not reside in the Word it would have no power to open the prison gates. . . . Yet men still sit in prison. In the facticity at issue here the facticity of imprisonment is included.

The same applies to the alien spirit that imprisons us and shuts us up. It is not just something outside that masters us, something merely transsubjective.

Luther dealt vividly with this problem in his work *The Bondage of the Will*. The question arose here whether we can renounce responsibility if an enslaving power seduces our will. How far are we agents of our own will? Luther replies that we cannot separate the alien power from our own identity. We have to identify ourselves with what we do in its name. The necessity to which we surrender is not for Luther a "coactio" that comes upon us from outside but an inner necessity (cf. Goethe's equation of will and necessity in his *Orphische Urworte*).[43] The alien thing can take the form of our own spirit. When the Pneuma takes the scales from the eyes of the obdurate (Isaiah 6:9ff.; Matthew 13:13–15; John 9:39), these cannot say in retrospect that an "it" came upon them and hardened them; they have to say that "they" were hardened. The transsubjective announces itself as our own subjectivity (to claim again the needed help of an inadequate terminology).

Who are the wise of this world, the representatives of the *sophia tou kosmou*, of whom Paul speaks in 1 Corinthians 1:18–30? Who are the Jews who ask for a sign? They are all prisoners caught in their own and another spirit. Bondage to one's own spirit means for the Greeks that they have in their wisdom a scale of values in which it is established in human fashion what is great and small, what is dignified and ridiculous. The divine can be at the head of this scale; it is at any rate on the list of human postulates. It can be the content only of a theology of glory:[44] God has to be the strongest of the strong, the loftiest of the lofty, the wisest of the wise.

Things are the same in principle among the Jews. For them the divine is conceivable only as a manifestation of power—of the supreme power that is expressed in miracles and evident to the eye. This, too, is an only too human postulate even though it is the by-product of a genuine event of revelation that has been perverted merely by a desire for signs (Matthew 12:39; 16:4; Luke 11:29f.).

Both Greeks and Jews, then, are caught in a schema which makes it impossible for them to see God where he really is, i.e., in the passion and cross of his Son. The preaching of the cross necessarily seems foolishness (*moria*). The categories of worldly wisdom rule out any other conclusion. What takes place here on the cognitive level—the unavoidable failure to diagnose what took place at the cross—implies at the same time a negative decision, the hardening of nonhearing and therefore of unwillingness and inability. How could the Jews see the majesty of God in him who could not help himself on the cross (Matthew 27:40, 42) and offered a picture of most ungodlike impotence?

Both Jews and Greeks want to "know" in their own ways. The Greeks want to perceive the divine in what is for them the definite superlative of wisdom.[45] The Jews demand that God open up knowledge to them by giving a visible demonstra-

---

[43]WA, 18, 634f.; LW, 33, 64f. Cf. ThE, I, §1438; E.T. I, p. 297.

[44]In his book *Luthers theologia crucis* W. von Loewenich develops this term especially in relation to the Heidelberg Disputation (E.T. *Luther's Theology of the Cross* [Minneapolis, 1975]).

[45]The early Apologists (Justin Martyr, Tatian) took a momentous step when with a tactical missionary purpose they accepted this and interpreted Christ as the fulfilment of the Greek concept of the logos. Cf. EG, I, pp. 88, 161f.; EF, I, pp. 79, 125f.

tion. Neither can see God in his alien being, in the foolishness of the cross which is a scandal to the wise, in the tormented sufferer who brings to nothing the strong (1 Corinthians 1:27). Because they want to "know," i.e., to lay hold of God as the conclusion of their own premises, the ability to believe is denied them. For faith can only go *against* appearances, *against* the evidence, in the power of a Nevertheless which is the basis of the presuppositions of life and thought. For Christ the claiming of a possibility of moving out of the dimension of faith into that of appearances and evidence could be nothing other than a satanic temptation and the abandonment of his messianic mission (Matthew 4:3–11).

This, then, is to be seen here as the bondage of the eyes, ears, and heart, as imprisonment to an alien spirit. This spirit simply expresses one's own spirit. But because one's own spirit does not control itself, because it cannot transcend itself or leave its own jurisdiction, the figure of binding by an alien spirit is unavoidable, as is also the need to identify oneself with this alien spirit. This means that I cannot possibly understand myself as an innocent victim, as the effect of an alien cause, as an object of violence.[46]

What delivers me from the zone that is occupied by my own and an alien spirit is not argument. For any conceivable argument would be determined by the table of categories which is closed to God's alien being and can find no place for either the impotent or the foolish God. What breaks the bonds of one's own and an alien spirit is simply the counterforce of God's own Spirit.[47]

Since I can know only what is analogous, but God is not analogous to me in virtue of his own alien being and my alienation, he is closed to me. The situation of the Jews and Greeks in 1 Corinthians 1 is simply an example of this. Only God is analogous to himself. Hence there is knowledge of God, as we have said, only as God's own knowledge of himself. Only *his* Spirit searches the depths of God (1 Corinthians 2:10) and knows what no eye has seen nor ear heard neither has it entered the heart of man (2:9). And if the context says that God has prepared these things that are not and cannot be heard and seen "for those who love him," this means that God so discloses himself as to let men share in his own self-knowledge. This, however, can be expressed only pneumatologically: God shares the Spirit in whom he knows himself. He does not heighten our natural knowledge nor extend the table of categories but sets us on another plane, where his Spirit tells us who he is and thus discloses to us what only he knows.

It would be a mistake to think of this form of revelation—for this is the issue— as an act of mere instruction. I can be taught only by way of contact with given presuppositions. Being non-analogous, as we have seen, these presuppositions are unable to grasp what is disclosed concerning the depths of God. For this reason the primary work of the Pneuma here is not to instruct but to change. The Word opened up by the Spirit also does things rather than just imparting. It "makes" the new creature; it "makes" an analogous existence. As we have seen, it is an active Word and not just an interpretative Word.[48] The Spirit of God is creative and

---

[46]It is characteristic that in the Bible satanic power (even in the story of the fall in Genesis 3) is never presented as forcing man, as the cause of evil.

[47]Cf. the chapter on theological epistemology in EF, I, pp. 193ff.

[48]Cf. EF, I, Index: Word of God, active and creative.

brings about change. He builds a bridge over the gulf between God and man, but he does so from God's side. This happens in such a way as to awaken faith.

On the cognitive level faith here means being freed from one's own presuppositions and no longer bound by them. In faith the Spirit is not one who comes but one who breaks in. We are put outside ourselves (which does not have to be understood psychologically as ecstasy). Our "I" becomes "ec-centric." We are delivered up to what happens to us and not to what we are. Yet that which receives "passively"(!) is our new I, our changed identity. I am this I and yet I am not—I live, yet not I—Christ lives in me (Galatians 2:20). The word I begins to flicker on the old table of categories and can no longer hold the new content.

The Pneuma, then, is an entity that our spirit cannot control. It is an object of prayer and expectation. It blows where it wills (John 3:8). It can also withhold itself—just as the faith which it effects is not for everybody (2 Thessalonians 3:2).

d. The Spirit Who Cannot Be Integrated

(1) The Spirit Who "Dwells in Us"
We have now seen what it means that the Spirit in relation to whom we are passive recipients cannot be controlled by us. Among other things this comes to view in the precise formulation of the Augsburg Confession that the Holy Spirit is not a created motion in the heart of the creature. The Word of God imparted by the Pneuma is certainly close to us (*engys:* on our lips and in our hearts) but it is not a part of us. It is not something that becomes spirit of our spirit, that is, as it were, transferred to our possession. The Spirit remains God's Spirit. Indeed, he is God himself. He is God imparting himself to us, entering our heart and understanding and will and action. He opens up himself to us as our Lord.

But what does this "entry" mean? What effect does it have on and in us?

This question is an urgent one in some sections of ecclesiastical and spiritual history. The church's history swarms with fanatics, spiritualists, and enthusiasts. Paul already had to wrestle with them. For all their variety the enduring core in all of them is faith in the immediacy of the reception, guidance, and possession of the Spirit, in the "inner light" as God's own presence in us. There is involved here a tendency not to let the Spirit come to us, or come to us any more, through the Word but to adopt instead a position of independence toward him as bearers of the Spirit.

In seeking historical analogies we need only recall Lessing's view of history. Humanity as a child is taught by the event and word of revelation until its own spirit takes over the leadership and appropriates by the autonomous insight of reason the truth that has hitherto been authoritatively imparted to it. In this eschatological age of fulfilment the Spirit of God seems as it were to be identical with the human spirit, just as we see the absolute spirit and the inner spirit merging according to Hegel's teaching.

In the doctrine of the Spirit of both enthusiasts and the Enlightenment it is not too bold to say that God has relinquished his Spirit to man. By letting his Spirit "enter" man he has treated man as an adult and given him control. As a rule enthusiasts do at least retain some remembrance of the Spirit's origin, whereas Enlightenment thinkers and the philosophers of identity strive after the complete emancipation of their own spirituality.

These historical observations force us to study the anthropological side of the impartation of the Spirit more closely. What does it mean that God binds himself to us by the Pneuma, that he grants the Pneuma to us and even causes those who are thus blessed to be "full" of the Holy Spirit[49] as one can also be full of cunning, roguery, envy, and anger (Acts 13:10, 45; 19:28)? What is to restrain us here from speaking of an integration of the Holy Spirit into our nature?

In reply to this question we had best begin with sayings which most seem to suggest such an integration. We remember what Paul says about the Spirit dwelling in you.[50] This sounds like an appropriation in which the Pneuma becomes ours. Even in its formulation is not this indwelling of the Spirit analogous to the indwelling of sin in me (Romans 7:17)?[51] Here sin wrests control of my acts from my will (Romans 7:19) and makes my will do what I do not will to do, so that for a moment it appears as an alien and binding power—so much so that I can differentiate it from my identity: It is not I who act here but sin dwelling in me (and possessing me) (7:17). But this differentiation is only for a moment. Only temporarily can sin have the form of an alien law in my members (7:23). The next moment Paul must take it back into his I and identify himself with it: "Wretched man that I am! Who will deliver me from this body of death?" (7:24). Since the statements are so closely parallel, why should the indwelling of the Spirit be any different? Does there not have to be an analogous identification, so that I have to say of the indwelling Spirit that it is now "my" spirit, that "I" am the bearer of the spirit?[52]

The decisive difference between the indwelling of the Spirit and that of sin is undoubtedly that sin enslaves me so that I am compelled to do what I do not will, whereas the Spirit of God does not compel me but frees me. He is not the Spirit of bondage but the Spirit of him who adopts us as sons (Romans 8:15) so that we may cry to him: "Abba, Father." Where the Spirit of the Lord is, there is liberty (2 Corinthians 3:17).

We still have the freedom, of course, to lose this freedom. We can miss it by not entering into it, by living contrary to the Spirit and not mortifying the things of the flesh as the impartation of the Spirit entails (Romans 8:13b). Thus we may "quench" the Spirit (1 Thessalonians 5:19). We may bar its path, blocking it with obstacles.[53] We entangle ourselves in a self-contradiction that is hostile to the Spirit when we think we know God but do not keep his commandments, when we think we are in the light but in fact we are living in the darkness of hate (1 John 2:4, 9). Yet even though we may again fall victim to contrary forces, as those

---

[49]Cf. esp. Acts 2:4, 31; 6:3, 5; 7:55; 11:24; 13:9, 52. Cf. also what is said about the fulness of the Godhead (and therefore of the Spirit) in relation to Christ in the *plērōma*-sayings of Colossians 1:19 and 2:9.

[50]Cf. Romans 8:9, 11, where there are three references to the *oikein* or *enoikein* of the Pneuma; cf. also 2 Timothy 1:14.

[51]Cf. EG, II, pp. 106f.; EF, II, pp. 88f. and also the discussion of different interpretations of Romans 7 in EG, II, pp. 284ff.; EF, II, pp. 234ff.

[52]On this question cf. also E. Käsemann, *An die Römer* (1973), pp. 213ff.; E.T. *Commentary on Romans* (Grand Rapids, 1980), pp. 223ff.; E. Gaugler, *Der Brief an die Römer* (1945), pp. 273ff. Cf. also EG, II, pp. 245ff.; EF, II, pp. 204ff.

[53]Cf. the discussion of *prohibitiva* and *impedimenta* (Ephesians 5:5 and 1 Corinthians 6:9ff.) in ThE, I, §§333ff.; E.T. I, pp. 87f.

whom the Pneuma has opened to himself we now have the freedom to do what we will.

That we now act, not by a new compulsion, but in freedom, is shown by the fact that the impartation of the Spirit always goes hand in hand with a call to responsibility. Not only in Romans 8:13 but in many other Pauline passages the indicative of what the Spirit has imparted to us is linked with imperatives: You have risen with Christ, therefore seek what is above. You have died with Christ, therefore mortify your members (Colossians 3:1-5). Become willingly what you are, live out what has been made yours. One might venture to say, then, that the Spirit makes us so free that he paradoxically makes us free in relation to himself, that he for his part exposes himself to the risk of this freedom. We can block him and reject his indwelling by resisting its implications and scorning its imperatives, i.e., by accepting other ties (such as idolatry or *porneia*) against which these seek to warn us. When we consider this ventured formulation that the Spirit gives us freedom even against himself, it is obvious that we are not happy owners who can identify ourselves with the Spirit and count upon it that he will automatically impel us toward what is posited in a new entelechy.[54]

If, then, the indwelling of the Spirit cannot mean that the Spirit becomes an immanent possession or even a quality, it can signify only a new and radical occupation,[55] a standing under the present Lord. The change of existence that the Spirit effects is based on the change of aeons.[56] We have a part in the new aeon that has dawned in Christ, and in the Spirit we have the first instalment of what will finally be given us in fulness (Romans 8:23; 2 Corinthians 1:22; Ephesians 1:14).

How little we can speak here of an enthusiastic immanentizing of the Spirit is especially clear when we consider that not only is the Spirit in *us* but we are also in the *Spirit* (*en pneumati*, Romans 8:9-11). Here the same dialectic is at work as in the double statement "I in Christ" and "Christ in me." That the Holy Spirit lodges in us, as the Pentecost hymn of Michael Schirmer puts it, is only half the truth. Innumerable biblical examples from the prophetic and NT periods, and especially the story of Pentecost in Acts 2:1ff., make it plain that the reverse movement corresponds to this lodging of the Spirit. The Holy Spirit "snatches us out of ourselves, out of our nature . . . and puts us outside our own being. He is the power of God coming upon us and changing us and sometimes changing the world through us."[57]

In contrast to the possession of the Spirit claimed by the enthusiasts we do not possess the heavenly but Christ possesses us.[58] Rather, our natural I is regarded as

---

[54]It is a mistake to take the "led by the Spirit" of Romans 8:14 (*agesthai*) to imply automatic impulsion. Käsemann (*An die Römer*, p. 216; E.T. p. 226) is right here when he says that Paul is here using enthusiastic terminology quite uninhibitedly and not uneasily as some of his expositors suppose on the ground that he took seriously the "Christ in us" of Galatians 2:20 and regarded the Spirit as an alien power. Paul took the "outside us" of grace very seriously and this corrective, which we shall have to discuss later, must always be kept in mind if we are to interpret the "led by the Spirit" aright.

[55]*Ibid.*, p. 213; E.T. p. 223.

[56]*Ibid.*, p. 214; E.T. p. 244.

[57]E. Heimann, *Theologie der Geschichte* (1966), p. 113; cf. pp. 109ff.

[58]Cf. Käsemann, p. 214; E.T. p. 224. If this is not seen, the one-sided understanding of the "Spirit in me" can lead to a theology of consciousness and self-understanding as well as to enthusiasm.

sōma, as a body that is indeed ordained for death (Romans 6:6; 7:24). What is meant, as in baptism, is the death of the body of sin, which as "flesh" is opposed to life in the Spirit. We are still in this carnal existence (*en sarki*) but we do not live according to it (*kata sarka*). Though still living a carnal existence in the old aeon, we are already through the Spirit citizens of the new and dawning world. To be in the Spirit, to be caught up into the Spirit, is to have a part in this new being, to stand under the lordship of God and no longer under the dictatorship of the "flesh." It is also to be put by the Spirit in permanent opposition to the restoration of this dictatorship (Galatians 3:1-3).[59] The "at one and the same time" (*simul*) which characterizes us as sinners and righteous applies also to our being in the flesh and our being in the Spirit (Romans 8:7ff.). The Holy Spirit does not create us out of nothing. He is not here the power of God that makes creation out of nothing. He is God's "generative power in created man."[60] He gives birth to the new creature within the old.

We thus have two thoughts. First, the Spirit takes us up into himself and orders us to his sphere of lordship. Second, we take part in this as those who still walk in the Adamic world and are citizens of the old aeon but who already have in the Spirit the pledge of the coming aeon. These two thoughts represent the sharp break between Paul's doctrine of the indwelling of the Spirit and the enthusiasts' doctrine of the possession of the Spirit. As God does not become identical with us, but even as Emmanuel, as the one who turns to us, still remains different from us, so the Spirit of God is the power of an "outside us" that calls and enlightens us, but even in enlightening us never becomes an inner light establishing itself within us and enforcing our emancipation.

(2) The Christological Link of the Spirit

The christological link between pneumatology and Christology is brought out *even* more sharply by this staying of the Spirit outside us. What we have in view is not just that the Pneuma is also the Spirit of Christ (Romans 8:9; 2 Corinthians 3:12)[61] but also the dialectic already mentioned, namely, that Christ is "in us" (Galatians 2:20; Romans 8:10) and we are also "in Christ." Though Christ as a personal figure would seem to be guaranteed in advance against non-identification with me (whereas the Spirit, understood as power, can be more easily integrated), neverthe-less, in the case of Christ too, the misunderstanding of a mystical union has constantly arisen in relation to both sides of the dialectic.

This mystical interpretation of the "in Christ" was developed in A. Deissmann's first work *Die neutestamentliche Formel "in Christo Jesu"* (1892), and it gave rise to a debate that continues today (T. Schmidt, *Der Leib Christi* [1919]; H. E. Weber, "Die Formel 'in Christo Jesu' und die paulinische Chris-

---

Thus G. Bornkamm ("Mythos und Evangelium," ThEx, n.s. 25) refers to Paul's decisive concern to proclaim a new history and existence in which I am taken up into Christ's history. It is not just a matter of the receiving of Christ into my self-understanding, of the Spirit in me, but also of my being planted in Christ's history. Without this theology will suffer from anthropological constriction as, e.g., in Bultmann.

[59]The correlation of indicative and imperative is a symptom of this.

[60]Heimann, *Theologie der Geschichte,* p. 112.

[61]In the history of dogma this link has been considered in relation to the *filioque;* cf. EG, II, esp. pp. 217f., 367f.; EF, II, pp. 182f., 298f.

tusmystik,'' *Neue kirchliche Zeitschrift,* 5th ed. [1920]; W. Weber, *Christusmystik. Eine religions-psychologische Darstellung der paulinischen Christusfrömmigkeit* [1924]; H. Conzelmann, *Grundriss der Theologie des NT* [1967], p. 233; E.T. *An Outline of the Theology of the NT* [New York, 1969], p. 210). He reached the conclusion that the expressions ''in the flesh'' and ''in Christ'' (Romans 9:1; Ephesians 2:22) are in contrast to each other. On the basis of 2 Corinthians 3:17 (''the Lord the Spirit'') he thus believed that ''in Christ'' signifies a local presence in the pneumatic Christ. As we live in the atmosphere, so Paul lives in the all-ensouling element of the Spirit and in God (W. Weber, *Christusmystik,* p. 53). There thus arises a mystical union with Christ or, as we would now say, an integration into the pneumatic Christ. The reciprocity of ''I in Christ'' and ''Christ in me'' is implicit in this understanding of the union.

In contrast to Deissmann's mystical union his followers brought about a radical change by a particular nuance. Thus Traugott Schmidt[62] emphasizes that ''in Christ'' cannot signify ''resting in'' but being impelled by his power. H. E. Weber goes further and in spite of the mystical components says that ''in Christ'' implies standing in his service and power.

This represents a decisive breakthrough inasmuch as Christ is seen here in his saving work upon us in the history which he traverses with us, in short, in his benefits (as Melanchthon put it). In particular such sayings as that we are justified in Christ (Galatians 2:17) show that in the Spirit we expect by faith the fulfilment of our hope of righteousness and *to that extent* are in Christ (Galatians 5:5f.). As the Spirit of the Lord works faith in us, we are incorporated into the history of his saving work and it can be mighty in us. Thus the saying: ''To know Christ is to know his benefits,'' could also be put as follows: ''To be in Christ is to be open to his work and presence in the Spirit.''

Thus Conzelmann has rightly noted that the ''*en* Christo'' becomes instrumental and takes on the force of a *dia* (through). In him love (*charis*) is given (1 Corinthians 1:4). In him the world is reconciled (2 Corinthians 5:19). In him we are pardoned (Galatians 2:17). All these things might indeed be said to have taken place ''through'' him,[63] and when we put it that way the transsubjective element in what takes place in Christ and the saving event fully accomplished on our behalf is brought out in a particularly vivid way. Recognition that the ''in'' and ''through'' are interchangeable here can be an antidote to the interpretation in terms of mystical union.

In the light of the salvation history which is fulfilled in us and takes us up into itself, the ''in Christ'' has, then, the significance that salvation has taken place there in him and not in me and for that reason it is true for me. Christ is God's instrument. God's love is displayed in him (Romans 8:9). We are called in him (Philippians 3:14). God says Yes in him (2 Corinthians 1:19f.). We have freedom in him (Galatians 2:4). We are sanctified in him (1 Corinthians 1:2).[64] As in faith I enter into what has taken place for me, I am taken out of myself. My I is no longer determined by what I see and feel of it, by its empirical identity, but by the fact

---

[62]*Der Leib Christi,* p. 88.
[63]Conzelmann, *Grundriss,* p. 234; E.T. *Outline,* p. 210.
[64]*Loc. cit.* (p. 211).

that I am the earthen vessel of this saving event (2 Corinthians 4:7), that I am "in Christ," and that he to that degree is also in me and at work in me. Thus it is no longer I that live, but Christ that lives in me (Galatians 2:20).

The twofold formula "Christ in me and I in Christ"[65] also describes the work of the Spirit, although in other words. It expresses as precisely as does Pneuma the way in which the saving event makes contact with us, the way in which we are incorporated into it and let it appropriate us. This can happen only as the Spirit helps our weakness (Romans 8:26), working, as it were, at our side and opening us up where we are closed (1 Corinthians 2:9). The same thing (really the same!) can be stated christologically by saying that Christ works in us, that he represents us—which can again be said of both Christ and the Spirit (Romans 8:26, 34).

To be noted especially here—and it perhaps contains the strongest opposition to the idea of mystical integration in relation to Christ and also the Spirit—is the role that is assigned to *faith* in all this.[66] To overlook the reference to faith is to disregard the Pneuma's christological link and thus to rob pneumatology of its point. If Christ lives in me, then, as Galatians 2:20 shows, I live "by faith in the Son of God" (cf. also Galatians 5:5f.). Faith, however, always stands opposed to the immediacy of sight and possession. It is the basis (*hypostasis*) of what one hopes for, the demonstration (*elenchos*) of things one cannot see (Hebrews 11:1). Faith believes against appearances and against what is directly visible. It calls from the depths, whereas God is on high (Psalm 130:1). As the faith given by the Spirit means the commitment of trust, as it is this faith that receives God's justification and his promise: "You are mine," faith still expresses distance and non-possession. And if the "in Christ" is related to faith, there is in it an indication that we now have Christ in the brokenness of our carnal existence, that we have him only and for the first time in this aeon, whereas it is said of *him* that he dwells in inaccessible light and no man has seen him or can see him (1 Timothy 6:16). Our darkness separates us from his light, and in this darkness we *believe*.

Thus faith is our comfort and hope. It lives by the Nevertheless which causes it to overcome the alienation and distance. We are comforted by it because we know that so long as our home is the body we live in a foreign land far from the Lord—for we walk by faith and not by sight—but we are of good courage and cling rather to the fact that our body is the foreign land and we dwell at home with the Lord (2 Corinthians 5:6-8). And we hope because this aeon with its separation is coming to its close, because being far from the Lord will have an end and will be terminated at his Parousia by eternal union with him. Even faith will cease one day when the brokenness of our being, of which it is a part, will be ended. The eschaton gives that "face to face" quality, that directness of fellowship and vision, in which love alone still abides (1 Corinthians 13:12f.).

We can express as follows the decisive point on which everything hinges. Just as Christ is and remains over against us, so does the Spirit, his Spirit. We stand toward both in the nearness and distance, the already and the not yet, of faith. If we are "in Christ" and he "in us," there still stands between us the "infinite

---

[65] As Lohmeyer rightly points out (*Grundlagen der paulinischen Theologie* [1929], p. 140), it never occurs in Paul in this direct combination, which would formally demand mysticism.
[66] *Ibid.*, pp. 139ff.

qualitative difference'' between the first Adam and the last, between the living soul and the life-giving Spirit, between him who is made and him who makes (1 Corinthians 15:45–49).

(3) The Spirit as Act-Word

That the Spirit is God's sovereign action which can never be transformed into our autonomy may also be seen plainly from the Johannine promises of the Paraclete. the Spirit-filled Word in which the exalted Christ will remain present among us is an *act*-word since it opens up to us possibilities that are not open to our natural existence. More pointedly one might even say that it snatches us out of the ''impossibility'' of this natural existence. The Paraclete is the Spirit of truth whom the world not only cannot give but cannot even *receive* of itself (John 14:17). For the world neither sees him nor knows him. He has to act to free us from our deafness and blindness. He not only has the hermeneutical function of elucidating and expounding the Christ event for us. He also performs the miracle of changing our existence from the old creature to the new. He puts us for the first time in the situation in which elucidation and exposition are possible. From this standpoint theological reflection, too, is a later possibility which needs the faith that is already imparted and has been effected in a miracle.

Thus the Spirit of truth is not just a teaching Spirit. For untruth is not just an intellectual error from which I can be freed by enlightenment and instruction. In both truth and untruth the real issue is my alienated life-situation, my existence in untruth. Because this existence is perverted and without analogy to God, we cannot hear the voice of truth. Conversely, only he who is ''of the truth'' hears this voice (John 18:37). Thus the Spirit does not teach us about the truth. He actively ''translates'' us into the new existence. He takes us out of perversion and untruth (John 15:26). In this way he transcends the possibility of the natural man and causes him to be ''outside himself.''

He may be seen as an act-word of this kind when he is manifest as the name and power in and by which a lame man is made to walk and witness is thus borne to both the name and the power (Acts 4:7f., 31). Again, when the Kyrios opens the heart of Lydia (Acts 16:14), this, too, is the work of the Pneuma, not *although* but just *because* the Kyrios himself is at work. The Spirit gives to the Word fulfilled by him more than the character of impartation. He makes it an efficacious Word which has the power of binding and loosing (John 20:22f.; 1 Corinthians 5:4f.). The power is the same as that which the Kyrios displayed as the bearer of the Spirit when he freed men from demonic bondage (Luke 4:36).

In the name of the risen Lord who breathed on them and imparted to them the Holy Spirit,[67] the disciples for their part exercise the power of binding and loosing. Through them, whom he claims as his instruments and channels, the Spirit effects something which no one can give himself. In this power to speak an efficacious

---

[67]Except in later confessions of Christ in which the community projected back the pentecostal Spirit-event to the pre-Easter Christ, there is little reference to the Spirit in connection with the earthly work of Jesus. F. Hahn finds in this a hint as to the interpretation of the puzzling saying about the unforgivable sin against the Holy Spirit: ''Sins from the pre-Easter period can be forgiven, . . . but sins against the revelation of the Spirit after Easter cannot be forgiven, i.e., salvation or perdition is decided in relation to the Spirit's work'' (in MD, V, p. 91).

Word the Pneuma's christological link may again be seen, and this in several respects.

First, the background of this story about the impartation of the Spirit is the fact that Jesus himself is the unique bearer of the Spirit. In relation to his baptism it is said that the Holy Spirit descended like a dove upon him and God confessed him as his Son.[68] In the different depictions of this event in the four gospels there is one common element, namely, the equipment of Jesus with the Spirit of God in accordance with messianic expectation.

Again, this gift of the Spirit at baptism is alluded to when Jesus later speaks at Nazareth and relates the saying about the Spirit in Isaiah 61:1 programmatically to his own mission, seeing it fulfilled in himself: "The Spirit of the Lord is upon me, because he has anointed me to preach good news to the poor, he has sent me to proclaim release to the captives and recovering of sight to the blind, to set at liberty those who are oppressed, to proclaim the acceptable year of the Lord" (Luke 4:18f.).[69] Here, too, the Pneuma is understood as the power which is the source of the authority to work the miracle of liberation and release, and therefore the basis of the act-word.

Finally, the link between the Christ-Spirit and the authoritative Word of the Kyrios as the primitive community saw it may be seen in the characteristic modification of a saying of Jesus. According to the older description of the authority to cast out demons which announces the dawn of God's kingdom, Christ broke the grip of demons "by the finger of God" (Luke 11:20). The saying about the finger of God evokes associations with Exodus 8:15, where Moses forces the Egyptian magicians whom he is combating to acknowledge that "this is the finger of God" that is superior to all the power of magic and darkness. There is also an echo here of the common OT image of the "hand of God" which directs and upholds all earthly activity. But later this saying about the finger of God is significantly changed into a reference to the Spirit of God through whom and by whom Jesus casts out demons (Matthew 12:28). The presence of the Spirit is, then, the presence of God himself who is in action here, who works in his Son, and who gives him a share in his divine sovereignty.

The Spirit of God who does not work within our possibilities but transcends them achieves his ultimate manifestation in the overcoming of death. This comes out vividly when we contrast what is said on the theme with what Plato says about immortality (*athanasia*).[70] For Plato immortality is a possibility posited in our psyche. We forfeit it but we can also claim it. For Paul, however, our life leads to death and our end in death can be overcome only by a Spirit-event which comes upon us and is outside our own control. The Spirit that raised Christ from the dead and has taken up his dwelling in us will also give life to our mortal bodies (Romans 8:11; 1 Corinthians 6:14; 2 Corinthians 4:14).[71] The history into which

---

[68] Luke 3:22, with a clear allusion to Psalm 2:7. There is a different nuance in Mark 1:11.

[69] Cf. as a supplement the message to John in prison in which his disciples are to tell him what they have seen and heard of the works of Jesus (Luke 7:22).

[70] Cf. the author's book *Tod und Leben* (Geneva, 1943; Tübingen, 1946).

[71] On the Spirit and the overcoming of death cf. E. Sjöberg and E. Schweizer, art. "Pneuma," TDNT, VI, pp. 377,33f.; 379,13; 389,20; TWNT, VI, pp. 376,1; 377,27; 387,31.

God has entered with us and we are incorporated by the Pneuma can as little come to an end as God himself can. We remain united to the last Adam as a life-giving Spirit (1 Corinthians 15:45). What is sown in corruption, dishonor, and weakness (15:42f.) does not engage in natural organic growth and finally bring forth the fruit of immortality. No, the producing of this fruit is not in "the power of our nature" (the *psychē zōsa*, 15:45) but is a miracle of the Spirit who raises up the pneumatic body (15:44, 46).

It is true once again, then, that the Spirit takes us out of a carnal psychic existence and sets us in the saving event in which death is a vanquished force that has been reduced to impotence. The christological determination of the Spirit may be seen here once more.

The point at issue is not a mystical union with Christ but incorporation into the saving event represented by him. The life-giving Spirit of the second Adam who remains faithful to us even to the overcoming of death and the resurrection world of the eschaton is no other than the Spirit in whom the exalted Christ is already present as the Paraclete, making us sure of his presence and leading us into all truth (John 16:13). And no matter what he may disclose to us or to what shores he might lead us, "he will take what is mine [Christ's]" (16:14) and "bear witness to me" (15:26). The Spirit will not lead us beyond what Christ has said in his Word and done in his work. He will not lead us to unknown shores. He will lead us into that Word and open up its depths to us. We will know what is familiar in a new form. The moment of faith and the moment of sight will thus be blended into a continuum which will open us to the same event in which salvation already meets us *now,* the blind are already made to see and the deaf to hear *now,* and the Word spoken to the men of the New Testament is fulfilled in us. Those with whom God has begun to speak, whether in wrath or grace, are truly immortal. The person of God who speaks and the Word of God show that we are creatures with whom God will speak forever and immortally, says Luther in his Genesis Commentary,[72] and in so doing he shows that it is the event that comes to us in the Word and Spirit from which we shall never be released and which even death itself cannot interrupt.

(4) The Hiddenness of the Holy Spirit

As the Pneuma thus makes us contemporary with the death and resurrection of Christ, causing us to participate in them as those who also die and rise again (Colossians 3:1ff.), we are conformed to the one who is hidden. The glory of God is concealed under its opposite in the form of a servant (*sub contrario absconditus*). Even the resurrection of Christ does not take place in full demonstration before the eyes of all but is certain only to faith.[73] The Spirit blows only where he wills (John 3:8) and has therefore the hiddenness of something incalculable which does not conform to our criteria of fair distribution. The blowing of the Spirit, however, is surpassed by the hiddenness of Christ. As in his two natures the human nature cannot be isolated and shown in its union with the divine,[74] so we

---

[72]WA, 43, 481 (LW, 5, 75f.). We shall discuss this statement more fully when we come to eschatology.

[73]EG, II, pp. 533ff.; EF, II, pp. 431ff.

[74]It is against speculations of this kind that Melanchthon directs the christological statement in the 1521 *Loci* which we have already quoted.

are not granted the possibility of defining the manner of the coming together of our nature and the Pneuma or of relating the two to one another in a kind of synthesis.

For this reason—that of this hiddenness—there is also no experience of the Spirit in the sense that we can diagnose the work of the Spirit in ourselves or others as a plain and demonstrable event and then base the certainty of our acceptance on this manifest and unequivocal experience and unequivocal symptom.[75] Just as we cannot believe in our faith but only "creep into Christ" with it and commit ourselves to the "outside us" (as in Luther's idea of the mathematical point), so we are prevented from believing in our Spirit-effected "inner life" and making it the basis of our certainty. Our psychic man is dead and our life—our Spirit-effected life—is hidden with Christ in God (Colossians 3:3). For this reason even the Spirit "in us" cannot bring about an introversion of view. He is simply the bridgehead which God's saving event has set up on the territory of the I in order to be able to take us into itself and thus cause us to be "outside ourselves."

This throws light on Romans 8:16, which says that God's Spirit bears witness with our spirit that we are God's children. Is our spirit here the "inner life identical with reason," so that what is at issue is the moment of dialogue between the Pneuma and our psychic I? According to the fairly unanimous view of New Testament scholars (apart from Käsemann, *An die Römer,* p. 218; E.T. p. 228), this is how we are to take it. Our gaze is thus directed to the correspondence which, as we have seen, is denied us as an object of experience.

Now Pneuma can indeed be taken in an anthropological sense in some passages. As examples we may refer to the clear sayings in 1 Corinthians 2:11; 16:18; 2 Corinthians 2:13; 7:13. Here, as Bultmann thinks, the term "pneuma" might be replaced by "I" (*Theologie des NT* [1953], pp. 202ff.; E.T. I, pp. 205ff.). In other places, however, one has to consider whether the pneumatic I might not be meant, e.g., in 1 Thessalonians 5:23; Philippians 1:27; Romans 8:16, etc. If so, we have to do with the Pneuma that works through us when there is reference to the Spirit-effected community and the communion of the saints is called the temple of God (e.g., Ephesians 2:22). In Romans 8, however, the Spirit who continually works on and through us is understood as God's Spirit and it is hard to see why the foreign body of a different, anthropologically understood pneuma should suddenly be introduced. I am thus inclined to think that Käsemann is right (p. 218; E.T. p. 228) when he takes the passage to mean that the Spirit who expresses himself liturgically bears witness to what the Spirit who dwells in us must acknowledge. In the metaphor that we are using this would mean that the liturgical Word lays claim to the bridgehead which the Spirit holds on the territory of our I.

The question of our true I and therefore of our identity has been wrongly put for a long time as though it were a question of our empirical I and its logical lines of connection with the possible work of the Spirit. This I, which is the normative theme of modern ideologies,[76] cannot possibly be the object of the question in Paul's pneumatology. It is relevant here only as the battleground of the Spirit of God and the alien spirit to which we are in bondage. Our true identity is the new creature which is the work of the Pneuma. "The justified does not seek the point

---

[75]Cf. G. Ebeling, "Die Klage über das Erfahrungsdefizit in der Theologie als Frage nach ihrer Sache," *Wort und Glaube,* III (1975), pp. 3ff., 186ff., 414ff., 567ff.

[76]Cf. Anthrop., *passim.*

and unity of his new life in himself but in the truthfulness of God who gives the promises. . . . Such a life has no positive definition [and for this reason already it cannot be a theme of its own: Author]; it simply knows what it is not.''[77] If we have to say, then, that the identity understood in this way is ''ec-centric'' and the exact opposite of an entelechy with its own center, it is also right for us to confess that the Spirit who works in this way brings man to *himself* by putting us in the ''outside us,'' that he draws out from him the true and buried original, that he does not make him someone else but makes him his true *self*.[78] For the old man is the alienated man, not the true man, whereas the spirit who is opened up by the Spirit and set in the saving event is the true man whom God had in mind and who is analogous to his plan at creation.

e. The Error of Osiander

(1) The ''Substantial'' Misunderstanding of the Holy Spirit
We will first summarize the previous findings upon which we now build. The heart of our pneumatological deliberations thus far, to which we were led from different angles, is the fact that the Holy Spirit cannot be ''integrated,'' as we have put it. The Pneuma as God's Spirit—God the Holy Spirit—is always the one who works on us. He never becomes an enacted quality which can be established as such. He never becomes a habitual form of holiness. Faith as the chief work of the Spirit-filled Word has paradigmatic significance in this regard inasmuch as it cannot be seen as the state of belief (credulity), or as a psychological habit, and cannot therefore be made the basis of salvation and assurance of salvation. Faith finds its essence in him in whom it believes and it is thus outward-directed. It exists in the ''outside itself.'' Understood thus, faith is neither a point nor does it automatically extend itself as a state of the soul. The correlation of indicative and imperative makes this plain. The Word imparted by the Holy Spirit claims us. It makes us responsible. It calls upon us to be what we are. There is also, as we have seen, a form of refusal, of non-entry, which can block the Spirit and cause what is grasped in faith to vanish again. There is, we might say, a degree of incongruence between what we are promised by the Spirit and what we actually are and how we actually behave. This is equivalent to the annulling of what is proffered and what is received in faith. To come to the altar in faith, but not to cleanse the disrupted relation to one's neighbor, is to renounce what is affirmed in faith (Matthew 5:23). To come to the Lord's table but to eat also at the table of idols, or to be a member of Christ's body and also to be the member of a harlot, is to be a slave to hypocrisy as an objective self-contradiction and to place oneself under a lordship which means separation from the Lord who is grasped in faith (1 Corinthians 8:1ff.; 6:16). To use the freedom of faith to give access to sin is to deny the Lord in whom one believes (or thinks one believes!). It is to miss the point that freedom exists only in commitment to the Lord who grants it. ''Do you not know that if you yield yourselves to any one as obedient slaves, you are slaves of that one?''; you cannot carry water on both shoulders. Freedom is the opposite of indifference (Romans 6:1ff., 15f.). Christ has no dealings with Belial.

---

[77]Iwand, *Rechtfertigungslehre und Christusglaube* (1930), p. 53.
[78]Cf. R. Luther, *Neutestamentliches Wörterbuch* (1932ff.), p. 89.

These forms of failure, which break again the union with God that is so close in faith, make it clear that the Holy Spirit is not a force (*dynamis*) that flows into me and establishes itself within as a habit of holiness, but that he is always a challenge and a claim, just as we are always the battleground between God's Spirit and the alien spirits that claim us for their lordship.

Now it is understandable that the resolute exclusiveness of the Reformation "by faith alone" should continually call attention to the incongruence mentioned above, to the discrepancy between the righteousness before God which is grasped in faith and the concrete state of unrighteousness in which we actually find ourselves. The extremely forensic doctrine of justification championed by Melanchthon necessarily arouses critical suspicion. All honor to Luther's "righteous and sinner at the same time"—but could it not be made a "pretext for evil" (1 Peter 2:16) just as the enthusiasts rebuked by Paul do with freedom? Could not the "sinner" side of it, as an unhappy infection of our Adamic existence (or even as the flowering of sin that it is to be enjoyed in part), offer free scope and open the door to an unrestricted laissez-faire?

We believe we have shown that there are no signs of this implication in Luther (or Calvin). Luther indeed exerted himself to protect the "by faith alone" against all kinds of libertinistic errors.[79] It is legitimate, and one of its valid implications, that a doctrine of justification which represents an alien righteousness, a righteousness of promise, should always raise the question of one's own state, of the way in which I either actually enter into the promise or sabotage it by what I really am and continue to be.

But this raises again the pneumatological question, this time with the nuance of how we are to think of the appropriation of God's righteousness as this is effected by the Spirit. Even if there is no doubt that the Spirit is the efficacious appropriating power, the question still arises whether that which works is not to be thought of also in terms of its work (or result), whether that which appropriates is not also to be thought of in terms of its appropriation. To put it metaphorically, what is the outcome of the battle between the Spirit of God and alien spirits?

This question is the central one for the controversial Reformation theologian Andreas Osiander (b. 1498), who is worth considering as an example.[80] Osiander is important because he saw himself as standing on the soil of Luther's theology and as its true interpreter. From this it may be seen at once that the question of the congruence or incongruence between the righteousness of faith and that of life is a problem immanent in the very principle of "by faith alone" and that it cannot be brushed aside merely by referring to the "righteous and sinner at one and the same time." If, as we have done, we understand the Spirit as act-word, as a creative power of change and liberation, then the question of the effect and verifiability of the Spirit-event arises of itself.

In Osiander this question does not occur expressly in pneumatology. For him it is more a question how far Christ takes up an essential dwelling in us by faith. It is

---

[79]Cf. as an example Luther's controversy with the Antinomians (ThE, I, §§624ff.; E.T. I, pp. 126ff.).
[80]For his most important writings cf. W. Möller, *Andreas Osianders Leben und ausgewählte Schriften* (Elberfeld, 1870). The best account is that of E. Hirsch, *Die Theologie des Andreas Osiander und ihre geschichtliche Voraussetzungen* (1919). On the ethical aspect of his theology cf. ThE, I, §§483ff.; E.T. I, pp. 82f.

obvious, however, that when the question is put in that way the problem of the Pneuma is implicitly posed. Osiander's Christology, even though it speaks of the effects of salvation, really lies even terminologically, by the use of such words as vivification, illumination, sanctification, and holiness, in the sphere of the third article of the creed.

This may be seen already in the introduction to his great work on justification.[81] His center of interest lies in the presentation (making present) of the salvation event and therefore in the core problem of pneumatology. He says at the outset that the decisive acts of the salvation event are separated in time by 1500 years. The first act took place between A.D. 1 and 30 in the Mediator's dealing with God; this is the act of redemption. He calls the second act the business of justification and regards it as a present event. It denotes the way in which the past event of salvation (Christ's life and work) becomes a force in me today and takes effect here and now. At issue, then, is the traditional question of the function of the Spirit which Osiander takes up explicitly in his *Guter Unterricht* . . . (1524) when he states that only works which the Holy Spirit works in us will stand in God's judgment.

Not what was *once* done by Christ brings us deliverance but what is done for us *today,* his act *made present,* saves us. The presentation is identical with a concrete and essential change. "When life is in the Word and the Word is in us, then life is in us and we live through this life."[82] By the mediation of this life-containing Word, and therefore of the Spirit, there comes about a real dwelling (Christ's dwelling) in us. Faith is the way in which we open the door of our heart to this indwelling.

The special accent that Osiander gives to this "Christ in us" (and that undoubtedly modifies Paul's similar formulations) lies in the directing of attention to the quality of the new being which is determined by the indwelling. Osiander finds in the indwelling of Christ in the believer the beginning already of the making righteous. To put it in our own terms, the Spirit as act-word brings about here and now the actual righteousness of our new being. The Christ who indwells us is our redemption to the extent that he daily kills off more and more of the sin that remains in us in spite of our justification, replacing it by vivification and illumination, and finally leading us in spotless purity through death to the resurrection.

In these statements one may plainly see a protest against Melanchthon's theory of imputation. According to Osiander this theory omits a decisive element. It leaves justification "outside" us. It does not let it be more than a forensic act. No qualitative renewal of the total I corresponds to it. Osiander tries to ground and secure this qualitative renewal with his thesis about Christ's indwelling in us.[83] For him justification is not just calling righteous but making righteous. To reckon or impute in the sense of calling righteous is to put to one's account the achievement or possession of another. This makes sense for Osiander only if it does not merely take place from outside as though we were no more than objects. Our involvement as subjects—Osiander does not himself use this term—presupposes that Christ works *in* us and *from within* us as well as *on* us. Only in this way can there be appropriation of his merits and righteousness.

---

[81] *Von dem einigen Mittler Jesu Christo und Rechtfertigung des Glaubens* (1551).
[82] Quoted by Hirsch, p. 185.
[83] On the confrontation between Osiander and Melanchthon cf. F. Blanke, RGG³, IV, p. 818.

Osiander thinks this is thoroughly in line with the Lutheran doctrine of justification, although the Thomistic idea of habit is suggested by the thought of indwelling (*inhabitatio*) and the real righteousness effected by it. Would not the Apology have to bring against Osiander the same objection as it does against papism when it complains that for papism faith is not justification but only its commencement and preparation? What makes us righteous is here the new beginning attested in our works.[84]

Osiander rebuts charges of this kind with the argument that this new being and the works produced by it are not our own act but are enacted on us and in us. Our righteousness is indeed grounded in an inner substantiality but this immanence is understood only as a kind of indication of place. Although it has entered us, it is not an integral part of us but is always a seed planted in us which is distinct from the soil in which it is planted.

Thus in real (or supposed)[85] distinction from Thomism the effect of making righteous does not lie in meritorious works of our own but in the righteousness of Christ himself which is grasped by faith, planted in us, and imparted to us.

At any rate, the event of redemption which is made present by the Spirit, grasped in faith, and realized by Christ's indwelling, produces according to Osiander a qualitatively new being, a making righteous which is based on our being pronounced righteous. The affinity of this to Luther's doctrine of justification, which he wants only to interpret and not to modify, is found by Osiander in the fact that this new state is received and not brought about by us, so that there seems to be a common front against the idea of merit. With his particular emphasis Osiander hopes especially to protect the Lutheran doctrine against deviations by correcting a certain imbalance. He finds distortions of this kind in Melanchthon's forensic teaching because this annuls the character of an efficacious act-word, lets the old Adam go on his way, and permits the threat of an intolerable discrepancy between our being in God's eyes and our actual state. He finds here a possible rushing into the dead end of the objective self-contradiction which the New Testament, as we have seen, describes as hypocrisy. His fear is that the nonrecognition of concrete regeneration will necessarily lead to indifference to the actual sinner, to a tolerance which leads to libertinism, and even perhaps to a dubious justification of sins.

Since Osiander's view of real righteousness on the basis of the indwelling of Christ and the Pneuma seizes on a material conflict in Luther's doctrine of justification, it is understandable that it should constantly recur in many variations right up to the present time. K. Holl's famous essay on Luther's teaching may be cited as an example (*Gesammelte Aufsätze*, I, 6th ed. [1932], pp. 119, 123, 128). Holl discerns an affinity not merely to Osiander but also to the Roman Catholic concept of habit against which Osiander carefully distinguishes his own view. As Holl interprets Luther's statements in his *Romans*, our reception into fellowship with

---

[84]Cf. LBK, I, p. 174, no. 71; Tappert, p. 116.

[85]We say "or supposed" because modern Roman Catholicism does not feel affected by Osiander's distinction. While differing from the Reformers in regard to "by faith alone," Roman Catholicism since Trent has explained "by grace alone" in such a way that simply to use the label "righteousness of habit or works" is a misrepresentation. Of the host of works on this cf. esp. Hans Küng's book on justification (*Justification* [1964]) and also G. Söhngen, *Die Einheit in der Theologie* (1952), pp. 324ff. and J. Ratzinger, *Einführung in das Christentum*, 5th ed. (1968), pp. 218ff.; E.T. *Introduction to Christianity* (New York, 1970).

God through justifying faith is simply a condition for the stripping away of our sinful being in a process of sanctification. It does not accomplish this. Renewal is rather the goal which God pursues in justification and which he anticipates when he pronounces us righteous. God foresees where man will go once the foundation of the state of justification is laid in him. That God does not do something definitive in justification but anticipates something still to come may be seen, Holl thinks, in the decisive significance of man's obedience to God's gracious purpose for him (*Romans*, p. 119). As in Osiander the complex of what he does in this obedience and how his actual regeneration is manifested is part of the event of justification.

In distinction from Osiander and Holl, A. Schlatter adopted *his* doctrine of making righteous not as an interpretation of Luther but as a polemic against him and against his idea of "righteous and sinner at the same time." Along these lines he thought that he could play off Paul against the Reformer ("'Luthers Deutung des Römerbriefs,'" *Schrift zum Gedächtnisjahr der Reformation* [1917]; *Kommentar zum Römerbrief "Gottes Gerechtigkeit"* [1935]; *Erlebtes* [1924], pp. 138f.). His son T. Schlatter followed in his steps ("'Für Gott lebendig in Christi Kraft . . . ,'" *Jahrbuch der theologischen Schule Bethel,* I [1930]; "'Tot für die Sünde, lebendig für Gott,'" *ibid.,* III [1932]). A. Ritschl interpreted Paul along similar lines (*Rechtfertigung und Versöhnung,* II, 3rd ed. [1899], pp. 365ff.).

The same thesis of essential righteousness and real infilling by the Spirit may also be found in Pietist schools and Holiness movements. Thus Zinzendorf finds a habitual-essential change of heart of such a kind that there can be no more conflict with sin, this being overcome at the moment of conversion. Full holiness of heart and life is championed by the Holiness theologian Charles Finney in the 19th century and O. S. von Bibra after World War II. Cf. ThE, I, §§495ff.; E.T. I, pp. 78ff.

When we spoke of an immanent conflict in the Reformation doctrine of justification, we were conceding that the question of the concrete state of man after justification, of his actual change and the presence of the Pneuma in him, is a valid one. What is the reason, then, for our suspicions regarding Osiander and his followers? Why are we unable to view their teaching as a permissible variation of the Reformation doctrine of justification?

The debate with Osiander must begin at two points.

First, the question arises how the relation between law and gospel (a central one in Reformation theology) is to be understood. For Luther, as we have seen, tension remains between the two. Only as we permanently experience under the law how much our actual state needs forgiveness does the gospel continue to be the expression of a miracle—the miracle of the forgiveness, the justifying pronouncement, which comes to us in the Word and the witness of the Holy Spirit. Without the contrapuntal function of the law the gospel would become the epitome of the "dear Lord" whose love is, as it were, a timeless state and ultimately a principle of indifference, the epitome of a state and not an efficacious act.

We will be content here with a simple statement and refer to our chapters on law and gospel in Volume II (EF, chapters XIV–XVII).[86] Any doctrine of essential

---

[86]Cf. also ThE, I, §§554–623; E.T. I, pp. 94ff.

righteousness, of sin that is negated as well as pardoned, has to ask itself whether it does not basically shift the relation of law and gospel and therefore latently and involuntarily replace the actuosity of the Pneuma by the description of a static state of man and even of God himself. We saw in Volume II how significant the dialectic of law and gospel is for the historicity of the divine action.

Second, the same questions have to be put to Osiander as we came across in our understanding of faith. If it is an error to try to deny that faith is also a psychic process, work, and experience, and therefore to disembody it in docetic fashion, we also miss its point if we ground it on this psychic dimension. Faith, as we have seen, does not live on itself but on the one in whom it believes. The same, it seems to us, has to be said about the inner events that follow appropriated faith. Do they not have to be prevented from becoming an object of special interest, of a theologically involved inquiry? Should they occur except only as we surrender confidently to the rule of the Spirit, trusting that he who has begun a good work in us will complete it (Philippians 1:6)? Will not a broader interest in the inner history, in the impartation, growth, and coming into being of a real righteousness, surreptitiously mean that these processes will cease to be understood as mere *results* of our justification and become instead *conditions* of our justification (as in Osiander)? In this way a new and spiritualized form of works righteousness can creep in again. There can also result once again the introversion of attention which studies the I-event and in so doing shatters assurance of salvation, the certitude that is grounded only in the "outside us."

It is very interesting to see how Luther within his doctrine of justification does speak of real effects, of the growth of righteousness in us after faith, yet in contrast to Osiander does so without making these results a *condition* of our justification.

Luther could often speak of our being made more and more righteous or of the believer always growing (WA, 56, 169, 29; 227, 3; LW, 25, 149 and 211) or of faith becoming incarnate in good works (40/I, 427, 11; LW, 26, 272) or of sin being purged so that there is a growing ontic righteousness (WA, 7, 337, 28; LW, 32, 24). This passage describes faith and the grace of the Spirit as a new leaven which not all at once but gradually makes us new as God's loaf. Our life, then, is not piety or health but becoming pious and healthy. It is not a being but a becoming. We are not as yet but we are becoming.

Thus the "righteous and sinner at one and the same time" does not lead to a fatal and fatalistic state of balance between the two, to an acceptance of the indestructibility of the old Adam. Instead there is sturdy reference to his being drowned and killed. Luther has a clear view of the process of spiritual progress, growth, and change, in short, of convalescence (cf. the great chapter on this in R. Hermann, *Gerecht und Sünder zugleich* [1930], pp. 234–89, esp. pp. 259f.). Although his statements often sound like those of Osiander, the difference lies simply in their rank, or, as one might say, in the presence alongside them of other statements that do not allow them to occupy any basic position in the salvation event.

The classical statement on their rank may be found in Luther's exposition of Psalm 91 (WA, 4, 350, 14; LW, 11, 477), which says that progress is no other than a continual beginning. It is very paradoxical that Luther defines progress here in terms of its starting point and not its goal. Normally the idea of progress sees us advancing with a goal in view. On the spiritual level this would be a state of perfection, of holiness, of essential righteousness. Theologically this would obviously mean that faith is a means to reach this state and the state of *being* righteous is necessarily the real basis of justification, as in Osiander.

Luther, however, reverses things. For him I advance only as I go back to the starting point, the beginning of faith. I have to go back to where I receive, where the gift is given, where the Spirit reaches and changes me in his Word. Being changed is the content of a trust that is won from me by the Word of promise. It is the object of faith but not of sight, not of observation, and certainly not of self-observation.

Not only can one fail to progress by reaching for an ideal spiritual state. One can also fail to begin by burying the talent that is received (Luke 19:13) instead of putting it to work, by stopping at the moment of endowment and not taking this moment up into one's own history. We should then have an abstract and unreal faith that is unworthy of the very name of faith. It would lead us backward to destruction. It would be no other than the fatal misunderstanding that Paul deals with in Romans 6:1, 15. We should view faith as an act in which we have received total absolution for the past and future, so that we can continue to blossom in our sins (to take up an earlier metaphor), arguing that we are saved and therefore nothing can affect us. This would be bringing down the curtain after the first act instead of continuing with the play and giving him who has begun the good work in me space to advance it.

Only as I thus go back to the beginning and constantly creep back into my baptism, but not, of course, stay there, can there be progress in my spiritual life. At the end there might well be the confession that Martin Kähler uttered as he lay dying: "There is now nothing more in me that is against God" (A. Kähler, *Theologe und Christ. Erinnerungen und Bekenntnisse von Martin Kähler* [1926], p. 282). This confession is not made in virtue of what has been attained but in virtue of faith in the promise that it will be attained. We do not grow away from the beginning of our faith but more and more into it.

Luther put this very vividly in his Third Disputation against the Antinomians (WA, 39/I, 519) when he said that a man who believes in Christ is already reckoned just and holy and already living in heaven, but as we are carried in the Father's bosom clothed in the best robe our feet stick out and Satan tries to bite them. We must tuck our feet under the mantle or we shall have no peace. We could give free rein to fancy and depict all the misunderstandings of the Reformation doctrine of justification in relation to this metaphor. Our peace, the final state of spiritual fulfilment, is not really that God's mantle completely covers us. This state of ontic righteousness is reserved for the eschaton when we shall see God face to face, whereas now we see through a glass darkly (1 Corinthians 13:12) and are exposed to temptation. We are already apprehended by Christ but our own apprehending is still in process (Philippians 3:12). We are already known by God but are only on the way to the goal of knowing him (1 Corinthians 13:12b). In the interim we fight the evil one who tries to nip our feet. No supposedly substantial righteousness exempts me from this conflict, as Osiander believed.

The opposite misunderstanding—that of work-righteousness—is also warded off by this metaphor of the mantle and the feet. When Satan tries to bite our feet, the struggle against him does not mean that I try to protect myself by kicking him. This would simply give him more chances to nip and bite. No, I must tuck my feet under the mantle. I must go back to where faith began and where the saying "You are mine" came to me in the witness of the Spirit as a saying valid for *me*, calling me to a new being. Within this power (so long as I shelter in it) nothing else can gain power over me.

The difference that we have noted here between Luther and Osiander could be vividly expressed in Osiander's lifetime in popular polemics, as in a song "To the Osiandrists in Prussia," which circulated in Königsberg and Leipzig. The second verse of this song said that there was no more terrible heresy than that of Osi, who was full of devilish cunning, and the fifth asked his supporters to help overcome Osi by their death (Hirsch, *Die Theologie des Andreas Osiander*, Appendix 2, p. 291).

f. Ecclesiological Implications

Bibliography: K. Adam, *Wesen des Katholizismus*, 9th ed. (1940); G. Ebeling, "Zur Frage nach dem Sinn des mariologischen Dogmas," *ZThK*, III (1950), pp. 383f.; H. Fries, art. "Kirche, systematisch," *Handbuch theologischer Grundbegriffe*, 2nd ed. (1974), pp. 455ff.; P. Gasparri, *Römischer Katechismus*, 2nd ed. (1939); Hampe, Vol. I; KKK; G. Maron, "Credo in Ecclesiam? Erwägungen zu den Arbeiten des 2. Vatikan Konzils," MD, I (1964), pp. 1ff.; Harding Meyer, "Das Wort Pius IX: Die Tradition bin ich," ThEx, CXXII (1965); J. Moltmann, *Kirche in der Kraft des Geistes* (1975); E.T. *The Church in the Power of the Spirit* (New York, 1977); Heribert Mühlen, "Der Kirchenbegriff des Konzils," Hampe, I, pp. 291-313; also "Das Christusereignis als Tat des Geistes," MS, III, 2 (1969), pp. 513ff.; Pius XII, encyclical "Mystici corporis (Christi)" (1943) and "Humani generis" (1950); K. Rahner, *Schriften zur Theologie*, II (1955), pp. 7-94; E.T. *Theological Investigations*, II (Baltimore, 1963), pp. 1-88; J. Ratzinger, *Das neue Volk Gottes. Entwürfe zur Ekklesiologie* (1969), esp. pp. 231ff.; E. Schlink, "Zehn Bemerkungen (zur Kirchenkonstitution)," Hampe, I, p. 313; E. Wolf, "Ekklesiologie und Mariologie nach dem 2. Vatikan," MD, II (1967), pp. 21ff.

(1) The Problem
It is not only to the individual believer, as in Osiander, that the reality of the Spirit cannot be attributed as an inherent quality. An institution, too, cannot be thought of as a possible vessel for such a Spirit-imparted quality. It is important to ask whether and how far the Roman Catholic understanding of the church involves an institutional inherence of the Spirit along these lines. To put it rather daringly, do we have here a kind of Osiandrian ecclesiology?

There is no doubt that when hunting around in Roman Catholic theologies one constantly comes across formulations which might suggest a positive answer to this question. Thus reference is made to the permanent help imparted by the Holy Spirit to the church. The Spirit is regarded as the "soul" which fills the visible institutional body as its invisible, spiritual, and supernatural principle of life.[87] Karl Adam can say that the introduction of the Spirit of Jesus into this-worldly reality takes place in the form of orders and offices which the fellowship rightly

---

[87]Gasparri, *Römischer Katechismus*, Q. 124f., p. 112.

generates as structural elements according to the will of Jesus.[88] To that extent Christ is the true I of the church. And the church is the body permeated by the saving powers of Jesus.[89]

One might also see the same habitual indwelling of the Holy Spirit in the institution when it is described christologically instead of pneumatologically. This is true of formulations which define the church as the continuing Christ and therefore assume the presence of his Spirit. We may recall Möhler's typical identification of Christ's body with the church. For him the church is the Son of God constantly manifested, permanently renewing himself, and eternally rejuvenating himself among men. It is his ongoing incarnation.[90] In this identification the Spirit of Christ is present in his institutional body. Here there is indeed a close relation to Osiander's concept of indwelling, although now in institutional form.

It would be unfair, however, to heap up such statements in detachment from their theological and historical context and to treat them as representative of Roman Catholic ecclesiology. They are controversial in the Roman Catholic world itself, and since Vatican II there has been with increasing clarity a critical movement away from them even when this concept of the church occurs in papal encyclicals and is codified in Denzinger. We shall have to speak about this.

(2) Inner Catholic Criticism of the Osiandrian Error
To begin with something positive, Vatican II and the theologians influenced by it oppose a simple identification of the Roman Catholic Church with the mystical body of Christ[91] and consequently they oppose a static and institutionally received possession of the Spirit.

A theologian like Ratzinger does, of course, think that he can find in Paul some references to a kind of identification of Christ and the church, as in 1 Corinthians 12:12: "For just as the body is one and has many members, and all the members of the body, though many, are one body, so it is with Christ." Here "Christ" is used in a passage where one would expect "church" or "community." Here (if one considers also v. 13) the interchanging of the terms Christ, body, and church seems explicitly to identify them,[92] although this obviously represents only one side of what the New Testament says. It is supplemented by other passages in which a separation and distinction is made between the church and its members (though here the church itself is never depicted as sinful).

As regards 1 Corinthians 12:12 Ratzinger seems to me to be exaggerating when he calls the terms Christ and church interchangeable and therefore finds hints of an identification. In a comparison (this is what we have) between the functioning of members in an organism and in the church we have to take note especially of the point of comparison. Here this is the unity displayed by the members in their joint

---

[88] *Wesen des Katholizimus*, p. 44.

[89] *Ibid.*, p. 26.

[90] J. R. Geiselmann, ed., *Symbolik* (1958), p. 389.

[91] For the distinction between a "romantic-organological" concept of the church as Christ's mystical organism and a "juristic-hierarchological" and static view cf. Ratzinger, *Das neue Volk Gottes*, pp. 231f.

[92] *Ibid.*, p. 238. Though I have doubts about Ratzinger's exegesis here I agree with the decisive lines of his ecclesiological thought and will continually take up his suggestions in what follows.

activity. When Paul says "so it is with Christ" where one would expect the church, he is leaping ahead (Schlatter, *Paulus der Bote Jesu,* 2nd ed. [1956], p. 345; also Wendland, *Der Brief an die Korinther* [1946], p. 74). But there is a theological reason for this. For not by itself is the community what it is. It cannot bind its members and direct them to unity in its own name. It is Christ's work and possession. As Barth says, "it is in the 'bodily nature,' in the simplicity and plurality of Jesus Christ Himself, that the Corinthians are to recognise the necessary order, the relatedness and the freedom of their life as His community" (CD, IV,1, p. 663). It is no mere question, then, of an idea of unity such as might be grounded in the entelechic organism. The unity of the members has an ec-centric basis. It is not the unity of *a* body but of *his* body, and it loses its force and focus if it is seen to be sociologically and institutionally grounded in itself.

The concept of the church is indeed attenuated to a mere idea and docetic abstraction if one accepts the possible falling away and separation of the members from Christ but does not view the church itself as open to a charge of sinfulness.[93] Can a church that is not seen as determined and characterized by its members be anything other than an ideal Platonic society which it is natural to equate with the kingdom of God? Such a church would not be waiting for the kingdom but would already represent it in the idea and in this sense would have at its disposal an ideal presence of the Spirit. The eschatological lacuna would be complete. That we are not just outlining the mere caricature of an eventuality but referring to a line of thinking which may in fact be found in Roman Catholic dogmatics will be seen later in the section on mariology.

To forestall a false interchangeability of Christ and the church and therewith the assumption of an institutionally guaranteed possession of the Spirit everything depends on maintaining the qualitative difference between the head and the body and the dominance of the head over the body. The relation between the head and the body runs one way from the former to the latter and is not reversible. Upholding this irreversibility forms the true barrier to the identifying of Christ and the church and to the idea that the church is a kind of renewed incarnation of Christ.

This irreversibility is especially prominent in relation to the idea of a disloyal membership of Christ's body. The locus classicus for this is what Paul says about *porneia* (fornication) in 1 Corinthians 6:15-20. *Porneia* here is not a moral phenomenon with an ascetic ideal in the background. The real issue is that Christ as Head exercises dominion over his members and unites them to him by his Spirit (cf. Romans 6:1-3, 15f.). Those who instead pander to *porneia* become one body with a harlot and thereby bind themselves to the alternative to being one spirit with Christ. Since the two attitudes are mutually exclusive, *porneia* involves no less than a change of lordship.

The member of the body has, then, the possibility of denying the head and therefore at the same time emancipating itself from the body. This denial does not have to take the form of an anti-Christian or atheistic confession. Institutional membership, and therefore membership in Christ's body, may well continue verbally and in intention. Liturgies can continue to be celebrated. Beneath the verbal

---

[93]There is—very naturally—an awareness of the sinfulness of members of the church; cf. "Lumen gentium," 14b (*Documents of Vatican II* [New York, 1963], p. 33).

and institutional level, however, the change of lordship has taken place and it has set up blocks (*impedimenta, prohibitiva*) to faith[94] which will then press for confessional renunciation.

A study of church history should cause us to hold back if we are inclined to find this possibility of disloyalty only among individuals or groups but not in "the" church or its officebearers. The loss of being one spirit with Christ is a threat to which the faith of the community as a whole is exposed. This is why there is a repeated call for watchfulness not only in Paul but throughout the New Testament.[95] This is why there are exhortations, the imperatives that are added to the indicatives of promise.[96]

It is hard to see why the reference should not be to the community, to "the" church in its concreteness,[97] when in the form of blame or exhortation we are told that believers may sever themselves in doctrine or conduct from the body of Christ whose members they are, that they may break away from the Spirit of Christ who dwells in them and seeks to permeate them.[98] The indwelling of the Spirit is not a habitual factor that is bound up constitutively with the "church" or "community."

Although in Ratzinger (and other post-conciliar theologians) we catch echoes that represent the traditional Roman Catholic thesis of the sinlessness of "the" church as one element in the complex of ecclesiological statements, the real accent is unmistakably placed on a dynamic and not a habitual and static union between Christ and the church, so that bulwarks are erected against the Osiandrian misunderstanding.[99] It is hard to see, however, how the two theses do not have to be exclusive of one another. It seems obvious that there is a latent controversy between the official view and its revision.

The dynamic element applies, although in different ways, to both partners in the relation: Christ *and* the church. On Christ's side his address is definitive. He made his sacrifice for us once and for all (*ephapax*). His promise is thus unconditional and forever (Romans 6:10; 1 Peter 3:18; Hebrews 7:27; 9:12; 10:10). According to Hebrews this is what distinguishes his offering from that of the priests of the old covenant. These had to sacrifice continuously because the guilt that needed expiation was constantly repeated. Whereas atonement was then conditional (on keeping the law), it is now pronounced unconditionally to those who believe the promise. Those who by baptism share in the Lord's death and resurrection will receive the gift of the Spirit (Acts 2:38). Constant as this address is, it takes

---

[94]Cf. ThE, I, §§333ff.; E.T. I, pp. 87f.

[95]E.g., 1 Corinthians 16:13; Matthew 26:41; 1 Thessalonians 5:6; 1 Peter 5:8.

[96]Cf. the "Shun..." of 1 Corinthians 6:18 in relation to *porneia*.

[97]The word "church" (*ekklēsia*) is not common in the NT. It occurs for certain only twice in Matthew (16:18; 18:17) and not at all in the other gospels. It is not common in the epistles. In Paul—and this is the most important point here—it is used mostly for the local community (e.g., Romans 16:1; 1 Corinthians 1:2; 2 Corinthians 1:1; in the plural, Galatians 1:2). It is not used for the church as a whole apart from the local communities. This is probably the reason why the church is never presented as sinful in the NT. The church "itself" in the presupposed Roman Catholic sense is not mentioned, so that asserting or denying its sinfulness (in spite of Ratzinger, *Das neue Volk Gottes*, p. 238) can find no place (K. L. Schmidt, TDNT, III, pp. 501ff.; TWNT, III, pp. 502ff.).

[98]Cf. Galatians 1:6; 3:1ff.; also the letters to the churches in Revelation 2 and 3.

[99]For this and for what follows cf. Ratzinger, *Das neue Volk Gottes*, pp. 239ff.

place—here is the dynamic element—in ever new actualizations, in an ever new self-declaration and knocking (Revelation 3:20), in an ever new demand that we accept the offer (John 3:5) and share in the once-for-allness of the Lord's death and resurrection.

Over against the constancy of the divine faithfulness there stands on the human side the instability of the community and the individual. In the church "between the times" faith is under assault. The possibility of sin and apostasy threatens. The church is not yet the kingdom of God in which God is "all in all." What makes the difference between Christ and his church is that the church is always a church of sinners who must be carried across an abyss. "While . . . the Logos has come down into a sinless human nature," H. Mühlen rightly says,[100] "the Spirit of Christ is sent into our hearts (Gal. 4:6), and therewith into a plurality of human persons who are fundamentally subject to sin."[101]

This dynamic element is so noticeable that our glance turns away from the habit of the institution to the actual condition of persons. Church membership as such does not (automatically) bring participation in the body of Christ and his Spirit. Participation involves not only claiming the means of grace and compliance with order but also possession of the Spirit of Christ. Hence even if we are made members of the church we are not saved unless we persevere in love and belong to the bosom of the church in heart as well as body (as Augustine expressly said).[102]

In fact we no longer have here the triumphalist, clericalist, and juridicalist identification of the Spirit of Christ and the church which Bishop E. J. De Smedt of Bruges alleged against the first and provisional council drafts.[103] Instead it is humbly acknowledged that the Spirit of Christ is very concretely sent into the plural reality of persons who are fundamentally subject to sin. In place of a static and timeless possession of the Spirit there enters in here a dynamic and historical element. We do not have a perfect state.[104] The church is still on the way, striving for the fulness which according to the Lord's will his body will attain to in the course of time.[105] In this sense the fulness of the Spirit, too, is the object of a promise and not a possession. To the degree that attention shifts from the institution to persons the dynamic understanding of the union of the head and the body of Christ grows. The gift of the Pneuma is actualized.

---

[100]Hampe, I, p. 292.

[101]Cf. "Lumen gentium," 8: The church embraces "sinners in its own bosom. It is both holy and always in need of cleansing, it continually goes the way of penitence and renewal" (cf. *Vatican II Documents*, pp. 22–24).

[102]*Ibid.*, 14 (E.T. pp. 32f.); KKK, pp. 139f. Augustine, *De Baptismo contra Donatistas*, V, xxviii, 39: One can still catch a soft echo of the identifying of Christ and the church: Without full membership in Christ's body there is no full membership in Christ. If I am right, the difference which Vatican II made between Christ and the church is here quietly withdrawn in the form of a negation. The church itself can be holy, sinless, and in possession of the Spirit. The lack which puts the identity of Christ and the church in question applies only to the members.

[103]Hampe, I, pp. 292, 301.

[104]Mühlen, e.g., refers to neglect of the theology of the Word.

[105]Cf. the ecumenical decree "Unitas redintegratio," 24, 1; KKK, p. 249. A certain problem, of course, may be seen here. The NT relates consummation and recapitulation (*anakephalaiosis*) solely to Christ's Parousia. It is not the result of a process of church growth or cosmic maturing (Moltmann, *Die Kirche in der Kraft des Geistes*, p. 90; E.T. *The Church in the Power of the Spirit*, p. 73).

A dubious point in this view, which might still awaken the Osiandrian misunderstanding, may be found perhaps in the understanding of the church as a sacrament. Vatican II adopted this view.[106] According to it the church in Christ is as it were the sacrament, i.e., the sign and instrument of the most inward union with God and also of the unity of all humanity. The church is, then, the basic sacrament of the salvation of the world insofar as it stands in relation and distinction and subjection to Christ as the primal historical sacrament in whom God's self-declaration achieves historical manifestation and irreversible fulfilment.[107] The church has sacramental significance because it is the historical sign which brings and therefore effects the historical manifestation in the world of the will of God that fashions salvation and unity.[108]

That the church is this efficacious sign is given a pneumatological basis in "Lumen gentium." The risen Lord has sent his life-giving Spirit into his disciples and through them made his body the church the all-embracing sacrament of salvation.[109]

Since Vatican II does not develop the ecclesiological concept of the sacrament we are confronted here by uncertainties of interpretation. If I understand aright the passage cited, it is noteworthy that there again seems to be a personal ring about the impartation of the Spirit. He is given to the disciples and not (or at least only indirectly and derivatively) to the church as an institution. H. Mühlen obviously shares this interpretation when he takes "sending" to mean that the Spirit of Christ is not just imparted to members of the church externally (i.e., in virtue of their institutional participation in Christ's body) but very inwardly, and that he thus forms the principle of the church's unity in them.[110] In Rahner,[111] too, the same personal emphasis occurs when the church has to be understood not merely as the proclaiming bearer of God's revealing Word but also as its listening and believing addressee to whom God's Word of salvation is directed in Christ.

This variously attested understanding of the church as it is sacramentally understood can hardly be accused of the Osiandrian misunderstanding. Indisputably the indwelling of the Spirit is not understood here in terms of an ontic habit that is proper to the institution. The impartation of the Spirit has instead an unquestionably actual (dynamic) reference, for it is related to the appropriation by persons, to their awakened faith and their practice of love.[112]

Nevertheless the question remains whether variations of this ecclesiological

---

[106] "Lumen gentium," 1 (KKK, p. 123; *Vatican II Documents*, 14f.); 9,3 (p. 133; p. 25); 48,2 (p. 180; p. 79). Cf. on this O. Semmelroth, *Die Kirche als Ursakrament*, 2nd ed. (1955), pp. 39ff.; E. Schillebeeckx, "Die Kirche als Dialogsakrament" *Gott—Die Zukunft des Menschen* (1969), pp. 100ff.; E.T. *God, the Future of Man* (New York, 1968), pp. 117ff.; K. Rahner, "Die Zeichenfunktion der Kirche," in E. Jüngel and K. Rahner, *Was ist ein Sakrament?* (1971), pp. 75ff.

[107] Rahner, *Was ist ein Sakrament?*, p. 75.

[108] *Ibid.*, p. 76.

[109] "Lumen gentium," 48,2 (*Vatican II Documents*, p. 79).

[110] Hampe, I, p. 300.

[111] *Was ist ein Sakrament?*, p. 77.

[112] We again recall the central passage "Lumen gentium," 14,2 (KKK, pp. 139f.; *Vatican II Documents*, p. 33).

concept of the sacrament might not secretly develop which would again be oriented to an automatic view and again press toward a habitual concept of the indwelling of the Spirit in the sacramental institution.[113]

That there are some dangerous elements in Vatican II in spite of its carefully differentiated theology of the Spirit may be seen clearly from the celebration of the four hundredth anniversary of Trent at the end of the second session (3/12/1963). The address by Cardinal Urbani, which he did not just give on his own responsibility, bore the title "Credo in ecclesiam" ("I believe in the church"). Here the ominous "in" implies that the church is set alongside the Father, Son, and Spirit as an object of faith and that it might thus be an autonomous bearer of the Spirit. This goes even beyond the understanding of the church at Trent. For the council which was being commemorated emphatically avoided placing a *credo in ecclesiam* alongside the *credo in Deum. . . , in Jesum Christum. . . , in Spiritum Sanctum*. The catechism which Pius V published in 1566 as a follow-up to the council expressly draws attention to the fact that *credo in* applies only to the Holy Trinity, whereas the works of the triune God, which include the church, are related to *credere* only by a simple accusative (cf. K. G. Steck, *Die katholische Lehre von der Kirche* [1955], pp. 51f.). The many assurances of Vatican II which delight Protestant theologians—assurances even against this understanding of the church—seem to suggest that forces are still at work in the background which constantly demand delimitations of this kind. Cf. E. Schlink, "Die Diskussion des Schemas 'De Ecclesia' in evangelischer Sicht," MD, VI (1963), p. 101 and on the Roman Catholic side O. Semmelroth, *Ich glaube an die Kirche. Erwägungen über das gottmenschliche Geheimnis der Kirche* (1959).

Even apart from a concept of the sacrament which may tend toward a material or automatic view, the question is whether there is not perceptible in Roman Catholic theology a certain thrust toward the autonomy of the institutional church, toward its possession of the Spirit. Is this just an invention? Those whose voices were heard but suppressed in the council debate seem to be pressing for a pneumatic habit of the church as an institution or for the substitution of the church for the Pneuma (cf. the section on mariology). Naturally we cannot regard what we have called the Osiandrian error in this sense as official Roman Catholic ecclesiology, as in popular Protestant polemics. We have seen how much antitoxin was mobilized against it in the council statements. Yet it would be a mistake, and not according to the mind of Roman Catholic theology as it is increasingly shaped by the Bible, to overlook a certain dogmatic potentiality which is present in the fulness and complexity of Roman Catholic ecclesiology. What has been often virulent in history can again break out of its incubation stage in the future. In order not to underrate Roman Catholicism in its full range we must face these possibilities—though hoping that the preventive measures taken against them will prevail.

---

[113]The automatic view seems to me to be rendered innocuous by Rahner when he says that it denotes no more than the victorious power that has been given by God to the exhibitive Word of faith which reaches its true fulness in the Word of the sacrament (*Was ist ein Sakrament?*, p. 80).

(3) The Mystical Identification of Christ and the Church

To the extent that the church is called a second Christ the conclusion seems unavoidable that the church defined in this way is the institutional vessel of the Spirit of Christ. The encyclical "Mystici corporis" of Pius XII does in fact speak to this effect. It says that all the gifts, virtues, and charisms which dwell in a supreme, rich, and efficacious way in the head are transferred to all(!) members of the church. The result is that the church is as it were the fulness and completion of the Redeemer and in this relation Christ finds fulfilment as it were in the church. The same encyclical agrees with Augustine when he says that the church as the second Christ is as it were his alter ego on earth through whom heaven and earth are related to the unceasing continuation of Christ's saving work on the cross. Only the union of the head with his body, only Christ *and* the church, form the whole Christ.[114] Hence we have to grow used to seeing Christ himself in the church.[115] The church whose identification with Christ's mystical body is at issue is the Roman Catholic Church.[116] The encyclical "Humani generis" underscores this identification once again with its thesis that the mystical body of Christ and the Roman Catholic Church are one and the same.[117]

That the organized church has a privileged possession of the Spirit is unmistakable according to these statements. How can we conceive of the institutional representation of the second Christ apart from the corresponding endowment with the Spirit of Christ? There may be detected here little or nothing of Rahner's differentiation when, as we have seen, he understands the church not only as the bearer of the Word of revelation but also as the *addressee* of the Word of proclamation who is called to faith and cannot refuse it. The church as Christ's alter ego can be understood only as the subject of the Word of revelation so that a far-reaching and dramatic form of the infallibility of its teaching office seems to be unavoidable.[118]

It is typical that Vatican II resists the identification of Christ and the church by putting the term *subsistere* in place of *esse:* The only church that we confess in the creed as the one, holy, catholic, and apostolic church is actualized (*subsistit*) in the catholic church.[119] What is substituted for identification here might be expressed as follows. How far the Roman Catholic Church is the body of Christ is left open; what is said is simply that Christ's body is to be sought here.

It seems to me that we see here what we have called a turning to the personal understanding of the church. The ecclesiological imperative which is set for the church as its goal depends on the way its members receive the Spirit and allow him to work in love.[120] Only to the degree that this happens does the empirical church

---

[114]Denz., 3813.

[115]"Mystici corporis," 54. In his commentary on Ephesians, 5th ed. (1969), pp. 206ff. H. Schlier tries to solidify this thought by saying that Christ needs the church, as it were, so that by its growth and extension as a world-body he may reach his own fulness.

[116]AAS, XXXV (1943), p. 199.

[117]Denz., 2319; E.T. 1309. The 1965 edition leaves out this passage. Does the omission denote reservations occasioned by the Vatican Council?

[118]Cf. Harding Meyer on Pius IX, "Vatican I," ThEx, CXXII, pp. 52ff.

[119]"Lumen gentium," 8,2; KKK, pp. 130f.; *Vatican II Documents*, pp. 22f.

[120]"Lumen gentium," 14,2; *Vatican II Documents*, p. 33.

approximate its model, the body of Christ. To put it pneumatologically, the church does not possess the Pneuma as an institution but reaches after him and lives by its prayer for the *coming* Spirit. Renouncing the identification of the church and Christ's body, one can only define the church quantitatively. It is Christ's body insofar as its fulfils its given imperative in faith, love, and hope.

H. U. von Balthasar is right, then, when in his essay "Wer ist die Kirche?"— the personal form of the question is itself worth noting[121]—he replies that the church is "most [!] there where there is most faith, love, and hope, most unself-ishness and the bearing of others' burdens." Only where the church achieves this is it most itself and does it find its true head and center, which lie in a completely different place from its center of government. Here, then, the organized empirical church is asked how far it is itself. It is not represented by its outward head to the extent that this thinks it has a monopoly of possession of the Spirit and therefore the ability to lead in the Spirit, but by its members to the extent that they measure up to the demand for holiness.

Only this break with the identification thesis can also modify a rigid understanding of the statement that outside the church there is no salvation. If the church is most there where there is most participation in Christ, then conversely the church is least self-enclosed and closed off where it is most itself.[122] Not being self-enclosed relates not merely to sinners who belong to it and toward whom Christ's holiness is not exclusive but sustaining. It relates also to Christians outside the church's walls. The inner and true head and center of which Balthasar spoke do indeed reach beyond the institutional limits of the organized church. That the separated church is the church is thus raised afresh as a question without being already answered *a priori* in the negative.

The new trends which emerged with the help of Vatican II can be presented, then, only as the wrestling of Roman Catholic theology with other trends which are deeply rooted in its tradition and constantly threaten to become virulent. These other trends, in virtue of the thesis that the empirical church is the second Christ, and therefore in virtue of the thesis of identification, want to give the monopoly of possession of the Spirit an institutional anchor and therefore extend the Osiandrian misunderstanding as it were collectively. The antithesis to this understanding of the church, which has become official since Vatican II, opens up new and promising ecumenical perspectives.

(4) The Mariological Identification

The second form of a triumphalist ecclesiology[123] which sees the church as habitually and not just actually endowed with the Pneuma, and which therefore helps to promote the *credo "in" ecclesiam* (I believe "in" the church) can insinuate itself by way of mariology.

Only the ecclesiological implications of the development of mariology interest

---

[121]In *Sponsa Verbi. Skizzen zur Theologie,* II (1961), p. 181; cf. Ratzinger, *Das neue Volk Gottes,* p. 243.

[122]Ratzinger, p. 244.

[123]Cf. again E. J. de Smedt's criticism of the first draft of the schema on the church (Hampe, I, p. 292).

us here. At first the virginity of Mary accented Jesus' birth outside the nexus of original sin. He was not conceived of male seed but of God's Spirit. As an extension of this, Mary herself as the God-bearer (*theotokos*) was also, by the immaculate conception, taken out of that nexus in perpetual virginity (cf. Ebeling, *Wort und Glaube,* III, pp. 384ff.). After some intervening dogmatic stages in which Mary's status in salvation history was defined (by Sixtus IV in 1477 [Denz., 1400 (E.T. 734)], and then Trent [Denz., 1516 (E.T. 792)]), Pius IX came to a definitive doctrinal decision in 1854, claiming for it the infallibility which was officially granted to the papacy only in 1870. According to this pronouncement Mary was without original sin from the moment of her conception (Denz., 2803 [E.T. 1641]). In spite of the analogy to Christ's own exceptional birth this "singular grace and privilege of almighty God" does not set her alongside Christ as a second redeemer. Rather, Christ's merits are anticipated here. It is in virtue of these that God preserves her from original sin. The "Christ alone" is thus upheld. Nevertheless, the figure of Mary, who originally was wholly integrated into Christology, has unmistakably achieved increasing autonomy even if there is a concern to maintain the primacy of Christology over mariology.

A decisive step toward this autonomy, oriented to Mary's role as co-redeemer, was taken by Leo XIII in his encyclical "Octobri mense" (9/22/1891) when he called Mary the representative and symbol of the human race in its readiness to accept grace. The eternal Son did not want to bind himself by union with the race before it was freely open to this act of grace. Mary representatively fulfilled the act of expectation and receptivity without any possibility of this act being stained by sin (Denz., 3274 [E.T. 1940a]). This vicarious role means that Mary is significant in the saving event, for only as her representation is inclusive and we let ourselves be taken up into her can Christ's mediatorial work be effective in us. As Leo XII puts it, she is the "mediatrix to the Mediator." If one cannot come to the Father except through the Son, no one can come to the Son more easily than through the mother" (Denz., 3274 [E.T. 1940a]).

Ebeling is probably right when he says that this development means that Mary with this mediatorial role is replacing the Holy Spirit on the one side, since it is he who opens up the possibility of acceptance, and the church on the other side when one recalls the saying of Cyprian that "no one can have God as Father who does not have the church as mother."

From here it is but a step to the setting of Mary's mediatorship alongside the saving work of Christ with no more than barely discernible nuances. In his encyclical "Ad diem illam" (2/2/1904) Piux X stated that through the fellowship of suffering and intention between her and Christ Mary earned the right to become the restorer of the lost world and the dispenser of all the blessings which he won for us by his death and blood. It is thus granted to the exalted virgin to be with her only son the most mighty mediator and reconciler for the whole earth (Denz., 3370 [E.T. 1978a]).

The nuance which preserves the primacy of Christ's work in spite of these very fulsome statements (at least among theologians if less so in popular piety) is to be found in the repeated assurance that these honorary titles (restorer, mediator, reconciler) should not lead to any questioning of the exclusive redemptive power of Christ's death or the ascribing to the God-bearer of any power to effect super-natural grace.

Nevertheless the encyclical shows how little these appended statements detract from the preceding mariological theses by using the metaphor of Bernard of Clairvaux that while Christ is the head, Mary is the neck. To be sure this metaphor is not taken to mean that the neck turns the head but simply that it is the member which joins the head to the body. Metaphors, however, have an autonomy of their own.

The hymn to Mary in the "Mystici corporis" of Pius XII (*Vatican II Documents*, p. 63) leads to a final summarizing and climaxing of these statements and suggests some ecclesiological perspectives. It was she who by her powerful inter-cession brought it about that the Spirit of the divine Redeemer already granted at the cross was shed forth on the newborn church at Pentecost with miraculous gifts. The connection of Mary with the Pentecostal event which founded the church is repeatedly mentioned at Vatican II. It is pointed out that prior to Pentecost we find the apostles at prayer with Mary the mother of Jesus and his brethren (Acts 1:14). She prays for the gift of the Spirit who had already overshadowed her at the annunciation (cf. "Lumen gentium," 59, 65 [*Vatican II Documents*, pp. 90, 93]; "Ad gentes," 4 [pp. 587ff.]; "Presbyterorum ordinis," 18 [pp. 569f.]; and "Evangelii nuntiandi," HK, III [1976], p. 151).

In sum, one may say that because of her availability for the Spirit Mary stands at the head of the line which leads to the pneumatological event of the founding of the church and its world mission. This means that Mary's presence in the church which moves toward the event of Pentecost takes her beyond the beginning to the praying center of the church which is the place of the possible sending of the Spirit and therefore the inner presupposition of the church's missionary service.

The actualizing formulation "possible sending of the Spirit" in which Mary exercises a kind of mediatorial function certainly corresponds to the intentions of the mariology of Vatican II. Yet the question arises whether the earlier mariologi-cal tradition whose basic features have just been sketched undergoes a (fortunate) dilution, whether there does not arise (or have to arise) out of the trend of tradition a *different* ontology of the church. If we have to answer these questions in the affirmative, this cannot imply that we are playing off tradition against the council or pressing on it a better understanding of its own prior history. This would obviously be ridiculous. Our concern is simply to make it clear that behind Roman Catholic thinking—and rightly suppressed—theological possibilities are in force which in the framework of mariology dispute the actualizing understanding of the Spirit and move toward what we have called the habitual Osiandrian misun-derstanding. This is given special significance by the dogma of the bodily assump-tion of Mary.[124] What is the bearing of this on our present problem?[125]

We have already pointed out that the mariological statements (especially in the 19th century) can be exchanged for statements about the Holy Spirit and the

---

[124]Cf. "Munificentissimus Deus," AAS, XLII (1950), pp. 753-73; H. Grass, *Die katholische Lehre von der heiligen Schrift und von der Tradition* (1954), pp. 55f.
[125]On what follows cf. Ebeling, *Wort und Glaube*, III, pp. 389f.

church. The church as well as Mary can be called the mediatrix of all graces and the mediatrix to the Mediator. It is the church, says Ebeling, that not only offers the daily sacrifice of the mass but already offered the Son of God on Golgotha—an extreme formulation of the congruence of ecclesiological and mariological statements. There is no way to Christ except through the church, i.e., Mary. Both are in exactly the same way co-redemptrix and mediatrix. In Mary the church is venerated. It is the object as well as the site of the cultus. This leads indeed to credo "in" ecclesiam.

In this light the force of the dogma of Mary's bodily assumption is plain. If both Christ and his mother are bodily exalted into heaven, this crowns the analogy between them which had previously been expressed in their common exemption from original sin and their cooperation in the salvation event (with the proviso that Christ's saving work has the primacy).

If the observed exchangeability of ecclesiological and mariological statements leads to the question what are the implications of this for the understanding of the church in more recent dogma, the answer is obvious. The church now sees itself as the exalted and ascended church. It is the perfected church and no longer the expectant church. It is the church triumphant. It no longer needs to wait for what is to come eschatologically. It is already revelation in permanence. It is the ongoing reality of incarnation in human historical nature.[126] As Mary represents the analogy of being, the reciprocity of receiving nature and self-imparting grace, the church, too, is the place of this synthesis. It is the locus of the essential presence of the Spirit.

If these implications of the dogma of the assumption determine the self-understanding of the church—and I see no argument that can restrain them—then the church is complete as the vessel of the Spirit, or, in our present vocabulary, it has the habit of Spirit possession and is in an Osiandrian sense the place of the institutional indwelling of the Spirit. If Alfred Loisy at the beginning of the century wrote in debate with A. von Harnack that Jesus proclaimed the kingdom of God and the church has come instead,[127] the irony in this saying has suddenly become pointless after the dogma of the assumption, for the distinction between the church and the kingdom of God has been removed and the consummation is already present.

The possibility of this self-understanding of the church is already posited and in some sense anticipated in the one-sided understanding of the church as the second Christ. This theology of identity presses toward a theology of glory in which the church regards itself as God's kingdom already present and therefore fundamentally forgets its eschatological future and becomes the foolish virgin who already uses the oil in her lamp to light up her own festivities instead of keeping it for the coming of the Lord to the marriage.[128] Even without the dogma of the assumption a Roman Catholic theologian can thus be exposed to the threat of an eschatological lacuna, of an illegitimate anticipation of the eschaton, which lies in wait in some

---

[126]Loc. cit.
[127]L'Evangile et l'Eglise, 3rd ed. (1904), p. 154; E.T. The Gospel and the Church (New York, 1912), p. 166; in interpretation cf. G. Gloege, Theologische Traktate, II (1967), pp. 318f.
[128]Cf. Ratzinger, Das neue Volk Gottes, pp. 240f.

theologies in his church (and in other churches, too). The dogma of the assumption shows in this regard that it is not just a matter of the aberration of individual theologians[129] but that there can be de-eschatologizing in official decisions of the teaching office as well.[130]

For all that, we cannot, as stated, describe this Osiandrian theology of glory as ''the'' catholic ecclesiology. We have seen that at Vatican II, in spite of an alien mariology and (restrained) references to the assumption,[131] there was no thought of a habitual possession of the Spirit by the church but the outpouring of the Spirit is actual and is an object of prayer and expectation if also the content of a reassuring promise.

Against a theology of triumph which allots possession of the Spirit to the church as an institution and identifies it as a second Christ—as whose body it must see itself—the decisive barrier is erected when we learn to grasp what Christ's body really means. If we understand the body only in terms of the incarnation, of Christ's entry into history, then an ecclesiological understanding suggests itself whereby the church is the institutional continuation of Christ's work in history, his permanent incarnation, and to that extent a second Christ. It is here that there lurk the theology of glory and the de-eschatologizing to which we referred and which come to a climax in the dogma of the assumption. What the body of Christ is, however, must be seen in the light of Easter as well as the incarnation. It is the spiritual body (*sōma pneumatikon*) of the second Adam. This last Adam is the life-giving spirit (*pneuma zōiopoioun*, 1 Corinthians 15:44f.). As the church is Christ's body in this sense, it is not a church triumphant possessing the Spirit but a church that waits for the Spirit, an anticipation of his eschatological fulness (*plērōma*). Yet precisely as the kingdom of God, though still coming, is already among us in the presence of the exalted Christ (Luke 17:21), so the church lives already by spiritual participation in the spiritual body whose image it will one day bear without imperfection (1 Corinthians 15:49). Until then its participation in the Spirit is hidden. It will only *become* manifest.

The church is a hidden church (*ecclesia abscondita*) which is still waiting for the full unity of the head and the body and therefore for the unity of its members.

---

[129]Ratzinger quotes as an example Ansgar Vonier, *Das Mysterium der Kirche* (1934).

[130]In order not to give the impression of using an author one-sidedly it may be expressly added that Ratzinger makes the opposite charge against the Reformers. Starting in an unfaithful church they reduced the concept of the church to OT terms while the Roman church was projecting itself into the eschaton (p. 241).

[131]Cf. ''Lumen gentium,'' 50, 62, referring to Mary's intercession at the throne of God (*Vatican II Documents*, pp. 90ff.).

II

The Holy Spirit as the Basis of Love

In the preceding cycle of themes on the Holy Spirit as the basis of faith we have taken a comprehensive look at pneumatology and also considered its controversial theological and ecclesiological aspects. With a pivotal concept like faith it was inevitable that we should hear something about the two other relations of the Pneuma, namely, to love and hope. We may thus presuppose that much of the material has been covered already and give a shorter form to what still remains to be said.

To speak about the Pneuma is to speak about its effects, namely, its power of presentation, but also the "fruits" that it causes to grow therefrom.[1] Among these fruits love is named first (Galatians 5:22).[2] Without this fruit, all the other gifts of the Spirit—the charisma of prophetic utterance, the possession of ever so lofty wisdom or strong faith or generous philanthropy (1 Corinthians 13:1-3)—are without value. They are as it were empty shells. Love as an implication of the faith that is the work of the Spirit is the chief fruit which bears decisive witness to the presence of the Spirit.

That we can speak about the Spirit only in relation to his effects, to the gifts he imparts, to the fruit he produces in us, we have expressed already in a formula borrowed from Melanchthon, namely, that to know the Spirit is to know his benefits. Statements about this self-impartation and work are the point of pneumatology as Luther puts it in the Larger Catechism when he says that the third article cannot be better described than by saying that here the Holy Spirit is expressed and depicted with his office, namely, that he sanctifies.[3] He comes to expression in our sanctification.[4] He is present in his work and can thus be called

---

[1] E. Brunner, *Vom Werk des heiligen Geistes* (1935); K. Barth, "Der heilige Geist und das christliche Leben," in K. Barth and H. Barth, *Zur Lehre von heiligen Geist*, Beiheft I, *Zwischen den Zeiten* (1930), pp. 39ff.; E.T. *The Holy Ghost and the Christian Life* (London, 1938); also CD, IV,2, §68; R. Prenter, *Schöpfung und Erlösung* (1960), pp. 449ff.; E.T. *Creation and Redemption* (Philadelphia, 1967), pp. 474ff.; G. Ebeling, *Wort und Glaube*, III (1975), pp. 388ff.
[2] Cf. Romans 15:30; 2 Corinthians 6:6; Colossians 1:8; 2 Timothy 1:7.
[3] LBK, II, p. 653,34; Tappert, p. 415.
[4] P. 653,33, 43; Tappert, p. 415.

the Sanctifier.[5] He does this work by bringing Christ's work close to us and making us open to it. The decisive thing is done, of course, in Christ's work of redemption. But what would it help us if this treasure were to remain buried? The Spirit as the Sanctifier brings this treasure and redemption to us and makes it ours.[6]

The Holy Spirit is exclusively and uniquely described as "holy." But this exclusiveness does not mean the erection of a "holy numinous" over against the profane. On the contrary, the holy does not withdraw to an inaccessible distance, but God wills to be there for us with all that he is and has. He has poured himself out wholly and utterly . . . and kept nothing back that he has not given us.[7]

The Pneuma is the medium through which he makes us open and ready to receive. The word "holy" loses here its so to speak general and traditional sense with its suggestion of distance. Like all biblical words it is defined solely in terms of him who declares himself by his Word. And he wills to be the one who pours himself out and holds nothing back.

This alone is the reason why the Holy Spirit can be understood only in terms of his office and work, of what he does to us and in us as the Sanctifier. As Luther in the second article defines Jesus Christ in terms of his work for me,[8] so he does with the Holy Spirit. If you are asked what you mean by the words: "I believe in the Holy Spirit," you may answer: "I believe that the Holy Spirit makes me holy, as his name is."[9]

It is within this framework—namely, that through the Pneuma God reveals to me what is most properly his and therefore himself—that we are to see what is said about the fruit of love. In it we have the clearest picture of how God sees himself and how he wants us to see him. We can thus say the same about love as we said about the word "holy." It does not disclose its content by etymological analysis or its traditional meaning but is characterized and defined by him who here reveals himself as the one who loves.

1. HOW DOES LOVE ARISE?

Love certainly does not arise out of obedience to the command: "Thou *shalt* love." The command to love is not a legalistic command. Where imperatives of this kind occur they always imply an indicative presupposition. The possibility that we can love God is opened up by the preceding fact that we have found in God the one who loves and that our love is thus no more than a reaction, a loving in return (1 John 4:19). The imperative simply states that we must claim the possibility that has opened up, that we must not delay or default. Thus in the passage in Galatians which speaks about the fruits of the Spirit and preeminently about love it is expressly stated that we already live in the Spirit, that he has already been given to us, and that "logically" for this reason we should also live according to the Spirit (Galatians 5:25).

---

[5]P. 654,3f.; Tappert, p. 415.
[6]P. 654,37; Tappert, p. 415.
[7]P. 651,13; Tappert, p. 413.
[8]P. 511,26f.; Tappert, p. 345.
[9]P. 654,47; Tappert, p. 416.

This presupposition that the Pneuma is already at work as the power that opens and directs us to God has to be viewed as implied even where it is not expressly stated, as in the parable of the vine when it speaks about the relation of the branch to the vine which is the specific work of the Spirit (John 15:1ff.). The same applies to the tree in Luke 6:43. In Paul's vocabulary these similes mean that there has been a transplanting from the dominion of the flesh to that of the Spirit—a transplanting that we have not done ourselves but that has been done to us.[10] Here, too, we find the imperative that we are to claim what has been given and to enter into it: "Abide in my love, keep my commandments" (John 15:10).

Love, then, is a result of presuppositions that are not at my disposal. Love in the sense of eros—to apply a test—is in contrast a form of love that is at my disposal. I expose myself to the attractiveness of another, or, better, I choose an object for my love according to the criterion of attractiveness, according to what the other means and offers to me, according to his or her worth.[11] The fact that I can love when there is no such attractiveness—and this is what agape means as openness and mercy to the suffering and the needy and enemies—brings me up against something that is not at my disposal. This is broken through and changed into my possibility by my learning to see others differently in the faith that is the work of the Spirit (and not at all, then, by my own will and resolve, by my own work). Whereas earlier there applied to our fellows what Paul on the basis of a prophetic text says about God,[12] namely, that no eye has seen him and no ear heard his true voice, by the intervention of the Spirit my eyes and ears and heart are now open to them, too. They are now open to me as those they ultimately are, those who are dearly bought and for whom Christ died.[13] I see them in the light of God now opened to me. As God is now present to me only in faith, I learn to believe in others, too. They bear the alien dignity of those whom God values. In my own eyes they have only functional value or usefulness, e.g., in an erotic, economic, or some other only too human sense. But I now see their infinite value, the alien worth with which they are invested even as those who are blind and spiritually sick.

What my natural eyes previously saw now seems to me like blindness. That I now see the alien dignity of others overwhelms me like the miracle of making the blind to see. As the Spirit gives me a part in God's self-knowledge (1 Corinthians 2:11), he also enables me to see my neighbor with God's eyes: Now "we regard no one from a human point of view" (2 Corinthians 5:16). We no longer view people from the immediate (fleshly) standpoint, whether they serve our interests or not. We value them to the degree that God values them. We no longer look at the dust where the pearl lies but at the pearl that lies in the dust. This is the opening of our eyes by the Spirit.

To see others with God's eyes and therefore to be freed for love is to see what is godly in them, to see that wherein they are called to be God's image. It is not as

---

[10]For this relation of the flesh and the spirit in the gospels cf. Mark 14:38; John 3:3, 6, 8.

[11]Cf. ThE, III, §§1775ff., 1845ff., 2287ff.; E.T. *The Ethics of Sex* (New York, 1964), pp. 3ff., 26ff.

[12]Isaiah 64:3; 1 Corinthians 2:9.

[13]Romans 14:15; 1 Corinthians 6:20; 7:23; 8:11; cf. Job 15:1-3; Psalm 8:5-9.

though God did not see the dust that covers the pearl. It is not as though he overlooked the fall and alienation. If in human style his love were bound to the attractiveness of what he created, we should have only his aversion and negation and judgment. That God in love turns to alienated man means that by his act-word, by the miracle of his Spirit, he takes the pearl out of the dust, that he *makes* us new creatures (2 Corinthians 5:17). God does not love us because we are of such worth but we are of worth—we bear the alien dignity—because God loves us. God does not assess our worthiness to be loved. No, it is his creative act that he makes us worthy of his love. This act shames us because it compels us to confess that we are unworthy of it and that it is his pity that causes him to confess us. Along these lines Luther describes as follows the difference between divine and human love. God's love does not find its object already there but creates it. Man's love, however, begins with its object.[14]

Pneumatologically, we might express in this way the new dimension of love that is disclosed here.

When God by his Spirit makes himself known as the one he is, this means that he makes himself known as the one who is manifested to us in love. We cannot receive the Holy Spirit except in faith, says the Apology for the Augsburg Confession. But faith enables us to know and grasp God's mercy. In this way God becomes for us a lovable object.[15] The same Spirit herewith enables us to see our neighbor. We now see in him one for whom God discloses himself, about whom he is concerned, and for whom he wills to be present. In this way our fellow-man becomes a lovable object, too. Our love responds to the prior love of God (cf. Matthew 18:23–35).

That love is not here act and work (as it would have to be if it arose as an act of obedience resting on a legal demand) may be seen clearly from its grounding in the being of God himself. I am a loving subject only insofar as God is a lovable object. Our love is just a reflection of his love. Here sanctification (to which our love belongs) is directly connected with justification. For what we said about our love being a reflection of God's love applies equally to the righteousness of faith that is imparted to us: It is a reflection of the justifying righteousness of God. In this sense the term "righteousness of faith" is two-sided. It means both God's justifying righteousness *and* enclosed in it the righteousness of man before him. On the one hand we have God's side, on the other man's. It is thus understandable that the term "love of God" should have the same double meaning. The genitive may be either subjective (God's love) or objective (man's love of God). This two-sidedness is expressed with singular precision by the phrase "lovable object."

This brings to light another characteristic of love for God according to this understanding. It cannot possibly be derived psychologically from the state of the I. It blocks the introversion of outlook which is interested in testing the emotions of love. Just as faith cannot be explained in terms of its subject and his state, but is exclusively determined by its intentionality, its orientation to its object, so our love for God is not characterized by our subjectivity, our capacity for emotional trans-

---

[14]Heidelberg Disputation, Thesis 28 (WA, 1, 354, 35; LW, 31, 41).
[15]CAApol, IV, pp. 128f.; LBK, I, pp. 185,49–186,7; Tappert, p. 125.

ports, or the intensity of our religious experience, but is exclusively determined by its object. Even the quantitative strength of love as an experience depends solely on the extent to which God is present as a lovable object. The same applies to the subject of love as to the subject of faith, according to Luther. It is to be understood, not as an extended psychological field, but as an unextended mathematical point.

The question of the origin of love is wrongly put if the sanctifying work of the Pneuma is sought only in the individual sphere. This work is fully related to the community, the assembly of holy Christendom, the church.[16] The only question is *how* we are to think of the relation of love to the supraindividual dimension of the community.

There is a temptation to think of this relation in terms of the love that is released in me seeking action, contact, and encounter, of its creating fellowship, so that the rise of the community seems to be a product of this impulse of love.[17] This is too nondialectical a view. For before love seeks the other and presses for fellowship—as it does—it already derives from the existing community. For this is already called together by the Holy Spirit in one faith, mind, and understanding . . . , harmonious in love.[18] It does not come into being because of the need of fellowship of those who are awakened to love but through the summoning Word of God. As I hear the same Word, I am incorporated into it by the Holy Spirit and become a part and member of it, sharing all the good things it has.[19]

Through participation in the community a change of lordship takes place, for whereas previously we were ''of the devil'' we now belong to the sphere of the Pneuma that is promised to the community.[20] The community does not have its basis in the love of its members triggering a kind of need to communicate. On the contrary, love has its basis in the community that is there before it. This is easily seen.

For it is through the community and its witness that I experience the evangelical Word about God as a lovable object. God's love always encounters me already as a love with form and body, for it is proclaimed by those who have been reached by it, who have come together in its name, and who incorporate me into themselves as a part and member.

Hence my love does not found the community but is again simply a responsive love that accepts the fact of the community. It listens with it to the Word that founds the community and it thus belongs to it by the Holy Spirit. Once again love

---

[16]Luther avoided the term ''church'' because in the popular mind it was too strongly associated with the building. He also regarded ''communion of saints'' as suspect, as ''bad and unintelligible'' (LC in LBK, II, p. 656,1–26; Tappert, pp. 416f.). He preferred the personal term ''congregation'' or ''community.''

[17]This idea is fairly close to Schleiermacher's view of the church. For with him the church arises when the regenerate find themselves in orderly interaction (*Christian Faith,* §115). This is even plainer in the concept of companions in religion (*Speeches on Religion,* 4). The *Christian Faith,* of course, sees this motif of communication to be limited by the idea that a sovereign divine election stands behind the regenerate and their common life (§§116f.).

[18]LC in LBK, II, p. 657,29ff.; Tappert, p. 417.

[19]*Ibid.,* p. 657,33ff.; Tappert, p. 417.

[20]LBK, p. 657,40ff; Tappert, p. 417.

is not a work that brings the community into being but a reflection of the Spirit-filled Word that calls the community and incorporates me into it.[21]

2. WHAT IS LOVE?

How the nature of love is to be understood is included for the most part in what has been said about its origin. Love is the sanctifying act of the Pneuma who causes us to see God as he sees himself, namely, as the one who loves and who thus frees for the response of love. Nevertheless, the question of the form of this response of love remains. That this question is not to be understood as an inquiry into the psychological state of the one who loves is already clear. The form of love can be understood only in relation to him who forms it, who has won it by first loving us (1 John 4:19). What is the form of love from this standpoint?

Love is at any rate spontaneous. It wells up in me. It is not the product of an act of will that has to prevail against other strivings of the ego. If we read in the commandment of love (Matthew 22:37) that the love of God holds sway only where all the heart and all the soul and all the thoughts are full of it, this implies that love is a total movement of the ego.

This means that in love no rival contents of the soul have to be suppressed, as in obedience to the law. Wherever there is an imperative, like the categorical imperative of Kant, it is a protest against rivals such as inclination, impulse, eudaemonism, etc. The law, then, gains only a partial mastery over the territory of the ego and can never take over the whole (cf. Romans 7:23).

Where we love, however, we will what we ought to do.[22] The will at work in love ceases to be only a partial impluse that is not coextensive with the totality of the ego. The magnetic needle not only *has* to point north but *wants* to do so. Freedom and necessity are identical. We have the same total movement of the I as Fichte refers to in his teaching on genius.[23]

This happens only when along the lines of Jeremiah 31:33 the law is removed from its outside position as a *heteros nomos* and placed in my heart, so that heart and mind are no longer claimed from without (and partial opposition always remains in us) but the law becomes an inner urge and we will what we ought to do, conformity thus arising with the will of God. This conformity is so strong that no teaching or indoctrination is needed to know God's will. For this will is already in our hearts. A legal formulation of this will would now be a beating of the air; it is thus superfluous (31:34). The transition of God's will from an outside claim to a motivation of our hearts, which in Jeremiah is an eschatological promise, is precisely the same as that which elsewhere (e.g., Joel 2:28) is described as the work of the Holy Spirit, the miracle of appropriation.

The form in which this conformity to God's will occurs is love. Only in love are

---

[21] *Ibid.*, p. 657,36; Tappert, p. 417. Cf. Ebeling, *Wort und Glaube,* III, p. 325: "That the Christian is never more than a part and member of the body of Christ implies primarily for the understanding of sanctification, not a shaping together but a being shaped together, participation in a common life to which each Christian owes his life."

[22] K. Holl, *Aufsätze zur Kirchengeschichte,* I, 6th ed. (1932), p. 179.

[23] Luther, too, can speak of a voluntary and happy necessity (WA, 6, 27, 10ff.).

we attracted and impelled by the object of love in such a way that the discrepancy between will and impulse is overcome. Only in love are we totally (and not just partially) brought into conformity with God's will, totally committed.

In relation to this conformity Augustine pointed out that a work can have value and be of merit before God only if it proceeds from love. For if I render only a legal obedience of the letter, I act grudgingly. I thus do my work as one who is not fully involved (part of me is not in it). It is done through me but I do not really do it. "What you do grudgingly is only done through you; you yourself do not do it."[24] According to Augustine a work can really be in harmony with God's will and therefore of merit only if we do it as subjects, in free spontaneity, out of love. Only when we praise God in love do we act freely, for "you love—in this context, you feel drawn to—what you praise." There is no compulsion here, only your own good pleasure.[25] In all other cases I am simply an object, the object of that which awakens in me fear and hope.[25]

In the same way Luther and Calvin point out that this love which unites me totally with God's love derives from the appropriation of the Spirit. Filial love, says Luther, does not come from our own nature but from the Holy Spirit.[26] Calvin in his exposition of Jeremiah 31:33 emphasizes the point that we have just made: All our senses are at war with God. They are in a state of opposition to him. It is a new world when man lets God rule him and a change of lordship takes place. This happens when the law is written on the heart. This means the forming of the heart in such a way that the law rules there and every impulse of the heart (our spontaneity) accepts and agrees with the teaching of the law. Obedience, then, is not something to which a man can be brought before he is born again by the Spirit of God and the Spirit gives life to the letter.[27]

It would be a fateful and unrealistic error if we were to interpret the conformity to God's will that is given in love as a static condition or an attained habit of unity. The path to an unequivocal love in which the totality of the person is involved will always lead through new fields of conflict. Only love itself as a "moment"—as one might say with Kierkegaard—is without conflict. In its fulfilment, then, it is an eschatological *promise*. Love will remain and will be the epitome of seeing when the conflict and nevertheless of faith are behind it (1 Corinthians 13:8).

In what sense the path of filial love leads constantly through the stages of disunity and conflict is made clear when Luther experiments with the idea of resignation to hell in his exegesis of Romans 9:3 (Ficker ed., II, pp. 218f.; LW, 25, 379ff.; he is using here a thought taken from Tauler).

When we trust in God's grace and love is released in us, might there not be here an element of eudaemonistic self-love (as one might put it today)? No one can know whether he is really proof against salvation egoism, against love of self instead of supposed love of God; no one knows whether he loves God without reserve, so long as he does not experience a readiness to give up his desire for

---

[24]Exposition of Psalm 91:5.
[25]Exposition of Psalm 134.
[26]Commentary on Romans (Ficker ed., II, 217,27; LW, 25, 378).
[27]Commentary on Jeremiah 31:33 (*Commentaries on Jeremiah and Lamentations* [Grand Rapids, 1950], IV, p. 132).

salvation and even to accept damnation should this be pleasing to God. But would we really do justice to God if trust in "by faith alone" brought us this disappointment and we found ourselves in hell instead of close to God in heaven?

Luther's experiment loses its monstrous character, however, if we get its point. If we are ready to praise God even in hell, then our conformity to God's will is proved to the uttermost. It has not the least trace of the salvation egoism which might disavow even the confession "by faith alone." But those who are thus united with God and declare it by praising him from hell cannot possibly stay in hell. Their filial love, thus demonstrated, will take them out of hell and confirm the nearness to God in which they really stand. For they will what God wills. They are thus pleasing to him. If pleasing to him they are loved, and if loved they are saved (218, 1ff.; LW, 27, 381).

We see clearly here that love of God is not a state of habitual oneness. Being always vulnerable, we are caught in perpetual tension between assurance of salvation and salvation egoism. Love must win its way out of this conflict. As we are righteous and sinners at one and the same time, in the age before the eschaton we can never escape the close proximity of conflict and love.

Yet love—whether achieved for a moment in time or as the eschatological fulfilment beyond our temporality—is always for Luther an unequivocal act in which the whole of the ego is integrated. He can illustrate this by the will of man which, as in his exposition of Psalm 1, represents the whole life of man and constitutes his source and guiding head (cf. *Operationes in psalmos* [WA, 5, 33; LW, 14, 294f.]). Where life is grasped by the Spirit there arises unequivocal love, pure good pleasure, and the delight of the heart in God's will. To be sure, the desire of the members of which Paul speaks in Romans 7 strives against the unequivocal will that is seized by love. (Even though the serpent's head has been bruised it still strikes with its tail.) Yet ineluctably the movement of love in the will draws to itself the other spheres of the ego, and the heart and body follow it. As the I is brought by love to rectitude, to conformity with God's will, the other members no longer need imperatives to spur them on; love draws everything to itself (cf. the Galatians Commentary of 1519 [WA, 2, 576; LW, 27, 349f.]). The spiritual will, shaped by the Spirit, is a loving willing with God's will; it is concord and conformity.

From different angles, then, it has become clear that love is not to be viewed as a state. It is either, as I boldly put it, the unequivocal "moment" which the Pneuma achieves in the strife of the members or it is the eschatological triumph. In both—in love in time or love beyond temporality—love is plainly not an attainment of our own nature. It is God's most proper work to write his law in this way in our hearts.[28]

Love is not, then, a psychogenic phenomenon; it is to be understood in terms of the external factor of the Spirit-filled Word. To that extent the spiritual life of the Christian is a hidden thing. It cannot be demonstrated as an empirical datum. It has no place that can be fixed psychologically. Even the heart is not a place of this kind. It is grounded in the invisible God himself. It is grounded solely in the

---

[28]Calvin, *Jeremiah and Lamentations*, p. 132.

hearing of the Word of promise and therewith in the Spirit who opens our ears to hear.[29]

3. LOVE IN STRUCTURES

We must look again at the question of the form of love that occupied us in the preceding section. As we have dealt with it thus far, it has met us in the internal zone of the ego. It represented harmony or conformity with God's will. This was correct so long as we depicted the external basis of the conformity, its basis in hearing, in the Word and Spirit.

It is a question, however, whether love does not press toward a form that lies beyond the internal zone of the ego. The elementary structure of love indicates that this is so. Purely formally, it comes from outside the ego. It orients itself to what is outside the ego. The Thou belongs constitutively to love: the Thou of God and the Thou of the neighbor. One may ask, however, whether this hint is enough.

The one who is called to agapic love must be there for his neighbor with mercy, help, and comfort. Necessarily this involves wanting to give the maximum of help to others. We can strive after this maximum only if we do not simply respond to their need for help in the form of spontaneous assistance (e.g., by gifts of money, soup kitchens, alms) but also inquire into the causes of their plight. Only then can we hope to do more than deal with the symptoms and momentary needs and get to the root of the evil.

An example may help.

The question of the causes of poverty can lead us to social roots. Mass poverty and proletarian suffering may be due to particular economic structures. They may also be related to the rise of crime, the failure to rehabilitate released prisoners, and many other things. In this regard the spontaneous assistance of the moment cannot bring any decisive cure. In some circumstances it might even contribute to the obscuring of the real seat of the disease.

If suffering is rooted in a certain social system, maximum help (and love) can be achieved only by going systematically to the root of the evil, altering the social structures, and thus seeing the tasks of love in a specific political attitude. There can be no doubt that the atheist Karl Marx—under very different banners—discovered this dimension of love. The motives that led him to this and his programmatic inferences from it are not at issue when we say this.

The story of the Good Samaritan who spontaneously aided the man who fell among thieves (Luke 10:30ff.) needs to be carried a step further to bring out these systematic implications of the commandment of love. Love has the task not merely of binding up wounds but of preventing them, i.e., creating circumstances which as far as possible will rule out the wicked acts of the thieves. The task of love has the goal of systematic and politically active prevention.

Does not the reference to this form of love extend essentially our understanding of the Pneuma and his work? If the Pneuma brings us close to God and opens us up

---

[29]Cf. On the Epistle to the Hebrews (WA, 37/III, 215, 1; LW, 29, 216).

to him through the conformity of love, this implies that he also opens our eyes to our neighbor as the one he ultimately is, the apple of God's eye (Psalm 17:8; Zechariah 2:12, etc.), the bearer of alien worth. That the Pneuma attests the neighbor to us in this way can only mean, however, that he also opens our eyes to the forces and powers which oppose our neighbor's worth, which alienate him from his destiny, which block his ability to hear and mar his image. If the Spirit searches the deep things of God, he also searches the deep and shallow things in the existence of the neighbor—or? The mere sight of the things that are disclosed to us therewith can bring us closer to the maximum of loving concern of which we have spoken. Thus the horizon of love extends to the political sphere, relates social structures and their alteration to the theme of love (and therefore also to the witness of the Spirit), and gives a Christian sense to the form of love that has been called "love in structures."[30]

We cannot speak of this structural dimension of love, of course, without emphatically pointing out how decisive it is what motive lies behind it. Does it go back to the testimony of the Holy Spirit who attests the neighbor to us and thus shows us what threatens to mar his image or does it derive primarily from an intention to improve the world structurally or from a political program? The two motives move in opposite directions. In what direction the socially and politically humanitarian thought moves is obvious. It is definitely not grounded in the external factor of the spiritual Word which gives birth to a new creature but presupposes the possibility of a self-production of the new man and it thus produces a distinctive modification of the idea of works righteousness. Since the identity of man is seen only in his social function, he can change and therefore "produce" himself by changing the social conditions of his existence. The apparently attainable perfection of final social conditions leads necessarily, then, to the vision of a correspondingly perfect man who is no longer beset by egoism, aggression, and crime.

The tragedy of this illusory conception is that it overlooks the destructive fact of the fall or interprets it as a false social development which can be reversed. In contrast it is an axiom of the Christian view of existence and history that man is radically enslaved to alienation in a way that he himself cannot reverse. This may be seen pneumatologically in the fact that the Spirit has to open blind eyes and deaf ears and hardened hearts (1 Corinthians 2:9) and that they cannot open themselves. The point of the doctrine of justification that lies behind this is that there is no self-liberation, no possibility of the self-production of man by his works. The questionable nature of man which social humanism overlooks is thus brought to light precisely in the way in which the fall cannot be overcome, and proves resistant as it were, in any system, even in the doctrine of structural redemption.

---

[30]The phrase seems to have been coined by the politician M. Kohnstamm (cf. W. D. Marsch, "Wie revolutionär sind Christen" in *Information der Evangelischen Zentralstelle für Weltanschauungsfragen*, No. 31, IV [1968], p. 12). It is related to the "theology of revolution initiated by Richard Shaull (cf. "Revolutionary Change in Theological Perspective," *Changing World* [New York/London, 1966], Vol. I). For surveys see H. E. Tödt, "Theologie der Revolution," *Ökumenische Rundschau*, I (1968), p. 1; J. Moltmann, "Gott in der Revolution," EK, X (1968), pp. 564ff.; R. Frieling, "Die lateinische Theologie der Befreiung," MD, II (1972), pp. 26ff.

Two examples will make this plain.

First, Milan Machovec has classically described the resistance of the fall in the Marxist-Leninist system (*Jesus für Atheisten* [1972], pp. 17f.; E.T. *A Marxist Looks at Jesus* [Philadelphia, 1976], pp. 29f.). As he points out, Marx and his first disciples sharply criticized the social system which left the alleviation of human suffering to private initiative and therefore to chance. Three or four generations of Socialists knew very well what G. B. Shaw portrayed in his plays, namely, that "private Samaritans" do not alter the foundations of exploitive capitalist society but simply promote the illusion of the pure and the pharisaism of the rich—a double deception that has to be radically dispelled. Socialist states, then, set up a system of social security to care for the sick and handicapped and unemployed. But how could these noble 19th-century Socialists foresee that in the 20th century a situation would arise in which thousands of people would believe that official institutions alone are responsible for the needy, that the state has taken over everything, that the compassionate and self-sacrificial heart has been replaced, and that in the last resort individuals would feel no discomfort at others suffering around them? Thus the ancient egoism and cowardice and pharisaism come back in a new garb. The devil cannot be banished or outplayed with the help of institutional safeguards. The fall cannot be organized away, for it transcends organizable structures. The resistance of the bad as it recurs in a new form gives the lie to the dream that love can be institutionalized and that this institutionalizing will give rise to non-alienated man.

Second, the dominance of the thought of structures and the underlying concept of an organized society that is an end in itself mean that fellow-humanity and love are tied to certain structural limits, i.e., to "class." This result is unavoidable when history is understood in Marxist fashion as a history of class conflict and man is understood as a function of the class situation. Thus Mao Tse-Tung (cf. *Reden an die Schriftsteller und Künstler im neuen China* [East Berlin, 1952], pp. 16, 59) opposes the ancient and Enlightenment view of love of humanity in general instead of class-conditioned love. Many comrades say that everything must be done out of love. But we must realize that in a society of classes there is only class-conditioned love. These comrades want a classless love of humanity, an abstract love, an abstract freedom, an abstract human nature. Since society split up into classes there has no longer been an all-embracing love of humanity. Confucius and Tolstoy could not establish the demands they made along these lines. True love of humanity will come only when classes are set aside. (For a similar attack on abstract and classless humanism cf. M. I. Petrosian, *Essay über den Humanismus* [East Berlin, 1966], quoted in A. Gehlen, *Moral and Hypermoral* [1969], p. 85.) Within this class-confined and -conditioned love we again see signs of the fall in the form of pharisaism, hatred, and aggression, the new mask being that these are now transformed into collective emotions, into the magnifying of one's own class and the despising of others or the attitude of members of socialist systems to members of (capitalistic) class societies.

Love, we might say in conclusion, is either determined from outside by the work of the Word and Spirit or it becomes the function of its immanent bearers. The same applies to the form of man and the neighbor. Either his worth is determined externally and is understood as an alien dignity or it changes secretly into the pragmatic predicate of usefulness, of suitability and functional competence in a specific social system. (This is not said with the East alone in view!) This downward movement threatens every secular humanism that has an immanent foundation. (On this whole problem of a structural production of the new man as works-righteousness cf. my discussion of Marcuse in Anthrop, pp. 53ff.)

III

The Holy Spirit as the Basis of Hope

Bibliography: E. Bloch, *Das Prinzip Hoffnung* (1959); H. Fries, "Spero ut intelligam," *Wahrheit und Verkündigung. Festschrift für M. Schmaus* (1967), I, pp. 353ff.; G. Marcel, *Homo Viator. Entwurf einer Phänomenologie und Metaphysik der Hoffnung* (1949); E.T. *Homo Viator* (New York, 1962); W. D. Marsch, *Zukunft* (1971); J. B. Metz, "Verantwortung der Hoffnung," *Stimmen der Zeit*, CLXXVII (1966); also "Gott vor uns," *Ernst Bloch zu Ehren* (1965), pp. 227ff.; J. Moltmann, *Theologie der Hoffnung*; E.T. *Theology of Hope* (New York, 1967); J. Pieper, *Über die Hoffnung*, 6th ed. (1961); J.-P. Sartre, "Die Zeitlichkeit bei William Faulkner," *Situationen* (1965), pp. 98ff.; G. Sauter, *Zukunft und Verheissung* (1965); H. Schlier, *Über die Hoffnung* (1964); P. Schütz, *Parusia. Hoffnung und Prophetie* (1960), esp. pp. 423ff., 592ff.; T. Wilder, *The Eighth Day of Creation* (1968), esp. pp. 67, 82.

1. PRESENT AND FUTURE ESCHATOLOGY

It is well known that the biblical and especially the prophetic understanding of history usually has had and has a part in the development of a concept of history which presents it as a closed process that is to be seen in its totality.[1] One of the most important reasons for the understanding of history as a meaningful continuum and not just a collection of individual histories is that by the reference to the Lord of history as Creator, Redeemer, and Consummator the three tenses of temporal occurrence are related to one another, not in the sense of a perceptible structure but in terms of a believed meaning. Not just the spatial spheres of east and west but the temporal epochs of past, present, and future "rest peacefully in his hands." The gifts that have been and will be given us, memory and hope, the then of what is

---

[1]Cf. H. Cohen, *Die Religion der Vernunft aus den Quellen des Judentums* (1919), pp. 307ff.: "The idea of history is a creation of Judaism"; K. Löwith, *Weltgeschichte und Heilsgeschehen* (1953), pp. 11ff.; E.T. *Meaning in History;* E. Meyer, *Geschichte des Altertums*, II, 2, 3 (1953), p. 285; H. W. Wolff, "Das Geschichtsverständnis der alttestamentlichen Prophetie," *EvTh*, V (1960), pp. 218ff.; *Anthrop* (1976), pp. 342ff.

behind us and the then of what is eschatologically promised, are all encircled by this peace.

If what is ahead, the promise of fulfilment, is given a special accent, this is connected with the nature of God as Yahweh, who says of himself: "I will be what I will be, I will be what I am."[2] God is always active. That he is "God in action" he demonstrates as the Holy Spirit who constantly moves from the past into the present and opens up the future. To this extent this disclosure of the times has a trinitarian character.[3]

At the same time the efficacious power of the Spirit is connected with motifs which are present in man's historical existence and which E. Bloch has impressively (if one-sidedly) formulated in his *Prinzip Hoffnung*. To be human is to be on the way to something else. It has to be described by an "ontology of the not yet." Asked to put his philosophy in a nutshell, Bloch can say: "S is not yet P." Sartre expresses this constitutive significance of the future for man's historicity in his criticism of W. Faulkner's understanding of temporality.[4]

Faulkner, he thinks, knows only a present that without cause is suddenly there and then fades again. There is in him nothing of the future. Nothing takes place; everything has already taken place. With no future all that we experience may be reduced to the pessimistic and destructive saying: "It cannot last." In contrast Sartre thinks that the present moment or tense can be preserved from its isolation only if we are aware of its openness to the future. A white page whose other side is hidden from us (though we can turn it over) and all the solid bodies around us develop their most direct and intensive qualities in the future. *"Man is not the sum of what he has but the totality of what he does not yet have but can have"* (italics mine).

What is here purely phenomenological, i.e., man's observed attitude of expectation, is given a theological basis, and integrated into the correlation of question and answer, by the work of the Spirit which is the ground of the future. We shall have to see later what significance the Pneuma has for the summing up of the times. First, however, it is important to consider the historicity of the salvation event in this sense. From it we may see that the tension between past and future does not just determine the understanding of the two Testaments but is already present within them.

In the classical prophecy of Israel the idea of possible possession of the Spirit by individuals (e.g., Moses, the seventy elders, the judges, and the kings) is replaced by consideration of the future promise that not just the messianic king or Servant of the Lord will bear the Spirit, but with the help of different metaphors the outpouring of the Spirit is promised to members of the messianic kingdom (Isaiah 32:15; 44:3; Ezekiel 11:9; 39:29). By the imparting of the Spirit God will change the stony heart into a heart of flesh (Ezekiel 36:26f.). The sudden coming of the Spirit (W. Eichrodt) as it now takes place in the case of individuals will never become the tranquil abiding and completing of an assured position. Indeed, there is only a

---

[2]See EG, II, pp. 132ff.; EF, II, pp. 109ff.
[3]This is why I presented the doctrine of the Trinity in EF, II in the chapter entitled "Revelation as a Word Which Posits History" (pp. 124ff.).
[4]J.-P. Sartre, in *Situationen*, pp. 98ff.

stretching in faith for what comes but is not seen as yet. The endowment of prophets with the Spirit is always seen only as sending, equipping, and guiding by Yahweh, as the disclosure of an unknown coming which can be only the advent of one and the selfsame God.[5] Only the community of the end-time and the fulfilled kingdom will be completely equipped with the Spirit along with the Messiah as *the* bearer of the Spirit.

The tension between what the promise of the Spirit causes us to wait for in the future and what is already present as a preliminary stage is even sharper in the primitive community and in Paul. Whereas prophetic expectation of the Spirit has an almost exclusively eschatological accent and is oriented to the messianic end-time, the NT is aware of an endowment with the Spirit before the end-time, not in the sudden and sporadic manner of the OT, but as a constitutive element in the Christian life. John the Baptist and presumably the historical Jesus were still waiting for the gift of the Spirit at the Parousia, at the coming of the Messiah in his glory. But the community at Pentecost is already given a first instalment of the expected Spirit. It is made into the Christian community only by this first instalment. This could not be foreseen in the program of end-time expectation found in the Jewish community. In this program it could never have happened to the Jewish community. The unique factor in the Christian community, that which gives it its own distinctive profile and marks it off both from the OT community and from the coming kingdom, might be described in this way. In the giving of the Spirit at Pentecost this community already receives the gifts of the coming kingdom even though the kingdom itself has not yet come.

This cannot mean, of course, that future eschatology is replaced by a present eschatology. The present imparting of the Spirit is only an anticipation or foretaste of the end-time event. It does confer a possession which is adequate in itself. Instead, it intensifies the promise by pointing, as a first instalment, to the coming fulness. What is already here has still to come in its fulness. What we already have always points beyond itself.

Thus the tension which permeates the NT, that of the now and the then, of present and future, leads on the one side to the praise of the God who is already here and on the other side to the petition: "Come, Lord Jesus" (Revelation 22:20). The reception of the Spirit at Pentecost is understood only as an advance on the final inheritance, as a firstfruits and deposit (*arrabōn*) (Romans 8:23; 2 Corinthians 1:22; 5:5). The coming aeon leaves traces of itself already in the ongoing age and thus points to what has still to come. The Spirit of him who raised Jesus from the dead and who thus brings to pass what lies ahead of our present grants us certainty that in his future "he will give life to your mortal bodies also through his Spirit which [already] dwells in you" (Romans 8:11). By baptism we are already "set in the sphere of the Spirit of God who has already become active in the community."[6]

---

[5]W. Eichrodt, *Theologie des AT*, I (1933), p. 208, cf. pp. 203ff.; E.T. *Theology of the OT* (Philadelphia, 1961).

[6]Cf. F. Hahn, MD, V, p. 93. Thus baptism and the giving of the Spirit are closely related. The Spirit does what baptism attests. He calls to sonship (Romans 8:15). But sons are heirs (8:17), and so the address of the Spirit points to the manifestation of the children of God (8:19; cf. Colossians 3:4;

In view of the fact that the endowment of the Spirit is a promise and deposit it is absurd to say that in the NT kerygma only the Spirit comes instead of the kingdom—just as absurd as Loisy's comment vis-à-vis Harnack that Jesus proclaimed the kingdom of God and the church came instead (A. Loisy, *L'Evangile et l'Eglise,* 3rd ed. [1904], p. 154; E.T. *The Gospel and the Church,* p. 166). The trust is that at *one* point in our world of death—at the point where Christ's community is—the power of life is already present and the *exousia* of sin has been broken in anticipation of what is to come. We are transferred from the dominion of sin, law, and death to the magnetic field of a new lordship. This is still partial (1 Corinthians 13:9). We are only partially liberated. The battle between the flesh and the Spirit continues (Romans 7:17ff.). Even though the heart is changed there are still within us unredeemed areas, numb members that are not yet renewed. We are still in a process of becoming, of growth and progress. We are far from perfect. Yet within the old world and our old being we are seized and summoned. A new history with us has begun. This miracle is the Spirit-promise of what is to come.

It is a mistake, then, to separate present and future eschatology and play off the one against the other. If we take from the presence of the Spirit its character as promise, and thus cease to view it as a mere instalment and pledge,[7] this means detaching the Spirit from him who gives him and who remains identical with him (2 Corinthians 3:17). The Spirit thus becomes a title of ownership for our existence, the dynamic of a power that is immanent within us. He has to be understood as a "quality" and loses his character as something outside that we cannot control. But the converse is also true. If the Spirit is seen *only* as the content of a promise, he is made into the docetic ghost of an impalpable future that is not present at all. He is thus robbed of that which makes the certainty of promise possible for us: the fact that he *already* opens and appropriates to us the Word which contains the promise, causing it to penetrate to our "inner man."[8] In Paul the connection between present and future eschatology is precisely that the Spirit is "*here* (already) the power of the assault of grace on the world which already gives eternal life *now* (Rom. 5-8) but whose goal is that everything *become* subject to Christ (1 Cor. 15:28)."[9]

The division of the gift of the Spirit into two stages, that of promise and that of fulfilment, shows that the Spirit *relates to time*, not just to present and future but also to past. There was a time without the Pneuma (John 7:39), a time in which the death-dealing letter reigned without the Spirit, opposing the appropriation of the Word—Calvin's penetration—and therefore operating as the power of destruction

---

1 John 3:2). In Acts 10 the outpouring of the Spirit precedes baptism whereas in Acts 8 and 19 the baptized have not yet received the Spirit. This is connected with a "dynamic understanding" of the Spirit (Hahn) but does not remove the basic relation to the incorporation into sonship which the Spirit effects at baptism.

[7]Firstfruits (*aparchē*): Romans 8:23; deposit (*arrabōn*): 2 Corinthians 1:22; 5:5; the Spirit of promise (*tēs epangelias*): Ephesians 1:13; "sealed" by the Spirit for the day of redemption (*esphragisthete*): Ephesians 4:30.

[8]On the basis of Ephesians 1:13 Calvin in this sense calls the Holy Spirit the "internal teacher" by whose work the promise of salvation penetrates our mind and without whom it would only beat the air or reach our ears (Inst., III, 1, 4).

[9]Käsemann, RGG³, II, p. 1174 (italics mine).

and death rather than the power of life. But *now* the Spirit has been given and has permeated our hearts with love (Romans 5:5), transferring us from the distance of servanthood to the immediacy of sonship (Romans 8:15; Galatians 4:6). The Spirit who makes present and yet also promises—a further reference to his relation to time—is connected with the exaltation of Christ. This is the decisive break after which the promised Paraclete is imparted to us (John 14:16; 15:26; 16:7). Even here, however, the reference back to the Word already given remains in force. Whatever the Spirit reveals to us eschatologically can only be exposition of what has already been said: "He will take of mine" (John 15:26; 16:13f.). To be sure, he will *also* lead into all truth and reveal what is now still concealed. But the truth which is to be revealed has already been given. It is manifest. The future can only be the unfolding of a perfect. *The truth does not grow but we grow in and into the truth.* Even if the coming kingdom of God is totally different from this aeon, the truth will still be the same. On the basis of what we have already perceived we shall recognize it even as we shall know again the voice of the Good Shepherd.[10] This is the new mode of *anamnēsis* understood in a Christian sense.

2. JUSTIFICATION AND SANCTIFICATION: THE FUTURE OF FAITH AS GROWTH

If the Holy Spirit binds past, present, and future together in this way, the problem of time emerges in a form which brings out structural analogies to the temporality of faith. Retrospectively faith is related to God's presence in the "mighty acts" that have taken place (Acts 2:11) and prospectively, by the hope dwelling within it, it is related to sight (1 Corinthians 13:12), to seeing him "as he is" (1 John 3:2). And if faith and sight are different modes of relationship, the one to whom they relate is always the same: he who was and is and is to come.

We have already noted the temporal structure of faith in the story of individual faith. Here, too, faith presses for a change of life, for sanctification.[11] If in so doing it links the indicative on which it rests with the imperative,[12] this imperative also contains the promise of the future. It has the ring not only of a "Thou shalt" but also of a "Thou shalt be."

Only on this presupposition—in terms of the tension of the already and the not yet—can one understand the concept of progressive sanctification, the growth element in faith. Luther, even though he says that the subject of faith is only a mathematical point with nothing of its own to develop, can still speak of growth and progress in the life of faith.[13] He talks of becoming more and more righteous and moving from the good to the better.[14] In these references, of course, the decisive stress is still explicitly on limitation. Advancing is always a new begin-

---

[10]On the interrelation of past, present, and future cf. EG, II, §15, pp. 238ff., 265ff.; EF, II, pp. 184ff., 199ff.

[11]On this cf. A. Köberle, *Rechtfertigung, Glaube und neues Leben* (1965), pp. 88ff.

[12]ThE, I, §§314ff.; E.T. I, pp. 72f., 83ff.

[13]On what follows cf. ThE, I, §§1097ff.; E.T. I, pp. 226f.

[14]Cf. the Romans Commentary (Ficker ed., II, 101, 20; 76, 30-77, 7; 267, 2-6, etc.; LW, 27, 225, 478).

ning; beginning without advancing means falling back.[15] The process of growth that looks to the future is always forced to refer back to what has happened, to the act of salvation and justification that has already been grasped in faith. This implies two things.

First, the concept of growing and unfolding life is unavoidable when we have personal life in view. We cannot think of personal life as a state of rest and balance in a static relation. A static view would be inevitable if we accepted the abstract alternative of either being in order or not, of either standing in faith or not. Even the idea of a mathematical point must not be isolated and thus made into an ideology which robs the believing ego of its own being and its own historicity. One must not overlook the fact that this epigrammatic term has a polemical meaning in Luther and serves no more than a defensive purpose, being designed to ward off a view of faith which sees in it a work or an experience. Faith may still be an act of man and take the form of a psychological emotion. Indeed, it certainly does so. But these phenomenologically demonstrable features in the ego are not what causes faith to bring justification. As we have seen, faith lives by him in whom it believes and not by itself. It is thus related to forgetfulness of self and makes the subject of faith in some sense a negligible quantity.

Second, there is tension between the two statements (1) that personal life can be thought of only dynamically and not statically, so that it necessarily finds itself in movement, growth, and progress, and (2) that faith cannot have its own center of action. Combining the two statements can lead to overemphasis on either the one or the other. Faced with this threat of conflict we can find a helpful corrective in Luther's thesis that advancing can take place only with a constant reference back to the beginning, to the origin of faith. This also contains a pneumatological reference. For it tells us that we cannot think of progress in the spiritual life as the mere unfolding of an inserted seed of sanctification. The Spirit is "in" us but he never becomes a quality or possession of ours in the Osiandrian sense. Being in us always means working on us. The reference back to the beginning takes up this understanding of the Spirit. It refers us to him who gives us a part in grace and justification and to our "first" reaction to this, namely, that we fear and love him.[16] It leads us to forgetfulness of self and directs us to him who works on us.

Now just as the backward look turns us away from ourselves and points us to him who works on us, so it is with the forward look to our future. The statement that we are at the same time both righteous and sinners, that we are now sinners in fact (*in re*) and righteous only in hope (*in spe*), is a complementary argument for the fact that in the growth of the spiritual life we do not have an "impressed form" which is engaged in vital self-development and which thus fixes attention on our inner history. No, because holiness has begun and increases daily we wait for our flesh to be put to death covered with dirt but also to come forth and to be raised up to full and total holiness in a new life.[17] As our new being has sprung from that which works on us, so our future trust is not for the self-development of a seed

---

[15]Exposition of Psalm 91 (WA, 4, 350, 14).
[16]Cf. Joest, *Gesetz und Freiheit*, 2nd ed. (1956), pp. 145ff.
[17]LC on the 3rd article (LBK, II, p. 659,1; Tappert, p. 418).

deposited in us but for what the Spirit will further do to us, increasingly overcoming the old ego and granting us new life.

The glance at self, insofar as it is not blocked by forgetfulness of self, can only cause us to see the sin that *de facto* is still in us and by this sobering sight prevent us from falling victim to the illusion of a spiritual transfiguration. For as yet we are only half pure and holy until the Holy Spirit by the Word and daily forgiveness brings us to the life where there will be no more forgiveness but people who are fully pure and holy . . . free from sin and death and all evil.[18] Our future, then, will not be the completion of our evolution but the history of God's Spirit with us to which we commit ourselves in faith and hope. As this history uses the Word that is proclaimed and addressed to us, it is not the history of our supposedly isolated personal individuality but the history of the church—a process which takes place in communication with the community to which the Word and Spirit are entrusted.[19] The community again is not thought of as a self-evolving institution, or, in modern terms, one that is shaped by group dynamics and social processes; it is always referred to him who by the spiritual Word called and gathered it and leads it to his coming kingdom. The church, too, is an instalment of this kingdom. For this reason it has not come in place of the kingdom. It is a *locum tenens* for the future. It lives by what has come and is still to come. It is to grow toward what is to come in faith, love, and hope. But in so doing it remembers that this growth does not result from the fruitfulness of its organic conditions but is due to the Spirit who empowers it for faith, love, and hope and who sets the goal of hope toward which it grows.

---

[18] *Ibid.*, p. 659,7; Tappert, p. 418.
[19] *Ibid.*, p. 659,19f.; Tappert, p. 418.

B. The Work of the Power of the Spirit

IV

The Gifts of the Spirit (Charismata)

1. THE DIVERSITY OF GIFTS

Bibliography: K. Barth, CD, IV,2, pp. 825ff.; R. Bultmann, *Theologie des NT* (1953), pp. 157f.; E.T. *Theology of the NT*, pp. 154ff.; H. von Campenhausen, *Kirchliches Amt und geistliche Vollmacht in den ersten drei Jahrhunderten* (1953), pp. 67ff.; E.T. *Ecclesiastical Authority*, pp. 62ff.; H. Conzelmann, art. "Charisma," TDNT, IX, pp. 402ff.; TWNT, IX, pp. 393ff.; H. Greeven, "Die Geistesgaben bei Paulus," *Wort und Dienst*, N.F. VI (1959), p. 111; H. Gunkel, *Die Wirkungen des Heiligen Geistes*, 3rd ed. (1909); E.T. *The Influence of the Holy Spirit* (Philadelphia, 1979); A. Schlatter, *Paulus, der Bote Jesu*, 2nd ed. (1956), pp. 331ff.; H. Schürmann, *Die geistliche Gnadengaben in den paulinischen Gemeinden* (1970), pp. 236-67; H. D. Wendland, "Das Wirken des heiligen Geistes in den Gläubigen nach Paulus," ThLZ, LXXVII (1952), pp. 457ff. For ecstatic phenomena in modern holiness movements, especially speaking in tongues, cf. D. J. Bennett, *The Holy Spirit and You* (Plainfield, N. J., 1973).

The derivation of the term "gifts of the Spirit or of grace" (*charismata*)[1] from *charis* and *charizomai* yields the sense of a "proof of favor," or "benefit," or "gift," although, as we shall see, with a constant reference to the one who gives the gifts. The gifts are the result of *charis* in action.[2] In Paul the same applies to *charis* as to *dikaiosynē*. The latter as active righteousness means God's justifying act as well as the state of the justified. Similarly *charis* means grace and proof of favor as well as the work in the one thus favored in the form of joy and gratitude. Both concepts refer to one thing but from different standpoints, first God's and then man's. They mean especially ecstatic gifts (prophecy and speaking in tongues) but also endowment for secular everyday service.[3]

The theological question posed for us by spiritual gifts consists primarily of the problem of understanding how the one Spirit who binds together all the members

---

[1] Apart from 1 Peter 4:10 the term occurs mostly in Paul; cf. Romans 11:29; 1 Corinthians 12–14.

[2] TDNT, IX, p. 403.

[3] *Ibid.*, p. 405.

of the community differentiates himself in diverse gifts, of thinking of the unity and plurality of the power of the Spirit in concert.

The special gifts mentioned in 1 Corinthians 12–14 make this an urgent question. If the Pneuma as we have understood him thus far is in man but never becomes a quality or an integral part of man, always working on him and remaining distinct from him, always being in fact the Lord himself, then even the idea of a gift of the Spirit raises problems. Can the work of the power of the Spirit be studied in terms of what it does? Can we try to know the Giver by his gifts?[4] Does not this approach, this apparent use of the empirical aspect, entail the danger of speaking of forms of possession of the Spirit, so that the gift can be detached from the Giver? Does not the very word "endowment" give rise to the same danger, since it usually suggests the intellectual or musical abilities of those who are endowed? Looking at the pounds that are given seems to obscure recollection of him who gave them.

We are certainly not doing hermeneutical violence to the passage if we find developed in 1 Corinthians 12 the very problem corresponding to the questions to which our own view of pneumatology has led.[5] It is important for Paul's argument that he limits the field within which there can be any reference to spiritual gifts at all. His indication that this field is exclusively the Christian community involves a reference to him to whom the community knows it is united as the Giver. The issue cannot be a mere phenomenology of the ecstatic or of diaconal service, for all that may be found in paganism, too. In Paul's sense, however, paganism is without the Spirit. This may be seen in his summons to the Corinthians to remember their pre-Christian past (12:2). Pagans are "led astray" (apagomenoi) to dumb idols. That the idols are "dumb" (aphōna) means that they are impersonal, that there is no encounter with them, that they can give no answer. That pagans are led astray to them expresses the fact that they blindly follow their emotions and do not know what they are doing (cf. Romans 1:21).

To describe the work of the Pneuma one must also oppose certain negative statements. The Spirit does not impel blindly but brings about conscious decision; he sets us before the personal God. The Spirit also summons us out of an unthinkingly compelling traditionalism which simply causes reflexes and, like legalism, does not affect the core of the person. In contrast to pagans, Christians receive a Spirit by whom God so moves the mind and will of men from within that they give themselves to him with their own faith and obey him with their own love.[6] While idols lead men astray and in so doing alienate them, the Spirit enables them to take on their true identity and leads to an involvement in which they are wholly themselves, i.e., the subjects of love and faith and not just the objects of injunctions that must be followed externally. Apagomenoi can also be the word for being led off to prison and execution. But the Spirit leads to freedom (2 Corinthians 3:17f.) and therefore to a new selfhood which cannot be had either in the law or in

---

[4]The saying "by their fruits you shall know them" (Matthew 7:15–20) does not imply a simple reference back to the giver, for what we have here is a polemical statement against false prophets whose deeds will unmask their hypocrisy.

[5]From this standpoint it is immaterial whether "peri . . . tōn pneumatikōn" (1 Corinthians 12:1) is taken in the masculine or the neuter.

[6]Schlatter, Paulus, p. 332.

idolatry. This awakening to selfhood, to originality, is particularly expressed in the depiction of the later multiplicity of gifts. The alienation from the Spirit that is found in paganism also means alienation from self, the loss of identity.

How the gift of the Spirit is here related to him who gives it can be seen in the criterion with whose help the Pneuma may be differentiated from alien and possessive spirits. No one who is apprehended by the Spirit of God can curse Jesus,[7] just as no one can call him Lord except by the Holy Spirit (1 Corinthians 12:3). God, Christ, Holy Spirit: This is the single divine reality which cannot bear witness contrary to itself.

Does not contrariness seem to arise, however, when the one Spirit is differentiated in terms of various "spiritual gifts, ministries, and operations" (*charismata, diakoniai, energēmata*) (12:4–6)? Is it not this threatened dissipation which causes the apostle constantly to appeal to the *one* Spirit within the diversity and to point to the uniting bond which holds together the members of an organism (12:12–26)? The Spirit at work is *one,* though that which he does is multiple.

This leads to the question why the Spirit distributes different gifts. Is this due to the difference in the individualities of those who receive him? And if so, can one say that the Spirit develops what is personal and original, whereas among pagans, to put it metaphorically, we have only copies of collective modes of conduct? In giving life to what is individual in man, does the Pneuma discharge as it were the function of a photographer developing a negative? Have we not seen already that the Spirit has an affinity to the finding of identity?

What suggests that this question should be given a positive answer is especially the fact that the Spirit does not act in the sense of creation out of nothing but rather in that of refashioning and renewing what is there.[8] If each has his own gifts, one this kind and another that (1 Corinthians 7:7), if some are called to teach, some to minister, some to the cure of souls (1 Corinthians 12:6ff.), we may indeed assume that in this regard natural presuppositions and gifts are not left out of account. Yet this cannot be carried to the point of inferring self-fulfilment (perhaps as an end in itself) and ascribing neo-humanistic tendencies (as in W. von Humboldt) to the Pneuma. The uniting of the old and new creature, like the rise of the new identity, is a subsidiary thought, the true point of the *charismata* being found in the unselfish motive of service. The orientation is not to personalities and their fulfilment but to the community as the body that embraces its members. The gifts are equipment for service, for the common good (*sympheron,* 12:7).

As concerns the *charismata,* then, the stress is not on *my* having them but on two things that point away from me: first, that they are given me by another, and second, that they relate to purposes that I do not control, the purposes of the kingdom of God. This is perhaps the reason why it seems to be a serious error, an illegitimate form of *kauchasthai* (boasting) from the NT standpoint, if I say of myself: I am endowed by the Spirit; I control gifts of grace. The impossibility of speaking in this way shows that the *charismata* are not personal qualities.

Paul himself makes it clear that there can be no question of possession when in opposition to some pneumatics who fancied they were in possession he told the

---

[7]Schlatter notes that the naming of the human name "Jesus" here bears a deliberate reference to the offense of the crucified Jew (*Paulus,* p. 334).
[8]EG, I, §8; III, esp. pp. 192ff. and §9; EF, I, c. VIII, esp. pp. 148ff., and c. IX.

church that Christ would sustain (*bebaiōsei*) them while they were waiting for his manifestation (1 Corinthians 1:8). To this extent the gifts are provisional.[9] They are not at all a habit or an indelible character. They are never more than an act that has to be continually prayed for and awaited—until the Parousia.

In this connection Paul, when he has enumerated the various gifts—apostleship, spiritual utterance, teaching, helping, administering, tongues (12:28f.)—demands that there should be striving for "the higher gifts" (*meizona*, 12:31), i.e., for those that transcend the present provisional charisms and will prove permanent. What he has in view is not so much the superiority of prophecy over the tongues that flourished in Corinth, or an emphasis on *gnōsis* or faith,[10] but rather love, to which the familiar hymn is addressed in 1 Corinthians 13 immediately after this exhortation (cf. 2 Corinthians 8:7). Love alone endures. It outlasts faith, which exists only in the Nevertheless opposed to the present age, and it still endures when hope is no longer needed because it has been fulfilled (13:8, 13).

In the light of what endures the provisional nature of the gifts connected with our pilgrim status in this aeon is more clearly etched. As God here and now gives to each his own (and thus brings each to selfhood), the gifts cannot be regarded as "the eternal already present today" but "rather represent our future possession in provisional form."[11] The more we, unlike the pneumatics, keep the giver of the gifts in view, the more we shall be expectant, not forgetting what is finally promised because of the deposit. For the coming of the Lord is still ahead.

2. LIST OF CHARISMS

The list of charisms in 1 Corinthians 12:8-11 (cf. 2 Corinthians 8:7) shows that their plurality corresponds to the diversity of ministries in the community (as also, we may suppose, to differences in natural endowment). To this degree the members of the one body have different functions. Since the list describes ministry, the description is based on the reality. (For this reason Paul does not, e.g., mention laying on of hands or anointing with oil in referring to healing.) Apart from the diversity of the ministry Paul puts the chief stress in his list on the *one* Lord and the *one* God in whom the plenitude of charisms has its common basis so that its indwelling thrust is toward communion and not separation. The many forms of the Spirit's operation may be distinguished but not divided.

The detailed charisms are as follows.

a. Knowledge (*gnōsis*)

The reference is probably to the forms of understanding and clarification that are indwelling implications of faith, just as we find faith and sight and knowledge interrelated in the Johannine writings (John 14:7, 9; 17:25; 1 John 3:6).[12] Faith presses on toward knowledge because it is not just commanded and hence does not

---

[9]Conzelmann, TDNT, IX, p. 405; TWNT, IX, p. 394.
[10]Barth, CD, IV,2, pp. 826f. (KD, IV,2, p. 938) on the basis of 1 Corinthians 14:1 and 13:12.
[11]Conzelmann, TDNT, IX, p. 405; TWNT, IX, p. 395.
[12]Bultmann, *Theologie des NT*, pp. 419, 475; E.T. II, pp. 73, 129f.

arise merely out of legal obedience but confidently and in free spontaneity responds to the call of God. This is possible, however, only when it knows to what it is responding, e.g., when it can differentiate—whether immediately and pre-theoretically or reflectively—between law and gospel. The gnosis-implications of faith mean also that we are led by it to right decisions in the concrete situations of life, e.g., in the difficult question of dealing with those who are weak in faith (Romans 14:13-23) or in the many practical issues that are dealt with in the paraenetic portions of Paul's epistles. Along the same lines we may read in Colossians that the recipients are filled with knowledge (*epignōsis*) of God's will in all wisdom and spiritual understanding (1:9). When the mind (*nous*) is transformed by renewal, the possibility arises of gaining sure judgment (*dokimazein*) on what the will of God is (Romans 12:2).

"Filling" with gifts of knowledge necessarily raises the question of more or less, of the quantitative amount of knowledge and therefore growth. Thus we read in Philippians: "And it is my prayer that your love may abound more and more [*mallon kai mallon*], with knowledge and all discernment, so that you may approve what is excellent . . . " (1:9f.). It may be connected with these different degrees of knowledge that within the charisms knowledge is a special manifestation which the one Spirit who imparts himself to all gives in a special way to one or another in order to serve the rest thereby. We may thus see here the possibility of a *theological* furtherance of the community by those who are particularly capable of interpreting Scripture and the tradition and therewith discharging as it were a vicarious function of knowledge for the community.[13]

b. Wisdom (*sophia*)

The terms *gnōsis* and *sophia* are often interchangeable in the NT, though the ambivalence between the divine and idolatrous character immanent in them is more marked in the case of *sophia*. This may be seen in Paul's distinction between the "wisdom of the world" (*sophia tou kosmou*) and the "wisdom of God" (1 Corinthians 1:20f.). Each seems to be "folly" to the other (1:19, 21). Yet when Paul makes it clear and even shows it to be necessary that the wisdom of God, especially the wisdom of the cross, has this aspect of folly—the Jews cannot help but find it an offense and the Greeks can do no other than see it as foolishness (1:23)—he still claims the word *sophia* for the "foolish" preaching of the cross even though this wisdom is accessible only to the mature (*teleioi*) and remains hidden from the world and especially the rulers of the world (2:6-8). This wisdom which searches the deep things of God (2:10) is not accessible to the rationality of the natural man and is even compromised in his eyes as folly (2:14). It is disclosed by the Pneuma only to those who open themselves to God's Spirit (2:11f.).

Worldly wisdom can, of course, fatally *mix* with the wisdom of God, as in some gnosticizing movements whose spokesmen Paul denounces as "false apostles" (2 Corinthians 11:6, 13). The danger lurking here, to which Paul is particularly sensitive because he himself can use gnostic terminology, manifests itself in much

---

[13]On the interpretation of the tradition (*paradosis*) cf. Bultmann, *Theologie des NT*, pp. 474f.

the same way as the heresy of the pneumatics with which he deals. Both regard the Spirit and the wisdom of God that derives from him as disposable possessions and imparted "qualities." They are thus marked by the same symptoms. Whereas the true community looks toward the Pneuma and his gifts in prayer and hope, the pneumatic and gnostic intruders *boast* of their wisdom and knowledge (1 Corinthians 1:29; 8:1f.). Those charismatically endowed with special *sophia* will realize instead that they are pledged to the *one* Spirit who discloses himself to them in this way and appoints them to ministry.

c. Faith (*pistis*)

When we first hear the list of gifts it might strike us as surprising that faith is put among them and is just one gift among others. This is odd because faith is the condition for the reception of all the gifts of the Spirit and to that extent is superior to them all. In fact Paul puts it at the head of another list of this kind (2 Corinthians 8:7).

It could be that Paul has another aspect of faith in view when he understands it as a charism. There are two possibilities.

First, he may be thinking of it as a force that moves mountains (Matthew 17:20) and of the special power which can be given to it (so H. D. Wendland). But we pause at once: Can we really speak of a special power and say that this "can" be given to faith, and that it is thus one of the extraordinary charisms? Do not this promise and this fulness of power belong to all faith, not just to an extraordinary faith but even to that which is only as a grain of mustard seed (Matthew 17:20; cf. Mark 11:23)? Schlatter tries to explain this idea of a supposedly special form of faith as an error on the part of some exegetes who interpret faith as simply the holding of pure doctrine[14] and thus illegitimately restrict it. For such a theoretical faith which understands itself simply as assent any kind of power will in fact have the character of the extraordinary.

Now undoubtedly this is a caricature of what Paul and the whole of the NT say about faith. In the NT faith is taken in a comprehensive sense as confident clinging to God's promise, as commitment to the truth, and also as sharing in the power of the Kyrios.

Yet it is no aberration if within this complex we should find certain accents and charismatic emphases. In this sense what might be in view in this accentuation is what is said about miracles in what follows in the list.

Second, such an emphasis on special gifts of faith seems likely when we do not think of faith only as faith that justifies us before God. So long as we have this distinctive sense in mind, the quantity of faith and other accompanying attributes are in fact irrelevant. As we have seen, the subject of faith with all that is his, including his gifts, is in the background here. But once we think of the phenomenology of the expressions of faith, of the way in which it manifests itself, there are indeed different degrees: little faith,[15] faith as a grain of mustard seed, and growth in faith.[16] We find the type of progress that Luther has in mind with his

---

[14]Schlatter, *Paulus*, p. 341.
[15]Matthew 6:30; 8:26; 14:31; 16:8.
[16]2 Thessalonians 1:3; cf. Ephesians 4:15; 2 Peter 3:18.

concepts of advancement, completion, and beginning, as well as becoming more and more righteous. We find the faith that is stronger or weaker, that is more pressured by temptation and doubt or not. Finally, then, we find the faith that has the advantage of the special riches of gifts of faith (*perisseuein*, 2 Corinthians 8:7). From this standpoint some gifts of faith might very well be listed among the *charismata*.

d. Miracles, Healing, and Authority over Powers (*charismata* and *energēmata dynameōn*, 1 Corinthians 12:9f.)

The gift of healing as a divinely given charismatic power of faith stands in opposition to the disruption of his creation by sickness, pain, and death. The Spirit of God in which it participates is the force that resists the powers of disorder. The Spirit, however, does more than heal. He manifests himself as authority over the powers.

The term "powers" is a genitive plural here (*dynameōn*). Schlatter and others construe it as a subjective genitive ("the operations of the powers"),[17] but *we* take it to be an objective genitive ("authority over the powers"). Behind this view lies the consideration that in Paul and the rest of the NT *dynamis* is usually the power of God or the power granted to believers—a power which is strong even in the weak (2 Corinthians 12:9f., etc.). Only by way of exception is *dynamis* used for forces that are ungodly or antigodly, e.g., those that might come between God and us (Romans 8:38), or the power of sin that lies in the law (1 Corinthians 15:56; cf. Ephesians 1:21). In this case the plural, being used of ungodly forces,[18] suggests an objective genitive, so that the reference is to a power given *over* the powers. The reference might be to *exousia* over demons (Matthew 7:22; Luke 9:1; 10:17) or in relation to the anathema (1 Corinthians 5:5).

e. Prophecy and the Discernment of Spirits (*diakriseis pneumatōn*)

Unlike other forms of proclamation the gift of prophecy is characterized by the fact that the prophet receives his message directly from God, that it is spoken "into" him and not mediated through men. In this sense inspiration is always treasured as a special gift of the Spirit. Here the Pneuma attests himself in his immediacy (*auto to pneuma*, Romans 8:16). Immediacy does not mean that the word of the prophecy has no reference to the Word that has been spoken or that it has an authority of its own. If this were so, the prophetic statements would contradict one another—and possibly stand in opposition to the Word—and they would thus be detached from the one and indivisible Spirit of God. This in turn would refute their validity. The prophetic element is integrated as a member into the organism of the community and its tradition. There is thus a chain of prophets whose members are interrelated. They cannot fail to be connected to one another. They will be ready to seek the manifestation of God's Spirit, and open to hear him, not only in themselves but in others, too.

---

[17] Schlatter, *Paulus*, p. 342.
[18] In the sense of divine power *dynamis* is rare in the plural; it occurs in relation to the *charismata* when governed by the thought of differentiation and multiplicity (1 Corinthians 12:28f.; Galatians 3:5).

Yet there are false and true prophets, pseudo-prophets and real ones. All that glitters is not gold and everyone who prophesies is not a prophet. The unconditional claim with which prophecy comes would leave us helpless in face of truth or falsehood if in addition to the gift of prophecy there were not also given the charism of the discernment of spirits.

That there are many spirits (of dubious origin, Ephesians 6:12) as well as the Holy Spirit means that we are confronted by the most varied claims and cannot therefore accept every spirit's appeal to God or validity as a prophetic authority. We are threatened by a similar confusion here as with the various wisdoms (*sophiai*) among which there may be worldly wisdom as well as the wisdom of the cross which is concealed as foolishness. The term Pneuma, especially in the plural, is clearly ambivalent. Even the self-validation of a supposed bearer of the Spirit by an appeal to God's Word may be a mere pretext and palpable camouflage. The classic instance of this is to be found in the story of the temptation of Jesus (Luke 4:1–13) where the satanic power practices its seductive skills with the help of quotations from Scripture. The devil, however, is not subject to the Word. He plays with it. He misuses it in deliberate opposition to its Author. Misused in this way on the lips of the devil, the Word of God can be constituted only by the Spirit who led Jesus to this place of conflict and messianic testing (4:1). Otherwise the "it is written again" which Jesus throws back at the devil could only produce an endless debate of one saying against another. There is no objective and legalistically applicable criterion by which to decide which of the two is right and has Scripture on his side. It is God's Spirit who unmasks the abuse of God's Word and validates the opposing Word.

The Word of Scripture, then, can be misused. It can be set in the service of an alien spirit. Churches, sects, and antichrists all appeal to the Bible. Whether it is the thesis of throne and altar, the principle of democracy, apartheid, or an ideology of state and society—they all want to find biblical support. Even pure doctrine is not exempt from the verdict that it may be appealing illegitimately to God's Word, e.g., when the Word of God is misunderstood legalistically (cf. the fundamentalist view of verbal inspiration) or detached from time and condemned to irrelevancy in an ivory tower (cf. some champions of orthodoxy under Hitler who were blind to the pseudo-Christian claim of the German Christians and their mixtures of theology and politics). The moment when the discernment of spirits helps is often the moment when mere argument is broken off (because it prolongs the discussion to infinity) and exorcism or the anathema of 1 Corinthians 5:5 must take over.

The dispute cannot be decided by debate but only in the power of the Spirit. For outwardly the demonic spirit can in fact validate itself, not only by quoting Scripture but even by deeds and miracles (Revelation 16:14). Outwardly it is an open question whether Christ casts out demons in the name of God or of Beelzebub (Luke 11:15–21). The ability to make distinctions at this level is a gift of the Spirit. It transcends all categories at the disposal of human reason.

f. Various Kinds of Tongues and the Gift of Interpretation (*genē glōssōn* and *hermeneia glōssōn*)

By tongues (glossolalia) we understand the form of "speech in which the tongue or the whole instrument of speech is not moved and directed by the will of the speaker but by some kind of inner impulse.'"[19] As an ecstatic phenomenon this is common in the pre-Christian and extra-Christian world and within Christianity it is viewed as an irruption of the divine Spirit whose power transcends fixed forms of speech and all other rational controls.

Instead of an irruption of the Spirit a snatching away *to* the Spirit may be seen.[20] Speaking in tongues in modern Pentecostalism may be completely inarticulate utterance (though more than mere baby-talk) but it may also be speaking in a foreign language which observes grammatical rules and syntax.[21] The ecstasy of speaking in tongues is usually described as an extreme blessing and even as a foretaste of the bliss of heaven.[22]

For Paul, however, the occurrence of glossolalia among the charisms is not without problems. He presupposes that those who speak in tongues are not speaking to men but to God (1 Corinthians 14:2). The difficulty here is that the decisive mark of the gifts of the Spirit is pushed in the background, namely, that of *serving* the community. Do those who speak in tongues meet this claim? This is the question. For as distinct from prophetic utterance which serves to edify the community, those who speak in tongues edify only themselves (14:4). They cannot communicate and so they make the hearers "foreigners" who do not understand them (14:9, 11). Communication breaks off because only the Pneuma in them prays and the understanding (*nous*), the organ which forms an intellectual link, plays no part (14:14). Hence the community cannot say Amen to what is spoken (14:16). Paul, then, asks for an interpreter who can translate what is not understood into what can be understood and in this way make it charismatic "service" and incorporate it into the organism of the community.

A criterion that the event of glossolalia is a work of the Pneuma and not some kind of—perhaps very pagan—ecstatic possession is its secret relation to the Word, which is concealed at first but then brought to light by the interpreter. In other words, one may see in this way whether speaking in tongues proceeds from the Word and can thus be put back into the verbal form of a saying of faith when the interpreter puts it into something articulate instead of something inarticulate and foreign. Since the Pneuma expresses himself in the Word and imparts himself through it—in distinction from purely ecstatic babblings—this is how it has to be.

Obviously the gift of discernment of spirits has enhanced significance in relation to phenomena of this kind. For the transcending of the Word in glossolalia threatens to evade only too easily the judicial relation to the Word. It can substitute emotional and ecstatic self-enjoyment (in God) for self-forgetful faith. It can also become the expression of a possession which the author has encountered in the cult of Spiritism in Brazil and syncretistic combinations of Christianity and animism in Africa.

---

[19]So H. Rust, RGG[2], p. 2142.

[20]Apart from 1 Corinthians 12 and 14 cf. the promise of glossolalia in Mark 16:17 and the operation of the Spirit of Pentecost in Acts 2:10, 46; 19:6.

[21]Cf. Bennett, *Nine O'Clock in the Morning*, pp. 21ff. Often an ancient or modern language is spoken—even Chinese—which the one who is caught up in tongue-speaking does not normally speak and has not learned.

[22]Bennett (*ibid.*, p. 35) asks what we shall do in heaven if we do not find intercourse with God the most beautiful experience on earth. Shall we play interplanetary golf or interlunar bridge or take up heavenly hobbies to relieve the tedium of "mere" fellowship with God?

Valid forms of glossolalia may be conceived of, if at all, as an emotional extension of worship, deriving from it and returning to it as a form of the Word and proclamation. Exemplary instances of this may be found in black congregations in North America. In such cases glossolalia can have the same significance as the rhythmic music which stimulates emotion (and the nerves) and the cultic dance which is also practiced.

As concerns our own culture the discerning of spirits must ask primarily what is the reason for speaking in tongues or using contemporary music such as jazz and rock. Is it the worship of God and the felicity of faith that impels us to choose this expression which is so close to our own taste and our own power of expression, or is it only a matter of progressive speculations designed to win contemporaries with refined psychological strategies? The first would be as legitimate as the demand to put the gospel in one's own words in order to confess it responsibly. The second, however, is a neo-pagan pragmatism which has renounced confidence in the Word's own activity and efficacy. It lies on the same plane as the changing of theology into sociology and praxiology as areas in which it is thought that contemporaries expose an open flank for Christian advance.

In the case of all the prominent and special gifts represented by the *charismata* the decisive point is their relation to diaconal service (1 Corinthians 12:4). The gifts of the Spirit are thus held aloof from the enjoyment and boasting (*kauchēma*) of those to whom they are given. The prophet cannot exalt himself above a deacon but is always related to him as a member in the same body (12:12–26) who has his gift from the same Lord, is empowered by the same Spirit, and works in the name of the love which is the common bond and which will abide when at the end of history and the dawn of the kingdom "provisional" gifts will no longer be needed.

V

Empowering for Prayer by the Pneuma

Bibliography: H. Beintker, "Zu Luthers Verständnis vom geistlichem Leben des Christen im Gebet," *Luther-Jahrbuch* (1964), pp. 47ff.; H. Benckert, "Das Gebet als Gegenstand der Dogmatik," EvTh, XV (1955), pp. 535ff.; H. von Campenhausen, "Gebetserhörung in den überlieferten Jesusworten und in der Reflexion des Johannischen," *Kerygma und Dogma,* III (1977), pp. 157ff.; F. Heiler, *Das Gebet,* 5th ed. (1932); E.T. *Prayer* (New York, 1958); also "Das Gebet in der Problematik des modernen Menschen," *Interpretation der Welt* (1965), pp. 227ff.; G. von Rad, *Theologie des AT,* I (1958), pp. 362ff.; E.T. *Theology of the OT,* I (New York, 1962), pp. 355ff.; K. Rahner, "Thesen über das Gebet 'im Namen der Kirche,'" in Rahner, V (1962), pp. 471ff.; E.T. *Theological Investigations,* V, pp. 419ff.; also *Von Not und Segen des Gebets,* 7th ed. (1965); J. Ratzinger, *Das neue Volk Gottes* (1969), pp. 225ff.; R. Schäfer, "Gott und Gebet," ZThK (1968), pp. 117ff.; H. Thielicke, "Das Amt des Beters," *Theologie der Anfechtung* (1949), pp. 180ff.; also *Das Gebet, das die Welt umspannt,* 13th ed. (1973); E.T. *Our Heavenly Father* (New York, 1960); F. Wulf, art. "Gebet," *Handbuch theologischer Grundbegriffe,* II, 2nd ed. (1974), pp. 50ff.

One cannot speak about the gifts of the Spirit without including prayer, for speaking with God is a testimony to the relating and presenting which is the work of the Pneuma. Even if we must focus here on the connection between the Spirit and prayer and thus be content to deal with only one aspect of prayer, this aspect is its true core. In the broad area of prayer there is hardly a region to which the pneumatological side will not give access.

1. PRAYER AS ANSWER

Perhaps the oldest Christian definition of prayer is that of Evagrius Ponticus:[1] "Prayer is the ascent of the mind to God."[2] The Neoplatonic background of this saying—that the spirit must free itself from matter, from the body—is plain to see

---

[1] A desert monk from Ibera in Pontus A.D. 346–399.

[2] *proseuche estin anabasis noos pros Theon, Patrologia graeca,* LXXIX, p. 1173.

and it threatens to restrict and even falsify the meaning of prayer. Similarly Augustine's remark in his commentary on the Psalms (on Psalm 75:7) that "your prayer is address to God" (*locutio ad Deum*) may perhaps give too much weight and initiative to the human side of prayer, although this impression is undoubtedly incorrect when we consider the total thrust of Augustine's theology. The nature of prayer from a Christian standpoint certainly cannot be understood unless we see it as an answer to the *command* of God: "Seek ye my face..." (Psalm 27:8; Jeremiah 33:3), and also to his *offer* to be open to my cry and to turn to me in grace (Psalm 4:3; 50:15).

Both points are made in the preface to Luther's Larger Catechism (III, xiii, 17f.) where prayer is spoken of as obedience to a strict command but there is reference also to the promise, to God's attracting and pulling, to his taking to heart our needs (21f.). Prayer is not action but reaction. It bases itself on the preceding Word of God which makes it possible. To bring out this aspect Calvin in his chapter on prayer in the *Institutes* (III, 20, 8) points to the motive behind Daniel's prayer: "We do not pour forth our prayers unto thee on the ground of our righteousness but on the ground of thy great mercy. O Lord, hear us; O Lord, be kindly unto us. Hear us, and do what we ask... for thine own sake" (Daniel 9:18f.).

Precisely in relation to this character of prayer as answer the work of the Pneuma is relevant. For to be certain of the command and the promise as *God's* summons, and to be able to reply to it, presentation is needed in a double sense— first, that of the Word coming to *me* so that I know I am called by "my" name (Isaiah 43:1, 3f.), and second, that of my being certain of the presence of God and my turning to him in freedom (*parrhēsia*). But this, as we have seen, is all the work of the Pneuma. The Spirit "makes the Father present in the heart of him who prays and thus evokes his strength and love (Romans 8:15; Galatians 4:6)."[3]

Since it is the Word that is made present here, prayer rests on presuppositions which this Word creates and places at its disposal. Among these we have in mind especially the manifestation of the incarnate Word which brings the Father close to us and us close to the Father. The most inward relation to Christ described in the parable of the vine (John 15:1–8) is also closeness to the Father. It enables us by his mediation to give thanks to the Father (Colossians 3:17) and to come before him "in the name of Jesus" (Mark 11:24; John 14:13f.; 15:7, 16; 16:23, 26). (Already in EF, II, pp. 181f., 298ff. we dealt with the significance in this regard of the filioque, which views the Spirit of presentation as proceeding from Christ as well.)

2. PRAYER AS UNION WITH THE WILL OF GOD (CONFORMITY)

Conversation with God, which as hearing and answering constitutes the essence of prayer, is possible only in confidence that he addresses me. Since, especially in petitionary prayer, we cannot assume a preexistent congruence between the human will and the divine, there is often conflict between them, and complaint about this conflict (Job). Hence there can be no conversation unless there is a readiness to surrender one's own will and yield to God's.

---

[3]Wulf, HThG, p. 61.

The petition in the Lord's Prayer that God's will be done (cf. Luke 22:42) has nothing whatever to do with the fatalism which capitulates to a superior impersonal fate. The one who prays knows to *whom* he yields and can yield—namely, that he is the one who will do better things for him than he himself can either desire or think (Romans 8:28). When we love and trust we can yield to the one we love and trust. To arrive at union or conformity with the will of God is the triumph of trust and therefore an expression of the certainty that the Spirit's act of presentation imparts to us.

We must now consider more closely the nature of presentation in making prayer possible.

Since prayer is always situational, we do not see in it only the distance from God which is implied in the basic status of sin and alienation and which needs to be bridged by the Pneuma. The situational reference points rather to a special form of alienation. We can pray, says Calvin,[4] only when we "turn the eye of the mind toward God" and "affection of heart has to follow," so that we concentrate on him to whom we turn. The situation in which we are and which weighs on us, however, so occupies us[5] that heart and mind fall far short of concentration and union with God's will, or, more plainly, "they faint and fail, or are carried in the opposite direction."[6] Need may teach us to pray, but only conditionally. On the one side it may impel us to cry to God for help, but on the other it focuses our thoughts and emotions more on our anxiety and plight than on him who is mightier than they are. "They who are truly trained in prayers are not unmindful that, perplexed by blind anxieties, they are so constrained as scarcely to find out what it is expedient for them to utter. Indeed, when they try to stammer, they are confused and hesitate."[7] Naturally a purely legalistic obedience, while it may drive us to prayer, will not overcome this situation which is hostile to prayer. Instead, the law will kill here, too (Romans 7:11; 2 Corinthians 3:6f.). By "law" we have in mind not merely the commanding Word of God, which may well play a role for the practicing Christian, but also the inert law of tradition and background. Legalistic obedience can remain externally when the inner man withdraws and does not participate. This leads to the destructive self-contradiction between inner situation and external act which the NT calls "hypocrisy."[8] A gesture of prayer is made but there is no prayer (Matthew 6:7). Part of prayer is the spontaneity which is possible only for the committed heart. This alone denotes a presentation which makes us certain of God's fatherly closeness and thus causes us to cry directly: "Abba, Father" (Romans 8:15; Galatians 4:6).

This directness of presentation which opens up the possibility of prayer is a work of the Pneuma. It is denoted by the term *parrhēsia*, which means freedom,

---

[4]Inst., III, 20, 5.

[5]Cf. the prayer of the Indian Johnson Gnanabaranam: "My Lord, speak louder! I cannot hear what you say. Your voice is unclear. My Lord, I need your directions, your warning." "My friend," God replies, "my word is very close. To hear my voice is not hard. Close your ears to the voice of evil. You cannot hear my voice and the call of evil at the same time. If you are deaf, come to me and be healed and you will hear my voice."

[6]Inst., III, 20, 5.

[7]*Loc. cit.*

[8]Cf. EG, II, pp. 247, 254f.; EF, II, pp. 206, 210f.

confidence, joy, or spontaneity. This alone signalizes the union of the Christian with Christ, the oneness of branch and vine (John 15:1ff.), and therefore the conformity of man's will with God's.

Where the Spirit fills believers, other and perhaps comparable forms of spontaneity are generated: "Address one another in psalms and hymns and spiritual songs" and "always and for everything give thanks in the name of our Lord Jesus Christ" (Ephesians 5:18–20). Ephesians links the call to pray in the Spirit with the promise that thereby access will be opened up to the mystery of the gospel and all this with *parrhēsia,* with immediacy and joyous freedom (6:18f.). What is here said to be a work of the Spirit can also, with an implicit if not an explicit pneumatological reference, be said of Christ. Faith in him gives joyful assurance (*parrhēsia*) and confident access to God (3:12).

As we have said, the indication that *parrhēsia* is a work of the Spirit makes it clear that we naturally do not control it and are thus incapable of prayer on our own. "Thus we see that God's saintly servants give proof of huge torments . . . when they utter their plaintive cry to the Lord from the deep abyss, and from the very jaws of death.'"[9] Quite apart from the fact that we cannot lift ourselves above our situation, we *ought* not to do so. No act of repression (as we should say today) is needed to smooth our hearts and make us ready for prayer. To be "released from every anxiety" and in "sweet and perfect repose"[10] is inimical to prayer because "great anxiety kindles in us the desire to pray.'"[11] "For the saints the occasion that best stimulates them to call upon God is when, distressed by their own need, they are troubled by the greatest unrest, and are almost driven out of their senses, until faith opportunely comes to their relief.'"[12]

The "almost" used by Calvin shows that the power of need as a spur to prayer is limited. As we have seen, the coming of *parrhēsia* is a work of the Spirit and not a product of our own nature or of natural distress. By nature our helplessness not only robs us of the power and joy of prayer but also—and this is a deeper crisis—fails to make us aware of what we ought to pray and ask for (Romans 8:26). If *all* things work for good to those who love God (8:28), how can we ourselves choose among these things and determine what God ought to give us? Do we not in fact continually ask for foolish things, for the granting of our own desires? And if we try to deck out our prayers with spiritual maturity and to get beyond childish and foolish talking with the Father, is not this hypocrisy of a high degree and even an ancient craft which should be pleasing to neither man nor God?

This is where the work of the Pneuma comes in as empowering for prayer. When we do not know what we should pray for, "the Spirit himself intercedes for us with sighs too deep for words" and "helps us in our weakness" (Romans 8:26). Through the Spirit God calls us into conversation with himself and gives us a share in his own self-knowledge.[13] Thus we are summoned into conformity with God's will, not by acts of sanctification and pious works, but by the act of the Spirit. God

---

[9]Inst., III, 20, 11.
[10]*Loc. cit.*
[11]Inst., III, 20, 4.
[12]Inst., III, 20, 11.
[13]Cf. EG, I, §11, pp. 262ff.; EF, I, pp. 193ff.

recognizes his own Spirit in us—a Spirit conformable to himself[14] and therefore effective in prayer. This conformity can also be called conformity (*symmorphos*) to the image of God's Son (8:29).

The union which the Pneuma effects with God's will transcends our human and natural possibilities. It does not stop any longer at our own wishes and it breaks free from the suggestions of the spirit of anxiety. For the fulfilment enclosed in this kind of prayer is no other than the certainty of conformity to which the coming of the Spirit calls us. The Spirit bears witness (*symmartyrei*) with our spirit that we are the children of God (Romans 8:16) and are thus in harmony with him. The situation of the servant and his external obedience has been overcome. In its place comes the freedom or *parrhēsia* of the child that with the Spirit of Jesus Christ in the heart can draw near to God with the cry: "Abba, Father" (Galatians 4:6). Here supreme readiness for conformity with the will of God as this comes to expression in the prayer: "Not my will but thine be done" can no longer carry with it any painful renunciation. On the contrary, it will be a confident letting go of self. In it we do not fall into an abyss or accept our fate. We commit ourselves to the counsel of a heart that confesses us.

Nevertheless the coming of the Pneuma as the subject of prayer in our place might evoke false associations in us. It might seem as though what we have is a kind of mystical union which expunges the active center of our humanity and dissolves it in the spiritual, eliminating our nature or concrete existence. We need only suggest this possibility of interpretation to see at once a lurking misunderstanding. For did we not maintain in agreement with the Reformers that we cry out of the depths and are oppressed by cares when we pray, that this provides the impulse to pray, and that this troubled state should not be repressed?[15]

This can only mean that the concreteness of our situation and our ego as it is determined by this must not be erased. The question thus arises how the depths which divide us from God and from which we cry (and which must always remain realistically present to us as these depths) can be reconciled with the fact that we let the Spirit of God pray in our place and bury our own will in the will of God.

To solve this problem the Lord's Prayer is our guide, especially with the context it provides for the prayer for union: "Thy will be done. . . ." If this petition stood alone, or were the only petition permitted me, there could hardly be any talk of an actualization by the Pneuma. We should have instead a union outside time, a timeless state of *being one* which, as I noted, is familiar to us from mysticism and leaves far behind the commitments of our existence in the limits of time and space. In it I should be snatched away from myself. In fact, however, the actualization or presentation which we have called a work of the Pneuma takes place in such a way that our temporality remains *relevant* (like the incarnation or condescension of the Word). The Pneuma brings the Word close to us and brings us close to the Word—*in* all the depths and distance. He comes into our every present. And if

---

[14]*kata theon*—his prayers thus being according to God's will (Romans 8:27).

[15]Apart from Calvin cf. the clear statement of Luther that we see and remember the necessity which should constantly compel and force us to pray. For those who would pray must bring and present and name something that they want. If they do not, there can be no prayer (LC, III, 24; Tappert, p. 423).

Ephesians says that we should always (*pantote*) and at all times (*en panti kairō*) pray in the Spirit (5:20; 6:18), it does not have in view a timeless "always" but rather that we are called upon to pray in every changing present. In the present that is always new, and in the situation shaped by it, we must be open to the coming of God which he effects by the Spirit.

The word "present" as an expression for our actual present does not denote, however, a mere moment in the chronological sense but as "my" present comprises the many circumstances that constitute my present situation. These circumstances may be a matter of joy or pain or merely indifferent. They include not merely the deep dimension of spiritual assault but also immediate everyday anxieties about food and clothes and examinations and friction with a colleague. From the rich multiplicity of these forms of the present my prayer will be directed from constantly changing situations and angles to one and the same goal: "Is any one among you suffering? Let him pray. Is any cheerful? Let him sing praise" (James 5:13).

Jesus' own prayers give evidence of this relation to the present and its situation. He calls on the Father at his baptism and the impartation of the Spirit (Luke 3:21), when he is oppressed by the people's need (Mark 1:35; 6:46), at the selection of his disciples (Luke 6:12), before Peter's confession at Caesarea Philippi (Luke 9:18), before the transfiguration (Luke 9:28), and before the beginning of the passion (Matthew 26:36ff.).

The Lord's Prayer is the decisive introduction to prayer inasmuch as it encompasses the whole span of possible situations out of which we pray. It focuses on the coming of the kingdom and the hallowing of the divine name but also on the supply of daily bread, on all that the body needs—food, drink, clothes, shoes, house, farm, fields, money, property, a devout wife and devout children, devout companions, a devout and loyal master, good government, good weather, peace, health, order, honor, good friends, true neighbors, and the like.[16] Within each present with its anxieties and temptations and hunger and guilt there is to be the union with God's will that the Spirit achieves. The individual petitions of the Lord's Prayer enable us to speak with God out of our given situation and mark the depths out of which we cry.

Only against this background can we make sense of the real goal of the Pneuma, namely, to bring us into conformity and union with the will of God. This is as it were at the center as the end toward which our praying moves and also as the beginning at which we confess our readiness to take all self-will, all the auxiliary conceptions that we bring to prayer, and bury them in the confidence that God will do the right no matter how he may hear or deny our requests. The fundamental answer that we are given the assurance of sonship (Romans 8:15f.; Galatians 3:26; 4:5) is in any case our portion.

The situation which thus plays a part in prayer as the locus of the praying subject is first and last determined by the fact that he is in the community, that he is surrounded by the church, and that he is not to be understood, then, as an isolated monad. This is especially true in the OT—so much so that one might say that the

---

[16]Luther, LC on the Fourth Petition.

people as a cultic community is here the true subject of prayer.[17] The individual Israelite is relevant only as a member of the covenant people. It is only in this sense that he, too, is called by Yahweh and answers him (Deuteronomy 4:1; 6:4). Abraham is a representative and prototype of his people (Genesis 12:1-3). But in the NT too, as we have seen, there is still a Spirit-effected membership in the body of the community (1 Corinthians 12:13; Ephesians 4:4). This underlies the admonition to pray with and for one another (Romans 15:6; 2 Corinthians 1:11f.; 4:15; Colossians 3:16).

For this reason it seems to me that in the usual statements about the marks of the church something is lacking even in the Reformation confessions when only right doctrine and the right administration of the sacraments are mentioned as criteria for the presence of the church.[18] The church is primarily there when "two or three are gathered in his name" (Matthew 18:20) and fulfil the edifying office of prayer as those who respond to the preaching of the Word and the sacraments.

Only when this note is added is justice done to the work of the Pneuma in the church. That is to say, it is not enough to mention the mere operation of preaching the Word and administering the sacraments (with all the magical misconceptions that might be lurking here). An eye should also be had to the answering community which is fashioned by the Spirit-filled and active Word. The true church is there, Luther can say, when it *prays,* when in faith and full earnest it prays: "Forgive us our debts as we forgive our debtors." Only here does there begin the "history" of the church which causes it to grow toward that to which the Word and Spirit would lead it. As yet it has received only the firstfruits of the Spirit and not yet the tithe and certainly not the fulness of the Spirit, at least in this life. We have not yet escaped or cast off the carnal (and institutional!) tie. We are still engaged in laying aside all this. But we are also being pulled forward (by the Spirit). We are on the march, marching ahead.[19] If the church is here the true subject of prayer, the word "church" is interchangeable with the word "we."

---

[17]G. von Rad, *Theologie des AT,* I, pp. 368ff.; E.T. *Theology of the OT,* I, pp. 370ff.
[18]CA, Art. VII; Tappert, p. 132.
[19]WA, 40/III, 506, 18; LW, 13, 87.

Part Two

THE MEANS OF PRESENTATION
The Word-Form of Presentation

Bibliography

In this list *Kanon*=E. Käsemann, ed., *Das NT als Kanon* (1970). P. Althaus, *Die christliche Wahrheit*, I, 1st ed. (1947), §§17-21; A. Beintker, *Die evangelische Lehre von der Schrift und von der Tradition* (1961); J. Beumer, *Die katholische Inspirationslehre zwischen Vaticanum I und II* (1966); G. Bornkamm, "Gotteswort und Menschenwort im NT," *Studien zu Antike und Urchristentum, Gesammelte Aufsätze*, II (1959), p. 223; C. H. Dodd, *The Bible Today* (1947); also *The Apostolic Preaching and Its Developments* (1936); H. Dietzfelbinger, ed., *Schrift, Theologie, Verkündigung* (1971): contributions by H. Gollwitzer, G. Ebeling, W. Zimmerli, C. Maurer, and K. Herbert; G. Ebeling, "Die Bedeutung der historisch-kritischen Methode für die protestantische Theologie und Kirche," *Wort und Glaube*, I (1960), pp. 1-49; E.T. *The Word and Faith* (Philadelphia, 1963), pp. 17-61; "Sola scriptura und das Problem der Tradition," *Kanon*, p. 282; "Das NT und die Vielheit der Konfessionen," *Wort Gottes und Tradition*, 2nd ed. (1966), pp. 144ff.; E.T. *The Word of God and Tradition* (Philadelphia, 1968), pp. 148ff.; and "Wort Gottes und Hermeneutik," *Wort und Glaube*, I, pp. 319-48; E.T. pp. 305ff.; J. R. Geiselmann, "Das Konzil von Trient über das Verhältnis der Heiligen Schrift und der nicht geschriebenen Traditionen," *Die mündliche Überlieferung*, ed. M. Schmaus (1951), pp. 123-206; G. Gloege, "Zur Geschichte des Schriftverständnisses," *Verkündigung und Verantwortung, Theologische Traktate*, II (1967), pp. 263ff.; B. Hägglund, *Die Heilige Schrift und ihre Deutung in der Theologie Johann Gerhards* (1951); C. A. Hase, *Hutterus redivivus*, 5th ed. (1842); R. Hermann, *Gotteswort und Menschenwort in der Bibel* (1956); K. Holl, "Luthers Bedeutung für den Fortschritt der Auslegungskunst," *Gesammelte Aufsätze*, I, 5th ed. (1927), pp. 544-82; M. Kähler, "Zur Bibelfrage," *Dogmatische Zeitfragen*, 2nd ed. (1907), new ed. (1937); also art. "Bibel," *RE³*, II, p. 686; K. Koch, *Was ist Formgeschichte?* (1964); E.T. *The Growth of the Biblical Tradition* (New York, 1969); H. J. Kraus, *Geschichte der historisch-kritischen Erforschung des AT* (1956); W. Kreck, "Wort und Geist bei Calvin," *Festschrift für G. Dehn* (1957), pp. 167-81; W. G. Kümmel, *Das NT. Geschichte der Erforschung seiner Probleme* (1958); E.T. *The New Testament* (Nashville, 1972); H. Küng, "Der Frühkatholizismus im NT als kontroverstheologisches Problem," *Kanon*, pp. 175-204; P. Lengsfeld, "Katholische Sicht von Schrift, Kanon und Tradition," *Kanon*, pp. 205-18; W. von Loewenich, *Luther als Ausleger der Synoptiker* (1954); W. Pannenberg, "Die Krise des Schriftprinzips," *Grundfragen der Systematischer Theologie* (1967), pp. 11ff.; E.T. *Basic Questions in Theology*, I (London, 1970), pp.

1ff.; F. Pieper and J. T. Mueller, *Christian Dogmatics* (St. Louis, Missouri, 1934); H. G. Pöhlmann, *Abriss der Dogmatik,* 2nd ed. (1975); K. Rahner, art. "Inspiration," *Handbuch theologischer Grundbegriffe,* II, 2nd ed. (1974), pp. 354ff.; G. Blaurock and H.-U. Kirchhoff (ed. for the Reformed Church of Holland), *Rechenschaft über Geschichte, Geheimnis und Autorität der Bibel* (1968); H. Rückert, "Schrift, Tradition und Kirche," *Vorträge und Aufsätze zur historischen Theologie* (1972), pp. 310-28; M. J. Scheeben, *Handbuch der katholischen Dogmatik,* I, *Gesammelte Schriften,* III, 2nd ed. (1948); O. Scheel, *Luthers Stellung zur Heiligen Schrift* (1902); K. E. Skydsgaard, "Schrift und Tradition," *Kerygma und Dogma,* I (1955), pp. 170ff.; H. E. Weber, *Reformation, Orthodoxie und Rationalismus,* I, 2 (1940), esp. pp. 260ff.; also *Historisch-kritische Schriftforschung und Bibelglaube,* 2nd ed. (1914); G. Wingren, *Die Predigt* (1955), esp. pp. 51ff.; E.T. *The Living Word,* esp. pp. 44ff.; H. W. Wolff, "Zur Hermeneutik des AT," EvTh (1956), pp. 337-70.

VI

Word and Spirit: Their Basic Relationship

Summary of Conclusions Reached Thus Far

The relationship between the Word and the Spirit has engaged us repeatedly from various angles. Before we deal with it systematically we shall briefly summarize the main points that have been made already, largely in EF, I.

1. The Word and the Spirit may be distinguished but not separated. The Spirit is concealed in the letter of the Word. The Word contains the Spirit.

2. What we say about the incarnation of the Word in relation to Christ (John 1:14), we must say about verbalization in relation to the Pneuma. "Holy Scripture," says Luther on this point, "is God's Word written and, as I might say, put in letters, for as Christ is held and handled in the world, so it is with God's written Word." To that extent the Spirit is concealed in the letter.[1]

3. The legitimate appeal to the Spirit and the legitimate appeal to what is written do not contradict one another so long as the Word is understood spiritually. But contradiction can arise when God's Word is understood as mere letter apart from the Spirit. This happens when it becomes legalistic compulsion and no longer impels me "from within," as the Spirit does. Then life-giving address is replaced by death-dealing force (2 Corinthians 3:6f.). It becomes law and as such takes the place of the Spirit. To this extent we fix the relation between letter and Spirit by the way in which we interpret the relation between law and gospel.[2]

---

[1]WA, 48, 31 (on Psalm 22).
[2]Cf. EG, II, pp. 219-321; EF, II, pp. 184-258.

4. The spiritual Word does not just teach but also and primarily effects. It is an active and not just an interpretative Word.[3] In addition to teaching me about forgiveness it effects it.

5. The Spirit also exercises a hermeneutical function in relation to the Word by disclosing and appropriating it to me by his inner testimony. Here again the efficacious character of the spiritual Word is clear. For this disclosure takes place in such a way that the Spirit makes a "new creature" and thus restores the lost analogy which alone makes understanding of the Word possible.

6. Our discussion of the gifts of the Spirit showed that the Spirit never works without the instrumentality of the Word, not even in the ecstasy of glossolalia.

This, then, is a summary of what we have said thus far about the relationship of Word and Spirit. We shall now supplement it.

1. THE RADICAL EMANCIPATION FROM THE WORD AND THE REFORMERS' REBUTTAL

The relationship between the Word and the Spirit is especially a theme in the Reformers when they find themselves compelled to reply to the provocations of the radicals. For these break the relationship because in supposed possession of the Spirit they let themselves be seduced into feeling superior to the Word and understanding it as only an interim instrument which they no longer need.[4]

Calvin is angry when he writes about the "frenzy" of these "giddy men." His anger is caused by their departure from something that the patriarchs and prophets and apostles all accepted unconditionally, namely, that we can never grow beyond the Word in the name of the Spirit but can only keep the two together. "By a heinous sacrilege these rascals tear apart those things which the prophet joined together with an inviolable bond" when he proclaimed as the Word of Yahweh: "My Spirit which is in you, and the words that I have put in your mouth, will not depart from your mouth, nor from the mouth of your seed . . . forever" (Isaiah 59:21). The scorn for the Word of which the radicals are guilty accords to it only "fleeting and temporal" validity. But nowhere does Scripture see itself as something that simply serves to exalt the Spirit and thus to render itself superfluous. The Spirit whom Christ has promised is one "that would speak not from himself" (John 16:13) but always points to the incarnate Word and can never go beyond him. As the Spirit agrees with the Word, his emancipation from it can only be an arrogant and lying doctrine. (Today we might speak of ideologies.) If the Spirit has written the law in the hearts of believers (Jeremiah 31:33), this does not mean liberation from the Word but the presence of the Word as willed by God. Its call from outside, which is, as we might put it by way of comment, a *heteros nomos,* comes into the inner heart, so that we are made one with the will of God in freedom. The Spirit with what he says does not call us away from the Word or lift us above it but forever calls us back to the hearing of the Word.

In the passage from Calvin quoted there is a place which—unintentionally—

---

[3]Cf. EF, I, Index, *s.v.* Word of God.
[4]On Luther cf. K. Holl, "Luther und die Schwärmer," *Gesammelte Aufsätze,* I, pp. 420ff.; for Calvin cf. Inst., I, 9, 1-3 (from which all quotations are taken unless otherwise noted).

contains an incipient prognosis for the future history of thought. Calvin accuses the radicals of being led by their emancipation to "seek the Spirit from themselves rather than from God" (I, 9, 2). But is this Spirit that is sought from themselves the Pneuma? Is he not reduced to the *nous*, to reason as the spirit of man?

In fact this way from the Pneuma to the *nous*, with the devaluation of the Word in the background, may be illustrated by many examples. I will select two particularly striking ones.

We recall the relation of reason and revelation (or the Word of revelation) in Lessing's *Education of the Human Race* (cf. *Lessing's Theological Writings* [London, 1956], pp. 82–98). (One might also cite the parable of the ring in his *Nathan the Wise;* on both cf. my book *Offenbarung, Vernunft und Existenz . . .* , 5th ed. [1967].) Here the revelation that encounters us in the Word has precisely the interim character that Calvin criticizes. It is just a pacemaker which, like a teacher, mediates truths of human reason in a preliminary, childlike, symbolical, and mythical form. If we are pupils in this educational process, being pupils is not the goal. The goal of the teacher is to make the pupils independent and himself superfluous. The human spirit or reason is simply stimulated by revelation until it comes to itself and attains maturity and then it can take over the mediated truth directly as its own insight. This stage of appropriation is also the moment of independence and emancipation from revelation.

In modern terms, the goal of revelation is secularization. This is thinking out on one's own and in one's own strength what can first be encountered and accepted only as heteronomy and on authority. Thus the Logos of God's Word becomes the logos of one's insight. The Pneuma has changed into *nous*. This Spirit is sought from ourselves and not from God. Calvin's demanded return to the Word to which the Pneuma points us is in Lessing's scheme a sorry return to childish immaturity, an impermissible nostalgia.

Whereas Lessing represents the Enlightenment variation of this emancipation, the young Schleiermacher represents the Romantic version. In his *Speeches* (1799) the Word is set aside, not by reason (as in Lessing), but by the religious I, by the contemplation and feeling of the Universe. The biblical Word and the doctrine derived from it are significant, not as an original message from God in the sense of a supposed *Deus dixit,* but as a verbalization of the religious experiences of the prophets and other "mediators." We have in them verbal projections of what religious people experience.

Like Lessing's, this understanding of the Word implies that it has only an interim role. It offers temporary stimulation by bringing us into touch with spiritually ablaze persons and causing sparks to leap over from them to us. In itself, however, it is hard and cooled off lava which simply points us to this original fiery state. The goal of the Word is again to make itself superfluous. It simply leads us to the point where the supreme power of religious experience can be released in us. The decisive act takes place in our own spirit. Holy Scripture and the Word written in it are no more than a springboard which our feet touch for a moment and which helps us to leap into the sphere of the inner spirit. As the Second Speech states, every holy writing is only the mausoleum of a religion, a monument that a great spirit was once there who is there no longer; for when he lived and worked, how could he have attached such great value to the dead letter which could give only a weak impression of him? The person who has religion is not the one who believes in a holy writing but the person who has no need of such or could make his own. We have here a dramatic fulfilment of Calvin's prophecy that the radicals' emancipation from the Word would lead them to their own spirit. (The fact that this represents only the young Schleiermacher and not Schleiermacher in his totality has been noted already in the christological discussions in Volume II [EG, pp. 336ff., 351ff.; EF, pp. 274ff., 284ff.]. *The Christian Faith* and especially the sermons suggest an essentially modified understanding of the Word.)

In Calvin as in Luther the Spirit does not replace the Word and then undergo a surreptitious transformation into the human spirit. Instead he points us to the Word. He brings it close to us. Being sealed by the Spirit of promise (Ephesians 1:13) means that the Pneuma becomes our "inner teacher by whose effort the promise of salvation penetrates into our minds" instead of just striking the air or beating upon the ear.[5] Thus the Spirit sees to it that the eternal blessings hidden in the Word come to us and that the incarnate Word dwells in us.[6] At issue here is what we earlier[7] called the subjective side of revelation, the miracle of its appropriation, empowering to hear and understand.

More important, however, is another nuance that should not be overlooked.

If the Pneuma does not break loose from the Word but remains tied to it as the instrument of impartation, this means more and other than that the Holy Spirit simply appropriates the Word to us. If that were all, the possibility of a radical coming of age apart from the Word would still be present. Also true, however, is the reverse direction of the Spirit's work, namely, that we are called into the Word and the saving event represented by it, that we are as it were called away from ourselves. The same problem occupied us already when we dealt with the christological relation of the Pneuma and pointed out that we have to speak not only of Christ "in us" but also of our being "in Christ." Only in this way is the decisive barrier set up against the misunderstanding that there might be an autarchy of our self-consciousness and an integration of theology into anthropology.[8] The very opposite is true, namely, that our new history accompanied by the Word and Spirit is taken up into Christ's history and that we members are incorporated into his body and into the continuity of the salvation event.[9]

When in the Parting Discourses of Jesus we read that after his departure the Spirit of truth will lead us into all truth (John 16:13), this stands in only apparent contradiction to the indissolubility of the relation of the Spirit to the Word. For it does not mean that the Word, especially the Word incarnated in him who proclaims it, contains only partial truth and must later be completed by the work of the Spirit. No development initiated by the Spirit can lead beyond the Word, for the text expressly adds that all the truth disclosed by the Pneuma will be taken from, and will thus refer to, what is proper to the incarnate Word (John 16:14f.). The Spirit, then, explicates the implications of the Word.

---

[5]Inst., III, 1, 4.

[6]Inst., III, 1, 1.

[7]EG, II, p. 44; EF, II, p. 38.

[8]For a clarification of this cf. the debate with Theology A in EG, I, pp. 62ff.; EF, I, pp. 62ff.

[9]G. Bornkamm has made this point very forcibly in his "Mythos und Evangelium," ThEx, N.E. 26, p. 25.

Provisional Note on the Roman Catholic Understanding of the Relation between Scripture and Dogma

This question has time and again occupied Roman Catholic theology when either critically from without or self-critically from within it has had to meet the accusation that the dogmas proclaimed by popes and councils (e.g., adoration of the saints, papal infallibility, and the assumption of Mary) have no support in the biblical Word. As the church claims to bear the Spirit of God and even to be the ongoing Christ, so the objection runs, it sets its own authority alongside that of the Word, understands itself and its tradition as a second source of revelation, makes its truth something more than that of the Word, and thus emancipates itself from the Word. (This argument was especially important for the Reformers.)

Modern Roman Catholic theology, which is closer to the Bible than in many previous generations, feels the force of this accusation because it obviously challenges the biblical normativity confessed by it. Historico-critical research into the Bible, which it also takes seriously, enables it to give up the view that every development of doctrine must be justified by quoting biblical texts as though everything were already there in the Bible.[10] Instead Karl Rahner, for example, points out that dogma is never final but is always a beginning. But it is still a development of what is already present as a seed in the biblical Word, although hidden in an earlier form so that there can be no direct quotation. Thus the history of dogma proclaims the infinitude of Holy Scripture, not going beyond it—how can one do that with what is infinite!—but expounding it and going beyond only the formal or seedlike aspect of its statements. Rahner then, if I am right, understands the relation between the dogmatic tradition and Scripture along the lines just suggested, namely, that we have here only the explication of biblical implications.

One may contest the explication. It is important to realize, however, that this cannot be done with direct biblical quotations as in the attacks of the Reformers on the church of their day. On both sides there can no longer be a direct consultation of the Bible. The question now is whether a dogma is really on the line of biblical thought, whether a branch on the dogmatic tree really stands in a "genetic" relation to the biblical seed. In spite of the shift in theme the debate about this question will be no less keen. But it can be more objective and take on the character of a dialogue between disputants who speak within a common attachment to the Bible that differs only in nuance.[11]

We shall return later and more expressly to the problem of the relation between Scripture and tradition which is no more than intimated here.

2. THE PLACE OF THE HOLY SPIRIT AS A SOURCE OF REVELATION

a. Trinitarian Order of the Sources of Revelation

---

[10]As one among innumerable examples it may be noted that in the 13th century Innocent IV claimed that purgatory had a biblical basis (Denz., 838; E.T. 456), and Trent upheld this against Luther's objections (Denz., 1487; E.T. 777).

[11]For Rahner's position cf. his essay "Chalkedon—Ende oder Anfang?" in *Das Konzil von Chalkedon*, III, 3 (1954), esp. pp. 3–11.

The Word of God exists only as an attested Word, attested by men.

As regards the media within and by which this attestation takes place, we may distinguish (though not separate) three media in a trinitarian order.

First comes the revelation of God the Creator, the Sustainer and Lord of history.

That this form of revelation is not "natural theology," i.e., a direct readability of the Creator from creation along the lines of an analogy of being, is something that we have continually pointed out in our deliberations.[12] The decisive reason why it is not this is that creation was called into being by the effective Word of the Creator, his "Let there be . . . ,'' so that there can be no access to creation without access to this creative Word. Relation to this Word constitutes the distinctiveness of man, for he is the only creature that can be addressed in the second person and summoned to the communication with the Creator which is set up by the Word.[13]

Even though Romans 1:18ff. says that God's "invisible nature," "his eternal power and deity,'' may be seen in the things that have been made (*poiēmata*), there is no contradiction here. For in background, unmentioned but presupposed, there stands the creative Word in which the Creator presents himself and opens himself for communication.

That this is so may be seen negatively from the failure of men to perceive God's creative work and their incurring thereby of the wrath of God. This blindness to the footprints of God in his creation is not an epistemologically conditioned lack of insight. It rests instead on an unwillingness to see. Men suppress (*katechein*) the truth that is held out to them because they do not want to understand themselves in their creatureliness. Since they aim at emancipation and autonomy they overlook the Creator who disturbs them in this attitude of theirs. In psychoanalytic terms, they "repress" him. Their blindness, then, is in truth blinding. Hence God's wrath is directed against people who are guilty and not just intellectually untalented or religiously "unmusical'' (as Schleiermacher might perhaps have put it). The problem is not a lack of reason or an inability to interpret the world religiously. Personal rejection, not noetic failure, is the issue. This can happen, however, only because the communication with the Creator established in the Word has been broken, or, more accurately, renounced by man (on Romans 1:18ff. cf. the Index of Scripture References in ThE and EF).

The Word, then, is the decisive basis of the revelation in creation.[14] The same applies to God's providential and judicial activity in history. Here, too, his traces are ambiguous and unrecognizable apart from his efficacious and interpretative Word.[15]

Second, the revelation of God the Redeemer brings out this relation to the Word in its most radical form. For Christ does not merely bear witness to the Word or authoritatively fulfil it; he *is* this Word. We thus have identity as well as witness and fulfilment (John 1:1ff.). Hence Christ as God's Word is the normative authority for every word of proclamation, whether that of prophecy in the prophets and the OT as a whole or that of witness and recollection in the evangelists and

---

[12]EF, I, Index, *s.v.* analogia entis; Creation, belief in.
[13]Cf. on this ThE, I, §§710ff.; E.T. I, p. 159.
[14]Cf. ThE, I, §§711ff.
[15]Cf. ThE, II, 1, §§2084ff.

apostles. The prophets and apostles are indeed the foundation (*themelion*) of the community and its attestation of the Word, but Christ is the cornerstone of the edifice built on this foundation (Ephesians 2:20). Hence he is the canon. He is the hermeneutical principle of all biblical witness. This is what Luther had in mind when he said that the OT is God's Word because and to the extent that it promotes Christ.

Third, the Holy Spirit is the power of the revelation and appropriation of the Word. This power—to deal with the biblical aspect—finds expression in the inspiration (*theopneustos*, 2 Timothy 3:16) of the Word of God mediated through Scripture and also—if I may use the well-known definition of the older Protestant orthodox theologians Hollaz, J. Gerhard, and others—in its perspicuity and clarity and its ability to be its own interpreter.

This faculty of Scripture points again to its normative center, to the incarnate Word and his hermeneutical function. The alternative to it would be its self-disclosure through imported criteria and its subjection to hermeneutical conditions of external derivation.[16]

We dealt with criteria of this kind in our debate with existentialist hermeneutics.[17]

To contest Scripture's ability to interpret itself is to contest or reduce the function of the Pneuma in giving it this faculty. For the presupposition of its having this faculty is that it makes itself analogous to the hearer by the testimony of the Holy Spirit and thus puts itself in a situation in which it can be understood. Where this presupposition does not exist, the analogy has to be set up by the hearer. But the hearer sees himself able and qualified to hear and understand and accept the Word only as he feels that it addresses his questions, that it meets the conditions of his understanding of the truth and himself, and only as it can be integrated into his existential situation.[18] Where the Word does not satisfy these conditions that have been elevated to the rank of criteria, it remains "outside" and is dismissed as irrelevant (e.g., the miracle-stories in the case of Bultmann).

To sum up, one might say that when Scripture's ability to interpret itself, and therefore the analogy, have to be set up from outside (e.g., by the reference to existence), there pneumatological reflection is superfluous, though the work of the Pneuma may frequently be dealt with ironically (and not altogether without reason) as supernatural aid when difficulties of thought and understanding occur or in the case of sheer indolence of thought. At any rate, the hermeneutical principle which is taken from the spheres of our own existence and its concerns and interests, and imported into Scripture from outside, can cut away the testimony of the Spirit and render it apparently superfluous. What usually happens then is that surreptitiously a hermeneutical function becomes one that is prejudiced and normative.[19]

---

[16]As an example, cf. Troeltsch's thesis that historical facts recorded in the text are verifiable only if they correspond to the criteria of causality, analogy, and immanence.

[17]EG, I, pp. 26ff., 50ff.; EF, I, pp. 40ff., 55ff.

[18]Cf. Bultmann's typical and much quoted dictum that to understand records of events as the work of God presupposes a prior understanding of what can be called the work of God (ZThK, I, p. 66).

[19]EG, I, pp. 155f.; EF, I, pp. 122f.

b. The Meaning of the Historical in This Regard

All three forms of God's self-disclosure have, then, a word-form. The sum of this Word is the Bible as Holy Scripture. To this extent the Bible is the means of salvation.

In this respect we must remember—and we shall have to look at this more closely later—that while the scriptural Word is the last source of revelation accessible to us, it is secondary to the oral proclamation of the prophets and apostles and especially to the "ontic" Word which is Christ. The transmission of the oral Word into the written Word takes place only by necessity (P. Brunner), and even then more incidentally than intentionally, and relatively late. Discussion of the problem of the canon in particular will bring us back to this.

Since the Bible is also a historical document—both in relation to its contents and its own development—the question arises with increased urgency what is the relation between God's work in it and man's. What role is played, e.g., by the individual and historical setting of the authors? What degree of independence do they have? Were they just writing machines whose personalities and situations had no part in the process of inspiration? Also at issue is the relation between the claim of God which is above time and time-conditioned forms in which it is understood and repeated. There can be no doubt that contemporary ideas, social structures, and customs (cf. 1 Corinthians 11:4ff.) formed the sphere (or schema of categories) within which its revealed statements were understood. Where is the boundary here between what is always binding and what is just a relative mode of expression? In the debate with Bultmann (cf. EF, I) we noted that his statement that myth brings transcendence (and therefore the divine) into reality gives point at once to the above question: Does the saying that the Word became flesh come under this verdict of the mythical? Is God brought into reality in this way?

The problem also arises concerning contradictions and discrepancies in biblical teaching, e.g., in Paul's doctrine of justification and that of James.[20] Here again a distinction must be made between material and situational reasons for the differences.[21] This question is particularly urgent because from the very first the kerygma presses for considered doctrinal statements. The gospel never has a nonhistorical form "in itself" but always exists in confrontation with false proclamation and teaching and this leads necessarily to confessions, theology, dogmatics, and therefore doctrine.[22]

A final issue in these matters of the relation between the divine and the human, the historical and the suprahistorical, is that of the absolutely binding or time-conditioned form in which the modes of understanding, expounding, and repeating take place on *our* side, that of the hearer and reader. We have only to look, for example, at the story of research into the life of Jesus to get some impression of the extent to which hearing is not objective but our own spirit worms its way into the act of hearing and projects itself into the text. Manipulations of the biblical mate-

---

[20]Cf. on this Joest, "Erwägungen zur kanonischen Bedeutung des NT," *Kanon*, pp. 277ff.

[21]Käsemann rightly points out that different christologies are not opposed to one another but rather supplement one another, stressing different aspects as occasion demands (*Kanon*, p. 404).

[22]*Ibid.*, p. 400.

rials do not just follow the act of hearing but are built into it and cause us to hear selectively and to change what we hear. A desire to be strictly objective in historico-critical research makes no basic difference in this respect. It is still exposed to the critical (and, we hope, self-critical) question whether completely time-conditioned presuppositions of interpretation are not at work in it as well.

With this question of the relation between the divine and the human we have reached the precise point around which all the controversies about the understanding, place, and value of the Bible as the vessel of God's Word revolve. In discussing critically the main issue in these controversies we shall also find the decisive thread which will lead us to our own understanding of the Bible.

A. Controversies about the Understanding of the Bible: A Critical Stance

Threats to the authority of the Bible usually come through discussion of its human elements. Outside the church reason is claimed as a criterion, as in the Enlightenment, and this is extended from the human elements to the whole of the Bible, which is then divided between the timeless and binding truths of reason on the one side and the accidental and nonbinding truths of history on the other. Within the church emphasis on the human factor can lead to the questioning of Scripture's position as the judge, norm, and rule of the tradition, i.e., of its supremacy over tradition.[1]

Consideration of the apparently very human development and form of Scripture—especially when it takes place simplistically and with no theological interpretation—leads to a series of further questions. Thus one might ask how far heretical human arrogance could have crept into biblical statements and therefore obscured the authority of Scripture; or again, how far legends could have attached themselves to historical facts in biblical proclamation, so that instead of factual records we have later products of the community or mythical embellishments; or again, how far we have the actual words of Jesus and therefore the normative, because original, figure of the "historical Jesus"; or finally, the question already mentioned, namely, where we are to draw the line between time-bound (and human) forms of expression and the irreducible kerygmatic core.

In principle the critical questions regarding the human side of the Bible are already put in the Bible itself. Thus in the OT false prophets and idolaters may be known by the fact that they proclaim innocuous things that people want to hear, that they carry only messages of peace; whereas the true God, who is the Judge of history, continually declares himself in the messages of disaster that his servants carry, being manifested in his opposition to all human wishes.[2] The prophets themselves can misuse their spiritual authority and for opportunistic reasons be-

---

[1]Epitome, LBK, p. 769,19–40; cf. Tappert, p. 465.
[2]1 Kings 22:15ff.; Isaiah 23:9ff.; 28:7; Jeremiah 2:8, 26; 5:31; 6:13f.; Ezekiel 13:1ff.; Micah 3:5ff.; on this whole theme cf. O. Procksch, *Theologie des AT* (1950), pp. 131ff.

come false prophets of peace who fail to speak about judgment. The legitimate prophecy of true men of God is aimed against this abuse of power. In the NT we recall the debates of Jesus with the Pharisees, who have made God's Word of none effect and substituted their own traditions for it (Matthew 15; Mark 7). The apostles contend against similar falsifications (Colossians 2:4). The true secret of NT proclamation is that God's Word does not hover "platonically" over man's word but enters into it, so that the authoritative Word of Jesus is wholly human, the Word of God in the simplest human word. Humanity has become the seal and sign of the deity of the Word. This is the unique authority of Jesus.[3]

This integration of the divine and human word makes it impossible for us to separate them and to say that what affects us in "human" fashion is not "divine." For this reason the human element in the Bible cannot be just a statistical matter. It needs theological interpretation. It has to be understood as the vessel of the incarnate Word. The normative sign of God's self-disclosure is that he encounters us in this human form. Conversely, it would be a mark of heresy to deny human embodiment to the divine Word after the manner of the Docetists and to try to have the divine element only "in itself." More than statistical criteria are needed to distinguish what is *truly* human about God's Word and its illegitimate humanizing (as in the false prophets and the Pharisees). Only the charism of discernment of spirits can make this differentiation.

All these critical questions that arise regarding the biblical Word give rise to various—legitimate and illegitimate—attempts to establish it by showing and proving the validity of the biblical statements against the different attacks. In all these attempts the question how to relate and also to distinguish the divine and human elements in the biblical Word recurs in different variations. In them we shall obviously meet different understandings of the incarnation, of God's entry into human form, and beyond that of the trinitarian schema of revelation.

Along these lines, then, we shall discuss the attempted establishment of the authority of Scripture by (1) the formation of the canon, (2) the separating or uniting of Scripture and tradition, (3) immanent scriptural criteria (the formal and material principles), (4) the doctrine of verbal inspiration, and (5) historico-critical research.

---

[3]Cf. G. Bornkamm, *Antike und Urchristentum,* pp. 227f.

VII

The Establishment of Scriptural Authority by the Formation of the Canon

Bibliography. *Das NT als Kanon,* ed. E. Käsemann = *Kanon.* K. Aland, "Das Problem des neutestamentlichen Kanons," *Kanon,* pp. 134ff.; N. Appel, *Kanon und Kirche . . .* (1964); K. Barth, CD, I,1, pp. 61ff.; H. Braun, "Hebt die heutige neutestamentliche Forschung den Kanon auf?" *Gesammelte Studien zum NT und seiner Umwelt* (1962), pp. 310ff.; H. von Campenhausen, "Die Entstehung des NT," *Heidelberger Jahrbücher,* VII (1863), pp. 1ff.; O. Cullmann, *Die Tradition als exegetisches, historisches und theologisches Problem* (1954); H. Diem, *Theologie als kirchliche Wissenschaft,* II: Dogmatik. Ihr Weg zwischen Historismus und Existentialismus, 2nd ed. (1957), pp. 196ff.; E.T. *Dogmatics* (Edinburgh, 1959), pp. 224ff.; "Die Einheit der Schrift," EvTh, IX (1953), pp. 385ff.; and "Das Problem des Schriftkanons," *Theologische Studien,* ed. K. Barth, No. 32 (1952); G. Ebeling, "Das NT und die Vielzahl der Konfessionen," *Wort Gottes und Tradition,* 2nd ed. (1966), pp. 155ff.; E.T. *The Word of God and Tradition,* pp. 148ff.; art. "Tradition," RGG[3], VI, pp. 976ff.; and " 'Sola scriptura' und das Problem der Tradition," *Kanon,* pp. 282ff.; G. Gloege, "Zur Geschichte des Schriftverständnisses," *Kanon,* pp. 13ff.; H. Grass, *Die katholische Lehre von der Schrift und von der Tradition* (1954); A. von Harnack, *Die Entstehung des NT und die wichtigsten Folgen der neuen Schöpfung* (1914); E.T. *The Origin of the NT . . .* (New York, 1925); A. Jepsen, "Kanon und Text des AT," ThLZ, LXXIV, pp. 65ff.; W. Joest, "Erwägungen zur kanonischen Bedeutung des NT," *Kanon,* pp. 258ff.; E. Käsemann, "Begründet der neutestamentliche Kanon die Einheit der Kirche?" *Exegetische Versuche und Besinnungen,* I (1964), pp. 214ff.; also "Kritische Analyse," *Kanon,* pp. 336ff.; J. Knox, *Marcion and the NT* (1942); W. G. Kümmel, *Das NT. Geschichte und Erforschung seiner Probleme* (1958); E.T. *The NT* (Nashville, 1942); also "Notwendigkeit und Grenze des neutestamentlichen Kanons," *Kanon,* pp. 62ff.; H. Küng, "Strukturen der Kirche," *Quaestiones disputatae,* XVII (1952); E.T. *Structures of the Church* (New York, 1964); also "Der Frühkatholizismus im NT als kontroverstheologisches Problem," *Kanon,* pp. 175ff.; P. Lengsfeld, *Überlieferung, Tradition und Schrift in der evangelischen und katholischen Theologie der Gegenwart* (1960); W. Marxsen, "Das Problem des neutestamentlichen Kanons aus der Sicht des Exegeten," *Der Exeget als Theologe* (1968), pp. 91ff.; C. H. Ratschow, "Zur Frage der

Begründung des neutestamentlichen Kanons aus der Sicht des systematischen Theologen," *Kanon*, pp. 247ff.; A. A. van Ruler, *Die christliche Kirche und das AT* (1955); E.T. *The Christian Church and the OT* (Grand Rapids, 1971); G. Söhngen, *Einheit in der Theologie* (1952), pp. 305ff.; H. Strathmann, "Die Krisis des Kanons der Kirche," ThBl, XX (1941), pp. 295ff. (*Kanon*, pp. 41ff.); also "Heilige Schrift, Tradition und der Einheit der Kirche," ThBl, II/III (1942), pp. 33ff.

The question of the formation of the canon and the canonical force of the Bible— especially in relation to the NT—has been for centuries the theme of innumerable learned investigations, reflections, criticisms, and apologies, so that from the standpoint of the difference between the quantitatively meager texts of the NT and the tremendous mass of the literature dealing with it one gets the impression of a gigantic ballet being danced in a saucer. In fact the systematic theologian is in a hopeless position at this point. As concerns the development of the canon, which cannot be detached from its significance and normativity, he is at the mercy of the documentary data of the historians and exegetes. He cannot subject the almost chaotic disorder of information and its interpretation to the control of his own material insights. His thinking can cover only five questions.

1. What can be the valid or invalid point of the canonical restriction of what counts as the gospel?

2. What significance may be attached in this regard to the (real or supposed) priority of the testimonies (i.e., their apostolicity)?

3. What is the position in relation to the unity and discrepancy of canonical statements and what does this imply for the limitation or relativity of these statements and the possibility of their being outdated?

4. Who or what is it that fixes the canon—the church or tradition?

5. Can a hermeneutical principle be found for the fixing and interpreting of the canon as in the distinction between "formal and material principles" or the concept of a "canon within the canon"?

1. THE WORD OF GOD AS LIVING VOICE AND HOLY SCRIPTURE

Any discussion of the canonical rank of the Bible will be determined by the question whether and how far Holy Scripture contains God's Word or is perhaps identical with it.[1]

To answer this question one must define more closely what is meant by the Word of God. Three forms may be distinguished with three degrees of authority.

1. There can be no doubt that according to the witness of the NT the proper and primal Word of God is the Word incarnate in Jesus Christ (John 1:1–14; cf. Revelation 19:13). Here the Word is a personal and not a purely verbal event. It is

---

[1]For identification cf. Lutheran orthodoxy, the theology of the Missouri Synod, and works such as those of H. Echternach, *"Es stehet geschrieben"* (1937), who even describes Luther's translation as binding and verbally inerrant, and G. Maier, *Das Ende der historisch-kritischen Methode,* 3rd ed. (1975); E.T. *The End of the Historical-Critical Method* (St. Louis, 1977), who demands a firm and full return to a form of verbal inspiration.

ontic, not spoken. It is identical with the person of the Redeemer and personified in him.

2. Apart from the primal Word, but in association with it, the Word of God is also that which passes on the message of the incarnate Word in the form of human witness, standing at its disposal as an instrument. Obviously this applies particularly to the original Christian witness which has come to us through the evangelists and apostles (no matter how these terms be defined either materially or historically) in the accounts and commentaries they wrote only a short time after what happened. More precisely one might say that in these documents there is not merely reference to the Word of God but the Word of God is actually present, that it reaches us in them, so that the Word that was incarnate at a particular point in time is here presented afresh.

3. A final form of the Word of God is the witness which on the basis and under the guidance of the kerygma is given in later ages by witnesses of the Word. Between this verbal form of past, present, and future witnesses and the original witness enshrined in the NT no qualitative distinction need be made, for both share the promise that in their Word no less and no other than God's Word is proclaimed and the Kyrios links his own ongoing presence with this proclamation (Matthew 18:20). The promise applies to the Word proclaimed today and always that it will be endowed with the Pneuma and become God's own Word in spite of the weakness of human lips and the fragility of earthen vessels.

If I thus contest any qualitative distinction between the biblical witness and that of later witnesses, I am arguing only against the one thesis that there was a direct presence of the Kyrios in the original Christian testimony but there is only an indirect and reduced presence later. This view rests on two presuppositions that we oppose. This chapter will show the reasons for our doing so.

The first presupposition is that the primitive Christian witness as it is given in the NT is to be understood as "the" Word of God and therefore the difference is erased between God the Word incarnate in Jesus Christ and the human testimony to it. This view may be found in its most consistent form in the doctrine of verbal inspiration.

The second and related presupposition is that there is a qualitative difference between the witness of the NT and later witness. The NT (or the whole Bible) is here understood as a kind of second incarnation of the Word. As W. Joest puts it in a felicitous phrase, the Word of God that was incarnated has now been "incodified."[2] Much more important than the difference between the original witness of the evangelists and apostles and that of later witnesses, we contend, is the difference between the incarnate Word and the human word that bears witness to it, no matter whether it be that of prophets, evangelists, and apostles, or the Word of God that is proclaimed today and tomorrow.

For all that, there is, of course, a difference between the original Christian testimony written down in the NT and all later testimony. Since the former is the first Word of God accessible to us—and no debate about "apostolic" and "non-apostolic" can alter this—it has a normative function in relation to all later forms

---

[2] "Erwägungen zur kanonischen Bedeutung des NT," *Kerygma and Dogma,* XII (1966), p. 33.

of proclamation. It is for them the criterion, focus, and place of appeal. It will prevent all later preachers who keep to it as the original form of God's Word from replacing the Pneuma by their own spirit and set forth instead the close connection between the Pneuma and the Word.

There is thus good reason for distinguishing between the canonical Word of the NT or the Bible and the later Word of witnesses, the one as primary norm and the other as derived and secondary, even though there is no difference in principle between the two forms of proclamation, since the Word that was published then and the Word that is preached today are one and the same Word of God. Naturally this does not apply to all proclamation or preaching, as is shown by much sad experience not only in the case of others but in one's own as well. Nor is it wholly unnecessary to point out that the traditional distinction between the primary norm and the derived (*norma normans* and *norma normata*) applies not only to the biblical Word and preaching but also to the biblical Word and the church's confessional writings and their character as subsidiary authorities. The confessional writings can be a criterion, focus, and place of appeal for the living voice of actual proclamation only as they for their part are measured by the original form of the Word of God.

The normative significance of the original testimony is in no way damaged by the fact that it does not have the form of a scientifically historical description of God's mighty acts (Acts 2:11) but is the confession of men who depict the Christ event in the light of the resurrection, so that it has an "after-the-event" character. Similarly the normative significance of this witness is valid even though a considered and interpretative Christology is interwoven into the canonical gospels and the influence of community theology may thus be traced.[3] The oldest accounts do not document what happened "in itself." They have already passed through the filter of the witnesses and their reflection. They thus carry the clear and definite profile of these witnesses. Yet this does not throw doubt on the thesis that Christ is the incarnate Word, God's own Word in person. Instead, it establishes the thesis, for the Word shows itself here to be an efficacious Word that calls forth witnesses and moves constantly on to new "corporeality."

The identity of the one Word of God which persists even in the difference between the NT and later witness is brought out most impressively by the circumstance that the original form of the NT witness, too, is that of the living voice, i.e., oral witness; its depositing in a written canon has a secondary and subsidiary character.

The Spirit is related to the Word and hidden in the letter, but while this applies to the written Word of the Bible it does not apply to it alone. For Luther God's own Word, the Word incarnate in Christ, is concealed and offers itself to us in the human word. Holy Scripture is the Word of God written and put in letters, just as Christ is God's eternal Word hidden in humanity. And as Christ is contained and dealt with in the world, so it is with God's written Word.[4] Nevertheless, the entry

---

[3]E. Käsemann, "Das Problem des historischen Jesus," *Exegetische Versuche und Besinnungen*, I (1964), pp. 193ff.
[4]WA, 48, 31.

of the Word of God into Scripture is only a transitional stage which is bounded behind and before by the living voice of oral proclamation.

Before Scripture and the fixing of a canon there already existed the oral preaching of the prophets and apostles and an oral tradition.[5] Depositing in Scripture followed because of the need to safeguard oral tradition and protect it against developing variations and falsifications.[6] The need for Scripture and the establishment of the canon has a partial basis, then, in human nature and its tendency to falsify God's Spirit by its own spirit. For Luther it is even a sign of the lessening of the activity of the Spirit. Before the biblical authors wrote, people preached and brought about conversions with the bodily voice which was their proper and NT work. This was the phase of the direct Word of God. That books had to be written is a great loss and it is a lack of the Spirit that brought about the need, not the nature of the NT.[7] Originally the gospel was not a written work but good tidings to be passed on by the lips and not the pen, just as Christ himself, the ontic Word, did not write anything but simply spoke.[8]

Having its origin in oral proclamation, Scripture presses back to its origin, i.e., to the presentation of its message by the spoken word. It seeks to be preached, being itself no more than the score which must be sounded out faithfully in living notes.

To preach it is to understand it. Sermons are not just recitation but exposition. Exposition is possible only when the scope and emphases of what is to be expounded are taken from the text and hermeneutically evaluated. In relation to the Bible this means especially understanding the Word of God inscribed on this score in terms of God's own Word incarnate in Christ. It was in this sense that by way of elucidation and criticism Luther regarded it as the point of Scripture to promote Christ.[9] As the message of Scripture presses to be put back into oral proclamation, it raises the question how it can be proclaimed, or, more precisely, how far God the Word himself is the sun that lights up the cosmos of Scripture (and perhaps falls on nooks and crannies that are still in shadow).

As Holy Scripture originates in the spoken Word which is indwelt by the certifying Pneuma, and as it leads back to the spoken Word which for its part has the promise of the Spirit, the Spirit is assigned to it, too, as the legitimation and power of presentation. If the need for a written deposit is in a sense an emergency measure deriving from the vulnerability and confusion of the human spirit which in self-will resists God's Spirit, the deduction cannot be made that Holy Scripture is a product of abandonment by the Spirit. On the contrary, there is fulfilled in it the wrestling of the Holy Spirit with the human spirit. Scripture is the most authoritative testimony to the presence of the Pneuma. Only thus does the *sola Scriptura*

---

[5]Form criticism was not the first to see this. Luther, e.g., finds in it the basis of God's presence in preaching. J. S. Semler (1725–91) also refers to it in his work *Von freier Untersuchung des Kanons* (1771ff.), I, pp. 216f., etc.

[6]H. von Campenhausen, *Kanon*, p. 122.

[7]WA, 10/I, 1, 626f.; LW, 52, 205f. The OT writings were gathered together canonically because the Spirit no longer spoke, the pseudonymous and highly inspired Enoch and the Patriarchs being apparently dubious if lively witnesses (cf. C. H. Ratschow, *Kanon*, pp. 248f.).

[8]WA, 10/I, 1, 17; LW, 35, 123.

[9]In the 1522 prefaces to James and Jude (LW, 35, 395f.).

(Scripture alone) attain the rank of a confession by which the church describes its basis.

In this assertion there also lies the decisive reference to the meaning and limit of the statement that Holy Scripture is "inspired." This can mean only that *God* was actively at work when he gave witness to his Word in Christ. It can also mean only that this witness, including its setting in the canon, was not produced by the church, or by man at all, but that it came from outside to the church, was disclosed and made audible to it by the Spirit, and was received by it, so that the church did not constitute the canonicity of Scripture but could only confirm it as the received Word of God. Here, too, the Spirit-effected Word of God precedes the written form, the canon. This is most important in fixing the relation between church and canon. It brings us up against the question of the nature of canonicity.

2. CONCEPT AND HISTORY OF THE CANON

a. The Concept of the Canon

According to the dictionaries canon means measure, rule, binding list. Legally it has the sense of basic legal principles which have normative significance for the statutes derived from them. In ancient literature it can be understood as the list of authors to whom the experts, the grammarians, ascribe normative significance as examples for the various types of poetry. In art it refers to the natural standard which fixes the proportions of parts of the human body. In ancient philosophy the rules of logic were regarded as valid norms of thought, so that Epicurus' logic could be called "canonics."

Always the same basic idea recurs. Canon is the epitome of binding norms. The collection of biblical writings has canonical rank in this sense, and in such a way that there is ascribed to it the divinely authorized authority of God's own Word.

This authority is general. It is not limited to a specific sphere like other authorities, e.g., political or academic authority. We may see this in the fact that the messages of the prophets, which were originally given to Israel, have achieved universal significance to the extent that they relate to the whole oikoumene, to the church as spiritual Israel. Even more plainly and dramatically it may be seen in the NT epistles. When the letters to the Romans, Corinthians, Thessalonians, etc. are declared to be canonical, it is conceded that even though they are sent to specific churches they have universal authority. This is true not merely in a spatial sense as their message traverses the earth but also in a temporal sense, since they are God's Word for coming generations as well as their specific recipients.

It cannot be said, of course, that the original authors cherished a kind of canonical purpose or were conscious of the corresponding significance of their works. One reason why such intentions could hardly arise is that an interest in canonical establishment would presuppose looking ahead to historical processes in which the authority of the entrusted Word would remain as an assured legacy. In view of the expectation of the imminent return, however, there could be no place for any such interest.[10] Only with the delay of the Parousia did people begin to

---

[10]W. Marxsen, "Das Problem des neutestamentlichen Kanons," *Kanon*, pp. 239f.

look ahead to the historical future. Behind the rise of the canon, then, we find the same eschatologically determined motifs as behind the establishment of the church and its ordinances. At any rate what was not originally intended to be canonical came to be understood and predicated in its canonical implications (not motivations).

This process of canonical interpretation may be seen already within the works that achieved canonical rank. The evangelists Matthew and Luke use Mark's gospel and modify it in terms of what they regard as the kerygma and therefore authoritative. The fourth evangelist deals even more radically with the traditions that he uses. The same applies to the epistles of Peter. We see here that the canon as we have it today does not just seek to be a norm for the history of proclamation but is itself already historical. Older "canonable" materials are developed in their implications, supplemented, revised, and brought closer, as it were, to the goal of their canonical expectancy. The ultimate formation of the canon is thus the—definitive or provisional—conclusion of a process of awakening consciousness. As the church uses this legacy of tradition in divine service, or as it puts itself in its service and thus fulfils it, it becomes increasingly aware of its rank as an original or validly interpreted Word of God and confesses it in the form of canonization. To the degree that in its confessional choice it sets aside interests and ulterior purposes and self-will, it achieves growing certainty that what prevails in this act of canonization is the Word itself and that for this reason the testimony of the Holy Spirit is at work in this Word and attests itself in the discovery of its canonical rank.

Since the rise of the canon is at all events a history of developing awareness, it leads on relentlessly to the same question as is posed by any historical document: Where do its emphases lie and what dominant motif is at work in the processes at whose end it occupies its authoritative position? Only as this question is answered can we understand the canon and accept its validity. Without this answer it can play only the role of an authoritative law which makes us mere objects and consumers of tradition.

When put to the canon, the question is no other than the well-known question of a canon within the canon. We are thus pushing our inquiry into the background of the canon. Since the canon is the result of a historical process, it cannot as a document be the final court that decides how normative its authority must be taken to be. Its position can be only that of an authorized norm which raises the question of the norm that authorizes it, of the final court behind which we cannot look but which is the organizing center of the canon.

From what we have said, this center can be no other than God's own Word as it takes form in Jesus Christ. To the extent that the biblical Word participates in this Word's becoming flesh and history, it manifests its canonical rank.

We cannot say this, however, without adding at once that in going back to the figure of Christ beyond whom we cannot go, there can be no question of any Christ "in himself," i.e., of any historical "in himself" as the historical Jesus.[11] In the

---

[11] The impossibility of this has been shown theologically by M. Kähler in his *The So-Called Historical Jesus and the Historic, Biblical Christ* (E.T. Philadelphia, 1964) and historically by A. Schweitzer in his *Quest of the Historical Jesus* (E.T. London, 1910). The new quest for the historical Jesus in Ebeling, Käsemann, and others does not alter this (or seek to do so).

NT documents we encounter only the Christ who is grasped in faith and proclaimed in faith.

But the Christ "in himself" in whom we believe cannot be grasped by us. Insofar as he appropriates himself in faith, he comes into the schema of understanding and thought which is at our disposal. My own appropriation on the basis of his self-appropriation can take place as I bring the Christ-kerygma into association with my own questions and concerns and hopes and rationality and concrete experience. The subjectivity which comes into play herewith is a phenomenon of perspective. The diamond sparkles with ever changing colors as it is reflected in and penetrates our consciousness. In the NT writings, then, we do not have before us the believed Christ "in himself" but faith that is already reflectively "worked over," i.e., implicit or explicit christologies.

This is the final reason why the question of a canon within the canon cannot be pressed beyond the indissoluble relation between the primitive community and Christ—a relation which can no longer be dissected into subject and object. In other words, we cannot go back beyond the first hearing of the spiritual Word. (This is how we have to formulate it theoretically even though historically it is an open question whether we can get back to this first hearing. The important thing for me is the principle of the relation behind which we cannot go, no matter at what early or later stage it meets us.)

This is probably what the philosopher, biblical scholar, and dogmatician Franz Buddeus (1667-1729) had in mind when in his *Compendium institutionum theologiae dogmaticae* (ed. J. G. Walch [1723], §31) he certainly found a basis for the authority of Scripture in inspiration and the testimony of the Holy Spirit but characteristically added: the testimony of the church assenting. In other words, the Word of God—including its canonical legitimation—always meets us in connection with the one who receives it, i.e., the church. We receive it, then, along with this recipient. This demonstrates the indissolubility of the relation to which we refer.

Three elements may thus be distinguished in the formation of the canon. First, there is the complex of orally transmitted witness-material which does not itself have any canonical intention. Second, there is the spiritual experience which the church has in its liturgical use of the transmitted texts and in which their kerygmatic evidence and implied canonicity are set forth. Third, there is the official proclamation that the traditional material is the canon in which God's Word is contained and the standard for all future proclamation is to be sought.

In the final process of proclaiming the canon we must again see two elements, although these cannot be separated and indeed permeate one another. The first is the background of the act of legitimation in inspiration, the second the human side of its background.

From the background in inspiration we learn that the act of legitimation was not an arbitrary and self-willed venture of the church in which it played the role of a subject in the formation of the canon. Instead the traditional material of the Word manifested itself in its kerygmatic evidence by the power of the testimony of the Holy Spirit. The church does not prove or uphold it. Instead it manifests itself *to* the church. Even though the Pneuma is promised to the church and it is thus put in hermeneutical analogy to the spiritual Word, this cannot mean that it is given here the role of a subject. Both as hearer of the Word and as bearer of the promise that it is empowered to hear, it is a recipient. Using the intrinsically dubious subject-object correlation for a moment, we have to say that it is the object of that which is imparted to it as the self-evidence of the Word, of that which it simply reflects and expresses in its proclamation of the canon. This is what I mean when I speak of the background in inspiration.

There is also a human element, an element of practical theology, in the formation of the canon. The Word of God is menaced by human falsifications, by sectarian teachings and acts of human self-will as well as by the rank growth of uncontrollable tradition, by extravagances of the imagination, and the like. The history of the formation of the canon shows plainly, as we shall see, how far the issue is that of defense against these threats. That the element of inspiration and the human element do not just stand alongside one another may be seen from the fact that even as a defensive institution—imperfect though it may be as such—the canon is not theologically conceivable without God's confessing and protecting his Word in its all too human aspects.[12] This does not excuse what is unsatisfactory nor sanction once and for all what is defined as canonical. On the contrary, it is a constant summons to test the authorized norm of the canon by its basis, the authorizing norm of God's own Word, the canon within the canon.

Encouragement, though not complacency, in relation to this summons is conferred by the expert opinion that as things were, a better selection could hardly have been expected or achieved. It will always be astonishing with what sure instinct Christians at the beginning of the 3rd century perceived and retained the original material. There is nothing to show that other material was then present which the church abandoned and rejected for dogmatic reasons. It did not set aside but accepted and acknowledged even Galatians, which Marcion had perhaps rediscovered and put at the head of his collection of Pauline letters, and whose contents were highly discomfiting (H. von Campenhausen, *Kanon*, p. 120). K. Aland believes that in spite of all the imperfections and questionable features that may be discerned in the formation of the canon we cannot improve on the decision of the early church so far as the extent of the NT canon is concerned. No noncanonical work from the early period can be regarded as a candidate for later addition. If revision is considered, it can take the form only of subtraction and not expansion (*Studien zur Überlieferung des NT und seines Textes* [1967], p. 17).

b. The History of the Canon (with Special Reference to the Relation between Scripture and Tradition)

In this brief account of the history of the canon no full treatment can be given. Our systematic discussions will focus instead on *one* question in this history—the

---

[12]These aspects, including the arbitrary and accidental elements, are usually given by theology the rather more respectable title of "contingency." Cf. W. G. Kümmel's discussion of Barth, *Kanon*, p. 86, n. 74.

question whether and how far the intentions stated may be seen in the motivations and execution of the formation of the canon.

1. In the NT itself only the OT canon[13] is called *graphē*. The NT does not describe itself in this way.

2. The central writings of the NT (the gospels, the longer Pauline epistles, etc.) were established in the second half of the 2nd century, while in relation to the exclusion or inclusion of more peripheral works different decisions were taken in the different geographical areas.

3. The real motive for setting up a NT canon was to meet the provocation of Gnosticism in the 2nd century. It was not just that Gnostic ideology threatened to manipulate and falsify the original kerygma but that the related appeal to an esoteric knowledge tried to validate itself by supposed apostolic traditions. The rivalry of sources necessarily raised the question of authenticity, of the criterion by which to determine it, and then of the official validation—or canonizing—of what was found to be authentic.

4. One of the criteria set up was that of the originality, i.e., the real or supposed apostolicity, of the material transmitted by the means then available.

5. The *historical* drift of the question raises necessarily the question of accuracy. We have better historical methods at our disposal today and can construct the original tradition more exactly than could the early church which defined the canon. In fact, it is hard to reconcile the ideas of what is original. In particular, that which was then regarded as apostolic may often turn out to be secondary (see below).

6. To the extent, then, that historical theses were normative in the early church in its formation of the canon, they throw doubt upon the canon. They thus seem to demand that with the historical methods available to us we should now revise the canon and replace it with writings which by modern insights may be called original.

7. The intention behind this kind of criticism and reconstruction of the canon would finally be the same as that which raised the question of the historical Jesus and set for it the criterion that only *he*—only the result of this later inquiry—could be the criterion for the legitimacy of the Christian kerygma. The reasons why this experiment and hypothesis came to grief are decisive when it comes to showing how hopeless would be a historically motivated revision of the canon. For what is left out of account is that the historical (or supposedly historical) definition of the canonizable original was only one—and not the most essential—element in the formation of the canon. Behind the defensive motive the real reason was that the transmitted texts were used as a basis for liturgical proclamation and were the objects of spiritual experiences, i.e., there was experience of their evidence as truth.

8. Naturally this is not an objectifiable judgment but neither is it a mere appeal to the Holy Spirit. It reaches back to the basic Christian experience with God's Word in general, namely, that it validates itself by the witness of the Spirit and has to that extent what was later called a self-interpreting and self-evidencing quality.

---

[13]On this cf. Aland, *Studien*, pp. 3ff.

The formation of the canon is thus the church's seal affixed to the spiritual experience of the texts. The historical question of originality or apostolicity is in comparison only a secondary and additional measure taken with a view to adding historical "certainty" to spiritual "assurance." In putting the two terms "certainty" and "assurance" together here, we intend to bring out their difference in rank and to call into question the motive of seeking certainty to the extent that (beyond legitimate scientific interests) this may be misunderstood as a presupposition of being able to believe.

9. The basic error in absolutizing the historical element, whether in relation to the historical Jesus or to the establishment of the canon by historical means, is that it entails dissolution of a correlation that results from the union of Word and Spirit, namely, that of Word and faith, kerygma and community, address and reception. It tries to get back to something to which in principle we cannot get back but which forms the final limit for any attempt to gain certainty about what is original.

10. In this sense the development of the canon is to be understood as a witness of faith which like all faith and all witness rests on reception and on letting the spiritual Word do its work. Even tactical and time-bound discussions which interrupt this spiritual process cannot overlook the spiritual character of the basic event.

11. For the sake of this basic event we should not take a merely pragmatic view of the defensive motive in the formation of the canon. We should rather say that it gives evidence of a dialectic that is analogous to what we find in the framing of confessions. The structure of confessional statements is usually such that to the positive thesis ("We believe . . .") there is added the negative rejection, the so-called anathema. It may be assumed that what produced these confessional statements was the provocation offered by the anathematized counterfronts (of Papists, Socinians, Docetists, and many others). One might go further, perhaps, and say that the positive statement was not just formulated but achieved material self-awareness under the pressure of this provocation. Yet one should not conclude from this that the opponents control all that is done and said and thought, so that confessional statements are derived from and produced by a specific situation and the purposes it generates. Even before this there was at least an implicit knowledge of what was seeking explication and awareness. A truth that was previously in the incubation stage suddenly becomes virulent when in face of a heretical thesis it comes to see that this cannot be, but why not? and what is then the truth? The consciousness of truth which is the impelling force in the formation of the canon probably arose by means of a similar dialectic.

12. That we have to take into account an implicit pre-canonical consciousness of truth is made plain by the struggle between the formation of the canon and tradition. On the one side the canon is in debt to tradition. For it canonizes what it has received. As I have already shown, however, definite criteria of selection and rejection are at work in the formation of the canon, especially the reference back to God's own Word incarnate in Christ, also the self-demonstration of the texts used in worship, and finally the question of originality or apostolicity. In the formation of the canon the church does not just receive tradition but also criticizes it, even though the standards by which it does this—by means of that self-attestation—are themselves taken from tradition.

13. On the basis of this implicit pre-canonical consciousness of truth the early

church defended itself against the uncontrolled expansion of oral tradition. It did so on two fronts.

14. First, it defended itself against the tradition from which it itself derived. Two strands may be discerned.

(1) By the act of forming the canon it opposed the uncertainty of tradition as tradition moved further and further away from the starting point by which it was to be measured. The only weapon against this was an unchanged preservation of the sources as they flowed at the beginning from the event itself.[14] The *paradosis* (tradition) seeks the original basis and the canonical definition without which it cannot be so naturally, easily, and completely maintained and validated.[15]

(2) By the act of forming the canon it also criticized and rejected heretical elements which had penetrated the tradition from within and without, especially Marcionitism, Gnostic influences, and Montanism.

Whereas Roman Catholic writers see essentially only an act of preservation in the transition from oral tradition to *graphē,* more may in fact be discerned. By forming the canon the early church also acknowledged that from that time on tradition could no longer be a criterion of truth.[16] The canon fixes valid tradition and thus becomes the criterion for all statements that come to us from it.

15. Secondly, then, along with the existing tradition that is validated by it, the canon also took over the function of acting as a criterion for all traditions that might arise in the future. It thus came to discharge the office of a watchman. The establishment of a canon implied a recognition that church tradition must henceforth be supervised. Every later tradition must be tested by the apostolic tradition defined in the canon.[17] Thus the twofold function of the canon in relation to tradition is that of critically preserving past tradition and controlling future tradition. Only within this framework does the Reformation principle of *sola Scriptura* make sense. This principle resists any possibility that a church which thinks it has the Spirit in Osiandrian fashion might set up its own authority, teachings, dogmas, and other statements that have no support in the biblical canon and are thus contrary to the Scripture principle. The very principle of the canon contains a protest against the error, no matter where it originates, that the church is itself the bearer of an active tradition, even though it does not see itself as an autonomous subject but as authorized by the Pneuma.

16. The early church's implicit consciousness of truth in its formation of the canon actualizes itself especially in the historicizing appeal to apostolicity and the derived validation of the originality of the kerygma.

The Muratorian Fragment, which may have come from Hippolytus, gives evidence of the related tensions in the limitation of the canon toward the end of the 2nd century. A basic canon of undisputed writings is offered. The legitimacy of others such as the *Shepherd of Hermas* and the *Apocalypse of Peter* is contested. The test whether a work may be admitted into the canon is whether it can be traced

---

[14]H. von Campenhausen, *Kanon,* p. 111.

[15]M. J. Scheeben, *Handbuch der katholischen Dogmatik,* I, 2nd ed., ed. M. Grabmann (1948), p. 147.

[16]O. Cullmann, *Die Tradition als exegetisches, historisches und theologisches Problem* (1964), p. 45.

[17]*Ibid.,* pp. 45f.

back to an apostle or the disciple of an apostle invested with his authority. The concern about apostolic origin shows that normative and historical concerns are interwoven. The first witnesses could claim normative rank because they were historically closest to the mighty acts of God and were best protected against any suspicion that the word they left behind had been adulterated by change, alien influence, or misunderstanding. Their (real or supposed) status as the first witnesses also conferred on them uniqueness and unrepeatability. This gave them precedence over all later developments.[18]

Yet it is also plain that the historical approach to apostolicity soon became less important—and not just on the basis of modern methods of testing. Mark and Luke were given undisputed authority but they were not apostles. The Gospel and Apocalypse of Peter were ascribed to an apostle—and what an apostle!—but they remained outside the canon. The claim to apostolic authorship did not ensure the conferring of canonical dignity, as the long debates about Hebrews and Revelation show. Another problem with apostolicity was that the first witnesses were not all apostles but were for the most part disciples unknown to us (Käsemann, *Kanon*, p. 343).

It is unmistakable, then, that the historical criterion of apostolicity and first witness was increasingly replaced by the normative approach, not only in the sense that the question of the competence of these writings as faith-directives came to the fore but also to the extent that their rank as incontestable, i.e., first witness, was determined more by their contents than their historical confirmation. (In the Syrian church, for example, the apostolic worth of Philemon as a supposed letter of Paul was denied during the 3rd and 4th centuries on the ground that it was unedifying and therefore neither inspired nor apostolic [J. Leipold, *Geschichte des neutestamentlichen Kanons*, I (1907), p. 209].) The question of apostolicity thus became a theological question rather than a historical one. The title apostolic is to that extent no longer a presupposition but the result of a test (H. von Campenhausen, *Kanon*, p. 121). The decision is material rather than chronological. The criterion at issue is that of ''inner apostolic authority'' which is still ''compelling'' today (Cullmann, *Die Tradition*, pp. 46f.). If this is so, then apostolicity is a mark of kerygmatic quality which implies a direct relation to the history of revelation rather than an indirect and derived relation. When Cullmann speaks in this connection of the ''compelling'' significance of the texts he is certainly not thinking of a psychological impression but of the testimony of the Holy Spirit which is at work in the liturgical use of the texts and which validates them as the Word of God. If this is granted, one might speak of a *postulate* of apostolicity. This is an apt term because it appropriately puts the historical derivation of the texts from the apostles in a secondary position and thereby relativizes any historical mistake in this derivation. The apostolic postulate which results from material criteria has only subsidiary significance as it adds the support of temporal priority to the theological priority of the texts.

17. If *this* form of historical validation does not satisfy modern methods of historical confirmation, and if its results cannot stand before these methods, we may still maintain that in the NT canon we have the earliest attainable witness to

---

[18]Cf. the claim made in 2 Peter 1:18–21.

what the early church took to be the Word of God in the new covenant. Instructed and warned by the problem of the historical Jesus, we have already seen that the situation of witness, i.e., the correlation of speaking and hearing, of message and community, of Word and faith, forms the last frontier beyond which we cannot go when we want to know what is to be understood by the "Word of God." That to which witness is given is hidden behind the witness so far as its historical "in itself" is concerned.

3. PROBLEMS OF CANONICITY[19]

a. The Threatening of the Canon by Open Differences

The materially most serious challenge to the biblical canon is based on problems which arise out of tensions and discrepancies that force themselves even on the non-theological reader of the Bible. It would be unrealistic to expect that texts which arose in so many different ways and were transmitted in so many different times and places would be in complete harmony. If they were, one would have to suspect editorial manipulation, whereas the tensions are a sign that the faith attested here was a living one and could not therefore be pressed into a rationally concocted book. The correlation of (God's) Word and (living) faith that we established earlier prepares us for dissonances. These denote originality, whereas we could as little trust later harmonizing and redaction as we could the statements of dishonest witnesses at a trial.[20]

The canon would lack credibility from the outset if canonization meant the one-sided selection of what agrees or seems to agree. This would place an intolerable weight on the human factor, the independent changing of the kerygma by theologoumena and the devices of the *sophia tou kosmou*. It would especially undermine the thesis that the canon was formed by the witness of the proclaimed Word to itself and that to that degree it participates in the testimony of the Holy Spirit.

In fact there is no harmonizing tendency. The individual parts of the canon display a broad spectrum of contents and theologies. They even display considerable differences, so that the NT itself seems to be an arena of basic theological controversy. Precisely because there is this conflict and division of opinion the tradition enshrined in the canon cannot be reduced to a single common denominator. No victorious theses emerge triumphantly from the debates with the definitive simplicity that the perennial theology of our dreams should have.

As examples of the different statements that have been put together in the canon we may mention here only some of the most obvious.

First, there is the fact that the NT canon contains not just one gospel but four gospels which differ considerably in order, selection, and presentation (Käsemann, "Begründet der neutestamentliche Kanon die Einheit der Kirche?" *Exegetische Versuche und Besinnungen*, I [1960], p. 214). This difference is based

---

[19]We shall not deal with historical problems here since we have discussed them already in relation to apostolicity.
[20]H. von Campenhausen, *Kanon*, p. 122.

on the correlation of Word and faith. Faith is related here to reflective self-interpretation so that the received tradition is open to individual theological permeation. Various theologies are at work which change what is received in common and introduce formal separation. Thus the kerygma of the divine sonship of Jesus is common to all but it is variously interpreted according to different theological trends (*ibid.*, p. 215). Rahner thinks similarly that even in the simplest kerygmatic statement there is already a beginning of theology and already in Scripture this undoubtedly covers a wide spectrum as reflection on, and deduction from, the most direct experience of revelation ("Was ist eine dogmatische Aussage?" Rahner, *Schriften*, V [1962], p. 76; E.T. *Theological Investigations*, V, p. 61). For in a revelation that is believed and heard there is always through understanding, acceptance, and assimilation a synthesis between the Word of God and the word of the man concerned which he specifically can and must speak out of his own position in his historical situation (*ibid.*, p. 75; E.T. p. 61).

Reference may also be made to the familiar and much discussed antitheses between Luke and Paul on the one side and (especially) Paul and James on the other. For Käsemann these and other differences are so important that he can introduce the essay mentioned above with the statement that because of the differences in the proclamation of the NT the historian has to deny that the NT canon can be a basis for church unity (*Exegetische Versuche*, I, p. 214).

Now differences of this kind can be evaluated in many different ways. They can be seen positively as living tensions and negatively as explosive issues that jeopardize the canon. The significance attached to them will vary not only according to the differences in the criteria used (which range from rationalistic and moral to historical and existential) but also and especially according to the materially varying importance which is ascribed to individual discrepancies. I shall try to make this difference clear through some examples.

b. Examples and Evaluations of Differences

(1) Law of Perspective

Many divergencies may be explained in terms of different situations and standpoints. In this connection we may also mention that the kerygma came into different complexes of inquiry and reflection. At issue is a process which is repeated a hundredfold in the history of theology and preaching and which indeed initiates the historical process. The one truth is not enshrined in a single formula that always remains the same (perennial theology). It is always accepted in different forms as situations change and differ in different places. It is constantly reinterpreted and then reformulated. One side of the truth may retreat into the background as (actually or apparently) irrelevant and another can take on surprising relevance. The law of perspective creates nearness and distance.

The ceremonial law of the OT and the NT attack on it seem remote from the modern Westerner, but they may be very close to an Indian candidate for baptism. The fact that Christ overcomes anxiety and has the power to forgive sins is a basic theme of the kerygma, but what is experienced as anxiety and what sin is in a given case are dependent on circumstances and may take constantly changing forms. The fact that we should obey God more than men (Acts 5:29) and remember this when we render to Caesar what is Caesar's and to God what is God's (Luke 20:25 and par.) is again a commandment that is substantially the same everywhere as a criterion, but how this ''more'' is to be apportioned to obedience as between God and men and how we are to distinguish what belongs to Caesar and what we owe to God can work out differently in every new situation. Different decisions will be taken in a free constitutional state on the one side and under an ideological tyranny on the other. A subjectively based element in the distinction will be provided already by the need to interpret each political and historical situation. In some circumstances the difference in perspective will make it impossible for a synod to achieve consensus even though the command itself, which gives rise to the differing interpretations, is unanimously recognized.

The divine command enters into new situations, has different thrusts, and does not strike home to those who take a bird's-eye view of these situations, staying aloof from them. In this sense the divergencies that arise must be tested by the question whether they are grounded in the difference of perspective and may thus be relativized materially. They must be tested especially by the question to what kerygmatic identity they are oriented.

(2) The Theological Tension between Paul and James
We have already pointed out that open theological differences may be related to situational differences. But here the matter is undoubtedly critical. This may be seen from the debates caused by the apparent difference between Paul's doctrine of justification and that of James. This antithesis seems to make it possible to appeal either to Romans to establish the Reformation doctrine of ''by faith alone'' and/or to James to validate a doctrine of good works and possible merits. Taken alone these would obviously lead at once to a basic material difference that shatters the unity of the canon. These possibilities, which took on reality in history, culminate in the question what rank or force we are to attribute to this difference between Paul and James. The way in which we tackle it theologically can also be significant for analogous cases.

How delicate this question can be for the unity or the possible challenging of the canon may be seen from Luther's freedom in his appreciation or disparagement of the biblical writings (WA DB, VI, 10f.; LW, 35, 361f.) when in his September Bible of 1522 he separated Hebrews, James, Jude, and Revelation in a negative sense from the rest of the NT, and especially Paul. In this context his description of James as a ''strawy epistle'' is well known. This does not prevent him from calling James himself a good and pious man who took and wrote down certain sayings from the disciples of the apostles. But this is still disparagement. For Luther it was intolerable to say that righteousness was reckoned to Abraham because of the offering of Isaac and that it was his works, therefore, that first brought his faith to its full reality (James 2:21f.). He could not set James among the gold, silver, and precious stones of Scripture but only among the wood, hay, and stubble which are sometimes mixed in with it (WA, 54, 3).

If Luther saw James in gross contradiction to Paul and therefore put it on the extreme edge of the canon, if not outside it, he could say on the other hand that Scripture never errs (WA, 23, 122; LW, 37, 50f.) and is never at odds with itself (*loc. cit.*), so that if it seems to be so, this is only to hardened hypocrites who have no understanding (WA, 40/I, 318f; LW, 26, 193f.). Are these apparently antithetical statements simple contradictions, or do we have here a dialectic of freedom and obligation which is essential if we are to understand the canon? This question will be with us constantly in the deliberations that follow.

Certainly divergencies will be evaluated in very different ways if on the one hand we see in the canon merely an accidental conglomerate of texts arbitrarily selected according to a given age, or on the other hand we find in them a collection of writings in which—according to the self-understanding of the church that forms the canon—the self-evidence of the divine Word is expressed by the liturgical event and guaranteed in the testimony of the Holy Spirit. To the degree that we start with the second alternative we will be ready in some sense to agree that the early church knew what it was doing when it did not exclude genuinely or apparently dissenting passages from the canon nor see the unity of the canon threatened by them. At any rate it is as well to begin by asking how far this assumption takes us and therefore to test what might be meant by a unity of the canon that covers the divergencies.

To take up again the case of the tension between Paul and James, the canon offers us here two texts that seem to be in some antithesis to one another. As Paul sees it, righteousness is given by faith alone without the works of the law (Romans 3:28). For James faith is qualified by the fact that it leads to good works, so that faith and works are together the condition of the event of justification (James 2:26). As it stands, this seems to be a disavowal of Paul's doctrine of justification.

The author confesses that he can appreciate the contradiction when the two positions are set over against one another as emancipated theses but that he has never been able to see how this contradiction can stand if they are set within the reciprocity of relations suggested by the canon. This approach is impossible, of course, so long as we openly or secretly pursue the intention of validating the unity of the canon by a uniform doctrinal system. Since that is not possible, the attempt to put Paul and James together under a comprehensive doctrinal formula is futile and leads to very artificial constructions.[21] I suspect that the same purpose and therefore a doubtful view of canonical unity lurk in the background when people speak of the irreconcilability of the two positions. But how in fact are they to be reconciled?

It is shocking for those who accept Paul's "by faith alone" and "by grace alone" to read in James of a faith that can lead to justification only in combination with good works. Yet it is undoubtedly erroneous to see here a correction of Paul's position. What seems to be the real truth is that the two are speaking in different situations and that one can discern geometrical fields which intersect at a common point, namely, where the two situations relate to the one fact of justification.

What has changed is that a new historical stage has been reached at which Paul's doctrine of justification has degenerated into something abstract, an ethically indifferent principle. No formulation of the gospel cannot surreptitiously become a law again. No description of the "event" of grace cannot surreptitiously decay

---

[21] As an example cf. the doctrine of Scripture held by the Missouri Synod (cf. F. Pieper and J. T. Mueller, *Christian Dogmatics*, pp. 90ff.).

into a principle of grace. This spiritual experience, which involves disobedience, emancipation, and especially alienation from the Spirit, is understood and addressed by Paul himself in Romans 6:1-4 and 15-17. He saw precisely what would happen if justification by faith alone were made into a principle. Understood thus, the principle of faith is equated with the status of justification. Controlling this status, I seem to be in a situation of permissiveness. I can sin and yield to every sort of libertinage, yet still be justified and accepted by God. Indeed, the more I renounce legal restraint and surrender to the magic of a springtime of sin, the more impressively I bear witness to the irrevocable state of justification by faith.[22] The assurance of being justified by faith without meritorious works becomes the security of standing under the patronage of a timeless principle. *Certitudo* degenerates into *securitas*.

We all know how Paul dealt with libertines who rested in such security. Those who are baptized—and baptism can claim justification—are baptized into Christ's death (Romans 6:4f.). But this can mean for them only that they have actually died to the old life and know that they are summoned to life as "new creatures" (Romans 6:4; Galatians 2:17f.; 5:16ff.; Philippians 3:12ff., etc.). Those who find shelter from the law in grace do not set themselves under the protection of a principle but subject themselves to obedience to a Lord (Romans 6:15ff.) whom their life and acts cannot oppose. Justification by faith is not a status. As such it would become an indifferent principle which would be the exact opposite of commitment. Faith, however, leads to commitment.

The sign of this is the constant uniting in Paul of promise and exhortation, or indicative and imperative.[23] The reason why the promise of justification is always followed by claims and ethical appeals is that I am still becoming. God has entered into a history with me which has opened but not yet ended. Hence Luther always gives a typically quantitative answer to the question whether and how far the redeemed person (*liberatus*) no longer needs the law, namely, to the extent that he is redeemed (*in quantum est talis*).[24] Since as a justified person I am always becoming, I have to *learn* how justification relates to all aspects of my life. There may still be unredeemed areas in me. Many of my members are still numb and bloodless.

Naturally these demands and imperatives do not mean for Paul that in addition to faith I must bring achievements if I am to share in justification. They rather imply the testing question whether I am living out what I am, whether I am moving in life toward that from which I already come. Hence I do not go beyond faith but I am required constantly to return to its source, to the Lord who wins faith from me. The demand to go forward is identical with an appeal to return to the beginning.[25]

When the grace of justification is changed into a principle this dialectic of being and becoming, of indicative and imperative, loses its point. The fact that this dialectic is a normative part of Paul's doctrine of justification shows how he takes

---

[22]Cf. Luther's controversy with the Antinomians, ThE, I, Index, "Antinomians."

[23]ThE, I, §§314ff.; E.T. I, pp. 72f.

[24]WA, 39/I, 528, 11ff.

[25]Cf. Luther's statement in WA, 4, 350, 14f.; LW, 11, 477 (quoted in EG, II, p. 282; EF, II, p. 232).

precautions against this threatened degeneration of faith into a principle, into the timeless state of an indelible habit.[26]

Does not James have exactly in view this situation of faith perverted into a principle, a status of believing? Does he not contemplate some of the ways in which Paul's understanding of justification has been worked out in history? He actually has in front of him people who appeal to faith but do not regard it as an act of commitment nor claim it as a force that molds their lives but view it as a fact which is now behind them and which as an indifferent principle lets them do as they like. They can rest in it as the Jews whom John the Baptist attacked reclined securely because they had Abraham for their father (Luke 3:8) and thus thought that they did not have to make any commitment.

Face to face with this threatened and experienced degeneration of the doctrine of "by faith alone," the intentions of Paul and James are the same. It may be admitted that James, whose thought is less nuanced, expresses himself in an essentially cruder way (and thus gives rise the more easily to misunderstandings) than Paul does with his sublime distinctions. Yet we must not treat their views as thesis and antithesis in the timeless rest of systematic relations. We must understand them rather as the expression of different stages in the history of the working out of the message of justification. The doctrine of justification reveals what we might call its guiding motif most clearly at the "moment" when the justifying work of God to the sinner cancels the value of human action and the promise of the gospel overcomes the claim of the law. This "moment" is in temporal terms the *kairos* of Paul's teaching. James, however, is referring to the moment when grace has been changed back into law and misunderstood accordingly. This law is not the law which demands action from us but a law which ascribes to grace a kind of automatic efficacy which does not need our cooperation. When faith has fulfilled its function as a receipt for grace received, it can be, not discarded, but put in the records like a deed of ownership which secures my property, so that I have no longer to struggle for recognition of my possession and need not worry about it anymore. What takes place in the movement from Paul to James (or rather in James' readers) is a typical process and a primary model in the general history of words and concepts.

New positions and breaks with tradition seldom produce a new vocabulary. What usually happens is that a modification of meaning takes place under the shelter of the same verbal structures. In the history of the church and dogmatics the root Christian vocabulary displays a relatively high degree of constancy but such terms as grace and works, justification and judgment, Moses and Christ can mean different things. Our own age is witness to perhaps the most radical transformation of sense under the cover of the same words. Marxist-Leninism accepts many traditional concepts (peace, justice, etc.) but they are given a totally different meaning so that it is hard to understand even those who speak the same language. This has often been the case in the church's doctrinal history.

It could well be, then, that the tension between Paul and James can be traced

---

[26]The hymnwriter Johann Heermann speaks of the experience of this constant threat to faith when he says that while God is always ready to meet the sinner with mercy there is no grace for those who sin in the name of grace.

back to different times and situations. It could well be that this double aspect is needed if we are to be able to see the event of justification plastically and in perspective as an "event." It could well be that the event is being defended on two different fronts: first, against the self-righteousness suggested by Paul's understanding of the law, namely, the illusion that man can achieve self-fulfillment, and second, against the corruption of the understanding of grace and faith which produces a new form of self-righteousness, namely, the degeneration of the promise of justification into a static quality or legal title.

If this is so—and the author believes that this is how we are to see it—then the placing of both Paul and James in the canon makes sense. It is also shown very pointedly that the unity of the canon is not a unity of systematic teaching but a historical unity, i.e., the result of counterbalancing positions which arise from different situations but belong to the same plane and look in the same direction. This structure of the canon, however, cannot be discerned unless it is realized that we are drawn into the same history and the same event that is permeated by this tension; that we cannot do without the aids in perspective which are indicated in model form by Paul and James. We, too, need tension-filled correctives. It is necessary for us too, if we espouse Pauline theologoumena, to preach after the manner of James when this is what the hearers in front of us need.

It makes sense, then, that both Romans and James are texts in the canon. The canonical link between them has the special significance that we are not to let any of the NT witnesses speak alone but to hear their voices among all the other witnesses and thus to be open to the corrective event of the history of proclamation. If we isolate one of the witnesses, no longer seeing him in the context of the canon, then he threatens to take over the job of confirming our own prejudices and exaggerations. Readers of Romans, perhaps, fail to notice that for them the event of justification has frozen into a static habit and a new form of self-righteousness, while readers of James who do not know Romans can overlook the fact that they are discrediting "by grace alone" and "by faith alone." G. Eichholz has felicitously phrased it as follows: "What have they to say to one another, James to Paul and Paul to James, and what have both of them together to say to us?"[27]

The tension between Paul and James, which we have used here as a model of fundamental significance, does not break the unity of the canon but is instead adapted to make clear to us the nature of this unity. The early church obviously found some point in offering us the epistles of both as texts for preaching. But we should preach on them very poorly if proclamation were to do what systematic theology for good reasons is forbidden to do, namely, level the texts down or treat them as totally unrelated to one another. If the texts are to be understood in terms of their *kairos,* their hour and situation, we must go to work in sermon preparation to bring out the historical profile and claim the materials of historico-critical research.[28]

---

[27]G. Eichholz, "Jakobus und Paulus. Ein Beitrag zum Problem des Kanons," ThEx, N.S. 39 (1953), p. 48; cf. H. Diem, *Dogmatik,* II (1953), p. 207; E.T. pp. 237f.

[28]Along these lines cf. Käsemann's thesis that different christologies do not have to be contradictory but can supplement one another or bring out different aspects as the situation demands (*Kanon*, p. 404).

(3) The Question of Canonical Revision
Some differences are related to different situations and some are differences of theological perspective. But it cannot be ruled out that there might be divergencies involving things that are materially irreconcilable. Even if we think that we can concede to the act of canonization a share in the self-evidence of God's Word and the testimony of the Holy Spirit, we should not overlook the earthen vessel of the human forms of reception (unless we champion verbal inspiration). We may assume that these irreconcilable features may be seen for the most part in the relation between the OT and the NT (e.g., with reference to the imprecatory psalms). Difficulties within the NT (e.g., in the genealogies of Jesus, the resurrection stories, or eschatological data) are hardly in the same class.

In face of things that seem to be irreconcilable with the central themes of the NT, especially the message of the justification of sinners,[29] we must be ready to put to ourselves the self-critical question whether it might not be due to our own fixity of perspective that we do not see the kerygmatic relevance of these texts.[30] Nor can we ignore the question whether we are perhaps restricting individualistically the hermeneutical principle that the Bible is God's Word only to the extent that it promotes Christ. In this case we can hardly grasp the cosmic relation of the figure of Christ (Ephesians 1:19ff.; Colossians 1:15ff.).[31]

If in spite of these measures a divergence still remains which seems to us to be incompatible with the unity of the canon, such exceptional cases hardly justify the postulate of a revision of the canon. Luther, who took offense at some passages, did not draw this conclusion but advised us to tip our hats to such texts and pass on. The respect which he is thereby ready to give relates undoubtedly to the greater wisdom of the decision of the whole church. Our discussion of the "dualism" between Paul and James has shown perhaps that there is something in this, and that Christianity would have lost something if it had revised the canon in accordance with Luther's criticisms of James, Hebrews, and Revelation.

The preacher, too, is constantly tempted to overlook some passages which at the present stage in his history of faith are to him remote and inaccessible. This is true not merely in relation to individuals but also to whole historical periods to which biblical texts have sometimes seemed close and sometimes distant.[32]

We cannot, of course, pay our respects and pass on when sects seize on marginal texts and make them the center of their teaching and preaching. It is in keeping with the sectarian mentality to blow up the partial and make an absolute of the relative. In face of this the central has to be defended against the peripheral and it has to be made clear that even the canon does not make the Word of God so secure that we can relax in confidence but that we are constantly referred back to the self-evidence of the Word which attests itself *in* the canon. Lessing's parable of

---

[29]I am not quite clear why people today prefer to say "the ungodly" instead of "sinners."

[30]E.g., in relation to the ceremonial law, cf. H. Iwand, *Nachgelassene Werke*, IV (1964), pp. 286ff.

[31]Cf. O. A. Dilschneider, *Christus Pantokrator* (1962), pp. 31ff.

[32]In the relatively peaceful 19th century Revelation was a closed book to many, not because criticism ignored it but because it seemed to be kerygmatically unfruitful. Christians living under ideological dictatorships in the 20th century find that it sheds light on their situation (cf. the role of the tension between Romans 13 and Revelation 13 in the Confessing Church under Hitler).

the ring in *Nathan* is right to the extent that the genuineness of the ring has to be proved and we cannot be sure of it on the mere strength of a certificate. It is probably wrong only in respect of the moral forms of its proof of authenticity.

For the rest the NT itself speaks of the discernment of spirits whose critical function Paul relates especially to the understanding of the OT (e.g., 2 Corinthians 3:7ff.). Käsemann is surely right when he believes that this discernment must be exercised in relation to the NT as well.[33] Along these lines we have been able to see in the controversy about James how a valid principle—that of "by faith alone"—can degenerate into a dubious doctrine of habit. Paul himself is aware of possible perversions of this kind, especially in the replacing of the Spirit by the letter (Galatians 3:1ff.). The Spirit certainly does not contest the saying: "It is written." He manifests himself in Scripture. But Scripture always can and does become letter when it is not authorized by the Spirit but tries to be an authority by its mere existence and in this way replaces the Spirit.[34] The Word of God does not lie statically in what is written; as the event of Word and Spirit it breaks out of the letter. It is God in action, an efficacious Word. It fashions the letter and incarnates itself in it. It appropriates itself to hearers and readers, and lets itself be appropriated by them, through the testimony of the Spirit.

---

[33] *Kanon*, p. 31.
[34] *Ibid.*, p. 133.

VIII

The Establishment of the Canon by the Uniting of Scripture and Tradition

1. STUDIES IN DEFINING THE RELATION BETWEEN THE TWO NORMS

Bibliography (apart from dictionaries, dogmatic works, and histories of dogma): H. Beintker, "Die evangelische Lehre von der heiligen Schrift und von der Tradition," *Quellenhefte zur Konfessionskunde,* II (1961); P. Brunner, "Schrift und Tradition," *Festschrift für H. Meiser* (1951), pp. 119ff.; H. Bultmann, "Reflexionen zum Thema Geschichte und Tradition," *Festschrift für E. Beutler* (1960), pp. 9ff.; Y. Congar, "Traditio und Sacra Doctrina bei Thomas von Aquin," *Festschrift für J. R. Geiselmann* (1965), pp. 170ff.; O. Cullmann, "'KYRIOS' as Designation for the Oral Tradition concerning Jesus (Paradosis and Kyrios)," *Scottish Journal of Theology,* III (1950), pp. 180ff.; H. Diem, *Theologie als kirchliche Wissenschaft,* II (1955), §§7, 11, 14; E.T. *Dogmatics,* cc. 7, 11, 14; G. Ebeling, "Die Bedeutung der historisch-kritischen Methode für die protestantische Theologie und Kirche," *Wort und Glaube,* I (1960), pp. 1ff.; E.T. *Word and Faith,* I, pp. 17ff.; J. R. Geiselmann, *Die lebendige Überlieferung als Norm des christlichen Glaubens . . .* (1958); H. Grass, "Die katholische Lehre von der heiligen Schrift und von der Tradition," *Quellen zur Konfessionskunde,* I (1954); M. Jacob, "Sacra Traditio und Sacra Scriptura. Eine dogmengeschichtliche Untersuchung zur Lehre des II Vaticanum von der Vermittlung der göttlichen Offenbarung," *Theologische Versuche,* V ([East] Berlin, 1975); W. Joest, *Fundamentaltheologie* (1974), pp. 164ff.; W. Kasper, *Die Lehre von der Tradition in der Römischen Schule* (1962); G. Krüger, "Geschichte und Tradition," *Freiheit und Weltverwaltung* (1968), pp. 71ff.; W. von Loewenich, *Der moderne Katholizismus vor und nach dem Konzil* (1970); J. H. Newman, *vide* J. Artz, *Newman-Lexikon* (1975), pp. 1066ff.; W. Pannenberg, "Die Krise des Schriftprinzips," *Grundfragen der systematischer Theologie* (1967), pp. 11ff.; E.T. *Basic Questions in Theology,* pp. 1ff.; J. Pieper, *Über den Begriff der Tradition* (1958); K. Rahner, "Chalkedon—Ende oder Anfang," *Das Konzil von Chalkedon,* III (1954), pp. 3ff.; H. Rückert, "Schrift, Tradition und Kirche," *Vorträge und Aufsätze zu historischer Theologie* (1972), pp. 310ff.; *Studium generale,* VI (1951) with contributions on tradition by A. Rüstow, T. Litt, F. Becker, K. Reinhardt, F. Snell, J. Ebbinghaus, H.

von Campenhausen, M. Schmaus; F. C. Viering, *Evangelische und katholische Schrift-auslegung* (Diss., Tübingen); E. Wolf, "Tradition und Redemption," EvTh, XXII (1962), p. 326.

Under this heading our special concern is with Roman Catholic theology and its special establishment—or relativization—of the authority of Scripture. The church by its infallible teaching office guarantees the validity of the biblical canon and the understanding of its statements. In the much-quoted words of Augustine: "I would not have believed the gospel if I had not believed the church," this relation between Scripture and church has been given precise formulation. If Luther in his work *Von Menschensatzungen zu meiden* opposes to Augustine's thesis the statement that "each must believe for himself that it is the Word of God and that he inwardly finds it to be the Word of God . . . even though the whole world preaches to the contrary," this simply shows that defining the relation between the authority of Scripture and that of the church is one of the most serious problems in controversial theology.

Since the relevant doctrinal statements constitute a historical chain of utterances, there is a tradition in the understanding and exposition of Scripture which for reasons that we have still to discuss can take on the rank of a second source of revelation alongside Scripture and beyond it. The final reason why Roman Catholicism tends toward this understanding of tradition is that for it the church and its representatives are as an institution bearers of the Spirit.[1] The manifestations of the Spirit are attested in twofold form, as Holy Scripture and the word of the church. Among leading Roman Catholics today, e.g., K. Rahner (especially after Vatican II), there is an unmistakable tendency to assert the primacy of Scripture over tradition. The Bible movement in the Roman Catholic world points in the same direction. Yet the question arises—we shall keep it in mind and deal with it later—whether a radical primacy of Scripture is possible within the Roman Catholic doctrine of the church. Will not at least a *conflict* of norms necessarily occur with its attempted establishment?

Though it cannot be our task to survey the whole development of the relation between Scripture and tradition, we shall have to look at some of its stages because the way in which the importance of tradition rises and the authority of Scripture declines offers us material insights into the relation between them. It will suffice if we make the 13th century the starting point of our study and deal only with some of the more critical points.

1. In Thomas Aquinas the rivalry in the claim to authority is not decided nor has it even broken out; it is only hinted at. More or less self-evidently Thomas finds faith to be exclusively grounded in the revelation imparted to the apostles and prophets as it is contained in the canon. Over against this one binding source of revelation he accords only secondary rank to the findings of reason and the teachings of the church. These stand in the service of faith and may be helpful in

---

[1]Cf. I 2 f (pp. 41ff.).

elucidating the truth which it gains elsewhere, but they are not in a position to prove this truth themselves.[2]

Sacred doctrine uses the arguments of reason only as extraneous and probable arguments. It finds its own authorities in the canonical writers whose statements give it an impregnable foundation. The statements of other teachers in the church come within its range but at best these can only serve to make a doctrine probable. For our faith rests on the revelation given to the apostles and prophets; these were the men who wrote the canonical books. This revelation does not rest on the revelation given to some other teacher. In reading other writers we do not assume that all they wrote is true no matter how distinguished they may be for holiness or learning (q. 1, 9; Grass, in *Quellen zur Konfessionskunde,* p. 18).

Thomas, of course, postulates an interpretative court, for in Holy Scripture the truth of faith is contained only in a scattered and varied way and it is obscure in many matters. The lengthy efforts and exercises needed to attain clarity are more than can be asked of most people. Hence the truth of faith contained in Scripture has to be put together in an orderly and intelligible way. The resultant teaching of the church (and its teaching tradition) is not, however, added to Sacred Scripture but simply taken from it.[3] One may thus say that an even more unequivocal primacy is given to Scripture here and that tradition, as a derived norm, is allotted only an expository function which clearly limits any growth beyond Scripture. Even though the right is granted to the papacy to settle doctrinal disputes authoritatively by setting up confessional formulations, and definitively to define the truth of faith, its authority is undoubtedly subject to the authorizing norm of the scriptural canon.[4]

2. Understandably the primacy of Scripture became a matter of theological controversy only when, as at the Reformation, it was played off against tradition and the self-evident harmony of the two, which was still present in Thomas, was shattered thereby. When the Council of Trent answered the Reformation attack in Session IV (April 8, 1546), it found itself obliged, in relation to traditions that go beyond the Bible as well as those that are validated by it, to abandon the subjection of tradition to Scripture that we see in Thomas, and to give to it an equal rank. The Reformation in the name of the principle of "Scripture alone" had drawn attention polemically to the traditions that go beyond Scripture and denounced their biblically unjustifiable claim to revelation. Hence Thomas's concept of a tradition which simply clarifies Scripture and makes it didactically more accessible by confessional formulae could no longer be upheld. For the Reformation contested Thomas's axiom that tradition does not add to Scripture but is simply taken from it. If there was a wish to validate as the truth of faith that which was in fact added to Scripture, that which went beyond it, this was possible only by according to tradition the rank of a second source of revelation *side by side* with Scripture and thus making out of the subordination of tradition to Scripture a coordination with it.

---

[2]*Summa theologiae,* I, q. 1, 8.
[3]*Summa theologiae,* II/II, q. 1, 9 (Grass, *Quellen,* pp. 18f.).
[4]*Ibid.,* q. 1, 10 (Grass, p. 19).

For this reason the holy ecumenical and universal synod of Trent maintained that along with the books of the OT and the NT, whose author is God, it wanted to see traditions that define faith and morals . . . "received and venerated with the same piety and reverence." For—and this is the decisive argument for raising the rank of tradition—they have been given "either from the lips of Christ himself or dictated by the Holy Spirit" and "preserved in unbroken succession in the catholic church."[5]

The according of equal rank to tradition and Scripture rests, then, on two arguments. First, God or Christ is the author of both. Second, later traditions as well as the biblical authors can appeal to inspiration by the Pneuma. Implicitly at first there is thus intimated an ecclesiology which understands the church not merely as the recipient of the revelation enshrined in Scripture but also as its direct bearer and to that extent as the body which continues the biblical revelation.

3. Inevitably this equal ranking of Scripture and tradition cannot maintain equilibrium for long and therefore the question of primacy arises afresh. This takes place already at the end of the same Tridentine session[6] when the church as the bearer of tradition is accorded a monopoly in the interpretation of Holy Scripture. No one must dare to interpret Holy Scripture in such a way that in matters of faith and morals, "relying on his own cleverness, he wrests it according to his own opinion and contrary to the opinion which the holy mother church has held and holds" . . . or in such a way that he interprets Holy Scripture contrary to "the unanimous view of the fathers" even though no declaration to this effect has been published. To the church alone is it given to decide the true meaning and interpretation of Holy Scripture. Hence anyone stands under anathema from the outset who believes with Luther that the Word of God is the truth simply because he finds it so inwardly and even though the whole world preaches to the contrary.

In another context—in debate with Bultmann—we have already shown that we control the text if we have at our disposal a hermeneutical principle that we bring to it. Even if the hermeneutical principle seems at the first stage to accept the servant function of an organic use, it threatens at the second stage to switch to a normative use so that it no longer stands under the text but over it (EG, I, pp. 59f., 155f.; EF, I, pp. 60f., 125). This makes the conclusion unavoidable that the church's monopoly of exposition implies the primacy of the church or tradition over Scripture.

4. A logical result is that the primacy of tradition over Scripture which the church's monopoly entails exerts pressure for explicit recognition. This came eighteen years later in the Tridentine Profession of Faith of 1564. The bull of Pius IV, "Injunctum nobis" (9/13/1564),[7] clearly puts tradition above Scripture in the name of the church's privilege in the interpretation of Scripture: "I most firmly acknowledge and embrace the apostolical and ecclesiastical traditions and other observances and constitutions of the same church and sacred scripture" according

---

[5]Denz., 1501; E.T. 783.
[6]Denz., 1507; E.T. 786.
[7]Denz., 1863; E.T. 995.

to that sense which the holy mother church decides and no other than that which accords "with the unanimous consent of the fathers."[8]

5. The next step was waiting to be taken. The increasing dominance of tradition expresses itself—especially in theological writings—in three theses which constantly recur. First, Scripture has many meanings so that the expository directives of the church's teaching office are needed in its interpretation. Second, the canon does not contain the whole truth of faith but needs to be supplemented. Third and finally, the authority of Scripture needs verification by the church.

As regards the first thesis, J. A. Möhler[9] points out that it is impossible to answer heretics from Scripture alone. They, too, appeal to Scripture. Hence authoritative exposition is needed.

The resultant monopoly of interpretation, which is taken up again with particular resoluteness by Vatican I (cf. Denz., 3007; E.T. 1788), goes back to an ancient tradition. Cf. Irenaeus, *Adversus omnes haereses,* IV, 26. Vincent of Lerins, *Commonitorium,* c. 2, asks why the norm of Scripture, which is perfect and adequate enough in itself, has to be linked with the authority of the church's insight. The reason is that because of its profundity Scripture is not understood in the same sense by everybody. Novatian, Sabellius, Arius, Pelagius, and Nestorius all expounded it in different ways. Because of the many possibilities of error it is necessary that in expounding the prophetic and apostolic writings the line of ecclesiastical and catholic interpretation be followed (cf. M. Schmaus, *Katholische Dogmatik,* I, 2nd ed. [1940], pp. 32f.). Here, of course, we find "only" the church's privilege in interpretation. Tradition does not yet embrace Scripture or press toward primacy. "As yet" the church has in relation to Scripture no more than the position of an expository norm.

As regards the second thesis, the canon contains only fragments of the truth of faith and needs to be completed. This view rests on the premise that the church existed prior to Scripture (as Reformation theology can agree) and that for this reason (here is where the debate begins) Scripture is to be regarded as an expression of the church's life. In it the consciousness of faith and the derived proclamation were enshrined with the help of the testimony of the Holy Spirit.[10] But it is only one expression, not the total expression, of the Christian consciousness of faith. The revelation that the apostles had to impart is not found exhaustively in the written documents. In a more comprehensive way they preached orally and they left this oral witness with the church so that it might live on in it for all ages.[11]

As Karl Adam puts it (*Das Wesen des Katholizismus,* 9th ed. [1940], pp. 175f.; E.T. *The Spirit of Catholicism* [London, 1929], pp. 147f.), the NT Bible is a significant but not an exhaustive deposit of the apostolic proclamation that fills and saturates the total consciousness of the church. Oral proclamation, the living

---

[8] "Apostolicas et ecclesiasticas *traditiones* reliquasque eiusdem ecclesiae observationes et *constitutiones* firmissime admitto et amplector. Idem (!) sacram *Scripturam....*"

[9] *Symbolik,* 5th ed. (1938), §39.

[10] Cf. M. Schmaus, *Katholische Dogmatik,* I (1938), §10.

[11] F. Diekamp, *Katholische Dogmatik nach den Grundsätzen des heiligen Thomas,* I, 10th and 11th ed. (1949), §§7, 24.

apostolic word that moves through the congregations, is older and more original than the Bible. It bears witness to the inspiration and canon of the Bible. It is more comprehensive than this, for it testifies to the wealth of cultic life and religious customs, practices, and institutions that are only alluded to in the NT. It has in it something which the Bible as the written word does not and cannot have and which constitutes its chief advantage. It is the living spirit of revelation; the urgent vitality of the concept of revelation; the instinct of faith that stands behind both the written and the unwritten word; the mind of the church (*phronēma ekklesiastikon*).

The biblical canon, then, needs to be supplemented by the fulness of tradition in which the Spirit-caused instinct of faith is more direct than in the dead word. This is shown especially by the fact that the canon is related to the church's faith as one sector is to the whole circle. On this view the significance of Scripture as an authorizing norm is clearly relativized if not annulled. Hence we have to keep before us the question whether the obvious tendency of modern Roman Catholicism (especially before and after Vatican II) to lay a stronger emphasis on the Bible does not find a limit here, so that within this understanding of tradition the principle of "Scripture alone" is out of reach. It seems to be doubtful whether there can be here an "encounter" between Holy Scripture and the church (especially a "critical" encounter). By way of its tradition is not the church engaged merely in a monologue? Is not its inspired total consciousness simply talking to one sector of the inspired material?

As regards the third thesis, Scripture is no longer to be regarded as an independent authority which certifies itself by its own self-evidence (its ability to interpret itself). As it is simply one sector of tradition, it draws its authority from this court or its representative, the church's teaching office. Scripture, then, is an authority which needs authorization and accreditation; it needs to be vouched for by the institutional church. We recall the saying of Augustine already quoted: He would not have believed the gospel if he had not believed the church.

Thus the church in its living teaching office is the direct and nearest source of faith and therefore of the knowledge of faith, while Scripture and tradition are the more distant rule of faith.[12] More precisely, tradition, being represented by the church, is the next closest rule of faith and only Scripture is really distant. The basis of authority which is here sought in the church rather than Scripture is understandable only against the background of the premise that the church as institution is the bearer of the Pneuma. (We dealt with this in connection with the Osiandrian problem.) In the church truth is present. The remembered "once," to which the statements of Scripture belong, is brought out of the past into the present only as it shares in this living presence of the truth in the church. Without this mode of presentation Scripture remains a dead letter which cannot present itself and become "evident" in the power of the Spirit that dwells within it.

It seems to me to be unmistakable that even Vatican II is still tied to this presupposition. The church's monopoly of interpretation remains intact. The authentic teaching office of the bishop of Rome claims religious obedience of will and understanding even when he does not speak with the highest teaching authority

---

[12]Schmaus, *Katholische Dogmatik*, p. 32; cf. Vatican I (Denz., 3011; E.T. 1792).

(Dogmatic Constitution on the Church, "Lumen gentium," 25; *Vatican II Documents,* p. 48).

6. According to what has been said tradition is not the abstract transmission of Christianity but the planting of it in its immediacy and life. It relates to the total content of Christianity whether this be contained in Scripture or not.[13] Tradition cannot be understood, then, as a kind of conveyor belt which carries faith and doctrine through the ages and toward whose goods the church simply has a receptive attitude. On the contrary, it continually develops a new productivity in virtue of the living Spirit of revelation that dwells within it. It is this living Spirit, working through the teaching office, which makes possible for this plenitude its inner vitality, its power of expansion, and its ability to take root in all times, cultures, and intellectual movements.[14] At issue, then, is an active tradition, whereas all other Christian communions, insofar as they have preserved essential parts of the early Christian legacy, rest on a dead and rigid principle: Lutheranism and Calvinism on the letter of the Bible, the schismatic churches of the East on the letter of Scripture and passive tradition, i.e., the traditions of the early fathers and councils. In contrast, active tradition as the Roman Catholic Church understands it is filled by the progressive vital forces that lie in revelation. These demand further development of the seeds sown in revelation.[15]

It is perfectly clear at this point that there is no longer any question of the equality of Scripture and tradition but that tradition raises and presses a claim to primacy. It does this not merely with the help of a monopoly of interpretation but even more so by representing the totality of the wealth of truth imparted by revelation, whereas Scripture is only one part of this wealth and has therefore no more than an authority that is constituted by tradition.

7. In spite of its rank, tradition cannot be the only authority for revealed truth. It, too, needs a criterion and the resultant accreditation. Left to itself tradition is ambiguous[16] and confusing. In ascertaining what is revealed truth and what is human addition it offers essentially more serious difficulties than Scripture. The individual Christian is also burdened by so much material that he cannot go into it all and evaluate it. Even scholarship cannot reach a consensus on the obligatory truth of faith since it can achieve no more than natural certainty.[17] Hence the truth dwelling in tradition calls out for the criterion of an infallible teaching office which can guarantee the truth as a final authority empowered by the Pneuma. Illuminated by the Spirit of God, the church's teaching office can unerringly pick out the real apostolic tradition from the records of later times.[18]

8. The question arises whether in the modern Roman Catholicism of the postconciliar period the undoubtedly enhanced authority of Holy Scripture has really altered at all this hierarchy of criteria and courts. We may certainly see some shifts of emphasis and even some attempts to move ahead and break free. In the problem

---

[13]Möhler, *Symbolik,* pp. 442f.
[14]Adam, *Das Wesen des Katholizismus*, p. 179; E.T. p. 151.
[15]*Loc. cit.*; Viering, *Evangelische und katholische Schriftauslegung,* pp. 50ff.
[16]Cf. Abelard's *Sic et Non.*
[17]Diekamp, *Katholische Dogmatik,* §16, 58f.
[18]Algermissen, *op. cit.,* §§229f.

area of Scripture and tradition some people think they could see even at the council itself some efforts at damping down or reemphasizing, or that they could even hear some rattling of the chains, although these were not broken and no more was achieved than claiming the maximum radius of action that they allow. This may be illustrated by some pertinent statements by a prominent council theologian like Karl Rahner.[19]

Although Rahner finds a beginning of theology in even the simplest kerygmatic statement, e.g., in the gospels (p. 76; E.T. p. 61), he sees a qualitative distinction between the original witness of faith and all later theological reflections such as we have in tradition. While he moves in this way toward the primacy of the biblical testimony, there may be seen in him a singular—and to an outsider almost tragic—alternation of backward and forward movements as though he were on a spring, if one may say this of so venerable a figure.

In a first leap ahead Rahner espouses the primacy of Scripture on the ground that we have in it definite and spatially fixed events in which this revelation which is destined for all later ages takes place in such a way that these later ages are permanently tied to this historical event and can really attain to the revelation of God only when and to the extent that they go back to it. Holy Scripture thus occupies a unique place as the constant and irreplaceable authorizing (not authorized) norm for all later dogmatic statements. Its own statements belong to the unique historical event of revelation itself to which all later proclamation and theology refer. They are not just one statement of faith but the statement which is always the permanent basis of all other and future statements (p. 77; E.T. p. 62).

If we find here an astonishing approximation to the "Scripture alone" of the Reformation, its point is immediately blunted, even "taken back." Rahner does not draw the logical conclusion that by reason of the self-evidence of Scripture the adult Christian should have direct access to it and that even church (and council) promulgations must be measured by it. Instead he argues that the later Christian cannot have this original statement directly. Rather, not wanting to be unhistorical or unchurchly, he must always listen to the teaching office of the church and its consciousness of faith (p. 77; E.T. pp. 62f.) and let the original be mediated through these. What we have called the hierarchy of courts and norms is thus upheld.

In spite of a threefold "even if" (even if, e.g., it is an open question—this makes no sense to me—whether tradition as understood at Trent is an additional source of material faith-content or simply a formal criterion for the purity of faith), the next step is again to assert the primacy of Holy Scripture. If it is asked in what form the original statement of faith is given to us as an authorizing (not authorized) norm, Rahner answers that we are simply to say: "in Holy Scripture." For the church has no other objective norm when out of the concrete totality of its factual tradition it wants to determine, with the gift of discernment, what in this tradition is the true tradition of revelation and what is simply human tradition (p. 79; E.T. p. 64). It seems plain, then, that the frontier is opened to a biblical criticism of tradition along the lines of the Reformation "Scripture alone." But appearances

---

[19] "Was ist eine theologische Aussage?" *Schriften zur Theologie,* V (1962), pp. 54ff., esp. pp. 76ff.; E.T. *Theological Investigations,* V, pp. 42ff., esp. pp. 61ff.

deceive. At the very next step there is a new retreat. For although we have an authorizing norm in Scripture, and although this original word of revelation and faith differs essentially from all the church's later theological statements, the witness of Scripture is not directed to individuals but only to the whole church's consciousness of faith and the church's teaching office (p. 79; E.T. p. 64). Since there is no authority outside the church which can be regarded as competent to understand Scripture in the name of its self-evidence, there can be no biblical criticism of the church. The encounter between Bible and church and the critical claiming of the Bible over against the church are avoided. The "duet" of Bible and church cannot be broken.

What is the significance of Rahner's advances, one might ask, when he finishes up again in the dogmatic enclosure of the Tridentine understanding of Scripture and tradition (cf. Denz., 1501 and 1507; E.T. 783 and 786)? One can recognize that some effort is made to break out in a new direction. But the chains of tradition are a restraint and it is unlikely that they will be broken. Yet the dialectical dance of forward and backward movement can evoke admiration as well as melancholy.

In Rahner—and this is not meant ironically—the chains of tradition can look like elastic bands which expand but always bring back those that they bind into the sphere enclosed by tradition. The authority of the norms posited by tradition can be seriously challenged only to the extent that the relevant decision lies within the authentic possibilities of the origin and does not contradict them, but not to the extent that this decision is the only possible one and the only one demanded by the starting point (Rahner, *Grundkurs des Glaubens*, 5th ed. [1976], p. 321; E.T. *Foundations of Christian Faith* [New York, 1978], p. 331). The Christian community remains true to its origins and foundation when it makes historical decisions in a development of structures which are chosen from a broad range of genuine and intrinsically abstract possibilities but which are still irreversible and authoritative for all future epochs (*Grundkurs*, p. 322; E.T. *Foundations*, p. 332).

Here again we see the distinctive dialectic in which Rahner understands Scripture as an authorizing norm and yet it is overshadowed by tradition. In the sentences referred to, Scripture is the place of both origin and norm. What follows by way of authorized norm is bound to this foundation and origin. References back, however, are not regarded as direct derivation but as a selection among several possibilities that have simply to be within the limits set by the origin. At least theoretically, then, the possibility opens up that the doctrine of Mary's assumption—to mention only one of many possible examples—corresponds to a doctrinal development which lies within these limits even though there are no direct scriptural references to it.

In this sense theology is competent to develop doctrines that actually go beyond the Bible. Now even on the Reformation side, as will be shown in another context, this is not contested. For it is beyond question that especially in ethics—although not only there—questions constantly demand that positions be adopted and criteria sought which are not to be found directly in the Bible. Of these, too, it may be said that they lie within the limits set by the origin. Nevertheless, they are "only" theological doctrines and inferences and as such they are bound up with the venture of faith whose deliberations are tied to specific historical situations and may thus be criticized, transcended, and revised.

This is where the difference from the Roman Catholic concept of tradition arises. Tradition's real primacy as a source of revelation, whether open or tacit, comes to light in the fact that it develops theological doctrines which cannot be revised but are irreversible and infallible, as though Christ himself were present and speaking in the church of the present. Indeed, even this ''as though'' reduces the claim and is thus an understatement. In reality there is identification. As Rahner says, Jesus is actually and necessarily risen for all ages in the faith of his disciples (*Grundkurs,* p. 320; E.T. p. 330). The church is the institutionalizing of these disciples and therefore the presence of the risen Lord. What is proclaimed by this institution and thereby becomes tradition may be regarded as irreversible. It has to be.

2. CONCLUDING APPRAISAL

The various critical discussions of the relation between Scripture and tradition which we have developed in progressive stages cannot be broken off without a consideration of what Roman Catholics call the seeds of truth which supposedly evolve in the ultimately unacceptable hierarchy of authorities and norms.

Reformation theology and Roman Catholic theology never confront one another as truth and falsehood but either as different forms of truth or, as here, as truth and ''altered truth.'' They stand on the same ground and draw upon the same sources. The conflict is only about the canals that are dug in the ground and the question whether and how these change the water or perhaps alter the quality of the source. The same possession and background of truth, however, can never give rise to the opposition of sheer antitheses (when Luther saw it this way he was wrong) but only to the battle for the same truth in its (more or less) pure form and (more or less) distorted form.

1. In the actual primacy of tradition over Scripture we have the corruption of a true basic datum—the existence at the first of living oral tradition, not Scripture (1 John 1:1). The NT writings—to take these alone as a paradigm—are simply the deposit of what was proclaimed and believed in primitive Christianity. The testimony of the Spirit at work in proclamation extends, as we have seen, to the fixed written form of the witness of revelation which is found in the outlines of the first theological reflections and situational references.

2. Undoubtedly the gospels and occasional writings like the epistles do not contain everything that the apostles and their followers said. To that extent we can speak with tongue in cheek of the fragmentary nature of the biblical canon. On the other hand, the attempt to assemble scattered sayings of the Lord and to complete the gospels[20] shows how far tradition was already subject to most serious obfuscation and how little these apocryphal additions lead to enrichment.

In no case does it seem possible to arrive by way of active tradition at a material expansion of what was originally given and therefore to rely on the witness of the Spirit that was promised to the church. This brings the Roman Catholic concept of tradition into paradoxical proximity to the radicals and their inner light. The principle of expansion on the basis of tradition robs the biblical canon of its

---

[20]Cf. the efforts of Papias in this direction in the 2nd century.

function as a critical court and leads ineluctably to an infallible teaching office which as the final factor is no longer subject to control.

That the church defined (but did not create) the canon in virtue of the latter's liturgical self-testimony implies agreement that it must acknowledge an essential distinction between pre-canonical and post-canonical tradition and thus confirm the fact that the canonical statements are complete and cannot be transcended.[21]

3. Something true is also seen when the Roman Catholic understanding of tradition appeals to things that are obscure and hard to understand in the canonical writings and when it thinks of the arbitrariness with which heretics and cranks and other groups have tried to justify their programs with quotations from Scripture. From the tension between Paul and James it is clear where one-sided appeals can lead. This state of things does in fact call for a criterion for the recognition of what is God's Word in the midst of apparent contradictions.

But is this criterion an authoritative court, institutionalized in an infallible teaching office, which as an institution can claim the power to discern spirits (and more)? In the name of the self-evidence of the Word of God do we not have to answer this question of a criterion by seeking it in the Word itself, i.e., in what has been called the material principle or the canon within the canon? The basic message of the justification of the sinner which is heard in the message of the incarnation, crucifixion, and resurrection of Christ is intrinsically unequivocal and forms a reliable standard by which not only the canonical texts but also their expositors and the expository traditions may be measured. Luther's statement that we are to regard as God's Word that which promotes Christ seems more in keeping with the self-evidence of the Word than the postulate of an authoritative teaching office.

4. That the canon is a definitive witness to revelation which can never be transcended, and that no tradition, therefore, can claim to supplement the truth deposited in it, cannot mean that it need only be quoted as it stands in order to actualize its truth. Although it cannot be transcended, it is capable of development and stands in need of it. What Rahner says of Chalcedon is true of the canon too—namely, that we have constantly to move away from it, not in order to renounce it but in order to understand it.[22] To move away from the canon can mean only to develop its implications instead of cleaving to its letter.

Thus there is in the NT no systematically developed Christology or eschatology or ethics or social teaching or ready-made doctrine of the relation of nature and grace. If we spoke of occasional writings in the NT and therefore of the time-related nature of its statements and the difference in their perspectives, this difference in standpoints and in the questions put to the kerygma is found to an even greater extent in later Christian generations. To the degree that our sense of history develops there is a need to make statements about God within the framework of a developing doctrine of the Trinity and not to be content with the mere hints of this to be found in the NT.[23] To the degree that Christianity becomes a public matter—from the time of Constantine—there is a need to find a compass for its attitude to the world which will point in the direction that is commended to us by the NT

---

[21]We recall the diagnosis of Cullmann in particular (*Kanon*, pp. 98f.).

[22]K. Rahner, *Chalkedon*, p. 4.

[23]Cf. EG, II, §§9–13; EF, II, cc. IX–XIII.

commandment of love. The nature of the action taken will vary a great deal according to whether I am in the church or the world or act privately or officially (as a judge, politician, teacher, etc.). Some form of a doctrine of the two kingdoms will be urgently needed, and under different names it has in fact developed in all denominations and not just in Lutheranism.[24]

Many problems shaped by the modern situation are not posed in the Bible. Hence the kerygma has to be (not expanded, but) developed in relation to them.

After a lecture on euthanasia in which I spoke about the ability of modern medicine to prolong death as well as life, one student told me bluntly that in the Bible he found only the command not to kill. Thus the Bible offered no support for theological opposition to the prolongation of life with all the medical resources at our disposal. Such opposition presupposes that God did not foresee modern problems when he gave his command and that we may thus bypass him. Unwittingly this student touched on our present problem. Biblical statements are not just to be quoted but their underlying intention is to be applied to new situations as they arise. (To avoid any misunderstanding of my position on euthanasia I may refer to my work *Wer darf sterben? Ethische Probleme der modernen Medizin* [1979].)

The didactic as well as the paraenetic portions of the Bible have thus to be developed in relation to the situations in which they actualize themselves. Hence doctrinal statements will be made by theologians and the church for which simple biblical quotations cannot be provided. Controversies will be stirred up about these in which loyalty to God's Word will not be shown merely by accepting allegiance to the Bible but by applying (or, better, trying to apply) it to the specific historical situation[25] or to the constellations of personal life.[26] In this process cases will arise in which the individual and subjective interpretation of a particular historical situation is so dominant that no (e.g., synodal) consensus will be achieved regarding the relation of the Bible to it.[27] This does not mean, however, that individual decisions do not have to be responsible to the Word of God. The only point is that the basis of such decisions has no significance in the forming or dividing of churches.

To the degree that in such questions the church is concerned about obedience to God's Word and reaches theological decisions in this obedience (e.g., in the two kingdoms doctrine, which materially does not occur in Scripture), it can be sure of the assistance of the Holy Spirit and also of the ability to discern spirits. This cannot mean, however, that the teaching traditions which are thus built up either expand or supplement the biblical canon, that they form an additional element with its own weight and possibly with competing authority. Instead they are just developments of the one Word and must be accountable to it.

Thus the church cannot brag about its teaching tradition as about a legal title

---

[24]ThE, I, §§1783ff.; E.T. I, pp. 359ff.; Anthrop, pp. 277ff.

[25]In this sense the Barmen Declaration of 1934, for example, is more than a mere quotation even though it does quote Scripture. By applying Scripture to a situation threatened by ideologies it became a critical court for the alternative of outside or inside the church.

[26]Cf. such problems as contraception, family planning, abortion, and remarriage after divorce, and on these ThE, III.

[27]As in the question of the church's attitude to the peaceful use of atomic energy.

which validates those instructed by it merely on the ground that the church as an institution is equipped with the full authority of the Holy Spirit. This power comes to it only actively and from the Word which mediates the Spirit and is at the same time the court to which answer must be made regarding action in the Spirit. If tradition, and with it the institutional church, assumes to itself the rank of an independent source of revelation with the power of material expansion[28]—a source which gushes out in the church itself insofar as it shares in the possession of the Spirit—then the fateful result threatens that the proclamation of the teaching office, which itself embodies Christ and the Holy Spirit, can only express a kind of self-conversation of the church and its tradition and can never be anything more than this simple monologue.[29]

This kind of criticism, however, can be made only within a bracket which embraces both the Roman Catholic *and* the Reformation churches and finally makes both of them members of the one church which is still empirically concealed (*abscondita*). No matter how decidedly we emphasize the mote of a mistaken understanding of tradition in the eye of the other (and, it is hoped, do not overlook the beam in our own eye), the important thing is that the Bible is open in both churches. This unifying factor is stronger than anything that divides. This is true even though we see the principle of "Scripture alone" obscured in the Roman Catholic sphere by the concepts of tradition and the monopoly of the teaching office in the exposition and expansion of Scripture.

At this point we are protected against moving on to an irenical veiling of issues by the Reformation understanding of Scripture. So long as the Bible remains open, we can trust in the self-evidential and penetrating force of the Word of God. What no controversial argument can achieve, the authority of this Word can do. There is a definitive break only when tradition and the teaching office stop up the source of the written word and go ahead alone in the supposed strength of their possession of the Spirit. But there are no signs of this. Instead, there are recognizable signals that point in the opposite direction.[30]

---

[28]I have in mind here dogmatic definitions in the field of mariology, e.g., the immaculate conception in the bull "Ineffabilis Deus" of 12/8/1854 (Denz., 2803f.; E.T. 1641) and the bodily assumption into heaven in the encyclical "Deiparae Virginis" (Pius XII) of 5/1/1946 and then the apostolic constitution "Munificentissimus Deus" of 11/1/1950 (Denz., 3900ff.; E.T. 2331ff.).

[29]Cf. H. Diem, "Das Problem des Schriftkanons," ThSt, XXXII (Zollikon, 1952), p. 11.

[30]As Dibelius points out, the church is divided but in all its branches it is the church of Jesus of Nazareth, the one holy catholic and apostolic church of Nicea. It everywhere proclaims what Jesus said and did. It everywhere accepts what the Bible says about God and Jesus Christ and the sin and redemption of man and the commands of God and our debt of love and gratitude to God. This is everywhere taught. Only when some part of the church does away with the Bible or some part of it like the OT, or alters the NT, is there basic disruption. In all its parts the church is the one true church. In each church one can find Jesus of Nazareth and be saved (O. Dibelius, *Bericht von der Kirche* [1941], pp. 102f.).

IX

The Establishment of the Bible as the Vessel of God's Word by Immanent Scriptural Criteria

1. THE PROBLEM OF THE MATERIAL PRINCIPLE

The principle of "Scripture alone" makes all Holy Scripture the norm of saving truth to which faith looks and which is set for every theological doctrine. The adjective "all" cannot mean that this normative rank applies to each portion of Scripture. In our discussion of its canonicity we have shown already, e.g., by means of the tension between Paul and James, that the part has to be seen in the context of the whole and can be criticized by it. Only the doctrine of verbal inspiration relaxes this tension between the part and the whole. (At what cost it does so has been noted already and will have to be discussed again later.)

Suitable criteria are needed to differentiate within the Bible between the Word of God and the time-bound vessel, between saving truth and its clothing in mythical and philosophical forms of expression (e.g., later Jewish apocalyptic or Gnostic schemes of thought). There has always been a search for such criteria and they have been continually reformulated.

The best-known criterion, which was adopted and repeatedly expounded by the Reformers, was stated by Luther in his principle that Scripture (he had the OT chiefly in view) is for us the Word of God insofar as it promotes Christ. When Althaus calls the gospel the criterion,[1] he has the same thing in mind.[2]

There are many other expressions of this search for a material center, a canon within the canon, which can be used as a critical principle. For Tillich the material norm is the new being in Jesus as the Christ, i.e., what is done by Christ (*Systematic Theology*, I, p. 50). For H. Braun the man who is radically challenged and

---

[1] *Die christliche Wahrheit*, I (1947), pp. 195, 211.

[2] So does Pannenberg when he calls Christ the one matter and true content of Scripture, "Was ist eine dogmatische Aussage?" *Grundfragen systematischer Theologie* (1967), p. 170; E.T. *Basic Questions in Theology*, I, p. 197.

questioned and radically upheld in the Jesus event, not in the sense of an idea or doctrine, but as an event, is the basic NT phenomenon, the canon within the canon, by which true canonicity is to be measured and judged (*Gesammelte Studien zum NT und seiner Umwelt* [1962], p. 322). Along the lines of this concern to incorporate the believer as well as the object of belief into the determining of biblical or NT truth, Käsemann—in spite of every other difference—can state that the justification of the ungodly is the center of all Christian proclamation and thereby of Scripture too. Hence the message of justification has to be viewed as the qualifying and dividing criterion of the NT and as indispensable to that extent (*Kanon*, pp. 405, 368). H. Diem, on the other hand, raises against such criteria—including so central a matter as justification—the objection that justification can become an interpretative principle which permits only a restricted view of the whole event of revelation (*Theologie als kirchliche Wissenschaft*, II [1955], pp. 200ff.; E.T. *Dogmatics*, pp. 229ff.). This difficulty seems to raise the question how we can find any criterion for the Word of God in the canon which does not become a dominating "principle" and fall victim to the modern habit of substituting a theologoumenon for the matter itself (*ibid.*, p. 204; E.T. p. 233).

As a mere principle Luther's criterion of promoting Christ obviously cannot be a perfect key to the door of Holy Scripture because the question arises at once what Christ is meant and whether the principle of interpretation does not itself need to be interpreted. May not the christological criterion become a bolt rather than a key if we have in mind a Christ who is the teacher of the new law or a cult-god or an ethical example, while the friend of sinners and the victim of crucifixion fade into an invisible background? Whom do we mean by Christ: the historical Jesus or the one who rose again the third day or the Christ who is present in the life of the church and made secure in its formulation of faith?

The same questions arise in relation to the other criteria mentioned. For example, what does justification mean? Does it mean justification by faith alone, or by infused grace, or what? One might continue along these lines for a long time. What is intended to interpret Scripture stands in need of interpretation itself. What is the criterion for the criterion?

A consensus at least seems to be present in answering this question, at least among those who seek to be biblical theologians. The hermeneutical criterion must not be imported from outside Scripture but taken from Scripture itself. This answer is in fact related indissolubly to the thesis that God's Word is able to be its own interpreter. The hermeneutical circle which confronts us here is that only in Scripture itself do I find the key which opens it up. Scripture is both the subject and object of the evangelical church.[3] The subject of this criticism is not the theologian but the gospel itself.[4]

It is paradoxical that I can find the key only in the room which it opens up. This paradox makes sense only if I assume that faith precedes theological reflection and that it only interprets itself with the help of this. Faith is won from me by the totality of the biblical message (or by a part that is first accessible to me). It asks for the key, and finds it in the room that it has already entered, when it asks

---

[3]Althaus, *Die christliche Wahrheit*, p. 195.
[4]*Ibid.*, p. 211; cf. Tillich, *Systematic Theology*, pp. 62f.

concerning itself and its basis, i.e., when it starts to reflect. The dialectic continues as follows.

If the criterion attained in this way is not to harden into a hermeneutical principle which restricts the fulness of the biblical message, it must be constantly transcended and revised by listening to the whole Bible. It has, then, the provisional nature of a heuristic principle and not the definitive nature of a dogmatic principle. The scientist uses a heuristic principle as a mere hypothesis, a question put to nature, which he will show to be true or false by experiment.[5] Plainly he has derived his question or hypothesis from a previous but relatively naive encounter with nature. Only by way of this dialectical play between question and answer, between being questioned and being open to new questioning, does there arise a readiness to hear which will be concerned about all the possibilities of critical understanding and which will seek to protect every possibility against being absolutized and dominating the text, subjecting it instead to constant revision by the text. Only in this way can the danger be met of trying to control the voice of Christ and ensure correct exposition with the help of an infallible hermeneutical principle,[6] especially as there is in the multiplicity of the biblical testimonies no master key which will open up the way to an understanding of every passage.[7] If the hermeneutical principle stands at a fixed subject–object distance from the text without seeing itself as an object of the kerygma and therefore subjecting itself to revision by the text, blindness to whole areas of the biblical message can result. It may even be that, e.g., the cosmic statements of the Christology of Colossians, or the protological and eschatological statements of Scripture, are not opened up by an absolutized principle of justification. A relativizing of Scripture can follow because the principle of interpretation will not let itself be relativized—even though it is taken from Scripture itself. Even a purified biblicism of this kind is no protection against stupidity. By this sublime detour the Word can be brought under the control of man simply because he wants to make it secure.[8]

The dialectic between hearing the text, receiving it, and taking back the principle of interpretation is not an automatic process of feedback. Each of its stations can be reached and left again only with the help of the Pneuma. After what we have said already about the hermeneutical function of the Holy Spirit, this hardly needs to be emphasized. "No prophecy ever came by the impulse of man, but men moved by the Holy Spirit spoke from God." Hence "no prophecy of scripture is a matter of one's own interpretation [idias epilyseōs]" (2 Peter 1:20f.). Interpretation, too, must be the work of the Spirit.

The book I quote, 2 Peter, is usually regarded as a later NT work and a testimony to primitive catholicism. Hence 1:20f. is often taken to mean that individual handling of Scripture must give place to the authoritative exegesis of the teaching office (Käsemann, Exegetische Versuche . . . , I, p. 220; Küng, Kirche

---

[5]Cf. the theoretical investigations of K. Popper, Logik der Forschung (1935), pp. 10ff.; E.T. The Logic of Scientific Discovery (New York, 1959) and W. Stegmüller, Das Wahrheitsproblem und die Idee der Semantik, 2nd ed. (1968), pp. 262ff.

[6]Diem, "Das Problem des Schriftkanons," ThSt, XXXII (1952), pp. 21f.

[7]Ibid., p. 22.

[8]Küng is thus right to warn against excessive subjectivism (Kanon, pp. 188ff.).

im Konzil, 2nd ed. [1964], p. 146). Without wishing to contest the primitive catholic character of 2 Peter, I see no reason to interpret the verses in question within this framework. The *idias* of verse 20 does not mean private interpretation which heretically parts company with the official church but suggests an arbitrariness which diverges from the leading of the Spirit. The question, then, is what is the opposite of *idias.*

Our findings on the relation between the formal and the material principle, between "Scripture alone" and the hermeneutical key, may be summed up as follows.

If it is agreed that the NT Christ (and the faith he evokes and the new creature formed in him) is the key to Scripture, this means that the encounter with Christ mediated by Scripture implies disclosure of the salvation event. Recognition of the formal principle, i.e., of Holy Scripture as an authorizing norm, is not itself this disclosure. On the contrary, it can be a kind of legal bondage or servile obedience. It presupposes a compulsory faith (a contradiction in terms) in Scripture itself which results in a doctrine of verbal inspiration. Only the encounter given with Scripture leads to the recognition of Scripture as the means whereby the encounter is granted to me. "Scripture alone" follows upon "Christ alone." Only in this sequence will "Scripture alone" not lead to a legal understanding of Scripture which leaves out Christ as its theme.[9] When Scripture opens up itself in this way and is thus believed as a source of revelation and remains its own interpreter through the witness of the Spirit, it can hold its ground in face of all acts of exposition, even those of the church. Hermeneutical principles neither can nor will succeed in mastering it nor will the distinction between it and exposition vanish. In contrast the Roman Catholic view—but not it alone—is in danger of making exposition a normative principle, whereas God's Word as the constitutive factor remains over the church and the latter is to be understood as a creature of the Word.[10]

In brief, the dialectical process of interpretation is as follows. From Scripture, which at first is just as unqualified as its expositor, an encounter with Christ is granted to me. Scripture then becomes an authority for me since Christ is mediated to me in it alone. Finally I find that Scripture is greater, not than Christ, but than what I first experienced of him as the reality that opens up Scripture. I thus let my basic hermeneutical experience be constantly renewed by the fulness of Scripture as a whole. Only in this way can I make the exclusive statement "by Scripture alone."

Many examples show how this dialectic is continually broken at other points. In the debate with Bultmann in EF, I we saw how the hermeneutical principle of existential interpretation threatens to dominate the text which in intention it wants to serve and open up. The dialectic is interrupted at another point by the Jesus people, among whom there is at first a very enthusiastic meeting with the figure of Christ and a close relating of this to their own life (e.g., in the overcoming of loneliness or drugs), but there threatens to be no relating of the figure of Christ to the whole of Scripture, so that an extremely subjectivistic view of Christ results.

---

[9]Ebeling, *Wort Gottes und Tradition,* 2nd ed. (1966), p. 131; E.T. p. 136.
[10]*Ibid.,* p. 132; E.T. p. 136.

More examples might be given. Even when the dialectic is basically recognized, every theologian and every Christian is in danger of becoming a victim of violent interruptions of it in this way.

2. THE SIGNIFICANCE OF THE MATERIAL PRINCIPLE FOR THE UNDERSTANDING OF THE OLD TESTAMENT

Bibliography: Among the many relevant works, apart from the OT theologies of O. Procksch, W. Eichrodt, and G. von Rad, and the various dogmatics, only those with an immediate bearing on the present problem are listed. E. Auerbach, *Mimesis...* (1946); E.T. *Mimesis* (Princeton, 1953); K. Barth, "Evangelium und Gesetz," ThEx, XXXII (1935); CD, I,2, pp. 75ff., 310ff.; II,1, pp. 501ff.; IV,1, pp. 347ff.; F. Baumgärtel, "Erwägungen zur Darstellung der Theologie des AT," ThLZ (1951), pp. 257ff.; also "Der Dissensus im Verständnis des AT," EvTh, VII/VIII (1954), pp. 298ff.; W. Brandt, *Das Gesetz Israel und die Gesetze der Heiden* (1934); R. Bultmann, "Weissagung und Erfüllung," *Glauben und Verstehen*, II (1952), pp. 162ff.; O. Cullmann, *Heil als Geschichte* (1965); E.T. *Salvation in History* (London, 1967); W. Eichrodt, "Zur Frage der theologischen Exegese des AT," ThBl (1938), IV, pp. 73ff.; also *Israel in der Weissagung des AT* (Zürich, 1951); L. Goppelt, *Typos...* (1939); E. Heimann, *Theologie der Geschichte* (1966); H. Hellbardt, "Die Auslegung des AT als theologische Disziplin," ThBl (1937), VII/VIII, pp. 129ff.; V. Herntrich, *Theologische Auslegung des AT? Zum Gespräch mit W. Vischer* (1936); F. Hesse, "Die Erforschung der Geschichte Israels als theologische Aufgabe," *Kerygma und Dogma* (1958), I, pp. 1ff.; "Kerygma oder geschichtliche Wirklichkeit?" ZThK (1960), pp. 17ff.; and "Zur Profanität der Geschichte Israels," ZThK, II (1974), pp. 262ff.; E. Hirsch, *Das AT und die Predigt des Evangeliums* (1936); J. C. Hofmann, *Weissagung und Erfüllung*, 2 vols. (1841–44); also *Der Schriftbeweis*, I, 2nd ed. (1857); A. Jepsen, "Das Verhältnis vom AT und NT," *Bericht von der Theologie* (Berlin [East], 1971), pp. 24ff.; K. Koch, "Der Tod des Religionsstifters," *Kerygma und Dogma* (1962), II, pp. 100ff. (reply to von Baumgärtel in *Kerygma und Dogma* [1963], pp. 223ff.); also "Spätisraelitisches Geschichtsdenken am Beispiel des Buches Daniel," *Historische Zeitschrift*, CXCIII (1961); H. J. Kraus, "Zum Gesetzesverständnis der nachprophetischen Zeit," *Biblisch-theologische Aufsätze* (1972), pp. 179ff.; W. G. Kümmel, *Verheissung und Erfüllung* (1945); E.T. *Promise and Fulfillment* (Naperville, 1957); K. Löwith, *Weltgeschichte und Heilsgeschehen* (1953); E.T. *Meaning in History* (Chicago, 1949); A. Oepke, *Jesus und das AT* (1938); W. Pannenberg, "Heilsgeschehen und Geschichte," *Grundfragen systematischer Theologie* (1967), pp. 22ff.; E.T. *Basic Questions in Theology*, pp. 15ff.; G. von Rad, "Das Christuszeugnis des AT" (in debate with W. Vischer), ThBl (1935), X, pp. 24f.; "Sensus scripturae sacrae duplex?" *op. cit.* (1936), II, pp. 30ff.; also "Typologische Auslegung des AT," EvTh (1952–53), pp. 1–2; A. A. van Ruler, *Die christliche Kirche und das AT* (1955); E.T. *The Christian Church and the OT* (Grand Rapids, 1971) (cf. ThE, II, 2, §4275; E.T. II, pp. 604ff.); K. G. Steck, "Die Idee der Heilsgeschichte; Hofmann, Schlatter, Cullmann," *Theologische Studien*, LVI (Zollikon, 1959); H. Thielicke, ThE, 1, §§554–623; E.T. I, pp. 126ff.; EG, II, §§14–17, pp. 289ff.; EF, II, cc. XIV–XVII, pp. 237ff.; Anthrop, 2nd ed. (1977), pp. 342ff.; A. Weiser, "Zum Verstehen des AT," *Zeitschrift für alttestamentliche Wissenschaft* (1949), pp. 17ff.; G. Weth, *Die Heilsgeschichte* (1931); W. Zimmerli, "Verheissung und Erfüllung," EvTh (1952–53), pp. 1–2.

The material principle—the incarnate Word Christ as the key to Holy Scripture—raises with particular urgency the question of the relation between the OT and NT.

For the Reformers, especially Luther,[11] this was a problem. There were two reasons why this was so.

For one thing the criterion for God's Word (how far it promotes Christ) necessarily led to different attitudes in relation to the two testaments. In the NT the incarnate Word was the direct theme and true kerygmatic content. In contrast the OT was only a type and shadow of what was to come (Colossians 2:17; Hebrews 8:5; 10:1) even if it did not stand in antithesis to it as the representative of the law (e.g., Romans 5:20; Matthew 5:21-48). Theological views that pit the OT against the NT may be found from Marcion to A. von Harnack.[12]

Secondly, the problem of the distinction between the OT and the NT was forced on the Reformers because they rejected as a wresting of God's Word the idea of a multiple sense of Scripture, and especially its allegorizing, which has been in vogue since the time of Origen.[13] This rejection deprived them of the comfortable possibility of levelling down the testaments and with the aid of allegorical exegesis claiming that Christ was proclaimed already in the OT. This truly puts the OT and the NT on the same level. It even minimizes the advance from promise to fulfilment, since there can be no real movement to anything new.[14] In the modern world we again find in a subsidiary branch of the Barthian school, e.g., in H. Hellbardt and W. Vischer,[15] an extreme allegorizing which fully equates the OT and NT and negates any historical distinction between them.[16]

At any rate, to the degree that the Reformers rejected the allegorizing method and thereby stressed that we have in the OT and NT two different epochs of salvation history, the question how far the OT promoted Christ became for them the decisive hermeneutical problem. This question in a kind of chain reaction triggered a whole series of new problems. Is not the acceptance of the OT by Christians surprising if they can no longer interpret it allegorically? What authority should it be given alongside the NT? Will not this authority be of different degrees according to the individual books and passages?[17]

The demand that the OT be read in the light of the NT and that the gospel be

---

[11]WA, 18, 62ff.; LW, 40, 79-223; cf. Melanchthon, *Loci,* "On the Distinction between the OT and the NT."

[12]A. von Harnack, *Marcion. Das Evangelium vom fremden Gott* (1924), p. 248. For the OT as a preliminary stage cf. E. Troeltsch, *Gesammelte Schriften,* IV (1925), pp. 34ff.

[13]Origen found three senses, the literal, moral, and mystical, corresponding to the threefold division of the human organism into body, soul, and spirit. In the third sense, which used allegorizing, he saw a solution to the problem of upholding the OT against pagans and Gnostic and Marcionite heretics (H. von Campenhausen, *Die griechischen Kirchenväter* [1955], p. 53; E.T. *The Fathers of the Greek Church* [New York, 1959], p. 50).

[14]H. von Campenhausen gives many examples of allegorical exegesis beginning with Justin Martyr, for whom the tree of life, Jacob's rods, anointed pillars, the rods of Aaron and Moses, and other rods in the OT are all clear references to the cross and types of it, so that they are prophecies of Christ himself (*ibid.,* p. 21; E.T. p. 18).

[15]Cf. ThE, I, §§573ff.; E.T. I, pp. 100ff.

[16]Incorrectly F. Baumgärtel accuses G. von Rad of typologizing. We shall return to this later.

[17]This question arose quite early in relation to the Apocrypha, which was in the canon of Hellenistic Judaism—in the Alexandrian synagogue—but not in that of Palestinian Judaism. Whereas most of the apocryphal writings were declared canonical by Trent, Luther would not equate them with Scripture, though he found them good and useful for reading; the Reformed churches excluded them completely.

used as a key and norm in relation to the OT books could only lead to the result of not claiming for these works the same rank as that of the gospels and apostolic writings. The OT law—for Luther—was in its moral, cultic, and legal form valid for Israel and other peoples only to the extent that it agreed with their own sense of norms.[18] Christ is the end of the law (Romans 10:4) and therefore of the OT insofar as this represents the legal religion of Israel. The same applies to the cultus. The two forms of this end are attested by Paul (law) and the author of Hebrews (cultus). But is the OT *only* law and *only* cultus? And even if it is, is there in the NT only a dissolving and ending and not also a fulfilling and actualizing of what was only a vague outline in the law and cultus (Matthew 5:17; Romans 3:31; Hebrews 9:1ff., etc.). What significance have promise and fulfilment for the correlation of the old and new covenants?

To these questions, which have never been settled since the Reformation, a final one may be added.

The gospel is the new thing (cf. Hebrews 8:13), which could not be postulated, in the resolve of the God who meets us in our old history which is already in motion under the influence of creation and the fall, and who thus moves into traditions that are already set. Since we have something new over against what is already there—the breaking of the new aeon into the old—the faith engendered by the NT obliges us to define the relation between this new thing of the gospel and that which is present already. (Does it transcend it, e.g., or totally stop it? How far is it linked with it?)

In some sense the new thing of the gospel demands an old thing with which to be related in continuity and discontinuity. If this old thing is not found in the biblical OT because this seems to be "judaizing"[19] and to be too specific in meaning, then another old thing will have to be found. It might be sought in the history of religions where primal typological phenomena may be seen in which that which is fulfilled in the gospel seems to be prefigured. In 1571 the Jesuit priest Franciscus Cabralis thought he saw in the Japanese debate between Amidha Buddhism and Zen Buddhism an earlier form of the controversy between the Reformation and Roman Catholicism.[20]

J. C. Hofmann, who certainly did not want to see the biblical OT crowded out by historical analogies, was prepared to go to world history in general for prefigurations on the ground that if all things serve to unite the world under Christ its head, then there is something divine in everything in history and nothing can be totally alien to prophecy (*Weissagung . . .* , I, p. 7).

Richard Rothe (b. 1799) can even call these pre-forms "unconscious Christianity." But the prophetic character of world history is perhaps expressed most clearly of all by the Indian theologian Raymond Panikkar in his book *The*

---

[18]H. Bornkamm, "Gesetz und Evangelium in Luthers Auslegung des AT," ZsysTh (1943); P. Althaus, *Die Ethik M. Luthers* (1965), pp. 32ff.; E.T. *The Ethics of Martin Luther* (Philadelphia, 1972), pp. 25ff.; B. Lohse, *Ratio und Fides. Eine Untersuchung über die ratio in der Theologie Luthers* (1958), pp. 82ff.

[19]Luther's term for Esther.

[20]H. Frick, *Vergleichende Religionswissenschaft* (1928), p. 94. Cf. also R. Otto, *Vischnu Narayana. Texte zur indischen Gottesmystik* (1917), pp. 122ff.

Unknown Christ of Hinduism (London, 1965). In another work he states his conviction that the implied confession of faith of every good believer in any religion is really oriented to the one, holy, catholic, and apostolic religion (*Religions and Religion* [1965]). Hence the OT is simply *one* strand in religious history and loses its canonical rank. It is one prefiguration among many. But even without this relativization of the OT Roman Catholic theology with its principle of analogy tends to see in the moral and religious consciousness of humanity a foundation of nature on which the grace of the gospel builds. A symptom of this tendency is K. Rahner's doctrine of anonymous Christianity (*Schriften zur Theologie*, VI [1965], pp. 545ff.; E.T. *Theological Investigations*, VI, pp. 390ff.; cf. on this E. Jüngel in ZThK, III [1975], pp. 337ff.). We shall return specifically to these problems in Part IV.

Like Lessing in his *Education of the Human Race*,[21] one may also seek prefigurations of this kind (cf. deism) in reason and its sense of norms, or one may seek them in natural theology, which is found everywhere,[22] or in a pre-understanding of our existence, which Bultmann found in Heidegger's ontology,[23] or in the general religious sense, which in Schleiermacher replaces the OT, the feeling of absolute dependence being the prophetic demonstration of that which meets us in Christ as fulfilment.[24]

At all events, the new thing of the gospel forces us to seek the old thing which demands and prepares for it and is then fulfilled and transcended by it. If these prefigurations are not sought in the biblical OT, they must be sought somewhere else. Once Christ is understood as the goal of a redemption of the cosmos,[25] the possibility seems to be offered of seeing in anything and everything a prophecy of this goal—not merely in the history of Israel and therefore in the OT but in any event in secular or religious history.

Is this conclusion correct? In the first instance we need only investigate the trend of the question. In particular we must ask to what old thing the new thing of the gospel is related.

No matter where the hermeneutical principle of promoting Christ may lead us regarding the relation between the OT and the NT, two things are clear.

First, the correlation will have to be a result and not a dogmatic *a priori*. It must be stated firmly that a christological hermeneutics of the old covenant cannot just be derived from an existing correlation of the OT and NT, e.g., an unchallengeable schema of prophecy and fulfilment. It must be itself the *a priori* criterion in terms of which the correlation of the OT and NT is to be defined.

Second, the nature and relevance of the OT for Christians must be brought to light only by the NT. For the new covenant makes the old one old (Hebrews 8:13).

---

[21]Cf. my book *Offenbarung, Vernunft und Existenz . . .* , 5th ed. (1967).

[22]Under Hitler this took the cruder form of a doctrine of the law of the people (cf. W. Stapel, E. Hirsch [for a period], and F. Gogarten). People could be evangelized only as they were related to this law, i.e., only as they regarded the gospel as its fulfilment.

[23]EG, I, pp. 52ff.; EF, I, pp. 56ff.

[24]Schleiermacher found the OT an alien book which at most simply supplied good texts for patriotic occasions.

[25]Romans 9:19ff.; 11:32ff.; cf. the "pantokrator" passages—2 Corinthians 6:18; Revelation 1:8; 4:8; 11:17, etc.

The old one's intimations of the new are disclosed only when the new is present and offers a mark by which to orient them. Who Christ is—to use the thought-forms of Hebrews—cannot be seen from the figure of Melchizedek, the king of Salem and priest of the Most High God (Hebrews 7:1; Genesis 14:17-20), at least if this figure is considered in himself and therefore within the circle of the ancient covenant. The reverse is true. The meaning of this figure is disclosed only when Christ becomes the presupposition of the possibility of interpreting him. The point of the march is revealed only by the goal.

Paul knew the OT very well before his conversion. Even as Saul he already read it as God's Word. But only in the light of his meeting with the risen Lord did light fall on the old covenant for him. Only then did he begin to see in it foreshadowings of the one who was to come, perceiving how it had been fulfilled and transcended.

To that degree it is Christ who opens up the meaning of Scripture (Luke 4:21; 22:32; Matthew 22:29; John 20:9). The NT is concealed in the OT and the OT is revealed in the NT, as the ancient saying has it.

Paul in 2 Corinthians 3:12-18 gives us the decisive hint for deriving the correlation of the OT and NT from the christological criterion, or, better, for knowing where to seek it. He discusses here the account of Moses' conduct when he came back to the people after meeting Yahweh (Exodus 34:29-35). The meeting with God left a radiance on Moses' face whose numinous force was obviously too much for those who saw him, so that he hid his face behind a priestly mask. (This is the only OT reference to such a mask and the interpretation of it differs from that current among other religions of the time, e.g., in Egypt, where the mask denotes that the priest takes on the face of his deity and identifies himself with it, not that the numinous traces of the radiant face must be concealed [M. Noth, *Das zweite Buch Mose, AT Deutsch,* V (1959), p. 220; E.T. *Exodus* (Philadelphia, 1962), p. 267]: an indication of the uniqueness of this revelation in its religious setting.) This procedure is for Paul a type. The glory of God shines here only in a weak and fading form. In Christ and the presence of the Spirit on the other hand, it has appeared with a radiant fulness that can never be dimmed (3:8ff., 18). Before this light of immediacy shines and is comprehended (John 1:5) a veil lies over the eyes of the synagogue so that even the reflection of God's glory in the old covenant is not perceived.

Paul's reasons for interpreting this story typologically, and almost more so his modifications of it, show clearly how he handles the christological interpretation of the OT, proclaiming a new understanding of it which is beyond his own self-understanding and concealed from those who cling to the sphere of what is now old and obsolete (Hebrews 8:13). The following points should be noted.

1. The old covenant knows the revelation of God and the glory of his majesty. Paul is thus dealing there with the same God as is present in Christ as the light of the world.

2. In the old covenant, however, the radiance is only a reflection, only moonlight as it were. Unlike the light that has appeared in Christ it fades again. To express this Paul typically modifies the text of Exodus. Moses hides his face, not so much to prevent its radiance from being so overpowering, but rather to conceal its fading (2 Corinthians 3:13b), i.e., to hide the fact that his ministry is coming to an end. Not the radiance but its end is the point.

There are analogies to this elsewhere in Paul. Originally the law (of Moses) was in a sense radiant. It was given for life (Romans 7:10). But the light becomes dark because the law, when isolated from its author, necessarily brings death to sinners (Romans 3:9–20, 22f.). This work of death on the part of the law is, however, ended with Christ's death and resurrection for those who under the dominion of the Pneuma see "with unveiled face the glory of the Lord as in a mirror and are being changed into his likeness" (2 Corinthians 3:18). What was passing becomes something that remains and the mere reflection of light is changed into immediacy. In the figure of the temporary offering of the priests and the permanent atoning sacrifice of Christ the same thought is taken up in Hebrews (9:9–15). If the blood of "bulls" and "goats" could bring cleansing, "how much more" can the blood of Christ (9:13f.). Regarding this "how much more" cf. also Matthew 6:30; Romans 5:9f., 15, 17; 11:12, 24; 2 Corinthians 3:8.

3. Paul modifies the OT figure again when, now that Christ has come, he speaks of the mask covering the face of the synagogue rather than the face of Moses (2 Corinthians 3:15f.). It is the stumbling-block which makes it impossible for Israel to discern the prefiguration of the revelation of the Father of Jesus Christ in the old covenant. The ban and hardening which hold the eyes of Israel can give way only when it is converted to Christ (Romans 11:25) and can thus achieve the sight which God already grants to those who through the Spirit attain to participation in God's eternal glory (2 Corinthians 3:11, 18). Only in Christ is the veil, the concealing mask, taken from our eyes (3:14).

An illustration might help to show how the OT is then opened up in this way to our understanding. Like is understood only by like (EG, I, pp. 284f.; EF, I, pp. 205f.). Only participation in the unconcealed glory of God that has appeared in Christ opens our eyes to the reflection of this glory in its mere intimations.

It is not only Israel, of course, that misses this analogy and can no more understand the OT than it can itself. This hardening threatens us all at all times as the "lord of the world" blinds our senses and makes us unable to see the radiance that streams forth from the glory of Christ, from the image of God that appears in him (4:3f.). The adversary has only to dim the light of Christ in order to obscure the OT. If this decisive source of light is cut off, no effort at interpretation, however penetrating, can detect in it the pre-forms of what the unconcealed faces of the witnesses know as promise in the old covenant. The promise is then imprisoned in the OT's pre-Christian understanding of itself.

In Christian theology only A. A. van Ruler occupies a special position in this regard (cf. the chapter on him in ThE, II, 2, §§4275ff.; E.T. II, pp. 604ff.). Van Ruler regards Christ as neither typologically nor directly the goal and content of the OT salvation event but rather as an interim means to bring about the desired rule of God over the earth. Is not Israel God's concern in Christ, and the nations of the earth in Israel, and the fulfilment of creation, the sanctification of the earth, in the nations (van Ruler, *Die christliche Kirche und das AT,* pp. 63ff.; E.T. *The Christian Church and the OT,* pp. 67ff.)? In salvation history, then, "there is concentration, from the nations to the nation, from the nation to the remnant, from the remnant to the individual. But this concentration becomes expansion, from the Messiah to the Spirit, from the Spirit to the conscience, from the conscience to the state, from the state to the cosmos" (p. 69). Here then, to put it briefly, the OT is not seen in the light of Christ but Christ in the light of the OT, so that Christ is a transitional stage in this view of the saving process. Possibly van Ruler is essentially influenced here by M. Buber and his "visionary faith in the possibility of the sanctification of the earth" (p. 91; cf. H. J. Kraus, "Gespräch mit M. Buber," EvTh, VII–VIII [1952]).

If and to the extent that the new covenant is the fulfilment of the old, the character of the OT as promise can be shown only in the light of the new covenant and therefore only with the help of the christological criterion. In correspondence with the order of Hebrew letters, the OT can be read only right to left, or backward. We shall pursue this thought that Christ is at the vanishing point of the OT perspective, and thus forms the place of orientation, by considering three classical relations in which theological tradition has always seen the connection between the OT and the NT: first, the relation of promise and fulfilment, then that of law and gospel, and finally that of letter and spirit.

Usually the first member in the three relations (promise, law, letter) is given the role of representing the OT whereas the second member (fulfilment, gospel, spirit) stands for the goal of the salvation event (even in the days of the old covenant), just as it forms the hermeneutical criterion by which the OT is ranked as the Word of God. This also raises the question whether the fulfilment does not mean that the early stages are outdated and irrelevant for Christian faith (i.e., whether the line of interpretation followed by Marcion, Harnack, and Hirsch might not have been right). For what can the promise mean when the fulfilment is present, or the law when we have the gospel, or the letter when we share in the Spirit? Does the God of history, who is one and the same in the saving event of both the old covenant and the new, cause a certain feedback in the relation between the Testaments, a co-relation in the strict sense which again makes the old covenant for its part an interpretative key to the new?

X

Promise and Fulfilment

1. THEIR CONNECTION WITH THE HISTORICAL TENSES AND ALSO WITH THE STAGES OF THE OLD AND NEW COVENANTS

When God is understood as the Lord of history a bracket is posited which embraces and gives common meaning to the complicated fulness of historical phenomena and all the irrational effects of human freedom, all that is designed and all that takes place by chance. Because the OT prophets viewed history in this theocentric way, the many histories become for them the unity of one history, so that by common consent they are accepted as the creators of what we today mean by the term "history."[1] Not only do east and west—the hemispheres of what history embraces universally—"rest in the peace of his hands," but also the tenses of past, present, and future proceed from these hands and are held by them. This in itself suggests the relation of promise and fulfilment. Since the Lord of history is one and the same, the future cannot bring a complete innovation that stands in only a negative and distant relation to what these hands sent earlier.

In this assurance the prophets promise the future. This promise cannot mean, of course, that we must understand it as detailed foretelling and can see the course of history as a logically transparent continuum. (This illusion was reserved for Hegel's reason in history in which the decisive premise of OT prophecy is abandoned.) The premise of words of promise is that the unity of history that resides in the thoughts of God is just as much an object of faith as God himself is. To penetrate these thoughts, to see God in the cards, and to try to equate our own reason with God's higher thoughts (Isaiah 55:8) is hybrid arrogance. Even believers cannot understand the individual steps by which God's thoughts are realized in history. They find comfort in facing puzzling things (e.g., the good fortune of the

---

[1] Eduard Meyer, *Geschichte des Altertums,* II, 2nd and 3rd ed. (1953), p. 285; H. Gese, "Geschichtliches Denken im Alten Orient und im AT," ZThK (1959), pp. 127ff.; K. Löwith, *Weltgeschichte . . . ;* G. von Rad, "Der Anfang des Geschichtsschreibung im alten Israel," *Gesammelte Studien zum AT* (1958), pp. 148ff.; H. W. Wolff, "Das Geschichtsverständnis der alttestamentlichen Prophetie," EvTh, X (1960), pp. 218ff.

wicked who swell with fatness and are praised by the mob [Psalm 73:7, 10] while the righteous suffer the fate of Job]—in facing these things in all their stringency and replying with a relieved ''Therefore''—but no, even for believers the only possibility is to say: ''Nevertheless I am continually with thee'' (Psalm 73:23). For they do not just believe *in* God. They also believe *in spite of* what they see and cannot understand. The unity of history and the mystery that it is in the peace of God's hands may be seen only with the assurance of trust and not the security of sight.

To believe in God as the author of all things is to be sure of the end to which he strangely leads all things (Isaiah 28:29), but the steps on the way are not known and their traces have been erased: ''Thy way was (and will be) through the sea, thy path through the great waters, yet thy footprints were (and will be) unseen'' (Psalm 77:19). Promise is above all looking to the end when God's will will be done, strange though the ways may seem which he takes to this end.

If it was the privilege of the prophets to know something about these ways, this was not due to their own perception but to God's disclosure. Yahweh ''does nothing without revealing his plan to his servants the prophets'' (Amos 3:7). What God reveals, however, is not a prognosis. Prognoses of how things will turn out are totally alien to OT prophecy. Things do not just turn out; future history is controlled by him who speaks to the prophets. The word *dabar* which is used for the revelation imparted to the prophets has in this sense a characteristic double meaning. It means word or saying but also the fulfilment of the word in an event. It is an efficacious word, an act-word: ''The word which I speak will be performed'' (Ezekiel 12:25, 28). I am not just the one who speaks but also the one who performs. The prophet who promises the future has to do, not with a prediction which he adopts and then discloses to others, but with a statement which he trusts and proclaims, the statement in the name of Yahweh that Yahweh will still be the same in the future too.

When God as the author of history guarantees its believed unity, then future and past are related to one another. There is prophetic disclosure of the past too— retrospective prophecy. The past is to be seen in the light of the end when God's ways will reach their goal and fulfilment. Hence the backward references of the prophets and later the gospels and epistles to the historical leading of Israel away from the fleshpots of Egypt and through the desert to the promised land, or to the conclusion and breaking of the covenant, or to righteous and apostate kings, are not meant as recorded statements or historical statistics but as the interpreted history of Israel with Yahweh. The theologies of history in J, D, and E are in this sense retrospective prophecy in which the real issue is the openness of the event to the work of God in it.

What is set forth as promise, then, does not have to have the form of words. Figures and events of the past can have prototypical significance and form the outlines of what is actualized in later fulfilments. To take an example, the exodus out of Egypt is an act of Yahweh in which past and future meet. It is both a fulfilment of a prediction by Joseph (Genesis 50:24) and also a prefiguration of Yahweh's liberating action in the future. Threatened by the Amorites Israel should remember the liberation from Egypt and be confident that the faithfulness of Yahweh will be proved in new perils (Judges 6:8). The same prefiguration can turn into calamity and judgment, i.e., when Israel casts off its trust in Yahweh's witness and gives way to unbelief and despair (Deuteronomy 8:14; 13:11).

Past and future are related, then, to the extent that the historical future is decisively determined by Israel's attitude to the past, whether it trusts in the words and events of promise and lives by what it is told *or* whether it rejects them and thus turns salvation into catastrophe. No matter which way the decision goes, the promise still rests over Israel's history. Thus Joshua, when he says farewell at his last assembly at Shechem, holds out before the people once again the promise-event of the exodus and asks them to "choose this day whom you will serve" ("if you are unwilling to serve the Lord"), "whether the gods whom your fathers served beyond the River, or the gods of the Amorites in whose land you dwell; but as for me and my house, we will serve the Lord" (Joshua 24:15). The route taken by the people at this crossroads decides whether the promise that was given in the past will still be grace or whether it will turn into judgment.

The figures of Abraham (Romans 4:3) and Melchizedek (Hebrews 7) can have a similar prototypical function and so, too, can the sacrificial system of the OT (Colossians 2:17; Hebrews 8–10).

From this angle tradition does not just mean historical recollection and continuation in what is recollected in this way. It carries with it the claim which is the real point of prophetically interpreted history. It implies a demand to confess (and for this reason alone to remember) the proofs and promises of grace which are manifested here. It also contains the statement that what once took place in sign is still in force now, and will be in the future, because the one who promises remains true to himself. For Yahweh, as he calls himself (Exodus 3:14), means "I am who I will be and—a meaningful addition—who I have been from the very first." Remaining true to himself and confessing his promises, Yahweh embraces past, present, and future.

The question that arises, then, is what this relation of promise and fulfilment means for the connection between the OT and the NT and whether and how far the schema of promise and fulfilment can integrate the gospel into itself. Even if it can perform this integration so that the gospel (according to the self-understanding of the NT) can be understood as fulfilment of the promise, theological history offers a large number of examples to show with what astonishing breadth of variations the gospel can be interpreted as the fulfilment of the OT event of promise.

At the beginning of these deliberations I will select two typical forms to show how very different the understanding of the two Testaments can be. The first is taken from J. C. Hofmann of Erlangen (1810–77), the second from R. Bultmann.

The relevant statements of Hofmann may be found in his works *Weissagung und Erfüllung* (W) and *Der Schriftbeweis* (S).

Expounded in the schema of prophecy and fulfilment, the link between the OT and the NT finds its true basis and continuity in the fact that Christ was already person, indeed the eternal God, before he became man. To that degree his prefiguration does not take place without him but in virtue of his fellowship with the one who will generate him as flesh (W, I, p. 39). Hence history is an ongoing self-representation of the God who is present in Christ. As it presses toward the fulfilment of final fellowship, all the pre-stages of its fulfilment are pre-presentations and prefigurations. History is modelled on Christ. The echoes of this may be heard in the ultimate self-identification of the world-spirit.[2] In all the fulfilment manifested later what precedes is taken up in Hegel's sense and thus acquires the character of prophecy.

Prophetic events are chiefly found in the old covenant and the history of Israel since we have here the direct pre-history and pre-presentation of the incarnate Word. Yet as the eternal God and pantokrator Christ declares himself in the *whole* cosmos and in world history, not just in salvation history. This is how religious analogies and prefigurations parallel to the OT prophecies arise. In this sense Caesar Augustus can be a prototype of the universal dominion of God. Every triumph through the streets of Rome was a prophecy of Caesar Augustus, for the victor on the day of glory represented God in man, Jupiter in the Roman. By giving its victors these honors Rome perceived its future, namely, that it would rule the world through the divinely venerated emperor (W, I, pp. 15f.). Thus pagans experienced Christ in creation and called him by many names, their only error being not to distinguish him as Creator from creation. For this very reason, however, they saw him perish with corruptible beings and thus arrived at analogies to his crucifixion. They called him Cadmillus and Dionysos and bewailed him too soon, long before he died on the cross. . . . Pagans knew sons of God too soon, long before Jesus was exalted as Son of God and Lord of all (W, I, p. 39).

Hofmann found the special advance presentation of the incarnate Word of the new covenant, not in teachings and prognoses, but in history (W, I, p. 42), i.e., in what we have called the efficacious Word (*dabar*). Thus the passover lamb is a prophetic representation of the sacrifice on the cross (W, I, p. 16). This pre-history and its fulfilment occur in three essential stages: first, in the pre-presentation of Christ in our human life, in created humanity as the image of God and Christ; second, in his manifestation and transfiguration in the flesh; and third, in the presentation of his transfigured nature in the personal lives of Christians. Thus his appearance in the flesh is on the one side the fulfilment of a prophetic pre-presentation and on the other it is itself a prophecy, namely, the anticipation of its presentation in the life of the community (W, I, pp. 40, 42).

The provisionally final (but pre-eschatological) fulfilment of all prophecies is the self-presentation of Christ in the personal lives of Christians and in his community. Only when we see how radical is this process, which moves from prophecy to fulfilment and then finds new prophecy in the fulfilment, can we get the point of Hofmann's total theological conception. When we see that the advance presentations or prototypical events can be perceived only in the light of the fulfilment— it was the plight of pagans not to have the orientation of this fulfilment and hence to achieve no more than analogies—then the final fulfilment necessarily offers us a standpoint from which the totality of the prophetic sequence of events is disclosed. This middle point that gives perspective is the self-presentation of Christ in us which takes place in regeneration. What is prophesied and fulfilled may be seen in

---

[2]Cf. E.-W. Wendebourg, "Die heilsgeschichtliche Theologie J. C. Hofmanns in ihrem Verhältnis zur romantischen Weltanschauung," ZThK (1955), I, pp. 64ff., esp. pp. 75ff. E. Hirsch (*Geschichte der neueren evangelischen Theologie*, V [1954], p. 421) points out that Hofmann had only a sense of something strange and unpalatable about Hegel but structurally took over more from him than might have been expected from his earlier and definite rejection.

us as in a microcosm. Hence theology must begin with regeneration, with our inner being.[3] The scientific work of the theologian is done in three stages, the common feature being that each deals with an independent existence (that comes from outside and is not effected in us). Theology must begin with the directly certain fact of the regeneration of Christians as the fulfilment granted to us. If I may venture to say so, the degree of this direct certainty may be compared with the self-certainty of Descartes' *Cogito, ergo sum*. From the fact of regeneration the theologian then turns to the history and existence of the church as the next closest pre-presentation of Christ in believers. Finally it turns to Holy Scripture as the first and prototypical actualization of the schema of prophecy and fulfilment (S, I, p. 23).

Note should be taken of the sequence, which sharply pleads the thesis that we should not begin at the historical beginning with prophecy and then move on to the fulfilment, but rather that the fulfilment, i.e., regeneration, should be the starting point and the point of orientation from which to look back and understand the prophetic event. Hence our theological task is neither to describe the religious states of Christians (against Schleiermacher) nor to reproduce the teaching of Scripture and the church . . . nor to derive Christian insights from a master principle (against Hegel) but to develop the simple fact which makes the Christian a Christian (S, I, p. 11). Only in this light can one understand the basic axiom of Hofmann's theology that "as a Christian I am myself the material of my research as a theologian" (S, I, p. 10). Only as we are thus gripped by prophecy and fulfilment do the preceding media of the divine self-attestation, the prophecies and the acts of God in salvation history, come into the picture (S, I, pp. 665, 669).

When Baumgärtel (*Verheissung*, p. 90) takes up Bultmann's question to Hofmann (Bultmann, *Glauben und Verstehen*, II, p. 170) what is the relevance of all this, and whether the sequence of pre-presentations does not leave us untouched and make of us mere spectators, the answer seems to have been given by what we have called the point of Hofmann's conception—something that the two questioners overlooked. Hofmann thinks—rightly or wrongly—that he sees a direct correspondence between the certainty of our regeneration and the preceding self-attestations of Christ in the old covenant and also—conditionally—among pagans. In terms of the hermeneutical system one might say that only to the extent that in regeneration the Christian places himself personally in relation to Christ's self-attestation is he put in a situation of analogy to the preceding self-attestations and thus enabled to accept and understand them. Only the middle point of the new birth, which gives perspective, makes it possible for faith to see the prototypical event. As he surveys the long chain of prophecies and fulfilments in their continuity, and sees that provisionally it ends with him, the believer understands regeneration as a new prophetic event pointing to the coming eschaton. The strict and full reference of the salvation event to Christian "existence" (as we would say today) makes it clear that the basic motif of this theological thinking is the pursuit of relevance.

---

[3]Only superficially does this sound like Schleiermacher. Whereas Schleiermacher has in mind the existing self-consciousness common to us all, Hofmann emphasizes that regeneration as Christ's self-presentation in us is a transcendent work.

Bultmann takes a different course in fixing the relation between the OT and the NT (Bultmann, *Glauben und Verstehen*, II, pp. 162ff.). He brings against Hofmann's schema of prophecy and fulfilment the rhetorical question: Is it not his mistake to try to set up this relation with the help of the philosophical idea of history as a process of development in which what was formerly a mere tendency finally achieves actualization (pp. 170f.)? According to the NT, however, Christ is the end of salvation history, not as the goal of historical development, but as its eschatological end (p. 171). With his use of the term "eschatological" Bultmann shows that the new covenant is not to be regarded as an empirical affair in this world. The community which replaces the historical people of Israel is no longer a people in the sense of a construct of secular history (p. 174). The individual is taken up by baptism and participation in the Lord's Supper into the new covenant set up by death. Christ calls us out of nationhood and founds a community which has no secular ties (p. 174). The new covenant is radically eschatological and therefore the thought of the people of God stands in sharp contradiction to that of an organized nation such as Israel was (p. 183).

The eschatological desecularization of the new covenant, of the new kingship of God, and of the new people of God (pp. 171, 176, 179) naturally sheds a totally different light on the relation between prophecy and fulfilment. The old prophecies had reference to secular realization in a historical people and are shattered as such. They have found in the new covenant their radical end and stand under the eschatological No of the new kingship of God. In contradiction to the old prophetic idea God and his work can no longer be equated with the empirical history of a people (p. 184). But this shattering, this impossibility of OT expectation, is the real promise (p. 184). For Bultmann this is true not only for Israel but for all. Nothing can be promised for anyone that is not the shattering of his way, recognition of the impossibility of having God directly in his history in this world, of identifying his history in this world directly with the work of God (p. 184). This is why we may rightly understand the OT history of catastrophe as the promise (p. 185). (In this regard Bultmann's view of the OT is close to that of E. Hirsch, *Geschichte der neueren . . . Theologie*.) God himself has brought the OT people to disaster, for the situation of the justified can arise only on this basis (p. 186). His faith needs to look back upon OT history as a history of defeat and therefore of promise (p. 186). The contradiction between the old and the new covenants is a spur in salvation history. The new is called for in the shattering of the old. The believer of the new covenant achieves assurance of deliverance as he looks at the abyss from which he has been rescued.

In spite of the different ways in which Hofmann and Bultmann interpret the OT as a promise and intimation of the NT, their two views are distinctively related. Both see in OT history an increasing concentration, a crescendo of promise. Both press toward a kind of Hegelian synthesis in the NT, although at opposite poles. For Hofmann synthesis arises in the gospel because in it there is a final outburst of the basic theme of the old covenant, namely, God's turning to us in the pre-existent Christ. For Bultmann the antithetical elements (e.g., man's literalistic faith and God's wrathful judgments) are merely disruptions or foreshadowings of the true and basic message.

Even for Bultmann, however, the dominant *anti*thesis (the this-worldliness, the presence of God in his historical acts, the uneschatological factor) causes a failure which takes on the function of the promise and is fulfilled in Christ. Hence the old covenant becomes the dark background against which the light of the gospel shines and which it needs to achieve its true brilliance.

Serious objections and questions arise in relation to both views.

a. Hofmann certainly made the schema of prophecy and fulfilment a theologically fruitful one by not stopping at individual sayings, e.g., the heavily stressed messianic prophecies, but understanding the history of God's people as an advance presentation of the coming fulfilments and bringing out the element of promise in it.[4] Yet the directness of the assumed ascent to the NT fulfilment implies a concept of evolution which is inspired by Hegel and which does not bring out the new factor in the new covenant, the revision expressed by Christ's "But I say unto you." Perhaps it might be permissible to say that for Hofmann the pre-existent Christ and the incarnate Christ are simply variations on one and the same basic reality—variations which simply describe the way from its first intimation to its full disclosure. Here the birth, death, and resurrection of Christ have ceased to be an unexpected miracle of God's saving work (which even the clever and the wise did not know)[5] and become a postulate which fits in with the inner logic of the saving process and can be understood *a priori*. Along these lines could we not regard van Ruler's view,[6] in which Christ becomes a phase in the saving event of the OT, as a kind of left-wing Hofmannism? Is there any place at all here for the NT dialectic of a fulfilling and especially a transcending of the promise that no one can postulate?

b. As for Bultmann, he is certainly right when he speaks about the eschatological desecularization of the new covenant, though there is reason to think that the new people of God does have a valid secular form even if it is given another rank. Here, too, there is (and has to be) institutionalizing and incorporation into historical entities.[7] One must also ask whether the OT promise to Israel as a people, even as an empirical and historical reality, is simply abandoned and eschatologically negated by desecularization?

There are two objections to this conclusion.

1. Paul in Romans 9-11 plainly denies that by rejecting the gospel of Christ Israel has been put out of the new covenant, God's history with it in the OT has come to an end, and continuity with the promise of the old covenant has been broken (cf. especially 11:1ff.). Even for an apostate people the promise is still in

---

[4]Bultmann recognizes this (*Glauben und Verstehen*, II, p. 170).

[5]Matthew 11:25; Luke 10:21; 1 Corinthians 1:19-21, 26-28; 2:7f.

[6]ThE, II, 2, §§4274ff.; E.T. II, pp. 604ff.

[7]Not least for this reason Melanchthon in the *Apology* (VII, 20; LBK, p. 238; Tappert, p. 171) rejects the idea that the church, the new people of God, is a Platonic *civitas,* an unworldly and incorporeal idea. Luther opposes this misunderstanding too (WA, 7, 693, 11; LW, 39, 218) and in his *Papacy to Rome* demands that the church manifested in the body not be sundered from the real church (6, 297, 3; LW, 39, 71). The church is always also an institution in historical form. Talk of the invisible church should not lead us to see in it only a spiritual entity (in Bultmann's sense of "desecularized"). W. Elert is right when he says that this church is not invisible in Plato's sense but *abscondita* (hidden) (*Morphologie des Luthertums,* I [1931], p. 2297; E.T. *The Structure of Lutheranism,* I, p. 261).

force, for "the gifts and the call of God are irrevocable" (11:29). They have an indelible character. To be sure, in view of the new situation they are valid in a changed form, so that the law of transcending and fulfilling may be seen again at this point. Whereas in the old covenant the promise applied to the people as a whole, it now applies to individuals within the people (Romans 11:23), for "not all who are descended from Israel belong to Israel" (9:6). Physical membership of the people is not the criterion for relating to oneself the ancient promises but only the faith that accepts the good news of the new covenant.

Thus far one can agree with Bultmann that the new covenant calls out of nationhood and founds a new community with no secular ties. This is why Jesus, to sanctify the people by his blood, suffered outside the gate and we are to go to him outside the camp bearing his shame (Hebrews 13:12f.).[8] The only question is—and in my view a negative answer has to be given—whether this calling out of nationhood in the new covenant breaks the continuity between the OT and the NT which is posited by the continued validity of the promise. Instead, is not this continuity strengthened precisely by analogy, distance, and variation along the lines of the Epistle to the Hebrews?

2. The OT promises certainly come to expression in earthly and sensory pictures. Thus some apocalyptic visions can say that in the end-time the wolf and the lamb will pasture together and the lion will eat straw like an ox (Isaiah 65:25; cf. 11:7, etc.). In these imaginative images the final state of paradisal peace is projected on to the horizon of secularity (as Bultmann would put it). In the NT sense eschatological statements of this kind seem to carry within themselves a self-contradiction insofar as they secularize the non-secular and change it into something that may be seen in this world.

As for what is done in such apocalypses, an Enlightenment theology like Lessing's makes sense when it sets a desecularized "eternal pure gospel of reason" in a definitely positive relation to the sensory figurations which are used by the divine Educator during the first stages of pedagogy.[9] Yet even on this path from promise to fulfilment the fulfilment—the *plērōsai* of Matthew 5:17—is still ambivalent. On the one hand the fulfilment is on the same lines as the promise but on the other hand the one who is the fulfilment in person, and who brings to light what was really intended, represents a new thing that transcends all the prefigurations of the promise-event, as he shows with his "But I say unto you." Thus he is prefigured in the OT priesthood but is also different and does not fit the analogies offered there (Hebrews 7:26–29). Hebrews views positively the manifestation of the promise in the sensory phenomena of this world when it finds in the material objects of the first tent made by men—the lampstand, the table, and the bread—something analogous to and yet also very different from "the more perfect tent not made with hands, i.e., not of this world," and hence in a sense "desecularized" (Hebrews 9:2, 11). The elements of analogy and difference, of the positive and the negative, in the relation between promise and fulfilment are linked by the use of the phrase "how much more." "How much more" than the old cultus "shall the blood of Christ . . . purify your conscience" (Hebrews 9:14).

---

[8] *Glauben und Verstehen,* II, p. 174.
[9] Here, too, a transcendent reason directed by God is at work, although at a pre-rational sensory level. Cf. my *Offenbarung, Vernunft und Existenz,* 5th ed. (1967), pp. 82ff.

3. What is fulfilled in the NT is prototypically indicated even in the OT law (Jeremiah 31:33; Ezekiel 36:26), although this fulfilment—which is uneschatological and inconsistent for Bultmann[10]—is expected within the empirical people of Israel. Can we really understand the law, therefore, only as a prison (Galatians 3:22) which, as Bultmann sees it, contains within itself the element of disaster and is thus a sign of disaster? Is it not also God's good will (Romans 7:12) which bears witness to the faithfulness of God in his identity? Both positions regarding the old covenant, which prove to be variations in continuity, are clearly established by Hebrews. On the one hand the old covenant is superseded, "obsolete and growing old" (Hebrews 8:13). The secular forms in which it presented itself and put its expectations are superfluous. Yet on the other hand what is coming in the new covenant is contained in its promises (8:10ff.; Jeremiah 31:33).

These discussions have led us to some first findings in which the relation between the OT and the NT is made plain. I shall try to formulate them by turning to another question in the next section.

2. HOW THE RELATION BETWEEN THE OLD AND THE NEW TESTAMENTS IS NOT TO BE DEFINED

Baumgärtel may well be right when he rejects a demonstrable correspondence between prophecy and fulfilment. The mistake in postulating such a correspondence lies in its equation of promise and prophecy. Promise, as we shall see, always has to do with the author of the promise and his identity. This identity remains constant on the historical path from the giving of the promise to its performance. In contrast, prophecy (or what is usually understood by it) refers literally, as we have seen, to events within history, especially the results of a definite attitude on the part of the people. To that extent it relates to secular or uneschatological forms of fulfilment.[11]

Along these lines the following results of obedience to the law are prophesied: possession of the land (Deuteronomy 11:8, 22f.; 30:5); life and prosperity (Deuteronomy 6:24; 7:12-16; 30:6, 9, 16; 32:47); good harvests (Deuteronomy 28:1-14; Leviticus 19:25; 25:21); blessing in the sense of general well-being (Leviticus 26:3-13; Deuteronomy 5:29; 6:3, 18, 24; 15:5f.; 29:9); victory over enemies (Deuteronomy 11:23; 28:7).

Obviously prophecies of this kind are not promises that are fulfilled in the new covenant and therefore unite the Testaments in terms of continuity in salvation history. They apply only to Israel and are irrelevant to members of the new covenant. This is true even if we assume with von Rad that very often in the presentation of facts there is something that transcends the actual event, so that tradition gives an added dimension to events as types. Something that has to be believed is obviously projected into history here. God's saving acts in relation to Israel are presented in their believed unity with God and what is believed is set forth as already fulfilled in history. Hence in spite of the secularity of the fulfilment one has to speak most precisely of an eschatological element in the depictions. They present a final act of God as something that is already actual in history.[12]

---

[10]*Glauben und Verstehen*, II,· p. 174.

[11]Baumgärtel, *Verheissung*, p. 133.

[12]"Typologische Auslegung des AT," EvTh, I–II (1952–53), p. 30.

Now even if in the Israel of the old covenant fulfilments expected in this world offer a glimpse of the final eschatological act of God, these shadowy intimations are of no significance for those who have in Christ a direct view which transcends and corrects such prophecies. In face of the fundamental thesis that the OT must be read in the light of the NT we have to be on guard against overinterpreting the traces of typological extension in the OT and thus finding a smooth correspondence between such prophecies and the NT fulfilment (as von Rad is perhaps inclined to do).

A basic problem, however, seems to be more important than this simplistic relating of the Testaments. This arises out of the assumed continuity of the Testaments in salvation history.

Von Rad, like Zimmerli, speaks of the kerygmatic intention of the OT.[13] What is in view is the way in which religious people in the OT understand facts in faith.[14] The question to which this gives rise is as follows: What is the divine action in salvation history which connects the Testaments and establishes their continuity? Does it lie in the verifiable words and historical deeds of Yahweh or does it lie in the kerygmatic interpretation of these by the devout? Is salvation history a real sequence of events or is it a history of interpretation? To put it in another way, how are we as members of the new covenant to read the OT? Must we stick to the facts of the salvation event and see in these the identity of the Father of Jesus Christ from beginning to end, or is this event relevant only insofar as it is an interpreted event, so that we have to adopt the interpretation and typological understanding of the devout, reinterpreted, corrected, and transcended, of course, in the light of the NT?

There is no doubt that historico-critical research with its distinction (especially in the NT) between fact and kerygma, history and community theology, has helped to increase the sharpness of this problem.

Precisely formulated, the question (which has to be put to von Rad) is to the following effect: What are we really to understand by facts in salvation history, by special acts of God? Since real facts are not the same as interpreted history, since the latter, to quote von Rad, is often projected into the former as an object of faith, a distinct cleavage seems to arise and the question has to be put whether the factual event of salvation does not retreat here before the interpretation. Since, however, historical research with its refined methods brings into relief what actually happened, the problem arises whether it does not force on us a reorientation in our understanding of the OT.

This question has been put most emphatically by F. Hesse.[15]

It may be that we have to recognize a theological quality in the history of Israel, but does the real history of Israel have this special worth of being salvation history, or does this function accrue to the history of the old covenant because of the way it is presented in the OT, i.e., as interpreted history (p. 3)? Seeing the real history, according to E. Sellin (pp. 6f.), opens up for us new aspects of what is called

---

[13] *Ibid.*, p. 31.

[14] Baumgärtel, *Verheissung,* p. 117.

[15] We shall be dealing here with his art. "Die Erforschung der Geschichte Israels als theologische Aufgabe," *Kerygma und Dogma,* I (1958), pp. 1ff.

revelation in the OT, for here we find phenomena like prophecy which do not derive causally or mechanistically from preceding stages but can be verified even by the historian as the breaking of God's revelation into history. In this way research into the history of Israel acquires the rank of a theological discipline (p. 7).

The impulse toward the reorientation proposed by Hesse is not provided, however, by these (apparent or real) interventions of revelation. It is released rather by the general impression that the gulf between real and interpreted history cannot be bridged. This is illustrated by the figure of Abraham (p. 11). According to the OT presentation, which is adopted in the NT, Israel came to be God's people because Yahweh called Abraham out of his Mesopotamian home and sent him to Canaan, where in spite of his age he was promised descendants and given them in fulfilment of the promise. But none of this really took place. We know that this picture of the early course of events is totally inaccurate. There was no patriarchal sequence of generations from Abraham to Isaac and then to Jacob and his twelve sons. All this is for Hesse the element that has to be believed; it has been projected into the history and then made out to be history. The facts depicted are not salvation *event*. At this level there is no salvation history which unites the OT and the NT. The NT understanding of Abraham cannot appeal to history itself but only to the OT kerygma. Only in this dimension is the message of the old covenant received.

Since, however, the OT is not a book of doctrines but purports to bear witness to the God of history and his mighty acts (Acts 2:11), the difficulty arises how in this situation we can sustain the reference to actual history, to the facts. Can we still preach about Abraham as the father of faith in the NT sense (Romans 4:1, 11) if we are convinced that he never existed?

Hesse thinks that the biblical passages which depict Abraham as the man of unconditional faith and obedience tell us nothing about the historical figure of Abraham or about Abraham as a datum in salvation history. He finds help, however, in the fact that they tell us a good deal about the believers who narrate all this about Abraham (p. 18). God raised up for himself in Israel believers whom he enabled to tell the early history of their people in such a way that it gained certainty for them as salvation history with a focus on persons.

When Hesse speaks about God intervening to raise up people, he is counting on a transcendent event of revelation which is not immediately accessible to the secular historian and to receive which (not being a systematic theologian, he does not expressly say this) he himself needs to be awakened and put in the same position as Paul was when he called Abraham the father of believers. For Hesse these awakenings by God are forms of the salvation event. They are history. They are not just interpretations of facts but facts. The only point is that the locus of the salvation event has shifted. The biblical record tells us nothing about the supposed historical point called Abraham. It tells us about the ancient narrator or narrators and their faith, in this case especially J. The historical point about which they tell us does not pass the historico-critical test. But the historical point at which the narrator stands and was awakened to his vision is and always will be valid witness. Believing Abraham is a reflection of believing J in the patriarchal age (p. 18).

If I read him aright, Hesse has three goals in view. First, he does not want to conceal the cleft between real history and interpreted history (as he thinks von Rad does). He wants to show how radical it is. Second, he wants to shift the locus of the salvation event from what is narrated to the narrator. Third, he does not want to throw doubt on the historicity of the OT.[16] On the contrary, he wants to establish it. The witnesses of the history of Israel are raised up by God to witness. They do not speak in a subjective interpretation. They are gripped by a salvation event which their natural eyes do not see (1 Corinthians 2:9).

All this is obviously an attempt to deal with the protest of modern historical criticism and to show OT theologians like von Rad and Zimmerli that they have obscured the cleft and passed off as factual history the history interpreted by Israel. In Hesse—as the author himself supposes—there is in contrast a clear separation between real and kerygmatic history.

To that extent consensus is sought with secular history and the objection to theological prejudices is dispersed. The only exception is that theological and secular history still part company when it is a matter of the qualification of the kerygma, e.g., in the story of Abraham in J. Here secular history finds only interpretation whereas an understanding based on the NT kerygma has to speak about an opening of eyes, or, as I would say more definitely, about the Holy Spirit and his illumination.

Furthermore, a green light can be offered without theological qualms to secular history and its critical destruction of the facticity of the patriarchal stories, for facts that do not stand up under criticism are theologically irrelevant and the relevance of the witness and his historical locus is to be affirmed instead. In spite of all their detailed protests von Rad and Hesse are thus much closer to one another in intention than they themselves think.

The question arises, of course, whether Hesse's basically illuminating view does not throw out the baby with the bath water when he radically separates real history from kerygmatically interpreted history. The baby is the core of historical facts that may be found in interpreted history too. Is it not possible—I would ask with von Rad and Zimmerli—that the patriarchal stories state something about what Israel experienced in its early days even if this statement differs qualitatively from the kind that would be made by a historian using Ranke's methods and even if the experiences of whole generations are collected here in a single narrative?[17] Do we have to conclude that the call of Abraham, his faith, the offering of Isaac, etc., never happened and are totally unhistorical? Is there no prejudice in what modern history with its methods thinks it can tell us is factual or in its view that a thing either has to be factual salvation history or it is theologically irrelevant? Is not its ability to lead us—this is the intellectual question—enormously overrated at this point? Does the real understanding of facts have to be updated after 2500 years?[18]

Von Rad, of course, misses the point in two respects in his controversy with Hesse.

1. Even the best-attested event of real history, he thinks, is ultimately silent in regard to God's direction of history. Its relevance for faith is in no way verifiable

---

[16]Von Rad mistakenly accuses him of doing this (*Theologie des AT*, II, pp. 8ff.).

[17]*Ibid.*, II, p. 8.

[18]*Ibid.*, p. 9.

objectively (p. 9). Hesse would not contest this and hence would not regard it as a cogent criticism. What is historically verifiable, e.g., the existence of prophecy in Israel, is indeed silent for any objectifying understanding. But it is given to the witness as material that can be witness to him. It is open to qualification as salvation history. To that extent historical facticity and theological relevance do not have to be in contradiction, as von Rad obviously supposes, not even when historical prejudice is taken into account. Historico-critical investigation of Scripture does not take up the task of theology but simply presents it with material. Hence there can also be personal union between the historian and the theologian.

2. Von Rad also raises this objection. To say that the capture of Jerusalem in 587 was a divine judgment is beyond the competence of historical science as it is now understood. Here, then, we have to follow the confession of Israel which in this regard undoubtedly had a more real view of things than the Babylonian general Nebuzaradan and Babylonian and modern chroniclers. The example given skirts the real problem. For the capture of Jerusalem is a historical fact and is thus on a different level from the things recorded in the remoter patriarchal sagas. The only question about the fall of Jerusalem is how one views something that is in itself indisputable: whether one ascribes it simply to historical processes or interprets it before God as an event of salvation and judgment. In regard to the stories of the patriarchs, which cannot be established so unequivocally (if at all) as historical data, the very different question arises of where we are to seek the saving event, whether in real experiences that were then personalized (e.g., in Abraham), or in later revelation that opened the eyes of the witness, or both together, as we ourselves think.

To sum up, relating the OT and NT as promise and fulfilment raises various problems.

1. The promise refers only indirectly to the fulfilment in the new covenant if we think of the many OT prophecies. Several of these are secular. This does not mean, as we have seen, that they may not enable us to see the God of history in his identity. But they are so provisional, shadowy, and in need of correction that they are irrelevant for those who share in the new covenant and its fulfilment, and their significance is limited to Israel.

2. The relation between the old covenant and the new also poses the question whether the saving event that unites the Testaments, and the identity of its author, are rooted in the factual givenness (or historicity) of the salvation event or in its kerygmatic interpretation. We have seen that we are not forced to choose here. Real experiences of Israel, even though their reality cannot be demonstrated historically in Ranke's sense, underlie the narrated history. Similarly the witness himself is in his historical place the instrument of a new event of revelation.

A further point is that verifiable history—I recall the fall of Jerusalem—can also be interpreted as the history of salvation and disaster.

Both modes of viewing the event of revelation and the OT promises are adopted in looking back from the new covenant to the old. (In this regard some dubious rabbinic methods of exegesis, e.g., in Galatians 4:21ff., may be disregarded.)[19]

---

[19]The same problem of facticity and kerygma arises in relation to the NT. We discussed it in the debate with Bultmann in EF, I.

3. POSITIVE ASPECTS OF THE RELATION BETWEEN THE TESTAMENTS

Our critical discussion of the debate concerning the salvation event in the OT has prepared us for some of the positive aspects. These do not come to light if we refer the fulfilment of the new covenant to prophecies that have meaning merely for Israel, but only if these prophecies are related to the basic promise of the old covenant: "I am the Lord thy God" (Exodus 20:2). This is the promise that God has turned to his people, his community, his man, that "I have no pleasure in the death of the wicked . . . but rather that he should turn from his way and live" (Ezekiel 18:23). The fulfilment in Christ is related to *this* promise.

With this ongoing promise (its prior fulfilments in the OT and its definitive fulfilment in the NT) three links between the Testaments may be seen.

First (1) comes the assurance that God is one and the same in both phases of the salvation event, that his identity as promised in his name—"I am that I will be"—is in fact maintained, that it is the Father of Jesus Christ who turned already to the patriarchs and prophets, who is the Alpha and Omega, who encompasses both the beginning and the end.[20] That the relation between the Testaments is theocentrically determined in this way, that it is related to the person of God, means negatively that it is not to be viewed, as in Hofmann and others of the salvation history school, merely in terms of a continuous and progressive history of salvation. Static constructions of such processes, as they occur and have occurred under the influence of Hegel, are artificial and theologically inappropriate. Between promise and fulfilment there is no fixed constructive relation, because God in his freedom forms the link between the two. God's freedom has certainly bound itself to his turning and promise: "I am the Lord thy God," but God is free in the mode of his address. The "higher thoughts" that move him cannot be imprisoned in human systematizations, e.g., in constructions of the saving process. They cannot be penetrated. Part of God's turning to us is his hiddenness. There thus corresponds to it on man's side the faith that holds fast to him in spite of his hiddenness and that is not only faith *in* him but also faith *against* appearances. That Jesus is the Messiah cannot be demonstrated by understanding the supposedly ongoing line of OT salvation history as a geometrical factor that points to him and equates him unequivocally with the expected fulfilment. The line is ambivalent. It can end in the NT but also in the Talmud. The Jews did not confess Christ even though they groped their way along the same line as they saw it. The freedom with which God brought about the fulfilment of the new covenant entailed surprises which could not be foreseen in any construction of a saving line.

What it means that the way from promise to fulfilment is not straight or plain, that it cannot be imprisoned in any static systematization, that it is grounded in the will and resolve of the person of God, finds illustration in the fact that God can "repent," that he stoops so low in his condescension that he makes himself dependent on human reactions to his Word and acts (on belief or unbelief, obedience or disobedience). Thus he takes back promises that are abused. The judg-

---

[20]Revelation 1:8. Cf. Isaiah 41:4; 44:6; 48:13. The Greek alphabet with its 24 letters corresponds to the 24 hours of the day. The first and last letters denote the beginning and end of the world-day.

ments of his wrath can also cause him to repent. In this sense he repents of abandoning his guilty people to judgment and therefore to the "logic" of guilt and retribution, as he first did (Exodus 32:14; Jeremiah 26:13; Amos 7:3, 6, etc.). The prophets do not shrink from massive anthropomorphisms in order to bear witness to the freedom of God's resolves. They even seem to relativize the omniscience of divine prevision. Ironic glosses like "God corrects himself" or "God slips up" do not suggest themselves to the prophets and their believing hearers, but they might well do so to readers with a Platonic or modern rationalistic orientation. Statements of this kind which are not afraid to seem anthropomorphic are in truth indications that the plan of salvation is not a fixed and static program which imprisons God himself and to whose normative compulsion he is subject. If his mercy is without end and new every morning (Lamentations 3:22), one cannot see to the "end" what ways it will take, so that one must be ready every morning for surprises, for what is beyond human calculation.

While God changes his decisions and does not let history unfold on the basis of fixed primal decrees or in deistic fashion, this does not mean vacillation in an all too human way, for behind the revisions stands the constant factor of his faithfulness. "His faithfulness is great" (Lamentations 3:23), even though it presents itself in a new way every morning, and we can hardly keep pace, so that God seems to be to us a hidden God. For the prophets, even obscure history is plain. Behind what presents itself to the human spectator as an irrational turbulence of events—of contradictory events—they see the unalterably constant factor that they call God's faithfulness. This factor, grounded in the person of God, forms the bracket around the old covenant and the incalculable new element in the new.

Second (2), a link between the Testaments may be seen in the situation of the forms of the two covenants. When in the original promise God makes himself known as God for man, necessarily the situation of the man to whom he relates in this way is permanently thematized. On all sides there are the strong and wise and clever who exalt themselves above the appointed limit and are cast down (Daniel 5:21; Colossians 2:15), while God is close to the weak and troubled and foolish and poor in spirit (Psalm 56:1ff.). On all sides there are sinners on whom the judgment but also the mercy of God comes. On all sides there are pious people in affliction, valleys of despair, but also the remembrance that God turns to good what men intend as evil (Genesis 50:20) and that he works all things for the best to those who love him (Romans 8:28).[21] In the Word given to Israel we again and again find promises, acceptances, rejections, judgments, blessings, leadings of the Spirit, consolations, and afflictions which are unparalleled in the world around but recur in the NT.

For this reason reference has been made to a "structural analogy" between the OT and the NT.[22] The most profound analogy lies perhaps in the experience of the hiddenness of God, especially as it results from his condescension and self-limitation and causes his majesty to be concealed under its opposite. Already his turning to Israel as "the fewest of all peoples" (Deuteronomy 7:7) hides his power in the world. That his promises may be delayed and not promptly fulfilled accord-

---

[21]Cf. the excellent parallels in Baumgärtel, *Verheissung*, p. 141, esp. p. 151.
[22]G. von Rad, *Theologie des AT*, II, pp. 376ff.; E.T. II, pp. 363ff.

ing to a human program can be a test even in the stories of Abraham, causing people to ask whether he really can fulfil them.[23] The way in which Yahweh deals with unbelievers and scoffers and deniers can cause him to be presented in the proclamation of the prophets almost as a caricature that hides his deity and exposes himself to supreme distortion: He is like a moth to Ephraim and like dry rot to the house of Judah (Hosea 5:12); he is a father who has adopted a wicked foundling (Ezekiel 16); he is a despised lover (Isaiah 5:1ff.); he is like one who helplessly searches the houses of Jerusalem with a lantern (Zephaniah 1:12).

The obscuring of the concept of God which is the result of his unselfish love and condescension culminates in the self-emptying of God that the new covenant proclaims with its theology of the cross. In the Crucified, God foregoes all the glory of his majesty—so much so that even the Son of God as he wrestles with death can ask why God has forsaken him. To human creatures the message of the cross obviously seems to be foolishness (1 Corinthians 1:18). The Greeks who seek wisdom and the Jews who want validation by miracles (1:22) find it all crazy and incomprehensible. Yet precisely this turning of God into the unknown is the revelation of his mystery, i.e., his turning to the lowly and lost, his descent into the depths. This is no game of hide and seek. It is not just an artistic use of paradoxes. It is the logic of his love. It is, then, an underlying wisdom (2:6).

Precisely in the lowest depths it is manifest that the natural eye can see nothing of him (2:9) and that only the Spirit of God can bring about the conformity with God which can perceive his glory in the scandalous picture of him who is humiliated and insulted (2:11, 14). Only the most serious crisis is also the fulfilment of that which is prefigured in shadowy outline in the old covenant to the extent that only the one who obeys and trusts overcomes the temptation of the hiddenness of God.

4. THE PROBLEM OF THE PREFIGURATION OF SALVATION HISTORY IN THE OLD TESTAMENT

These analogies give rise to the question whether in looking back from the NT (and this alone!) one does not see certain prefigurations in words, figures, and historical constellations which the NT gospel seems to fulfil and transcend,[24] so that the analogy is established as well as the difference. We shall give a number of examples to illustrate this ambivalence of the relation between promise and fulfilment.

a. The exodus from Egypt is an event of liberation which is not only predicted by Joseph (Genesis 50:24) and set in noteworthy conjunction with the original promise (Exodus 20:2) but which is also a model of the acts of Yahweh. When Israel finds itself threatened by the Amorites, it should remember the miracle of the exodus and trust that God's faithful act will be manifested in the approaching troubles as well (Judges 6:8ff.). In the same way what is prefigured can also be an announcement of doom, namely, if Israel does not understand the prior act of

---

[23]Cf. 2 Thessalonians, esp. c. 2.

[24]We have in view the "how much more" of Hebrews.

liberation as a divine assurance in which it may trust but allows hesitation, anxiety, or indifference to gain the mastery over it (Deuteronomy 8:14; 13:11).

What comes, then, is decided by Israel's relation to the salvation event that it experienced in the past. The promise may be fulfilled or it may be blocked and turn to hurt as an avenging law. Either way—in the good it does or the harm it brings—it is still in force. It is in this sense that Joshua at his last assembly reminds the people of the exodus and its promise. They must decide in *what* way they want it to be fulfilled (Joshua 24:17ff.).

When Hebrews refers to the exodus (11:29), it seizes on its character as promise and as in other instances taken from the OT brings out both aspects of promise and fulfilment, both the analogy and the difference.

The *analogy* is that the patriarchs had to and did believe in God's Word of promise in the same way as the members of the new covenant. They were accompanied by this Word of promise when they were sent into the unknown and unforeseeable. Only the promise could be grasped with certainty in faith. The *difference* finds expression in the fact that salvation is accomplished in the new covenant, that it has definitively come, yet that it is not actualized in earthly things, that it is not to be understood as the fulfilment of the people's destiny in history, but that it is ensured for believers as their heavenly future (Hebrews 11:1). This heavenly future is already present now in the dawning of God's kingdom as it is here in Christ.[25]

b. We have already seen that throughout the NT, and especially in Paul, Abraham is viewed in his prototypical significance as the father of believers. The righteousness which was imputed to Abraham (Romans 4:3) is now present in Christ. What is directly revealed in Christ's death and resurrection was parabolically prefigured in the story of Abraham (Hebrews 11:17–19). The promise-event counts as fulfilled when Christ's act of redemption opens up for us direct access to God (Hebrews 9:2–11) and frees us from the conditions that the law of achievement laid on us (Hebrews 7:19; cf. James 2:23).

c. Hebrews interprets the sacrificial ministry of the old covenant as an advance presentation and promise of what is later fulfilled in the passion and crucifixion of Christ (Hebrews 8–10). Here, too, the past is simply a shadow of the future (Hebrews 10:1; cf. Colossians 2:17). The structural analogy is that of the gulf between God and the sin of his people or the whole human race. This gulf can be bridged only by atonement. Atonement is the theme of both covenants. The basic difference in the making of atonement is, of course, unmistakable. The sacrificial ministry of the OT is a provisional and interim matter which has significance as a shadowy pre-form of what will be definitive but is still to come and is to find fulfilment at the cross.

One may see this element of distance and superiority from three angles. 1. The priests of the OT offer only bulls and goats and scatter the ashes of a heifer, but Christ offers himself (Hebrews 9:12–14). We see in him the self-offering of God, his solidarity with sinners and condescension to them. 2. The priests had first to

---

[25]Hebrews 10:14. In clarification one may refer to the theology of the Pneuma which tells us that in the gift of the Spirit we have already received the first instalment (the guarantee, *arrabōn*) of that which is to come (Colossians 1:22; Ephesians 1:14). What we hope for is already present.

purify themselves and had thus to offer atoning sacrifices for their own sin and weakness and fallibility, but Christ, who is eternal and perfect, does not need self-purification and offers only for others (7:27f.). 3. The priests of the old covenant continually had to repeat the expiatory sacrifices since they constantly sank back into the fallen state, but Christ offered his sacrifice once and for all and set up a new situation before God.[26]

The threefold "but" is a decisive catchword. It shows that in the fulfilment there can be something quite different from what one might gather from the Word of promise or the prototypical event (at least when seen in isolation). The fulfilment transcends the promise. When Christ says: "I come to do thy will," he sets aside the first (the shadowy prior analogical event of the promise) in order to bring the second into force (Hebrews 10:9). The prophets themselves did not know (at least entirely) *what* they were saying in their words of promise. The words have deeper meanings than disclosed by those who spoke them. Their true content is revealed only in the light of the fulfilment. In this light they take on a different aspect.

The hermeneutical rule which they force upon us is that the promise is to be understood only in the light of the fulfilment, that the OT may be truly seen only in the light of the NT. This rule has a deeper and more general basis. One can know the significance of the individual part only when one knows the whole to which it belongs and in which it has its proper rank. This is why it is only in eschatological "sight," in which the panorama of the whole will present itself, that the point will be disclosed of that which now in its obscurity demands of us the Nevertheless of faith and in this way grants victory over the problem of the hiddenness of God. The coming of the eschaton has already become an event in Christ. Proleptically the whole of God's plan of salvation is manifest in him. For this reason the individual part of the promise, which was necessarily obscure in its own time, or could be no more than a shadowy outline of what was to come, may now be seen in its true content.

d. The OT prophecies of calamity also display eschatological structures that unite the two Testaments. Every historical visitation that the prophets proclaimed (e.g., Joel 3:9–21) is an anticipation of the final destruction. Nor is it to be regarded as a mistake that the prophets proclaimed the end and then when the prophetic visitation was over the world carried on as usual. On the contrary, as in Joel's vision of the plague of locusts, the shadow of the last judgment is seen lying over the provisional judgments of history. This sense of analogy and advance presentation is the point of the "Alas" of Joel: "Alas, alas, alas for the day! For the day of the Lord is near. As destruction from the Almighty it comes . . ." (Joel 1:15–20). One of these judgments will be the last, but for the moment no one can say which. What is called the last here involves the full collapse and destruction of Jerusalem, the end of Israel, and therefore an event of secular history. In the light of NT eschatology this is simply the advance presentation of what is last in the *fulfilled* sense: the end of the world and an event that transcends history. If Joel was proclaiming the coming of the "northerner" under Antiochus, who suppressed

---

[26]On the concept of "once and for all" (*ephapax*) cf. Hebrews 7:27; 9:12; 10:10–12; also Romans 6:10; 1 Corinthians 15:6; 1 Peter 3:18.

the temple ministry for a time, this could count as an advance presentation of the definitive disaster that overtook Jerusalem in 70 and 135. The averted onslaught of the ''northerner'' was for Israel a kind of prefiguration of the final attack from the north that Ezekiel prophesied.

Metaphorically one might say that the big hand of the world clock continually stands at twelve and then creeps on. Each time the little hand moves on a little until it too will definitively indicate twelve, the goal of time. This metaphor[27] makes it plain that the visitations are not just symbols of judgment outside time. They are also the unrest which pushes the world clock on until it finally runs down. Time will have an end. History presses on to the shore of eternity.

As the OT prophecies of the end were not mistaken when time ran on, so it is with the NT.[28] When the hope of an early parousia is disappointed, this brings no shattering crisis, even though the community has waited in vain for the end (calculated by some like J. A. Bengel).[29] The reason why, especially in apocalyptic epochs, anticipation of the end can so easily be taken for the end itself, but just as easily disappointment vanishes and slips into new expectation, is perhaps not to be sought so much in the explanations that are given, e.g., in 2 Thessalonians 2:6, 7, namely, that a divinely ordained power of restraint (*katechon*) is the reason for the delay.[30] The reasons that lie in the central kerygma of the NT are more illuminating. The essential point is that in the war between God and Satan the decisive battle has already been fought. The anti-godly forces have already been overcome in Christ's resurrection. There can thus be real anticipation of the end. What we have now are only the final death throes on minor battlefields. The final Victory Day will bring the hidden but already operative triumph of God to the whole world and present it to sight as well as faith.[31]

The fact that further history is simply an echo or aftershock of the decisive battle leads constantly to the familiar phenomenon of a prophetic shortening of perspective which overlooks the interim of the aftershock and regards Victory Day as directly present. Mistaken dates for the end have a basis of faith, then, in the resurrection of Christ. This justifies the sense of victory as self-fulfilling hope and causes disappointment to yield to renewed expectation. In this sense eschatological tension knows no serious reverses, for the basis on which it is erected stands unshakably firm.

e. A final link between promise and fulfilment and therefore between the Testaments has always been seen in the chapter in Isaiah which speaks about the servant of the Lord and his vicarious suffering (Isaiah 53:2–12). Now we undoubtedly have a distorted view of the dominant typological foreshadowing here, and we thus miss the appropriate movement, if we say with Baumgärtel that the

---

[27] I have seen it somewhere but cannot say where.

[28] See c. XXXIV.

[29] Bengel expected the millennium to begin on June 18, 1836.

[30] Reference has constantly been seen to the Roman state as a function of order which staves off the coming of antichrist. Other exegetes, thinking of the statement in Mark 13:10 that the gospel must first be preached to the nations, suggest the ongoing missionary work of the church. Cf. O. Cullmann, *Christus und die Zeit* (1946), pp. 145f.; E.T. *Christ and Time* (Philadelphia, 1950), pp. 164ff.

[31] *Ibid.;* E.T. pp. 84, 141f.

primitive Christian community did not just draw its faith in Christ's worth from Isaiah 53.[32] Of course it did not! This would be impossible in any case in view of the basic structure of promise and fulfilment. For the fulfilment, as we have seen, is the hermeneutical key to an understanding of the promise, not vice versa. Faith is not based on the prefiguration of Christ's passion by the servant of the Lord. It is based on the figuration of the suffering and crucified Christ himself and only in this light does it apply to the "pre."

It also seems to be most banal if we allow the analogies between the servant of the Lord and Christ to be destroyed by noting that the prophecy that the servant of the Lord will have progeny and share his spoil with the strong does not apply to Jesus of Nazareth.[33] As though these were not just traditional expressions[34] and as though—if we read the OT in the light of the NT—they do not come to have a changed reference to the succeeding community and the rank of the eschatological Kyrios as pantokrator. Nor is it easy to see why the uncertainty that still prevails as to the identity of the historical 'ebed Yahweh (cf. also Acts 8:34) should be any obstacle to fitting Jesus of Nazareth into the contours of the OT analogy. Philip does this when he expounds the chapter to the Ethiopian eunuch without any "theory" of identification.

The real material analogies between Isaiah 53 and the story of the passion and the NT understanding of suffering, the analogies which make it understandable why the primitive community should have interpreted the hymn to the servant of the Lord prototypically, may be approached from three angles.

First, the servant of the Lord symbolizes vicarious suffering and is thus to be understood as an advance presentation of the suffering of Christ on the cross; the more so as many of the details correspond.

(1) "We esteemed him stricken, smitten by God" (Isaiah 53:4). Externally the crucifixion, too, seems to be a punishment for claiming divine likeness, an expression of the wrath of God.

(2) The suffering of the servant of the Lord, whether it be viewed as wounding or sickness, is to be regarded as caused by other men, as physical violence.[35] It is persecution or martyrdom (cf. also Jeremiah 11:19). He did not open his mouth to complain (53:7) but bore the suffering on behalf of those who persecuted him.

(3) The atoning significance of his suffering applied vicariously to both the sin and the punishment of others: "Upon him was the chastisement that made peace for us, and with his stripes we are healed" (53:5).[36]

(4) The suffering of the servant of the Lord condenses an experience which was startlingly new for Israel, which was not in continuity with its history, and which could thus be interpreted as an advance presentation of the new thing in the new covenant. Although there is repeatedly in the salvation event of the OT some kind of vicarious event, the outrageous and unheard-of thing here is that the saving significance of the vicarious suffering is related to a completely unimportant,

---

[32]Cf. P. Volz, *Jesaja II* (1932), p. 191 (quoting Baumgärtel, *Verheissung*, p. 139).
[33]Baumgärtel, *Verheissung*, p. 139.
[34]C. Westermann, *Jesaja 40–66* (1966), p. 215; E.T. London, 1969.
[35]C. R. North, *The Second Isaiah* (1964), *ad loc.*
[36]Cf. the thought of wounds healing wounds in passion hymns, esp. the chorales of J. Heermann, J. Gesenius, A. Thebesius, etc.

ordinary, and needy figure who evokes only abhorrence and scorn among his contemporaries,[37] and certainly not the dread of lofty tragedy. The parallel to the non-prominence of the crucified Jesus is obvious.

Second, the suffering of the servant of the Lord has the character of unconditional uniqueness,[38] as does also the atoning work that he does. This uniqueness stands in contrast to the constant compulsion to repeat the act and reminds us of the "once and for all" (*ephapax*) by which Hebrews differentiates Christ's atoning death from the sacrificial ritual of the OT, the more so as the expiatory suffering of the servant of the Lord seems to be "desacralized" like that of the new covenant, which does not take place in the temple precincts but outside the gate (Hebrews 13:12).

Finally there is a parallel between the exalting of the servant of the Lord and that of the crucified Jesus (53:10-12). In both cases this takes place only after they have been through the stages of deepest humiliation (Philippians 2:5-11). As stated already, nothing essential in the analogy is disturbed by the use of conventional terms to describe the exalted status of the servant—terms which undergo desecularization in the eschatology of the NT.

f. As a final example of OT events that are prototypes in the salvation event we may refer to Psalm 22, the psalm of the suffering Christ. This is not only quoted in what is according to the oldest account the last saying on the cross (Mark 15:34). It takes on decisive significance by showing that Christ's death finds its final point in dereliction. The crucified Jesus does not express his dereliction in the empty night of Golgotha. He does not complain against an unknown God or confess that he has been mistaken.[39] He complains of his affliction to God himself. He addresses him as Thou. In spite of the dereliction he thus counts on his presence. But above all—and here the significance of Psalm 22 begins—he complains with a quotation from Holy Scripture, i.e., with a saying of God himself, so that the circle in the relation with the Father closes again, and the final saying of Christ in John: "It is finished" (John 19:30), is filled with meaning.

What we have in Psalm 22 is not a prophecy which refers directly to the crucified Jesus. Regard should be had to the difference between the dereliction of the author of Psalm 22 and that of Jesus. But the structural analogy is unmistakable: the assault upon the righteous from whom God's nearness slips away and who, like Job, does not understand in the moment of suffering. In the case of the author of Psalm 22 there can only be again a shadow of what is ahead. His affliction is only a pale copy of that of Jesus when he is abandoned on the cross. Here again the fulfilment goes far beyond what is foreshadowed in the promise. But the foreshadowing corresponds to the NT's understanding of itself. This is because Jesus sees himself to be in line with the afflicted and persecuted prophets (Luke 13:33f.; cf. Matthew 5:12; Luke 6:23; Acts 7:52). And yet he is more than a prophet.[40]

The same analogy and difference apply to the hope of the author of Psalm 22 for

---

[37]Cf. on this Auerbach, *Mimesis,* pp. 494ff.

[38]Westermann, *Jesaja 40-66,* p. 216.

[39]As in Jean Paul's Sermon of the Dead Christ; cf. EG, I, pp. 331f.; EF, I, pp. 236ff.

[40]This can be said even of John the Baptist (Matthew 11:9; Luke 7:26; cf. also Matthew 12:41f.).

the fulfilment of his faith, namely, the conversion of the earth (Psalm 22:28f.). This hope includes the author's identification of his cause with God and therefore reasons for his triumphant expectation. Here again the promise is transcended in the NT, for in Christ we not only have an identity of cause but an actual identity of person. Christ is in person the pantokrator at whose feet the earth will lie. It is thus understandable that in the NT texts the situation of the author of Psalm 22 is seen to be in structural analogy to that of the crucified Jesus. Even though the modern concept of history has made the difference deeper within the union of promise and fulfilment, it still makes sense that the community finds in the sufferings and trials of the servant of the Lord a type of that which only by the events of the gospel fulfils and transcends the indicatory outlines of what took place earlier.

5. CONCLUDING REMARKS ON THE QUESTION OF PREFIGURATION (ILLUSTRATED BY THE MODEL OF DEATH AND ITS OVERCOMING IN THE OLD TESTAMENT AND THE NEW TESTAMENT)

From all that has been said this postulate of prefiguration is not to be understood in the sense of the older typologizing and allegorizing, i.e., in such a way (or in the illusion) that we can find in the OT prophecies objective signs of the coming fulfilment in Christ. This kind of proof from prophecy is in fact impossible. If there are any to whom this is not theologically clear, they will (finally) have to let themselves be convinced by the historico-critical investigation of Scripture. The promise does not prove the fulfilment. This was the doubtful element in the older proof from prophecy. The reverse is true. The fulfilment confirms and qualifies the promise. It brings to light in it a dimension of meaning which was still obscure at the time of its promulgation. The final ground of our thesis is that the prefigurations are revealed only in the light of the NT. They are, as it were, evoked by association. The powers from which Christ redeems (guilt, pain, and death) are accepted and suffered by the devout of the OT and worked into the framework of the history with God and God's history with men. The saying: "Nevertheless I am continually with thee" (Psalm 73:23), which the devout say to the hidden God but God, keeping to his promises, says also to his unfaithful people and to all men everywhere, recurs in deeper and more radical form in the NT. The crucified Jesus utters this Nevertheless in his cry of dereliction on the cross. God's Nevertheless to man also persists and comes to fulfilment in the offering of his Son (John 3:16). The question even arises whether a life in fulfilment of the gospel is possible at all unless a backward look at the salvation event of the preceding old covenant evokes such associations and brings to light the "type" in the structurally analogous situations of the devout of the OT.[41] One might indeed be inclined to fear that looking back from the gospel to the salvation event of the old covenant would indicate certain docetic features and remain strangely unfulfilled in the fulfilment

---

[41] A particularly good example which falls short of typologizing may be found in von Rad's exegesis of the Joseph stories, esp. their climax in Genesis 50:20 (*Theologie des AT*, II, pp. 382ff.; E.T. II, pp. 369ff.; *Weisheit in Israel* [1970], pp. 255ff.; E.T. *Wisdom in Israel* [Nashville, 1972], pp. 198ff.; *Gottes Wirken in Israel* [1974], pp. 285ff.).

if these associations were not evoked and we remained blind to the advance presentation.[42]

At the end of this section, then, it will be as well to illustrate the relation of continuity and discontinuity on the way from promise to fulfilment by an example of a special kind, namely, the wrestling of Israel with the riddle of death and the rise of a first hope of resurrection—a hope of promise.[43]

Those who completed their lives in the pre-Christian old covenant died old and full of years and were gathered to their fathers (Genesis 25:8; Job 5:26). Wächter (quoted by Kellermann, ZThK, III, p. 259) points out that dying, like sexual intercourse, was a natural part of life and the same phrase was used for it: "going the way of all flesh."

The supposed or real absence of any problem regarding death in ancient Israel has been given a sociological explanation. Nomadic peoples had no religious relation to death because they moved away from their burying places and thus did not remember death for long.

In later Wisdom texts death becomes increasingly a problem. It is here a masterful limit to the life-relationships that God has instituted: "I am taken from the land of the living and I shall look upon man no more among the inhabitants of the world" (Isaiah 38:11); "my dwelling is plucked up" (v. 12). The worst feature is that in the grave the righteous can no longer think about God (Psalm 88:6), so that the basic relationship which sustains all others is ended. Those who ignore death and imagine they will live on are foolish. Hence the psalmist prays: "Teach us to number our days that we may get a heart of wisdom" (Psalm 90:12). Pictures of resignation occur which compare dying with waters that sink into the earth or the withering of grass and flowers (e.g., Psalm 90:6; Job 14:10ff.). Man can be even more radically exposed to destruction than plants, for even a tree, when it is felled, is not without hope of coming up again (Job 14:7).

A first "consolation" is that the individual is part of his clan and the memory of him lives on in it. He continues to live on in his progeny, in whom his own life under the promise returns as it were. Praise of the dead is thus an intermediary stage in which the question of overcoming death is intimated (2 Samuel 14:7; Sirach 44:10ff.). Some analogies may be found here to Germanic religion in which the tribe was the medium of the hero's continued life (W. Grönbech, *Kultur und Religion der Germanen* [1937]).

A further step is the idea that Yahweh's remembrance and promises continue after death. What remains is the accompanying blessing (C. Westermann, *Der Segen in der Bibel und im Handeln der Kirche* [1968]; E.T. *Blessing in the Bible . . .* [Philadelphia, 1978]). Thus the dying Jacob when he says farewell to Joseph bears witness to the promise of Yahweh that after his death God's blessing

---

[42]This is especially true if we overlook the analogies between the transcending of the promise in the NT fulfilment and the same process in the OT (cf. O. Cullmann, *Heil als Geschichte* [1965], pp. 70ff.; E.T. *Salvation in History*, pp. 81ff.).

[43]In what follows I am indebted to suggestions in U. Kellermann, "Überwindung des Todesgeschicks in der alttestamentlichen Frömmigkeit vor und neben dem Auferstehungsglauben," ZThK, III (1976), pp. 259ff. Cf. also my *Tod und Leben, Studien zur christlichen Anthropologie* (Geneva and Tübingen [1943 and 1946]); E.T. *Death and Life* (Philadelphia, 1970). Another important work is L. Wächter's *Der Tod im AT* (1967).

will be on his descendants and they will go back to the land of their fathers (Genesis 48:21).

If I am right there is here a decisive breakthrough which transcends the original similarity between the understanding of death in Israel and that in the Near East (and among the Germans). In the OT that which overcomes death does not lie in an immortal substance in the ego (e.g., Plato's psyche), nor in a clan that is above the individual and lives on after him, but in something outside man, in the memory of God himself, who knows our name and has written it in the book of life (as the idea is developed in the NT [Revelation 17:8; 20:12, 15]). In God's remembrance we have a name that will never perish (Isaiah 56:5).

Here are the first hints of what we called earlier man's alien dignity. In distinction from our own worthiness this means being regarded as worthy by God. The identity of man does not lie in a personal core, no matter how we define it, but in a partnership or history with God which can never stop because God's remembrance never stops. What is called the divine likeness on the basis of Genesis 1:27 needs to be reinterpreted in this light. The *imago Dei* does not consist, as many theologians have thought, in special human qualities such as reason or conscience or walking upright. It is finally the image that God has of us (cf. ThE, I, §§700ff., 763ff.; E.T. I, pp. 150ff., 152ff.). In this sense the prodigal son in the far country had lost his recognizable identity and all his demonstrable qualities. But his identity was maintained in the image that his father had of him, in his thoughts of him (Luke 15:11ff.). The parable of Jesus is inseparably related to this OT background. Indeed, there is more here than a mere structural analogy.

Israel really has to struggle for this thought that it is the relationship with God that survives death and does not abandon those who go down into the grave. The idea finally prevails and forms a prelude to the certainty of resurrection in the gospel.

This struggle takes the form of wrestling with Sheol, the realm of the dead and of shades. Two antiphonal voices may be heard here. The one voice bewails the remoteness of Sheol from God. Death separates us from the cultus. Above all it removes us from the level where God does his mighty acts. It removes us from history and the salvation event (cf. Hezekiah's song of thanksgiving [Isaiah 38:10–17]). Since God is in the OT a God of history, the taking of the dead out of history threatens to take them out of God's sphere of power. Sheol seems as it were to be outside the territory of God's sovereignty. In it there is only supreme dereliction (Psalm 88:6ff.; Job 14:13).

Over against this voice of complaint the other voice is a doxological one which extols Yahweh's triumph over Sheol. It rejects the dualism in which the living are related to God as they share in history but the dead are set at a distance from God. Sheol, too, is under God's sovereignty and the abyss has no cover (Job 26:6f.). Hell and the abyss are uncovered before God (Proverbs 15:11). God is in Sheol as well. There is no place where one can hide from him (Psalm 139:8).

Thus the old complaint that death erases our relation to God is vanquished by the triumphant certainty that the faithfulness of God is without end. Even the dead in Sheol praise it (Psalm 22:30) and it can liberate them out of Sheol (Amos 9:2).

That God is mighty in Sheol, too, may be seen especially in the fact that he is identical with himself in judgment and grace. We see this clearly in the ongoing distinction between the righteous and unbelievers in Sheol. The nothingness of shadowy existence is never reduced to nothing. Those who forsake and scorn Yahweh cannot escape his wrath even in Sheol. Sheol is no longer a foreign land outside God's sovereignty. In the Wisdom Psalm 49 we thus read: "Truly no man can ransom himself, or give to God the price of his life, for the ransom of his life is costly, and can never suffice, that he should live on for ever" (49:7f.).

Even in Sheol, then, the question of ransom, of liberation from guilt, is a pertinent one. In face of this the psalmist can confess his confidence that the promises of God remain faithful to him in the realm of the dead and are still in force in this sphere: "But God will ransom my soul from the power of Sheol, for he will receive me" (49:16). The dead, then, are not taken out of salvation history. They *remain* hidden in it (cf. Job 19:25; Psalm 16:9; 73:23ff.).

Even if not a few of the resurrection sayings in the OT refer to the rising again of Israel and therewith to the making possible of what was held to be impossible (e.g., Isaiah 26:13ff.; Ezekiel 37:1ff.; cf. Kellermann, p. 282), and even if eschatological reality is thus projected once again into the present world (G. von Rad, TDNT, II, p. 848 with reference to Isaiah 26:19), nevertheless, especially in individual hope, we can see here the first indications of what the Johannine Jesus will tell his disciples in the parting discourses when he says that in dying he will prepare a place of refuge for them (John 14:1–4).

We see, then, that the OT does not have a uniform message concerning death and its overcoming. We note instead a choir of many voices within which the definitiveness of death is treated with resignation but the triumph of Yahweh's lordship over Sheol is also extolled and there are even hints of a belief in resurrection which come to fulfilment in the NT.

The picture of a choir, however, is not quite accurate, for the voices that are heard here do not sing at the same time but follow one another. There is a historical process in which the message of the overcoming of death gradually develops on into the NT. This does not mean, of course, that the NT message of resurrection simply dots the "i" and has the character of a logical deduction. No one could postulate that what was heard as promise would be fulfilled in this way or that the risen Jesus of Nazareth would be declared the prince of life by God. Surprise and apprehension were caused. A new thing took place. Yet there as elsewhere it all comes within the schema of promise and fulfilment. Looking back from the situation of fulfilment in the gospel one may see earlier lines that point clearly in the direction from which the new thing comes.

The essential thing here is that we cannot speak of an evolution propelled by immanent forces. The point of the process of preparation is better understood if we keep one thing clearly in view. What we have here is a history with and under God, a dialogic history. Israel learns only gradually what it means to be the partner in a covenant with Yahweh. It realizes only gradually that what it calls God's faithfulness—his covenant faithfulness—has no temporal limits and therefore cannot end when we are called away from this temporal scene.

Growing certainty about the overcoming of death is not, then, an automatic evolution but the increasing discovery of a mystery which is posited from the very first in the partnership with the covenant God. This mystery is simply liberated from its state of incubation. It becomes increasingly virulent.

This virulence does not imply an evolution in progressive human knowledge. It implies the work of the Spirit through whom God reveals himself and under whose impulses the heart becomes new (Ezekiel 11:19; 36:26f.). God *makes* himself known. Trust in the Spirit, who creates and creates anew, but whose absence plunges into nothingness (Psalm 104:29f.), leads more and more to the certainty that the spirit returns to God while the body crumbles to dust (as can be said in later Judaism [Ecclesiastes 12:7]). Here, too, the eschatological miracle of the Spirit can be expressed—as we noted earlier—in terms of the present world, in the work of the newly creating Spirit who gives life to the valley of dry bones and causes Israel to rise up out of the dust (Ezekiel 37:1-14). The faithfulness of God can make the impossible possible, so that there is no limit to God's relationship with his elect. From a great distance there may be seen already the outlines of a new promise which rings out in the new covenant: "Death shall be no more" (Revelation 21:4).[44]

---

[44]Cf. G. von Rad, TDNT, II, pp. 843-49; also *Weisheit in Israel* (1970), pp. 386ff.; E.T. *Wisdom in Israel,* pp. 304ff.; P. Stuhlmacher in ZThK, IV (1973), pp. 365ff., esp. pp. 373ff.; G. Wingren, *Die Predigt* (1955), pp. 156ff.; E.T. *The Living Word,* pp. 121ff.

XI

Law and Gospel[1]

1. THE SIGNIFICANCE OF THIS DIFFERENCE FOR THE UNDERSTANDING OF THE TWO TESTAMENTS (LUTHER AND CALVIN)

To the extent that the OT represents Moses, Luther sees in it very largely, although not exclusively, the law which came in because of transgressions.[2] Insofar as it represents the law it has been done away. In the new covenant even the Ten Commandments are at an end, or, more accurately, the office of Moses comes to an end inasmuch as it no longer makes sin strong by the Ten Commandments, and sin is no longer the sting of death. For through Christ sin is forgiven, God is reconciled, and the heart has begun to incline to the law.[3] Furthermore the law of Moses, unlike the prophets (e.g., Isaiah 42:6; 49:6; 60:3), applies only to the Jews and is not binding on the Gentiles.[4] The law is primarily understood here in its elenchtic use (as in Paul). Sin is strengthened by the law, i.e., made more virulent (Romans 5:20). The law is an occasion for it (*aphormē*, Romans 7:8f., 13). This is why we are now dead to the law (7:4). It is no longer relevant for us.[5]

For Luther, however, this relativizing applies only with a definite limitation. The law of Moses is given its decisive significance by the first commandment: "I am the Lord thy God." The law stands here under the sign of God's gracious

---

[1]In what follows the relation between law and gospel is viewed from the special angle of its bearing on the relation between the OT and the NT. The general theme has already been systematically developed in ThE, I, §§554–623; E.T. pp. 94–125 and EG, II, §§14–17, pp. 219–317; EF, II, pp. 184–258), which should be consulted.

[2]Cf. Commentary on Galatians 3:19 (WA, 40/I, 479; LW, 26, 308).

[3]Preface to the OT (1523) in H. E. Bindseil and H. A. Niemeyer, ed., *Dr. M. Luthers Bibelübersetzung nach der letzten Originalausgabe* (1845–55), 7, 303ff.; LW, 35, 244.

[4]Sermon on Exodus 19–20 (WA, 16, 363ff., esp. 371; LW, 35, 161ff., esp. 164). Cf. also H. Bornkamm, "Gesetz und Evangelium in Luthers Auslegung des AT," ZsysTh (1943). Althaus (*Die christliche Wahrheit*, I, p. 227) rightly points out that the OT religion of law in this sense is doubly abolished in the NT: by Paul with direct reference to the law; by Hebrews with reference to the cultus that justifies only "legally."

[5]WA, 40/I, 478ff.; LW, 26, 308.

approach, so that the identity of the author of the law and the gospel is maintained for Luther. To that extent Christ is not only he who fulfils the law but also the fulfilment of the promise contained in it.[6]

This idea that the law of Moses contains reference to the Emmanuel who will appear as he truly is only in the gospel leads Luther to issue a warning against disparaging the OT. For what is the NT but a public preaching and proclaiming of Christ, posited by OT sayings and fulfilled by Christ. You will find here the swaddling hands and the crib in which Christ lies and to which the angel directs the shepherds.[7]

Looking at the evangelical content of the OT can sometimes lead Luther to formulations which speak about Christ's presence in the old covenant and emphasize the unity of the community of patriarchs, prophets, and apostles.

One faith, one Spirit, one Christ, one fellowship of all the saints who before and after follow Christ. Here, the patriarchs with us, we have all believed in the same common faith in one Christ and we all still believe in him though in different ways (Sermon on Romans 3:11f. [WA, 10/I, 2, 4f.]). The little children who go before Christ sing Hosanna like the patriarchs. But we follow, with the whole world, and we sing the same song that we have from Christ; they go ahead and we follow behind (WA, 47, 163; LW, 22, 449).

In this way, even if only occasionally, Luther tends to find the same message in both Testaments and to use expressions similar to Calvin's. He can compare the OT to a letter which is opened in the NT, so that the latter is an act of making public, not an act with new content.[8] This reminds us of the way in which Calvin relates the Testaments, finding an identity of substance and a difference only in matter.

In the name of a radical diastasis of law and gospel E. Hirsch diametrically opposes this closer relating of the Testaments. He sees, of course, that the OT has things to say about God's grace and condescension but finds no references to the fulfilment of promised grace in the new covenant because grace and forgiveness stand under legal conditions in OT religion (*Das AT und die Predigt des Evangeliums*, p. 76). Here in fact is the difference which Paul brought to light with his justification apart from the works of the law and his emphasis on the unconditionality of grace in the new covenant. Except in the borderline sayings quoted above, Luther noted this difference and constantly spoke about it, though neither the apostle nor the Reformer questioned the unity of the author of both law and gospel in the two Testaments nor doubted the character of the OT as the Word of God. E. Hirsch, however, can see the Testaments only in radical antithesis: law here and gospel there. In these circumstances only an artificial dialectic can enable us to see them united in the one Bible. Because the OT is historically the strongest counterpart of the NT it fits in well as the first part of the Christian Bible. It must be preserved by Christians as an eternal portrait of the legal religion which is

---

[6]WA, 14, 640, 24; 40, 3, 161ff. Cf. P. Althaus, "Gottes Gottheit als Sinn der Rechtfertigungslehre Luthers (vor allem exemplifiziert im Ersten Gebot)," *Theologische Aufsätze,* II (1935), pp. 1ff.; H. Bornkamm, *Luther und das AT* (1948), pp. 140ff.; E.T. *Luther and the OT* (Philadelphia, 1969).
[7]Preface to the OT.
[8]Sermon on John 1:1f. (WA, 10/I, 1, 181, 15; LW, 52, 41).

negated (and not just modified) in the gospel, and therefore as a spur to Christian self-understanding before God (p. 83).

To the degree that Calvin softens the antithesis between law and gospel the Testaments necessarily come closer to one another. Everything depends on keeping intact the relation between law and gospel which many have unthinkingly dissolved.[9]

The nature of this relation is important. The dialectic of law and gospel that we find in Luther is replaced by a relation of complementarity. Calvin speaks of an agreement between law and gospel. This can confirm faith in the gospel if we hear that the gospel is no other than a complement of the law, so that in mutual agreement they enable us to see God as their common author, and thus bear witness to the God of the old and new covenants in his identity. In this way the gospel is distinguished from the law, and the NT from the OT, only in a quantitative and not a qualitative way. The one is simply a literal teaching and the other a spiritual teaching. The one is simply carved on stone tablets, the other is written on the heart.[10]

Even when Calvin, quoting Scripture, has to speak of the qualitative difference between law and gospel, as when he says that the law preaches death and perdition but the gospel preaches life and righteousness (Inst., II, 11, 7), he still tends to give this a quantitative turn. The apparently negative definitions of the law do not mean that it is of lesser worth in the sense of having no positive effects. On the contrary it has a productive function. By pricking the conscience it forces the people of the old covenant to look to the gospel for refuge (II, 11, 9). The law did not thrust them into despair but produced a holy unrest which opened them up to the gospel. To that extent it is the backward shadow of the gospel. It disposes us to receive it. Law and gospel, then, are logically related. The law has a demonstrable teleological purpose.

A purely quantitative difference may be seen also in the fact that the gospel is seen only in part in the law and therefore needs to be supplemented. For although the law has evangelical content, it does not achieve the fulness of the gospel, which gives full and exclusive grace and comfort. The unconditionality of the antithesis of law and gospel is thus relativized. We are left with a mere comparison. While the two confront each other as death and life, the fulness of grace in the gospel is clarified by its particular nature in the law. The quantitative aspect is that law and gospel are related to one another as the totality of grace is to a part. There is no longer contradiction between them but dissimilitude (II, 11, 7–8). The quantitative relation that arises is perspicuous, calculable, and teleologically determined.

As seen in this way, the difference between letter and spirit, or law and gospel, is for Calvin the difference between the Testaments too. The distinction between old and new is relativized along the same lines. The new thing in the new covenant is no longer totally new. It is simply a development of what God's primal decrees (that played so big a role in later Calvinism) had contained from the very first and

---

[9]*Harmony of the Gospels* (1555) on Matthew 5:17 (CR, LXXIII, pp. 170f.; E.T. p. 180). The quotations that follow are taken from this passage unless otherwise noted.
[10]Inst., II, 11, 7.

of what had been disclosed in part prior to the opening up of the whole fulness of grace. Instead of a line of salvation history which leads to really new points we seem to have here the graphic picture of two concentric circles. The smaller, particular circle simply extends its radius. It may look as though something new comes. In fact, however, we simply have the making present of something that was contained already in the past age of law. We are not to infer from the difference between letter and spirit that the Lord gave his law to the Jews unprofitably, as though there were in it no possibility of their turning to him. The difference is simply a comparison that is designed to commend the riches of the grace with which the same Lawgiver has honored the preaching of the gospel, as though he had put on a new person (II, 11, 8).

Now other traditions, e.g., the Lutheran, do not contest the identity of the Father of Jesus Christ in both Testaments. Yet we must not miss the special nuance in Calvin. Here, too, the "as though" which presents God as a new person in the new covenant relates to the difference between the Testaments. The NT simply seems to be a new one but in fact is only a development of the OT. What is in Luther only an occasional extreme formulation (e.g., that the closed letter of the OT is merely opened in the NT but is the same letter with the same message) becomes in Calvin an axiom which decisively determines the whole relation between law and gospel. This teleological relation between law and gospel, and therefore between the OT and the NT, is adopted and radicalized by Karl Barth. The law lies in the ark and therefore serves the promise of the covenant of grace (cf. "Evangelium und Gesetz," ThEx, XXXII; CD, I,2, pp. 76ff., 310ff.). We must be content here simply to refer to our explicit discussion of the positions of Barth and Calvin in ThE, I, §§594ff.; E.T. I, pp. 100ff.

We may sum up as follows the difference between Luther and Calvin in their relating of the Testaments from the angle of law and gospel.

Calvin finds in the law and gospel coordinated parts of the one will of God which we may know as such. He thus starts with the master concept of a Word of God which is then subdivided as law and gospel but which is in itself *beyond* both.

When I say that it is beyond both, I am alluding to H. Iwand's criticisms of Barth's CD, I under the title "Jenseits von Gesetz und Evangelium?" ThBl, III–IV (1935), pp. 65ff. Iwand here puts Barth in the Calvinist tradition. In contrast Luther contested the proposed teleological relating of law and gospel because this opposes the elenchtic use of the law (softening it with the happy ending of the gospel) and in so doing robs the gospel of its point, namely, that of being God's gracious turning to us with *no* legal conditions. For this reason law and gospel cannot be regarded as interrelated and demonstrably complementary parts of the one Word of God as a master-concept. The difference between them neither can nor may be logically transcended if the bearing of both is not to be lost. We do not and we should not know how the two go together. Only the Holy Spirit can see this. As Luther says in his 1531 Table Talks (WA Tischreden, II, 1234; LW, 54, 127, No. 1234), no one on earth can distinguish between law and gospel (in the sense of being able to show their teleological relation). Only the Holy Spirit knows how to do this. Christ the man failed to do it on the Mount of Olives, so that an angel had to comfort him. And he was a teacher from heaven. I thought I could do it because I wrote so long and so much about it. But when it comes to the point,

I see that I failed by a long way. God alone must be the most holy Master (i.e., because he alone knows how to relate law and gospel).

Luther himself had to enter into debate with Carlstadt precisely because a perspicuous relating of law and gospel, or law and grace, underlay the latter's defection to the radicals. This was influenced by Augustine's definition of the relation, namely, that law is given in order that we might seek grace and grace is given in order that we might fulfil the law (*De spiritu et littera*, XIX, 14). Cf. B. Lohse, "Luther und der Radikalismus," *Luther-Jahrbuch* (1977), p. 13; also "Die Bedeutung Augustins für den jungen Luther," *Kerygma und Dogma* (1965), pp. 116ff.

Calvin, unlike Luther, starts with the Word of God as something beyond law and gospel. He thus finds in law and gospel only different modes of dispensing the one Word—a secondary phenomenon. As a result the old and the new covenants are close to each other. The one bears especially the sign of law and the other that of gospel, but this is no longer a fundamental distinction. Both are marked by the identity of the one Word of God and differ only in its administration. The new covenant is not fundamentally new but simply a new stage in the unfolding of one and the same primal decree.

In contrast Luther starts with the given antithesis of law and gospel. In other words, he starts with the gospel as the actual, nondeducible miracle that saves us from the judgment of the law. Just because this is a miracle he has to refrain from demonstrating the teleological relations between law and gospel as a presupposition for deducing the new from the old. The identity of the author of law and gospel is an item of faith but it cannot be seen and is not meant to be seen. The same applies to the identity of God in the old covenant and the new.

2. THE OLD TESTAMENT: ONLY A REPRESENTATIVE OF THE LAW?

The Calvinist line in relation to the OT, for all the reservations about it that we have just listed, does contain one element of truth. The OT law cannot be understood merely as a negative counterpart of the gospel, even though it cannot be identified with it either.[11] Moses, when he receives the new tablets of the law, calls God "a merciful and gracious God, slow to anger, and abounding in steadfast love and faithfulness" (Exodus 34:6f.; cf. Psalm 103:8ff.). The revelation granted to Moses relates from the very first to Yahweh's saving acts (Psalm 103:8) which cause him to stay close to the guilty in spite of every failure to meet his demands (v. 9). This is all grounded in the covenant faithfulness of Yahweh and his constant readiness to save (1 Samuel 12:7; Micah 6:5; Jeremiah 3:12).[12] The covenant of Yahweh is the seal of his prevenient grace which precedes the claim of the law and underlies it.

From this standpoint one can indeed say that even in the OT the gospel has

---

[11] Luther, as we have seen, finds in the OT not only law but gospel too (in the form of grace and forgiveness). But the two are distinct here too. His attitude to the law of Moses shows that he does not find grace *in* the law but *in opposition to* it (in a divine Nevertheless).

[12] H. J. Kraus, *Psalmen* (1960), p. 703.

primacy over the law and the law, to use Barth's figure of speech, is laid up in the ark. But we can say this only with the limitation that the gospel that may be heard in the OT is bound to the condition of fulfilment of the law.[13] Certainly covenant grace is prevenient. But it comes into effect only when the covenant is ratified in the form of human obedience. This "when" is the condition for the coming into force of the covenant (Exodus 19:5; Deuteronomy 7:9, 12). Those addressed, as the many testimonies to remorse and repentance illustrate, are tied to their status as sinners and are thus commended to the mercy of God. Their longing, as it were, is that Yahweh's covenant will not be broken by their guilt. This differentiates them from the Gentiles and permits them to stand under the rainbow of reconciliation.

It is precisely at this point that the difference between the old and the new covenants is plain. The radical nature of the understanding of sin and grace in the NT leads to a qualitatively different situation before God. In the OT sin seems to be the sum of individual acts which are set under a positive sign. He who confesses himself to be a sinner is in status one who "fears God," separated from the ungodly by a great gulf (e.g., Psalm 14:1-7). This distinction falls to the ground, however, once sin, as in Paul (Romans 3:10-18), is seen as the sign of our whole status and not just of sinful acts. This radicalizing of the understanding of sin enables Paul to find in the witness of Psalm 14:1-7 a reference to the status of sin which the passage did not originally have (Romans 3:10). There is now no distinction; all are sinners (Romans 3:23; 10:12).

This ends any possibility of the gracious condescension of God being tied to the condition of fulfilment of the law. Such a possibility cannot be realized. Also entailed is a radicalizing of the understanding of grace. Grace is now man's unconditional acceptance. When the prodigal returns home from the far country he does not have to prove first that he will be accepted by his father. He is received at once with no conditions. The debt is paid. The note of indebtedness has been fixed to the cross (Colossians 2:14; Ephesians 2:14-16).

Yet it would be a mistake, or at least imprecise, if we were to interpret the qualitatively new thing of the gospel in such a way as to regard the radicalized and unconditional understanding of grace as a consequence of the radicalized understanding of sin. The reverse is true. The extent to which we are sinners is made clear to us in this radicalized way by the gospel. We are all sinners who do *not* live by grace, who are our own lords, who trust in our own wisdom (Romans 1:21-23). The deepest sin, related to our status, is not that we refuse a law but that we refuse a gift, the mercy of God.[14] Grace must have primacy if we want to understand the new thing of the NT, even the new thing of the NT understanding of sin.

This new thing—grace radically understood—may be seen in another broad difference that separates the Testaments. For this grace is a creative power. It does not just cover transgressions (Psalm 32:1; 85:3; Romans 4:7). It fashions a new heart and true repentance. This leads to a reversing of the old relations. The repentance and conversion of the righteous are no longer the condition of God's

---

[13]Cf. the statement of E. Hirsch that in the law grace and forgiveness stand under legal conditions.
[14]At *this* point Thomas Müntzer possibly had a correct insight when in *Protestation oder Erbietung* he said that in the gospel Christ by his kindness seriously declared the kindness of the Father (B. Lohse, "Luther und der Radikalismus," *Luther-Jahrbuch* [1977], p. 19).

covenant grace coming into force. Grace leads on to repentance and true fear of God (2 Corinthians 7:10). It makes us friends and doers of the law, as Augustine says.[15]

3. THE SPIRIT OF GOD AS THE BRACKET AROUND BOTH TESTAMENTS

The basis of sin and the goal of its conquest, of course, are at least indicated in the OT, especially when we think of the Deuteronomic tradition, the Torah as we find it not merely in the last book of the Pentateuch but also in post-exilic psalms and prophetic utterances.[16]

The ultimate basis of sin is the deceitfulness and darkness of the human heart and its estrangement from God. It thus develops, as we would say today, out of a personal center. "The sin of Judah is written with a pen of iron; with a point of diamond it is engraved on the tablet of their heart" (Jeremiah 17:1). "The heart is deceitful above all things, and desperately corrupt; who can understand it?" (17:9; cf. Genesis 6:5).

Hence the goal of the Torah is to start by changing this heart, which can only mean taking possession of it and writing its own words in it instead of sin (Deuteronomy 6:6). This involves the most inward form of appropriation, so that the will of God becomes man's second nature and determines his motivation. The prophetic promise of the renewal of the covenant points in this direction. This renewal is meant to bring about a change of heart. It seems to be characteristic that what is in view is not an intensified preaching of the law which will hammer home God's will on the heart but renewal by the offering of covenant grace and the gift of the Spirit (Jeremiah 31:33f.).

Here already the pardoning grace of the covenant which no longer remembers sin is not tied to legal conditions, to the achievement of obedience to the law. The very opposite is true. God's turning in the new covenant which renews the heart gives rise to conformity with God's will and thus leads to a new spontaneity in observance of the law. The law that is written in the heart strives against that which is carved on tablets and no longer feels it to be the dictate of a command that comes from outside and above. Thus people become lovers of the law, as Augustine puts it later. The external law loses its function, as it were, in this eschatological promise. The demand that one should know the Lord becomes superfluous, for this knowledge will already dwell in the heart. How can one be asked to admit what is already inside?

What is described here as the new spontaneity of faith and the result of the new grace of the covenant is in the most meaningful sense the same as what met us earlier as the testimony of the Holy Spirit. We have here, indeed, the eschatological promise of the Spirit as Ezekiel explicitly formulated it in adoption and development of the oracle of Jeremiah: "A new heart will I give you and a new spirit I will put within you; and I will take out of your flesh the heart of stone and give

---

[15]Ernest Kähler, *Karlstadt und Augustin. Der Kommentar Karlstadts zu Augustins Schrift "De spiritu et littera"* (Halle, 1952), p. 25.
[16]On what follows cf. H. J. Kraus, *Biblisch-theologische Aufsätze* (1972), pp. 179ff.

you a heart of flesh. And I will put my spirit within you and cause you to walk in my statutes and be careful to observe my ordinances'' (36:26f.).

What is seen here from afar in the form of promise, but cannot be expressed and prophesied in the ''how'' of its fulfilment, finds this fulfilment in the new covenant and the imparting of the Spirit of Jesus. This is how the NT understands it. Those who have received the promised Spirit know what is given to us by God (1 Corinthians 2:12). They are taken out of the situation of the natural man who knows nothing about the Spirit of God and who therefore experiences the will of this God only as claim and counterclaim (2:14). They are taken out of the servant-relation to God and set by Christ in the relation of children in which they cry ''Abba, Father'' and live in unity with the Father's will (Romans 8:15; Galatians 4:6).

In the promise of Ezekiel, then, one may see in outline the gates to a kingdom of freedom, to a kingdom in which the law of God no longer provokes resistance as a will that is alien to our own (Romans 7:11; Hebrews 3:15f.), but in which the Spirit of God dwells in us and our heart forms a bridgehead where God rules. In Jesus Christ this promise of freedom, of the new spontaneity, is fulfilled. Here if anywhere the Testaments are close together.

Now there can be no doubt that the Torah is already aiming at this renewal of the heart and is not content with the role of being an external authority of the letter. Even if the goal is not set so fully as in the promises of Jeremiah and Ezekiel, the renewal of the heart is already seen to be present as a first instalment or deposit wherever there is reference to delight in the law, or praise of it as a gift that is more precious than gold and sweeter than honey (Psalm 19:8–11; Psalm 119). The only way to understand the love of the law that is dominant here is to see that the Pneuma—in Ezekiel's sense—has already begun to take possession of the heart. The Spirit of God at whose impartation the Torah aims is thus the decisive bracket around the law and the gospel, around the promise and the fulfilment, and consequently around the two Testaments themselves.

This bracket stands out the more clearly because one may see also a first indication of the desecularization which Bultmann calls the mark of NT eschatology and which he denies to the OT, although less categorically in relation to Jeremiah and Ezekiel.[17] Desecularization comes to expression in the impossibility of regarding the historical people of Israel as a whole as the subject of these joyful testimonies or objects of the eschatological promise of the Spirit. More and more in the Deuteronomic period *individual* address and *confession* become the rule (Psalm 1; 19; 119). The relation of God and people is increasingly replaced by the I-Thou relation between God and the righteous individual within this people.

The special situation of Israel is undoubtedly at stake in and after the exile. The historically developed structure of the people is shattered. Yet it would be a mistake to explain the increasing accent on the individual purely in genetic terms or in terms of historical evolution. What takes place historically with the exile is more of a trigger. If it is true that the Torah is not just an external letter but pierces the heart and seeks to bring about renewal, then personal decision is demanded and a tendency toward individualism is introduced. Here is the first movement toward a new history of God's people, which presses beyond its identity with historical

---

[17] *Glauben und Verstehen,* II, pp. 174f.

Israel and according to the words of Jesus will find recruits among those who come from the east and the west and will recline at table with Abraham, Isaac, and Jacob in the kingdom of heaven, while the children of the kingdom will be cast into outer darkness (Matthew 8:11f.).

Emphasis on the individual in his relation to God means emphasis on a Thou to Thou relation toward God. But this is possible only if the *nomos,* as in the Torah-psalms, is not isolated as letter, nor objectified, nor detached from God. It is possible only if the *nomos* allows us to see through it the author of the law and the heart of God which turns to the petitioner. There is awareness that the point of the address is its author and that I must grasp him as a Thou. A sign of this is the recurrent Thou of the second person. We have to do with ''the torah of *thy* mouth'' (Psalm 119:72). ''I do not forget *thy* torah'' (119:61, 109). ''Graciously teach me *thy* torah'' (119:29).

The Torah is not, then, a stone tablet which gets between God and the righteous. Instead of blocking access to God it opens it up.[18] Only in the framework of a Thou to Thou relation to God can there be an anticipation of what the promise of the Spirit in Ezekiel declares for the future, namely, that the law has already seized the heart and that the spontaneity of the children of God is already present. ''I delight to do thy will, O my God; thy law is within my heart'' (Psalm 40:8).[19] Here the psalmist is already coming under the shadow of the new covenant.

Kraus points out why we can speak only of the shadow of the new covenant. In the Fourth Apocalypse of Esdras (9:36) we are told that because of our sins we who have received the Torah will perish with the heart in which it is set, though the Torah itself will not perish but will remain in its glory. The Torah is in our hearts but we are still aware of faults that cause us to perish. Thus the relation between Torah and heart is ambivalent. The Torah aims at the heart and the heart has received it. But the two are seen to be different. The heart cannot overcome its guilt and perishes. The Torah remains in its glory (Kraus, p. 190).

The light of reconciliation with God had shed some of its rays on some people who with their delight in the law seemed to anticipate the promise of Jeremiah and Ezekiel. But this light had not yet become definitive. It does so only with him who is the light of the world (John 8:12; 9:5) and who lightens the darkness once and for all (John 1:5; cf. also 2 Corinthians 4:16; Ephesians 5:6; 1 Peter 2:9). Previously the shadow of death persists. But so long as it still lies over the devout of the old covenant, the psalmist can only wait for the promise of Ezekiel and pray to God that he will bring about what none of us can give to ourselves, a pure heart in which God's Spirit is not just present erratically but which cannot retain this Spirit itself (Psalm 51:10f.). The righteous in Israel still do not have what the reconciliation of the new covenant will bring. They live still in anticipation.

4. THE GOSPEL AS THE DISSOLUTION AND FULFILMENT OF THE OLD TESTAMENT LAW

With all this we have already said implicitly how the gospel presupposes, dissolves, and fulfils the message of the OT. We can now sum this up thematically.

---

[18]Kraus, *Biblisch-theologische Aufsätze,* p. 187.

[19]Cf. the exposition of this in Barth, CD, II,2, pp. 604ff.

1. In the gospel there is fulfilled that which was only promise in the prophecy of Jeremiah and Ezekiel and which still lay in twilight[20] in its limited and sporadic individual fulfilments. Whereas we read in 4 Esdras that we can perish because of the superior power of sin, though the glory of the Torah remains, a decisive nuance may be seen in the new covenant: Though we may perish under the accusation of conscience, the gospel remains. The fundamental difference between the two statements is plain when we realize that the Torah that remains in its glory accuses the heart that is unfaithful to it and thus confirms its lostness, but the gospel that remains in spite of the accusation of conscience deprives the denunciation of guilt of its power to destroy us and to take away the peace of God. ''If our hearts condemn us, God is greater than our hearts'' (1 John 3:20). The debt has been definitively attached to the cross (Colossians 2:14). Nothing can now separate us from the love which is in Christ Jesus (Romans 8:38f.).

Luther, who also alludes to 1 John 3:20, deals with this radical change in his Romans Commentary (LW, 25, 188f.). Christ takes to himself my whole burden and makes his righteousness mine. Whereas under the law God is the accuser and conscience the defender (*Deus accusator, cor defensor*), the opposite is true under the gospel. Here my conscience accuses me but God is greater than my heart and becomes defender (*cor accusator, Deus defensor*).

2. The God who is manifested in Christ shows himself to be one who loves us unconditionally. Jesus leaves us in no doubt as to the identity of his Father with the God of the OT. There is no occasion for a Marcionite distinction between two gods. What distinguishes the once and the now of the gospel is rather the way in which the coming of Jesus has removed the cover (2 Corinthians 3:14–16) under which it was previously concealed, so that it is now declared in a manner that is astonishingly new. The cover consisted of the conditions that partially hid its merciful address and allowed us only to hope for the definitiveness of unbroken reconciliation. This definitiveness came with the self-offering of Christ. Whereas for Moses the manifestation of God was fearful so that he had to cry out: ''I tremble with fear,'' ''*you*''—the people of the new covenant—''have come to Mount Zion, and to the city of the living God, the heavenly Jerusalem, and to innumerable angels in festal gathering, and to the assembly of the first-born who are enrolled in heaven, and to the spirits of just men made perfect, and to Jesus, the mediator of a new covenant, and to the sprinkled blood that speaks more graciously than the blood of Abel'' (Hebrews 12:21–24).

The unconditionality of the love that we experience in the gospel summons us, too, into the freedom to be able to love (1 John 4:19) and therefore to fulfil the law. If the Torah simply aimed at the heart and sought to be appropriated by it, Christ has now appropriated us. And if love is the fulfilment of the law (Romans 13:10), the gospel grants us this fulfilment. The heart that is freed to love is really the new heart for which the Torah-psalms prayed. For love does not have to be commanded

---

[20]The twilight is that of the threat of new separation from God, a new staining of the clean or cleansed heart (Psalm 51). Thus the psalmist prays always for new reconciliation. This reminds us of the interpretation of the OT situation in Hebrews. In the old covenant the sacrifice had to be constantly repeated but Christ's offering of himself has brought about a reconciliation that is once and for all.

any more. It is an expression of the spontaneity of our hearts which see themselves impelled toward God in reaction to his movement toward us.

We have already referred to the classic formulation of this new element in the Apology for the Augsburg Confession. As God's righteousness has two sides in Paul and Luther, denoting both God's making righteous and our being made righteous, so it is with God's love. The genitive here is both subjective and objective. As God loves us in Christ he is worthy of our love and we love him. When God loves we apprehend his mercy by faith and he thus becomes a lovable object (LBK, pp. 185,55–186,2; Tappert, p. 125).

3. The gospel grants us immediacy to God (which the Torah was striving after with its Thou to Thou relation, its reflecting of the author of the law, and its directing of the renewed heart to him). The radical nature of this immediacy, and therefore of the presence of God, radicalizes also his requirements. These are not limited to the letter but bring out in extreme form the alienation of the people of this aeon from the manifested majesty of God (Matthew 15:18f.). They are not according to the world. They do not relate to the radius of action which is attainable for our activity within secular structures. They are according to the kingdom of God. They are eschatological. To that extent the radicalized commands of the Sermon on the Mount treat us as though we were still in the original paradisal state before the fall[21] and as though the eschaton of the kingdom of God were already present in fulness.

Although the gospel seems in this way to complete the OT and to continue some basic themes in its understanding of the law, there is also a total change. The radicalizing of the Mosaic *nomos* does not lead to enhanced fear, as it would have to do if seen in isolation, but things are now seen against the background of an accomplished reconciliation. The overture is the repeated "Blessed are . . ." (Matthew 5:3–12). The storm of the broken relation to God is seen from the sheltering harbor. It is only a backward look to a situation from which we have now been rescued. As those who were far away from God we have now been brought near by the death of Christ (Ephesians 2:13). We are blessed as those for whom there can be no accusation in the shelter of his peace (2:14). The Beatitudes of the Sermon on the Mount are in this sense a pre-form of what the Preacher did by his death.

A final question must be answered as we look back on the way that we have come. It is the question whether Pauline theology understands the OT law properly in presenting it as a counterpart of the gospel. We believe, indeed OT scholars have taught us, that there may be found in the Torah many features which point to the NT rather than the Talmud and hold evangelical contents, at least in shadowy prototype. Is not this character of the law as promise concealed in Paul when he sees in it only the elements of accusation and judgment? Somewhat epigrammatically, we might even ask, Whose understanding of the law is correct, that of Paul or that of the modern OT scholar?

Paul's understanding of the *nomos* does not really characterize the understanding of the law in the OT but only the specific possibility of a rigidity of the letter

---

[21]Cf. what Jesus says about divorce. It did not exist in the beginning before the spoiling of creation but arose because of the hardness of heart (*sklērokardia*) of fallen humanity (Matthew 19:8).

which is contrary to the immediacy of the relation to God that is imparted to faith. This rigidity is not inherent in the law, for as God's demand it is holy, just, and good (Romans 7:12, 14). It comes upon the law through human sin. The flesh attacks the spirit and sin triumphs (7:13f.). Man seizes the law and makes of it a legalism that is opposed to the will of God. But this process is by no means confined to the OT. It may be seen in many forms in the morality of the natural man. Within Christianity it can corrupt and misuse the gospel and produce the very opposite of faith. It was because Luther saw this danger that he regarded the right distinction of law and gospel as the criterion of Christian theology and viewed the mixing of the two as a surrender of the doctrine of justification.

For Paul legalistic perversion could be seen especially in the assumption of many believers that the status of justification meant freedom to sin and dissolved all commitment to the author of the law (Romans 6:1, 15).

In Lutheranism, as Luther saw already and often warned against, legalism may be seen in the surreptitious making of faith into a meritorious work instead of understanding it as a response to God's offer of grace (cf. on this EG, II, pp. 44, 53; EF, II, pp. 34, 44f.). It may also be seen in the treating of faith as something to be tasted and felt, so that instead of grasping the grace that is outside us it curves in upon itself (Schott, *Fleisch und Geist nach Luthers Lehre* [1928], pp. 9ff., 44).

Along similar lines one might see some kind of slide into legalism in all Christian confessions and theological schools. It might also be noted that the legalistic Christian is everywhere found to be unattractive as a type. Not merely if not least in the sects, he may be recognized by his adoption of negative criteria for defining Christians (not smoking, drinking, dancing, etc.) and also by his inclination toward bigotry and hypocrisy in order to present the required image of sanctity.

In this sense we do not have in Paul a historical interpretation of the OT understanding of the law. Seeing Paul historically we should have to accuse him of extreme one-sidedness, since there is no single OT understanding of the law but a broad spectrum. When Paul sees the law as a foil for the gospel, his concern is not to give a historical portrait of the Mosaic *nomos* but to offer a systematic presentation of the basic phenomenon of legalism. For this he can provide paradigms which derive from some understandings of the law and which are actually present among those with whom he has to deal in his letters. The backward reference to the Mosaic *nomos* has, then, the special function of making it plain that those whom he addresses are in danger of sinking back into a state from which the gospel has delivered them. They are "reactionary" (Galatians 3:1ff.; 4:8ff.).

5. SUMMARY

We recall in what context the question of the understanding of the OT arose.

We are thinking about the "material principle," i.e., the question how far the OT promotes Christ, how far the Word incarnate in Christ forms the hermeneutical key to what encounters us in the old covenant as the Word of God.

The decisive questions by which we let ourselves be led were as follows. How far does the OT have the character of promise and how far is it fulfilled in the gospel? In what relation does the gospel stand to the law of the covenant? How far is the OT to be understood as a legal religion?

To answer these questions it seemed essential first to realize that for the NT the identity of God persists in the two Testaments. The Father of Jesus Christ is the one who encounters the people of the old covenant as Yahweh. We had also to remember and establish, second, that the promise is to be understood in the light of the fulfilment, the Word of the old covenant in the light of the personal Word of God in the figure of Jesus. The reverse attempt to reach the NT by way of the salvation event of the OT is an impossible one. As Judaism shows, it can end only in the Talmud and not the NT.

For the relation of promise and fulfilment this means first (1) that there is no equality of the two covenants as though God's final Word were already in the OT but becomes plain (noetically) only in the new covenant. (We remember the problem which arises when we try to picture the OT as a closed letter which contains the whole of God's message but is only opened in the gospel.)

It means further (2) that the way from promise to fulfilment must not be taken to mean that we have an evolution—as Hofmann saw it under Hegel's influence—which leads on to the gospel in such a way that this is simply the final climax and consummation of what is contained in the preceding prefigurations and prophecies.

On the contrary, God's own Word in the gospel brings a new thing which could not be postulated and which in retrospect sets the Testaments in a unique relation of continuity and discontinuity. When Paul calls the gospel the *telos* of the law (*telos nomou,* Romans 10:4), the word *telos* suggests both goal and end. In the sense of goal it honors the character of the law as promise and concedes to it elements which already contain that which is to come. In the sense of end the law is abolished as outdated and has to yield to what is new; it is obsolete. The new begins where the old ends (Hebrews 8:13).

It is because of this dialectic of continuity and discontinuity that the NT can refer back to the OT and understand it as promise but can also claim the freedom that is proper to the stage of fulfilment in relation to these earlier stages: The Son of man is lord even of the sabbath and the sabbath commandments (Mark 2:23–28; Luke 14:1–6). The repeated "But I say unto you . . ." radicalizes the Mosaic *nomos,* takes it up, fulfils it, yet also stands in antithesis to it (Matthew 5:21ff.). It is the same God but he comes to us in a wholly new way. We have noted the same ambivalence of adopting and abolishing in Hebrews.

As regards the relation of law and gospel the result is that the OT is not just law in the elenchtic sense but has evangelical contents as well. The author of the law is also the forgiving and faithful God. This God says to the apostate people and individuals: "Yet I will be with you always. . . ." This forgiveness, however, is always under the conditions of the law, whereas the gospel brings unconditionally God's turning to us and thus makes possible an unconditional response of love which brings about the fulfilment of the law by love (Romans 13:10).

When Luther said that the OT is God's Word to the extent that it promotes Christ—the material principle—this cannot mean that we may find Christ himself in the OT (W. Vischer). It means that when we look back from the gospel associations arise which bring to light the shadow of good things to come and enable us to see their prefiguration (Hebrews 10:1; Ephesians 1:3). In this backward glance those who are under the gospel can be sure that it is the same God who freed Israel from slavery in Egypt and in Christ redeems us from slavery to sin, who spoke provisionally in the OT and then by his presence in Christ spoke once-for-all and definitively.[22] It is the same Spirit of God who before the beginning of creation hovered over the primal waters (Genesis 1:2), came upon God's people in the old covenant (Numbers 24:2; Judges 3:10; 1 Samuel 19:20, 23, etc.), and then as the Paraclete of the new covenant was manifested in the outpouring of Pentecost and as the power of participation in the self-knowledge of God (1 Corinthians 2:10f.). On every hand, both in the old covenant and the new, he is a Spirit of promise, a first instalment and deposit of that which is to come. In this sense even the fulfilment of the new covenant is a new promise of that which is still ahead eschatologically.[23] In his identity, the Spirit has different stages and forms. He is both prophecy of future fulfilments and also new prophecy in enacted fulfilments. In both forms he embraces both the old and the new covenants, now as faith and one day as sight.

To speak fully about the way in which the OT and NT are related, we should have to deal with letter and spirit as well as promise and fulfilment and law and gospel. Cf. the discussion of this aspect in EF, I, c. X.

---

[22]Pöhlmann, *Abriss der Dogmatik*, p. 52.
[23]We have already dealt with this kind of prophecy in Jeremiah and Ezekiel. In the NT the words *aparchē* and *arrabōn* express the prophetic character of the impartation of the Spirit (cf. Romans 8:23; 1 Corinthians 1:22; 5:5; Ephesians 1:14.

XII

The Establishment of the Authority of Scripture by the Doctrine of Verbal Inspiration

Sources: A. Calov, *Systema locorum theologicorum* (1655ff.), I, pp. 528ff.; J. Gerhard, *Loci communes theologici* (1610ff.), II, pp. 13ff.; C. A. Hase, *Hutterus redivivus,* 5th ed. (1842), pp. 38–49; D. Hollaz, *Examen theologicum acroaticum,* 8th ed. (1763), pp. 83ff.; F. Pieper, *Christian Dogmatics,* ed. J. T. Mueller (St. Louis, 1934), pp. 90–142, esp. pp. 101ff.

Secondary Literature: G. Ebeling, "Die Bedeutung der historisch-kritischen Methode für die protestantische Theologie und Kirche," *Wort und Glaube,* I (1960), pp. 1ff.; E.T. *Word and Faith,* pp. 17ff.; C. H. Ratschow, *Lutherische Dogmatik zwischen Reformation und Aufklärung,* I (1964), pp. 77f.; H. Thielicke, *Gespräche über Himmel und Erde,* 2nd ed. (1965); E.T. *Between Heaven and Earth* (New York, 1965); arts. on "Inspiration" in RE, IX, pp. 183ff.; RGG³, 775ff.; *Handbuch theologischer Grundbegriffe,* 2nd ed. (1974), pp. 354ff.

In the Lutheran and Reformed orthodoxy of the 17th and 18th centuries—and still today in some denominations[1]—the doctrine of verbal inspiration is designed to offer certain forms of legalistic security. This is shown by the historical process whereby the concept of inspiration came to move away from the imparting of the Spirit to persons and to focus on the divine authorship of the letter.

In the doctrine of Scripture in earlier phases of Lutheran orthodoxy, e.g., in Gerhard and Calixtus, there was little emphasis on a doctrine of verbal inspiration. A distinction was still made here between inspiration, which relates to the truths of salvation, and divine direction, which applies in matters that are not generally accessible to sense and reason. We thus have an understanding of the Bible which presupposed a readiness to use hermeneutical criteria and to seek inspired contents

---

[1]Cf. especially the fundamentalism of the Missouri Synod and the rift in 1973 between President J. A. O. Preus and J. Tietjen, the former President of Concordia Seminary.

in Scripture. But this sublime differentiation between degrees of authority was increasingly felt to be an element of insecurity and triggered a need for a more legally unequivocal position and a (supposedly) impregnable definition of the authority of the Bible. This goal was thought to have been attained with the formulation of the dogma of plenary inspiration and the removal of all differentiation in authority.

Along these lines Calov argued that there is no word in Scripture which was not divinely suggested to the authors and therefore inspired. This could not be unequivocally maintained, however, so long as it was assumed that even the tiniest part of the Bible derived from human knowledge, memory, or discovery, whether or not an element of divine direction was also presupposed.

What we see here is a need to establish Scripture which does not dare any longer to seek God's Word in it with the help of the testimony of the Holy Spirit but in the passive attitude of a consumer wants to find God's Word in book form. This need has important implications. For Baier, Hollaz, and Quenstedt the authors of the Bible are not people who presume to allocate to the divine content only such words as they have sought out according to their judgment. Instead it was proper for them to follow the dictation of the Holy Spirit. They did not distinguish between what they thought was inspired and what they and their age contributed (cf. 1 Corinthians 7:10, 25, 40) but regarded themselves as passive objects of a dictation which made the Holy Spirit the author of Scripture.

This starting point led ineluctably to further consequences. Even the choice of words could no longer be individual but was ascribed to the Spirit's dictation. Thus Quenstedt could say that if the authors used these phrases or words and not others, this was solely due to divine impulsion and inspiration.[2]

Naturally, too, the Holy Spirit could not be charged with linguistic barbarisms. An attempt was made, then, to say that what seems to be common idiom is popular speech in the best sense and accords with the genius of the Greek language.[3] The Reformed theologians Johann Buxtorf senior and junior—there was no generation gap here—could even claim that the vowel points were inspired, as did Gisbertus Voetius.

Voetius did find two degrees of authority, historical and normative. But he regarded all Scripture as authentic on account of its historical authenticity. The Bible contains inerrant inspired truth in all its parts, each statement being made, not by personal impulse or choice, but at the dictation of the Holy Spirit, both in content and in phrasing. The only exceptions are some private utterances and instructions of the prophets and apostles which do not serve to teach. The vowel points, being inspired, are part of authoritative Scripture (*Selectae Disputationes theologiae* [1648ff.], I, pp. 30ff., esp. p. 33, quoted in H. Heppe, *Reformed Dogmatics* [London, 1950], p. 27).

The strength of this need for security is shown by the inability of historico-critical research either to soften the doctrine of verbal inspiration in some denominations and sects or to open up to them the concept of the historicity of revelation

---

[2]Although most of the time we find differentiation in Luther, he, too, could occasionally speak along similar lines; cf. his Commentary on Psalm 127:3 (1533–34) (WA, 40/III, 254).

[3]Pieper, *Christian Dogmatics*, p. 121.

and its written testimonies. Indeed, the opposite reaction may be noted. The historical analysis of the texts of Scripture, being felt to be a threat, has provoked a stronger defensive movement and an increased hardening, as may be seen in the Missouri Synod and especially in the scholastic dogmatics of Pieper.

Even historical, geographical, physical, and similar statements, which through astronomical research and the modern sense of history seem to have different degrees of authority and to oppose the levelling tendency of verbal inspiration, are placed expressly under the taboo of inspiration. There is, of course, a trace of differentiation here. It is not the real point of Scripture to teach such things. But incidentally, because God entered human history in his Word, historical observations occur in his Word, and these are inspired and infallible because they are part of Scripture.[4] Thus the full inerrancy of Scripture is maintained in all its words and parts.[5]

A fascinating witness to the consistent application of this view of inspiration may be seen in relation to the interpretation of OT passages in the NT. Naturally there can be no question of the hermeneutical technique of rabbinic exposition or of a modification of the words of promise by the corrective of the fulfilment. This would call in question the mechanism of verbal inspiration. No, in OT quotations the Holy Spirit is quoting himself and he has power and free control over his own words. Thus in expounding sayings from the OT he makes a new text out of them.[6]

There is here a strange ambivalence in the underlying pneumatology. On the one hand the older theologians cannot abandon the basic thought of the Bible that the Pneuma is a power that is granted to and fills the authors. Thus Quenstedt[7] emphasizes that there is no mechanical or impersonal dictation in which the authors write unwittingly and unwillingly. They render their service as authors with a full sense and understanding that they are writing God's Word.[8] But Pieper, who suspects even the mild criticism that "positive" theology brought against the doctrine of inspiration at the turn of the century, thinks he can see latent dangers in this kind of personal inspiration. With its help one might speak of certain time-bound statements and subjective limitations. Hence the whole system of verbal inspiration might be destroyed. The personal relation of the Spirit is reduced, then, and Pieper goes on to make the incredible statement that Holy Scripture, not the writers, is the object of inspiration. This is what is breathed by God according to 2 Timothy 3:16. To reject verbal inspiration in favor of an inspiration of the matter or persons is to deny the biblical doctrine of inspiration.[9]

We may summarize this understanding of the Spirit and of inspiration as follows.

1. The incarnation of the Word becomes its inscripturation.[10] The way from the

---

[4]Pieper, p. 104.

[5]*Ibid.*, p. 105.

[6]*Ibid.*, p. 118.

[7]*Systema,* I, pp. 57, 82ff.

[8]Pieper, p. 107.

[9]*Ibid.*, pp. 101f. One can imagine, and then see clearly in Pieper (pp. 116ff.), what reinterpretations are needed to make Luther the chief witness for this doctrine of inspiration.

[10]Pöhlmann, *Abriss der Dogmatik,* p. 46.

kerygma to Scripture, as a sign of the incarnation of the Word and its entrance into history, is reversed.

2. The Bible becomes the legalistic letter whose *a priori* recognition is the presupposition of hearing the gospel. There results an unholy mingling of law and gospel which misses the point of the new covenant. Even the need to distinguish law and gospel later, which is unavoidable if we follow Paul,[11] can no longer gain the mastery over legalism, since the presentation of the gospel has already been forced into a distorting legalistic framework.

3. The dominant pneumatology here is intolerably one-sided. The Holy Spirit simply has the function of mechanically directing a process of writing. He cannot agree that with the help of his testimony the authors have received the gift of discerning spirits and the right of criticism. Even less can this gift be conceded to those who read Holy Scripture so as to find in it what promotes Christ and makes it the authoritative Word of God.

---

[11]Pieper, pp. 44ff.

XIII

The Establishment of the Authority of Scripture by Historico-Critical Research

Discussions of the historico-critical investigation of Scripture do not usually occur under the heading of "The Establishment of the Authority of Scripture." There is instead an inclination to see in this activity an unsettling of faith. As its history shows, it has in fact shattered the idea that faith is self-evident. Within it (I need only mention Reimarus, quite apart from later figures) there has often been an unmistakable intention of radically challenging the credibility of the Bible. And when E. Troeltsch included among modern historical criteria for the verification of facts the principles of causality and analogy (i.e., non-uniqueness),[1] it is obvious that a transcendentally grounded salvation event cannot meet, or, better, remain outside, the resultant process of historical control.

At the same time it would be a mistake to think that the critical investigation of the Bible conducted by such theologians is dominated by these tendencies. Their positive intention is rather to establish how the biblical claim to truth can stand in a situation which is convinced of the historicity of this claim to truth and thus comes under the pressure of the relativism that this historicity entails. How can we still speak of the absolute in a world of relativities? This question was undoubtedly the main impulse behind the work of Troeltsch. To put the question of truth to the Bible under this pressure, certain preliminary questions have to be dealt with first.

To begin with, there are matters of textual criticism. We cannot accept the texts as they stand (as in the theory of verbal inspiration). We have to seek the original form of texts which have been much revised and worked over and altered by oral traditions.

Then there is the matter of understanding the original texts. What did they mean to say? Here we have to be ready to take a self-critical attitude to our own (dogmatic) presuppositions with which we usually approach the texts. Most readers of the Bible come with a fixed tradition of biblical understanding, e.g., in

---

[1]EG, II, pp. 342, 373, 380; EF, II, pp. 279, 303, 338.

relation to the messianic prophecies. We must be ready, then, to stop seeking self-confirmation by the biblical texts and instead accept their strangeness. If we dare to enter a zone of insecurity in this way, we can be governed by the motive of finding a solid and secure truth thereby. For we begin with the fact that God's truth—to the extent that it may be found—is a unique truth which gives the lie to the previous sense of truth, challenging the wisdom of the Greeks and the desire of the Jews for a sign by the theology of the cross (1 Corinthians 1 and 2).

This cannot mean, of course, that the openness of unprejudiced seeking for what is strange will necessarily find the truth of God. If we were right when in our doctrine of the Pneuma we said that God by the Spirit gives us a share in his self-knowledge, and that this is to be understood as revelation, there can be no autonomous or automatic form of finding. The point is rather that the testimony of the Holy Spirit uses this historico-critical confrontation with what is strange to make what is distant closer. The truth of God has not been seen by any eye nor has it entered any human heart. It is opened up by that testimony or it stays unrecognized. This applies also to the critical investigation of the biblical texts.

Finally, the question of fact—naturally—raises special problems in the historical analysis of the Bible. What basis of reality do the biblical records have in actual or supposed events? This is a particularly urgent question when we come to the historical Jesus.[2] Originally—from Reimarus to Harnack—the point was to establish the reality. There was a desire to strip away the additions and accretions of community tradition, to get back to the original Jesus, and to find the unshakable basis of faith in what he was and said. As Schweitzer pointed out, however, in his *Quest of the Historical Jesus,* this attempt to go back beyond the kerygma and to find the real historical facts was bound to fail. Quite apart from the shattering of the attempt by the element that is beyond our experience, and quite apart from the fact that after stripping away accretions we seem to be left with an eschatological ghost, a stranger, and an enigma[3] which blocks the historical detour to Jesus,[4] there is an insoluble methodological problem which Kähler has formulated most sharply. It would be absurd, he says, to base an unconditional faith on the conditionalities of an example of historical subtraction and to make it dependent on the good or bad judgment of historians and their constantly changing views (cf. M. Kähler, *Der sogenannte historische Jesus und der geschichtliche, biblische Christus,* 2nd ed. [1928], p. 4; E.T. *The So-Called Historical Jesus and the Historic, Biblical Christ* [Philadelphia, 1964]).

From this sceptical experience there developed later the thesis of Bultmann that the historical pre-Easter Jesus does not form the basis of our faith and that only with the post-Easter kerygma of the primitive community does theological thinking, the theology of the NT, begin.[5]

---

[2]Cf. EG, II, pp. 372ff.; EF, II, pp. 302ff.

[3]A. Schweitzer, *Geschichte der Leben-Jesu-Forschung,* 1st ed. (1892), p. 397; E.T. *Quest of the Historical Jesus* (London, 1910).

[4]*Ibid.,* p. 398.

[5]Bultmann, *Theologie des NT* (1953), p. 2; E.T. *NT Theology,* p. 3. For the later return of the Bultmann school to the question of the historical Jesus cf. Käsemann, *Exegetische Versuche . . . ,* I, pp. 187ff.; II, pp. 31ff.; H. Diem, *Dogmatik,* II (1955), pp. 120ff.; E.T. pp. 133ff.; W. Schmithals, *Die Theologie R. Bultmanns* (1966), pp. 200ff.; E.T. *An Introduction to the Theology of Rudolf Bultmann* (London, 1968), pp. 195ff.

If it can be said—and this is the prevailing view no matter how the problem of the historical Jesus is dealt with in detail—that the pre-Easter Jesus of Nazareth cannot be detached from the post-Easter Christ, a related thesis is that all the accounts of the historical life of Jesus took shape in retrospect, i.e., in the light of the faith of the post-Easter community, and that the contents of this faith have influenced the story of the earthly Jesus, being projected back into it. Hence the records are kerygmatic, not historical. The life of promise is recorded in terms of the fulfilment. If the record is a true interpretation of the promises, as we tried to show earlier; if the commitment of the (post-Easter) community obviously permits no other view; if, then, formally correct historical accounts with their objectivizing tendency would be totally inadequate, then we have discovered the theological reason why it is impossible to make a distinction between history and kerygma or the historical and the suprahistorical.[6]

But this raises with full urgency the question what theological function can historico-critical research fill in these circumstances by way of elucidation of the biblical texts. It cannot, by verifying the stories of miracles and the resurrection, provide a secure historical basis for faith. Nor can it take away the basis of faith by contesting the facts. It cannot do either of these things because we are not dealing here with historical facticity in the sense that Troeltsch, e.g., had in mind with his principles of verification. For it is obviously part of the nature of kerygmatic forms of statement that historical records of this kind are permeated by nonhistorical factors in the presentation of events and the recording of the sayings of Jesus—factors which expressed the understanding of faith to which the community attained in the light of the Easter experience of Jesus and his mission as the Christ.[7]

Does this mean that in the strict sense historical inquiry is pointless? The dilemma that seems to confront us here may be stated as follows. If we fail to put the historical question at all, Christ becomes a mythologoumenon, a personified idea, and we fall into the docetic error. But if we do, we reach the dead-end that the historical information enables us to see only a man who is stripped of all his divine predicates (which exist only in his imagination and an eschatological dream).[8] This would lead to the kenotic error.

In its faith-relation to Christ the primitive community saw that it could not present the story of Jesus apart from its faith. The result was that it saw the abased and exalted Lord in his identity—and it had to do so if he was to be for it the presence of divinely enacted salvation. Yet it refused to put a myth in the place of history or a heavenly being in the place of the Nazarene.[9] It did not seek God's salvation in timeless ideas but in God's mighty acts (Acts 2:11) which he performed in historical events and people. In fact, then, primitive Christianity fought against both an emotional docetism on the one side and a historical kenoticism on the other.[10] Bultmann may well be right when he says that its very nondemonstrability safeguards the Christian message against the charge of being mythology.[11]

---

[6]So Kähler.

[7]Joest, *Kanon*, p. 273.

[8]So A. Schweitzer.

[9]Käsemann, "Das Problem des historischen Jesus," *Exegetische Versuche . . .* , I, p. 196.

[10]*Loc. cit.*

[11]*Kerygma und Mythos* (1951), p. 49; E.T. London, 1953, pp. 39f.

But he undoubtedly has to change Christology into mythology when he detaches it from the question of its historical background. For this means that the kerygma, as a final layer of proclamation behind which we cannot go, is itself a kind of "heavenly being" which stands in no definable relation to the historical figure. This is mythology and emotional docetism.

For this reason no Christology can evade the effort to find a foothold in the accounts of Jesus of Nazareth. If in fact the quest for the historical Jesus were to prove that faith in Jesus has no foothold in Jesus himself, this would be the end of Christology.[12] The task of historico-critical research, then, does not come upon theology from outside. It is not a concession that it must make to the spirit of the age. It is posed by its own relation to its object. It sees God's action in historical events even though the actual events may have a different structure from that which may be seen in their kerygmatic interpretation.[13] Everything depends on God's self-revelation being understood as a historical action.

This poses the task of historico-critical inquiry even if its limits cannot be fixed. These limits do not lie only in the historical obscurity to which the question of fact always leads. They lie especially in the inability of the results of critical subtraction, of the verification of facticity in the case of miracles and the resurrection, to provide any secure basis for faith. Faith can never be an "aha" experience on the basis of historical findings. It is always a gift in virtue of which the Pneuma-Word opens up the facts to us and lets them speak.

The theological legitimacy of historico-critical research is related to its being conducted in the name and framework of the same intention as was at work in primitive Christianity when with its view of the history of Jesus it could not abstract from faith but in the name of faith it also refused to abstract from history and see in Christ only a heavenly being or nonhistorical mythologoumenon.

Seen thus, the theological legitimacy of historical work means that the testimony of the Holy Spirit does not operate in such a way that the result of historical subtraction illumines it (or its absence obscures it). It is in fact already at work in the dominant interest of the one who does the research. It is as one who is seized (by the Word and Spirit) that he asks concerning the historical corporeality of his Lord and the mighty acts of God.

There are two ways of doing this work. Earlier an attempt was made to interpret the historical Jesus with the help of the primitive Christian kerygma. The attempt today is to interpret the primitive Christian kerygma with the help of the historical Jesus. The two approaches complement one another.[14]

---

[12]Ebeling, "Jesus und Glaube," *Wort und Glaube,* I (1960), p. 208; E.T. *Word and Faith,* p. 205.
[13]We have dealt with this question in relation to the OT, taking issue with F. Hesse's essay "Die Erforschung der Geschichte Israels als theologische Aufgabe," *Kerygma und Dogma* (1958), p. 1.
[14]E. Fuchs, Preface to his *Gesammelte Aufsätze,* II.

Part Three

THE FORM OF PRESENTATION: THE CHURCH

Bibliography

Out of the vast literature we list here only the works which have played an explicit or implicit part in the composition of the following chapter. P. Althaus, *Communio sanctorum* (1929); also "M. Luther über die Autorität der Kirche," *Festschrift H. Lilje* (1959), pp. 98ff.; K. Barth, CD, IV,1, pp. 643ff.; N. Berdyaev, *Freedom and the Spirit* (London, 1935), pp. 328ff.; D. Bonhoeffer, *Communio sanctorum, Dogmatische Untersuchungen zur Soziologie der Kirche* (1954); E.T. New York, 1963; E. Brunner, *Das Missverständnis der Kirche* (1951); E.T. *The Misunderstanding of the Church* (1952); H. H. Brunner, "Irrelevantes Reden von der Kirche?" *Reformatio*, IV (1964), pp. 204ff.; H. von Campenhausen, *Kirchliches Amt und geistlische Vollmacht in den ersten drei Jahrhunderten* (1953); E.T. *Ecclesiastical Authority* (Stanford, 1969); also "Einheit und Einigkeit in der alten Kirche," *EvTh*, III (1973), pp. 280ff.; H. Diem, *Theologie als kirchliche Wissenschaft*, III (1963); G. Ebeling, "Leitsätze zur Ekklesiologie," *Theologie und Verkündigung* (1962), pp. 93ff.; E.T. *Theology and Proclamation* (Philadelphia, 1966), pp. 94ff.; also "Zur Ekklesiologie," *Wort und Glaube*, III (1974), pp. 463ff.; cf. also pp. 322–27; F. Harnack, *Die Kirche, ihr Amt, ihr Regiment* (1862); J. Heckel, *Lex charitatis* (1953), pp. 167ff.; F. Holböck and T. Sartory, ed., *Mysterium Kirche*, 2 vols. (Salzburg, 1962); K. Holl, "Die Entstehung von Luthers Kirchenbegriffe," *Gesammelte Aufsätze*, I, 6th ed. (1932), pp. 288ff. (cf. *Festschrift für G. Dehn*, pp. 145ff.); E. Käsemann, "Amt und Gemeinde im NT," *Exegetische Versuche . . .* , I (1960), pp. 109ff.; W. Kasper and G. Sauter, *Kirche—Ort des Geistes* (1976); Statement of the Anglican/Roman Catholic Commission, HK, IV (1977), pp. 191ff.; H. Küng, *Die Kirche* (1967); E.T. *The Church* (London, 1967); J. Moltmann, *Kirche in der Kraft des Geistes* (1975); E.T. *The Church in the Power of the Spirit* (New York, 1977); A. M. Klaus Müller, *Die präparierte Zeit* (1972), pp. 464ff.; H. R. Niebuhr, *The Kingdom of God in America* (1937); Pius XII, encyclical "Mystici corporis" (1943); K. Rahner, "Anonyme Christen," *Schriften zur Theologie*, VI (1965), pp. 545ff.; E.T. *Theological Investigations*, VI, pp. 390ff.; "Anonymer und expliziter Glaube," *ibid.*, XII (1975), pp. 76ff.; and *Grundkurs des Glaubens*, 5th ed. (1976), pp. 313ff.; E.T. *Foundations of Christian Faith* (New York, 1978), pp. 322ff.; J. Ratzinger, *Das neue Volk Gottes. Entwürfe zu Ekklesiologie* (1969); T. Rendtorff, *Kirche und Theologie. Die systematische Funktion des Kirchenbegriffs in der neueren Theologie* (1966); J. Rohde, *Urchristliche und frühkatholische Ämter* (1976); J. Roloff, *Apostolat—Verkündigung —Kirche* (1966); K. L. Schmidt, art. "ekklēsia," TDNT, III, pp. 501ff. (TWNT,

III, pp. 502ff.); W. Schneemelcher, "Confessio Augustana, VIII im Luthertum des 19. Jahrhunderts," EvTh, VII/VIII (1950), pp. 308ff.; E. Schweizer, "Die Neutestamentliche Gemeindeordnung," EvTh, VII/VIII, pp. 338ff.; L. P. Tapaninen, "Luthers Kirchenbegriff," *Theologia Fennica,* III (Helsinki, 1943), pp. 48ff.; V. Vajta, ed., *Die Einheit der Kirche* (1958); G. Wehrung, *Kirche nach evangelischem Verständnis* (1945); E. Wolf, "Sanctorum communio," *Peregrinatio,* I (1954), pp. 279ff.; also "Der Mensch und die Kirche im katholischen Denken," *ibid.,* pp. 302ff.

XIV

The Concept of the Church[1]

In his *Xenien* Goethe once said that he had little time for church history since it dealt only with the clergy and he could find in it little about ordinary Christians.[2] What he missed in church history, and in the underlying concept of the church, was the human factor. He did not think he could see how faith was lived out concretely, how it deals with its object in Yes and No, in agreement and denial. Instead we meet only dogmas and their official representatives, the clergy.

Without having them in view, Goethe points us to some christological analogies which have long been noticeable in ecclesiology. There is first the heretical docetic trend which begins with God's abstract being as the Infinite and has thus to keep the divine nature of Christ apart from the finite processes of suffering and dying and indeed of the incarnation in general. To this view there corresponds a concept of the church such as that parodied by Goethe. The body of Christ, the church, does not enter fully into the humanity of history. It never becomes an institution that is subject to the immanent rules of ordinary life, e.g., church law. It remains a transcendental structure which keeps the blessings of revelation high above history.

Second, there is heretical Ebionite Christology which begins with Christ as finite man and then sees him elevated to divine or near divine honor. To this there corresponds an ecclesiology which begins with the church as an empirical institution, with its establishment, with its sociological reality, or even with the religious people who constitute a fellowship within it. These aberrant ecclesiologies are

---

[1]For earlier discussions of ecclesiology cf. above, chapter I, 6 for the christological and mariological aspects; ThE, III for the church in the changed world (§§762ff.) and especially church law (1598ff.), and ThE II, 1 for false conservative and revolutionary thinking in the church (§§1981–2001; E.T. II, pp. 627ff.), the church in the east–west conflict (§§2002–2010; E.T. II, pp. 632ff.), the church and politics (§§2002–2083; E.T. II, pp. 632–48), the church in time and above the times (§§1963–1980; E.T. II, pp. 622ff.), and the church's office as watchman (§§2298–2306). Cf. also the author's monographs *Leiden an der Kirche,* 2nd ed. (1966); E.T. *The Trouble with the Church* (New York, 1965); and *Notwendigkeit und Begrenzung des politischen Auftrags der Kirche* (1974).
[2]Cotta ed., I, p. 1122.

especially well calculated to clarify the essential relation between our understanding of Christ and our understanding of the church. In both—in ecclesiology too!—the problem of the doctrine of the two natures is at issue.

One might illustrate the confrontation of the two ecclesiologies in many ways. We will simply mention here two models. The first is the view of A. Vilmar (*Dogmatik,* II, ed. K. W. Piderit [1874], ed. 1937), which focuses only on the transcendental dimension (including sacral institutionality) and disregards or even rejects the human and personal side (pp. 186ff.). The church is simply the institution by which the blessings of salvation are passed on unchanged to all succeeding generations up to the coming again of Christ (p. 271).

In contrast to this docetic ecclesiology stands the personalist concept of Schleiermacher. Here the church is the fellowship of believers and the regenerate who let the Holy Spirit work in them (*The Christian Faith,* §126). There is a certain piquancy in the fact that Emil Brunner, the great opponent of Schleiermacher, is quite close to Schleiermacher in his personalistic view of the church, even though he does offer some safeguards and his personalism is primarily anti-institutional and directed against a dubious concept of the ministry (*Truth as Encounter* [Philadelphia, 1964]; *The Misunderstanding of the Church, passim*).

The doctrine of the church in the Smalkaldic Articles consciously puts together the two dimensions which meet in the church, as in Christ, and which are torn apart by docetic and Ebionite conceptions. Justice is done here to Goethe's human and personal corrective in the understanding of church history and the church when we read that even a child of seven knows what the church is—holy believers and the little sheep who hear the voice of the shepherd—so that children can pray: "I believe one holy Christian church."[3] A small child lives by sense-impressions and the church presents itself to it as a gathering of people. As is required in Christology, and as we tried to work it out,[4] the understanding of the church, too, must be developed from below upward and from outside inward.

Church history should not be found, then, merely in the clergy with their robes and tonsures and long coats and ceremonies.[5]

Although we begin by looking at the church as a gathering of people, we cannot stop there. Our glance moves up to the higher field of the religious concern or interest of the people thus assembled. Even the seven-year-old child knows that a call has gone out to this gathering and that they have met because of this call and not because of human motives. For as little children believe one holy Christian church, they believe the church which is grounded in the Word of God and right faith.[6]

The visible assembly and fellowship of people *and* the Word of God that constitutes it belong together. This correlation is indissoluble.

The church may be defined, then, only in terms of a relation that arises when the faith and prayer of those addressed by the efficacious and creative Word of God

---

[3]LBK, pp. 459,20–460,2; Tappert, p. 315.
[4]EG, II, pp. 331ff.; EF, II, pp. 302ff.
[5]LBK, p. 460,2; Tappert, p. 315.
[6]LBK, p. 460,4; Tappert, p. 315.

respond to it. This fundamental relation constitutes the church—the relation between the transcendent Word and the empirical historical reality in which faith in this Word arises and living people respond audibly and visibly to it. The two elements in a definition of the nature of the church are origin in the Word on the one side and historical being on the other. The mark of all christological and ecclesiological heresies is either the disruption of this basic relation or undue emphasis upon one element at the expense of the other.

Since this basic relation underlies all Christian existence, the church in any form and irrespective of its constitution is part of the question of human salvation and fundamentally co-constitutive for the human relation to God.[7] Negatively stated, there is no completely self-enclosed Christian monad with no windows opening on the world outside. To the Word there belongs the fellowship that it founds and within which alone it can be heard. To the resultant faith in this Word there belongs the fellowship of believers. This is not just because believers seek out those of like mind and are thus brought into fellowship, although this motive undoubtedly plays a part.[8] The fellowship of the church precedes faith.[9] I have not myself produced it; I have received it from the proclamation of the Word. This proclamation presupposes witnesses whom I will meet and who will mediate to me that to which I will react.

Hence the fundamental relation is already set up which is the essential condition of faith. Since faith is not a habit of implanted belief, but is always under attack and constantly needs to be renewed and strengthened, it is directed to the fellowship of brothers and sisters, to the community of witnesses. Nor am I an end in myself as one who is addressed and who hears. I do not find my own faith enough. I am simply a transitional point and by my life and witness I owe to others what I have received. This gives rise to the communicative aspect.

Although the church is co-constitutive for being a Christian, it obviously becomes an explicit dogmatic theme only at the Reformation. This calls for explanation. Neither in Thomas nor in the *Sentences* of Peter Lombard is the church dealt with independently. The obvious reason for this is that it formed a self-evident presupposition of theological thinking and one does not define the self-evident, as R. Grosche says.[10] Only the rift of the sixteenth century and the question that it raised as to the true church and its members made the theme of ecclesiology an increasingly urgent one[11]—increasingly because in the course of the centuries right up to the present day the question of the self-understanding of the church has been extended by new dimensions of the problem, e.g., by the historical evaluation of tradition, by the relation between state, society, and church, by the subjectivism of Romanticism, and naturally by new variations of the opposing theological conceptions as well.

---

[7]Rahner, *Grundkurs*, p. 332; E.T. *Foundations*, p. 342.

[8]The young Schleiermacher concentrates almost exclusively on this idea that religion triggers a need for fellowship (cf. *Speeches on Religion*, Speech III).

[9]Cf. the beginning of Calvin's chapter on the church (Inst., IV, 1, 1).

[10]H. Weissgerber, *op. cit.*, p. 10.

[11]As K. Holl rightly points out, this does not mean that Luther's view of the church was merely a "reaction" (cf. *Gesammelte Aufsätze*, I [1932], pp. 288f.).

Excursus on the Change in Meaning of the Term "Church"

In what follows I shall be repeatedly referring to the important essay of K. Berger, "Volksversammlung und Gemeinde Gottes. Zu den Anfängen der christlichen Verwendung von ecclesia," ZThK, II (1976), pp. 167ff. and K. L. Schmidt's art. "ekkēsia," TDNT, III, pp. 501ff.

Whether the word *ekklēsia*, as K. L. Schmidt supposes, is related etymologically to *kalein* and by way of this verb to the Hebrew *qahal*, is obviously open to question. In Greek the *ekklēsia* is a popular political assembly. In Hellenism it was the custom for kings to have their proclamations read in public gatherings. In Hellenistic Judaism the letters of the prophets were read before the *ekklēsia*.

In primitive Christianity certain analogies to this idea of the popular assembly lead to the use of the term *ekklēsia* for the community. In this cultic gathering God is praised (1 Corinthians 14:26; Ephesians 3:21; 5:19) and reference to his saving word and deed is central. As in the public meetings of Hellenism the question of order (*eukosmia*) plays a part (1 Corinthians 14:40). So do the questions of valid membership and possible expulsion (Matthew 18:17).

The primitive Christian use of *ekklēsia* is unquestionably related to the Jewish use of synagogue for the cultic assembly. Paul differentiates from this when he emphatically states that he has in mind the *ekklēsia* of Jesus Christ or of God as the Father of Jesus Christ (Galatians 1:22 and esp. 1 Thessalonians 1:1; 2:14; 2 Thessalonians 1:1).

Berger finds a decisive change of meaning when *ekklēsia* increasingly comes to denote a group rather than a specific meeting (*op. cit.*, pp. 187ff.). This leads the word away from its original historical reference. When Paul speaks of attacking the *ekklēsia* in his anti-Christian period (Galatians 1:13; Philippians 3:6) he is already thinking, not of an actual assembly, but of a group united by its common faith.

This extended meaning of *ekklēsia* may be seen in the LXX version of Psalm 89(88):5, where it is the heavenly assembly of angels and saints that praises the wonders and truth of the Kyrios. Earthly Israel simply stands in analogy to this assembly when it joins in the praise (v. 14). The same eschatological extension beyond all institutional palpability may be seen in Hebrews 12:22-24. We have reference here to a supra-empirical group composed of the firstborn who from the beginning of the world are enrolled in heaven and not in the registers of an earthly institution. This eschatological aspect is emphasized when it is said of Christians that they do not come as the fathers did to an earthly site like Mt. Sinai but are associated with the holy and immediate presence of God himself in heaven (U. Wilckens, *Das NT*, pp. 907f.). In Hebrews 12:23, then, we do not have an empirical assembly which meets at different times and places—the heavenly choirs are always in session!—but an eschatological and transcendent identity which can be grasped only in visions and expressed only theologically (Berger, *op. cit.*, p. 197).

We see here the continuity and discontinuity of the *ekklēsia* as the true Israel in its relation to the salvation history of the OT. It is obvious how little the concept has in mind an empirical assembly or union. The emphasis is that the *ekklēsia* begins in heaven, that it reaches back to an election before the foundation of the world, that it is not then a product of faith (as in Schleiermacher), but that it precedes faith and assimilates itself to an eternally existent choir singing the praise of God.

This view of the *ekklēsia* is not docetic in the sense previously discussed. The summons of Hebrews to the concrete Christian community, which is to see itself as a branch of this group of the elect that embraces heaven and earth, is that it is to realize that it has here its basis and goal, but that it is also to become an earthly assembly and fellowship and exist in analogy to this universal *ekklēsia*. Only thus does it understand and achieve its eschatological identity.

Hence *ekklēsia* can be rendered simply (but not simplistically) by "people of God." This people of God has no limits in time and space, for it embraces heaven and earth, the beginning of the world and its end. The *ekklēsia*, then, cannot be thought of institutionally. The institutional side can be only an expression and analogy of that which transcends it. The *ekklēsia* is an anticipation of the *basileia*, which is its eschatological realization. We have here only different aspects of the same thing. The *ekklēsia* is present, the *basileia* future.

It may be this non-institutional element in the original concept of the *ekklēsia* which still echoes in R. Sohm with his criticism of church law (cf. ThE, III, §§1611–36; E.T. III, pp. 134f.) and E. Brunner in his *Misunderstanding of the Church*. For the rest, the understanding of the church as the people of God cannot be restricted to the sphere of the term *ekklēsia*. In the loci of the NT concerning the church it is often described by "you" (the recipients) or "we" (the senders). The reference in both instances is to those who are grasped by the Word and put themselves under it. The people of God can also be called the body of Christ or those who are united in Christ's name.

XV

The Essence of the Church

No matter how the church be defined in detail, any basic statement must begin by relating it to Christ and understanding it as a presentation of his being and work. But this raises at once the question what is meant by this reference back to him. Is Christ to be understood historically in the sense that he founded the church, so that we are to think of him as we do of the founder of a society?

Naturally there is no evading this question as to the historical side of the reference even though it is no real part of the sphere of systematic theology. One might mention that even if no references can be found to suggest that Jesus meant to start an institutional church, and even if this lack of references might be connected with immanent eschatological expectation, lines may be traced which indicate an assembling and fellowship of believers in him—lines which constantly recur as constitutive factors in the later self-understanding of the church.

Among these we may mention the gathering of the disciples who represent God's people and whose number (twelve) points to the eschatological Israel which will be called together. This community of disciples is prepared by Jesus for assurance of their call even in persecution and trial and for perseverance in the new covenant (the institution of the Lord's Supper). The warning to Peter also suggests that the fellowship of those who are to be strengthened and sustained by him is to continue (Luke 22:31f.).

Whatever might be the institutional form of those who are united in Christ's name, they are given the authority of the Word to bind and loose (Matthew 16:19; 18:18; John 20:23). The "you" of the address, which denotes the disciples then and in the future, suggests that in the conflict those addressed are not to represent God on their own responsibility but that God himself is with them and will act through them. Hence they need not worry what to say when they are called to account before human courts, for "it is not you who speak, but the Spirit of your Father speaking through you" (Matthew 10:19f.; Mark 13:11). Even the hostile anti-Christian state has to reckon with God himself when it oppresses the fellowship of those who believe in him.

Something more and other is prognosticated, then, than a mere society of like-minded people which is summoned to be loyal to its cause because this cause will not deceive it. The cause at issue here is God himself who upholds his people and is present among them by his Word and Spirit, entrusting both to them. There can be no church of Christ which does not regard as its Magna Carta the founding document of this commitment and promise for all the future.

If we want to ask and know historically whether and how far the historical Jesus was the founder of his church, we come up against the limit of the historical aspect. At its first stage the question forces us back to the past, but the next moment it confronts us with the higher reality that the church has to do with the Christ who is present. Hence the question of the church's founding turns into that of the ground on which it stands, of the grounding word-event which is still taking place afresh here and now.[1] Where two or three are gathered in his name, he is forever in the midst of them as he is among his disciples when he says this (Matthew 18:20). What enables him to be present in his Word is the Spirit, the Paraclete, whom he will send (John 16:5ff.).

In a further relativizing of the reference to a historical founding, this means that only the one who has departed, the risen one who promises this presence among his people, is the one who will be with them all the days until this aeon (of our temporality) is completed (Matthew 28:20b). If we ask about the historical founding of the church we run up against the post-Easter Christ to whom "all authority in heaven and on earth has been given" (Matthew 28:18) and who by reason of this exaltation of his embraces time and space in the power of the Spirit and can thus assure his people of his presence. The essence of the church is grounded in this promise and commitment of the present Christ. This is why the historical question cannot be its ground. The ground of the church is the presence of Christ, or, more precisely, the presentation of his Word and work achieved by the Spirit. The point of the question concerning a valid founding by Jesus, but also the limit of its competence, is simply that it arises out of the identity of this present Christ with the Jesus of Nazareth who walked this earth. Hence the only way to describe the essence of the church is to say that it has its basis in the word and attitude and work of this earthly Jesus.[2]

All the NT statements about the essence of the church rest on this kind of reference, i.e., to the identity of Jesus and Christ.

Jesus is the author (Hebrews 12:10) and foundation (1 Corinthians 3:11f.). He is also present in the church as his body and makes his people members of this body (Romans 6:13, 19; 12:4ff.; 1 Corinthians 6:15; 12:2ff.; Ephesians 1:23; 4:15f.; Colossians 1:18). Finally, especially in Matthew's version of Psalm 118:22, he is the keystone of the whole building (Matthew 21:42; Acts 4:11; 1 Peter 2:7). By his cross he is our peace, so that in his community the opposition of Jews and Gentiles and the opposition of both to God is overcome (Ephesians 2:14–22). The loving relation between Christ and his church carries over to the relation between husband

---

[1] The church's appeal to its basis does not consist of a proof that Jesus founded it and in virtue of his authority delegated authority to it (cf. Ebeling, *Theologie und Verkündigung* [1962], p. 95; E.T. *Theology and Proclamation,* p. 96; cf. also *Wort und Glaube,* III, pp. 464f.).

[2] As T. Harnack points out (*Die Kirche,* §12), Christ creates the church by the outpouring of the Holy Spirit who shows himself to be Christ's Spirit by closely relating his work to the historical work of the incarnate Lord, and subjecting it to this.

and wife (Ephesians 5:25). As Christ lives from all eternity even though he was incarnate in time, so in him his community was elected from all eternity (Ephesians 1:4ff.; 2 Thessalonians 2:13). The Holy Spirit brings individuals to Christ (Romans 8:14; Ephesians 2:22) and by way of him they are joined to the community (Acts 9:31; 2 Corinthians 13:13; Philippians 2:1). (In NT exegesis the profiles of different ecclesiologies may be worked out in Luke, Matthew, Paul, and others but here we are simply giving some supplementary christological statements. For a survey of the profiles cf. K. Rahner, *Grundkurs,* pp. 326ff.; E.T. *Foundations,* pp. 335ff.)

The church as Christ's presence in his word and work means that there also belongs to the essence of the church the connection between the presence of Christ's Spirit by proclamation in word and sacrament and the effects of this activity and the responses to it in faith, love, and hope. It would be abstract (and docetic) objectivism to speak of the presence and activity of the Spirit if we did not also describe the setting of this presence and activity, the place of its mediation in the preaching and hearing church, and the hearts that receive the message in faith. Only thus do we have the gracious presence of the crucified and exalted Lord and only thus can the fellowship of believers become the instrument of his continued activity in the world.[3]

The term "connection" means negatively that one cannot separate the two essential elements that constitute the essence of the church. Neither the divinely conditioning side (Harnack) nor the act of faith on the human side can be set in isolation. Christ is not the church but the one who calls and seeks and woos it for faith and discipleship. The Holy Spirit is not the church but the presence of Christ which is mediated by the Word and gives soul to his body. Because God is Emmanuel and Christ is Christ for us, we can never mention the divinely conditioning side without also mentioning the "we" in whom something is done, who are won to faith, and who are assimilated into Christ's body as members.

But just as the divinely conditioning side cannot be isolated in defining the church, so it is impossible to isolate the human acts which it engenders. Such a one-sided view makes of faith a psychological state of believing which later finds a source in a human concept of God. It makes of love a mere act of social fellow-humanity and of hope the principle of hope (as in E. Bloch). It finally reduces the community to a socially relevant society in which is seen only what may be seen from outside. This empirical aspect is totally unable to grasp the mystery of the church. It involves the absurd attempt to base the rainbow on the earth that it touches. If restriction to the divinely conditioning side leads to Docetism, restriction to the participating human acts leads to a new Ebionitism. There are plenty of examples of both errors in orthodoxy and secularism.

We can maintain the connection, then, only if we see the church in those who are grasped by the presence of the Spirit of Christ in his Word and who consequently gather around this Word as a community. The people of God does in truth constitute the essence of the church.

CAApol states this and begins its ecclesiology with God's people. It thus describes the *ekklēsia* as the true congregation of the saints (pp. 236,36; 240,30;

---

[3] *Ibid.*, §17.

Tappert, pp. 171f.). But it takes care not to let this communion be understood as an external if distinctive polity (pp. 235,57; 236,47; Tappert, p. 170). In defining the church as the community of believers, and thus starting with those assembled in it, regard must be had to the transcendent origin of the faith stirred up by the Word and Spirit. This is a spiritual people, i.e., a people regenerated by the Holy Spirit (p. 236,48; Tappert, p. 17C).

It is very typical that the Apology expressly distinguishes the church of Christ from the people of the law in Paul's sense (p. 236,43,46; Tappert, p. 170), a people which bases itself on its own works and fabricates itself. The Holy Spirit is at work in the true people of God and our attitude is that of recipients. Hence this people can be defined only "ec-centrically" as those who accept the gospel and have among them Christ and the Spirit and the sacraments (p. 236,1; Tappert, p. 170).

Hence the communion of saints does not receive the fellowship and unity from a consensus of human ideas, sympathies, interests, purposes, or other common features (p. 236,3; Tappert, p. 170) but from the one object and origin of faith, from the same Christ, the same Spirit, the same Word and sacraments.

It is against this background that we are to understand the famous definition of the church in CA, VII as the congregation of the saints in which the gospel is purely taught and the sacraments are rightly administered (p. 59,17; Tappert, p. 32). The qualification of the words "congregation" and "saints" does not rest on an empirically verifiable proof, e.g., in the form of an obvious holiness and unity. The truth of both depends on whether the purity of the gospel that is set up here, measured by its biblical origin, leaves room for the presence of Christ.

Only in this "ec-centric" sense may the church be defined on the human side as the people of God. Only thus is the connection respected. Only thus can the pardoned and justified publican become a representative of the church (Luke 18:14). But along these lines one can really say that the church consists of the fellowship of faith and prayer, for the whence of faith and the whither of prayer are both kept in view. In this sense Luther in his Commentary on the Psalms says that there can be no dispute about the church. The true church is present where there is the earnest prayer of faith. But if we begin in this way with the human side, pursuing an ecclesiology as well as a Christology from below,[4] a further mystery of the church is set before us. In spite of Christ's presence with it, it often presents a disappointing appearance. Empirically its essence is hidden, not just because the object of its faith is hidden from this kind of sight, but also because the marred empirical image of the church conceals its object even more and turns people away from it. This is so because God's people is still his pilgrim people, far from the perfecting of its faith. It is so because the fellowship of believers as well as the individual believer has to be described as righteous and sinful at one and the same time. The church, too, lives by the promise that it has to become in fact what it already is by God's promise, that as yet it is righteous only in hope. Like the individual, as Luther says, the church is moving toward the goal but has not yet reached it. It is to put on the new man and put off the old, but it is still doing this. If

---

[4]This is not meant, of course, in an Ebionite sense but within a commitment to the transcendental reference of the community of faith and prayer.

we can already speak of a spiritual *ekklēsia* and of Christ's presence by the Spirit, we have to say that in this life we receive only the Spirit's firstfruits, not all the tithes, let alone the fulness of the Spirit. We are not yet freed from our flesh. Even the church is still all too human. But we are engaged in the act of putting off, of pressing ahead, of marching forward.

So then, as Luther says later, we cannot find the church in its appearance but only where the pure Word is preached and the sacraments are rightly administered. Here we come across people who love the Word and bear witness to it in the world. Where you find that, there is the church, whether it be few or many who keep to it and act accordingly (cf. WA, 40/III, 506, 18–507, 12; LW, 13, 89f.).

Though the church's face is full of spots and wrinkles, though it is imperfect and sinful in fact, this does not weaken the promise that it is the place of the Word, the presence of Christ's Spirit, the body of Christ. Thus it can be given the power to handle the efficacious Word in the form of binding and loosing. There is entrusted to it the active Word which is for life or death.[5] In distinction from the Word of teaching which tells us about the guilt that remains or is forgiven, and in distinction from the Word of recollection which recalls the judging and pardoning work of the earthly Jesus, the power of the Word of action makes it plain that it has its origin only in Christ as he is present and active in the church, that it presupposes his resurrection and exaltation.

Only in connection with the presence of Christ in his Word is there any basis for the thesis, found also in different forms in the Lutheran confessional writings, that outside the church is no salvation. The argument is a simple one. Where Christ is, the church is, and only where the church is, is Christ in his Word. To be outside the church is to be outside the means of grace entrusted to the church, i.e., the Word and sacraments (CAApol, p. 247,14; Tappert, p. 178). Apart from the church, then, there can be no faith in the heart nor righteousness of the heart before God (p. 241,14; Tappert, p. 173). The LC points in the same direction. Since the Spirit cannot be separated from the Word, but the church is constituted by the Word, it follows that no one can come to Christ the Lord outside the church, for outside the church the forgiveness granted by the Word is not to be found. Whether and how far those who are outside may not be far from the kingdom of God and therefore touched by the Pneuma in some way apart from the Word (Matthew 12:34) is a question that we shall have to discuss in the chapter on "The Exclusiveness of Presentation."

The Reformation view of "outside the church" differs from the Roman Catholic view. The latter relates it not only to the Word that constitutes the church but also to institutional membership in the Roman Catholic Church. It bases the church on other things apart from the Word, e.g., the Spirit who works in tradition and the teaching office. This is still true in the "Constitution on the Church" of Vatican II, though this reflects two different trends. It begins by saying that Christ is the only Mediator and way of salvation as he is present to us in his body the church ("Lumen gentium," 14; E.T. *Vatican II Documents*, pp. 32ff.). It thus suggests

---

[5] According to the Reformation view the power of binding and loosing is given to Peter as a representative of the community. The community has the power, not Peter or his papal successors in the chair of Peter (Matthew 16:19; cf. Matthew 18:18; John 20:23; also Luke 24:47).

that inside or outside is decided by *him*. But it then adds that union with this present Christ is possible only and exclusively by attachment to this one institution (the Roman Catholic Church) and its ordinances. Those are full members of the fellowship of the church who, having Christ's Spirit, accept its total order and the means of grace set up in it and are united in its visible link with Christ, who directs it by the pope and bishops—and this by the bonds of the creed, the sacraments, and ecclesiastical leadership and fellowship.

Fairness demands, however, that we admit that there is a certain dissatisfaction with these institutional definitions and that some non-institutional criteria for inside and outside are also set up. Thus even some who are full members of the ecclesiastical institution may be excluded from salvation. This applies to those who within the bosom of the church belong only to the body and not to the heart, not persevering in love. Here the way opens up to the relation between the Word and faith. The institutional "outside" can also be softened from this angle. Those who through no fault of their own do not know the gospel of Christ and his church, but honestly seek God and conscientiously try to do his will under the influence of grace, can be saved. So, then, at this difficult point in the debate, that of ecclesiology, we can see a sublime softening of the institutional criterion and a correspondingly enhanced importance of the Word and Spirit which offers hope of new impulses toward closer relations and mutual self-discovery.

No matter how definitely the church be grounded in the resurrection life or presence of Christ, it is in no way to be identified with Christ, as we said earlier. It is distinct from him as the body is from the head. Until its eschatological consummation the church will not attain to its full identity, at least in fact. Empirically it may be seen only in its defects and scandals.[6] Like justified man, it is characterized by an alien dignity and not its own. Empirically it is a hidden (*abscondita*) church—so hidden that it exists only in the eyes of God, that its face is only as it is seen by God and not as it is presented to human eyes, that only a single justified man like Elijah may represent it.[7]

Connected with this difference between the being of the church in reality and its being in hope is the fact that it can be believed only as the Word that constitutes it is believed and not as the Holy Trinity is the object of faith. Whereas the creed speaks of believing *in* the Father, Son, and Holy Spirit, it leaves out the *in* when it comes to the church. We do not believe *in* the church but believe it, reckoning it to be a reality in faith. This sharp nuance shows that in the sphere of faith the church is not an end in itself but simply the vehicle that carries our faith and mediates its true object to us. It is the means to an end. As Augustine says, it is founded for the worship of God.[8]

Augustine presupposes the distinction when he emphasizes that the church cannot be paid the veneration that applies to God alone. Neither the church as a whole nor any part of it wants to be worshipped as God is, nor to be God to those who belong to the temple of God, which is being built up of the "gods" whom the

---

[6]Cf. Luther on Psalm 90 (LW, 13, 88ff.).

[7]Cf. Luther in his Commentary on the Psalms (WA, 30/III, 505; LW, 13, 88f.). The church is truly present only where the Word of God is preached and is received in faith.

[8]Cf. E. Wolf, *Peregrinatio,* I (1954), p. 281.

uncreated God created (*Enchiridion*, XV, 56). In the realm of saving faith the church has only the rank of a secondary cause.

Calvin rejects the ''in'' in the same way and refers to Augustine and Cyprian, who held the same view and regarded the common use of ''in'' by the fathers as a loose form of expression. The same applies, Calvin thinks, to the Nicene Creed (Inst., IV, 1, 2). Wollebius lays special emphasis on this instrumental significance of the church and distinguishes it from the operation of the Holy Spirit. We do not believe the church on its own account, as we do the Holy Spirit. The church urges (*suadet*), the Spirit persuades (*persuadet*) (*Compendium of Christian Theology* [1629]; cf. *Reformed Dogmatics*, ed. J. W. Beardslee [New York, 1965]).

XVI

Where Is the Church?

Since one cannot describe the essence of the church without saying where it is to be found, what really matters has already been said in answer to this question. Hence we need only underline the decisive points and occasionally expand them.

1. The question of the "where" is to be answered along the lines of CA, VII (Tappert, p. 32). The church is to be found where there is true preaching of the gospel and a similar administration of the sacraments. Negatively this means that one cannot see it empirically in the state of believers. Nietzsche's charge that Christians should look more redeemed if one is to believe in their Redeemer gives evidence of this error.

2. We should have a docetic view of the church if there were not bound up with the preaching of the Word and administration of the sacraments an assurance that where the Word of God is, there is the people of God. Luther expresses this assurance in his constant citing of Isaiah 55:11, which attaches to the Word of God the promise that it will not return empty.

As Luther says, we can be sure that it is impossible that there should be no Christians when the gospel goes forth, no matter how few or sinful or frail they may be, just as it is impossible that there should be Christians and not pagans where the gospel does not go forth. This is the reason why the existence of Christians, i.e., the church, may be inferred from the preaching of the gospel. Similarly, Melanchthon says that the visible church is to be sought as a gathering around the Word (CR, XXI, pp. 825f.); it is not to be understood as an impalpable Platonic idea (CR, XXIII, pp. 37f.). The preaching of the Word is the answer to this question of the "where," Luther maintains, even though, as in the century of the Arians, hardly five sound bishops could be found and they were exiled, whereas the Arians reigned everywhere under the official name of the church. Even then Christ maintained his church among heretics, though it was not regarded and believed as a church.

The "where" of the church is not, then, a matter of statistics, as though all who hear the Word were to be counted as real members and Christians. Those who gather around the Word are a mixed company of believers, hypocrites, and apostates, as may be seen from the examples of Cain and Abel, Ishmael and Isaac, Esau and Jacob (Otto Clemen, *Bonner Studentenausgabe,* 139,2). Nevertheless there can be certainty that a holy remnant is hidden in the mass of perdition. Hidden does not imply Platonic invisibility, for this would be based on the false criterion that faith is a non-objectifiable inner process, so that empirically there could be no group of true believers and therefore no *ekklēsia* in the strict sense. Faith, however, cannot be defined as subjective believing. Its subject is a mathematical point (WA, II, 527, 9; LW, 27, 276). It is constituted by its object and origin. Hence God alone knows believers. The blind and ambiguous word "church" is not without responsibility for the misunderstandings mentioned (WA, 50, 624ff.; LW, 41, 143ff.). The church is not Platonically invisible but theologically hidden. Like all else in the Word and faith, it is known only by God (WA, 23, 189, 8; LW, 37, 92).

In Calvin this hiddenness, this being known only by God, is intensified by the special stress on the doctrine of predestination. Though there is a visible church with distinctive marks, the counsel of God is hidden. If we have in mind the company of those whom God has accepted for salvation by his secret election, this church is neither seen with the eyes nor distinguished by signs (Geneva Catechism of 1541/42; H. A. Niemeyer, *Collectio confessionum*... [1840], p. 136). Invisible to us, it is "visible to the eyes of God alone" (Inst., IV, 1, 7).

3. Since the Word contains the promise that it will not return empty, the question of the church's "where" can be answered only in terms of the relation between God's Word and its work through the Spirit. Its work is not just the common assembling of believers around the Word, even though they be an externally small remnant. The Word works through the Spirit and therefore they will be also fruits of the Spirit (Galatians 5:22; Ephesians 5:9). The essential fruit of the Spirit is love, which thinks the best of everyone, which is not mistrustful, which expects good from neighbors.[1] In this evaluation of fruits Luther—yes, Luther—assumes that the "where" of the church may be defined by the rule of love as well as faith.

This needs more detailed interpretation, for works (of love) as a criterion of the church instead of faith might be misunderstood, and the hidden being of the church seems to give place here to demonstrable signs. This is not so. Love in the power of the Spirit can never be an objective sign of the being of the church, for the basis of love—that we are first loved (1 John 4:19) and can pass on only what we have received—is not manifest to sight but only to faith. Hence love is not a sign but a witness and it thus shares with witness its unavoidable ambivalence for a neutral observer. Lack of this witness, of course, can be a negative test and can block access to the mystery of the church. There are hindrances (*impedimenta, prohibitiva*) to faith which choke it at the very core—and this applies to believing the church too (cf. ThE, I, §§333ff.; E.T. I, pp. 87f.). The witness of love does not in itself produce faith but lack of this witness can rob the church of its credibility. The church can change its hiddenness into obscurity.

In this sense the Word that works by the Spirit is not to be claimed without its work, without the act of the active Word. The promise that it will not return empty

---

[1]*The Bondage of the Will* (Clemen, *Bonner Studentenausgabe,* III, 140, 14).

cannot mean only its passive acceptance. It brings about Christ's saving presence through the Spirit and becomes active through awakened faith. Faith cannot exist without works. It has to become a faith that is formed by love.

How love does in fact become a criterion for the "where" of the church, the presence of Christ, may be seen in the parable of the judgment in Matthew 25:31ff.[2] At his coming the Son of Man will gather all nations around his throne and separate them as a shepherd separates the sheep from the goats. He will welcome the sheep on his right hand into his kingdom as those who are blessed by his father, for they have fed him when hungry, given him drink when thirsty, sheltered and clothed and visited him in prison. To their astonished question when and where he met them thus without their knowing it, he answers: "Truly, I say to you, as you did it to one of the least of these my brethren, you did it to me" (25:40). Similarly those who refused to help the least of his brethren learn that they had refused to help him.

Whether or not the Pneuma really makes the (incarnate) Word present; whether or not it summons the present Christ into the midst of those who hear; whether they are really gathered in his name (Matthew 18:20); whether he is really in the midst of them so that the church is there: this is all decided by the love which not only unites those who are gathered together but which is also directed to the poor and needy and oppressed both near and distant.

There is twofold Christian power in this love. Through it the hearer of the Word becomes a "Christ" to the other. But the one to whom it is directed also becomes a "Christ" to him who loves, for the Kyrios seeks to meet us in him and will remind us of this at the judgment day. Accepted salvation not only works itself out as love but is also a work of this love.

This can be so—and for this reason it is not even remotely like a righteousness of works—only when the love thus shown sees itself as a response to what is previously given by Christ and when it thus constitutes merely one aspect of faith, its embodiment. Again, this spiritual background of acts of love sees to it that love is a sign of the "where" of the church but as a fruit of the Spirit it shares the church's hiddenness and is thus exposed to misunderstanding and offense. Externally, the diaconate can hardly be distinguished from humanistically or socially motivated action, or else it may be wrongly distinguished (e.g., by attributing the holy egoism of meriting heaven to the diaconate, but ascribing social action to philanthropic or pragmatic motives).

In his work *On the Freedom of a Christian Man* (1520) Luther discusses the spiritual background of love. The Christian will become a servant helping his neighbor, but he can be a "Christ" to him only because he has first experienced Christ's grace to himself in his own need.

The missionary-theological constitution of Vatican II expresses this love that derives from Christ in chapters 11 and 12. The soul of the presence of Christ in human societies must be the love with which God has loved us and with which he wants us to love one another. Christian love extends to all without distinction, for as God turned to us with undeserved love, so are Christians to do in their love for others ("Ad gentes," 12; *Vatican II Documents,* p. 598).

---

[2]Cf. Moltmann, *Die Kirche . . .* , pp. 145f.; E.T. *The Church in the Power of the Spirit*, pp. 126ff.

4. A quantitative aspect is bound up with love as a means to locate the church. In the being of the church there are degrees in the appropriation and embodiment of faith, just as there is growth in faith itself. If, however, the church is most present where there is most faith and turning to neighbors and openness to society, where there is most participation in Christ, this means that the church is most an event where—for all its unequivocal safeguarding of the message and its fidelity to the Word—it is still not at all exclusive. It addresses[3] sinners, too, both inside and outside its fellowship. It seeks those who are in error and gives its voice to the deaf. It is not a society of plaster saints but a very mixed group of justified sinners and hypocritical fellow-travellers and very dubious figures of all kinds. It has much material on which to exercise its non-exclusiveness in both evangelistic and missionary work.

In contrast the church is least present where it stays in pious ghettos and enjoys those of like tastes, where it speaks the language of Canaan (a sign that betrays at once a dubious church) and does not learn the contemporary idioms by which alone true appropriation and true dedication may be discerned.

5. Borrowing a phrase from Y. Congar,[4] one might say along the lines of Reformation theology that we must stretch the warp but the woof is also needed. The church builds up itself like a fabric involving two factors, the warp of the preaching of the Word from generation to generation beginning with Christ's incarnation and extending to the end of this aeon, and the woof which brings afresh each day the efficacious gifts of the Spirit in the form of faith, love, and hope. The fact of the church derives from the warp, for the Word will not return empty. The manner of the church—in the quantitative sense—derives from the woof, from the degree to which faith finds embodiment as love.

6. As the fellowship of those who gather around the preached Word and to whom the presence of the Lord is given through the Spirit, the church is also the fellowship of the called who have received a glad liberation from the ungodly bonds of this world for free and grateful service to God's creatures.[5] This means that the church is sent into the world but is not "of the world" (John 17:15–18). It cannot be integrated into the world but stands at a distance from it. It receives its commission from its Lord and not from the world. It is open to the world in the sense of non-exclusiveness but it does not belong to the world.

We oppose various trends in saying this. The most immediate is a tendency to see in the church only an agency for social service. This entails emancipation from the constitutive Word and the changing of theology into praxiology. More impressive than these aberrations, however, are some classical ways of overcoming the distance between the church and the world. Two very different ones may be selected as examples.

1. First is the Russian-Orthodox doctrine of the deification of the world (cf. N. Berdyaev, *Freedom and the Spirit* [1935]). On this view the church is the christianized cosmos (pp. 328ff.) and the body of Christ is the cosmic body which embraces the full infinitude of cosmic life (p. 332). Until the fulfilment of God's

---

[3]Cf. J. Ratzinger, *Das neue Volk Gottes* (1969), pp. 243f.
[4]*Der Laie* (1952), p. 538.
[5]The Barmen Declaration of 1934, Thesis 2.

kingdom the church must rise above the non-enlightened elements of the world and not mix with them (pp. 331ff.). Nevertheless it is already true that the circle of the potential church is much broader and richer than that of the actual empirical church (p. 332). It is already an anticipation of the christianized cosmos.

The reason why the church, in spite of an interim distance from the world, potentially and proleptically embraces all humanity and the whole cosmos, is that it rests not merely on Christ and divine grace but also on the virgin Mary . . . the soul of the cosmos representing creation in its purity and chastity. In the virgin Mary . . . the world and men attain free deification. She is the cosmically feminine soul of humanity (pp. 334ff.).

While distant from the world during the interim, and rising above the non-enlightened elements in it, the church does not just wait for the eschaton nor will it be summoned from faith to sight only at the end. Because creation is already sanctified in Mary it already represents deified humanity. This universal potential identity must be maintained in face of Roman Catholicism. Whereas this sets up a closed sacral circle through the sanctifying of a bit of the finite by the breaking in of the infinite, the orthodox church sees what is finite and relative yielding to what is absolute and infinite. It sees the initiation of a creative movement toward the sanctification of the whole cosmos (pp. 335f.).

This potential equation of church and cosmos may be related to the fact that the eastern church hardly ever raises the ethical problems which arise for a church of the Word in relation to its commitment to the world and distance from it, as in the natural law of Roman Catholicism and the two-kingdom doctrine of Luther. The eschatological radicalness of the demands of the Sermon on the Mount in relation to the autonomy of worldly structures, the tension between them, and the problem of compromise can hardly cause any difficulty for a humanity that is summoned to deification. (Thus Bishop Makarios of Cyprus could not understand the question when he was asked how he could fulfil his double function as churchman and statesman.) This is why there is little in the way of theological ethics in the eastern church, though one would think that the related problems can hardly be avoided in a church that so often has to work with totalitarian governments.

2. A completely different potential equation of church and world may be found in R. Rothe (1799–1863). The idealism of Hegel and Schelling and the theosophy of Böhme and Oetinger form its background. Christianity, Rothe says, aims essentially at increasing secularization, at putting off the form of church which it had to assume when entering the world and putting on the more generally human form of moral life (p. 379). Here too—this is the point of comparison with the orthodox view—it is a matter of the world becoming the church, or its deification. If the life-process of the second Adam is one of steadily increasing normal (i.e., good and holy) spiritualizing, there takes place in it also a steadily increasing specific suitability for God's indwelling (p. 536). This process means the sanctification of the cosmos whose proleptic form the second Adam is. Even now it is already true that we can see Christianity not only in its ecclesiastical and conscious and programmatic form but also wherever Christian culture has become man's second nature and entered into him suprapersonally. Rothe is the first to discover "unconscious Christianity," i.e., a humanity directed by pure motives. Christianity in its church form is only an interim entity illustrating and promoting the process

of cosmic sanctification. (Cf. the similar theme in A. A. van Ruler, ThE, II, 2, §§4275ff.; E.T. II, pp. 604ff.). It is God's task to produce spirit out of matter. This is the content of world evolution. The Christ event is a phase in this. The end product is a christianized world in which the church has made itself super-fluous (cf. M. Kähler, *Geschichte der protestantischen Dogmatik im 19. Jahr-hundert,* ed. E. Kähler [1962], p. 105).

We do an injustice to Rothe if we find a motive of secularization or assimilation behind his view. It is no more present than in the Eastern Orthodox doctrine of deification. What made the greatest impression on his readers was his uniting of a doctrine of the cosmos and pietism (which made him in some sense a predecessor of K. Heim). From this standpoint he was moved by a definitely theological and even pastoral concern. His outlook on the world caused him to shrink back from the idea that God was the Lord only of his own little group and that Christ did his redeeming work only for a trivial minority. "I cannot believe," he said, "that my Savior exists only for pietists. My Savior is too big not to exist for the whole world" (*Ethik,* p. 116). It is perhaps of a piece with his view of a historical process aiming at christianization that his ethics had in his thinking a value quite different from what it could be allotted in Eastern Orthodoxy and its potentially given identity of church and world. Involuntarily, however, Rothe could not help but prepare the way for an assimilation of church and world such as may be seen later in a totally ethical Christianity, or, better, a Christianity of social ethics.

7. One of the marks of the church's distance from the world is that it represents a minority. The circle of the true church (Psalm 12:2), of real believers, is never the same as the institutional church and the number of the baptized (especially in state churches). The institutional church for its part is never the same as the whole of the human race.

Thus Luther in his work on government in 1523 (WA, 11, 251, 33; LW, 45, 91) can say that the world and the masses remain non-Christian even though they are baptized and are called Christians. Christians live at a distance from one another so that the world is not afraid of Christian rule over all the world or even one country. The wicked are much more numerous than the righteous. Ruling the whole world or one country with the gospel would be like a shepherd putting wolves and lions and eagles and sheep all together in one fold and letting them move about free-ly. . . . The sheep would be at peace here and would graze peacefully but they would not live long (cf. also WA, 12, 329, 3; LW, 30, 74).

The church's role as a minority has two implications.

First, it sets up a barrier against a false belief in expansion and the erroneous idea that the church will win the earth and set up God's kingdom in this aeon. Awareness that it is a minority reminds the church that the kingdom of God comes from God—it does not develop; it comes—and that the church is not an end in itself but is only provisional.[6]

Second, the idea of being a minority expresses the contradiction between the essence of the church and a theocracy in the sense of the church's rule over the world. The church is the salt in the soup of the world, not the soup itself. It can be this, however, only so long as it "has not lost its taste" (Matthew 5:13). It must be

---

[6]Küng, *Christ sein,* p. 495; E.T. *On Being a Christian* (Garden City, N.Y., 1976).

oriented to the substance of its message and must seriously keep its distance from the world instead of being assimilated to it. As this minority it also has the promise that it has a vicarious function for the non-understanding world and delays judgment on it, as the five or ten righteous might have done in Sodom and Gomorrah at the request of Abraham (Genesis 18:22, 32). There is such a thing as representative expiation and representative intercession.[7] (This dimension of the church's ministry is much better represented in the spirituality of the Roman Catholic Church, especially its orders, than in Protestantism.) God has not so abandoned the human race, says Luther in a prayer, that he has not left the church in its midst and held it ready as a refuge.[8]

8. If the church is a despised minority under the cross, this relates not merely to its statistical proportions, to the lack of relation between the littleness of its numbers and the greatness of its task, but also to its qualitative marks. To the extent that it follows its despised Lord it joins and accepts the despised.[9] It makes itself the voice that no one hears anywhere else. It does not limit itself to caring for the righteous who do not need a doctor (Luke 5:31). In the name of God's kindness to men it turns to the poor and weak, to innocent sufferers, to those who are mocked, to the anxious and disquieted. It calls to those who are wandering abroad and invites them back home. It preaches the Savior to the lost. It does not threaten sinners but offers them forgiveness in the Savior's name.

For this reason it does not try to adorn itself with a representative elite who can vindicate its rank before the forum of the world. No, as the church under the cross it sees itself confirmed by the fact that not many wise or strong or noble according to the flesh are called, but God has chosen what is foolish in the world's eyes to put the wise to shame (1 Corinthians 1:26ff.). What is said about the essence and marks of the church describes, of course, what it ought to be, not (God knows!) what it is as the empirical church. For this church the cross of the despised is its judgment which recalls, and calls it to repentance for, its omissions, its search for power and influence, its opportunistic flirting with the elite of the wise and strong and noble. Attempts to dominate and hierarchical privileges within its own ranks are also brought under judgment. Within it the question who is great should not arise. In the world princes reign and the strong are in power, but it should not be so in the church. Those who want to be great must serve, as the Son of Man did (Mark 10:35-45; cf. Matthew 18:1ff.; Mark 9:33ff.).

It would be a mistake to conclude from this overthrow of current values, from this interchanging of the great and the small, the honored and despised, rulers and servants, that there is in the gospel, and therefore in the church, a general levelling down and equalizing. All these emphases on value and the reverse take place in specific relationships, and it matters a great deal whether they are asserted and claimed before men or before God. Before men there is undoubtedly a difference between Jews and Greeks. Before God, however, they stand in the same condemnation and the same need and promise of redemption (Romans 10:12). The same applies to the sexes (Galatians 3:28). To extend equality before God in the name of

---

[7]Cf. my book *Theologie der Anfechtung* (1949), pp. 180ff.
[8]Cf. his exposition of Psalm 90.
[9]Mark 9:35; 10:44; John 13:16; 15:20.

the gospel to secular differentiations is a mark of extremism. (This problem arises in the secular sphere itself, for equality before the law does not remove everyday differences.)

The two aspects can sometimes lead to conflict in the church. For instance, does the equality of men and women before God mean that women can be ordained to spiritual office as pastors or priests? Does only the "before God" apply here and therefore the same commission? Can we leave differences of sex out of account? (Cf. ThE, III, §§2491–2510. Cf. also the attempt to find biblical reasons for the impossibility of women priests [HK, III (1977), pp. 151ff.] and the rather milder version [HK, IV (1977), pp. 206ff.].)

XVII

The Dualism of Roman Catholic and Evangelical in Ecclesiology
Theological Issues of Separation

Bibliography: H. Küng, *Rechtfertigung,* 4th ed. (1964); E.T. *Justification* (New York, 1964); H. von Loewenich, *Der moderne Katholizismus vor und nach dem Konzil* (1970), pp. 119ff., 302ff.; H. Rückert, "Promereri. Eine Studie zum tridentischen Rechtfertigungs-Dekret als Antwort an H. A. Oberman" (cf. ZThK, LXI [1964], pp. 251ff.), *Vorträge und Aufsätze zur historischen Theologie* (1972), pp. 264ff.; also "Die Rechtfertigungslehre als Kontroverstheologisches Problem," *ibid.,* pp. 295ff.

1. THE UNDERSTANDING OF JUSTIFICATION

As it seems to me, the difficulties in overcoming the separation between the Roman Catholic and Reformation churches lie chiefly in the understanding of what the church is. Ecclesiology as we have developed it thus far has been implicitly controversial. We must now lay special stress on some aspects of this. In so doing we do best to begin with some negative statements which tell us why outside ecclesiology the confessional division has been much reduced since the time of the Reformation and has become not much more than a difference between theological schools.

We may begin by saying that the decisive difference of the Reformation period, that relating to justification, has lost its divisive significance in post-Tridentine Roman Catholicism. The Roman Catholic theology that confronted Luther was a nominalistic doctrine of grace which in spite of anti-Pelagian statements counted on man's cooperation in the attainment of justifying grace and therefore brought "grace alone" into question. Since Trent, however, we can hardly accuse Roman Catholicism of being dominated by nominalism or of identifying itself with what was for Luther his papist enemy.

The question also arises whether the Reformation "grace alone" is still confessionally exclusive. The sixth session of Trent with its decree on justification[1] no longer espouses Occam's nominalistic view of grace but takes up Thomistic themes and ascribes complete dominance to prevenient grace. Even though free will is stressed, there is no idea that man's supernatural goal of divine sonship can be reached with its help. It is one of man's natural endowments and all it can do is meet some moral claims and correspond to what Luther calls civil righteousness. For the true destiny of man, i.e., being accepted by God and given a part in salvation, grace alone is decisive. The idea of cooperation hardly arises in this regard, for strictly speaking what man can do with his works is not his own activity but is triggered by the granting of grace.

At two points—cautiously expressed—we do, of course, find hints that man is a kind of partner in relation to grace. But the serious question arises whether this form of partnership is not also found in Reformation theology and its exclusive articles.

First the Aristotelian thought-form underlying Thomistic theology provides for a preceding disposition to receive grace on the part of man. In Aristotle this lies in the primal relation between form (*eidos*) and matter (*hylē*). Matter seeks to be formed by idea and logos just as pure and empty form seeks material filling and content. Thus the matter of body is formed by the *eidos* of psyche. Psyche plays the role of grace in relation to matter. The entity functioning as matter (body or indeed soul) offers naturally, as its contribution, a disposition for form. Thus the artist chooses specific materials (stone, metal, etc.) for his figure because by their constitution they correspond to the goal of his creative work.

Does not this schema call in question the exclusiveness of grace by positing a disposition or premise for the work of grace? This is very possible if we absolutize the formal schema but not necessarily so if we use it only as an instrument and link it to the thought that God himself has already set up this disposition and that preparation for grace is a preliminary work of grace itself.[2] In what Reformation theology—except that of the younger Barth when he was so full of animosity against Schleiermacher and E. Brunner[3]—do we not find a search for some similar point of contact in human nature? Where is it ignored that we do not receive the gracious gift of revelation as stocks and blocks but as human beings, and that there is therefore a bridgehead for this gift in our natural endowment?

Here, too, we find a schema of analogy and disposition, and here, too, the real point is what rank is accorded to the schema. Is it absolutized, and is an attempt then made, with the help of natural theology, to define this disposition and to make it a condition for what grace can do in it, the salvation event being thus constructed from below? Or is it in the light of revelation that we inquire into the promises and responsibilities that reside in human nature? Different understandings of the analogy between nature and grace will arise according to the rank granted to the schema; it will be either an analogy of being[4] or an analogy of faith and relation.[5]

---

[1]Denz., 1520ff.; E.T. 792aff.

[2]Rückert, *Rechtfertigungslehre*, p. 301.

[3]Cf. EG, I, pp. 186–91; EF, I, pp. 144–47.

[4]E. Przywara, *Religionsphilosophie katholischer Theologie* (1927).

[5]K.-D. Nörenberg, *Analogia imaginis. Der Symbolbegriff in der Theologie P. Tillichs* (1966).

Secondly, the responsibility of man as a partner is part of the event of justification. In Roman Catholic-Thomistic thinking this is set in motion solely by prevenient, justifying, and operating grace. This frees man from the fetters of original sin in the sense of making him ready and able to grasp the supernatural goal that he is offered. Here a cooperative element is at work, then, to the extent that on the basis of unconditionally imparted grace man's own responsible work is initiated and it exerts itself to make of grace that which it grants him as his goal. Here then, if we will, a new disposition is available with the help of grace. This can either be claimed or forfeited, the responsibility being ours. Thus a relic of the idea of merit can remain.

It should not be overlooked, however, that since the time of Thomas this rather dubious idea has been strictly controlled and limited in Roman Catholic thinking. An effort has been made not to let the rivalry of human works suppress the supremacy of grace. A sign of this is Thomas' distinction between merits of congruence and merits of condignity (STh, I/II, 114, 3). The former are in no way commensurate with divine grace and depend on God's generosity. God magnanimously accepts our feeble attempts. In the latter there is a balance between achievement and reward. But they arise for Thomas only when grace itself does this meritorious work in me, so that no harm is done, or is meant to be done, to "grace alone." This thought of the omnicausality of grace is given an even stronger emphasis at Trent when it appeals to Augustine's statement that it is the goodness of God to allow his own gifts to be counted as merits (Tridentine Session VI, c. 16; Denz., 1548).

Here again we undoubtedly find in Reformation theology analogies which bring out the importance of an active relation to the new life (in the form of works) on the part of those who are regenerated and renewed by grace. Luther spoke not only of justification but also of a progressive making righteous. In the Larger Commentary on Galatians he depicted a judgment by works. We are referred in this connection to the Pauline relating of the indicative and the imperative.[6] We should also bear in mind the negative significance for the justified of a lack of good works. This lack can block the ability to believe and call in question the status of the justified.[7]

Notwithstanding all the parallels we should not overlook some different nuances in the understanding of justification.

1. Even though in Thomism human merits are grounded in the gift of grace, a final element of claim seems to be unavoidable on this level. It has its basis in the autonomy of the idea of merit and can be developed in new ways as occasion offers, i.e., in certain theologies. Luther's opposition to nominalism led him to a doctrine of justification whose point lies in the exclusiveness with which the justified are referred to forgiveness. Works are futile even in the best of lives.

2. The ontological schema of thought which dominates the scholastic tradition makes it unavoidable that God's grace should not only be viewed as personified in the gracious God, God's favor,[8] but that its material form should also be

---

[6]ThE, I, §§314ff.; E.T. I, pp. 72f., 83ff. (cf. p. 99, n. 12).

[7]Cf. ThE, I, §§333ff., 356ff.; E.T. I, pp. 83ff., 92f.

[8]Cf. Luther's Preface to Romans and Magnificat (1520/21).

thematized, e.g., in the different ways in which it is at work in us as infused grace. This produces a tendency toward introspection in which it is a matter of whether and how far the water level of grace rises and produces a corresponding advance in righteousness. It seems to me that the idea of merit, even though only relics of it are left, is a symptom of this introversion. In contrast it is typical that Luther's experience of justification (under the influence of Staupitz) is liberating just because it is delivered from introspection and focuses on what is done by Christ's act on the cross.

The question arises, then, whether there are not still confessional differences. Even if "grace alone" no longer divides us, are not different emphases put on the concept of grace? This does not have to mean that the two schemas of thought—the ontological and the personal—have to separate the churches. It should be noted, however, that the Reformation schema contains possibilities which can make it more than a mere mode of statement and can define the actual content of the statement.

That the schema of thought can achieve in Roman Catholic theology a rank and importance which come near to absolutizing is shown by the papal reaction to some attempts, especially by French theologians, to overthrow the ontological scholastic forms of thought and to state the old truth in new and existential terms. Henri de Lubac and Jean Daniélou were representatives of this new theology. Pius XII had them in view when in his encyclical "Humani generis" of 8/12/1950 he actually canonized the scholastic terminology and the accompanying ontological thinking and found in other forms of thought a sabotaging of material truth (von Loewenich, *Der moderne Katholizismus* . . . , pp. 279ff.). If the ontological form is so important there is good reason for concern lest the autonomy of this form should lead again to a view of grace which hides the gracious God behind the forms and functions of his grace. These are just possibilities which, if appearances do not deceive, have been blocked off in post-conciliar Roman Catholicism, but which still lurk in the background. The author hopes that Roman Catholic readers will not see suspicion here, but concern.

3. This concern is not reduced when one remembers that the Thomistic exposition of Trent and its thesis of "grace alone" is as yet only a theological opinion and not a decision of the teaching office. One *may* hold and teach this view, and it is up-to-date to do so, but what guarantee is there that something else will not then become up-to-date?[9] The Reformation churches deliberately take the one-sided view that for them there can be no changes in teaching at this point.

We may sum up our findings by saying that the post-Tridentine development of Roman Catholicism has outdated the antithesis of the Reformation period and that apart from different nuances the understanding of justification is no longer a reason for disunity.

2. THE PAPAL PRIMACY

The papacy, which Luther regarded as antichrist, and which has been a particular stone of stumbling for Protestant thinking since the infallibility decree of Vatican

---

[9]Rückert, *Rechtfertigungslehre*, pp. 303f.

I, does not have to be a reason for disunity either. Why should not the church be represented by a figure that symbolically incorporates its truth and task and ministry? But if this happens or should happen, the Reformation understanding of Word and Spirit will feel that it is injured so long as the legitimation of such a figure is achieved with the help of what are often historico-exegetical manipulations and everything is made to depend on an unbroken Petrine succession. Apart from historical considerations, the privilege of descent which is sought in this way is just as dubious theologically as is the Jewish claim to salvation on the basis of circumcision (Romans 2:28; cf. 1 Corinthians 7:19), even granting a proven genealogy and unequivocal succession.

Petrine descent can be validated only if the bearer of the office is not a temporal successor of Peter but is with Peter a follower of the common Lord. When we look at someone like John XXIII we are shown what a head of Christianity looks like who does not compete with the true Head of the church (even in popular piety) but who bows before him and as this bowed head cannot be overlooked even by skeptics.[10] If John XXIII enjoyed authority not only in his own church but ecumenically, it was not because people were impressed by the succession that validated him but because his authority was obviously authorized by the Lord of the church and because he demonstrated a credible discipleship. And when he used to greet believers and nonbelievers alike with the biblical statement: "I am Joseph, your brother" (Genesis 45:3f.), he abandoned the style of hierarchical lordship and accepted solidarity with all whom his Lord wished to serve.

The chief shepherd who discharges his office in the name and as the representative of the supreme Shepherd must also measure himself by Peter as the disciple who was not only distinguished by Jesus but also particularly subject to temptation and danger. Precisely when he received the greatest promises Peter showed himself also not to be a match for them. Precisely when the fervor of his mission threatened to elevate him he came into judgment and his need for forgiveness was made plain.

The gospels give us three illustrations of this.

1. He had just been called Peter (the rock) on which the community of Jesus would be built, he had just received the power of binding and loosing (Matthew 16:18f.), when immediately he ignorantly opposed the Lord's prediction of his passion and championed his own view of salvation, so that the one who had been distinguished was now rebuffed: "Get behind me, Satan! You are a hindrance to me; for you are not on the side of God, but of men" (Matthew 16:21-23). On Peter's way there lurked the temptation of not building a church of the cross but surreptitiously championing a theology of glory and a church triumphant.

2. The prayer of Jesus that his faith should not fail had just strengthened him and he had just given the assurance that he was ready to go to prison or death with his Lord (Luke 22:32f.) when the very next moment Jesus foretold that he would deny him three times before the cock crowed (22:34)—and this did in fact happen (22:60f.).

3. The triple question of Jesus to Peter: "Do you love me?" (John 21:15-17)

---

[10]I am not disparaging other popes but simply indicating the special symbolical significance which this pope had.

shows how threatened this love was and to what temptations it was subject. Nevertheless (not because there was any reliance on his strength or overlooking of his denials) he was entrusted with the shepherd's office and a hint was given that he, too, would go to the cross as a disciple of his Lord.

Now while it is true that Vatican II can point out that officebearers in the church are called to the service of the poor and suffering and not to rule and honor ("Optatam totius," 9; "Lumen gentium," 8; E.T. *Vatican II Documents*, pp. 446, 23f.) and this undoubtedly applies to the holder of the highest pastoral office, there is hardly any indication of the solidarity of the latter with the weakness of Peter. This aspect plainly takes second place to the hierarchical primacy and privileges based on Peter (cf. "Lumen gentium," 8, 22; E.T. pp. 22f., 42ff.).

In real union with the Peter of the gospels the pope should include himself in the "both righteous and sinner" which applies to all believers and move away from the dominant statements about his hierarchical primacy and monopoly of infallibility. This could not help but affect the self-understanding of bishops and priests as well.

At any rate, profound division in the church is not caused by a papal office that appeals to Peter but only by a specific form of the appeal to the apostle—one which seeks (doubtful) historical and theological support in succession, stylizes Peter as the prince of the apostles, overlooks his failings, and uses his leading position in the apostolic band as a reason for hierarchical privileges. The papacy has to face the question, then, whether it is uniting Christianity—as is possible if it follows Peter—or whether it has divisive import.

3. THE CONCEPT OF THE CHURCH ITSELF

The obstacles to reunion most often mentioned in discussion seem to have been essentially overcome, or at least there is a basic possibility of overcoming them. More difficult, however, is the question of the understanding of the church itself.

We have already come up against the decisive problems in relation to the canon and tradition. Within the triad of Scripture, tradition, and the church, the church prevails, as we have seen, in the sense that Scripture can never become a critical argument against the church but must always serve to justify it.[11] This does not apply to individual theologians but to official church documents, in short, to "Denzinger." Because of its expository monopoly the church is the real rule of faith. Represented by its leading officers, especially the pope, it is the bearer of the Spirit. It can thus teach obligatory doctrine with an authority that is not validated by the Word nor referred to it. All this implies that the church has the rank of a source of revelation that is coordinated with Scripture or superior to it. (We have illustrated this earlier by "Osiandrian" elements in Roman Catholic ecclesiology.) Along these lines Reformation theologians find a strange affinity between Roman Catholics and Radicals. In both, although in different ways and on the basis of different forms of reflection, the Spirit can break free from the Word and achieve autonomy.[12]

---

[11]Rückert, p. 322. Cf. also H. Diem, *Dogmatik*, II (1955), pp. 190ff.; E.T. pp. 216ff.; G. Ebeling, *Wort und Glaube*, I (1950), pp. 39ff., n. 4; E.T. pp. 52ff., n. 1.
[12]Cf. the Smalkaldic Articles (LBK, p. 454,7 and 27; cf. Jacobs, *Book of Concord*, p. 332, no. 4).

Although the Bible has lately become increasingly important for Roman Catholic theology, as in K. Rahner, the church still maintains a certain autarchy, a freedom from the claim of Scripture to normative rank. The most dramatic example of this was offered when Pius XII proclaimed the Assumption of Mary in his bull ''Munificentissimus Deus'' of 1950. The reference to Scripture here is a halfhearted performance of duty, since a biblical proof can be given only by the most preposterous allegorizing, which no reputable Roman Catholic exegete could possibly allow. In fact the basis is not Scripture but tradition and therefore the church's possession of the Spirit. Even this raises difficulties, for the first four centuries offer no testimonies to Mary's bodily assumption. The only possible basis for it is to claim the concept of active tradition, of adding to the structure under the guidance of the Spirit without any need to follow the biblical plans. The dogma of the immaculate conception proclaimed in 1854 was already an addition in this sense. From this cleansing from sin it is only a step to the conclusion that death, the wages of sin (Romans 6:23), had no power over her. H. M. Köster can actually say in this connection that we need a concept of revelation and its history which can explain the gradual development of beliefs that have no historically controllable connection with the legacy of apostolic truths but may still be infallibly proclaimed and confidently accepted (''Das theologische Gewissen und die marianische Frage,'' *Theologie und Kirche,* XL [1950], pp. 399f.).

It is an open question, not answered without some difficulty, whether trends which represent a return to Holy Scripture, and which have left their mark in Vatican II, can modify these traditionally established ecclesiological principles relating to the teaching office. What awakens hope is the concept behind our own doctrine of Scripture. The Word of God as a spiritual Word has transforming and evidential power. For this reason hope can fade only when the Bible is closed and traditions multiply parthegenetically.

Such a radical emancipation of tradition, however, would be an absurd notion in Roman Catholic ecclesiology. It is blocked off already by the simple doctrine that Holy Scripture is the first link in tradition and can never be disregarded as a (co-)determinative force in the formulation of doctrine (even though it may have to be manipulated and allegorized as in the case of the assumption of Mary). If in spite of confessional limits we can still talk together over the open book, we give the Word space to work. Conversation around the Word needs to be continued between individuals and groups where it is already taking place. If we will first pay heed to the hearing of the Word, all other things will come to us, including institutions as constructs based on experience.

XVIII

Ministries and Offices

1. THE RELATION BETWEEN CHURCH AND OFFICE

The Spirit is one, but he distributes different gifts according to the many functions which he has for members of the body and also according to the many individuals with their different talents and backgrounds. Thus Paul, to whom we owe our knowledge of the structure of the earliest churches, can speak of the many charisms and tasks embodied in the different offices and ministries: the apostles, prophets, evangelists, pastors, teachers, and others (1 Corinthians 12:28; Ephesians 4:11f.). We are always dealing with mutually supplementary, cooperative, and integrated tasks in the body of Christ. They are related because those who perform them—though differing in themselves as Jews or Greeks, bond or free (1 Corinthians 12:13)—all work together to serve the same body (12:1–11).

It is doubtful whether the word "office" corresponds to these functions. It is not a biblical word and carries a suggestion of rule, hierarchy, and government. Closer to the NT is the term *diakonia,* which implies discipleship and has the promise of the assistance of the Spirit for those who are called to it, so that *diakonia* and *charisma* correspond to one another.

The call to minister to Christ's body raises the question of the relation of those who bear this office to the community as a whole. Are they set apart? Is there a distinction between officers and the community, between those who have a ministry and those who are the object of their ministry? Or are these variations within one and the same community? The hierarchical distinction of some offices and officebearers in church history—and we do not refer only to popes and bishops—forces us to discuss this question.

We shall attempt to answer it in three theses.

First Thesis. Ministries to Christ's body are not only instituted by God but are also means of his own working.

The decisive thing about preaching is not that this office was historically founded by Christ and that the proclamation of the gospel was entrusted to it but that it has the promise that with the preached Word the Holy Spirit will be given who produces faith when and where he wills.[1] Christ himself wills to be present in the Word of his witnesses: "He who hears you hears me" (Luke 10:16); "He who receives you receives me" (Matthew 10:40).[2] The presence of Christ in his Word attests itself especially in the office of the keys, i.e., in the fact that his Word is an efficacious one, that it has the power to bind and loose (Matthew 16:19; 18:18).[3] In what is often man's feeble word God's Word will be present and will exercise its authority. One might say that in the ministry of proclamation man's word does not describe or give information about God's own Word but speaks it. It does not just talk about the forgiveness of sins but forgives. It is God's own Word made present by the Spirit. We cannot speak, then, about an official power that is in the possession of the efficacious Word. Such a power is not entrusted to the bearer of an office as character. It is entrusted to his word to which God ascribes the quality of his own Word. The officebearer can act only as one who serves this Word. His is a ministry of the Word.

We may not objectifyingly infer from this a simple equation of the human word and the divine. Every poor, garrulous, and nonsensical sermon shows how absurd this would be. Often we only talk about the gospel and do not address it to people in the Spirit. Pious phraseology and easy cliches can hardly claim the promise of the Spirit's presence. This is simply an offer to the preacher and the congregation. The preacher can pray for the Spirit and trust that in the discipline of the Spirit and his own self-forgetful work on the text the message will shine through his weak human word. The congregation must pray that it will not ask for subjective edification of inspiring pulpit oratory or self-confirmation but for a real work of judgment and grace. The identity of God's Word and man's is an object of prayer and promise and not the content of an abstract equation.

Second Thesis. The ministry of the Word—which we are using here to represent all ministries and offices—is not committed to special persons who then as officebearers have an exclusive hierarchical position in relation to the community. It is entrusted to the church as a whole. Thus the Lutheran confessions emphasize that the power of binding and loosing, and therefore God's Word in all its efficacy, is not given to Peter alone but to all the disciples and therefore to the whole community.[4] In the normative NT passages,[5] T. Harnack states,[6] the special prerogatives of the apostles who founded the church are not given prominence but instead the preaching of the Word, the administration of the sacraments, and the forgiveness of sins, i.e., only those rights and powers which are common to both the office that serves to uphold the church and the apostolic office that founded it.

Since the full power of the Word is entrusted to the whole church as a common legacy, and since the whole church is itself the true officebearer commissioned for ministry, office is not connected with specific people. It is defined instead by functions that are allotted to individuals through their relation as members to the

---

[1]CA, V, pp. 1f.
[2]CAApol, pp. 240,45; 401,26; cf. Jacobs, *Book of Concord*, p. 167, no. 28; p. 298, no. 19.
[3]Smalkaldic Articles, p. 478,21; Jacobs, p. 342, no. 24.
[4]So Melanchthon in connection with the Smalkaldic Articles (LBK, p. 478,24ff.; Jacobs, p. 342, no. 24).
[5]John 20:21ff.; Mark 16:15; Matthew 18:18ff.; Luke 24:47.
[6]*Op. cit.*, No. 80.

Head and the whole body.[7] The NT function differs from the Levitical ministry of the OT to the extent that conditions of tribe and status and the like do not determine the ability to act but there is a freedom for calling to service.[8] The ministry of the Word is simply given by the Word itself. Since the Word is God's (and not a word about God), the ministers do not represent themselves but speak as representatives of the Lord himself (vice Christi) according to the saying: "Who hears you hears me."[9]

This speaking for Christ and ignoring of self can go so far that even hypocrites and the ungodly can be said to have a valid ministry. The question how far this validity extends is decided by what these people say, not by what they are. The hearers and recipients must be on guard against false prophets and must pay heed to the warning: "If anyone is preaching to you another gospel, let him be accursed" (Matthew 7:15; Galatians 1:9).

The reason why there neither can nor should be any hierarchical distinction of persons is that all members of the church (in the strict sense) are commissioned for service and proclamation and this leaves no place for privileged intermediaries. In the name of the universal priesthood all are equal in principle. All who have come crawling from baptism, says Luther, can boast of being already consecrated as priests and bishops and popes.[10] But this equality, he adds, cannot mean that it is seemly for all to discharge their office, though they enjoy it potentially. We are all priests and the same power is entrusted to all of us but we may not infer from this that there is a collective priesthood with no specific officebearers. What may be inferred is that there are no personal rights. Since all are priests, nobody must thrust himself forward and undertake to do without our consent and selection what we all have power to do.[11]

It would undoubtedly be a mistake to find only a sociological basis for this line of thinking—as though hopeless chaos would ensue and there could be no more order if all potential officebearers in the universal priesthood were to begin preaching and administering the sacraments and taking occasional services at the same time. Alarming though freedom of this kind might be, it is not the decisive reason why the spiritual capacity of all believers does not rule out the existence of specific officebearers (pastors, deacons, bishops, and the like). There are instead theological reasons for this. Just because the task of preaching and serving is that of the whole church no one should take up the common task without the will and command of the community. What belongs to the community must be done representatively. The commission, then, is to a function, to a representation of the fact that the body of Christ is made up of many members.

That the members are defined exclusively by their functionality in the body means a relativizing of the person. Officebearers have no specially privileged spirituality such as is supposedly expressed in the indelible character received at

---

[7]Ibid., No. 83.
[8]Melanchthon (LBK, p. 479,26ff.; Jacobs, p. 343, no. 26).
[9]CAApol, IX (LBK, p. 246,16; Jacobs, p. 172, no. 27).
[10]Luther, To the Christian Nobility, Three Treatises (1970), p. 14.
[11]Loc. cit.

ordination. No, if an officebearer is deposed or his function ceases, he is an ordinary member like all the rest. There can be no equating of office and person. This occurs only in Christ himself.

If ordination confers no indelible character and gives the person no special qualities except that of serving the body of Christ, Melanchthon is obviously guilty of regression when he calls priestly ordination a sacrament (CAApol, XIII; LBK, p. 293,29ff.; Jacobs, p. 214, no. 8). He remedies this when in his *Tractate on the Power of the Pope* he points out that the people originally chose their pastors and that ordination was simply a confirmation of their choice (LBK, p. 491,73ff.; Jacobs, p. 350, no. 70).

Naturally certain qualities and gifts are taken into account in the selection and confirmation of an officebearer. A stutterer will not be ordained to the preaching office. It is also legitimate to link the assumption of an office or ministry with certain cultural qualifications. But there must be limits to practical considerations and no fixed law should be established. If the Spirit of God moves when and where he wills, this applies also to the imparting of his gifts. These are not subject to human calculation or disposition. Room must be left in the church for charisms. On the other hand charismatics cannot infer personal rights from the entrusting of special graces to them. They cannot oppose a whole congregation to which the body-function is granted. They must not choose themselves but be chosen. Readiness for this will, of course, be exposed to situations of critical conflict when the congregation is riveted to legalism and sensitivity to the freedom of the Spirit's moving has been lost.

Understood in this way, charismata that qualify for service may make people independent of ordinary gifts and talents. In the Confessing Church of the Hitler period there were some who, humanly speaking, had few gifts and were anything but qualified theologians but who as "weaker brothers" fulfilled the function of pillars which the strong and qualified were unable to fulfil. Not infrequently they were able with words that did not reach the level of current worldly wisdom to shake whole synods out of confusion and weakness and lead them to the barricades in the spiritual battle. Charismatic treasures can be hidden in earthen vessels (2 Corinthians 4:7). Hence the claim that charismatics should not choose themselves but be chosen must be balanced by the claim that the church should discern the spirits and remember that there can be done here what no eye has seen nor ear heard. Our natural senses cannot see through the earthen vessels.

With the fact that ministry is tied to function and its discharge, and in both senses presupposes universal priesthood, is connected the further fact that the priest occupies no special position between God and man (P. Brunner, "Sacerdotium und Ministerium," *Kerygma und Dogma,* II [1972], pp. 101ff., esp. p. 107). Only Christ himself as High Priest exercises this mediatorship. If Paul can use the term *leitourgos* (Romans 15:16), he emphatically does not use it in the sense of the priestly mediator. His priestly service of the gospel is his winning of the Gentiles as sacrifices and not his bringing an offering for them to mediate between them and God. What Paul is thus describing is his mission as a preacher and evangelist, not as a priestly mediator. The OT term is used only with tongue in cheek and undergoes typical modification.

2. SUMMARY AND CONSIDERATION OF NEW LINES OF INQUIRY

a. Over against the unity of grace stands a plurality of gifts of grace corresponding to the differentiation of ministries and offices within the one service of discipleship. "There are varieties of gifts, but the same Spirit; and there are varieties of service, but the same Lord" (1 Corinthians 12:4f.). The reason why there is the same grace, the same Spirit, and the same Lord behind the many gifts is that we are always dealing with the gracious God. What is meant by this is God's attitude toward us.

The idea of grace has something a little dubious about it because it can break free from the gracious God and become autonomous. (Material concepts of grace such as one often finds in Roman Catholic dogmatics, e.g., infused grace, suggest that there is a certain inclination toward this emancipation.) This is why Luther underlines the personal character of grace and always defines it as God's favor. For him the basis of the unity of grace is that God gives *himself* to us in Christ. The gifts of grace are simply outworkings of this attitude which in relation to the variety of individuals and the required ministries have the appearance of parts or portions, i.e., a plural representation of the one basic divine attitude.

Thus in his Preface to Romans (1522) Luther sees the following difference between grace and gift. Grace is God's favor toward us out of which he is pleased to put Christ or the Spirit into us with his gifts. Although these outworkings of grace seem to be broken and partial, grace itself brings it about that we are accounted wholly righteous before God so that grace does not break up into parts as the gifts do. It takes us up totally into God's favor for the sake of Christ our mediator and advocate and in order that there might be a beginning of the gifts in us. So we must always look away from ourselves and the arrival of the gifts in us and look back at the beginning when we realized that we were the objects of divine favor (LW, 35, 369f.; cf. also the application of all this to the understanding of the church in the exposition of Psalm 90 [WA, 40/III, 506, 20ff.; LW, 13, 90]).

b. Over against the unity of faith in the divine favor stands the multiplicity of theological ministries, i.e., of forms of reflection on this faith.

Although this pluralism is limited, there are valid reasons for the multiplicity of theologies and schools, for the gospel of God's favor which gives rise to faith is an addressed message and reaches people of differing individualities in different times and situations. The result is that the required ministry of theology necessarily breaks up into different parts and pieces.

This variety can be conditioned by the different forms of thought that are available in the different intellectual periods, e.g., ontological Aristotelian forms in the scholastic age or personalistic concepts in Luther's theology. We have already had repeated occasion to say how profoundly aspects of the gospel are modified by current categories of thought. It is one of the legitimate intellectual (and spiritual) forms of appropriation to be able to express what needs to be understood in our own words and with our own thought-forms.

Each variation is, of course, limited—a part. This should suggest to us that the danger in theological thinking is not that it can deal only with partial aspects but that it may absolutize these aspects. The gospel is always more than the limited form of reflection in which we express it. Faith is always more than its development in thought. The legacy of the church's teaching is always more comprehensive than the output of a theological school. Theological *diakonia*, then, must have the humility to remember that while it cannot avoid distinctions and polemics its own aspect is limited. It needs to maintain a feeling for complementarity in the relations between individual theologies. This complementarity is particularly relevant to the relation between ontological and personalistic thought-forms.

That the differentiation of the gospel into various modes of theological ministry is connected with the different situations in which we receive God's Word has found classic expression in Paul Tillich's principle of correlation. Tillich has shown that the word "God" acquires different and new meanings according to the situation of our inquiry or concern. When the concept seems to stand in correlation with the threatening of our existence by non-being, God will have to be called the infinite power of being which withstands this threat. When anxiety is understood as awareness of finitude, God will have to be called the infinite basis of courage (cf. *Systematic Theology*, I [1955], p. 64). This topic was more fully discussed in EF, I, especially c. 1 and c. 3.)

The differentiation of theological ministries reaches extreme forms where there is reflection on one's own (political or social) situation, i.e., in ethics. In taking a theological position relative to political problems[12] psychological, sociological, and conventional "pre"-judgments will inevitably play a normative part in diagnosis of the situation, and its theological evaluation will at most achieve the rank of a judgment. Hence a consensus of the whole church fellowship (e.g., a synod) can hardly be expected, the evaluation will bear very strikingly the character of a partial theological aspect, and the concept of the limited nature of such statements will take on enhanced urgency.[13]

In Roman Catholic theology the gradated structure of man and grace (*analogia entis*) and the resultant doctrine of natural law (ThE, I, §§2010ff.) make possible a far-reaching casuistry and an authoritarian leadership such as one finds in the corresponding encyclicals. This decisiveness in detailed instruction which makes decisions and frees from conflicts meets the natural desires of vast numbers of people. One might almost say that it links up with the needs of human nature. It was along these lines that G. K. Chesterton justified his transition from the Anglican to the Roman Catholic Church. He found in the former no unity or agreement, no single answer to people who wanted an authoritative judgment. He could find no use for a church unequipped to fight, or even to lead its troops in the same direction, in the great issues of spiritual conflict and morality. In relation to the most important questions of life he found clarity and resoluteness only in the Roman Catholic Church and for this reason he became a Roman Catholic (*The Defendants*).

---

[12]Cf. in Germany such questions as rearmament after World War II or the question of the eastern frontier.
[13]For a more detailed discussion cf. my *Notwendigkeit und Begrenzung des politischen Auftrags der Kirche* (1974) and Anthrop (1976).

c. There are illegitimate and legitimate forms of this multiplicity of ministries and offices.

1. An illegitimate form is that of forming parties, i.e., of claiming absoluteness for a partial aspect, and the resultant and necessary rejection of other standpoints. This involves the adopting of a confessional stance with its anathemas. An absolute attitude is taken up toward what is relative. In sectarian style an individual member suffers from elephantiosis. A single theological school claims to represent *the* truth and thus tries to take on the rank of *the* church. Paul criticizes the parties at Corinth along these lines. One says "I am for Paul," another "I am for Apollos," another "I am for Cephas," another "I am for Christ." "Is Christ divided then?" (1 Corinthians 1:11f.; 3:12-15).[14] The unity of the communion of saints[15] is grounded in the one Lord. It can be destroyed only by denial of this Lord. Only the core of Christian truth can be the criterion by which to measure its destruction. This core can consist only of fundamental confessional statements, e.g., the threefold "alone" of the Reformation: grace alone, faith alone, and Scripture alone. Disunity cannot be measured by the criterion of secondary opinions, external customs and usages (in the observance of human traditions), or ceremonies.[16]

Yet even when the divisive anathema seems to be unavoidable, as at the Reformation, the wound of the divided body must not close. It must be kept open by gauze. Those who do not suffer from it will at once become a party which absolutizes itself. For the sake of truth, which is also truth *for* others, love may be forced to accept divisions. But it will not be able to cease seeking those on the other side. It will not be able to cease putting the self-critical question whether the division is really over essentials or over relative matters. It will also be ready for the further question whether and how far the circumstances that produced the division have changed, so that a revision of positions is necessary. Suffering under the division can never be without an awareness of guilt, or at least of possible guilt. It will also see that there is need for forgiveness in theological controversies, for we can see only what is before us, and our reason—even our theological reason—recognizes only the arguments of reason, whereas God knows the heart and notes the doubtful motives that stand behind or at least play some part in the arguments (1 Samuel 16:7).

2. Legitimate forms of multiplicity in ministry are characterized by the fact that in them equals render their service together: rich and poor, prominent and unknown, people of different race, nationality, and social status, groups with different and even antithetical interests, the enthusiasts and the more restrained. They do this because they are all disciples of the same Lord. For all of them the criterion of church membership is ministry to the body of Christ. The church itself is validated as such by being a serving and not a ruling church, by addressing itself to

---

[14]H. Küng, "Parteien in der Kirche?" *Concilium*, IX (1973), pp. 594ff.; E.T. "Parties in the Church?... , *Concilium*, LXXXVIII (New York, 1973), pp. 133ff.

[15]On the communion of saints cf. Althaus, *Communio sanctorum* (1929); E. Wolf, *Peregrinatio*, I, pp. 279ff.; Schmaus, *Dogmatik*, III, 1, pp. 128ff.; Moltmann, *Kirche . . .* , p. 341; E.T. pp. 314ff. On the unity of the church cf. H. von Campenhausen, "Einheit und Einigkeit in der Kirche," EvTh, III (1973), pp. 280ff.

[16]CA, VII, p. 3; Apol, VII/VIII, pp. 33f.

those who are anonymous, who have no voice, who are a poor and perhaps a despised minority. As a church under the cross it will not link itself to the glory of worldly prominence nor seek conformity with those who rule. The poor and humble and hurt are its treasure. It is here that the multiplicity of its ministry reaches true fulfilment.

The story of the martyr St. Lawrence (d. 258 in Rome) answers the question where the treasures of the church may be found. When asked by the emperor to produce the church's supposed secret wealth Lawrence collected the blind, lame, crippled, epileptic, and leprous, who all ventured to come before the emperor, and said: "The gold you want is the cause of many crimes; its glitter is deceptive. The true gold is the light of the world, Jesus Christ. These"—and he now pointed to the poor around him—"are the children of the light and the real treasures of the church, its gold and pearls and precious stones."

d. If in Paul's theology no problems arise in the grouping together of ministries and charisms, so that one can speak of the grace of service and of participation in Christ's body, problems arose in this regard in the early catholic church. Already in the Pastoral Epistles and Luke we find a structured order instead of the more charismatically determined Pauline communities. Conflict between organization and the free moving of the Spirit seems to be unavoidable, and openly or hiddenly it runs through the whole history of the church. The tendency to institutionalize the Pneuma in offices and to understand him as the spirit of office is often the result of self-defense against Gnostic and other ecstatic movements which threaten to break up the unity of the body through individual or collective introversion.[17] The institutionalizing of the Spirit, which we dealt with in connection with the "Osian-drian" relating of church and Spirit, uses the help of law—in this case the law of church organization—in its attempt to control the chaotic trends which result from a separation of the Spirit from the Word and the corresponding pneumatic practices.

The intervention of law is always a sign of weakness. The church itself is so little in possession of the Word and Spirit that it cannot use these alone to contain those who are in error. We do not intend this as a Pharisaic accusation. There are perhaps times and situations in which the church's need of forgiveness has to be evident in this way and all that it can do is to replace its lack of the Spirit by the legal use of order and church law. But it should do so in a readiness to repent which recognizes its own lack of spiritual power and which thus relativizes the substitute power of the spirit of office. To the extent that it is ready to do this it will preserve a measure of openness to charismatics and not (at least in this instance) quench the Spirit (1 Thessalonians 5:19; 1 Corinthians 14:30, 39).

e. The limitation of institutionality indicated hereby takes on particular significance in the Protestant state churches. If the church as the communion of saints is present where the gospel is purely preached and the holy sacraments of the gospel are administered,[18] then the question is put to the church's organization—especially to the local congregation and its officebearers—whether it really meets

---

[17]Cf. E. Käsemann, "Amt und Gemeinde im NT," *Exegetische Versuche* . . . , I (1960), pp. 109–34. On this cf. H. Küng, *Kanon,* pp. 193ff.; cf. also J. Rohde, *Urchristliche und frühkatholische Ämter* (East Berlin, 1976).

[18]CA, VII.

this criterion. The structural relationships of the national church leave it more susceptible and vulnerable to ideological penetration than a free church. With some exceptions its preachers have an official position which makes them to some degree independent of the congregations. This certainly protects them against questionable claims and desires and to that extent it makes sense.[19] On the other hand, the local congregation can be intolerably victimized by erroneous, heretical, and ideologically pervasive preaching. The helplessness of the local church is all the greater because disciplinary procedures are very hard to set in motion and above all because they are resisted, and accused of intolerance, by a pluralism which has almost come to be regarded as natural common sense. Since the national church refers the individual to his local church, and since the being of the church depends on the relation of its preaching to Scripture, the individual can find himself in the sorry situation of being the member of a non-church whose dubious status is supported by his taxes. The institutional church is even more open to question today because many of its officebearers are false—political—teachers and its churches are for the most part made up, not of true believers, but of indifferent taxpayers and mere names on the rolls.

Increasingly within the national churches, therefore, one finds alongside the official congregations smaller and unofficial groups which constitute the communion of saints as societies of different kinds[20] or as house churches.[21] The direct event of proclamation does not always have to be at the center. Contemporary questions—the generation gap, social tasks, etc.—may be discussed in the light of the gospel, so that a spiritual and intellectual work is done which often fails to offer the church correct if perhaps overtraditional preaching. In the latter case especially the danger that members will regard themselves as an elite, and will therefore set up a little church within the church, is not the real threat. There will be no claim to spiritual superiority but only the offering of emergency solutions to the spiritual deficiency of the official church, or a concern to actualize the gospel, to make it present, in the concrete problems of the day.

The question that arises at once in such cases is why not leave the empty husk of the official church, which may now be filled with an alien spirit, and why not set up an independent church (although there have been departures enough in the name of the gospel and not in renunciation of it). We came up against this question when we asked where the church is to be found and we now come up against it once more, though this time from a different angle.

The local congregation is, of course, the primary place to find the church. For here we have, or ought to have, the Word and sacrament, the living voice of the gospel. If the local congregation were the only form of the church, its ideological or heretical perversion should hardly lead to any other result than that of leaving it.[22] But the local congregation is only a niche in the larger building of the church.

---

[19] A comparison with free churches e.g., in the United States, helps us to appreciate this positive side. Here pastors can be dependent on influential groups within the church who can "fire" them at any time. There are problems either way, no institution offering protection against the devil.

[20] Cf. the pietist groups in Württemberg, etc.

[21] These may result from evangelistic work or arise spontaneously.

[22] In some cases this might be justified but it would not have to mean leaving the church as a whole.

Even if one niche becomes unusable, to leave the whole building is not a suitable response. The concrete delivering of the message is direct. It takes place in obedience to the gospel without being determined or mediated by any institution. Yet it takes place within the whole communion of saints which overarches the local church. This communion also overarches the centuries. It extends from the church of the patriarchs, prophets, and apostles to the community of the end-time. No individual group can live apart from this totality or without longing to be one with it and as best it can to make it felt in a given place.

This has to mean that one cannot leave a dubious local congregation too lightly. One should be concerned to further the alternative or supplementary work of a group within it. By concrete discipleship and proclamation one should seek to overcome its doubtful features.

A. Worship, Word, and Sacraments

Bibliography (apart from dogmatic, historical, and homiletical works): P. Althaus, "Luthers Abendmahlslehre," *Luther-Jahrbuch* (1929); W. Andersen, "Möglichkeiten und Grenzen der Abendmahlsgemeinschaft heute," ThEx, N.F. 7 (1949). Arnoldshain Theses on the Lord's Supper: G. Niemeier, H. Gollwitzer, H. Meyer, W. Kreck, P. Brunner, E. Sommerlath, F. Heidler, and K. Halaski, *Gespräch über das Abendmahl* (East Berlin); E. Barnikol, "Der Bruch der Arnoldshainer Abendmahlsthesen mit der Heilsgeschichte des Evangeliums," *Wissenschaftliche Zeitschrift der Martin Luther-Universität Halle-Wittenberg* (November, 1962), pp. 147f.; "Die Arnoldshainer Abendmahlsthesen," *Lutherischer Rundblick*, IV (1958), pp. 142f.; K. Kirsten, H. Laabs, W. M. Oesch *et al.*, "Theologische Feststellungen zu den Arnoldshainer Abendmahlsthesen," *ibid.*, p. 134. H. Benckert, *Die Stofflichkeit der Abendmahlsgabe* (1961); G. Bornkamm, art. "Mystērion," TDNT, IV, pp. 802ff. (TWNT, IV, pp. 809ff.); W. Dantine, "Kirche und Sakrament," MD, III/IV (1967), pp. 41ff.; also "Gedanken über Funktion und Sinn der Leuenberger Konkordie," *Bericht der Kommission für Glauben und Kirchenverfassung*, II (8/12/71), pp. 202ff.; H. Diem, *Dogmatik,* III: "Die Kirche und ihre Praxis" (1963); H. Echternach, "'Ist'—als Kopula und Kategorie," *Kerygma und Dogma,* III (1975), pp. 193ff.; H. Gollwitzer, *Coena Domini* (1937); also "Die Abendmahlsfrage als Aufgabe kirchlicher Lehre," *Theologische Aufsätze, K. Barth zum 50. Geburtstag* (1936); H. Grass, *Die Abendmahlslehre bei Luther und Calvin,* 2nd ed. (1964); J. Groot, "Welt und Sakrament," *Concilium,* IV (1968), pp. 24ff.; E.T. "The Church as Sacrament of the World," *Concilium,* XXXI (New York, 1968), pp. 51ff.; P. Jacobs, E. Kinder, and F. Viering, *Gegenwart Christi* (1959); W. Joest, *Ontologie der Person . . .* (1967), pp. 355ff.; E. Jüngel (with K. Rahner), *Was ist ein Sakrament?* (1971), pp. 9ff.; E. Käsemann, "Anliegen und Eigenart der paulinischen Abendmahlslehre," EvTh, IX/X (1948), pp. 263ff.; E. Kinder, E. Sommerlath, and W. Kreck, art. "Sakramente," RGG³, V, pp. 1321ff.; G. Kretschmar, "Die Geschichte des Taufgottesdienstes in der alten Kirche," *Leitourgia,* V, pp. 1–346; R. Leuenberger, *Taufe in der Krise* (1973); Leuenburg Concord (Lutheran-Reformed discussion): H. G. Geyer and M. Lienhard, "Gemeinschaft der reformatorischen Kirche," *Polis,* XLI (1971), pp. 5–176; on the eucharistic controversy, pp. 69ff.; W. von Loewenich, *Vom Abendmahl Christi* (1938); J. P. Michael, "Personalität und Heilsverständnis. Vom Seinsgehalt protestantischer Glaubensaussagen," *Wort und Wahrheit,* VII (1954), pp. 495ff.; J. Moltmann, *Kirche in der Kraft des Geistes* (1975), §§3–5; E.T. *The Church in the Power of the Spirit,* III–V; K. F. Müller and W. Blankenburg, ed., *Leitourgia. Handbuch des evangelischen Gottesdienstes,* 5 vols. (1954ff.); P. Neuenzeit and H. R. Schlette, art. "Sakrament," *Handbuch theologischer Grundbegriffe,* IV (1970); W. M. Oesch, "Zur Krise des Opferbegriffs beim Abendmahl," *Lutherischer Rundblick,* IV (1958), pp. 143ff.; O. H. Pesch, "Besinnung auf die Sakramente," *Freiburger Zeitschrift für Philosophie und Theologie,* XVIII (1971), pp. 266ff.; R. Prenter, "Die Realpräsenz als Mitte des christlichen Gottesdienstes," *Gedenkschrift für Elert* (1955); K. Rahner, "Wort und Eucharistie," *Schriften zur Theologie,* IV, 3rd ed. (1962), pp. 313ff.; E.T. *Theological Investigations,* IV, pp. 253ff.; also "Die Gegenwart Christi in Sakrament des Herrenmahls," *ibid.,* pp. 357ff. (E.T. pp. 287ff.); also (with E. Jüngel) *Was ist ein Sakrament?* (1971), pp. 67ff.; E. Schillebeeckx, *De sacramentele heilseconomie* (Antwerp, 1952); also "Die Kirche als Dialog-sakrament," *Gott—die Zukunft des Menschen* (1969), pp. 100ff.; E.T. *God, the Future of Man* (New York, 1968), pp. 117ff.; E. Schlink, "Die Lehre von der Taufe," *Leitourgia,* V, pp. 642–808; E.T. *The Doctrine of Baptism* (St. Louis, 1972); R. Slenczka, "Abendmahlspraxis, Abendmahlslehre, Abendmahlsgemeinschaft," *Bericht der Kommission für Glauben und Kirchenverfassung* (1971), pp. 186ff.; C. Stange, *Die Lehre von der Sakramenten* (1958); H. Thielicke, *Leiden an der Kirche,* 2nd ed. (1966); E.T. *The Trouble with the Church* (New York, 1965); Vatican Council, "Lumen gentium," 1, 7, etc. (Index); E.T. *The Documents of Vatican II,* pp. 20ff.

XIX

Worship, Preaching, and Liturgy

All ministries and the ministry of all come together in divine service or worship. For all receive their call and promise from common hearing. All answer what is heard in common prayer. All join in festal praise of him who calls them. All bow in common repentance in confession of their continuing guilt. Through the gospel all receive together remission from their guilt and bondage. All begin their way together in baptismal calling and all celebrate fellowship with their Lord and with one another at his table. Strengthened by commissioning and promise all are sent out together, with a parting blessing, to tasks and burdens and joys and even loneliness and enforced inactivity (in age or sickness). The Christian life begins, continues, and ends in worship.

1. THE REMOTENESS OF WORSHIP FROM THE WORLD AND ITS PROXIMITY TO IT

1. Worship is twofold. It takes place at a distance from daily life in the form of contemplation and celebration. Its special orientation to Sunday emphasizes this withdrawal even temporally. The gathering for worship is also, however, a departing fellowship which is sent back from celebration into the everyday world with the assurance of continuing fellowship with the Lord.

The meditation practiced in worship and triggered by it has the same twofold character. It takes us out of the stress and strain of daily life by way of reflection on what is essential, on the one thing that is fundamentally "needful" in the midst of every necessity or distraction (Luke 10:42). It does this, however, in order that we may be brought back from a sacral distance (that of Sunday worship) to the beginning, middle, and end of our working days. Meditation and prayer at the bench or desk or in the car can constantly actualize afresh the relation of the everyday to the one who gives both promise and commission. In this sense household work and childbearing and all daily tasks become worship.[1] If worship is hearing and doing God's Word, praising God, singing, praying, confessing sin, and seeking forgiveness,[2] the gap between the sacral and the secular dimension, between remoteness from the world and proximity to it, is constantly overcome.

2. Proximity and remoteness are made present by the eschatological reference of worship. If praising God means seeing the salvation event from its beginning to its end in the final victory of God, then this includes the eschatological depth of worship. Worship celebrates and anticipates the coming again of the Lord. It moves in the shadow of this future event even when it does not expressly deal with it. This consideration of God's coming kingdom and the Lord's Parousia lends consoling distance vis-à-vis the inscrutability of the moment and of the processes of this aeon, whether in the cosmic sphere or the personal and biographical sphere. This consoling distance is supported by the certainty that the saving meaning of all the obscure and trying things that now confront us will one day be disclosed (John 13:7; cf. Genesis 15:20). But with this eschatological distance we are given the task of setting up in this passing aeon the sign of that which comes and endures.

This is what Bishop W. Krusche of Magdeburg meant when he said that worship is the renewal of the promise for the task that is so questionable in the world of experience. In it the horizon of promise is newly opened up, in the name of the crucified and risen Lord, over the secular experience of death. Thus along with complaint: "Why? How long? Where art thou, God?" there is also praise of him who pronounced his creation good and who at the end will inaugurate his kingdom (Krusche at the Conference of European Churches at Nyborg [*Documents,* 24/71, pp. 12f.]).

3. Remoteness and proximity may also be seen in the festal side of worship, as at the great feasts of the Christian year. When Christmas tells us that God's coming in the flesh is a miracle of condescension, it shows how distant and alien and unreachable God's majesty would be if he had not performed this miracle of the incarnation. Easter, which celebrates the overcoming of death by resurrection, takes place against the background of a death which as the "wages of sin" snatches after us (Romans 6:23; Genesis 3:22) but is now shown to be powerless. Pentecost as the feast of the outpouring of the Spirit stands under the sign of the antithesis between God's Spirit and our spirit, between worldly wisdom and the folly of the cross (1 Corinthians 1:18–31).

With this remoteness there is also the proximity of festal worship. Human everyday events stand in its magnetic field; with its help birth and death, the seasons, political celebrations, birthdays, and jubilees are all seen (or ought to be) from the standpoint of eternity.

2. PREACHING AND LITURGY

The ritual of worship also suggests proximity and remoteness. This is mainly due to the contrapuntal functions of preaching and liturgy. To borrow a metaphor, one

---

[1]Cf. LBK, p. 118, No. 57; p. 404; Jacobs, *Book of Concord,* p. 60, no. 57.
[2]*Ibid.,* pp. 581,84; 190,33; 220,189; Jacobs, p. 402, no. 84; p. 108, no. 33; p. 143, no. 189.

might say that liturgy is the supporting leg of worship and preaching the free leg.

Even when preaching centers on teaching[3] it is preaching only to the extent that it does not just speak about God but speaks the Word of God and is thus the efficacious Word of pardon.

It can do justice to the given immediacy of the hearer only by being an addressed message, by making the message present to the hearer and his age in the power of the Spirit. It has to be relevant. It has to correspond to its time. As a living voice, it is thus tied to the venture of the witness who trusts the Spirit that moves where he wills. It has before it a biblical text. But the job of the witness is to interpret, address, and actualize this, putting his own cause in the service of God's cause. Because it is a venture and has to be bold, e.g., in avoiding cliches, it may err in detail or sound the wrong note or vary in quality. Preaching also depends on things like the situation of the preacher, on his experiences, on how fresh or tired he is, on his spiritual and human disposition. The degree of his theological insight and human maturity can also play a part. Finally we should not underestimate the contribution of the theological and more general spirit of the age, including its ideological influence.

Above all, what might be called the history of preaching has a hand in the hermeneutical cooperation of the preacher in expounding the text.[4] Anyone who reads older collections of sermons will note at once that we could not preach them unchanged today even though they are the work of great preachers whom we still honor (e.g., Luther or Schleiermacher). But we often hear sermons that could just as well have been preached in 1880. Such apparent timelessness is not an advantage. It implies a degeneration of preaching. If preaching is no more than quoting and paraphrasing biblical and liturgical idioms and combining traditional concepts in new forms as though they were glass beads, then paradoxically we can find no theological fault just because such sermons suffer from a lack of theology, i.e., of original interpretation and daring actualization. The impression of timelessness is achieved only by ignoring the age and not allowing the Word to be incarnate in it.

The text that is expounded is a bulwark against the danger that a sermon will belong to the age instead of being close to it. The ceremonial rule about the relation of text and sermon has always been controversial. The problem comes out in the choice between basing the sermon on a text or on a theme.[5]

There are two ways of proceeding.

1. The first asks whether the legitimate form of evangelical preaching is not the homily, a meditation which works through the text verse by verse and word by word.

If this thesis, which is championed especially by Barth and his followers, opposes a thematic form of preaching, it sets itself in the half-light between right

---

[3]Teaching is much neglected in the pulpit and is very much needed today; cf. my *Der Glaube der Christenheit*, 5th ed. (1965); cf. *Man in God's World* (New York, 1963); *Woran ich glaube . . .* , 5th ed. (1976); *Theologisches Denken und verunsicherter Glaube*, 3rd ed. (1974).

[4]Cf. M. Schian, RE[3], XV, pp. 623-747.

[5]Cf. H. Diem, *Warum Textpredigt?* (1939); W. Trillhaas, *Evangelische Predigtlehre*, 2nd ed. (1936), pp. 84ff., 124ff.; G. Wingren, *Die Predigt* (1955), pp. 21ff., 31ff.; E.T. *The Living Word*, pp. 16ff., 25ff.

and wrong. It is right if an extraneous theme which is imported into the text becomes the dominating factor and the biblical text is reduced to conventional decoration or Christian coloring or a mere refrain. This danger is an obvious one, especially on national and other anniversaries and so forth. It can also be very serious when striving for secular relevance or the achievement of psychological effects causes the preacher to put the main stress on what he regards as up-to-date, so that he constricts the text and forces it to serve his rhetorical purposes. Here its content as God's Word necessarily degenerates into a purely human word.

But the homily-thesis is wrong if the thematic emphasis simply brings out one or more important points in the text itself, if the theme is actually taken from the text and simply represents what is technically called its "scope." In this regard we have to remember that the intellectual processes of understanding take place in such a way that the hearer or reader finds particular emphases in a text, distinguishes between what is important and what is secondary, and thus brings order into the chaotic mass of that which encounters and addresses him. It is a basic thesis of all "divinatory" understanding (cf. Schleiermacher and W. Dilthey) that we first find in the text that we seek to understand a bridgehead of our own pre-understanding and that then a dialectical process begins in which this pre-understanding is self-transcended, self-corrected, or self-extended. To this extent no fault can be found with the old-fashioned way of announcing three points so long as these are important emphases in the text itself. (Even here the text is not protected against misuse because alien cliches can creep into the divisions, as in the famous New Year sermon "Backward with Thanksgiving, Onward with Cheerfulness, Upward with Faith.")

The function of thematic points in a text is to produce intellectual order. Methodologically, then, it can be a great help which the purely homiletical preacher has to give up. Experience shows that good preachers can do without it, though not their disciples. Karl Barth could preach homiletical sermons because his ability to order things intellectually guided him unconsciously even though he did not claim it consciously, methodologically, or programmatically. In lesser preachers the homily entails a levelling down of the proximity and distance, a relaxing of the tension these produce, and a feeble repetition of thoughts with neither contours nor structure. The sermon will be tedious and hard to follow. Instead of the thematically misused text the refrain will now be an incidental and often very artificial contemporary reference.

2. The second procedure is found especially in missionary or secular preaching. In conventional worship the congregation assembled on Sunday can take it for granted that a regular or specially chosen reading from Scripture will precede the sermon and that preaching will take place, as it were, with an open Bible. In missionary or evangelistic services or in addresses to a secular audience, e.g., at certain funerals, some freedom can be claimed from ceremonial rules and the order of text and sermon may have to be reversed.

The usual order shows that the preacher is aware of being under the authority of Scripture and of preaching only in its name. Before a secular audience, however, he has to consider that this sign of biblical authority may not be understood because Holy Scripture is not—or is not yet—an authority for his hearers. Thus an introduction relating to the situation of the hearers is needed (e.g., the riddle of death or the special theme of a conference). This will lead up to a biblical saying or truth. The aim is to produce an "aha" experience: We come with our questions and troubles; we are not subjected to a dogmatic authority as expected; we find instead that our situation is lit up by a hitherto unknown light.

Here again, of course, a biblical text is latently presupposed. It may not form an express preamble to the sermon. Theological and ethical reflections can be proclamation in a special mode. But it is already there in the mind and heart of the preacher. From the very first he puts his message under its light. Only in this way can he discover it. He is using Socratic concealment when he refrains from announcing it at the beginning.[6]

Common to all the forms of preaching discussed thus far is that they seek to be proclamation of God's addressed Word. Address means following God's way to man in the incarnation of the Word. It means turning to real hearers. The Spirit of God with his testimony is a Spirit of presentation, of disclosure. Yet in effecting proximity, he takes precautions—as God's Spirit—against assimilation to the age, against accommodations to its spirit and desires, against tickling the ears of the hearers. The Holy Spirit of presentation is not the Spirit of quotation and mere repetition, as in timeless dogmatic preaching. The statements made in presentation may be out of date in a few years or decades, in form though not in content. Changes in joys and anxieties and problems mean changes in address. The preacher is responsible only for his own age. When he has run his own stretch he hands over the baton to others.

Because preaching is a venture, and even an adventure, which has to be undertaken on the narrow and dangerous ridge between proximity to the age and belonging to the age, it needs to be corrected by liturgy and the fixed element in it. Here Holy Scripture is read directly and the ancient prayers of the church are repeated. Here there are responses in which the congregation is the subject of worship. These have become the common legacy of the church, at least when they are not introduced artificially and synthetically or made into a work of liturgical art, like the paper flowers about which Bernanos speaks. Here the voice of the venturing witness is accompanied by the suprapersonal voice, the "we" of the community, which includes patriarchs, prophets, apostles, the people of our own age, and the people of the end-time.

Where this dominant note is clear and firm the counterpoint, says Bonhoeffer, can be strong. The two are as undivided as are Christ's divine and human natures according to Chalcedon.[7] The dominant note is the liturgy, the counterpoint is preaching. Worship is an indivisible whole.

Another musical comparison might illustrate the relation between liturgy and preaching. As liturgy recites the classical biblical and traditional texts, it brings what is canonically established to worship. It is as it were the score, while preaching is the musical interpretation, which includes the subjectivity of the witness. The union of God's Spirit and man's in the witness of presentation needs constant reference back to the Word, which as the score is the fixed element amid the many

---

[6]For an example of exposition preceding the text cf. the new readings for secular use in connection with the *Schott-Messbuch* (Herder-Verlag).

[7]*Widerstand . . .* (1951), p. 193.

different interpretations (even though it, too, came by way of human witnesses).

An impressive illustration of what this combination of preaching and liturgy means for worship is offered by the Enlightenment. The things then preached from the pulpit can only amuse us today. (Cf. my *Fröhliche Grablieder zur Laute des Pfarrers M. von Jung* [Herderbücherei No. 599 (1976)].) Typical rationalists of the age spoke about all kinds of matters but they did not speak the Word of God. They spoke about fresh air and husbandry and the art of living. If there had been only preaching, Christianity would have been preached to death by their aberrant subjectivity. But in the liturgy the old texts were still read even if watered down and "improved" a little. They did not fit in with the sermons but they were still there. Almost choked by the pulpit twaddle and to a large extent not understood, they were hidden in a state of incubation. But one day they came to life again when the Spirit came into the valley of dry bones. The stalk left to winter in the cellar of the liturgy began to grow green again and at last a new and living preaching came into association with it. The gravestone of degenerate preaching was not heavy enough to hold down the living among the dead. An "idea" would not have survived this drastic treatment but the risen Christ waited for his new day in the stronghold of the liturgy.

This is the first promise of the liturgy. That it is the fixed element in worship, of course, cannot mean that it is just antiquated and does not have to be understood. The Roman Catholic Church knows what it is doing when when alongside the Latin mass it is issuing translations of the liturgy and adding commentaries to make comprehension possible. Ancient texts that cannot be comprehended and become Word do not include the hearers but exclude them. To represent the constant element means for the liturgy something other than just transmitting antiquated material and merely going through motions that remain at the distance of non-involvement.

For this reason the liturgy needs significant corrections and modernizations. But these are just modifications. The constant element will gather up contemporary hearers to itself and make itself present through them. As the constant element, the liturgy of the contemporary community has to become "flesh and blood." It can do so only on two conditions. First, it must be understood. Second, it must be repeated from youth to age, e.g., in the Christian year, so that it becomes just as familiar as one's mother's voice.

It is thus a fatal thing when some liturgical experts make crude alterations and destroy what is familiar, when even the hymnbooks are exposed to radical attacks, this time in an antiquarian direction, so that worshippers not only have to master (partially) alien tunes and texts but also explanatory footnotes. The matter is no better, but it is all a sorry paradox, when these innovations are made in the name of the past, when long-forgotten treasures are brought to light, often dusty and illegible, like the labels on old bottles of wine. One can break the continuity enshrined in the liturgy not only by being too novel and progressive but also by being too reactionary. No matter whether we leap ahead or backward, the work of destruction is done.

There is nothing against ancient treasures. But as I have said, we have to allow things to grow in this field; only the devil has no time. To change or add some pictures carefully and in the right stages is a different matter from iconoclasm.

Luther can say that it is better for love's sake to delay correction of the liturgy if people are not ready for it, i.e., cannot understand and accept it (WA, 10, 3, 3f.5.7.9.16; LW, 51, 71ff., 76). The opposite of love is the legalism which for historical or musical reasons dictates to the community. The inclination of liturgical reformers (and many church musicians) to act dictatorially is well known. For an unhappy example we have only to turn to the archaic forms of Rite I of the United Evangelical Lutheran Church in Germany which Martin Walser criticized so forcefully in *Halbzeit,* p. 347. Originally the long introductory addresses to God were meant to take us out of ourselves and our everyday world and lead us into the dimension of prayer. But today many people who are not used to meditation have not the time for them, especially when they are taken from the Latin Mass and with their use of relative clauses ("O God, who...") seem too grotesquely different from the way that a child talks to its father.

Concern for intelligibility and acceptance naturally raises the question whether radical liturgical reforms of another kind are not needed. Should we not replace Gregorian chants and similar music with modern idioms (jazz, rock, etc.)? Should we not use trumpets, saxophones, and the like instead of organs? Certainly such a break with traditional worship is not permissible if a secular group is used merely for the sake of being modern and of tickling the ears of (young) people. Psycho-strategy is the worst enemy of the spiritual and self-evident Word, quite apart from the fact that the aim is noticed and is missed for this very reason. On the other hand, it is one of the basic truths of Christian hymnology that we must all praise God with our own voices and in our own ways.

One of the less pleasing secondary phenomena of much missionary activity is that many Africans and Asians have not put their own choral and musical styles to Christian use but have been content to import tunes and texts from the West. The demand for one's own idioms must be made over against the styles of modern music too, even in subcultural spheres. But these idioms must develop as an expression of the young community itself.

The same applies to the concern of young Christians to formulate liturgical prayers in their own language and from the standpoint of their own sense of— especially social and political—guilt. I add by way of example a fine prayer composed by Berlin students (with reference to the then problem of Biafra):

> Lord, thou hast created us—why are we all called Cain? Lord, thou hast created light—why do we not see? Lord, thou hast offered up thy Son—why do we do nothing? Lord, thou hast given us a conscience—why does it not cry out? Lord, thou hast fed us—why have we forgotten what hunger is? Why, Lord? O Lord, hear us when we cry. Amen. (In its total compass the prayer is much longer. In spite of some concrete allusions it is definitely liturgical in structure; that is, it uses biblical models and it can be repeated again and again.)

XX

Worship and the Sacraments

To clarify the term "sacrament" it is important to remember that the term is not used in the NT, at least to denote baptism and the Lord's Supper.

In the Itala and Vulgate it is synonymous with *mysterium* and is the translation of the Greek *mystērion* (cf. G. Bornkamm, TDNT, IV, pp. 802ff.; TWNT, IV, pp. 809ff.). In its rare appearances in the NT it does not refer to baptism and the Lord's Supper but occurs in eschatological and christological statements (TDNT, IV, pp. 817ff.; TWNT, IV, pp. 831ff.). Only in the early church did *mystērion* come to denote the sacraments. In Luther one may detect some reserve in relation to the ecclesiastical term. Going back beyond tradition to Scripture he can say that there is only one sacrament in the Holy Scriptures, Christ the Lord himself (WA, 6, 86, 5). In his work on the sacraments (*The Babylonian Captivity, Three Treatises,* pp. 123ff.) the things that the church calls sacraments (baptism, penance, the Lord's Supper) are, strictly speaking, sacramental signs.

Since for hundreds of years there has been confusion about the concept of the sacraments, it is an almost impossible task to give a critical account of the extensive debates about them in a single chapter of dogmatics. We can only cut a path through the original forest which will serve the end of clarifying why there has to be much reserve in relation to the concept.

1. THE EXTREMES BETWEEN WHICH THE UNDERSTANDING OF THE SACRAMENTS MOVES

The central theme in controversies about the sacraments is always that of the relation of Word and sacrament, or, better, of Word and signs (water, bread, and wine). Can the two go together, and if so, how? Is the sacrament just another form of the Word or is it more? This crude alternative might be heuristically fruitful as our first line of inquiry.

The relation of Word and sacrament—relative both to the operation of the sacrament and its biblical validity—is at the heart of the tortuous arguments against the medieval idea of seven sacraments in CAApol, XIII. We cannot go into the details of this instructive controversy and recommend the thorough presentation and criticism in H. Diem (*Dogmatik*, pp. 116ff.). In criticism of a historical appeal to institution by Christ, cf. G. Ebeling, "Erwägungen zum evangelischen Sakramentsverständnis," *Wort und Tradition*, p. 225 (E.T. p. 234), who argues as follows: That Jesus is the foundation of the church does not stand or fall by whether he founded the church by an express act. . . . So it is with the sacraments. They come from Jesus in the sense that they bear witness to him as the sum and compendium of the gospel.

If we study the differences in relating Word and sacrament only in their extreme forms, two types may be discerned.

1. According to the first extreme the sacrament has some privileges when compared to the Word. In it we not only have a personal presence, as in the Word, but a real presence. The reason is to be found in the elements that are added to the Word (the reference is especially to the Lord's Supper). The transubstantiation or consubstantiality of these elements means that they contain within them the ontic, bodily, and palpable presence of Christ. They thus give the sacrament a quality of transcending the mere Word.

Readers might expect that I would illustrate the real presence from Roman Catholic teaching (e.g., that of Radbert [831/33] or Cardinal Humbert of Silva [1059]). But I cannot resist the need to come closer to home and show that this extreme can still be found occasionally in modern Lutheranism. Thus Regin Prenter (*Realpräsenz*, p. 308) says that Christ's presence in the eucharist is the presence of a thing (*res*, "Ding"), namely, his sacrificed body and blood. By the words of institution an event under Pontius Pilate becomes a substance or thing that century upon century one can hand to others to eat and drink (p. 316). The body on the cross is identical with the bread and wine on the altar as a sacrificial gift (pp. 468f.). This crassly magical view is hardly softened by the occasional hint (p. 316) that our ontological categories are transcended here. This suggests logical inconsistency—or an unhelpful fear of the logical implications. A danger which afflicts Roman Catholic theologians exists here too, namely, that the gracious personal God will become a substantial grace and that the salvation granted to us will become an entity, or entitative habit, which is detached from God and lies at our disposal (Pesch, *Freiburger Zeitschrift*, p. 303).

There can be no doubt that the *est* ("this *is* my body") which Luther stressed over against Zwingli sowed the seeds of this extreme view. For it involved an obvious fight for "presentation" in the elements instead of a purely personal presence. (Cf. the crass explanation in *Against the Heavenly Prophets* [WA, 18, 159ff.; LW, 40, 169ff.].) Luther, of course, surrounds such statements by correctives which describe the eucharistic gift in terms of personal salvation, "for you." This theme is normative for the emphasis on the ontic *est* (cf. CA, X and XII). For the point of this is Luther's concern that salvation comes from outside us, that it is offered to us and not grasped or produced by us. Luther thinks the "from outside" is best denoted by the corporeal *est*. It is certainly no mistake to suppose that Luther belonged to a sacramental tradition which chiefly used ontological categories. In his works the partly unresolved tension between this mode of thought—which tends to slip into substance-*res* categories—and the new and personal way of depicting God's favor is quite unmistakable. W. Joest has developed it in his great work *Ontologie der Person*.

2. The second extreme is the approach represented especially by Zwingli. Here the elements do not have inherently any special quality but have purely symbolical rank as illustrations. The Lord's Supper is a meal of remembrance and represents fellowship with the exalted Lord. It is simply a sensory exposition of the Word and in relation to this it has purely instrumental significance with no special privileges.

This line of thought, too, extends by way of the Enlightenment, which found it most congenial, to our own day. A. von Harnack carried it so far as to recommend, in the name of the sole normativity of the Word, that it might be best to drop the sacrament from divine service. Only God's Word and prayer really have a place in worship (*What is Christianity?*, p. 291). Everything apart from the Word and faith is a matter of indifference (p. 313). The classical theologians of Erlangen Lutheranism reduced the sacrament to simply another form of the Word. While the Word speaks to the person, the sacrament with its appeal to the senses speaks more to our "nature" (G. Thomasius, *Christi Person und Werk* [1850], III, 1, p. 357; on this and on what follows cf. Pöhlmann, *Abriss der Dogmatik*, pp. 236f.).

This thought could hardly help being psychologized in our own day. By nature we have eyes as well as ears and in the sacrament we are given something to see as well as hear (E. Brunner, *Unser Glaube* [1934], p. 120). Tillich refers to the subconscious in our nature which is not reached by the Word but by sacramental processes, the two together corresponding to our multidimensional unity (*Systematic Theology*, III [1966], pp. 120f.). Along similar lines H. Stephan thinks that the sacrament strengthens the working of the Word, appealing not to the intellect as the Word does, but to our "natural" life by way of sense and imagination (*Glaubenslehre*, 3rd ed. [1941], p. 220).

The history of theology presents us with many different interpretations between these extremes. (We shall deal with that of Calvin in the section on the Lord's Supper.) We are particularly pleased to mention the synthetic view of Thomas which embraces both extremes in itself. Characteristically Thomas thinks the sacraments have two functions. First they impart the gift of salvation. Second, they have the psychological task of seeking out man in the sensory sphere, raising him up from below, and leading him to the spiritual background of what is presented in sensory form. Thomas sees three reasons why the sacraments are needed.

(1) It is an essential part of human nature to be led by what is bodily and visible to what is spiritual and intelligible. We have been given the sacraments to meet this need.

(2) Since man has become subject to bodily things through sin, the healing medicine needs to be applied to the source of the sickness. Thus spiritual medicine is not given directly. The spirit which is bound to the senses could not take it in this form. It is given in bodily signs.

(3) Man needs the humbling reminder that by the fall he belongs to the sensory world of sin. The fact that in order not to be overtaxed he must be helped by bodily gifts serves as such a reminder. It seems here that the sacraments are almost a kind of punishment. Man must first pass through these forecourts because he is not ready for the true gift (the Word??). There almost seems to be here an immanent criticism of sacramentalism—an indication that the newer and much stronger emphasis on the Word and its sacramental sense (cf. Rahner, Ratzinger, Pesch,

etc.) can find a place in this tradition (cf. Thomas, STh, III, q. 61, a. 1; Michael, *Wort und Wahrheit,* VII, pp. 501f.; Pesch, *Freiburger Zeitschrift,* p. 278).

As a first finding we can say that the two contrasting extremes in the understanding of the sacraments are not to be regarded as deriving pathologically from subjective errors on the part of those who hold them but rest instead on the immanent obscurity of the term ''sacrament.'' In spite of and even *in* the official definitions on the Roman Catholic side, the concept remains indistinct. Its great plasticity may be seen in the broad range of more recent theological interpretations from, shall we say, Diekamp to Rahner. On the Protestant side the range is even wider, embracing both Zwingli's doctrine of signifying at one pole and that of an ontic presence in the elements at the other.[1]

The multiplicity may be attributed to the effect of the obscure genealogy of the term and the impact of its many ideological origins. Thus the decisive word *mystērion* ceases to be restricted to apocalyptic statements, as in the NT. It is moved to the sphere of antiquity's concept of mystery, even in relation to the Christian sacraments.[2] The imprecise and indistinct definition of the term sacraments carries permanently within itself a latent threat to evangelical theology and the evangelical church.[3] One might indeed ask whether the Ansbacher Ratschlag of 1524[4] was not right to threaten the sacrament with punishment as a human invention.[5]

If we want to keep the word sacrament, we can do so only on two conditions.

First, it cannot play the part of a master concept from which our sacramental understanding of baptism and the Lord's Supper is to be deduced. Taking this course exposes us to both of the ideologizings mentioned and lets the dubious genealogy of the term sacrament affect our view of baptism and the Supper. What a sacrament is can only be known inductively from a formulation of the features common to baptism and the Supper. (We shall deal only with the two Reformation sacraments without entering into debate with Roman Catholicism over the additional five.)[6]

Second, the term sacrament is theologically valid only if its relation to the Word is cleared up, i.e., only if it is stated that the term does not imply any transcending or relativizing of the Word but simply denotes another mode of the same definitive Word.

Augustine seems to meet these conditions in his view of the sacraments, which is clearly adopted by Melanchthon in CAApol, XIII and which is often claimed by Luther.[7] The precedence of the Word is denoted in Augustine by his treatment of the sacrament simply as a visible Word. Only when the Word is added to the elements is there a sacrament.[8] The only question that might arise in this regard is whether one should not reverse the statement and say that in the sacrament the

---

[1]Cf. Diem, *Dogmatik,* III, p. 48.

[2]Bornkamm, TWNT, IV, pp. 832ff.; TDNT, IV, pp. 824ff.

[3]Jüngel, *Was ist ein Sakrament?,* p. 13.

[4]Not to be confused with the ''German Christian'' travesty of the same name in 1934.

[5]Elert, *Morphologie,* I, p. 526; E.T. *The Structure of Lutheranism,* p. 293.

[6]Cf. Diem, *Dogmatik,* III, pp. 117ff.

[7]Cf. LC (LBK, p. 694; Jacobs, *Book of Concord,* pp. 467ff.).

[8]Augustine, *In Johannis,* LXXX, 3. On what follows cf. R. Seeberg, *Dogmengeschichte,* II, 3rd ed., pp. 452ff., esp. p. 454.

element is added to the Word, so that it has only "accidental" significance in relation to it. Augustine himself recognizes this reduced importance of the element when he says: "Take the Word away and what is the water (of baptism) but water," or, as we might say even more sharply today, "What is the water but H_2O?"

That the Word is for Augustine the decisive factor in the sacrament may be seen from the fact that he makes everything depend on the *virtus* (power or effectiveness) of the act.[9] This is no other than the *virtus* of the efficacious Word itself (*verbum faciens*). In what does this consist? In the producing of faith. Only thus does the baptismal water which touches the body and washes the heart achieve its purpose.[10] The Word does not change the elements; it changes the heart by producing faith.[11] This stands in sharp antithesis to any magical operation (*opus operatum*). For the decisive *virtus* of the sacrament is the sanctification of invisible grace[12] and this is no other than faith.

The correlation of Word and faith is thus the constitutive element in the sacrament. This is the true *res* which is symbolically clarified and brought home to the consciousness by the sign, as can happen only because the sign has in it something analogous to the *res* that it signifies.[13] Thus far the elements have only a symbolical or demonstrative significance.

Yet the problem of the signs is not solved hereby. The word "sign," which Roman Catholics, Luther, Zwingli, and Calvin all use in their sacramental theology, has itself a broad range of meaning with many nuances. This shows that the understanding of "sign" is part of the problem of multiplicity in the understanding of sacraments. Has the sign an effective or a purely significative character? If the latter, is the sign a fixed mark by which believers recognize one another?[14] Or is it a sign and witness that God's will toward us is to awaken and strengthen our faith? These variations in the understanding of sign could easily be multiplied.[15]

We need, then, to examine the term "sign" more thoroughly.

2. THE PROBLEM OF "SIGN"

For Luther the sacramental sign, as he shows in his *Babylonian Captivity,* has two characteristics. First, it does not just signify and expound but effects what it signifies. The sacraments are efficacious signs of grace.[16] Second, the sacramental sign characterizes what it signifies. There are improper sacraments which may signify and effect but do not signify and effect that which can be ascribed only to the Christian sacraments. These alone signify the grace of God and by it the faith which brings grace. Moses gave signs in the form of priestly rites such as robes,

---

[9]*In Johannis,* XXVI, 11.

[10]*In Johannis,* LXXX, 3.

[11]*De baptismo,* VI, xxv, 47.

[12]In *heptatione,* III, q. 84; Seeberg, *Dogmengeschichte,* p. 454.

[13]*Epistulae,* XCVIII, 9.

[14]Cf. CA, XIII in implicit criticism of Zwingli.

[15]Cf. Q. 66 of the Heidelberg Catechism, Luther's understanding in *The Babylonian Captivity* (pp. 162ff.), and Calvin's view of spiritual eating (Inst., IV, 17).

[16]*Babylonian Captivity,* pp. 186ff.

vessels, foods, houses, and the like.[17] Luther rather boldly calls these sacraments of works.[18] The point of comparison between the sacraments of the old covenant and those of the new is that there is in both something to be achieved. The difference is that in the former the "power and nature" refers to works,[19] while in the latter it refers to faith.

If, however, the sacramental signs of the new covenant are marked by what they signify and effect—grace and faith—one can speak of sacraments in the OT as well, and it is hard to distinguish between the old and the new sacraments, since they have the same power of the sign and signify the same thing.[19] The God who now grants us salvation through baptism and the bread is the same as the God who saved Abel by sacrifice, Noah by the rainbow, Abraham by circumcision, and others by their own signs.[20]

In both the OT and the NT, then, we find signs of law and signs of the gospel. Or perhaps we should say that both are found in the OT but in the NT there is only the *one* sign of justifying grace. Hence we find sacraments of justifying faith but not of (legal) achievement.[21] Only as we follow the traces of the righteousness of faith in the old covenant shall we perceive the continuity of the OT and NT with respect to sacramental signs.

If the sign denotes God's justifying grace and its efficacy consists of the awakening of faith which enables us to receive grace, the implication is that the sacrament as such does not justify but faith in the sacrament or faith in the sense of the sacrament.[22]

If we understand Luther correctly, the concept of sign comprises for him a relation within which something takes place. The sign denotes that which effects and also that which is effected, i.e., justifying grace as the former and corresponding to it on man's side justifying faith as the latter. Only along these lines can Augustine's thesis be adopted that it is faith that fulfils the saving intention of the sacrament. This saving intention is the Word of promise which it denotes and to which the only proper response is trust.[23]

No autonomy is ascribed to the sacrament or its sign in the sense of automatic operation (*opus operatum*). It effects nothing merely by being performed. It never makes the recipient a mere object or, as we might say today, a mere consumer. It does not merely let him participate in the sacramental administration. It lets him "communicate" in the strict sense. It calls him to communion with God whose Word promises him salvation in the sign, who makes him dependent on the Yes of his faith, and who thus makes him a partner. The relation of Word and sacrament is to this extent determinative for the sacramental process. At no point does the latter transcend this relation.

Calvin appeals explicitly to Augustine in his definition of a sacrament (Inst., IV,

---

[17]*Ibid.*, p. 187.
[18]*Ibid.*, p. 188.
[19]*Ibid.*, p. 187.
[20]*Loc. cit.*
[21]*Ibid.*, p. 188.
[22]Literally "faith of the sacrament"; the genitive may be either subjective or objective (*ibid.*, p. 188).
[23]For the annexed word of promise cf. *loc. cit.*

14, 1): It is "an outward sign (*symbolum*) by which the Lord seals on our consciences the promises of his good will (*benevolentia*) toward us in order to sustain the weakness of our faith; and we in turn attest our piety toward him in the presence of the Lord and of his angels and before men." More briefly it is "a testimony of divine grace toward us, confirmed by an outward sign, with mutual attestation of our piety toward him."

Here again we may see the relation between the divine Word-act and our response in faith. What rank is accorded to the Word is shown by two supplementary considerations.

First, the confirming function of the sacrament does not relate to the Word, which needs no confirmation, but to our faith in the Word, which can be strengthened by symbolical elucidation (IV, 14, 3). Hence the work of the sacrament does not rest on a power that transcends the Word but takes place in the subjective sphere of the recipient as a confirmation of faith.

Second, the Word which the sacrament serves does not itself work automatically (*ex opere operato*) (Calvin raises this charge against the magical priestly incantations used in transubstantiating the elements); it is a preached Word which as a visible sign as well claims our understanding and commitment, our faith (IV, 14, 4). Only when the faith that it effects follows the Word that is represented by the sacramental sign can the sacrament take over the further function of a witness of faith, of showing the flag as it were, to other men.

In sum, the sign has three aspects for Calvin. First, it signifies that God is friendly and open toward us. Second, it signifies that we respond in faith, thus rounding off the relation that constitutes the sacrament. Third, it signifies that we confess our faith to others. (Why H. Diem, *Dogmatik*, III, pp. 116f., objects to CA, XIII in this connection, and can even see in it approximations to the Roman Catholic view of sacrifice, I do not understand.)

Even if there are unmistakably some strange magical features in Roman Catholic sacramental teaching[24]—and Calvin described them much more vividly than we could—these are in tension with opposite tendencies which are close to what the Reformers regarded as the point of the sacraments. Thomas expresses these tendencies when, adducing Augustine, he can say that the Word does not work in the sacrament because it is uttered—the "mere noise" that Calvin censures—but because it is *believed* (STh, III, 60, 7, ad 1). The parallel to Luther (cf. the 1517/18 Lectures. on Hebrews) is obvious, for he, too, says that what justifies is not the sacrament itself but faith in the sacrament (*Babylonian Captivity*, p. 188).

Yet there are subtle differences whose discovery shows why faith's role in the sacramental operation still leaves a flank exposed to the idea of an automatic work. O. H. Pesch, who stresses the parallel between Thomas and Luther (*Freiburger Zeitschrift*, pp. 307f.), is surprised that Luther ignores the distinction between the form (Word) and matter (elements) of the sacrament which is so essential for Thomas. It seems to me that this Aristotelian distinction is the reason why Word (understood as form) has for Thomas a ranking in the sacrament which Luther and

---

[24]Rahner himself breaks a somewhat blunted lance for *opus operatum* (Jüngel/Rahner, *Was ist ein Sakrament?*, p. 80).

the other Reformers could not accept. Form in the Aristotelian sense is the essential determinant which impresses and changes matter; it thus prepares the ground for the possibility of transubstantiation. The Word as form also makes an impress—automatically—on the one who receives it in the sacrament. (At least there is the possibility of a movement in this direction.) With this line of thought the personal involvement of the recipient or his faith is not needed. It is enough if there is no bar, or opposition, or if there is at least undisturbed consumption. This is precisely what Luther rejects in many places, including the very next passage to that quoted above (*Babylonian Captivity,* p. 189).

Nevertheless, we must also say that in opposition to the tendency suggested by the Aristotelian mode of thought faith as the personal involvement of the recipient is the goal in the Thomistic understanding even when the proclamation of the Word in worship is regarded primarily as preparatory instruction (STh, III, 64, 1, ad 1; 67, 1, ad 1; cf. Pesch, p. 308, n. 101). The only point is that the ontological schema which works with the terms form and matter can obscure this goal and a certain autonomy can take over in which the concept of form in particular can become a self-evident one. Pius XII in his ''Humani generis'' of 1950 expressly validated this scholastic terminology and did not wish it to be subordinated to otherwise justifiable changes in the vocabulary of philosophy (W. von Loewenich, *Der moderne Katholizismus,* 2nd ed. [1970], p. 287). If appearances do not deceive, there has been a clear loosening up in more recent Roman Catholic theology, especially after Vatican II, so that the personal relation of Word and faith can and does achieve increasing prominence.

3. WORD AND SACRAMENT

From all this it follows that in understanding the sacrament everything depends on defining its relation to the Word. In this respect one may say that it signifies the Word or, as F. Brunstäd puts it,[25] that as an actual Word it sums up the Word or event in a binding and definitive act. In Luther's terms it is the seal on a document or the handshake that gives force to an agreement. The seal and handshake do not add anything new to what is said. They ratify it and express it symbolically. The sign serves the thing signified.

This thing signified that is expressed in the Word is not just a preparatory thing, a march toward the goal which is followed by the symbolical act of the sacrament as the climax, the true point of the salvation event. The thing signified is the gospel, the Word, and this is the real end and goal and everything else. The sacramental sign is thus an instrumental sign of the Word. It is a mode in which the Word presents itself because the superabundant wealth of grace extended to us in the gospel takes several forms in which to come to our aid in our fight against sin.[26]

This relating of the sacrament to the Word is the real breakthrough of the Reformation in contrast to the previous sacramental tradition. Yet we have to say

---

[25]*Theologie der lutherischen Bekenntnisschriften* (1951), p. 139.
[26]As the Smalkaldic Articles (LBK, 449,24) say, God is superabundantly rich and his grace and goodness are lavish (cf. Jacobs, *Book of Concord,* p. 330).

that it is not consistently carried through, especially in Luther and Lutheranism. Relics of the tradition remain unconquered, particularly in the Lord's Supper. For this reason everything depends on continuing to think along this line of relationship to the Word, on keeping to it without deviation, and on resisting the remnants of the tradition (e.g., the Lutheran *est*), not with the arguments of the Enlightenment, but with the basic thought of the Reformation that the sacrament is a form of the Word.

Several fundamental principles make it plain that this is the real point of the Lutheran view of the sacraments.

1. The enumeration of acts of worship indicates the primacy of the Word over the sacraments. God turns to us first in the oral Word which is the preaching of forgiveness of sins, the true office of the gospel; then in baptism; then in the holy sacrament of the altar; then in the power of the keys (Smalkaldic Articles [LBK, p. 449,8; Jacobs, p. 330]).

2. Luther deals with the sacraments in such a way as to put all the stress on the Word. The point of the sacrament is the Word that we hear (on Psalm 51 [WA, 40/II, 411, 4]).

3. This primacy of the Word over or *in* the sacraments can be given extreme emphasis, as in the question whether we can infer the existence of the church from the administration of the sacraments. Where there is no gospel, there is undoubtedly no church. There may be baptism and eating of the bread, but the gospel, before the bread and baptism, is the one most sure and principal sign of the church, for it is by the gospel alone that the church is conceived, formed, nourished, born, trained, fed, clothed, adorned, strengthened, armed, upheld. Its whole life and being is in the Word, not the written but the spoken Word (WA, 7, 720). Thus the words of institution did not just found the sacraments but they are its basis, for they contain the promises of the gospel (*Babylonian Captivity,* pp. 156ff.).

4. Because of this primacy of the Word faith can live without the sacraments, but not without the Word. The sign of the gospel is only added. We have to regard the Word as the real testament. The efficacy that is given to the Word is greater in the testament than in the sacrament. Hence we can claim the Word or testament apart from the sign or sacrament (*ibid.,* p. 162). Cf. also *Von der Winkelmasse* (1533): For the sacrament cannot exist without the Word, but the Word can without the sacrament. If need be we can be saved without the sacrament, but not without the Word. Cf. Mark 16:16.

The priority of the Word over the sacrament shows that the sacrament is a Word-event, an actual Word. But this implies a very definite understanding of the Word. It would make no sense and be misleading if the Word were viewed merely as information or doctrine and the sign were viewed as a didactic aid or illustration. In this case the Word would be interpretative, would appeal only to the understanding, and would be functionally dependent on the possibility of understanding. As we have expressly shown, however, this Word is an act-word or word-event which brings about change.[27] It has itself, if one will, a sacramental determination.

We can elucidate this relation of Word and sacrament by Luther's extreme

---

[27]See EF, I and II, Index "Word of God."

teaching about the eating of unbelievers or the unworthy.[28] This idea is developed especially in relation to the real presence of Christ's body and blood at the Supper. Luther's intention was to maintain that the saving reality of Christ's presence is not dependent on our faith and cannot, therefore, be undone by unbelief.[29] It is oriented to the transsubjective fact of the presence. The question at once arises: What does the sacrament do in unbelievers if it is not annulled by their unbelief? Appealing to the saying in Isaiah 55:11 that the Word never returns empty, Luther understands the work in unbelievers to be judgment (Luke 10:10ff.; 10:16; 2 Corinthians 2:15).

Hence the objective real presence of Christ always does something. In opposition to Zwingli this must be set forth as its real effect. For if the Lord's Supper is simply recollection and demonstration, nothing really takes place if the event does not touch the consciousness and is rejected in unbelief. It is thus made dependent on the subjective state of the recipient. The point of Luther's protest against Zwingli and his doctrine of the eating of the unworthy lies in a definite understanding of the salvation event. This is present here and now in the real presence in the sacrament and to that extent it always accomplishes something, whether salvation in faith or judgment in unbelief.

Undoubtedly the debate with Zwingli forced Luther to focus the real presence of the salvation event on the presence of Christ's body and blood in the eucharistic elements and therefore to insist on the ''is.'' The polemical vehemence of the controversy undoubtedly obscured its true point, namely, the difference in the understanding of the Word itself. It has thus left the impression that the real presence of Christ depends on the sign—the elements—and not on the Word that it signifies. Our own task, starting from the center of Lutheran theology in its understanding of the Word, is to shift the accent, to undertake an immanent correction. A new definition of the priorities is needed.

The essential point is that Christ's real presence is not only in the sacrament but also in the Word (the spoken Word) of the gospel. When we gather around the Word, Christ is in the midst (Matthew 18:20). What is said about the sacramental form of the Word is true of the Word itself. It effects grace and judgment. It does not return empty. It is wrong to say that Christ's body is of no use (i.e., that it is not efficacious, that it does nothing). It is always of use, even though it is of no use to me because of my unbelief. The sun always shines even though the blind do not see it. God's Word is always to salvation even though it is poison and the savor of death to the ungodly. Christ's body is always in the sacrament even though it is not in these blind and foolish spirits.[30] Here the Word and the body of Christ are used synonymously as regards their transsubjective character. What applies to the feeding of the unworthy applies also to the speaking of the Word.

Does this mean that we must renounce our previous relating of Word and faith or sacrament and faith? Must we revoke the statement borrowed from Augustine

---

[28]WA, 26, 491, 4ff.; Wittenberg Concordat (1536) (LBK, p. 451, n. 1); Smalkaldic Articles, II, 6 (LBK, pp. 450f.; cf. also pp. 250,62; 799,16; 990,57); cf. Jacobs, pp. 330ff.; p. 176, no. 62; p. 513, no. 16; pp. 611f., no. 57.

[29]Cf. the Solida Declaratio (LBK, pp. 980,25; 982,22; Jacobs, pp. 605f., nos. 25, 32).

[30]WA, 18, 194, 28.

that faith in the sacrament, not the sacrament itself, makes it what it is meant to be? The impression might arise that an automatic efficacy is being ascribed to both Word and sacrament which is independent of faith or its opposite.

This would be mistaken. Two considerations show why this is so.

(1) For Luther everything depends on maintaining the externality of the salvation event, as shown. In no way does salvation depend functionally on our subjectivity, not even our believing subjectivity. The sun shines even though we in our blindness cannot see it.

(2) This forces us to understand our faith more precisely. If it is regarded as a power which constitutes the salvation event, it becomes one of the works that it is meant to exclude. It suffers from the illusion of setting up our fellowship with God instead of receiving it from outside. The basis of faith is not in subjectivity, where it simply occurs,[31] but in its object. This is why we are not to dwell on ourselves or our faith but to "creep into Christ."[32] Faith does not rise up to go to God; God comes to faith and makes himself present to it by his Spirit.

The situation of faith as something that receives instead of rising up is depicted in the debate with Carlstadt. The devil cries "Spirit, spirit," yet he does not teach that the Spirit should come to you but that you should come to the Spirit.[33] Part of the diabolical strategy is to make faith a vehicle which human autonomy uses to take the initiative in the attainment of salvation. Here again Luther's concern is the externality of salvation which comes to us from outside without our cooperation and which we cannot win for ourselves, not even by mobilizing our faith.

It is precisely this that shows us how decisive the role of faith is. It is not excluded here as something of no account. It is pointed to its true function. Faith is the attitude of trusting acceptance to which God's salvation can be granted without condition. The very fact that we have here something external whose efficacy does not depend on faith as a constitutive factor; the very fact that faith is itself owed to this external factor and brought into being by it—this is the comfort of faith. This is the thing that causes it to confess: "Thou, O Lord, art everything."

In fact, then, everything depends on the relation of faith and sacrament—of faith to the extent that it sees itself to be receptive and an effect, while the Spirit is for us the power of presentation. The real presence, which takes place transsubjectively and is independent of faith or unbelief, applies to both Word and sacrament. But because the Word is primary, there is no need to focus the real presence on the bodily presence of Christ in the sacramental elements. Such a focus can direct our attention away from the true presence in the Spirit-borne Word and give force to the tradition whose sacramental understanding is overcome only by the priority of the Word. It is only occasionally even in the debate with Zwingli that we see that what makes the difference between Luther and Zwingli is in fact the understanding of the efficacious and Spirit-filled Word. Even then we can see it only in the controversy concerning the real presence in the sacramental elements, as when Luther scoffs at Zwingli's distinctions between the Word of command, of permis-

---

[31]Cf. E. Schott, *Fleisch und Geist bei Luther* (1928), pp. 44ff.
[32]WA, 10/I, 1, 126, 14.
[33]WA, 18, 137, 11; LW, 40, 147.

sion, and so forth, adding that in the Supper the Word is not an afterword but a Word of power that does what it says (Psalm 33). God speaks and it is done.

One might say that the real presence in relation to the elements threatens to remove the priority of the Word over the sign and gives both of them the same rank. This actually seems to be the case in what the older dogmatics called the sacramental union, i.e., "the concurrence of a divine and human, an inward and outward, an invisible and visible operation and reception of grace in the 'sacramental' actions of baptism and the Lord's Supper."[34] Here the sign and thing signified melt together in an inseparable unity, so that the sign is no longer something added or accidental, but has an equal share in the quality of the Word-act.

If we express it in this way, we at once effect the relation to the Word which was incarnate in Christ and which is the basis of every other Word. For here and here alone the sign—that of incarnation—is more and other than a mere designation which points to the thing designated. Here and here alone the sign is God's own act, his condescension. What has been called the sacramental union and related to the Lord's Supper, took place in the miracle of Christmas.

Only Christ is a sacrament in the strict sense of a union of sign and thing. For this reason it is a serious question whether the term should not be reserved for Christ. In view of the many misunderstandings and erroneous traditions, should we not stop using it for baptism and the Lord's Supper? These are both liturgical celebrations in which we celebrate the presence of the Lord in his Word with the help of his Spirit and by means of the appointed signs.

As regards the relation between Christology and the understanding of the sacraments it is noteworthy that these are parallel and also intersecting themes in the debate between Luther and Zwingli. The classical account of the relationship in Thomasius' *Christi Person und Werk*, II (1857), pp. 209ff. is still worth reading. There is hardly a problem in Chalcedonian Christology that does not arise in eucharistic discussion.

The idea that Christ is the only sacrament occurs in Luther and Melanchthon. Biblically, says Luther, we have one sacrament and three sacramental signs (WA, 6, 501; LW, 36, 18). The Scriptures contain only one sacrament, Christ the Lord himself (6, 86). What Luther has in mind is the NT *mystērion* which is used only in christological and eschatological contexts. Similarly Melanchthon says in his *Loci* that by sacrament Paul means Christ. In sacramental theology the term is used for what are strictly signs or sacramental signs.

While we have had to criticize the term sacrament very radically, and would prefer to see its replacement by celebration, our coolness toward it is on a different level from that of Barth when in his baptismal teaching he is sorry that he did not fully juggle it away in his earlier statements on baptism.[35] Barth ascribes to water baptism—as distinct from baptism with the Spirit—only the character of a human work which serves as a cognitive clarification[36] and is for the believer "the binding

---

[34]Barth, CD, IV,2, pp. 54f.

[35]Barth, CD, IV,4, p. ix referring to I,1, §3.

[36]Cf. the earlier work of Barth, *The Teaching of the Church regarding Baptism* (1943), pp. 25f.

confession of his obedience, conversion and hope, made in prayer for God's grace."[37] What we have here is a different understanding not merely of the sacrament but also of the sacramental Word, which, it seems to me, has for Barth only demonstrative rank and no efficacy.[38]

It is true that even linguistically what Barth says here is ambivalent and hard to grasp, so that we can speak only of a general tendency with many exceptions. Thus in relation to the resurrection of Christ Barth says that the revelation that takes place here is not to be understood only noetically: "The divine noetic, God's self-declaration as the One He is in the being and action of Jesus Christ, the prophecy of the divine-human Mediator, has the full force of the divine ontic. The Word of God does not return to Him void (Isaiah 55:11), but is effected as it is spoken and stands fast as He commands (Psalm 33:9)" (CD, IV,3, p. 298).

4. CONCLUSION

As we have pointed out, one reason why the term sacrament is a doubtful one is that it is exposed historically (even in the history of the Reformation) to the danger that the sign will become autonomous and challenge the primacy of the Word. But there is a second reason too. Two diametrically opposed possibilities of interpretation arise. The one is universalist, the other sacral and esoteric.

1. Tillich (and in some sense Wycliffe) represents the universalist interpretation. His principle of analogy and correlation forces us to understand the totality of being symbolically and to bring to light the participation of every form of being in its ground.[39] Thus all forms of being take on sacramental rank as pointers and signs. There are not just seven sacraments but an infinite number. Everything transitory is a likeness.

The complete dissolving of the contours of a Christian view of the sacraments can hardly be preserved by two obvious restrictions.

First, one might point out, as Augustine did,[40] that the symbol bears some resemblance to the thing symbolized. Thus, bread, wine, and water stand in a *special* analogy to the saving event expressed in them. In reply it can be argued, of course, that similarities of this type can be expressed even in the biblical texts by other forms of being, e.g., the sun, birds, lilies, doves, lions, etc. But a sacramental universalism of this type necessarily rests on a presupposed analogy of being and therefore on natural theology. It makes being the subject of religious interpretation and thus severs the basic relation between Word and faith. Here again, then, the crisis in understanding the sacrament results from a crisis in understanding the Word.

Second, one might try to separate the specifically Christian sacraments from this general symbolism by pointing to their institution by Christ himself. But this is open to question both historically and theologically. Neither church nor sacraments can be validated by historical acts of foundation but only by the fact that

---

[37]The thesis of CD, IV,4.
[38]I have described this view of the Word as nonhistorical in ThE, I, pp. 203ff.; E.T. I, pp. 98ff.
[39]K. D. Nörenberg, *Analogia imaginis* (1966), pp. 161ff., 219ff.
[40]*Epistulae*, XCVIII,9; Seeberg, *Dogmengeschichte*, p. 454.

both make the figure and message of Christ present by the testimony of the Spirit in his Word.

What Ebeling said about the church in this regard applies equally to the sacraments. They derive from Jesus in the sense of bearing witness to him as a sum and compendium of the gospel (*Wort Gottes und Tradition. Studien zu einer Hermeneutik der Konfessionen,* 2nd ed. [1966], p. 225, cf. p. 130; E.T. *The Word of God and Tradition,* p. 234, cf. p. 135).

2. In contrast the sacral and esoteric interpretation of the sacraments involves the emancipation of a sacred sphere from every secular field and the establishment of a "religious province." Buber has very impressively shown how this can come about.[41] As he sees it, the real purpose of worship is to prepare us for communion with God in the world. The primal and most extreme danger is "religion," in which a special side of life is sanctified rather than everyday life. The God of this kind of worship is only an appearance, so that the partner in communion is missing and the gestures are empty. What was meant to bring fulness of life is cut off from it (*loc. cit.*).

Here again the crisis of the sacrament in the form of sacral remoteness from life arises out of a denial of the Word and its priority. For the Word is always a Word of sending and the fellowship of the Lord's Supper is a departing fellowship[42] like that of the Passover to which it is linked. The Word interprets the world and history as the sphere of God's working and it summons us to service in this sphere. It constantly causes the border between the kingdom on the right hand and that on the left to be crossed.[43] The sacramental esotericism and cultic autarchy of a core community which does not see itself as a center of proclamation, but consists only of the devout, are the result of a renunciation of the Word of sending. The sacrament ceases to be a sign (CA, XIII) of God's will toward us to awaken and strengthen our faith thereby. It is simply a sign by which to recognize an exclusive group, an emancipated religious sphere.[44]

We may sum up our deliberations as follows.

1. Even though we use the traditional word "sacrament," we have expressed clear reservations concerning it. We prefer to speak of the celebration of baptism and the Lord's Supper in order to characterize both as special forms of a Word-event and to obviate rivalry between Word and sacrament.

2. In this sense the sacrament, alongside preaching as the proclamation of the Word, has a special liturgical function. It is distinct from the homiletical venture—we have already discussed this—and it expresses directly the central intention of the gospel as the promise of the Lord's presence and the task of mission. In this sense it is not just direction but provision for the way.[45] It is a sign of God to exercise and strengthen our faith.[46]

3. In the strict sense Jesus Christ as the incarnate Word is the only true sacra-

---

[41]*Chassidische Botschaft,* p. 14; cf. K. Kerenyi, *Umgang mit dem Göttlichen,* 2nd ed. (1961), p. 19.

[42]See EG, II, pp. 483ff.; EF, II, pp. 395f.

[43]ThE, I, §§1783ff.; E.T. I, pp. 359ff.

[44]Tokens of our profession among men (CA, XIII).

[45]I owe this felicitous phrase to Pöhlmann, *Abriss der Dogmatik,* p. 240.

[46]Clemen, *Bonner Studentenausgabe,* I, 170, 26.

ment. In him alone thing signified and sign have equal rank and significance in their union, the sign being not just a demonstration (significatively) but the act (efficaciously) of the self-giving and self-sacrificing love of God.

4. As the sacrament points to Christ as the incarnate Word and to the union of his divine and human natures, its aim is that the divine and human natures of the sacrament (thing signified and sign) should be known only as Christ himself is known, i.e., as we focus on their gifts and benefits.

This statement, modelled on that of Melanchthon, means in practice that eucharistic fellowship does not depend on one's understanding of the eucharist, as though Zwinglians, Calvinists, and Lutherans had to exclude one another. It depends solely on readiness or openness to God's gift of salvation and agreement that it is given to us without merit or worth (Luke 18:13). As the Word of the gospel calls those blessed who hunger and thirst after righteousness (Matthew 5:6), hunger and thirst qualify also for reception of the Word accompanied by the sacramental signs.

5. Not the elements alone are signs but also the fellowship within which the sacrament is dispensed and received. The "naked" Word establishes togetherness and refers us to the ministry of passing on to others. But the Word accompanied by the sign is already an act in fellowship.

This includes rather than excludes a constant theme in Luther, namely, that the sacrament, unlike preaching which is to everybody, sets the individual Christian personally before the offer of salvation with no possibility of being represented by another. He himself comes as an individual, receives the sacrament, and thus makes and attests his individual decision. Yet this is only a matter of difference in clarity, not of a basic distinction between Word and sacrament. For the Word is personal too, though in preaching it is not spoken to the individual alone, as it is in penance (WA, 15, 486; cf. Formula of Concord, Solida Declaratio, XI, 36f. [Jacobs, pp. 655f., nos. 36f.]; for further references cf. O. H. Pesch, *Theologie der Rechtfertigung bei M. Luther und Thomas von Aquino* [1967], pp. 331ff., 340).

6. With the sign that accompanies the Word the sacrament addresses the *whole* person. It touches us bodily, affects various senses, and transcends reason as the sphere of intellectual apprehension. It need not imply any mystification or psychologizing to say that it also addresses the zones of the subconscious. But we may say all this only if we add that the Word, too, addresses the *whole* person, so that once again there is no fundamental difference, only a pedagogic clarification appropriate to human nature.

5. EPILOGUE: NEW ROMAN CATHOLIC STATEMENTS ON THE RELATION BETWEEN WORD AND SACRAMENT

If appearances do not deceive, intensified dialogue between Protestants and Roman Catholics in the last decades has contributed essentially to some rethinking of sacramental theology on the Roman Catholic side; these deliberations begin characteristically with some new thoughts about the theological status of the Word. At this decisive point, which strategically is even more important than the important and controversial one of ecclesiology, some real barriers seem to have been broken down. In illustration we shall discuss the pertinent reflections of Karl Rahner.[47]

That the relation of Word and sacrament should be seen and treated as the central problem of sacramental theology is itself a surprise. If we ask what the Word of God is on the lips of the church, how it operates, what God speaks in it, what it seeks to do in those addressed by it, statements about God's Word result which are astonishingly parallel to those usually made about the sacraments. Both the power of the Word and that of the sacraments characterize the essence of the church in a basic way.[48]

The astonishing thing about the Roman Catholic teaching tradition (and the suspicious thing—though Rahner would not say this!) is that it has to fill up some gaps relative to an explicit theology of the Word. There is an urgent need for make-up work. In average teaching, in the Latin textbooks, no place is provided for a theology of the Word.[49] The index to Denzinger has no heading "Word of God."[50] In practice the Word has thus far been dealt with only as an unavoidable preparation for the sacraments and not as something independently efficacious in and alongside the sacraments.[51]

But this seems to be changing in modern Roman Catholic theology.[52] This change, Rahner thinks, is not due to criticism of the previous view of the sacraments (though such criticism may have been a result of the change). It arises out of a concern to give the Word its proper place. So long as the Word serves only to prepare for reception of the sacrament, it is in the main instruction (*didache*).[53] But the Word is really proclamation in which what is proclaimed is at work. It is the mighty, creative *dabar* of God to man in which the proclaimed reality is present for us.[54] To this degree God's Word is not just teaching about God's gracious act. It is itself an act of grace, an active revelation, and it has an unquestioned share in the character of God's saving action in Christ. It is itself a salvation event.[55]

In the light of this view the traditional privilege of the sacraments can be maintained only with difficulty (if at all) unless parallelism of Word and sacrament is later limited again or abandoned. In fact Rahner's own attempt to stay with the tradition shows signs of strain and is open to further infiltration.

In trying to adjust the new relation of Word and sacrament to the existing tradition Rahner follows two approaches.

First, he views the sacraments as the climax of the exhibitive Word of grace in the church.[56] Two points are to be noted here. First, the sacrament is granted only

---

[47] "Wort und Eucharistie," *Schriften zur Theologie,* IV, 3rd ed. (1963), pp. 313ff.; *Theological Investigations,* IV, pp. 253ff. (cited as "Word"); Jüngel/Rahner, *Was ist ein Sakrament?,* pp. 55ff. (cited as *Sacrament*).
[48] "Word," p. 314 (254).
[49] P. 315 (255).
[50] P. 316 (255).
[51] P. 317 (256).
[52] P. 315 (255).
[53] P. 323 (261).
[54] P. 323 (261).
[55] P. 321 (260).
[56] *Sacrament,* p. 79.

a quantitatively higher rank than the spoken Word: it is the climax. Second, the higher position relates only to exhibitive rank (as Rahner constantly stresses). The superiority is not grounded in the "matter" but only in pedagogic accommodation, in the demonstrative force of the saving offer.

In his concern to prove the unbroken continuity between this view and the previous understanding of the sacrament Rahner meets with even more difficulty when he tries to rescue the concept of automatic sacramental efficacy. He makes a very forced statement when he says that at root this concept implies only the victorious power which God grants to the exhibitive Word of faith when it reaches its fulness in the Word of the sacrament (*Sacrament*, p. 80). Here we have an obvious generalizing which is not the real point of the older doctrine. In relating the automatic efficacy to the exhibitive Word of faith, the Word of the sacrament, he puts the doctrine in the context of his interrelating of the Word and faith. But does not this juggle away the older doctrine, which ignores the relation between the Word and faith? Why does he not accept this? What is he afraid of?

Formally Rahner wants to integrate his theology of the Word into the tradition. Unmistakably, however, his new understanding of the Word[57] causes repercussions which disturb many of the traditional rankings. Here at the center a movement has started whose bearing on the debate between the Reformation and Roman Catholicism cannot as yet be calculated.

Second, Rahner tries to integrate his relating of Word and sacrament into the tradition by using ecclesiological arguments. Following the Dogmatic Constitution on the Church of Vatican II,[58] he calls Christ the primal sacrament and the church the basic sacrament.[59] It is natural that the church should have sacramental significance because sign and thing signified are united in it. The church is a sign and instrument both of inner union with God and also of the unity of the human race.[60] We can be hesitant to accept this only to the degree that we may suspect that there lurks in the background an equation of the church with the present Christ, which we have already rejected. But apart from that another consideration seems to me to be especially significant.

The new emphasis on the Word as the presentation of salvation can make the relating of the Word and faith fruitful in ecclesiology too and bring about several notable shifts of accent. One example might be given to show in what direction there could be modifications.[61]

In our ecclesiological deliberations we pointed out that according to the Roman Catholic view the church as the subject of both canon and tradition is prior to both as the rule of faith. Hence Scripture cannot be used as a critical argument against the church but can only serve to justify it.[62] The question arises then: Will the

---

[57]Rahner is only one of many in this regard. See the art. "Wort" in the Roman Catholic *Handbuch theologischer Grundbegriffe*, IV (1970), pp. 406–49 and the bibliography (pp. 448f.).

[58]"Lumen gentium," 1, c. 1 (*Vatican II Documents*, pp. 14f.; KKK, p. 123).

[59]*Sacrament*, p. 75.

[60]"Lumen gentium," 1 (*Vatican II Documents*, p. 15; KKK, p. 123).

[61]I realize that Roman Catholics would not use the word "modifications." Their tendency toward synthesis would lead them to argue that what I call modifications are already present in the tradition as possibilities and are therefore only specific implications.

[62]Cf. H. Rückert, *Vorträge und Aufsätze zu historischer Theologie* (1972), pp. 321f.

enhanced position given to the relation of Word and faith by modern Roman Catholicism, especially after Vatican II, open up new dimensions for the understanding of the church as the basic sacrament? It seems to do so in Rahner when he says that while the church is the sign which historically manifests and effects God's will for the world, and while it is thus the proclaiming agent of God's revealing Word as the message of salvation to the world, nevertheless it is also to be regarded as the hearing and believing addressee to whom God's saving Word in Christ is directed. It is thus the hearing church as well as the teaching church. It hears God's Word, so that fundamentally even its supreme authority knows that it is bound to this Word.[63]

Even though these theses have never been denied, the new emphasis on the Word and hearing is unmistakable. Hence one may ask whether in the foreseeable future the accusation that the church has control of the Word and evades its criticism will not lose its point. That the church in rediscovering and redefining the rank of the Word sees itself not merely as the subject but also as the target of proclamation means at least that something that had been forgotten or almost forgotten has been brought to light again and has taken on new vigor. In putting it thus we are recognizing that this does not mean any challenge in principle to the Roman Catholic commitment to tradition but rather that something previously implicit is now explicit. In any case the new understanding of the Word and its theological rank will lead to important and influential nuances in the relation of Word and sacrament, of Bible, tradition, and church. There open up here some new ecumenical horizons.

---

[63]O. Karrer, art. "Wort," HThG, III, pp. 288f.

XXI

On the Understanding of Baptism

Supplementary Bibliography: K. Aland, *Taufe und Kindertaufe* (1971); K. Barth, "Die kirchliche Lehre von der Taufe," *ThEx,* N.F. 1943; E.T. *The Teaching of the Church regarding Baptism* (1948); also CD, IV,4; M. Barth, *Die Taufe—ein Sakrament?* (1951); G. Bornkamm, "Taufe und neues Leben bei Paulus," *Das Ende des Gesetzes. Paulus-studien* (1952), pp. 34ff.; E.T. *Early Christian Experience* (New York, 1969), pp. 71ff.; R. Hermann, "Kindertaufe bei Luther," LMH, II (1962), pp. 67ff.; J. Jeremias, *Hat die Urkirche die Kindertaufe geübt?* (1949); also *Die Kindertaufe in den ersten vier Jahrhunderten* (1958); E.T. *Infant Baptism in the First Four Centuries* (London, 1960); E. Jüngel, "K. Barths Lehre von der Taufe," ThSt, No. 98 (1968); W. Kasper, ed., *Christsein ohne Entscheidung—oder: Soll die Kirche Kinder taufen?* (1970); W. Kreck, "K. Barths Tauflehre," ThLZ, VI (1969), pp. 402ff.; J. Moltmann, *Kirche in der Kraft der Geistes* (1975), pp. 252ff.; E.T. *The Church in the Power of the Spirit,* pp. 226ff.; A. Oepke, art. "Baptō, baptizō," TDNT, I, pp. 529ff. (TWNT, I, pp. 527ff.); C. H. Ratschow, *Die ein christliche Taufe* (1972); H. Schlier, "Zur kirchlichen Lehre von der Taufe," *Die Zeit der Kirche,* 2nd ed. (1958); O. Semmelroth, *Wirkendes Wort. Zur Theologie der Verkündigung* (1962); E.T. *The Preaching Word* (New York, 1965); P. Stuhlmacher, "Erwägungen zum ontologischen Charakter der *kainē ktisis* bei Paulus," EvTh, XXVII (1967), p. 20; Theological Faculty of Tübingen, "Gutachten über die Taufordnung," ZThK, II (1950), pp. 265ff.

1. THE MESSAGE OF BAPTISM

In what follows we shall not be dealing with such historical questions as that of the baptismal command in Matthew 28:18-20, the relation to John's baptism, the baptism of Jesus (Mark 1:9-11; John 1:31-34), the fact that Jesus himself did not baptize, proselyte baptism, and baptism as it was practiced after Pentecost.[1] Instead we shall limit ourselves to some specific systematic problems that our preceding chapter on the sacraments has suggested. We shall not be asking, then,

---

[1]Cf. the summary in Schlink, *Leitourgia,* V, pp. 648-73, esp. pp. 661ff. (E.T. pp. 9-41, esp. pp. 26ff.) with bibliography, pp. 643-47; also Moltmann, *Kirche,* pp. 262ff. (E.T. pp. 236ff.).

whether baptism goes back to a charge of Jesus after the resurrection and has thus a rather dubious historical validity. We shall be asking instead whether and how far the exalted Lord presents himself in baptism by Word, Spirit, and sign, and wills to be with us "to the close of the age" (Matthew 18:20; 28:20). What value has baptism for the discipleship that Christ had in view?

The right to ask this type of question is provided by the distinctive transitive use of *mathēteuō* ("make disciples") in Matthew 28:19 (K. H. Rengstorf, TDNT, IV, p. 461; TWNT, IV, p. 465). The fact that the triune formula is used here instead of the formula "into the name of Christ" is no reason for historical scepticism regarding the pericope. For it is in keeping with the NT kerygma in general that the Holy Spirit should play a part in the calling to discipleship. In this sense baptism into the name of Jesus means that the one Son of God has been manifested who is himself the Spirit and who gives God's Spirit, so that God himself is present and active here, killing and making alive (J. Schniewind, *Das Evangelium nach Matthäus, NT Deutsch, ad loc.*). The fulfilment of the promise of the Spirit in Christ to which reference is made here is intimated in John's baptism (Matthew 3:11). In this sense, according to Schniewind, the Trinity is not a new dogma that suddenly appears at this point. The OT too, as we have seen, speaks of the Spirit of God as the presence of God. If those who are baptized are brought into the context of salvation, they become disciples of him who is the Son and learn from him to call upon God as Father; as disciples of Jesus they also become his brethren (28:10) and therewith the children of God (5:9, 45); as they are aware, this is all the work of the Holy Spirit (cf. Romans 8:15; Galatians 4:6) (Grundmann, *Das Evangelium nach Matthäus* [1971], p. 579). Thus the triadic formula fits into the traditional context.

2. Having established the priority of the Word in the doctrine of the sacrament, we have first to define the element of proclamation in baptism. It consists of the message that those who are called to discipleship are buried, crucified, and risen with Christ and have begun to live a new life (Romans 6:5ff.; Galatians 2:20f.). They have died to sin, being dead and buried, so that no power has any more claim over them. The fellowship with Christ attested and effected thereby relates not only to his death, however, but also to his resurrection. The head does not leave the members behind. We have a share in the Lord's resurrection.

At the point of the baptismal message this christological reference so dominates the scene that it makes no essential difference who baptizes (1 Corinthians 1:12, 14f.). Baptism binds us to the Kyrios and not to man. To this extent baptism means a change of lordship. We are no longer (*ouketi*) under the dominion of sin and death but by the death and resurrection of the Lord have come to belong to him who has overcome sin and death once and for all (*ephapax*). Hence when Paul says: "Consider yourselves (*logizesthe*) dead to sin and alive to God in Jesus Christ" (Romans 6:11), this is no mere metaphor but is a conclusion ("so"). Nor is it a mere "as if." The saying means that there opens up before believers the reality which is disclosed to them in Christ, in terms of which they see their own existence in faith, and in orientation to which they may now lead their lives.[2]

---

[2] G. Bornkamm, *Das Ende des Gesetzes*, p. 44; E.T. *Early Christian Experience*, p. 79.

Baptism expresses in a sign this change of lordship by dying and rising again with Christ. It does so in such a way that it ascribes to the baptized this relation to Christ, this incorporation into his body.

Because baptism symbolizes death and resurrection, Luther viewed it as a powerful sign and not a weak and cautious one as in mere sprinkling with water. He liked full dipping into the water. He added that while this was not essential to the validity of baptism, it was a good thing to offer a full and complete sign for so full and complete a thing (*Babylonian Captivity;* LW, 36, 68).

Because of this significance of the Word, of the message of baptism, it includes not only the trinitarian formula ("I baptize thee in the name of the Father, the Son, and the Holy Spirit") but also preaching which expounds the baptismal act as a promise. Since baptism belongs to the christological heart of the gospel, all Christian preaching deals implicitly or explicitly with it and can be understood as a follow-up of baptism in verbal form. Although baptism itself is given only once—more of this later—the thing signified is permanently relevant until death and the last day.[3] For the presence of the Lord expressed in the spiritual Word and sign, incorporation into his body, and the change of lordship achieved thereby, are all part of the ongoing follow-up in faith. The relation of acceptance and appropriation determines the whole of the new life initiated by baptism.

3. The efficacious Word by which Christ is appropriated to us in baptism is also expressed by the sign of baptism to the extent that it underscores the "outside us" aspect of the salvation event enacted here. If something also happens to us, we ourselves cannot perform it. If it then leads to something in us, especially the faith which receives and determines the new life, that which triggers and sustains everything is what happens outside us and to us. In temptation then, when all inner feelings and certainties vanish, Luther could find comfort in baptism: I am baptized. He sought refuge in the "outside him" which was untouched by changing psychological moods and always stood firm. Along the same lines Calvin appealed to baptism as the given sign and seal of "the initiation by which we are received into the society of the church, in order that, engrafted in Christ, we may be reckoned among God's children."[4]

In pointing to the "outside us" of something that happens to us, baptism stresses two elements which are prominent again in Calvin. In the first place it reminds us of the distance between us who belong to other lords and Christ who has overcome the world. This distance is so great that we cannot overcome it. An act of God is needed to do this. This act is the work of the Pneuma. In him Christ appropriates us by descending and making himself present to us. In the Spirit he makes us his and draws us up to himself so that we are united and belong to him body, soul, and spirit.[5]

4. The "outside us" that is proclaimed in this way attests itself also in its independence of our state of faith. We do not believe in our faith, so that we are not grounded in the state of our faith. We do not believe in the faith of our fathers, so that tradition does not come between us and Christ. Instead, we say with the

---

[3] We are always being baptized and dying and living (*ibid.*).
[4] Inst., IV, 15, 1.
[5] Cf. Inst., IV, 14, 7; 15, 6.

Reformers that faith grants immediacy to the Kyrios and so we are told not to stop at ourselves or our faith but to "creep into Christ." As the baptismal message— and with it the whole of baptism—refers us to the "outside us" of the death and resurrection that have taken place in Christ, it gives our faith a firm and irremovable foundation on which we can always build and to which we can always return from every crisis or failure of faith. The access to Christ that has been opened up remains open. Hence baptism always stands, and although we all fall from it and sin, we always have access to it, and can thus subject the old man to us. Repentance is simply a return to baptism in which we come back to the point at which we began but which we had left.[6]

Baptism, then, takes us up into an eternal covenant of grace and promises us a salvation that has been achieved once and for all by Jesus Christ. This is why there is only one baptism. In a way that cannot be reversed, it sets us in relation to him who has claimed us as his own. Crises and failures of faith are no reason for repeating baptism when we repent and come back. We can only return to baptism itself and to the acceptance into the covenant of grace that has taken place in it.

Luther saw a kinship between the Anabaptists and the Roman Catholics in this area. Both put the accent in baptism on subjective conditions and thus denied the "outside us," whether by making conversion the condition (the Anabaptists) or by seeing in baptism an ontic change and viewing the reception of justifying faith as a supernatural habit and a cleansing from original sin (the Roman Catholics). (Cf. *Tübinger Gutachten*, p. 266.) Thus Luther can accuse Rome of the Anabaptist heresy, for while it does not repeat baptism it seeks to restore the baptismal grace that has been lost by works and by new sacraments (Diem, *Dogmatik*, III, p. 138).

Once subjective conditions come into play, the definitiveness of baptismal grace on the basis of the "outside us" seems to be ridiculous and is itself regarded as a heresy. For on this assumption the definitiveness claimed by the Reformers seems to be that of a subjective state. It was not meant as such but "merely" as that of the promise received in baptism, which can constantly be claimed afresh even when we return from the far country. That the Reformation thesis of definitiveness was in fact misunderstood by Rome may be seen from the anathemas of Trent in this regard. Thus the position that we cannot lose baptismal grace even though we sin and lose our faith is anathematized (Denz., 1619; E.T. 862), as is also the position that all postbaptismal sins are remitted or become remissible merely by the recollection of baptism or by faith in it (Denz., 1623; E.T. 866).

One may see here how the use of ontological schemas of thought on the one hand and personalist schemas on the other necessarily provokes misunderstandings of this kind. The ontological schema of scholasticism has to begin with the ontic subjective state, with being and habit, its changeability, and the need for its revision (by sacraments and works). In contrast the personalist schema begins with a relation which is established once and for all and whose grounding in the "outside us" is independent of any subjective state. Misunderstandings of this type may be seen in all the themes of dogmatics. One has only to think of the Roman Catholic understanding of the Reformation doctrine of original sin as the total ruin of man when what is meant is "only" the ruining of his relation to God.

---

[6]LC (LBK, p. 706,78f.; Jacobs, p. 475, nos. 76, 79); cf. *Babylonian Captivity* (LW, 36, 68f.).

The doctrine of baptism is a classical example of how we can talk past one another because of differences in approach. In this regard it is an open question what is cause and what is effect. Is the ontological schema of thought the great temptress (even the personalist schema is no safeguard against the devil!) that leads autonomously to dogmatic statements? Or are the dogmatic statements already there looking for a suitable schema of thought?

However that may be, in controversial theology dogmatic method is the decisive question and the main reason for self-criticism. The debate between Pius XII and French Roman Catholic existentialists, to which we have already referred and in which the conceptual framework of dogmatic statements is the issue, bears on this crucial matter. Apart from the existentialist aspect it can hardly rank as controversial theology.

5. When we insist on the "outside us" of the baptismal grace promised to us, this *in*cludes rather than *ex*cludes the fact that the "outside" becomes an "inside." Here again the relation of Word and faith implies that the promise will be accepted and that there will be a dying and rising again with Christ. It is typical, however, that Luther does not say that baptismal grace has to "creep" into us (to give birth to a habit) but that we have to "creep" into baptism, willingly and believingly entering into the covenant of grace that has been made. If life is to be a constant penitence or return to baptism, one might say that our life must be a constant ratification of the baptismal covenant. The alien righteousness of Christ becomes our own righteousness in this way. It is not just outside us but also in us because God is what he is, not for himself alone, but for us too.[7]

For this reason we can never say within the christological relation that God is righteous but we are not, that he is holy but we are not. Because God in his righteousness and holiness is for us, because he wills to be Emmanuel, the sinner is *in*cluded and not *ex*cluded. Christ's vicariate expresses more than anything else what happens to and outside me but it differs from—most—human vicariates by including me within it and by coming into force only with the follow-up, the ratification. It is an inclusive and not an exclusive vicariate. This question is a particularly important one in infant baptism, as we shall see.

Representative action in the human and social sphere offers only poor examples of this relation between the outside and the inside aspects. For it is for the most part exclusive. The engineer who drives a train acts on behalf of the passengers and does not want their participation. This exclusiveness may be traced through almost all relations from the manual worker to the artist (ThE, II, 1, §§1615ff.). Things can be different in the personal sphere (hence the question of sponsors in infant baptism). Parental instruction takes over many functions that are beyond the capacities of children, but only to make itself superfluous and not to exclude the children—except in such pathological cases as that of the urge to dominate or perverted mother-love. Here, then, we may find an example of inclusive representation.

---

[7]Cf. Iwand, "Glaubensgerechtigkeit nach Luthers Lehre," ThEx, LXXV (1941), p. 56; cf. WA, 54, 186; LW, 34, 337, where Luther describes God's work as his work in us, the strength of God whereby he makes us strong, the wisdom of God whereby he makes us wise, his power and salvation and glory.

The concept of "inclusive representation" appears in P. Althaus ("Das Kreuz Christi," *Theologische Aufsätze* [1929], pp. 35ff.) and before him in B. Steffen (*Das Dogma vom Kreuz* [1920], pp. 41ff.). Materially, though not under this name, we find it also in M. Kähler when he speaks of an "expiation offered by God to man for his appropriation . . . not a substitute which makes the gift of one's own will to God superfluous, but one which makes it possible." It is not, then, a substitute which, because it is offered by God, releases us from the relation to God, but one by which we enter into this relation to him (*Die Wissenschaft der christlichen Lehre* [1960, a reprint of the 1905 ed.], §428, p. 369).

2. WORD AND SIGN: THE PROBLEM OF CAUSATIVE OR COGNITIVE

1. Baptism is not just teaching about integration into Christ. It does not just illustrate justification. It accomplishes these things.[8] That it does so is grounded solely in the Word that performs what it says and makes God's saving action present by the Pneuma. (Making present means here both bringing it to us and bringing us to it.)

Naturally baptism has an illustrative and cognitive side. But this *in*cludes rather than *ex*cludes its causative character. Illustration alone is not enough, as one may see from what Jesus says about his illustrative parables in Matthew 13:13-15. If we are far from the thing depicted in the sign, the sign will simply depict this distance and not give us access. In denoting the thing signified it will also signify and seal the distance and thus lead to hardening. Nor will the sign overcome indifference. The sign is not creative and efficacious. This is true only of the Spirit of God who makes it a sign, who makes its deciphering possible, and who performs the miracle of accessibility.

The cognitive side of baptism which leads us from the sign to its message is more than mere instruction. It is the promise of participation in the divine covenant of grace. If even Socratic knowledge can change life, the knowledge of Christ mediated in this way can certainly do so. Hence the antithesis of causative and cognitive is a false one. Being mediated by the Spirit, baptism makes us the temple of the Holy Spirit (1 Corinthians 3:16; 6:19; 2 Corinthians 6:16). It sets us in the covenant of grace.

This work of presentation was what caused Luther to champion the real presence of Christ in the eucharistic elements. Under the pressure of traditional teaching—and additionally stimulated by the extreme opposition of Zwingli—he yielded to the temptation to give the sign an inappropriate ranking over against the Word. In relation to baptism, however, he did not overvalue the sign or ascribe to the water a special quality. Hence the renewal of his sacramental understanding is plainer here than in his view of the Lord's Supper.

It seems to me that Barth misunderstands Luther, and Diem after him (*Dogmatik*, III, p. 140), when he accuses him of ascribing a sacramental quality to the water of baptism, quoting in support Luther's reference (on Matthew 3:13-17 [WA, 52, 102]) to the divine water "which takes away sin and death and all evil

---

[8]Barth in CD, IV,4 distinguishes between baptism with water and baptism with the Spirit, ascribing to the former only illustrative and demonstrative significance.

and helps us to heaven and eternal life,'' this water being a precious medicine which God himself has mixed, ''the true water of life that banishes death and hell and makes eternally alive.''

One should not isolate such sayings but put them in context. Luther elsewhere compares the baptismal water to parents (LC [LBK, pp. 694f.; Jacobs, pp. 467f.). Parents are human beings like others. Like Turks and heathen, they have noses, eyes, skin, hair, flesh, and bones. Why, then, should we respect them more than others? But when there is added the command—the Word of God—that we should honor our fathers and mothers we see them as people who are adorned and robed with the majesty and glory of God. The command is thus the gold chain around the father's neck and the crown on his head showing us why we should honor this particular flesh and blood. Similarly, it is because the Word is added that the water takes on significance and is exalted to the same rank as the father with the gold chain even though the latter is no different from a heathen or Turk in his natural quality. Apart from the Word the water is like any other water, like the water with which the servant cooks. The Word is what does it (Sermon on 1/15/1531 [WA, 34/I, 88]).

If we view Barth's quotation in the light of this passage, the dignity of the water is clearly not an immanent quality or an infused grace. It is an alien dignity, to use a familiar phrase of Luther's. Hence focusing on the water makes no sense and any other use of it, e.g., for healing, is magic and superstitious.

Calvin avoids even more fully any presence of Christ in the elements, especially with Luther's eucharistic teaching in view. His argument is that instead of a static presence we have a making present by the Holy Spirit. This argument points to his underlying Christology. This causes him to distinguish sharply between Christ's divine and human natures both ontologically and functionally, and therefore to reject Luther's ubiquitarianism (Inst., IV, 17, 30; also W. Kratz, ''Christus—Gott und Mensch. Fragen an Calvins Christologie,'' EvTh, V [1959], pp. 209ff.).

2. From what has been said, it makes no sense to contrast the terms ''causative'' and ''cognitive'' in our understanding of baptism. ''Causative'' presupposes correlation with a demonstrable effect, a real change in the baptized person so that he is something that he previously was not, a habitual change. This is not what is meant in the NT or the Reformers. ''Cognitive'' makes the sign, in Zwinglian fashion, a mere illustration of the Word, which itself is purely descriptive and not efficacious.[9]

Neither term is adequate to describe what goes on in baptism—our appropriation by Christ, our inclusion in the covenant of grace.[10] Here is an act which is efficacious without being causative and the disclosure of an act which goes beyond the cognitive.[11]

---

[9]Cf. Abelard's view of the birth, crucifixion, and resurrection of Christ as simply a demonstration of the love of God (F. Nitzsch, RE, I, pp. 24f.; K. Heim, *Jesus der Weltvollender* [1937], p. 110; E.T. *Jesus the World's Perfecter* [Edinburgh, 1959], pp. 96f.).

[10]Cf. WA, 17, 338, 4.

[11]That water baptism has for Barth only cognitive significance is part of his whole theological system, which is decisively shaped by Christ's having put all people into relation to God (cf. CD, IV,2, pp. 45f. and ThE, I, §596; E.T. pp. 100ff.). As this has taken place once and for all in Christ the Word can no longer do it. It has, therefore, only the function of a reference, as does also the sacrament (cf. Jüngel, *Sacrament,* pp. 26f., 35).

We cannot ignore the question whether the NT does not in fact say more and speak of an actual change, so that there is a causative element. This seems especially to be so because of the close relation between baptism and the reception of the Spirit. Hence we must survey some of the main points in this relation.

Chronologically the relation between baptism and the reception of the Spirit is varied. In the story of Cornelius in Acts 10 the Spirit precedes baptism. The Samaritans, however, are first baptized by Philip and then receive the Spirit later through the apostolic laying on of hands (Acts 8:15–17). In Acts 19:5f. the two acts are a single whole but in the case of the Ethiopian eunuch in Acts 8:36 there is no mention of the Pneuma. In Paul, since baptism promises a share in Christ's death and resurrection (Romans 6:1ff.; Galatians 3:27), the implication is that this union with Christ and incorporation into his body is accomplished by the Spirit (1 Corinthians 12:12f.).

We gather from these references that the union between baptism and reception of the Spirit becomes increasingly closer. In John's baptism water baptism is sharply differentiated from the coming Spirit baptism of the Messiah (Matthew 3:11; Luke 3:16; John 1:33). Eschatological significance is ascribed to the latter. "To baptize" is figurative in this context and it has nothing to do with water baptism. It denotes the outpouring of the Spirit (Joel 2:28ff.; Zechariah 12:10).

In the other baptismal references baptism and the imparting of the Spirit gradually come closer together, so that the eschatological future is already present, although baptism still retains an element of promise and its eschatological dimension is not completely lost. Water baptism and Spirit baptism are seen as one, though the nature of the union is still an open question.

The indefiniteness of the nature of the relation, which comes to expression in the varied chronology, is an essential matter. It is removed if we take the causative view that baptism accomplishes a demonstrable change. As we noted, however, in the chapters on the Pneuma (Part I), and especially in discussing the charismata, the Pneuma is the power of disclosure which makes God's Word efficacious, and the Spirit never becomes our own possession. Hence incorporation into Christ's body takes place as efficacious proclamation and it is a pneumatic event (1 Corinthians 12:13; Titus 3:5).

The point of receiving (*lambanein*, Acts 8:17) the Spirit is not to be sought in the recipient or in processes in the subjective sphere but in the act of address. This alone maintains the correspondence which we found in the relation between Spirit-mediated Word and receiving faith.

3. If in Word and sign baptism imparts incorporation into Christ's body, is it necessary to salvation? Is it a *sine qua non* of the Christian life? In this context this is almost a superfluous question. If the sign annexed to the Word means sealing, it confirms the Spirit-mediated promise of the Word without adding anything that is not already contained in the Word. In churches that practice adult baptism no one will deny to confessing but unbaptized Christians their status as members of Christ's body. In Reformed churches no one could ever imagine that infants dying without baptism are consigned to eternal perdition or the milder *limbus* of infants.[12]

Baptism is not, of course, an option or an adiaphoron. The seal on a document

---

[12]We shall deal with the related question of emergency baptism later.

that has to do with life and death is hardly a matter of indifference.[13] To that extent we shall desire baptism. If we do not want it or despise it, this works against salvation. The statement that baptism is not necessary to salvation is true only if the Word is received in faith even though for some reason it has to remain without the seal of water baptism.

Apart from this, baptism by origin and unbroken and universal use throughout Christian history has become a sacred obligation. It is binding in the same way as the church membership which incorporates us into the Lord's body and which is conferred and also confessed by baptism.[14] In adults it is a solemn and explicit answer to the offer of the covenant of grace. It is thus a confession before God and men and a reception of the distinguishing human mark.[15]

3. INFANT BAPTISM

a. Problems and Traditional Solutions

As concerns biblical support, the problem of infant baptism differs from that of baptism in general. Schleiermacher's observation is still true that if we are to find traces of infant baptism in the NT we must first import them.[16] Even if we recall that the early church never debated the issue nor made any synodal decisions about it, so that the practice seems simply to have developed, we face a different situation today. Once infant baptism was perhaps so self-evident that no basis was needed for it,[17] but changed conditions no longer allow us to pass it on in the same uncritical way. The noticeable abuse of infant baptism is at most the occasion for the necessary investigation, not the deeper reason.

The abuse is obvious: the formalism of mass baptisms at clinics, baptisms administered like compulsory inoculation on the occasion of family celebrations, the syncretistic implications as with the forced baptism of imported African slaves in South America, the common practice in national churches.

Behind this deterioration of infant baptism into a formal act which is often viewed as magical, there is undoubtedly a decline into the secularism which replaces the church by Christendom. Whereas in primitive Christianity and in missionary churches an awakening to faith is the normative motive for the reception of new members, in Christendom infant baptism sees to it that birth and tradition constitute the spiritual link between the generations. The question inevitably arises whether infant baptism is legitimate on this basis. But the question is really a rhetorical one. Scepticism as to the continued existence of Christendom gives it a sociological twist. In our pluralistic and secularized society the claim of an institution that at the great points of life, especially birth and death, it can take over the patriarchally inserted function of giving meaning is more than doubtful (Moltmann, *Kirche*, pp. 254-57; E.T. pp. 228-32).

---

[13]At the same time, I cannot share Luther's view that in temptation one may find refuge in the seal: "I am baptized." If we cease to trust the Word and its author, the seal can bring little relief.

[14]Leuenberger, *Taufe in der Krise*, pp. 58ff.

[15]In intention confirmation serves the same purpose, however inadequately.

[16]*The Christian Faith*, §138; E.T. 1928, pp. 633ff.

[17]Schlink, *Leitourgia*, V, p. 750; E.T. p. 137.

Even in the past history of the church we find arguments for infant baptism that are only partially relevant or acceptable for us today. Tertullian raises the modern problem when in his work *On Baptism* he relates baptism to conscious acceptance in faith and reserves it for an age when one may know Christ. He also refers to the innocence of infants and asks what the forgiveness of sins can mean for them at their age (*De baptismo*, 18).

In contrast, the argument that baptism is a remedy against original sin (e.g., in Origen, Cyprian, Augustine, and Thomas) has an alien and unacceptable ring. To claim that infant baptism is a defensive rite that wards off sin in its state of incubation is to misunderstand original sin as a latent genetic defect against which preventive action must be taken in good time and also to misunderstand baptism as a magical medicine which works independently of individual awareness. It is also a bad sign that Thomas brings in the doctrine of habit when he tries to support infant baptism and deal with unconsciousness at its reception. Baptism, he thinks, confers habitual grace which then becomes actual at maturity, just as those who are asleep possess habitual virtues which are prevented by sleep from becoming actual (STh, III, q. 69, 6). Baptism accomplishes an ontic change by mediating what nominalists called infused faith.

This sacramental-ontic alteration of the person is opposed by the "outside us" of the Reformers, which represents an act on the hearers of the Word and recipients of the sacrament, an act which draws them into itself and thus directs attention away from habitual changes *in* them. This is particularly clear in Calvin's understanding of infant baptism, which rests entirely on his view of the covenant. The old and new covenants are identical in substance and different only in outer form and administration. Thus Christian children receive the same promise of covenant grace as children of the old covenant do through circumcision (Inst., II, 10, 2). "But if the covenant remains firm and steadfast, it applies no less today to the children of Christians than in the Old Testament it pertained to the infants of the Jews. Yet if they are participants in the thing signified, why shall they be debarred from the sign?" (Inst., IV, 16, 5). The "outside us" of baptism here is reception into a covenant and the promise of prior covenant grace to the children of Christian parents. The doctrine of habit is a foreign body that cannot be absorbed into this view.

Behind this list of interpretations of infant baptism, which could easily be extended, there stands the decisive question raised by the relation of Word, sacrament, and faith which is no problem in adult baptism. To use the different extremes by way of illustration, it arises for us both in the doctrine of habit, where faith is actualization of the habit, and in the covenant theology of Calvin, where the promise precedes faith but also includes it as the later ratification of the covenant by the baptized. During and after the Reformation this anticipatory divine promise constantly stimulated the thought that infant baptism signifies this anticipation and demonstrates it in the baptized infant, we being only recipients in relation to God's saving act. If baptism and faith are God's saving acts, faith cannot be one-sidedly demanded as a prerequisite and condition for receiving baptism. It can also be expected as an effect of God's saving act through baptism.[18]

---

[18]Schlink, *Leitourgia*, V, p. 766; E.T. p. 143.

It is obvious that the relation of Word, sacrament, and baptism is upheld here on the one condition that instead of the simultaneity of baptism and faith, as in the NT accounts, there is a temporal postponement of faith, which with the growth of consciousness "creeps" into baptism and ratifies the baptismal covenant. This act of ratification can be given ritual form in confirmation.

This kind of anticipation of the baptism covenant, which is accepted and confirmed by faith, makes sense, however, only if the baptized infant is from the very first placed in the relation of Word, sacrament, and faith even though the child itself is not the believer; but the faith of parents and godparents plays a kind of vicarious role in the establishment of the relation. The baptismal covenant has to be ratified and responsibly put into practice at some point. The administration of infant baptism must stand under the guarantee that the saving act of God is not just an isolated promise but is continuously actualized in the life of the baptized and instruction follows in expectation of the faith, or the decision of faith, which is engendered by God's saving promise. This means concretely that while the statement that God's saving act precedes and demands faith is not a condition, it is also not a farce only so long as the saving act is made present, i.e., is proclaimed and lived out as the parents, godparents, and congregation surround, treat, and address the baptized infant in the name of this saving act, so that with the testimony of the Holy Spirit the act becomes one that he himself can believe.

If the baptized infant is not put in this relation, baptism is an empty rite whose curse will fall on those who knowingly perform it.

Infant baptism can be justified then, at least in principle. But what does "in principle" mean here? The problem is still whether these irrevocable conditions can be met in a secularized society and a national church in which the doors are wide open to abuse. The main question is not whether infant baptism is possible in principle but whether in circumstances such as these it is practicable, whether it is a possibility that can be recommended with a good conscience. It would be fatal if under the pressure of secularism our only alternatives were either to appeal to an infused habit which persists in spite of utter indifference[19] or to allow infant baptism to become an empty formality.

The constitutive relation of baptism and faith, quite irrespective of the chronological order, poses a constant question to all those who have to administer infant baptism responsibly, whether as ministers, parents, or sponsors.

This relation helps us to see why the question persists whether the vicarious faith of adults can really cause us to forget about the faith of the baptized in the name of the priority of God's saving act. Luther was not content with this and advanced instead the dubious theory of infant faith (K. Brinkel, *Die Lehre Luthers von der "fides infantium" bei der Kindertaufe* [1958]). In his LC he says that we should leave this question to scholars, and he does not try to define this faith more precisely. This is understandable, for infant faith does not measure up to the usual criteria for faith as a grasping of the divine promise. In fact, he nowhere describes this faith, which would be absurd. What can he have meant by it? His only way out seems to be that of the abandoned doctrine of habit. In his *Babylonian Captivity* he says

---

[19]Cf. the highly respected Roman Catholic J. Sellmair, who claims that even if East Germany were to seal off many people from all Christian influences those baptized as infants would keep the habit, which stamps them in spite of everything.

that the mighty Word of God through the prayer of the offering and praying church brings about a change and renewal of the small child by infused faith. Here the faith of those who bring the infant is not vicarious but simply helps to awaken the (infused) faith of the child.

In WA, 17/II, 81 Luther expressly rejects the idea that infant baptism is based, not on the present faith of the child, but on the promise of its future faith. There has to be faith before or in baptism if the child is to be rid of the devil and sins. When the question is put whether the child believes and desires baptism, the answer Yes is given on its behalf.

This daring view is obviously in keeping with the whole tenor of Luther's sacramental teaching and its relating of the Word and faith. As he sees it, infancy is no barrier to faith, only to its confession. It is here that the sponsors step in. They alone can verbalize the silent faith of infants. But the fact that this faith is silent and unconscious forces Luther to describe it in ontological categories which he elsewhere rejects in the name of the relation of the Word and faith, namely, as infused faith.

The same ontological schema may be seen in the exorcisms in his baptismal office (LBK, p. 536). The formulae of renunciation have here a suspiciously magical ring. Against this Reformed theology utters a decisive No (cf. the Confessio Sigismundi [Salnar's *Harmonia confessionum fidei* (1887)], p. 167). Along the lines of our own understanding of baptism as promise, which seeks to do justice to the ''outside us'' of the address of grace and thus rejects the ''inside us'' of the ontic doctrine of habit, exorcism must be replaced by telling the child about the promise that Christ gives him a share in his body and kingdom and thus proclaims to him a change of lordship. Luther's doctrine of infant faith, while paradoxically in keeping with his starting point, implies a return to the ontological schemas of nominalist scholasticism which seriously disrupt his understanding of grace, faith, and original sin. At this point Luther needs to be corrected by Luther himself.

Zwingli's theology of consciousness spares him entanglements of this kind. If baptism is primarily a sign of commitment and confession among men and before God (Schlink, p. 758; E.T. pp. 146f.), it presupposes faith and ability to speak in the baptized. This led Zwingli to criticize infant baptism (G. W. Locher, RGG, VI [1966]; Schlink, *ad loc.*). If he illogically retained it, he was led to do so by two arguments. According to *Fidei ratio* (Art. 7; P. Wernle, *Zwingli* [1919], p. 321) baptism does not bring faith causatively or ontically, but the church bears witness that grace is already proffered to the baptized. Thus faith does not precede in infant baptism but what precedes is the promise of God that this child belongs to the church of God. Again, Christian children are not worse off than Israelite children. As the children of Christian parents they, too, must have a share in the sign of the covenant. This line of thought, which Wernle calls ''terribly artificial'' (p. 207), makes it clear that in debate with the Anabaptists Zwingli developed an apology for infant baptism which was confusingly contrary to his original intentions.

Karl Barth logically follows up Zwingli's original point in his repudiation of infant baptism in CD, IV,4. Rejecting totally the causative sacramental understanding of baptism and even its significance as a confirmatory sign that God has given, he describes it as the first step of a life that is faithful to God, i.e., a Christian life. The Christian by his own decision asks the community for water baptism, and the community gives it, as the required confession of his obedience, conversion, and hope, made with prayer for God's grace in which he respects its freedom. Baptism, then, is an act of obedience and confession of faith. The relation of the Word and faith is preserved here inasmuch as faith is the work of the spiritual Word. But baptism is taken out of the relation, for it is not a visible Word, a Word that comes to us in the sign, but, with a one-sided stress on faith, it is simply a sign of faith before God and among men. Infant baptism is thus a theological impossibility. The inconsistency of Zwingli is corrected, but traces of it remain. Thus I fail to see why Barth rejects the rebaptism of baptized infants and calls infant baptism questionable and irregular but not invalid (p. 189). In view of his basic criticism that infant baptism misses the point and involves an idolatrous sacramentalism, it is unconvincing for him to locate the problem in abuse of the practice.

In making infants the objects of baptism the church has not only come up against theological objections based on the nature of baptism in relation to the Word. It has also given rise to the very secular suspicion that it is manipulating helpless beings and usurping their power of decision in its own favor. It would be unfair to attribute to critics of this kind only an unjustifiable cynicism. In view of some of the crass abuses of the practice one can understand the outside impression that we have here only tactical maneuvers and empty traditional ceremonies that have nothing to do with the Word, or faith, or indeed the Holy Spirit. While the thing signified in baptism does not support the charge of manipulation, its concrete perversion may.

Why does the charge not affect the thing signified? What does manipulation mean anyway?

Lexically, manipulation is the direction of the conduct of others in such a way that those concerned are not aware of it and it serves the interests of those who do the directing. The secular criticism finds some support in this definition. But there is also an element of manipulation in the processes of learning both by the influences of models (imitation or learning by observing) and also by instrumental conditioning through reward and punishment. In this sense therapy, too, makes positive use of manipulation, e.g., in fighting phobias.

It is incontestable that every form of instruction, especially in the case of small children, involves some degree of manipulation along these lines. Birth itself is manipulation, for none of us is asked whether he wants to be born. Social status, domestic setting, speech, and innumerable other factors to which children are simply subject may be mentioned in this regard. Parents constantly make decisions representatively for their children.

Nevertheless the question arises whether infant baptism does not mean exerting more influence than in the ordinary affairs of life just mentioned. It includes Christian education, as we have seen. Does not infant baptism mean manipulation in spheres in which the decision is emphatically our own (apart from the testimony of the Holy Spirit which makes it possible)? Do not parents exceed their representative function at this point?

I offer two considerations in reply to this question.

First, when it is a matter of final questions of meaning, of the rise of a sense of values and norms, in short, of philosophical questions, the child is always exposed to outside influences. Its ideas in such matters are fostered by impressions at home and at school, among friends of the same age, by books and television. The vacuum of its psyche, as one might somewhat unguardedly say, is filled by these imports from outside and it is the more defenseless against them the less it has criteria of selection, of acceptance or rejection, at its disposal.

From this standpoint it would be unreasonable for parents not to offer their children materials and criteria which they themselves have found essential and supportive, including their faith. If they did not do this, they would abandon them to diffuse and uncontrollable outside influences which would not give them the safeguard of a standpoint from which to make their own adult decisions.

There are, of course, forms of Christian education which hardly seem to offer a standpoint of this kind but are more like an intolerant drilling. Yet what we have here is not manipulation but indoctrination, or, in modern terms, an ideologizing of Christianity. This is inimical not only to infant baptism but to faith in general. For the promise of salvation seeks always personal faith and decision. And the promised imparting of the Spirit grants an immediacy of the individual to God. Indeed, it creates the individual and causes him to "creep into Christ" with his own faith instead of into the faith of others. Infant baptism should initiate the story of Christians who are prepared for a personal adult follow-up of their baptism—or who can reject it.

Second, we remember what we said earlier about inclusive representation. The role of parents and godparents at baptism is of this nature. It is interim in character and aims at transferring the confession taken on their behalf to the baptized themselves so that they may ratify or recall it in person.

b. Borderline Cases: Emergency Baptism and the Postponement of Baptism

(1) Emergency Baptism
Borderline cases take us to the heart of a matter, just as the instinct for what is to be anathematized as heresy usually awakens the decisive theological reflection that leads to the formulation of positive confessions. From this standpoint we shall take a brief look at the problem of emergency baptism.

In the tradition that espouses this, the starting point is that the dead who are not sacramentally released from original sin suffer damnation, although they may be freed from the positive penalties of hell and may enjoy a certain natural felicity if they do not commit serious personal sin. Later theology called the resting-place of those who are excluded from heaven in this way the *limbus puerorum* or *infantium*.[20] This is a place of lesser felicity where unbaptized infants reside.

I introduce these crass references deliberately in order to show what extravagant speculation lies behind the postulate of emergency baptism and also to draw attention to the related magically causative misunderstanding of baptism.[21] Although the idea of the *limbus* of infants softens the shocking idea of infant damnation, the church is clearly on a dangerous path in this regard.[22] More important

---

[20]Diekamp, *Katholische Dogmatik nach den Grundsätzen des heiligen Thomas,* III (1942), p. 445.
[21]K. Rahner in an interview clearly diverged from this view, so that it would not be right to call it *the* Roman Catholic position. If there is a heaven, he said, unbaptized infants will be there. He described the problem as more difficult than it seemed to be to Roman Catholic and Evangelical biblicists fifty years ago. He could not himself simply and non-dialectically consign an unbaptized infant to *limbus* rather than heaven as would have been done then.
[22]*Tübinger Taufgutachten,* pp. 268f.

than the eschatological apocalypse, however, is the implied understanding of baptism. Emergency baptism is given to infants when death is expected. It is not assumed, then, that infant baptism is acceptance into the covenant of grace and initiates a history which can ratify the covenant by the faith of the baptized. What we have called the point of infant baptism is missing. The Word that underlies baptism is never accepted. Baptism remains isolated from justification by faith alone, which is its point on the Reformation view. The quasi-magical concept of baptismal operation, its causative effect, is what is dubious here. We had better ignore the underlying concept of a God who will not let infants near him without ritual validation. That the Father of Jesus Christ accepts dying infants is surely beyond question in the light of Matthew 19:14 and par. Instead of emergency baptism they should be given the blessing of the congregation which commends them to this Father.

(2) Postponement of Baptism
The repeatedly discussed abuse of baptism usually raises the question whether it should not wait until people ask for it on the basis of their own decision of faith. We are not dealing here with the secular objection which would leave children exposed without protection to a pluralism of values in which they would have to find their own way without guidance. Often enough it is those who want to be serious Christians, and are aware of the relation between Word, baptism, and faith, that because of their *respect* for baptism are plagued by the idea of restoring validity to baptismal practice. The objection can be, then, to the thing signified by infant baptism, as in the arguments of Karl Barth.

We must begin with this objection and the church's reaction to it. We ourselves accept the validity of the traditional understanding of infant baptism and the relationship implied. We cannot regard the simultaneity of baptism and faith as necessary. Nevertheless it seems to us that we have here differences in theological interpretation rather than differences that divide the church. So long as variations in the understanding of baptism move within the essential article of justification by faith and the implied relation between the Word and Spirit, so long as they are advanced in the name of these things, the theological debate must continue, but it must undoubtedly do so within the church in the form of an inner conversation of the communion of saints. In a community in which infant baptism is the prevailing practice adult baptism is needed as an admonitory corrective.[23] On the basis of Mark 10:14 blessing infants suggests itself as an alternative at the beginning of life with baptism as a future goal. Blessing of this kind must be linked, of course, to Christian parentage and a commitment to Christian upbringing.

How to initiate and practice this alternative is a matter still to be considered. Whether parents should be given the alternative of baptism or blessing for a newly born child, as in the Reformed Church of Geneva (R. Leuenberger, *Taufe in der Krise,* p. 81), is debatable. In spite of intentions to the contrary, the free choice of baptism as one among other possibilities might lead psychologically to its disparagement. The perverse situation might also result that those who take baptism more seriously choose blessing while the indifferent choose the intrinsically more binding form of baptism (p. 84). Thus confusion threatens.

---

[23]*Ibid.,* p. 271.

A better solution in the author's eyes is that the church should propose baptism where this is the dominant practice. Since the relation of Word, baptism, and faith makes necessary an interview with the parents and sponsors (or at least the parents) and demands that reference be made to their responsibility, any doubts about infant baptism can be brought to light in the discussion. If the choice of baptism or blessing is proposed at this point, it is early enough.

c. Results

The many confusions and formalisms in baptismal practice, especially in popular usage in a secularized age, call out for reforms of different kinds if the event and proclamation of baptism are not to lose their credibility. We need not discuss here the desirable structuring of the act and its liturgical form.[24] Part of its signification is that it should take place within divine service in order to bear witness to incorporation into the body of Christ and to the responsibility of the congregation. Since we have seen that the aim of baptism is faith, and that the speaking of the Word and promise of the Spirit belong to its essential nature, we shall limit ourselves in these systematic deliberations to reforms that are calculated to emphasize this aspect.

The most necessary thing from this standpoint is the preparatory, accompanying, and succeeding proclamation of the Word. If baptism aims at faith it demands above all things an understanding of baptism itself on the part of those who accept responsibility for the child. As from the very first a catechumenate has been required for those awaiting baptism, so now in the framework of infant baptism there should be a catechumenate for young parents who are ready to engage in discussion. The initiative of setting up groups for this purpose must be taken. Concentration on this task is demanded.

Something of this kind was attempted in the *Information on the Faith Project* when we tried to give information about baptism in letters to young parents. These suggested the formation of groups and offered know-how on how to implement the suggestion. Among specific considerations underlying this action was especially the idea that the questions of upbringing that face young parents, precisely in the context of baptism, are definitely related to the view of man found in the gospel. We have not only to clothe and feed children and care for their physical well-being but above all to be concerned about the one necessary thing. Upbringing also raises questions of guilt and forgiveness, love and understanding, fellowship and temptation. To this extent the situation of young parents offers striking points of contact for orientation of the message. Hence a baptismal catechumenate need not be limited to dogmatic problems and information in the narrower sense but can embrace the broader field of the relation between the generations. Since young adults sometimes tend to be less strongly represented in the church, the formation of parent groups (or something like them) can also open up for the church an important sphere of work. Infant baptism can be a normal peg on which to hang this kind of catechumenate of parents. It can thus bring to light the relation of Word, baptism, and faith and help to establish a new credibility in opposition to abuses.

---

[24]For some useful suggestions cf. Leuenberger, pp. 87ff., 160ff. and bibliography.

XXII

On the Understanding of the Lord's Supper

Supplementary Bibliography: H. Grass, *Die Abendmahlslehre bei Luther und Calvin* (1954); J. Jeremias, *Die Abendmahlsworte Jesu,* 2nd ed. (1940); E.T. *The Eucharistic Words of Jesus* (Oxford, 1955); W. Joest, *Ontologie des Person bei Luther* (1967), esp. pp. 12, 395ff., 421ff.; E. Käsemann, "Anliegen und Eigenart der paulinischen Abendmahlslehre," *Exegetische Versuche und Besinnungen,* I, 3rd ed. (1964), p. 11; W. Kreck, "Die reformatorische Abendmahlslehre angesichts der heutigen exegetischen Situation," EvTh, V (1954), pp. 193ff.; W. von Loewenich, *Vom Abendmahl Christi* (1938); E. Lohmeyer, "Vom urchristlichen Abendmahl," ThR, N.F. 1937, Nos. 3–5; W. Niesel, *Calvins Lehre vom Abendmahl,* 2nd ed. (1936); A. Schweitzer, *Das Abendmahlsproblem auf Grund der wissenschaftlichen Forschung des 19. Jahrhunderts und der historischen Berichte,* 2nd ed. (1929); also *Geschichte der Leben-Jesu-Forschung,* 2nd ed. (1913); E.T. *Quest of the Historical Jesus* (1910); E. Schweizer, "Das johannische Zeugnis vom Herrenmahl," EvTh, XII (1952–53), p. 341; also with H. Grass, E. Sommerlath, G. Kretschmar, and W. Jannasch, art. "Abendmahl," RGG, I, p. 10; H. Thielicke, EG, II, pp. 399ff., 483ff.; EF, II, pp. 324ff., 393f.; G. Thomasius, *Christi Person und Werk,* II (1857), esp. pp. 209ff., 307ff.

1. THE IDENTITY OF BASIC OUTLINE. ORIGIN AND FORM OF REFLECTION

Many theological doctrines of the Lord's Supper have appeared over the last nineteen hundred years. Debates, divisions, and schisms have taken place over them. Nevertheless, according to the biblical material and beneath the level of reflective distinction the basic outlines are constant. We may thus begin by trying to sketch these outlines and fix on the agreed elements. We do not do this ironically but with the conviction that only against this background can we establish the material relation between the identical outline and the variations in reflection.[1]

---

[1]The relevant texts are Matthew 26:26–29; Mark 14:22–25; Luke 22:15–20; 1 Corinthians 11:23–26.

1. At the Supper the Kyrios gathers his people together for table fellowship and with bread and wine (his body and his blood) gives them a share in himself and unites them to himself.

2. The broken bread and shed blood are signs of his passion and especially of its fruit, the remission of sins. In the Fourth Gospel, in which there is no account of the institution, Christ is the bread of life: "He who eats this bread will live for ever" (John 6:48–58). Against the background of the forgiveness of sins life here means divine life as it has appeared in Christ and will be given to the disciples in fellowship with him (John 11:25; 14:6). In the Lord's Supper salvation comes through the presence and promise of the Savior.

3. Unlike baptism the Supper is a feast that is repeated (1 Corinthians 11:25b; cf. Acts 2:46; 20:7). Like the word of proclamation it must go forth afresh as address, claim, comfort, and promise.

As Luther says, the Lord's Supper is food for the soul which nourishes and strengthens the new man. Through baptism we are born again . . . but we still have the old skin in flesh and blood . . . and so we grow tired and faint and sometimes stumble. For this reason God has given us the Lord's Supper as daily food and nourishment, so that faith may be refreshed and fortified and may not fall back in the battle but become stronger and stronger (LC [LBK, p. 712, no. 23; Jacobs, p. 478, no. 23]). This argument for repetition falls within the sphere of common consent.

4. The Lord's Supper is a memorial feast pointing back to Christ's passion and death—which were still ahead at the time of institution—and also reminding us of his remoteness, of the end of earthly and visible fellowship with him. At the same time it is an eschatological feast which directs our attention to his coming again, for even though he will no longer drink the fruit of the vine with them, the day is coming when "I drink it new with you in my Father's kingdom" (Matthew 26:29 and par.). This reference to Easter includes the promise that the exalted Lord will be with us "always, to the close of the age" (Matthew 28:20) and that ongoing table fellowship is the pledge of this presence of his.

5. Table fellowship with Jesus, who with his closeness and communion mediates forgiveness, salvation, and new life, is not to be understood apart from his table fellowship with publicans and sinners which bound them to himself but caused such offense to the "righteous" (Luke 15:2; 5:30). Thus the sacrament does not depend on our worthiness.[2] It is for the sick and not the healthy (Luke 5:31). It is the feast of the forgiveness of sins.

To this extent it anticipates the joyous eschatological banquet of the nations when on Mt. Zion the veil will be removed which now conceals him from the Gentiles (Isaiah 25:6ff.). The parable of the great supper (Matthew 22:2ff.) points ahead to the eschatological fulfilment when table fellowship will be celebrated in God's kingdom. To this supper the poor and handicapped and lame and blind are invited (Luke 14:21). This is not a banquet for the elite, the "righteous," the core community. Those who will come are the lost whom the host seeks (Matthew 18:11).

6. Instead of our own worthiness there is required only the grateful acceptance

---

[2]LBK, p. 720, no. 61; Jacobs, p. 483, no. 61.

of an undeserved invitation and trust in the one who grants this fellowship with himself. Only believers, even though they be publicans and sinners, can be worthy to share this fellowship. But if faith is readiness to be accepted without merit, the question arises whether it can take the form of "belief," i.e., whether it is tied to the condition of certain forms of insight and knowledge, whether certain eucharistic doctrines must be held if we are to have access to the fellowship, whether the readiness of the heart is not enough.[3]

Naturally this basic fellowship with the Lord and with one another, which later came to be called a "sacrament," is subject to many different interpretations and reflections. These involve controversies and differences of opinion, so that what was meant to establish fellowship led to breach of fellowship. The result is the confusion that met us in our survey of the history of sacramental interpretation. But for all the statements and counterstatements, for all the theological divisions and ecclesiastical schisms—Luther, Zwingli, the Radicals, the Roman mass—it is still true that the administration itself came first, not merely the institution by Jesus, but also the primitive Christian practice of breaking of bread. Reflection follows practice. It is reflection which first raises the question of the "how" of the Lord's presence: his real presence in the event, the symbolical meaning of the rite, consubstantiation and transubstantiation, and the various christological theories.

Practice—the celebration of the Supper, the acceptance of forgiveness of sins as a result of the passion, hope of the eschatological banquet—cannot be dependent on theory. Nor can the church have its basis in theological theses. Its basis is the proclamation of the Word itself. Theological theory follows this.

This brings us back to the question raised above whether we can make the blessing of the celebration and the possibility of participation dependent on certain interpretations of the Supper instead of on faith alone (which will then call for understanding). We must be concerned at the very outset to get our emphases and priorities straight in understanding the Lord's Supper.

With regard to the Supper, too, we shall focus on the relation of Word (Spirit), sacrament, and faith which has been the basic systematic principle in all our deliberations. In the eucharist as in baptism the important thing is the primacy of the Word which sustains the action, embodies itself in it, and awakens faith through the Pneuma.

Luther expressly maintained this primacy, and in the light of it one might question the famous "is" which he asserted against Zwingli as a basis for Christ's real presence in the elements. For the Word that has the primacy is not the literal "is" but the efficacious Word, sustained by the Pneuma, in which the present Christ meets us, which declares the forgiveness of sins, and which gives us the promise of the coming feast in the kingdom of God. These words are for Luther much more important than the sacrament and more attention should be paid to them. To disparage them is to disparage the sacrament itself and to show that we do not understand it. It is a perversion to want the sacrament and not to want even more the sacramental words, especially in the heart (WA, 11, 432, 25). What is meant here is the efficacious Word, as is made plain a few lines lower down where Luther says that claiming Christ's body and blood apart from the Word is work-

---

[3]LBK, p. 715, nos. 36–38; Jacobs, p. 480, nos. 36–38.

righteousness that directs attention away from the faith that receives. The Word is first, then bread and wine. The words teach us why Christ is present and cause us to forget our own works and wait only upon his. The sacrament is a matter of faith, for God's work should be within us and should be done through his Word (WA, 11, 488, 26).

The dominance of the relation between the Word and faith offers us some criteria by which to assess the inner Protestant divisions and splits over sacramental teaching between Luther, Carlstadt, Zwingli, and Calvin. Since Luther was at the heart of the controversies we do best not to begin, as many do, with his polemical works, and thus become entangled (at least in part) in his anachronistic metaphysics. Instead we shall turn first to the soteriologically accented outline of his eucharistic doctrine in the catechisms.[4] Here his initial intention is less obscured than in controversial writings in which the decisive point, the presence of the Lord in Word and sacrament, is engulfed by reflections on the mode of the presence.

There is a similar return to the real eucharistic issues in modern Roman Catholic theology, especially in its handling of transubstantiation (cf. Hampe, I, pp. 598f.). A pastoral letter from the Netherlands (1965) is a good example. This distinguishes implicitly but clearly between the present Christ whom we meet in celebrating the eucharist and theological discussions of the mode of this presence. It is expressly stated that understanding of the modality is theologically controversial and there can be debate about it without in any way challenging faith in the present Christ. Discussion of that kind "has nothing whatever to do with the question whether the Lord is really present." It relates only to understanding and describing this mystery of faith. "We are of the opinion that this question of the mode of the presence of Christ may be left to theologians for free discussion" (*ibid.*, pp. 599f.).

The discussion is not *so* free, of course, that one may think of Christ's presence in any other way than as the change of the elements of bread and wine into the Lord's body and blood. But transubstantiation is not blindly accepted nor made an object of faith synonymously with Christ's presence. As in E. Schillebeeckx, it is historically relativized. On the level of natural philosophy Christ's real presence can be *expressed* in terms of the historically conditioned Aristotelian concept of transubstantiation (*ibid.*, p. 600; cf. E. Schillebeeckx, *Die eucharistische Gegenwart*, 2nd ed. [1968]; E.T. *The Eucharist* [New York, 1968]; also *Jesus*, 3rd ed. [1976], pp. 494ff.; E.T. *Jesus* [New York, 1979], pp. 559ff.).

The Dutch theologian L. Smits goes even further when he says that the original content of the term transubstantiation is shattered when it has to express Christ's presence, which cannot be expressed in Aristotelian ontology, for while the substances of the body and blood remain and only the accidents change, the accidents of the elements are left without a substance. Smit himself thinks it would be better to use the concept of "person" which derives from existentialist phenomenology. He makes it clear, however, that we should not fix Christ's eucharistic presence conceptually so that the concept, too, becomes an object of faith, but that faith can and should use elastic and variable concepts (*Vragen rondom de eucharistie*

---

[4]In this regard we have the support of W. von Loewenich, *Vom Abendmahl Christi*, p. 105.

[1965], pp. 21ff.; Hampe, I, p. 602). A reality of faith which cannot be permanently grasped in reflection will constantly take new conceptual lines, so that the conceptual instruments must be strictly differentiated from what they are designed to express and must be kept subject to the question of priority as demanded (cf. on this whole matter L. van Hout, *Fragen zur Eucharistielehre;* Hampe, I, pp. 598–607).

This distinction between concerns of faith and forms of reflection is often a dubious one, but because theological concepts are relative, inadequate, and time-conditioned it is unavoidable in relation to the historical eucharistic controversies. The Reformation distinctions—whether we be dealing with Luther's defiant ''is'' at Marburg or the various modes of the real presence or the humanist irony of Zwingli—may often seem to be hair-splitting to us today but they are exciting and significant the moment we see in them the fundamental and insoluble conflict between the ineffability of a mystery of faith and its necessary reflective and verbal description, the antagonism between concern and explanation of the concern. In this respect eucharistic debate is a model that shows us both the possibility and the limits of theological statement. We can see this properly only when we accept the priority of the revelation of the Word over its theological presentation and the priority of table fellowship with the Lord over this or that understanding of the mode of the presence.

2. THE QUESTION OF THE BIBLICAL BASIS

In our preliminary methodological discussions we have already taken up a position regarding the essence of the Supper, especially in our attempt to set forth the identity of the celebration and its purpose behind all the differences in understanding. We have linked the message of the Supper—present fellowship with Christ and the promise of future fellowship—with the insights that we gained in discussing the understanding of the sacraments and the question of baptism. In what follows, then, we can restrict ourselves to the main points and work with almost thetic brevity.

With a view to the later debates we must first look at the biblical texts. Since our main interest is the systematic one of purpose we may leave to exegetical research such detailed historical questions as the relation of the Supper to the Passover or the influence of hellenistic mysteries.[5]

The first question to concern us is that of the meaning of the giving of bread and wine at the first Supper. It can be understood only in relation to a double future: the approaching death of Jesus and the eschatological feast in God's kingdom. In terms of the former it is a parting meal, of the latter a meal of promise and hope.

If we think first of the departure of Jesus, the use of bread and wine has the simple and obvious sense that what is on the table, and is usual on such occasions, is consumed.[6] It is true that bread and wine also have a symbolical sense and kindle (as they should) associations with biblical analogies, but this has often led

---

[5]On the latter question cf. W. Heitmüller but also A. Schlatter and J. Jeremias, who relate the Supper to Jewish traditions.

[6]von Loewenich, *Vom Abendmahl Christi*, p. 26.

to overmuch symbolical mystification. The bread in particular has given rise to speculations of this type because it is so readily symbolized. The cup which is open at the top and which is to be received can have similar associations. But symbolical considerations of this nature become misleading the moment the meaning of the Supper is derived from this type of philosophy of the elements. Instead of an analogy of being which construes salvation in terms of created elements we need here an analogy of faith in which the choice and meaning of the elements is determined by the *telos* of the celebration of the Supper, not vice versa. This principle will be important when we come to the Lutheran-Reformed debate about the significance of the elements, and especially to Luther's famous "is."

This relativizing of the elements in the name of the meaning of the Supper is important in another respect too. Bread and wine have their own biblically attested aptitude as symbols. But the similitude must always yield to the original. Hence the use of wine is not absolutely necessary, e.g., in the case of alcoholics. Because of the symbolism we will use only similar drinks, e.g., grape juice, and rightly refrain from using artificial or synthetic products. No one would suggest Coca Cola. But the servant-role of the elements, and therefore their relativity, permits us to use almost anything in emergency situations such as imprisonment.

We come up against this question of relativity on the mission fields. Thus bread and wine are foreign to the Japanese. In the interests of freeing Christianity from the charge of being a foreign import, should we not leave the choice of elements open in such cases, just as in church music we must leave room for other melodies and rhythms and instruments in place of translated chorales and the related organ music?

In fact bread and wine are not intrinsically symbolical. They become so by being set in the service of the message. They owe their symbolism to this relation. Thus the Johannine Christ calls himself the bread of life (John 6:35, 41, 50) and after the miracle of feeding the multitude blames those who do not see behind the physical provision a symbolical reference to himself (6:26). Bread has a similar symbolical reference in the Passover. Its unleavened form recalls the haste of the exodus. Similarly the wine has an affinity to christological statements. Christ calls himself the vine and his disciples the branches (John 15:1ff.). The sight of vines might have suggested the comparison, as the wine on the table did at the Last Supper. The path to Gethsemane leads past vines. For geographical reasons the vineyard often supplies symbolical material. God is commonly the owner of a vineyard (cf. Psalm 80:8ff.; Isaiah 5:1ff.; Matthew 21:33).

As in the parallelism of Hebrew poetry, bread and wine both represent the same thing, i.e., table fellowship with the dying and returning Lord. That the same thing is expressed in two ways without its identity being affected may be the reason why only bread was used in the primitive community (Acts 2:42, 46; 20:7). Either symbol may be used in view of the unchangeability of what is symbolized.

Bread and wine signify the broken body and shed blood. In view of the link between the first Supper and the Passover it is natural to see an allusion to the sacrifice of the "Lamb of God."

With the reference to his death Jesus also celebrates the Supper as an advance presentation (*prolepsis*) of the coming banquet with his people at the end of the times. He refers to the fulfilment of the new covenant (Matthew 26:28; cf. Jeremiah 31:31) which embraces "many" among the nations of the world, as the parable of the great supper also suggests (Matthew 22:2ff.; 8:11f.; Luke 14:15ff.; cf. Isaiah 52 and 53). The new covenant is no longer restricted to Israel. The new people of God is recruited from the ends of the earth. The death of Jesus is a vicarious atonement which results in his eschatological community assembled from all peoples. As the meal of hope which looks beyond the parting it is celebrated by the primitive community with jubilation (Acts 2:46f.).[7]

As a meal of parting and expectation the Supper has an interim character corresponding to the imminent but not yet consummated kingdom of God. The old aeon is "no more" but the new is "not yet" present in fulness. Everything that takes place in the community of Jesus is determined by this "no more" and "not yet." Christ's miracles are signs of the lordship of God which has still to come but which has come already in him who brings about the change of aeons (Matthew 12:28; Luke 17:21). The ministry of the Holy Spirit suggests this interim, for, as we have seen, he is the deposit or first instalment of what is to come. The Sermon on the Mount especially shows the present hour to be an interim period. It commands us as though we were *still* living in the primal state and also as though God's kingdom were *already* present (cf. Matthew 19:8). This makes it plain to those to whom it addresses its radical demands that their Now is a time of transition.

Thus the Lord's Supper is inconceivable without the expectant prayer: "Amen. Come, Lord Jesus" (Revelation 22:20). This celebration, too, is simply a pledge, anticipation, and sign of what is still to come.[8]

The symbolical character of the Last Supper led Luther in the Reformation debates to make a sharp distinction between being and meaning. His anti-Zwinglian stress on the "is" at Marburg was meant to express the fact that the sayings of Jesus: "This is my body—this is my blood," not merely contained a symbolical reference in the sense of meaning but expressed his ontic or real presence in the elements. But the controversy between Luther's "is" and Zwingli's "signifies" finds no place in the texts. It is just as time-bound in the one-sided symbolism of Zwingli as it is in the sacramental realism of Luther, who detected an alien spirit in Zwingli but who tried to meet him with a traditional ontologism that contrapuntally tied him, too, to his own age.

The incarnation of the Word in Christ forces us to take seriously the concrete and very human circumstances under which the first Lord's Supper took place. Just before his death Jesus gathered with his disciples around a table on which were set bread and wine. To suppose that prior to his departure he handed them his own flesh and blood to eat in an ontic sense would be ridiculous. We do not say this on rationalistic grounds but because it takes the situation seriously. When this

---

[7]The author has often experienced the joy of festal celebration in the United States (and not just in black churches) in contrast to the liturgical solemnity and joyless seriousness of many European celebrations.

[8]In evangelical hymns we find only traces of this eschatological background of the eucharist, as when Philipp Nicolai speaks of going into the banqueting hall.

is not done the incarnation itself is not serious. This threat always arises when later doctrines and dogmas of all kinds project themselves back into the original narratives in order that a biblical foundation might be gained. The ontic view does precisely this. A real meal, a very human event in the life of Jesus, is docetically evaporated and rendered inconceivable. Events have to remain close to the ground if they are to be taken seriously. And when they become parables, as here, the ground has to be recognizable, just as the parables of Jesus bear witness to the circumstances that gave rise to the stories in his travels and encounters.

Only on this presupposition can one say that the symbolism of the bread and wine mediates a reality, the presence of the Lord. "Signifies" and "is" are not alternatives as Luther and Zwingli thought. In contrast to modern usage biblical thought does not distinguish between thing and sign, between the ontic and the noetic, between signifying and effecting. The thing signified is present in the sign.

Thus the parabolic action in which Christ hands his disciples bread and wine means that he is not just setting up a memorial sign (in the sense of "signifies") but that he is also giving them a share in his sacrifice and placing them in the new covenant. The signifying Word is an efficacious Word. For this reason Luther is closer to the meaning of the saying than Zwingli in spite of his fixation on the elements. Zwingli misses the efficacious character of the Word. What Luther wants to confess with his impossible "is" is the real presence of Christ among those who in his name gather around his table and his Word. He was not content with a mere remembrance of the past life and death of Christ (Matthew 18:20).

Luther put this badly because he regarded a merely modified theory of transubstantiation as a suitable ontological way of giving force to the real content of the "is." This forced him to relate the real presence of Christ to his flesh and blood as they are given in the eucharistic elements.

One might say that Zwingli perceived the symbolical nature of the Supper but did not do justice to the thing signified—real participation in the sacrifice of Christ. On the other hand Luther grasped the thing signified but with his ontological concentration on the elements destroyed the symbolical nature of the first Supper, where Christ was the living host and certainly could not have given the disciples his own flesh and blood. "This is my body" and "this is my blood" simply mean: "This am I," or, more precisely: "With this food and drink I give you a share in the new covenant which will come into being in me and by my death, for my death is for you and for many"; or: "As I here give you bread and wine, so I give myself for you."

Even in his ontological distortion of these words of institution Luther seems to be closer to their saving promise than Zwingli was, for in intention he had in view real acceptance into the new covenant and the real presence of the Lord. Nevertheless the ontological distortion leaves the impression that Christ gives a special sacramental gift apart from his own person. This distinction between person and gift is alien to the text. It disturbs the primacy of the Word over the sacrament, for to the advantage of the sacramental gift it takes from the Word its efficacy and the spiritual presentation of the Lord.

Might it not be, however, that Paul goes beyond the synoptic words of institution and offers the basis for an appeal to the real presence of Christ in the eucharistic elements?[9]

There are four arguments against this.

1. The controlling factor in the Pauline variant is the qualitative difference in time between the synoptic situation and that of the primitive community. Between the two stand Easter and Pentecost. The Bible does not give us abstract and timelessly valid teachings. It bears witness to the process of a salvation event. It thus offers us narratives instead of inculcating ideas. For this reason the historical location of a saying is of basic importance. The break of Easter and Pentecost between the sayings is vital. The same thing has to be said differently on the one side of the break than on the other.

At the first Supper the body of Jesus has not yet been given nor his blood shed. He is still present in the body with his disciples. (As we have seen, this prevents an ontic equation of the bread and wine with his body and blood.) The first Supper has something in view that must still come, something that is directly and eschatologically future. Jesus has not yet been offered up or exalted. After the resurrection, however, the situation is fundamentally different. For Paul the Kyrios is no longer present with his people "according to the flesh" (2 Corinthians 5:16). The exalted Lord is present as the Spirit and works in this way among them (Acts 2:1ff.; 2 Corinthians 3:17). The Spirit moves where he wills (John 3:8) and is above space and time. Thus the celebration of the Lord's Supper is detached from the parting hour of the first celebration. It can be repeated at any time. When bread and wine are distributed in the celebration, the exalted Lord is present as the Spirit. The issue is not the ontic quality of the elements but the presence of the person of the Kyrios.

2. That it is a matter of fellowship with his person may be seen especially in references to the exclusiveness of this fellowship. Fellowship at the table of demons, i.e., eating idol meats (1 Corinthians 10:20ff.), is ruled out. The basis of this exclusiveness is not the magic of hellenistic mysteries[10] but the idea that the (old *and* new) covenant releases us from all ungodly obligations and commits us to the Lord. There can be no unequal yoke with unbelievers, for how can Christ agree with Belial and what is there in common between the temple of God and idols (2 Corinthians 6:15f.)? The exclusiveness of the covenant does not point to some special quality in the elements but to an exclusive commitment to the Lord who is present at the celebration and who in giving himself wholly to us claims us wholly and undividedly for himself.

3. A supposed argument for the real presence of Christ in the elements has been constantly found since Luther's day in the warning of Paul against eating this bread and drinking this cup of the Lord unworthily (*anaxios*), because to do this is to incur guilt in relation to the Lord's body and blood (1 Corinthians 11:27–29). Luther's doctrine of the eating of the wicked, which is based on this, finds a reference here to an ontic presence in the elements, for only on this view, he

---

[9]Some Gnesiolutheran groups have taken this view, appealing to Luther's work *Against the Heavenly Prophets* (WA, 18, 159ff.; LW, 40, 169ff.) and in opposition to the Arnoldshain Theses (LR, IV [1958], p. 133).

[10]Heitmüller thinks this had some impact (RGG, I, art. "Abendmahl").

thinks, does it make sense that what takes place in unworthy eating and drinking is not nothing but an offense against the Lord's presence in the misused elements. In fact, however, there is no indication whatever that the presence of Christ at the Supper as Paul accepted and proclaimed it was in any way related to the elements. It is rather his being made present by the Word and Spirit among those who gather in his name. The possibility of unworthy and therefore guilty eating and drinking presupposes that it is not just our faith that makes Christ present, which would mean that his presence is not real but is simply a presence in our consciousness (in remembrance or trust), as Zwingli thought. No, Christ makes himself present in his community. He does this by the Word and Spirit and at the celebration of his meal.

This is why there is the possibility of unworthy reception and misuse of the presence by the "halfheartedness" that is partly committed at the same time to false gods and ideological claims. If judgment comes on the unworthy, it is not because some supposedly celestial matter becomes poisonously diabolical but because the unworthy despise the person and saving offer of the Lord and therefore his presence too.

If the accusation is made that the unworthy eater does not discern (*diakrinōn,* 11:29) the Lord's body, this does not refer to his material presence. What Paul has in mind is rather that anyone should treat the Lord's Supper as a normal meal which is simply meant to satisfy him, so that he has no concern for others but only lovelessly and selfishly for himself (11:33f.). In doing this he profanes the presence of the Lord who calls us together in loving fellowship. The charge against him is that of the Johannine Christ after the feeding of the five thousand, namely, that the people do not seek him because they have been given a sign but because they have been fed. They accepted the meal but did not discern the one who in it made himself known as the "bread of life" (John 6:26). Instead of giving God all the glory they thought only of the physical side and said: "A meal." They failed to distinguish between the physical side of eating and its symbolism. The presence of him who placed himself at their disposal as the bread of life passed unnoticed.

In this light the eating of the wicked loses its magical-sacramental sense. We have already pointed out that even in Luther this real presence of Christ is seen in his Word. This Word that is made present by the testimony of the Spirit carries the reality of salvation and effects the real presence of the Lord. It is not just a sound (an acoustic means of communication), just as the Holy Spirit is not just a motion in creatures[11] and the Lord's Supper is not just an ordinary meal. This "filled" Word is not for Luther a Word that simply rings out into the void and returns empty where it is rejected and not understood. It is always an efficacious Word, whether in grace or judgment. The mouth of the unworthy can eat judgment and the ear of the unworthy can hear it. In both cases the Lord is present to judge as well as bless.

4. An analysis of what Paul means by the "body" of Christ in his eucharistic statements also makes it clear that he is not thinking of an identification with the elements. The word *sōma* has for him two related dimensions of meaning. Following the symbolism of the synoptic accounts he finds in the bread a symbol of Christ's

---

[11]A misunderstanding avoided in CA, I, No. 6.

body. But for him the body is predominantly the community (Romans 12:4f.; cf. Ephesians 1:23; 4:12; 5:30). Both meanings are typically united in 1 Corinthians 10:16f.

On the one hand the consecrated cup and bread bring us into fellowship with the blood and body of Christ. Like baptism (Romans 6:3; Galatians 3:27), these give us a share in his death and its fruit. But there also takes place a kind of transfiguration. The one bread eaten in common makes the many one body, the body of the community whose head is Christ (10:17). This change in meaning is not a change into another genus. The two senses complement one another.

The communion of saints as Christ's body is grounded in communion with Christ. At the same time it is only this body of Christ that grants communion with the head. Here the covenant promise is again actualized. Communion with the body and blood of Christ means being taken up into the new covenant sealed by Christ's death and becoming a member of his body. This has nothing whatever to do with any celestial matter or any special quality in the elements. Ideas of this kind rest on the ontologizing and metaphysicizing of a simple theological fact and are the product of projection back into the biblical text. On the other hand, along the lines of Luther's theology of the Word and thinking in terms of benefits, the eucharistic elements should be given the same rank as the water of baptism. The efficacious Word which establishes the covenant makes both the baptismal and the eucharistic elements signs that denote the presence, the real presence, of the Lord.[12]

3. INNER PROTESTANT CONTROVERSIES

Our inquiry into the biblical basis of the Lord's Supper was guided by insights which were the subject of controversy during the Reformation. In the light of the NT texts we had thus to take up positions on the main items of debate. Behind a textually unsupported attachment to Christ's real presence in the elements we found at work in Luther the decisive thought that in Word and sacrament, made present by the Spirit, there is a presence of Christ, that salvation is declared for us, and that we are assured of reception into the new covenant.

In contrast we have noted that Zwingli, under cover of a contextual interpretation of the first Supper as a symbolic action, makes a nontextual distinction being "being" and "signifying" and chooses the latter. In this way the presence of Christ is robbed of its ontic character. Christ is not essentially present but present only in the consciousness, in the mind, in remembrance. Whereas in Luther certain ontologisms of the sacramental tradition predominate, Zwingli is influenced by newer humanist forms of thought which bring in the unbiblical differentiation between a symbolic and a real act.

In what follows we can give only a rough outline of the main points at issue. The debate cannot be understood apart from the different underlying christologies. These have been dealt with explicitly in the christological chapters (EG, II, pp. 399ff.; EF, II, pp. 324ff.) and need only be referred to here.

---

[12]For the relation between the Lord's Supper and the Passover cf. EG, II, pp. 483ff.; EF, II, pp. 383f.

Luther's view of the Lord's Supper develops in two clearly differentiated phases. The first is shaped by his debate on the Roman mass, the second by his debate with the radicals, especially Carlstadt. His statements are thus made in answer to challenges and take a polemical form. This is not the least important reason why his time-bound thought-forms can sometimes obscure his real intention and force us to distinguish between his concern and its conceptual explanation. We arrive at what is Lutheran not just by quoting Luther but by an interpretation which sets his polemical statements in the light of the core of his thought.

a. The Battle against the Mass

In the early writings of 1518 (WA, 1, 329) and 1519 (WA, 2, 742; LW, 35, 49) Luther was not specifically opposing the doctrine of transubstantiation, although in the *Babylonian Captivity* he would have liked to have seen it replaced by con-substantiation: As in heated iron both iron and fire are present, so bread and wine *and also* Christ's body and blood are present in the eucharistic elements (WA, 6, 508-10). The starting point of his criticism is thinking in terms of blessings. This means that in all cases—in his theology of Word and sacrament as well as his Christology—Luther starts, not with the saving event as such, but with the gift mediated by it, with its effect, its benefits. Early pre-polemical works (and the catechisms) make this plain.

From this standpoint Word and sacrament are closely related. The Word in which the benefits are expressly allotted to us takes the lead. In the *Sermon on the NT* this applies to the words of institution which with the forgiveness of sins impart to us "so great and eternal and indescribable a treasure" (WA, 6, 358; 18, 204, 5ff.; LW, 36, 28-33; 40, 214). We receive precisely what the Word says, no more. Much more depends on the words than the signs (WA, 6, 363, 7; LW, 36, 91). "I could do without the signs," Luther says, "if only I have the words and feed and strengthen my soul on them" (WA, 6, 358, 11; LW, 36, 85). The sign is a seal and legal mark even though in it we have Christ's real body and blood under the bread and wine (WA, 6, 359; LW, 35, 86). The text that is sealed is valid without the seal but it cannot be appropriated without faith (WA, 6, 518, 16; 18, 294, 15ff.; LW, 36, 44; 40, 214).

This acceptance of Augustine's "believe and thou hast eaten" rules out an *opus operatum* which eliminates the relation between Word and faith (WA, 2, 751, 4; LW, 35, 62). Luther unthinkingly takes over from the tradition the idea of Christ's real presence in the elements, but this idea is not emphasized and it stands in the shadow of the promise and benefit of the sacrament, of the Word. In the name of the Christ who is present in the Word and Spirit sins are forgiven and unity of heart and membership in Christ's body are declared (WA, 1, 329, 11).

Luther's main emphasis in his criticisms of the mass is based on these benefits. We may ignore at this point our earlier questions whether Luther really understood the Thomistic (and modern) interpretation of the mass. Our only concern is how far his own view is articulated in his polemical statements. His criticism of the mass, or at least of its practice, is that in it the benefits of forgiveness and justification by faith alone are denied, for it (supposedly) carries with it an idea of sacrifice which crowds out Christ's self-sacrifice (WA, 6, 355ff.; LW, 35, 80ff.), makes the priest a mediator (WA, 6, 370; LW, 35, 100f.), and thus makes the offering made in it a "good work" (WA, 6, 512; LW, 36, 35). The heart of his criticism does not lie in the field of a doctrine of the elements or the theory of transubstantiation or consubstantiation, but in the field of the doctrine of justification and the "grace alone" of the declaration of the Word.

b. The Debate with the Radicals and Zwingli

Radical Christianity of the Spirit is marked by the spiritual autarchy of the Christian through the impartation of the Spirit. The Christian does not need any additional external authorities, not even Holy Scripture. Filled with the Spirit, he can produce this himself, as Schleiermacher would later say in his *Speeches*.

Luther could not recognize this claim of the radicals to be bearers of the Spirit because it offered no criterion by which to distinguish between the human spirit and God's Spirit. Such a criterion can be found only in something "outside" that comes from God and meets us in the form of Word and sacrament. For Luther the Spirit is constitutively bound to the Word. As he says in *Against the Heavenly Prophets* (1525), God will give no one the Spirit or faith apart from the external Word and sign appointed for the purpose (WA, 18, 136; LW, 40, 146). The inner parts (reception of the Spirit, remission of sins, etc.) *follow* the external.

Here again we can see Luther's thinking in terms of benefits. He emphasizes the justifying grace that comes from outside. To look within is to obscure pure reception and to define man in terms of works.

In fact Carlstadt, as Luther says, knows Christ only as an example or an embodied law and not as a gift of grace, so that he relapses from faith to works (WA, 18, 197; LW, 40, 207). Certainly Christ is an example, but this is his least important feature, in which he is like other saints (*Letter to Strassburg* [1524] [WA, 15, 396, 18; LW, 40, 70]). As an example he cannot help us any more than other saints. He can only produce dissemblers and not Christians, just as doing the works of the law produces hypocrisy (*Christmas Postil* [1522] [WA, 10/I, 1, 33, 8]).

Over against Carlstadt's idea of an example Luther sets that of an exemplar. Christ is the exemplar and epitome of all the works of God in which he turns to us in grace (Romans).

There are thus two radically different ways of imitating Christ. To imitate him as an example of the moral law is to fall into work-righteousness and the opposite of justification by grace alone. Legitimate imitation begins by accepting Christ's exemplary work of salvation (calling to divine sonship) and derives its impulse from this, so that the imperative (what should be done) arises out of the indicative (what has been done) (cf. ThE, I, pp. 87ff.; E.T. I, pp. 51ff.). Hence Luther can say epigrammatically in his *Galatians:* "Imitation does not make sons but sonship makes imitators" (WA, 2, 518, 16; LW, 27, 263).

Here as elsewhere the point is that God's work from outside is the precondition of being a Christian. Although this is adequately covered by the "outside" Word and the Spirit (as person), Luther seems to find an additional safeguard for it in Christ's real presence in the elements, especially as he thinks he can play off obedience to the Word (of institution) against Carlstadt's theology of the Spirit apart from the Word (WA, 18, 161, 3ff.; 166, 7ff.; LW, 40, 171 and 176).

In opposition to Zwingli, whose eucharistic teaching went through different stages but had one fixed point, Luther's concern was to avoid a spiritualizing attenuation of Christ's presence. This takes place when Christ is present only in the consciousness and the Supper is only a memorial meal. Luther also argues against Zwingli that there corresponds to this spiritualizing a Christology which divides the unity of Christ's person and connects his presence only to the divine nature. He himself in his *Confession of the Lord's Supper* (1528) makes the famous statement that God and the humanity cannot be divided, for Christ became one person and he does not take off his humanity as Hans takes off and lays aside his coat when he goes to sleep (WA, 26, 333, 6; LW, 37, 219). This leads Luther to his thesis that Christ is bodily present in the elements. It also leads him to speculations on the ubiquity of this body and to the corresponding theories of space (WA, 26, 327-36; LW, 37, 205-23). An ontological schema of thought is taken for granted here and it results in excesses which weaken Luther's initial concern for Christ's saving presence.

When Zwingli replies with his concept of *alloiosis* and pours scorn on the absurdity of an omnipresent body (cf. EG, II, pp. 399ff.; EF, II, pp. 324ff.), it would be unfair to see here only rationalistic objections. These may play a part, but Zwingli has a theological basis for his resistance to Luther's doctrine of ubiquity. He finds in it a docetic volatization. A body that is not limited in time and space loses its quality as a body. The incarnation is no longer taken seriously.

In sum one might say that the debate between Luther and Zwingli is predominantly, although not exclusively, a battle of thought schemas which cannot adequately express the mystery of the real presence and which in their autonomous development lead us to the very edge of absurdity. The only enduring antithesis is that of the basic positions: the real presence of Christ in person (which Luther dubiously ties to the elements), and the presence of Christ in mental recollection (CR, V, p. 587). In discussing the biblical basis we believe that we found support for Luther's basic teaching.

c. Calvin's Doctrine of the Lord's Supper

As a biblical exegete Calvin is the Reformer who is least subject to the metaphysical and ontological thought-forms of his day. He thus avoids both Zwingli's symbolism and Luther's sacramental realism, having noted and rejected the humanistic and scholastic schemata that influence and distort them. There is an unmistakable affinity to Luther's real presence, as Luther himself saw (cf. von Loewenich, p. 89; J. Köstlin/G. Kawerau, *M. Luther,* II [1903], pp. 577, 603f.). On the surface there are differences only in respect of the mode of the presence. Calvin's discussions lead into theological depths of Christology and pneumatology that make it understandable that his eucharistic teaching could not be just a synthesis of Luther and Zwingli but would lead to later Lutheran/Reformed controversies about these underlying themes. (One may ask again, however, whether these differences were not due in part to the inadequacy of the thought-forms used; cf. EG, II, p. 402; EF, II, p. 327.)

It can be said at once, however, that Luther's intentions, as we see them in his earlier works, were adopted and developed in purified form in Calvin's teaching. To this extent Calvin, unlike Zwingli, poses a permanent and productive question to Lutheranism. He can force it into purifying self-criticism which will take as its criterion its own principle of thinking in terms of benefits.

In his chapter on the Lord's Supper in the *Institutes* (IV, 17) Calvin takes issue with Zwingli when he expressly rejects the thesis that participation in Christ by eating his body and drinking his blood is nothing more than believing in Christ (17, 5). He plainly fears here a shifting of the salvation event to the subject of faith. One of the two mistakes one might make is that of showing ''too little regard'' for the signs and ''divorcing them from the mysteries to which they are attached.'' The mystery of the eucharistic gift along with the sign is the transsubjective factor—Luther's ''outside us''—which faith must *follow*. ''This mystery of Christ's secret union . . . is by nature incomprehensible'' (17, 1). Thus guarantees and tokens which can ''penetrate even the dullest minds'' are necessary, for they assure us that ''just as bread and wine sustain physical life, so are souls fed by Christ'' (*loc. cit.*).

In the Lord's Supper, then, there is not just remembrance of a past event which is simply made present in the mind (Zwingli). There is real union with Christ and to that extent the real presence of Christ is proffered to faith and awakens it. This real presence embraces both the past event of Christ's one act of redemption on the cross and ever new union with him when we let the promise of the gospel be sealed by table fellowship with the exalted Lord. He gave his body once so that it might be bread. He gave it for the redemption of the world in the death of the cross. As this crucified body he also offers it to us daily in the Word of the gospel so that we might partake of it. He gives it to us where he seals this self-presentation by the sacrament (mystery) of the Supper. He also gives it when he fulfils inwardly what he thus designates outwardly in the sign (17, 5). In the efficacious Word that is sealed by the sign Calvin thus sees the real presence which by presenting Christ's saving work and making it effective establishes union with him here and now. This is a plain renunciation of the symbolism of Zwingli.

Yet Calvin opposes no less forcefully the way in which Luther ties Christ's presence to the elements. He here advances pneumatological and christological arguments which are often aimed at Lutherans too (17, 7), even though they are brought against others, especially papists, e.g., Nicholas II (17, 12).

The pneumatological argument is as follows. It is a perverse error to tie Christ's body to the elements (17, 12). To overestimate the elements and their significance is to obscure the mysteries themselves (17, 5), especially the mystery that the Spirit and not the elements confers the blessing on us, making us one with Christ in body, soul, and spirit. He, the Spirit of Christ, is the bond (*vinculum*) by which we are united with him, the channel by which all that Christ is and has is conducted to us (17, 12). This Spirit works like the sun which engenders and nourishes and gives life to new buds. Is not the Spirit of Christ fully able to grant us fellowship with him (17, 12)? Paul says that it is through his Spirit that Christ dwells in us (Romans 8:9) (17, 12). We thus despise this bond when we consign Christ's body to the elements and when Nicholas II forced a man like Berengar of Tours to confess that the spatial presence of Christ in the eucharist is such that we touch him with our hands, chew him with our teeth, and swallow him with our mouths (17, 12).

This doctrine of a physical presence (17, 13) and a crass ''enclosing'' of Christ in the elements (17, 16), which sins against the Holy Spirit, applies only in part to Luther, for the concept of consubstantiation undoubtedly softens the enclosing, to which supreme testimony is given in the elevation of the host. Nevertheless Calvin is warning us here against a path which Lutherans are suspiciously close to taking.

The christological argument relates especially to Luther's doctrine of ubiquity. Calvin calls this "monstrous" (17, 30). An omnipresent body is simply a phantasm (17, 17). Luther's famous "is" on which it rests is exegetically in error (17, 20, 22). A body of this kind denies the ascension, overthrows real corporeality and with it the incarnation, and thus opens the door to Docetism (17, 17). What only the Spirit can do as the bond between Christ and us is here ascribed to the body. Hence the body has to take over a function which is beyond its competence and contradicts its nature. In so doing it becomes a docetic phantasm.

A vital point in all this is that Calvin is not moved by rationalistic considerations when he resists the absurdity of Luther's ubiquitarianism. This is what distinguishes him from Zwingli. For Zwingli the rationalistic background is determinative. Reason can more easily grasp a being of Christ in the consciousness, a mental presence in recollection, than the miracle or mystery of his real presence. We can see that Calvin's criticism is definitely theological, not rationalistic, when he teaches the miracle of presentation. Christ comes down to us in his Spirit as well as in the outward symbol truly to give life to our souls with the substance of his flesh and blood (17, 24). Calvin adopts (instead of attacking) Luther's point that there is real union with the Lord who is really present in the Supper. Here if anywhere it is plain that Calvin's quarrel is with the rampant ontological schema of thought in Luther, not with the intention behind his eucharistic teaching.

If Calvin rejects the real presence of Christ in the elements (ubiquitarianism), but accepts the blessing of his presence (vivification and union [17, 24]), what alternative does he offer to the real presence in the elements? His alternative is the spiritual presence of Christ and the spiritual fruit of his eucharistic gifts.

We must not take the word "spiritual" to have the intellectual sense of a presence only in the mind (Zwingli). The spiritual has nothing whatever to do with the mental products of our consciousness. It refers to God's real acts toward us, the mystery of something that happens. Having set aside some "absurdities" in the Lutheran doctrine (17, 19), Calvin protects himself against a misunderstanding of his attack. In opposing the Lutheran "is" he does not mean to say that believers grasp Christ's body and blood merely with the imagination or the understanding. Far from supporting the Zwinglian error he is teaching that believers do in fact partake of Christ's body and blood as the food of everlasting life (17, 19).

To the spiritual event of the Supper there thus corresponds on man's side, not the mental act of insight and recollection, but the spiritual act of faith. Appealing to Augustine, Calvin argues that man does not receive more from the sacrament than from the vessel of faith (17, 33). At issue is the eating of faith (17, 5). To take the flesh and blood of Christ is simply to have faith in him (*loc. cit.*). The offer of Christ's presence and its reception in faith are both included in the one spiritual event.

It is not surprising, then, to catch echoes in Calvin of Luther's doctrine of the eating of the unworthy, although this is not connected here with any sacral quality in the elements (as against Niesel, *Calvins Lehre vom Abendmahl*, pp. 87ff.).

Even though a distinction must be made between the offer and its reception (17, 33), and even though it is true that only faith receives, nevertheless the power of the sacrament remains intact no matter how much unbelievers exert themselves to nullify it (17, 33).

At this point Calvin unmistakably parts company with Zwingli and comes close to Luther. If the presentation of Christ were simply a mental recollection, then nothing would happen if through indifference or rejection this mental recollection did not take place. If, however, Christ himself is present in his saving offer through Word, Spirit, and sacrament, then rejection of the offer means that it becomes "deadly poison" for those who will not let themselves be fed and strengthened by it (17, 40). The Lord was near and was despised. It was not the transformed elements that were near. An eating of the unworthy which is related to the elements is rejected as idolatrous by Calvin. This is illustrated by adoration of the host as an extreme form of the tying of Christ to the elements. What is idolatry but the revering of the gifts instead of the Giver (17, 36)? The Giver is present, not in virtue of our spirit, but in his own Spirit. When the ungodly deny this presence and offer, what takes place is not *nothing* but judgment (1 Corinthians 11:27).

To sum up, there are two aspects to the union with Christ which is the benefit of his presence in the Supper.

Christ *comes down* to us in his Spirit as well as in the outward symbol to give life to our souls with the substance of his body and blood (17, 24). He does this in such a way, however, that he also takes us and *lifts us up* to himself (17, 16). A wonderful exchange has taken place. Christ became the Son of man with us and made us the sons of God with him. He came down to earth and thereby opened to us the way to heaven. He took to himself our mortal nature and in so doing imparted to us his immortality (17, 2).

As this double benefit is received in the Lord's Supper—the *descent* of Christ in our flesh and blood and the *ascent* in exaltation—the symbol obviously coincides for Calvin with the real fulfilment of union, so that in opposition to the mere symbolism of Zwingli he gives theological precision to the basic concern of Luther: the efficacious promise of salvation to faith. In the sacred meal Christ commands us to receive his body and blood under the symbols of bread and wine. We have no reason to doubt that he himself truly offers these and we receive them (17, 32).

Calvin's discussion shows particularly clearly how far scholastic thought-forms gave rise to the eucharistic controversy. The fact that the antithesis between the Lutherans and Reformed could be reduced to the well-known formula that Luther championed the principle that the finite can grasp the infinite while the Reformed took the opposite view makes it plain that abstract principles were striving for mastery here. It would be a fatal mistake to let these principles stand and thus to ideologize the confessional differences. They, too, must be understood in terms of the concern which is at work but very inadequately expressed in them. What Luther wanted to say with his principle that the finite can grasp the infinite is that we should take seriously the full and unconditional entry of the eternal Word into our limited humanity. Calvin did not dispute this but with his opposite principle he wanted to say that since the incarnate Logos resolved upon this, then as the subject of this act of condescension he is also more than the finite form that he assumed.

This gave rise to the so-called Calvinistic *extra*. We may refer to the express discussion of this in Volume I and especially to the serious results of ideologizing the principles in later theological history (cf. EG, I, pp. 423ff., 548f.; EF, I, pp. 292ff., 374f. and II, pp. 399ff.; EF, II, pp. 324ff.).

4. SUMMARY, RESULTS, AND EVALUATION

Now that we have pierced through the time-bound concepts of the traditional eucharistic doctrines and reached their theological core, we are in a position to sift out the nonnegotiable element in our statements about the Lord's Supper. Reduced to a single formula, this may be described as the real personal presence of Christ in feeding through Word, bread, and wine. Since the real presence is not meant as presence "in itself" but as presence "for us," one might also use for this nonnegotiable element in the eucharist an adaptation of Melanchthon's famous saying: "To know the Lord's Supper is to know its benefits." These benefits are participation in the Lord's death and resurrection through the work of the Spirit, the declaration of forgiveness of sins, and incorporation into Christ's body through the bond of love.[13]

Only this acceptance in faith of the presence of Christ and its gifts constitutes the church. This is the bond which binds the communion of saints together. In contrast to this constitutive factor the understanding of the mode of the presence is to be set in the sphere of interpretative and descriptive teaching. The firmer the main theme of the benefits, the better this teaching can serve as counterpoint.

Admission to the Lord's Supper should not be tied to a specific confessional understanding of it. It should depend solely on the hungering and thirsting (Matthew 5:6; John 6:35) of those who seek it, for to them the promise is given that by the Spirit the hungry can receive the nearness and fellowship of the Lord. The only criterion for worthiness is preparedness by faith in the present Lord—or in the Lord whose presence is simply sought and who is timidly invoked in a developing faith—to receive the gift of fellowship with him. The unworthy might well be those who on the ground of their supposedly legitimate understanding arrogate to themselves the right of fellowship and refuse it to others. To encumber eucharistic communion with the burden of confessional exclusiveness is for this reason not only incomprehensible but a definite sin. The Lord's table should in a very special sense represent the gift of a fellowship that transcends all traditional, historical, and confessional limits.[14]

This does not mean that theological differences in understanding are unimportant or may be relativized. In our attempts at interpretation we have seen how far they can stand for different views of faith, Christ, and the Spirit, and also how far they can conceal differences and relationships, so that we need to challenge them

---

[13]For a more precise theological expression of this nonnegotiable element cf. the Arnoldshain Eucharistic Theses (1957) in which Lutheran and Reformed theologians attempted a common statement.

[14]This way of relating faith and understanding suggests that children, too, should be allowed to participate. Whether they are given the bread and wine or are simply blessed is a secondary question. Either way, the main motif in infant baptism is here taken up again, namely, reception into the fellowship of believers and incorporation into the body of Christ.

as hindrances. Readiness to relativize can be protected against blind iconoclasm only if it goes through a stage in which the forms of reflection are understood in terms of their central affirmations. Only thus can they retain their importance.

The decisive point for me is something which I have constantly stated in all three volumes of this work and which receives enhanced relevance when applied to the place of eucharistic teaching as distinct from eucharistic practice.

The gospel as declaration has radical priority over theological reflection. It does so in every form—as preached Word, as festal meal, as sacrament. Reflection arises out of encounter with the Word. Eucharistic theology follows celebration of the eucharist. It is the rendering of an account and the offering of praise by our spirit. Hence we do not have to complete theological reflection and reach certain conclusions before there can be access to the Lord's table. This is why the doors to the eucharistic banqueting hall cannot be opened too wide.

This might be regarded as a tolerance which is related to indifference[15] and which would then be a new way of despising the Lord's Supper. But this charge cannot stand so long as it is the community that receives the guest at the Lord's table and does not leave him to his subjective and perhaps erroneous ideas but sets him under its accompanying Word, under proclamation, teaching, and pastoral care.

---

[15] We shall discuss the problem of toleration in the next chapter in relation to the religions.

Part Four

THE EXCLUSIVENESS OF PRESENTATION

The Gospel and the World of Religions

Bibliography

P. Althaus, "Mission und Religionsgeschichte," ZsysTh, V (1928), p. 550; H. U. von Balthasar, "Geist und Feuer (Interview)," HK, II (1976), p. 72; K. Barth, *Christliche Dogmatik* (1927), pp. 316ff.; KD, I,2, pp. 309ff.; CD, I,2, pp. 280ff.; E. Benz, *Ideen zu einer Theologie der Religionsgeschichte* (1960); also "Das Anliegen der Menschheit und die Religionen," *Studium generale*, XV (1962), p. 767; P. Beyerhaus, "Zur Theologie der Religionen im Protestantismus," *Kerygma und Dogma*, II (1969), p. 87; D. Bonhoeffer, *Widerstand und Ergebung*, 10th ed. (1961), esp. pp. 178ff.; E.T. *Letters and Papers from Prison* (New York, 1967); C. C. Bry, *Die verkappten Religionen* (1924); M. Buber, "Christus, Chassidismus, Gnosis," *Merkur*, LXXX (1954), p. 923; H. Bürkle, "Die Missionstheologie in der gegenwärtigen Diskussion," *Die Verantwortung der Kirche in der Gesellschaft* (1973), esp. pp. 179ff.; also "Die Herausforderung der Kirche durch den heutigen Hinduismus," *Kirchentag* (1973), p. 752; also "Der christliche Anspruch angesichts der Weltreligionen heute," *Absolutheit des Christentums*, ed. W. Kasper (1977), pp. 83ff.; J. A. Cuttat, *La rencontre des religions* (Paris, 1943); E.T. *The Encounter of Religions* (New York, 1960); G. Ebeling, "Evangelium und Religion," ZThK, II (1976), p. 241; M. Eliade, *Die Religion und das Heilige* (G.T. 1954); E. Fahlbusch, "Das Heil der Nichtchristen. Die Erklärung *Nostra aetate* des II Vatikan Konzils," MD, XIX (1968), p. 1; also "Theologie und Religion—Überblick zu einem Thema römisch-katholischer Theologie," *Kerygma und Dogma*, II (1969), p. 73; E. Feil, "Zur Wiederkehr der Religions-kritischen Problembericht," HK, I (1978), pp. 30ff.; H. Frick, *Vergleichende Religionswissenschaft* (1928); P. Frostin, "Marx und Bonhoeffers Religionskritik," ZThK, III (1976), p. 315; F. Heiler, *Erscheinungsformen und Wesen der Religion* (1961); W. Holsten, *Christentum und nichtchristliche Religion nach der Auffassung Luthers* (1932); E. Jüngel, "*Extra Christum nulla salus*—als Grundsatz der naturlichen Theologie?" ZThK, III (1975), p. 337; also *Gott als Geheimnis der Welt. Zur Begründung der Theologie des Gekreuzigten im Streit zwischen Theismus und Atheismus* (1977); S. Kierkegaard, *Concluding Unscientific Postscript* (Princeton, 1944); K. Koch, "Der Tod des Religionsstifters," *Kerygma und Dogma*, II (1962), p. 100; H. Kraemer, *The Christian Message in a Non-Christian World* (1938); H. Kruse, "Die anonymen Christen, exegetisch gesehen," *Münchener theologische Zeitschrift*, XVIII (1967), p. 2; G. van der Leeuw, *Der Mensch und die Religion* (1941); also *Phänomenologie der Religion* (1956); E.T. *Religion in Essence and Manifestation* (New York, 1963); T. van Leeuwen, *Christianity in World History. The Meeting of the Faiths of East and West* (1964); P. Löffler, "Die Herausforderung der Kirche durch den heutigen Islam," *Kirchentag* (1973), p. 773; T. Luckmann, *Das Problem der Religion in der modernen Gesellschaft* (1963); E.T. *The Invisible Religion* (New York, 1967); "Lumen gentium," Dogmatic Constitution of the Second Vatican Council, esp. art. 16; U. Mann, *Theologische Religionsphilosophie im Grundriss* (1961); *Vorspiel des Heils* (1962); *Theogonische Tage* (1970); and *Das Christentum als absolute Religion* (1971); H. J. Margull, "Die Herausforderung der Kirche durch den heutigen Buddhismus," *Kirchentag* (1973), p. 761; A. Nygren, *Die Gültigkeit der religiösen Erfahrung* (über das religiöse apriori) (1922); E.T. *Essence of Christianity* (Philadelphia, 1960), pp. 11–78; R. Otto, *Das Heilige* (1917); E.T. *The Idea of the Holy* (Oxford, 1925); W. F. Otto, *Die Götter Griechenlands,* 2nd ed. (1934); E.T. *The Homeric Gods* (London, 1954); R. Pannikkar, *Christus, der Unbekannte des Hinduismus* (1965); E.T. *The Unknown Christ of Hinduism* (London, 1964); W. Pannenberg, "Erwägungen zu einer Theologie der Religionsgeschichte," *Grundfragen systematischer Theologie* (1967), p. 252; E.T. *Basic Questions in Theology* (London, 1971), pp. 65ff.; also *Wissenschaftstheorie und Theologie* (1973); E.T. *Theology and the Philosophy of Science* (London, 1976); S. Radhakrishnan, *Die Gemeinschaft des Geistes. Östliche Religion und westliches Denken* (1952); K. Rahner, "Weltgeschichte und Heilsgeschichte," *Schriften zur Theologie,* V (1962); E.T. *Theological Investigations,* V (1966); "Die anonymen Christen," VI (1965); E.T. VI (1969), pp. 310ff.; "Christentum und nichtchristliche Religionen," Hampe, III, p. 568; more fully *Schriften zur Theologie,* V (1962), pp. 136ff.; E.T. V (1966), pp. 115ff.; C. H. Ratschow, "Der christlichen Glaube und die Religionen," *Evangelischer Theologen-Kongress Wien, Hauptvorträge* (1967), p. 88; J. Ratzinger, *Das neue Volk Gottes* (1969), esp. pp. 325ff.; C. M. Rogers, "Hindu and Christian," *Religion and Society,* Vol. XII, No. 1, p. 35; G. Rosenkranz, *Der christliche Glaube angesichts der Weltreligionen* (1967); H. R. Schlette, *Die Religionen als Thema der Theologie* (1963); E.T. *Towards a Theology of Religions* (New York, 1966); N. Söderblom, *Das Werden des Gottesglaubens,* 2nd ed. (1926); also *Der lebendige Gott im Zeugnis der Religionsgeschichte* (1942); E.T. *The Living God* (Boston, 1966); H. F. Steiner, *Marxisten-Leninisten über den Sinn des Lebens* (1970); R. Stoeckle, "Der ausserbiblische Menschheit und die Weltreligionen," *Mysterium,* II, pp. 1049ff.; N. Takenaka, "Christentum und nichtchristliche Religionen in Japan," *Areopag,* II (1973), p. 143; H. Tenbruck, "Wahrheit und Mission," *Freiheit und Sachzwang. Festschrift für H. Schelsky* (1977); H. Thielicke, "Das Ende der Religion (on Bonhoeffer)," ThLZ, V/VI (1956), p. 307; *Offenbarung, Vernunft und Existenz,* 5th ed. (1967); and Anthrop (1976); P. Tillich, *Biblical Religion and the Search for Ultimate Reality* (1952); and "The Significance of the History of Religions for the Systematic Theologian," *The Future of Religions* (1966), p. 80; E. Troeltsch, *Gesammelte Schriften,* II (1922); *Die Absolutheit des Christentums* (Siebenstern No. 138 [1969]); E.T. *The Absoluteness of Christianity* (New York, 1958); and *Glaubenslehre,* ed. M. Troeltsch (1925); W. A. Visser 't Hooft, "Gläubiges neues Heidentum," LMH, XI (1977), p. 634; H. Vossberg, *Luthers Kritik aller Religionen* (1922); J. Wach, *Vergleichende Religionsforschung* (1962); E.T. *The Comparative Study of Religions* (New York, 1958).

XXIII

Debates about the Concept of Religion

1. THE SIGNIFICANCE OF THE PROBLEM OF EXCLUSIVENESS IN THE PRESENT SYSTEMATIC CONTEXT

The presentation of God in the Spirit-mediated Word, in what we have called revelation in the objective and subjective sense,[1] implies two things: first, the making known of its truth through the biblically recorded event of salvation (the objective dimension), and second, the effect in the lives of those who experience this truth (the subjective dimension). These people participate in "being in the truth" (John 18:37; 14:6). They are freed from the corrupting outlook of their lives which suppresses and blocks the truth (Romans 1:18, 21, 25). They are placed back in the lost analogy to God as his children.[2]

Since this truth comes to us in an event and is not attainable in our own reason or strength,[3] it claims a monopoly, refusing coordination with other truths that arise within this sphere of our own reason and strength. Indeed, it describes itself as at odds with these other truths and says that in relation to the one truth, the truth of God, they are simply means of suppression (*katechein*) and obscuration and instruments of human self-defense and pride (Romans 1:18ff.; 1 Corinthians 1:20f.).

Thus *exclusive* significance is attached to this truth. The Word incarnate in Christ is proclaimed as *the* truth (Acts 4:12). The truth of God is thus linked to the judging and liberating Word. Since biblical and Christian tradition regards the Pneuma as the presentation of the Word, so that the Spirit is bound to the Word as his vehicle, the exclusiveness of the revelation of truth applies also to the sphere of operation of this Word. Thus claiming the Pneuma for a revelation outside the Word comes under the suspicion (or the verdict) of confusing our own spirit with God's Spirit and doing something that is a characteristic mark of radical enthusiasm.

---

[1] EF, II, cc. I–III.
[2] EG, II, p. 21; EF, II, pp. 18f.
[3] SC, article 3.

Theological reflection that tackles the question of exclusivism has to face two tasks.

First, if this exclusivism is not to come under the suspicion of being a dogma that refuses to be investigated, a basis must be found for it. This means finding criteria which will make a decision possible among competing claims to truth. We must raise the question of a material legitimation of exclusiveness even though the result may be that this cannot have the character of a "proof."

Second, since religious claims are among the competing claims to truth, the question arises whether we are ever dealing with claims that are made in our own reason and strength. Might it not be that there is some kind of revelation in all the religions—perhaps a preparatory form along the lines of the *logos spermatikos* of the early apologists—God being behind them as in some way their author, not having left himself without a witness (*amartyron*, Acts 14:17)?

To this extent encounter with the religions raises the question of the exclusiveness of Christian truth in its most urgent form. It raises it in the form of a questioning.

2. THE POLARITY IN THE UNDERSTANDING OF THE RELIGIONS

This questioning is even sharper when we consider the following:

a. Does not the exclusiveness of Christian truth seem to reach the limit of absurdity when we remember that Christianity is as it were a latecomer in history, that it might enjoy only a limited historical span, and that it is not therefore one of the inalienable and essential human characteristics?[4]

b. The spirit of the age is opposed to making an unconditional claim to truth, to uncompromisingly championing a single truth, whether in the dubious fields of ideology or in that of very general and therefore attenuated basic rights. In a time marked by relativism we are bewitched by the attractive word "pluralism." Many views must coexist, tolerating and not challenging one another. The white flag of "live and let live" is a virtuous sign of liberalism. We live in an open society. A claim to absoluteness finds itself confronted not only by competing claims but also by a commonsense view which has to regard all claims as relative, as conditioned by time and place and society, as being in principle beyond any possibility of decision. The very idea of exclusiveness is contrary to the age in which we live.

c. Above all, it is very hard to grasp concretely what is meant by the religions because they are so many and so heterogeneous.

For example, in an intensive discussion with the Zen-Master S. Hisamatsu, called Hoseki, in Japan, I was left with the impression that in the Zen exercises there are realities which cannot be conceptualized and which elude dogmatic debate, so that we are confronted here with a "wholly other" with which comparison is impossible, since the Christian kerygma and the Zen-Buddhist doctrine of salvation have no common basis. In this case, how can there be criteria for, e.g., exclusiveness (cf. my *Voyage to the Far East* [Philadelphia, 1962], pp. 149ff.)?

Even within non-Christian religions there seem to be similar differences. Thus it

---

[4]Ebeling, ZThK, II, p. 242.

is impossible to compare one of the main religions, with its long tradition, and the new religions of mass communications (Tenri and Omoto) which have sprung up in Japan.

In Africa, on the other hand, one may see primitive animism and black magic which awaken anxiety and panic in face of demonic encirclement. In Brazil we find the ecstatic cult of the spiritists, the terrors of magic, and the follies of religious frenzy within a daring syncretistic conglomerate of African gods and Christian saints on neighboring altars.

I mention these examples in order to warn the systematic theologian against the temptation overhastily to coordinate and conceptualize the hetereogeneous aspects, whether as synthesis or antithesis. The need to think out the exclusiveness of the Christian claim to truth forces us to seek criteria for debate. Even dialogue— and mission is more than that—would make this necessary. But we want readers to see that under the burden of experienced heterogeneity we recognize the almost impossible difficulty of this task and cannot understand the dogmatic simplicity with which dialectical theology denounces the religions wholesale as ungodly (more of this later).

The problem is not just that the multiplicity of the positive religions leaves an impression of heterogeneity. The very concept of religion is problematical. Does it refer to something identical in all religions, as though the one light of primal religion were now split up into many colors? If so, the religions should remember what is common to them all instead of attacking one another and raising claims to exclusiveness. On this view they would all be complementary to one another.

Radhakrishnan (*Die Gemeinschaft des Geistes,* p. 8) thinks that only *one* truth lies behind the different religions. This cannot be expressed in any one faith or limited to any one church or temple. It is our duty to rise up to this truth by overcoming the limitation of our way, the contingency of our inheritance, and the one-sidedness of our understanding.

Religion is thus seen here as the epitome of a final truth which is eternally valid beyond the restricted and accidental truths of history. It is natural to claim that reason is the organ of what is eternally valid. Not by chance, then, rational religion became the shibboleth of the Enlightenment. We remember Lessing's parable of the ring, which makes virtue the identical core in Judaism, Christianity, and Islam: Do what is right and pleasing before God and man. On this view the positive religions, as in Lessing's *Education of the Human Race,* are the mythical husks of this kernel, modes of expression suitable to the given stage of human consciousness, accommodations in space and time (J. Semler), relative, and significant only insofar as the timeless core may be seen through them.[5]

But this identical core does not have to be moral, as in the Enlightenment. It can be the unconditional element, the final dimension, in all reality, of which reality itself is a likeness. Along these lines the religions, as in Goethe, can be complementary descriptions of this identical element and as such stages on the way to the ultimate dimension.

Thus Goethe can coordinate the religions in a schema which is determined by

---

[5]Cf. my book on Lessing, *Offenbarung, Vernunft und Existenz.*

the subjective way in which we relate to or even see this final dimension. The object of reverence and our attitude to it show this. Reverence is here the slogan for the basic religious attitude.

In ethnic religions reverence for what is "over us" is normative. In these religions there is a first happy release from abject fear.

At the second stage we find reverence for what is "like us." This leads to philosophical religion in which we bring down what is higher and raise up what is lower to our own level.

The Christian religion is characterized by reverence for what is "beneath us" in compassion and mercy. It has brought something into the world that can never be banished again.

All three forms of reverence or religion are united in "trinitarian" fashion, being complementary to one another and in their totality representing religion (cf. *Wilhelm Meisters Wanderjahre*).

Goethe makes this even plainer in a letter to F. H. Jacobi dated 1/6/1813. He says here that one religion is not enough for him. The various areas of his life need different religious attitudes. As an artist he is a polytheist, as a scientist a pantheist, in morality a monotheist. Here again one may speak of a "trinitarian" order. The various expressions of religion relate to different geometric planes which meet at a point that cannot be grasped. They are transitional stages on the way to the one truth. None must be made an end in itself or absolutized.

The conviction that the religions are relative is a persistent one. Lessing, Goethe, and Radhakrishnan represent many others who hold it. The "history of religions" school gave it the support of empirical data.

d. From this type of religious understanding, which uses anthropological criteria, whether with reason (Lessing) or religious man (Goethe) as the focus, it is only a step to the point where religion is a mere category or way of looking at things with no relation at all to any concrete proclamation of truth. Schleiermacher develops this view of religion as a category in his *Speeches*, especially the second.

Here religion is found wherever we consider finite things from the eternal standpoint and this consideration is in tune with the "contemplation and sense of the Universe." There is, then, a special religious view of the world and even of its so-called profane spheres.[6] This must be sharply distinguished from the philosophical and moral approaches which signalize a qualitatively different relation to the universe. To genuinely religious forms of experience there corresponds a distinct category of seeing which is independent and cannot be subjected to criteria taken from other intellectual spheres. This function of religion, which is anchored in the human subject, leads later to the view (e.g., in Troeltsch) that we construct our own religious *a priori*. On an individual table of categories it serves the purpose of giving to religious statements the same validity as other statements which according to Kant are also grounded in the epistemological possibilities of the human subject.[7]

e. Indicative of the great range of the term "religion" is the fact that even its etymological basis is contested. Some trace it back to *relego*, which means "to

---

[6]EG, I, pp. 30ff.; EF, I, pp. 43ff.
[7]Cf. A. Nygren, *Die Gültigkeit der Religiösen Erfahrung.*

keep reading" or "to be reflective." Here the emphasis is on meditative consideration of canonical texts, so that the term applies to only one distinct stage in religious history, that of book religion, and not to primitive stages, e.g., those of animism and magic.

Another and more common derivation is from *religari,* which means "being related to" or "dependent on." The very formal character of this interpretation enables us to subsume under it very different forms of religion, both theistic and atheistic (Buddhism). Luther himself alludes at least indirectly to this understanding when in his Larger Catechism he calls God that "on which man may hang or lay his heart."[8] This general statement raises the question whether he is hereby trusting in the true God or an idol (e.g., mammon).[9]

The fact that the formal term leaves open and undecided this question of God or idol makes necessary the distinction which Augustine was the first to make between true and false religion,[10] which then raises the question of truth. It is on the assumption that they are the champions of true religion that Zwingli and Calvin can write their books *On True and False Religion* and *Institutes of the Christian Religion.*

Even today it is still debated whether the gospel can be subsumed under this general concept of religion or is to be held aloof from it with an infinite qualitative distinction, as the exclusiveness of Christian truth would seem to suggest. We shall discuss this question in what follows.

---

[8]LC, "The First Commandment," 6.
[9]Cf. WA, 40/I, 604, 3–605, 3; LW, 26, 397.
[10]*City of God,* X, 1ff.: "On True Religion."

XXIV

Paradigms of the Controversy about the Question of the Gospel and Religion

In sketching representative paradigms of this kind, we are not motivated by historical interest but aim to discover from critical analysis of these models some insights which will be useful to us when we attempt our own definition of the relation between the gospel and religion.

1. HEGEL'S IDEA OF A SYNTHESIS

Lessing found a wide and ugly ditch between the timeless necessary truths of reason and the accidental truths of history, i.e., between his reason and the historical revelation of Christianity. Hegel thought he could bridge this ditch with his thesis that everything historical, including the historical manifestation of a religion, is rational. The accidental element is overcome because the world-spirit is actualizing himself in the historical process, coming to himself through it, and thus making it a spiritual event and enabling it to participate in logic and dialectic.[1] In religion the spirit who knows himself is directly his own pure self-consciousness.[2] Thus the finite spirit has a part in the self-consciousness of the absolute spirit. It is the vessel in which the latter actualizes knowledge of himself. The absolute spirit knows himself in finite knowledge and vice versa. The finite spirit knows his knowledge as absolute spirit. This is the general concept of religion.[3] In religion the spirit knows (in the medium of finite consciousness) and is also known.[4]

Part of Hegel's view of history as the self-actualization of the spirit in a process is that religion has a share in it. The individual religious stages represent different

---

[1]Cf. *Lectures on the Philosophy of History* (New York, 1956).
[2]*Phenomenology of the Spirit* (Oxford, 1977) and *Lectures on the Philosophy of Religion* (London, 1895).
[3]*Lectures on the Philosophy of Religion.*
[4]*Ibid.*

degrees in the relation of the finite spirit to the absolute spirit. From this standpoint Hegel portrays each of the great religions as a specific and typical variation on religion in general. The total typology shows historical development from natural religion to spiritual religion. This process raises religion up from dull and dream-like stages of spiritual self-consciousness to increasing clarity and adequacy.

The goal of the spirit's coming to himself is reached in absolute religion, in Christianity. Absolute religion is revealed religion which has itself as its content and fulfilment. It is perfected religion which is the spirit's being for itself, the religion which has become objective to itself, the Christian religion. In it the general and the individual spirit, the infinite and the finite, are inseparable.[5]

In the process of religious history Christianity represents the hour when religion comes fully to itself (as a person does when awakening out of unconsciousness or semi-consciousness). It is the absolute religion because in it the historical being of religion has become congruent with the concept.

In this short sketch we need not go into what is said about such individual topics as creation, the fall, Christology, the Trinity, and eschatology. Our task is rather to show how the concept of the self-knowing and historically self-actualizing idea makes it possible to view revelation as the mark of all religious history, to see in Christianity the absolute instance, and—to use our own terms—to understand the gospel as religion.

Like Hegel, A. von Harnack weaves the gospel into the history of religion, not as one of the religions, but as the representative of the goal and fulfilment of all religion: the union of God and man. The whole message of Jesus can be summed up in two points: God is Father and the soul is so ennobled that it can and does enter into union with him. This shows that the gospel is not a positive religion like others. Not that it has no place in religious history. Rather, it is religion itself (*What is Christianity?*, p. 63). Harnack, too, finds in Christianity a congruence between the idea of religion and its historical manifestation—the Christian and the human being in this case equated. There can be no further question of any tension between the gospel and religion.

It is plain that a synthesis which Christianity proclaims as the fulfilment of the history of religion and a disclosure of its content presupposes certain criteria by which its status is measured. The dialectic of the spirit in a Hegelian sense might be the assumption on the basis of which the Christian idea of the Trinity contains the adequate sum of religion. Or moral standards might seem to show that Christianity meets the highest demands and makes any transcending of its normative content unthinkable.

This observation ought to make us apprehensive in regard to any such attempts at ranking and synthesis. The theological question that arises here raises the problem whether a religion of revelation is not contradicted from the very first if it is judged by norms that derive from outside. To adopt an expression of Luther's,[6] might not a secret human religion be at work here to regulate God's religion, and to do so even though it assigns to it the rank of the climax of religious history? If the gospel is really understood as revelation and the Word and Spirit are viewed as

---

[5]*Ibid.*
[6]E. Wolf, "M. Luther. Das Evangelium und die Religion," ThEx, VI (1934), pp. 8ff.

an event from without, there must be no evaluating of it by given norms but it itself must contain the criteria or standards which judge human religion, as it does in Paul.

In Chapter I of Volume II we dealt with the problem of revelation. We made it clear there that God as the author of revelation cannot be objectified in terms of given premises, for man in contradiction is not analogous to him. For this reason, we argued, only God himself is the adequate subject of the knowledge of God. Only the Spirit searches the depths of God (1 Corinthians 2:10f.).[7] This means that this knowledge of God contains the criteria for the knowledge of what is not God and therefore of the most appropriate godlike predicates. It means that man himself—in his religion too—is subject to this norm. This shows how far man forms God in his own image. Feuerbach was not the first to suspect this. Luther perceived the possibility in his early commentary on Romans:[8] As we are, so is God for us.

Hence we can meet positive or negative evaluations of Christianity only with the theological proviso that the principle used is contrary to the self-understanding of revelation, that it is subject to the criticism of inadequacy, and that it gives a high place to human religion instead of exposing it to questioning by divine religion.

By way of illustration we shall take a more drastic case of the well-meant regimenting of revelation than that of Hegel. In a hymn on the OT R. Kittel describes it as the blossoming of all ancient religions and the instrument by which the master could achieve *the* absolute religion. The OT is the climax of all ancient religion. If we realize with what purity and majesty the idea of God is expressed in Israel, namely, the idea of God as moral will; if we consider how there develops out of that the ideal of personality which has real worth only when moral and holy; if finally we open ourselves to the influence of the moral and social universalism in virtue of which humanity itself becomes a moral community, a great international union of moral and religious personalities or a kingdom of God, then we have to admit that the OT is religion as such (Hegel's absolute religion) and in spite of individual weaknesses we have to maintain its truth and enduring worth (R. Kittel, "Die Zukunft der alttestamentlichen Wissenschaft," ZAW [1921], pp. 84ff., esp. pp. 96-98).

A similar picture may be seen in the field of comparative religion when we turn to H. Gressmann, who thinks that in evaluating and ranking religions what is needed is not scholarship but ripe understanding and profound love even for the revelations in what is called paganism. In fact the humanistic categories that are assumed to be universally valid here make it impossible for revelation to claim exclusiveness and the difference between Christians and pagans disappears. Gressmann also thinks that we can no longer speak of a revelation of God in history in the biblical sense. Christianity is at the very most the absolute religion, though we have to realize that this absolute religion is only an abstraction which covers all religions in virtue of the religious element in them (H. Gressmann, "Die Aufgaben der alttestamentlichen Forschung," ZAW [1924], pp. 30f.). Both these assessments naively betray the fact that Hegel's concept of absoluteness is the background of a normative human religion.

---

[7] EG, II, pp. 21f.; EF, II, pp. 18ff.
[8] Ficker ed., II, 72, 6; LW, 25, 219.

One might perhaps say that post-Hegelian attempts to understand religion and the religions are like a broad spectrum in which Hegel's synthesis of reason or religion and history, or of religion and the gospel, breaks up again.[9] Without regard to chronological sequence we shall first offer two instances of this: first, opposition to the synthesis from the standpoint of the history of religion, then from that of anthropology and materialism.

2. OPPOSITION TO THIS SYNTHESIS FROM THE STANDPOINT OF THE HISTORY OF RELIGION (TROELTSCH)

For Troeltsch with his far wider knowledge of empirical religions than that of Hegel, a speculative synthesis of the world of religion was impossible. It could not be considered because the epistemological situation had changed. Trust in metaphysical deduction was no longer convincing to the positivistic science of the 19th century which was impressed by the individual, contingent, and therefore nondeducible character of the historical world.[10] History stood opposed to any conceptual levelling down or generalizing. If Hegel had covered up Lessing's broad and ugly ditch between universal validity and historical relativity, Troeltsch reopened it, though he himself was not seeking rational truth as the common ground in religious history but only certain impulses toward the ultimate.

In any case Troeltsch could not accept the abstract construction of an absolute religion in history. History knows no general concept which covers the succession of all the contents of history and also contains an evolutionary law by which these contents unfold and achieve self-realization.[11] Religious history knows no essential ground common to all religions. It presents only concrete individual phenomena. All these have their own profiles and all stand within their own historical constellations.

This is also true of Christianity, which shows no suprahistorical absoluteness but is always time-related, first to later Jewish apocalyptic with its eschatological fixations, then to Hellenism (Plato, Stoicism, Aristotle).[12] Troeltsch accepts the famous thesis of D. F. Strauss[13] that the idea does not realize itself by pouring its whole fulness into a single instance which it favors above all others but likes to spread its wealth abroad in a multiplicity of examples which complement one another.[14] Troeltsch's point is that revelation can exist only in an infinite series of finite forms and not as a specific historical case.

Troeltsch examined closely the rational and normative premises that give rise to the idea of a general concept of religion and then offer a scale by which to measure the religions and portray Christianity as a concretion of the general concept. He finds in these speculative premises an inappropriate attitude to history (especially

---

[9]Except of course in theological Hegelians like A. E. Biedermann and P. K. Marheineke and theological Liberals like A. von Harnack.
[10]For the philosophical basis cf. esp. W. Windelband and H. Rickert; cf. also ThE, III, §2045 (E.T. III, p. 86) and Troeltsch, *Absolutheit*, p. 29 n.; E.T. *The Absoluteness of Christianity*, p. 45.
[11]*Absolutheit*, p. 47.
[12]Pp. 52ff.
[13]*Life of Jesus* (London, 1973).
[14]Quoted in *Absolutheit*, p. 50, n. 14.

in their orthodox manifestations).[15] This is part of his scholarly vehemence in resisting any dogmatic authority. For him fixed presuppositions of this kind rest on manipulations of weaker natures which are afraid of anything alien and fear to lose themselves in a commitment to history.[16]

If we are ready for an unconditional confrontation with historical phenomena as they really are, the first principle is that Christianity itself in all the elements of its history is like all other religions a purely historical phenomenon with all the time-bound features which this entails.[17] This seems at first to involve the surrender of any distinctive normative claims, since historical and relative are identical for Troeltsch.[18] History is no place for absolute religions or absolute personalities.[19] All religion is truth from God even if according to the general level of spiritual development.[20]

This concept of the relative, which seems to deliver us up to fear of the uncertain and insecure and aimless,[21] ceases to be a threat when we see what it really implies, namely, that all historical phenomena are individual forms in the outworking of a nearer or more distant total nexus and they all point us to the totality in the context of which alone we can view them together and evaluate them.[22] For Troeltsch the totality which sustains the relativity is an absolute, but it cannot be a phenomenon in history. Kant would have called it a postulate.

Only when we have overcome the fear of relativity and not been forced into an overhasty vote for the exclusiveness of Christianity[23] can we try to build a new temple on the ruins of the old. The presupposition must be an abandonment of the antithesis of absolute and relative as one that does not do justice to historical reality. Not the juxtaposition of absolute and relative, but their mixture, the development of movements toward absolute goals out of the relative, is the problem of history. History places us before the sense of mere approximation to true and final and valid values which it does not itself realize but to which it points.[24]

This leads us to the most difficult point in Troeltsch's view. We have to find our way in the confusing world of religions. If it is a matter of movements toward absolute goals or approximations to final values, then the decisive question arises where the clearer direction or the greater approximation is to be found and how Christianity stands in this regard. Naturally, to answer this question, there have to be norms. But how can there be norms when the rank of individual religions can be established only in the light of the whole, of the total nexus which is not yet available to us, which is still ahead, which is not a fixed point in history? Is not Troeltsch merely reaching out here? He himself would accept this if by such norms

---

[15] *Ibid.*, pp. 29ff. (E.T. pp. 45ff.).
[16] P. 66 (E.T. p. 87).
[17] P. 66 (E.T. pp. 87f.).
[18] P. 65 (E.T. p. 85).
[19] P. 59 (E.T. pp. 70ff.).
[20] P. 38 (E.T. p. 54).
[21] P. 65 (E.T. p. 86).
[22] P. 68 (E.T. p. 89).
[23] W. Köhler, *E. Troeltsch* (1941), p. 106 tells how after a lecture on the concept of relativism one pastor said in a loud voice that he would resign at once if Christianity were not the absolute religion.
[24] *Absolutheit*, p. 69 (E.T. p. 90).

are meant, not static surveying rods, but norms that have to be sought in daring encounters with history.

His first demand is in fact that standards should not be imported in the form of scholastic theories of order but must be reached of themselves.[25] The norm can arise only in the free play of ideas.[26] It must emerge from the depths of history and make itself evident as we move into the play of forces and give ourselves to a careful survey, impartial appreciation, and conscientious evaluation,[27] not claiming to know everything in advance on account of some hermeneutical principle.

If we encounter history with this openness, we shall not, as the fear of relativism caused us to think, come up against a chaotic sea of values in religious history nor find ourselves abandoned to nihilism.[28] Instead we shall find only a limited number of basic values which make decision easier. It is astounding by how few thoughts the human race has really lived, how little true content history has thus far engendered.[29]

These various schemes of value undoubtedly have something in common which forces us with inner necessity to weigh the one against the other.[30] The great sustaining values worked out in history may be clearly differentiated and seen in their interrelatedness.[31] Among the special values by which Troeltsch's generation was guided we no longer find the question of the Reformation: "How shall I find a gracious God?" but: "How shall I rediscover the soul and love?" or: "How shall I (in a mortally infected humanity) find a higher personal life from God?"[32]

Perhaps the traumatic fear of Troeltsch was that even criteria won in dialogue with religious history might be cumbered by the verdict of dogmatic prejudices or might themselves become such if he did not attach even to them certain criticisms and restrictions.

We have seen already that the standard by which these differences are to be assessed could not be a religious theory deduced *a priori* from somewhere else, nor could it be the common factor in these religious constructs.[33] But the criterion could not be any objective principle. We find that it is subjectively conditioned and have to take this into account. What we have here is a matter of personal conviction and an axiomatic act.[34] This is related to the fact that decisions have to be made for values that exist only as goals and ideals[35] and de facto only in individual actualizations that are bound up with temporal historical circumstances. For this reason the claiming of a specific religious construct for one of these final values and its corresponding ranking in the hierarchy of values rests on a daring and subjective evaluative decision (though Troeltsch himself does not seem to use this concept).

---

[25]P. 12 (E.T. p. 26).
[26]P. 74 (E.T. p. 96).
[27]P. 75 (E.T. p. 97).
[28]P. 72 (E.T. p. 94).
[29]P. 72 (E.T. p. 94).
[30]P. 68 (E.T. p. 89).
[31]P. 75 (E.T. pp. 97f.).
[32]*Gesammelte Schriften*, II (1913), pp. 522 and 840.
[33]*Absolutheit*, pp. 73f. (E.T. p. 95).
[34]Pp. 74f. (E.T. pp. 96f.).
[35]P. 76 (E.T. p. 98).

A second critical restriction of value-norms is connected with the first. Because the goals and ideals occur historically only in individualized forms (like gold in gravel as it were), absolute unchanging value, which is not conditioned by time, does not occur in history at all, but only on the far side of history which is accessible only to longing and faith.[36] It is under the heaven of Platonic ideas, after which we daringly grasp, that there unfolds the confusion of earth in which we seek impure copies of those ideas and which permits us to give only subjective approval to our findings. In this Platonic type of construction may it not be that Troeltsch is positing a new dogmatic *a priori* which from a concealed background directs his choice of standards and the subsuming of the religions under these standards?

However that may be, Troeltsch, having been burned by dogmatic and ideological traditions, knows how provisional is that which he responsibly tries to see and assess and evaluate. He also accepts the limit set on him—that of having to sit in front of the Platonic cave, unable, in Goethe's words, to enter the land of ideas, but allowed us to weigh anchor by the shore.[37]

He weighs anchor in this way when he makes the attempt to bring Christianity into his ventured scale of values and to allot it a supreme place. By experience we find in all the great religions related common thoughts and powers and impulses. Basically there are only four groups of ideas: God, the world, the soul, and a related higher life beyond the present world.[38] If we measure religions by these fundamental thoughts, it is clear that the goals that are sought are attained with fullest autonomy and force in Christianity,[39] whereas deficient elements may be seen in non-Christian religions of law and redemption.

Is not Troeltsch arriving here, from the other side, at the same concept of an absolute religion inasmuch as Christianity adequately covers the obligatory content that is contained in the idea of religion? In the end do not the impartial appreciation and conscientious evaluation of the battle of ideas come to the same conclusion as that which theological and philosophical dogmaticians believed they knew at the very beginning as a premise, namely, that the much attacked concept of absolute religion is ultimately unavoidable and is in fact posited by religious history itself?

At the same time it is plain that the empirical training to which Troeltsch subjected himself and the risk of relativism which he ran produced a different sort of absoluteness from that of the dogmaticians. Since absolute truth unburdened by individual temporal conditioning does not occur in history, we are exposed to new surprises in history. The future constellations of the historical sphere of relativism cannot be foreseen (unless we regard as fixed premises the experiences of value that we have had thus far). For this reason it cannot be proved with any strict certainty that Christianity will have to be the final climax and can never be surpassed.[40] What is certain is only that the future alone will bring absolute truth in

---

[36]P. 69 (E.T. p. 90).
[37]P. 84 (E.T. p. 106).
[38]P. 89 (E.T. p. 113).
[39]P. 89 (E.T. p. 113).
[40]P. 90 (E.T. pp. 114f.)

the judgment of God and the end of the present world.[41] Absolute truth is reserved for the eschaton, which is no longer of this world and for which we wait. We wait to see the whole which alone will give final validity to standards of value.[42]

Confidence that Christianity is not just the climax but also the point of convergence of all known developmental tendencies in religion is thus exposed to the relativizing interim of this world and its historical relationships. Perhaps it is not too bold to say that Troeltsch's faith is finally a nevertheless-faith which cannot see how to overcome relativism but still confidently resists it. For Troeltsch senses and experiences a trend in religious history whose provisionally knowable goal is fulfilled with provisionally knowable perfection in Christianity.

Troeltsch realizes that the figure of Christ himself finally inspires this confidence. For the personality of Christ is the authority on the basis of which the Christian belief in God is experienced as truth (*Glaubenslehre*, p. 345). Even it cannot be seen as an absolutely normative and fixed point in history. Like any other historically limited individuality it is subject to the limitations of nationality and time, which include a one-sided focus on religion, a will fixed on the approaching end, and a related aloofness to the goods and tasks of this world (pp. 346f.). Does this mean that even Christ is subject to historical relativism? Can he then be an absolute authority for the future?

The way in which Troeltsch finally says that he can characterizes his historical thinking. Christ is not just a historical figure. His death has released the Spirit within this historical phenomenon as an ongoing principle which accompanies time and its needs (p. 347). This Spirit of Christ is related to the historical figure and takes all his basic thoughts from it but he keeps alive its basic direction and leads into all truth by responding to new problems and situations with new disclosures (p. 347).

By appealing to the Spirit of Christ and his dynamism Troeltsch tries to show that the living stream of history is not arrested by Christ as by the pillar of a bridge but that Christ himself flows with the stream. He thus remains a unique authority but does not stop history. He remains normative without putting an end to the march of norms and values.

Troeltsch's concept of religious history provokes critical discussions which we shall formulate first as questions.

Is the exclusiveness of the Christian claim to truth as we have theologically represented and argued it merely to be denounced as dogmatic prejudice? Naturally there can be no question that an axiom which cannot be further investigated has frequently been used, and will continue to be used, as a starting point. On the other hand, approaches of a very different kind must be considered when the claim appears on the horizon of Troeltsch's destruction of the theory of absoluteness. We shall be content to deal here only with two points which take up what we said earlier on the theme.

---

[41]P. 91 (E.T. p. 115).

[42]Cf. the similar view of Schleiermacher who in his *Speeches* (the Fifth, p. 242) says that Christ never claimed to be the only object of the application of his idea of being the only mediator. There are traces of the same thought in *The Christian Faith*, but in his sermons Schleiermacher speaks of the definitiveness of Christ (cf. *Werke*, IV, p. 836 and VII, pp. 4ff.).

1. Discussions of the testimony of the Holy Spirit have shown us that the self-evidence of the truth (of revelation) does not occur merely with the passive acceptance of Christian commonsense assertions or mere compliance with the law of tradition. No person achieves adult faith by merely believing in the belief of others, e.g., parents. Truth is attained only as it is experienced as a liberation from previous bondage for certainty—a liberation that is brought about by the efficacious Word. This certainly does not rest on the acceptance of a static axiom but arises in a living historical struggle between the divine and the human, or, if we will, the absolute and the relative. Luther's famous saying that only temptation makes a theologian applies here too. Faith has to pass through the field of temptation in order to come to itself. Untested faith which simply hangs on artificially as childhood faith is a product of sloth and indifference. The believer will relate to it only as object and not as subject. Only those who face nothingness can attain to their own faith.[43]

2. It should also be considered that later, with experienced certainty, we can understand why a Spirit-mediated certainty of this kind necessarily takes on its own normative significance. Its function as a standard, however, does not apply in controversy with other religions but in debate with the empirical distortions of Christianity itself, which is often enough no more than the sum of misunderstandings which have clustered around Jesus of Nazareth.

This normativeness is not to be understood as static or once for all. It will have to prove its claim in ever new encounters and in a readiness for dialogical questioning. Without this readiness, for example, there can never be the historico-critical investigation of Scripture that theologians engage in, for it would constantly be blocked by a static fundamentalism. Faith is always a venture—or else it is an assertion of supposed truth which is motivated by legalism and anxiety.

3. OPPOSITION FROM THE STANDPOINT OF ANTHROPOLOGY AND MATERIALISM (FEUERBACH)

a. Feuerbach's Anti-Hegelianism

As a paradigm of the materialistic opposition we shall use Feuerbach and not Marx, although the latter's concept of ideology[44] has won for Feuerbach's theory of projection its greatest historical effectiveness, and this not merely in the spheres of Marxist-Leninist domination. We choose Feuerbach because the question of religion was for him life's real problem[45] and because he pursued theology in a negative mode—M. Stirner calls him a pious atheist[46]—and posed the most consistent antithesis to religion.

---

[43]In his exposition of the seven penitential psalms, Luther says that it is God's nature to create out of nothing, so that God can make nothing out of those who are not nothing (WA, 1, 183, 39–184, 3).

[44]On this cf. ThE, II, 2, §§154–422 (E.T. II, pp. 26–70) and the chapter on Marxist anthropology in *The Hidden Question of God* (1977), pp. 35ff.

[45]All my writings have "strictly a single goal, will, thought, and theme. This theme is religion and theology and the things related thereto" (*Vorlesungen über der Wesen der Religion, Werke*, VII [1908], p. 6; E.T. *Lectures on the Essence of Religion* [New York, 1967]).

[46]Stirner meant this as a criticism, the word "pious" indicating that Feuerbach stopped halfway in his criticism of religion and was one of the many fieldmice still scampering around in the darkness of the "beyond" (A. Kohut, *L. Feuerbach* [1909], p. 184).

The apologetic helplessness of the theology of his day against this antithesis shows that his theory of projection received essential impulses from tendencies in this theology and to that extent forced it into self-critical inquiry.[47]

In saying that Marx accepted Feuerbach's theory of projection we do not mean that he uncritically copied him. In his *German Ideology* Marx attacked the Hegelian element in this left-wing Hegelian with some basic objections. But this disagreement did not affect his assent to the decisive thesis that God is merely a projection of man.

Marx has three criticisms of Feuerbach.

1. With Hegel Feuerbach adopts the attitude of a spectator toward history. He does not consider human activity as an intervention in the world. He is thus one of the philosophers who interpret the world instead of changing it (*Deutsche Ideologie, Thesen über Feuerbach,* in K. Marx, *Die Frühschriften,* ed. S. Landshut [1953], pp. 339, 341).

2. He agrees with Feuerbach that the illusionary element in religion ("the fact of religious self-alienation") consists of its splitting of the world into religious and secular spheres, so that God is man's alter ego. Feuerbach wants to dissolve the religious world in its secular basis but he fails to reach the true core of the problem, that of the secular basis itself. For only out of the disruption and self-contradiction of this basis can one explain the fixing of an independent kingdom in the clouds. In other words, if man's relation to the material basis is unclear or perverted, there will necessarily arise a religious "cloud-cuckoo-land" with its false consolations and palliatives. Feuerbach criticizes heaven but does not criticize earth and bring to light the motives behind projection (Thesis 4).

3. While Marx agrees with Feuerbach in merging man's religious nature into his general human nature, he does not find in him the concrete question of the material constitution of this general nature. Here again Feuerbach fails to raise the question of "earth." His concept of man is generalized. What he calls human nature is an abstraction not found in any individual. In its material reality human nature is the ensemble of social relationships. Only when man is seen to be socially and economically conditioned do we arrive at real man and understand why he dreams of that kingdom in the clouds (Thesis 6). The resultant religious disposition is a social product. Feuerbach does not see this (Thesis 7; cf. the parallel criticism of F. Engels, *L. Feuerbach und der Ausgang klassischer deutscher Philosophie* [1888; new ed. 1946]; E.T. *Ludwig Feuerbach and the Outcome of Classical German Philosophy* [New York]).

It was ultimately because of his break with Hegel, and especially with Hegel's philosophy of nature, that Feuerbach arrived at his thesis that religion, including Christianity, has no transcendent origin in revelation but is a reflection of man himself which man has produced and projected. For Feuerbach the weakness in this chapter of Hegel's thought is that he sees nature only very generally as a "being of the idea outside itself" and is not able, as in his philosophy of history, to deduce the plenitude of phenomena and gather them together in his concept. Hegel

---

[47]Barth is right here, although I do not feel that he really advanced the debate with Feuerbach. He does not put what seems to me to be the fundamental question that ought to be put (cf. K. Barth, *Die protestantische Theologie im 19. Jahrhunderts* [1947], pp. 486, 489; E.T. *Protestant Theology* [London 1959], pp. 536ff.; KD, IV,3, pp. 79ff.; CD, IV,3, pp. 72ff.).

explained his failure here, not by the weakness of his conceptual understanding, e.g., the unsatisfactory nature of his category of spirit, but by the weakness of nature, its alienation from spirit, its contingency, which resists the concept. It is odd that Feuerbach should find the weakness of Hegel's philosophy, its inability to think of the individual and its constant generalization, not in the philosophy of history but in the philosophy of nature.

In contrast Feuerbach sees in the individual and concrete the true sustaining reality. In his *Criticism of Hegelian Philosophy* (1839) he thus reverses the conception of his master. The reality of nature is not out of tune with the concept but vice versa. Hegel's concept cannot grasp reality. In the conflict between reality and the concept of reality, reality is right. In his *Principles of Future Philosophy* (1843) he thus develops the thesis that only the sensory individual, man in his reality, is authentic reality, while the general is an abstraction and even an illusion of his own formation. Whereas for Hegel the spirit, which is general, is true reality, and by bifurcation it develops through several stages of the particular, Feuerbach reverses the process. The spirit is simply the doubling of the real individual. The general idea is simply a later projection of this basic reality.

We cannot understand Feuerbach's criticism of religion if we fail to note this anti-Hegelian impulse and therefore do not consider that his theory of projection is simply a final result of what Marx calls the "decomposition" of the absolute spirit. Thus Feuerbach radicalizes the criticism of religion and Christianity by D. F. Strauss, another left-wing Hegelian. Strauss fought Christianity's claim to truth with the weapons of history and philosophy and his aim was simply to free some of its normative ideas from their historical ballast and to establish them in purer form. Feuerbach presses the criticism to its abrupt end with psychological weapons. The idea of religion is an illusion which is obviously produced by psychological mechanisms.[48] We must see how the illusion arises in order to free ourselves from it.

The basic thoughts in Feuerbach's theory of projection are so well known that we need only outline them here. They may be found especially in his works *The Essence of Christianity* ([New York, 1957], pp. 12ff.) and *Das Wesen der Religion, Werke* (VI–VIII).

The gods are projections of fear and hope. "As men's wishes are, so are their gods" (VII, p. 503). Consciousness of God is consciousness of self and knowledge of God is self-knowledge. God is the revealed inner part of man, his expressed self (VI, p. 15). Religion, or at least the Christian religion, is thus man's attitude to himself, or, more correctly, to his being, his being as another (VI, p. 17). The illusion is that we think we are meeting another when in fact we are meeting ourselves. God's apparent otherness rests on the fact that while the divine nature is nothing but a projection of the human it is detached from the limits of individual corporeal humanity. This objectification creates the illusion of another nature but in fact it is man's own nature seen apart from man, freed from what seems to be limitation or evil to the individual, either in feeling or in thought. Similarly the other world is nothing but this world freed from what seems to be limitation or evil (p. 219).

The materialistic starting point of this view may be seen even in its linguistic

---

[48]For the development of this thesis by Freud cf. Anthrop, pp. 435ff.

formulation, which constantly uses the reductionist expression: "is nothing but. . . ." Thus man is nothing but a process of oxidation. Values are nothing but defense mechanisms and reaction formations. Man is nothing but a biochemical mechanism (cf. V. E. Frankl, *Universitas, IV* [1970], pp. 369ff.; Anthrop, pp. 458ff.). Similarly, God is for Feuerbach nothing but a reflection of the opposite of man. God is perfect, man imperfect; God is eternal, man temporal; God and man are extremes. God is the positive side, the epitome of all reality, while man is the negative side, the epitome of all nonreality (p. 41).

What Feuerbach seeks is psychologically motivated disclosure. He does not simply want to show religion to be illusory but also to disclose the reality of man, who in his projections expresses his own most secret longings and anxieties. (This is why Feuerbach is a welcome point of contact for psycho-analytical anthropology.) Feuerbach does not have only a destructive purpose. On his planned level he has an ethical goal, liberation *for* as well as liberation *from*. The aim of his works is to make men anthropologists instead of theologians, lovers of man instead of lovers of God, students of this world instead of candidates for the next, free citizens of earth instead of religious and political valets of a heavenly and earthly monarchy and aristocracy (VIII, pp. 28f.).

Subjectively, then, he has a positive purpose. By showing what is false he wants to lead to the truth. This truth is the new humanity which makes human communication a religious relation in a new and realistic sense—a relation in which, as a turning point in world history, the basic principle is that man is the God of man (VI, p. 326) and not a wolf as Hobbes said and Machiavelli in his own way thought (cf. ThE, I, §§1984ff.). This intention made an impression on the young Marx even though he was concerned to eliminate the religious remnants which he still saw in Feuerbach's act of liberation.

Only recently has the humanism which Feuerbach distilled out of religion been heralded. This has taken place in the new theological left for whom God has become a cipher of fellow-humanity. Feuerbach coined its decisive shibboleth when he said that "man with man—the unity of I and Thou, is God" (*Philosophie der Zukunft,* Thesis 59, *Werke,* II, p. 318).

b. In Criticism of Feuerbach

The fundamentally simple concept of reversal, which recurs with endless variations, betrays its suspect character even by the boredom which its monotony produces. Yet Feuerbach cannot be refuted by a foolish apologetics that focuses on details and tries to show that this or that, e.g., Christ's crucifixion, cannot be subsumed under the sum of all longings and is thus contrary to the theory of projection.[49] What is to prevent psychiatry from explaining even Kierkegaard's theology of the cross by negative complexes which his distorted relation to his father engendered?[50] A certain instinct for the uselessness of this kind of approach may explain why almost all dogmaticians have avoided it, being agreed, in spite of the extreme differences that exist between a K. Barth and an H. Stephan, that the

---

[49]Even the *Adult Catechism* of 1975 does not avoid popular apologetics at this point.
[50]Cf. Anthrop, p. 442.

theology of the time, with its anthropocentric or eudaemonistic orientation, was responsible for Feuerbach's reaction.

The primary criticism of Feuerbach must probe more deeply and should be conducted from two main angles.

First, it must begin with the theological question how the doubling of man in religion comes about and why man projects an alter ego in heaven in whom he sees his desired image of himself in enhanced and purified form. Feuerbach himself did not put this basic question. Marx made good the defect and answered it, as shown, by tracing back the doubling to the disruption and self-contradiction of the world, i.e., man's social situation. By his unresolved, distorting, and alienating wrestling with the material basis of things he arrives at religion as a promise of illusory consolation for the misery of the world. The rise and continuation of this illusion is naturally convenient to rulers because as "opium" it stills the revolutionary impulses of the exploited.[51]

By seeking the reason for projection Marx undoubtedly radicalizes the problem of Feuerbach. Yet we have to go deeper than Marx, too, and ask how it is that man lives by hope—even though it be false and illusory—and thus produces visions of hope.

These impulses are obviously related to the quality of the human, the *specific* element in human nature. This element consists of man's relation to time, which fundamentally distinguishes him from animals.[52] Animals live for the moment but man surveys the whole of his finite span of time and sees that he moves toward death. He is thus projected toward the future and shaped by the existential elements of fear and hope. But this qualitative distinction and burden of man cannot be seen only in terms of his social situation. This situation does not *produce* disruption and alienation—the wrong diagnosis of historical materialism. At most it only reproduces it. It is its occasion, not its cause. It releases something that belongs to man's presocial quality but would be unintelligible if it did not become virulent as disruption, hope, and projection. Society and the situations to which it gives rise can only draw out of man something that is already potential in him. Already by nature man is a being who is torn, who can sin, and who has to plan, decide, and transcend himself.[53] This is plain from the task which is laid upon him by creation according to the biblical account. He has a charge and he can also fall.

Feuerbach disregards this basic state of the human from which the ability to fear and hope and project derives. He simply notes man's factual being and his apparently factual processes of projection. This is what makes his enterprise so simplistic and banal. If he had worked through the phenomena to the basic state his initial question would have arisen afresh. Can man really be understood as the subject that produces his projections of fear and hope? Is he not rather in a given situation which can first *cause* him to play this role of subject?

This question implies a further one. Does not man have to see himself as one who does not control this being of his and whose self-fashioning does not relate to

---

[51]Marx took the phrase "opium of the people" from Herder (cf. E. Benz, "Das Anliegen . . . ," *Studium generale,* XII [1962], p. 767).

[52]Cf. the chapter on "Man and Time" in Anthrop, pp. 327ff. (also p. 384).

[53]Anthrop, pp. 218, 339 and *passim.*

his basic state. He can fashion himself but not create himself. To an overhasty hypothesis of projection the question thus poses itself whether there is not a source of his being to which one might trace back his possibility of projecting and of producing hope.

Put thus, the question obviously cannot be regarded as a first Socratic step toward the reality of religious truth or a proof of God. It relates simply to the nature of projecting man and questions the process of projection without ruling out in advance a negative answer. Our first criticism of Feuerbach, then, is that he does not put these fundamental questions of anthropology before proceeding to theology.

Second,[54] might it not be that projection is oriented to something other than the one who projects? One may at least suspect or assume this if in projection certain basic facts may be seen which have perhaps, or in fact, been previously imported. Thus the meaning of the universe which is projected into heaven as God might be a universally comprehensive meaning which includes man. This would suddenly give the theory of projection a wholly new turn. It would mean that man can project the logos on the white screen of the universe only because the universe contains the logos and takes up man himself into this content.

This would bring us to an insight which constantly recurs in the history of philosophy. We may take Stoicism as an example. This sees reason as thinking rationally and as treating the world which is thought by it as rational. In some sense it projects itself into the universe (if we may adjust it to Feuerbach's theme). But for it the universe *is* rational. It is subject to the logic of the laws of nature. This is why reason comes up against this logic and can describe and influence the world accordingly.

We thus confront the fact of correspondence between noetic reason and the ontic logos which obtains in the universe. The hermeneutical presupposition of all knowledge of the world is this analogy between the structure of thought and the structure of being.

Modern science and mathematics rest on this presupposition. With no empirical investigation of nature a mathematician can construct mathematical universes which come into his mind as pure productions of reason.[55] The astonishing thing is that these projections can later be verified empirically by astronomers. This can be explained only by the fact that ultimately nature is obviously a web of mathematical relations. Only on this assumption can noetic reason and ontic reason—the logos that thinks in man and the thought logos of being—coincide. There are thus fundamental affinities between the structure of our consciousness and the structures of the empirical world.

The question that we have to put to Feuerbach is obvious. Might it not be that whatever causes us to project the idea of perfection or the purified ideal of the human is grounded in the fact that the necessary content of the human is imparted to us as a gift in the form of our appointed goal so that here again there may be a correspondence between what comes into our mind as projection and

---

[54]For what follows I am especially indebted to P. L. Berger, *The Social Reality of Religion* (1959), pp. 179ff.; *A Rumor of Angels* . . . (1969), pp. 57ff.
[55]Cf. Berger, *A Rumor of Angels* . . ., pp. 58f.

what our mind already grasps as reality? Might it not be that God as our heavenly Father is not just an anthropomorphic projection based on the concept of our earthly father but that conversely the concept of our earthly father is simply a theomorphic reflection of our heavenly Father? If religious projections correspond to a suprahuman and supranatural reality, it is only logical to seek traces of it in the nature of the one who does the projecting.[56]

We do not ask Feuerbach simply to abandon his theory—at any rate as a first step. If he were still alive we should simply ask him to pursue his own anthropological theme in his own field of experimentation. We should simply ask what it is that causes him to project and whether this does not give a wholly different look to the theory of projection.

The problem of exclusiveness could not arise in Feuerbach, at least in the sense of a possible absolute religion. Since he reversed Hegel's concept of spirit, one might have expected him to speak of an absolute *anthropology,* i.e., an anthropology that had found its absolutely adequate and exhaustive projection in a certain religion (Christianity?). But even this would have been inappropriate. For the psychological approach is by nature relativizing. It does not let us seek the truth of underlying existence or what we have called the basic state of the human. It does not let us seek correspondence between the noetic and ontic logos. It is interested only in the process of reflection and reduplication in self-projection. Hence it has no standard by which to evaluate the legitimacy of this process (its source and nature). It has no criterion for the appropriateness of the reflection. How can it have when it does not ask about what is reflected, when it does not put the question of ultimate anthropological truth?

We are thus forced to say paradoxically that the only thing for which Feuerbach claims exclusiveness is his own position, which is exclusive in respect to the asserted impossibility of raising the question of exclusiveness. Being thus exclusive it is outside the sphere of all previous history and criticism of religion. Only at one point is it familiar to us and not without analogy. As relativism relativizes everything except itself, so Feuerbach says that everything religious (and spiritual) is projection without asking what projection of what existential basis his own theory might be. He cannot investigate this because to do so would presuppose a prior investigation of this basis, i.e., of the basic state of the human.

If, then, we are to oppose Feuerbach we must begin, not with his statements about theology, but with an investigation of his anthropology.

4. OPPOSITION FROM DIALECTICAL THEOLOGY (BARTH AND BONHOEFFER)

a. Feuerbach Transcended

One might almost have guessed that Hegel's dialectic of history, however haltingly, would live on in matters of religious understanding, that having gone through the stage of antithesis in Feuerbach it would reach in Barth a phase that at

---

[56]*Loc. cit.*

least views the synthesis from afar. Feuerbach's antithesis is transcended (*aufgehoben*) in Barth's view of religion; it is superseded and yet also retained.

It is retained inasmuch as Feuerbach is an ally in the theological condemnation of all religion and its denunciation as a human work.

It is part of the underlying mischievousness of Barth—one of the few predilections that he shared with his intimate friend E. Hirsch—that he prefers to associate with notorious heretics rather than lukewarm theologians, e.g., with Feuerbach and P. de Lagarde rather than Schleiermacher, R. Otto, and a host of others from the 19th and 20th centuries.

The antithesis is also overcome, however, inasmuch as Barth does not criticize religion in the name of an unmasking theory of projection but in the name of true religion,[57] of the Word of God declared in the biblical revelation. There thus returns here, materially at least, the concept of an exclusive absolute which Feuerbach had erased, so that Barth's relation to Feuerbach is an ambivalent one of both analogy and antithesis. He does not use psychological categories to relativize religion but the absolute of a unique and once-for-all revelation.

Barth does, of course, avoid the word "absolute" which Hegel and many theists had overburdened. In particular he does not try to deduce a claim to exclusiveness from it. I, too, shun the word, as will have become clear in the chapter on Hegel. Yet because of the historical contexts in which it occurs we cannot completely avoid it. Even behind Barth's theology a metaphysical schema is undoubtedly at work in which there is a place for the concept of the absolute.

In this respect I accept (with reservations) the analysis of F. Gogarten (*Gericht oder Skepsis* [1937]). (For the reservations cf. my article "Krisis der Theologie," ThLZ, XXIII [1937] and my book *Theologie der Anfechtung* [1949], pp. 59ff.) On the metaphysical background of Barth's theology cf. the analysis of his monism in ThE, I, §596 a-x; E.T. I, pp. 108-17.

Without engaging in an empirical study of religious history, Barth takes issue with religion throughout his work. He first systematizes his criticism in his *Christliche Dogmatik* of 1927 (the first draft of Volume I of *Church Dogmatics*). Here he distinguishes radically between religion and revelation. We must not be deceived by the reverence for another being with whom religious man has found superior strength and help and to whom he then, as subject, shows gratitude and dedication. Man in contradiction does not deny himself even in this piety of his.

"It should not be overlooked . . . that precisely in the event of religion man finds himself most powerfully and flagrantly engaged and entangled in this contradiction." Religion is "the final and deepest act of contradiction against God" (*Christliche Dogmatik*, pp. 316, 302).

The form of this contradiction and apostasy is that man changes into its precise opposite the event of salvation and revelation which God has authored. He makes himself God's creator. He thus degrades God as man's God and makes him a mere predicate of his own being and life.[58]

We see here the direct affinity of this view of religion to Feuerbach's interpreta-

---

[57]Thus Barth can say paradoxically *both* that no religion is true *and* that the Christian religion is true religion (KD, I,2, pp. 356f.; CD, I,2, pp. 325f.).

[58]*Christliche Dogmatik*, p. 316.

tion. Man creates his own alter ego who can no longer question him but only confirm and stabilize him in all his questionability. The difference, however, is that for Barth it is an illusion to think that religious man can unmask the process of projection by psychological self-analysis. The perverted psyche is precisely what manifests itself in the process. The psyche is thus an interested party. It cannot be objective in relation to itself. Objectivity can obviously come only from outside, from revelation. Hence revelation encounters religious man primarily as judgment. It accuses him of his arrogant attempt to seize God and form him according to his own image. Religion is unmasked as unbelief, as "a concern, indeed, the one great concern of godless man."[59]

Hence religion, from the standpoint of revelation, "is clearly seen to be a human attempt to anticipate what God in His revelation wills to do and does do. It is the attempted replacement of the divine work by a human manufacture. The divine reality offered and manifested to us in revelation is replaced by a concept of God arbitrarily chosen and wilfully evolved by man" (CD, I,2, p. 302).

Although we have no references to prove it, it seems probable that the completely different criticisms of religion by Feuerbach and Kierkegaard meet in Barth. It is perhaps a sign of this that Barth on his side champions a normative theme of the Dane, namely, that revelation criticizes not only religion but the Christian religion as well, in which the autonomy of religious man is particularly strong. What is usually called Christianity is in many areas (e.g., in forms of society and order, in efforts to fashion a Christian life both individually and socially, in Christian strategy and tactics in favor of the cause) a thoroughly "human work" that stands "on the same level as the human work in other religions."[60]

Yet in spite of the difference between revelation and religion Barth can still include a subsection on "True Religion."[61]

There are three reasons, all with corresponding reservations, why Barth decides to make the dubious concept of religion a—much conditioned—term for the truth of revelation.

1. Barth admits that we cannot consider revelation only in itself but that it is also "an event which encounters man" and has "the form of human competence, experience and activity." On the side of the recipient, then, revelation has to do with the given factor of religion.[62] It constitutes, as one might say, the schema and category within which the truth of revelation is received and perceived. Once man as the recipient of revelation is emphasized thematically, Barth cannot avoid treating the existing state of religious man as the "point of contact" of understanding, although he cannot bring himself to use this to him pejorative expression.

---

[59]KD, I,2, p. 327; CD, I,2, pp. 299f.
[60]*Ibid.*, p. 327. Cf. Barth's discussion of the law of religion in his *Commentary on Romans* (c. 7). Here the law represents religion in a struggle with the final possibility of religious man. The law stimulates this possibility and launches an attack on the freedom of grace. Later Barth changed his concept of the law (CD, II,2, pp. 509ff.). As the law of religion it is a human work but as the gospel it belongs to divine revelation. In the one case it relates to human religion, in the other to divine religion. For a discussion of law and gospel and dialogue with Barth cf. ThE, I, pp. 87–244; E.T. I, pp. 30–53; EG, II, §§14–17; EF, II, cc. XIV-XVII.
[61]CD, I,2, pp. 325ff.
[62]CD, I,2, pp. 280f.

2. As history teaches, when revelation and religion meet there at once take place, according to Barth, some fatal false developments. Beginning in the 16th century, and constantly escalating, there is a tendency to see and explain revelation in terms of religion instead of the other way around.[63] What ought to be just a category for the understanding and receiving of revelation takes on normative rank.[64] A general concept of religion is formed and Christianity is subsumed under it, so that the concept becomes normative. Whether or not Christianity is given a good rating, the standard of evaluation is not found in revelation, but revelation is subjected to this standard. This is why Neo-Protestantism is for Barth "religionism" and Christian theology is, as R. Seeberg called it, "religious science." This development is "a more serious symptom than the very worst pages in the books of a Strauss or a Feuerbach,"[65] for it enables these rabid destroyers to see revelation and religion in the same condemnation and to do away with both of them. Thus Barth's initial thesis is still valid. The critical place for the criticism of religion is revelation itself. Revelation cannot be absorbed in religion. It confronts it at a distance.

3. The decisive reservation which must be kept in mind when we describe the Christian truth of revelation as "true religion" is now plain. "We can speak of 'true religion' only in the sense in which we speak of a 'justified sinner.'"[66] We can do so only as we say that religion is transcended by revelation not merely in the sense of being negated but also in the sense of being exalted, i.e., upheld and hidden, justified and sanctified. "Revelation can adopt religion and mark it off as true religion."[67] Only if religion is understood in this sense as a religion that is judged and graciously accepted by revelation can the paradoxical formulation "true religion" stand. Only then is the movement from revelation to religion preserved and the perverse ascendancy of religion over revelation halted.

There is no doubt that with this criticism of the Promethean nature of religion Barth has also in mind the Thomistically understood analogy of nature and grace (the analogy of being in the sense of E. Przywara). Thomas is present indeed in this parade of heretics (CD, I,2, p. 284); he is seen as being in the same darkness as the orthodox Lutherans. One might perhaps summarize Barth's criticism of Roman Catholic terminology in this way: Grace does not perfect the nature of religion but destroys it (*tollere* ["to destroy"]) having the same ambivalence as Hegel's "aufheben," since it can also mean "to raise up" [cf. I,2, p. 326]).

P. Tillich, whom Barth does not mention here, or much at all, makes the positive relation between revelation and religion, which Barth touches on only lightly, into his predominant theme. He views the two as correlative. While revelation comes from God to man, religion expresses the human situation into which it is received. Barth might have said the same, but in him the question of the subjectivity of the recipient, of his "who" and "why," is at once swallowed up by the fact that what is at issue is the justification of the sinner, the reception of

---

[63]CD, I,2, pp. 284ff., 291.
[64]Cf. our discussion of Theology A in EF, I.
[65]CD, I,2, p. 291.
[66]CD, I,2, p. 325.
[67]CD, I,2, p. 326.

the prodigal son. And what interest can there be in the recipient's state, in his old life? Instead of looking back at himself he can only look ahead to the experience of his justification, his welcome back home.

In contrast Tillich's idea of correlation gives lasting and equal significance to God who imparts revelation and man who receives it. The situation of the recipient helps to shape his understanding of revelation and to determine the words in which he bears witness to it. Those who receive revelation witness to it according to their individuality and the social and intellectual situation in which it is imparted to them. They do so in terms shaped by their religion (*Biblical Religion . . .* , pp. 3f.). Thus the Bible is a document both of God's self-manifestation and of the way in which people have received revelation. Those who tell about it also tell about their own religion (*loc. cit.*). In the OT and the NT men bear witness to their reception of revelation and therefore every passage is both revelation and religion. In a thousand different ways a call is heard (A. M. K. Müller, *Die präparierte Zeit* [1972], pp. 467ff.) which resists any dogmatic systematization insofar as we consider the breadth of variation in perception and reception. To hear and understand the biblical text we must also hear and understand the religious individuality and its situation to which revelation is directed and in which it took on the form of its witness. There can be no question of the indifference or irrelevance of the being of the recipient at the moment of justification. The issue of a point of contact for revelation is not superfluous.

One has to ask, of course, whether Tillich is right to call the situation of the recipient his *religious* situation. Are the theological profiles of the synoptic gospels to be explained only in terms of religious differences (cf. G. Bornkamm, art. "Evangelien," RGG³, II, pp. 753ff.)? Do they not rest rather on different interpretations of the kerygma with the help of criteria deriving from different approaches and theological intentions? The basis, then, is in specific traditions of salvation history which already have to do with revelation and are not adequately described by the term religion. It is better to say, then, that where the kerygma is heard it does not always have the same shape but is at once interpreted and taken up into a specific theological schema (cf. Käsemann, *Exegetische Versuche und Besinnungen* [1964], pp. 192ff.). It is better to speak of the different theological contours of biblical statements than of their religious differences.

b. Implications for the Understanding of the Religions

In Barth revelation confronts religion and the religions as a "wholly other." This absolute of revealed truth (as we may cautiously put it) unmasks them as phenomena of revolt and ungodliness. If in the God who for Barth stands behind revelation as its author one can hardly help seeing an abstract and speculative God in himself—unconditional lordship and freedom[68]—the human work of religion is in contrast levelled down to a faceless mass of perdition. The polarity of the divine and the human which lies behind this view[69] remains abstract inasmuch as Barth

---

[68]Cf. the chapter "Der freie oder der isolierte Gott in Gogarten, *Gericht oder Skepsis*, pp. 80ff., 90.

[69]We still see this polarity in the later Barth even though he does build bridges to a better concept of analogy (that of faith and relation). In spite of such acts of sublimation he himself referred constantly to the identity of his basic conception.

does not deal concretely with religious phenomenology nor enter the field of religious history. At this distance from the empirical it is easy to overlook the monstrous implication of his tendency to level down. He has to lump together without distinction Buddhism, animism, and the new religions of Korea and Japan[70] as well as philosophies of all kinds with their atheistic variations. His negative slogan applies to all. It hardly need be shown that this implies the total impossibility of dialogue or debate.

In an express monograph on Barth we should have to trace this levelling-down tendency in broader areas. Of a piece with Barth's view of faith as (essentially) recognition and acknowledgment is a paradoxical relating of Christians and non-Christians. The only difference is that there is knowledge of God among Christians but not yet among non-Christians. But this is not a decisive difference, for it is outweighed and encircled by a fundamental common feature which Barth develops in his doctrine of election. Christians are not elect and non-Christians reprobate. There is no absolute preference for the former nor passing over of the latter (CD, II,2, p. 327). All are elect without distinction in Jesus Christ. Any difference is within this common reality. In every person the community has to do with a potential Christian, a *Christianus designatus*, a Christian in hope, a creature "ordained to know and realise his membership of Christ's body" (CD, IV,3, p. 810).

This levelling down in the name of salvation history and universal grace raises again the question of the metaphysical background of Barth's theology and especially the question whether we may see in this universal determination the old Reformed doctrine of the original decrees. According to these decrees and their monism of grace all later saving events, including Christ's return and the dividing of the race into Christians and non-Christians, are simply executive interim events which move toward the eschatological *telos* posited in the original decrees. In ThE, I (§§568, 612f.; E.T. I, pp. 99f.) we have tried to show that the influence of Hegelian monism on Barth's thought may be seen supremely in the central significance which he accords to the equation of law and gospel (cf. esp. CD, II,2, pp. 509ff.).

It is obvious that from this standpoint atheism (cf. also Jüngel, *Gott als Geheimnis der Welt*, pp. 135ff.) is relatively not very serious theologically. It is no massive anti-Christian force.

For one thing, it does not relate to the God of revelation, whom it does not know, but to the perversion of God in religion, to the figure of theistic reflection, to the projected God above us. The radical distinction between revelation and religion seems to offer Christian theology the possibility of not feeling affected by the atheistic attack. There is room for doubt, however, whether we have here a correct interpretation of atheism in its various forms, whether it will accept the differentiation, and whether, when suitably enlightened, it will recognize faith in the crucified God as a twin (Jüngel, *loc. cit.*). Have we not to consider the possibility that the crucifixion will deepen the offense?

Again, atheism is ultimately a negligible quantity because it, too, is included in

---

[70]Cf. W. Kohler, *Die Lotus-Lehre und die modernen Religionen in Japan* (1962); R. Italiaander, *Sokagakkai. Japans neue Buddhisten* (1973); San Myung Mun, *Ein Prophet spricht heute* (1976).

the election in Christ which embraces all men even though the atheist does not (yet) know it. The atheist, too, is a potential Christian.

Abstraction produces generalization. It subsumes empirically different things under a single concept, in this case that of universal election. The one who generalizes denies the need to take into account the fulness of empirical phenomena, in this case the breadth of religious history. Levelling down or generalizing leads to snap judgments and is content with them. This is the rather sad result of Barth's theory of religion. It does in the opposite direction exactly the same as that of Feuerbach, for whom all religious phenomena are under the same condemnation, and whose theory of projection brings about the same undifferentiated lumping together.

The same tendency on the same monistic basis necessarily applies in ethics too. Existing situations in which and on which we have to act can no longer be distinguished as good and bad or as relatively acceptable or not. Specific defects which might be remedied show us instead that everything is bad. Total corruption of this kind means that it makes no sense to fight it, since fighting it is caught in the same corruption. The man who thinks he can cast off evil by fighting it is the revolutionary man who simply puts new wrong in place of that which he fights.[71] The possibility of ethical decision is thus blocked. It is set in the ambivalence of "perhaps and perhaps not." This challenging of the whole complex of our existence and nature, this final "perhaps and perhaps not," which is laid as an ax at the root of the trees, is the freedom which we have in God beyond the law, "the freedom of God himself" (*Romans*, p. 292; cf. ThE, I, §80; E.T. I, p. 28, n. 1).

In "all-encompassing darkness" in which "all cats are gray" we cannot grasp this freedom, or can only grasp after it. Whatever we do stands in a negative bracket. The tendency toward levelling down in religion is in ethics a tendency toward indifference.

Barth later spoke out very decisively in ethics, and more particularly in political ethics, under National Socialism. But this was for other reasons. Theological indifference in ethical decisions hands over a wide sphere to rational judgment and grants it a kind of emancipation. (Cf. my book *Geschichte und Existenz*, 2nd ed. [1964], VIII.) Here, then, decision is possible. All cats are not gray for human reason.

The division of ethics into two spheres under different criteria becomes especially questionable when rational decisions in politics are later given theological weight with some suggestion of a theology of the cross (as in the appeal to the Czechs in 1938, *Eine Schweizer Stimme* [1948], pp. 58f.). We see here what happens when a radical and unbridgeable gulf between God's kingdom and the world's, between revelation and religion, releases earthly relations from theological control, so that not infrequently there is vacillation between theological and rational judgment. The passionate rejection of Luther's two-kingdom doctrine—which is certainly not immune to criticism (cf. ThE, I, §§1783ff.; E.T. I, p. 359)—and also of the distinction between law and gospel is simply a symptom of this helplessness. The relevant hesitation may be seen in a later letter of Barth to J. L. Hromádka (1962) which is diametrically opposed to the letter mentioned above (1938). Cf. Barth's *Letters: 1961–1968*, Swiss ed. 1975, pp. 114ff.; E.T. 1981, Letter 68.

---

[71] *Romans*, p. 480.

c. Continuation of the Criticism of Religion in Bonhoeffer

Bonhoeffer's famous letters from the Tegel prison[72] try to think through Barth's distinction between the gospel and religion and pose the question how the Christian message can be passed on in a completely religionless secularism in which it can no longer be linked to religious presuppositions. In order to find an analogical relation for modern man and therefore to make understanding possible, Bonhoeffer has the idea of a nonreligious (secular) interpretation of biblical concepts and even of a religionless Christianity. The trend of modern development is toward man's increasing sense of autonomy,[73] toward a maturity which can do without the "working hypothesis of God" and establish itself in a world of values which does not need to validate itself by appealing to the authority of God because it is self-evident.[74] For Bonhoeffer this trend is irreversible. If, then, Christian proclamation tries to lead adult and emancipated man to the gospel by way of a regeneration of religion, this will correspond to the wrong intention of some members of the primitive community to bring new Christians under the yoke of Mosaic legalism (Acts 15:1-32).[75]

For all the resemblance to Barth's criticism of religion we see at this point an essential difference. According to Bonhoeffer religion is not a constitutive part of human life. It belongs only to given epochs.[76] There are religionless times as well, our own secularistic age being a case in point. Behind this diagnosis there necessarily stands a different concept of religion from that of Barth. In fact Bonhoeffer does not begin by finding the religious phenomenon predominantly or exclusively in the arrogance of man or the interchanging of Creator and creature. He has a more differentiated if no less dubious view.

There are for him three marks of religion.

1. Religion is characterized by a certain metaphysical theism which is united with inner devotion and celebrated cultically.[77] The underlying motive is to make something of oneself (sinner, penitent, or saint).[78] In contrast, to be a Christian is to be a human being. Christ creates humanity in us.[79]

2. Religion has an esoteric vocabulary, a language of Canaan which relates to non- and supraterrestrial spheres and has no affinity to our secular concerns, to what interests man come-of-age.[80]

3. Religious people speak of God only when human knowledge (often through mental laziness) can do no more or when human resources fail. Hence God has the role of a *Deus ex machina*. He is allowed to emerge either to offer apparent solutions to insoluble problems or to supply strength in human weakness, making the most of this weakness in human emergencies.[81] This is what shows the interim

---

[72]*Widerstand und Ergebung* (1951); E.T. *Letters and Papers from Prison* (1971).

[73]*Ibid.*, p. 325 (1971 ed.).

[74]Bonhoeffer makes a rather dubious appeal here to natural law in Grotius (p. 325).

[75]Paul's question whether circumcision is a condition of justification is today the question whether religion is a condition of salvation (cf. p. 281).

[76]Ebeling draws attention to this in "Evangelium und Religion," ZThK, II (1976), pp. 243f.

[77]P. 280.

[78]*Loc. cit.*

[79]*Loc. cit.*

[80]P. 281.

[81]Pp. 281f.

character of religion, its restriction to particular epochs. For one can be religious only so long as one feels the limits of knowledge and power to be narrow and constricting. As the horizon of knowledge widens and adult man feels the strength of his autonomy, no place is left for the *Deus ex machina*. Religion becomes superfluous. In contrast to this self-discharging religion, Bonhoeffer in the name of the gospel wants to look for God, not on the borders of human life but in the middle, not in weakness but in strength, not in death and guilt but in man's life and good.[82] In this way God will be freed from the role of the God of the gaps that religion forces on him. He will no longer be a mere "working hypothesis."

Questions need to be put to all three of these supposed marks of religion. By way of example, we will content ourselves with criticism of the first and third.

As regards the first, Bonhoeffer may be right in his attack on the religiosity of Schleiermacher and the religious subjectivism of 19th-century theology. Yet faith in the gospel undoubtedly leads to a kind of inner piety. If Christ wants our whole person, and we are to be undivided members of his body, how can an essential part of us be excluded, that of our inwardness and imagination and emotional life? Even sociologists speak of "internalizing" when it is a matter of the sense of values and norms. Damage is done—as some forms of Pietism show[83]—only when inwardness becomes an end in itself, when pious subjectivism as experience becomes the focus of interest, when faith is no longer determined by its object but is subjectivized as the psychological state of believing.

At any rate it is hard to see why inwardness is in principle made a mark of religion and separated from Christian faith. A more likely view is that piety, as R. Otto describes it phenomenologically, is a connecting element between the gospel and religion (Acts 17:22f.) and that the two have at least a formal relation to one another.

As regards the third mark, is it really religion that makes God the God of the gaps when we are unable to cope with emergency situations? In this respect I see both an illegitimate form and a legitimate form in which God is actualized in these experiences. Neither is determined by *religion*. Both are constitutively connected to the *Christian* experience of salvation.

a. The illegitimate form arises because the historical character of biblical revelation carries with it the possible danger of confusing the kerygma with the time-bound view of the world in which it is presented in the Bible. The biblical kerygma is undoubtedly clothed in the ancient view of the world. Modern historical and scientific inquiries under the guidance of the principle of immanent causality undoubtedly play no role, or only an accidental role, in this framework. The attitude to knowledge as well as the range of empirical knowledge is unmistakably different from ours.

The narrower horizon and the different attitude make it natural that God should be more rapidly and directly invoked as the original cause of natural and historical events than he is by us moderns. But this does not in any way rule out the fact (a) that what we see expressed here is the transparency of world events to God's working, and (b) that we ourselves are required to discover this in some other way

---

[82]P. 282.

[83]I refer intentionally only to some forms of Pietism, not to Pietism as such.

of our own. Trouble arises in our relation to the Bible only when—as in some fundamentalist thinking—the time-bound world-view of the Bible is thought to be covered as well by its revelatory claim and is thus accorded the same normative rank. This locks us up again in a narrow horizon of knowledge[84] and makes God the one who fills the gaps in our restricted knowledge. It prevents us from making the venture of faith whereby God is the Lord of a changed world which is incomparably better understood, at least from the rational standpoint if not from that of meaning.

But is this role of God of the gaps and *Deus ex machina* really to be put to the account of religion? Is it not an internal problem of Christianity which does not confront the religious man of Schleiermacher? Does it not rest on a falsification of the understanding of revelation which identifies the historicity of God's self-disclosure with the historical media of this self-disclosure as though the conceptual framework of the kerygma were just as revealed as the kerygma itself? It is a mistake to make religion the representative and spokesman of ignorance. Other themes are at work, at least for those of us who are shaped by Christian culture.

b. The legitimate side of the fact that Christian faith has to do with frontier experiences and not just or chiefly with the center, the power and good of man, is omnipresent in the biblical testimonies and the Christian tradition. We can understand Bonhoeffer's statements here only if we see that they are aimed against some pressuring conversion-practices with their coloring of everything in black and white. Apart from that the question arises[85] whether without further experiences man could hear and appropriate the Word of God at all. One may ask with R. Röhricht whether it is really a matter of man in the so-called center of his life. Does not preaching of the kingdom live precisely by the fact that we neither have nor are the kingdom of God but it comes to us? Do we not have to admit that we are in need—not of the fulfilment of our life but of its changing into full reality? To that extent the Christian message and Christian faith exist only in the medium of the negative,[86] or at least in transition through this medium. One might say in Luther's sense that there is no faith without testing, without the experiences of holy Job (Tobit 2:12, 14). Here, too, frontier experience is the shadow-side of the faith which follows or precedes it. It is this on the basis of biblical (not religious) encounters with God. For the promise that God will be my God and grant me salvation brings fear of such experiences—the suffering of the innocent and triumph of the wicked (Psalm 73:3–11), in short, the apparent contradiction between what happens in the world and the promises of salvation. That faith in the biblical sense is not only faith *in* God but also faith *against* appearance demonstrates its basic structure. Here, too, to denounce the religious as the real cause of frontier experiences is mistaken.

In Bonhoeffer's polemic against religion his guiding concern is not to let Christian life be reduced to a religious province, a particular state of the ego. He does

---

[84]Cf. the dating of creation in 4134 or 4135 B.C. (T. Flügge, *Affenmensch, Weltall, Bibel* [1958], p. 60).

[85]Cf. R. Röhricht, "Der Name Gottes," in *Leben angesichts des Todes*, ed. B. Lohse and H. P. Schmidt (1968), p. 1.

[86]*Ibid.*, p. 177.

not want faith to be provincialized in this way. Part of his defense against such reductionism is that he does not want to see Christian proclamation limited to religious epochs but wrestles with the question how it can be shown to be relevant to religionless man.

The concept of religion which he uses is, as we have seen, arbitrary and untenable. But it is not only here that Bonhoeffer's terminology is hard to grasp. The same applies to his nonreligious interpretation of biblical concepts. Apart from the avoidance of the language of Canaan and a concern for ordinary speech, it is not clear what form this should take.[87] He could not have had in mind Bultmann's existential interpretation since this is not nonreligious. Possibly L. Kolakowski shows why he could not realize his purpose when in another context he says that religious experience can never be translated into secular speech.[88] Where this has been attempted, e.g., with the use of "lucky" for "blessed" or "girl" for the virgin, it has produced only damp squibs. Fundamental terms like sin and grace are untranslatable. They demand exposition, but not verbal replacement.

To do justice to Bonhoeffer we must remember his situation in prison. The representatives of the regime and the officials whom he met were not only nonreligious but also "de-platonized" people who had broken loose from all the traditional norms and values of the West. His problem was how to write the eternal Word on these blank slates. Furthermore, in letters to his friend H. Bethge he could not give a systematic account of his thoughts. They had to take the form of aphorisms and cries from prison. It is because these thoughts had not been fully developed but were only fragmentary that they have had such an extraordinary impact even to our own time. They contain a Socratic power of release such as can come only from what is original but incomplete.

Because Bonhoeffer's definition of religion is untenable, so, too, is his prognosis that religion will disappear altogether. On the contrary, both within Christianity and without we have seen an escalating interest in religion, though this will certainly not bring any Christian triumph (to use a horrible paradox) but can only be noted with scepticism and surprise in many circles. It looks like a flight from the drabness and rational coldness of the concrete world with its impersonal structures when the spheres of the irrational are sought in the form of every type of mysticism and ecstasy. Eastern practices of meditation are borrowed. Cultic inclinations are cultivated. Herman Hesse is read (especially in America). Charismatic movements are founded.[89] The rhythm of the Negro spiritual carries people away.

More important, however, is that the religious question crops up in ciphered

---

[87]Just how unclear everything is may be seen from the various interpretations of Bonhoeffer in which even prayer has been brought under the verdict of being religious and outdated (cf. Ebeling, *Wort und Glaube*, III [1975], pp. 420f., 546f.). Bonhoeffer himself was well aware that he had not found all the new terms (cf. Hanfried Müller, *Von der Kirche zur Welt* [1961], pp. 409ff.).

[88]"Der Mythos, das Christentum und die Realität des Bösen. Gespräch mit L. Kolakowski," HK, X (1977), p. 501.

[89]Cf. the books of D. J. Bennett: *Nine O'Clock in the Morning* (1970); *The Holy Spirit and You* (1971).

form outside these clearly labeled forms. It does so as the question of meaning, or as despair at lack of meaning, or at any rate as an attempt to transcend the world of provisional goals.[90] The almost "indelible character" of religion seems to be demonsrated both in its open practice and the ciphered question. Here again Kolakowski appears to be right when he says that the need for religion is always present as a need for meaning. It is unavoidable even if it hides under different names.[91] Obviously man is incurably religious.

d. Summary and Results

1. Bonhoeffer starts, as we have seen, with some statistical observations concerning religion which, grieving him personally and challenging him as a Christian, seem to indicate a decline into total indifference. Consideration of this decline forces upon him the question how the gospel can be proclaimed in a radically secular world without an existing correlation to the religious which causes faith, in defense and relationship, to experience its own different identity.

2. But the lack of religion takes a limited, distinctive, and one-sided form in Bonhoeffer, namely, that of the complete disappearance of the consciousness and sense of a final relation, e.g., a sense of "absolute dependence." His real shock is at finding people who have freed themselves from both religious and humanistic ties, who are not just nonreligious but also, as we have said, de-platonized.[92] He met such people at terrifyingly close quarters in Tegel.

3. The God who has thus disappeared from consciousness[93] covers only one particular nuance of the word *Theos*. This God is the God of theism, the supra-terrestrial God, who has become in reflection the "God of the philosophers" and left the sphere of immanence.[94]

Long after Bonhoeffer, and with no special reference to him, this view of God has found a committed and aggressive presentation in T. Moser's work *Gottesver-giftung* (1976). In this religious autobiography the Almighty, the supernatural God, awakens the feeling of anguished subjection in face of an all-powerful leader. God's inaccessible but omnipresent countenance reminds us of the all-controlling eye of "big brother" in Orwell's *1984*. But here, too, we see how religious impulses are not eliminated by resistance to this idea of God but can be stimulated, so that the indelible character of the religious is again confirmed. Moser can speak of a "God-trip" which he has taken because religious hopes are so dry and gloomy in everyday life.

In conclusion we may say that in Bonhoeffer (as in Barth) the exclusiveness of

---

[90]Cf. my book *Die geheime Frage nach Gott*, 3rd ed. (1976), esp. pp. 11ff.; E.T. *The Hidden Question of God* (1977), esp. pp. 9ff.

[91]Kolakowski, p. 503.

[92]Cf. my essay "Das Ende der Religion," ThLZ (1956), pp. 311ff.

[93]The death-of-God theology built on a misunderstanding of this thesis of Bonhoeffer. Cf. P. M. van Buren, *The Secular Meaning of the Gospel* (New York, 1963), pp. 188ff. and for a discussion EG, I, §§13-15, pp. 307-453; EF, I, cc. XIII-XV, pp. 221-311.

[94]We recall the famous phrase of Pascal. On this whole problem cf. W. Weischedel, *Der Gott der Philosophen*, 2 vols. (1971-72).

the gospel is that of the self-declared truth of God in contrast to the impulses and stimuli of human subjectivity and autonomy. It is the exclusiveness of the act of salvation accomplished in and by Christ in contrast to human dreams of salvation and human projections. Finally it is the exclusiveness of an eternal truth which is for all times in contrast to the time-bound interim stages of religious epochs.

We have seen at what cost this thesis of exclusiveness is won—the cost of a reduction and even perhaps a caricature of the concept of religion.

XXV

An Attempt at a Theological Synthesis (Tillich and Pannenberg)

1. THE NEW SITUATION

The question of the absoluteness or exclusiveness of Christian revelation in relation to religious history cannot be made credible by the attempt of Barth and Bonhoeffer to say that the gospel is not religion and thereby to snatch it out of the mass of perdition of the history of religion. Our critical analysis should have made this evident. As we have seen, to approach religious history with this thesis is first to refuse to face it, second to refuse to let it question our own claim to truth and thereby to refuse to win through to the assurance of faith through testing, and third to level down the positive and secularly disguised religions in intolerable fashion.

If we think that the gospel naturally implies a claim to exclusiveness, then we must demonstrate this in the encounter with other religions, no matter what form the demonstration may take. It is obvious in advance that no *proof* can be given. For a proof as a synthetic judgment *a priori* and *a posteriori* would mean that we have a timelessly valid principle at our disposal as a standard by which to measure the religions and show the superiority of Christianity, its fulfilment of the religions (in the Hegelian sense), or its total difference from them. But to presuppose that there is such a normative principle would contradict at the outset the self-evidence of the claim of revelation, first because this principle would be set above both revelation and its author, then because revelation discloses itself by the testimony of the Holy Spirit and not by rational insight, and finally because faith and not sight or insight corresponds to revelation on man's side. In the encounter with religious history, too, assurance of the exclusiveness of the gospel is still a gift which is imparted to the decision of faith and which remains inaccessible to rational assault.[1]

---

[1] Cf. Althaus, ZsysTh (1928), pp. 585ff. When J. Wach (ZsysTh, VI [1929], pp. 484ff.) accuses Althaus of subjectivism he either does not understand or does not acknowledge the pneumatological background of Althaus' argument.

Even if so simple a way of measuring cannot do justice to the gospel's claim to exclusiveness, the postulate remains that this claim must offer demonstration in religious history, for the biblical tradition is part of that of the Near East and the Mediterranean; it adopted materials from religious history, and in some sense conquered them.[2] We for our part have to do what the Bible itself did in relation to religious history—to receive, change, and conquer. We have to expose ourselves to encounter with this history.

We are thus brought face to face *again* with the question of Troeltsch and must reverse the evasive maneuver of Barth and Bonhoeffer. But since we have to regard as questionable and inadequate Troeltsch's massive attempt to prove absoluteness, we seem to be confronted by a serious dilemma. To advance we shall examine two conceptions—those of Tillich and Pannenberg—which in common rejection of the criticism of religion in dialectical theology take the history of religion seriously but are concerned to put the question of absoluteness in a theologically and biblically oriented sense and thus abandon the religio-historical immanence of Troeltsch.

2. ON TILLICH AND PANNENBERG

Tillich begins with a definition of religion which tries to embrace the whole range of its history, including Christianity understood as religion. The universal basis of religion is for him the experience of the holy within the finite.[3] The holy appears universally in everything finite and particular, always in a distinctive form. Although it appears in the finite, it lies beyond all its embodiments. Tillich brings all the characteristics of religion, which need not be listed here, under the concept of a religion of the concrete Spirit[4] which transcends its individuations, i.e., is exhausted by none of them. This religion of the concrete Spirit cannot be equated with any of the real religions, not even Christianity as a religion. Hegel's concept of absoluteness may be seen in the distance here—in the distance because Hegel has in mind the idea of Christianity and from this standpoint can view it as absolute religion, i.e., equivalent to the idea of religion. Tillich, in much greater affinity to the empirical religious world, has in view the concretion and individuation of the Spirit and makes it clear that the Spirit cannot be exhausted by this but contains something more.

Religious history is the setting of a dynamic event, of processes which deal with the tension between the holy and its finite element which is posited by the religion of the concrete Spirit.

This tension constantly threatens to be resolved in such a way that the holy is swallowed up in the finite element, which Tillich calls the sacramental basis, so that the transcendent element is lost in a false equation. For Tillich this is a

---

[2]Cf. Tillich, *Werk und Wirken*, pp. 191f.; E.T. *The Future of Religions*, p. 84. Tillich recalls how liberating it was for him to find universal motifs from the creation story, Hellenistic existentialism, and Persian eschatology in the later parts of the OT and in the NT. Symbols for the redeemer and redemption had been created which shaped the picture of the person and work of Jesus in the NT.
[3]*Ibid.*, p. 194 (E.T. p. 86).
[4]P. 195 (E.T. p. 87).

demonic process. The same demonism is present when the tension is heightened by a secularizing of the sacramental basis in which the finite loses its relation to the holy.[5] In the sense of a present and not just a future *telos* of religious history one may say that it aims to overcome these demonic deviations—the swallowing up of the holy by the finite and the desanctifying or secularizing of the finite.

The key to an understanding of what seems to be the chaos of religious history is to see that there is played out in it a struggle for the religion of the concrete Spirit, a conflict between God and religion within religion. In protecting the inviolateness of the holy, God himself is at work even in religious history. In opposition to Barth's theory of revolt and pride the religions have their own theological significance.

We again see Hegel at a distance when Tillich tries to hack a path through the jungle of religious history in the hope that it will give us a glimpse of the conditioned exclusiveness or absoluteness of Christianity. (Tillich avoids explicit use of these terms, and in our interpretation we shall have to show why we think we may apply them to him.)

For Tillich "Christus Victor" is the model of the victory over demonic claims within religious history. As the NT tells us, he overcomes the astrological forces which as finite things appropriate the numen. What took place symbolically in the victory of the cross took place and still takes place fragmentarily in other places and at other times, and will continue to do so in the future even with no historical or empirical link to the crucifixion.[6] In this sense one might see in Tillich a peculiar mixture of Hegel and the early Apologists (Justin Martyr, Tatian). There is approximation to Hegel insofar as the victory over the demonic that is symbolized in the cross represents in pure form the basic thrust of religious history and is thus the absolute instance of religion—an instance which as a historical event may be completely and not just fragmentarily equated with the idea of religion. There is approximation to the Apologists, it seems to me, insofar as these concede fragments of truth (*logoi spermatikoi*) to the Greek philosophers, who were in some sense religious prophets. From this standpoint Socrates and Heraclitus as well as Abraham were Christians for the Apologists, since they already had these germs of truth. The whole Logos, however, is manifested in Christ. He offers in unabbreviated fulness what the religions and philosophies contain only in fragments.

Perhaps it is not unnecessary to point out that in antithesis to Hegel this special position of the gospel is not "proved" in Tillich. We catch a note of positivistic relativism when Tillich says that this special position is true for us Christians. Might it not be due to the limitation of our own horizons in time and space that this is so (pp. 196f.; E.T. pp. 88f.)?

In spite of his greater closeness to the concrete phenomena of religious history, has Tillich really advanced beyond Hegel?[7] Obviously not. The only point is that encounter with the religions has produced in him the touch of relativism which affected Troeltsch, too, as he made his way through religious history. To be sure,

---

[5] Pp. 196f. (E.T. p. 88).
[6] Pp. 196f. (E.T. pp. 88f.).
[7] It is not so important here that Tillich is closer to German Idealism than, by way of Hegel, to Schelling's philosophy of identity.

the victory over the demonic is only fragmentary and isolated in religious history, whereas in model form it is complete in "Christus Victor." But since religious history goes on, one cannot foresee what it will bring either with or without a historical and empirical link to the cross.[8] For us Christians, i.e., for our place in religious history, the exclusiveness of the model holds good. But the question must remain an open one whether this is only a relative and temporary exclusiveness which will be equalled and even surpassed by other religions. The unconditionality of the Christian experience of truth in faith has to be sought in some other place and not where Tillich seeks it. The attempt to use a hermeneutical principle—even though it be victory over the demonic—to understand and evaluate the religions involves surrender of observation of the incalculable openness of history. (We have seen this already in the case of Schleiermacher.) It is no wonder that Tillich avoids the terms exclusiveness and absoluteness, which for him belong to the dubious sphere of an asserted "true religion."[9] But this should not prevent us from using these terms in a critical investigation of his view of things.

This makes us all the more eager to see how Pannenberg, who holds aloof from Hegel and Tillich, answers the question of the absoluteness and exclusiveness of the gospel. He will have nothing whatever to do with the easy way in which dialectical theology handles this matter without facing religious history. But his academic listing of theology as a discipline within the science of religion arouses some skepticism.[10]

Pannenberg is impressed by the mostly disparate juxtaposition of the religions. He thus rejects the Hegelian view which relates them by way of the common *telos* of the religion of Spirit.[11] Yet he makes a supposedly empirically demonstrated unity of religious history his starting point. This does not mean that he begins by presupposing a speculative principle of unity. In intention at least this would be opposed to what he has in mind. He believes that empirical study of religious history establishes this unity. He finds witness to it in various forms of common growth, of a process of integration among various religious traditions.

Appealing to K. Koch's "Tod des Religionsstifters" (*Kerygma and Dogma,* II [1962]), he shows how the figure of Yahweh develops out of different traditions: the Kenitic Yahweh of Sinai, the God of the exodus, the patriarchal deities (the God of Abraham, Isaac, and Jacob), and El, the God of heaven. Even some functions of Baal have a part in the syncretistic process. Similar syncretisms and integrations may be seen in the development of the Egyptian Amun and the Babylonian Marduk (*loc. cit.*).

Yet these integrative processes did not take place in empirical freedom but under the direction of a speculative slogan—the unity of divine reality itself.[12] The paradigm of primitive Christianity makes this plain. Is this just a fusion of the Judaic and Christian heritages? Does the Logos of John's Gospel express such a

---

[8] *Op. cit.,* p. 197 (E.T. p. 89).

[9] P. 187 (E.T. p. 80).

[10] Pannenberg, *Wissenschaftstheorie und Theologie* (1973), pp. 316ff. and *passim;* E.T. *Theology and the Philosophy of Science* (London, 1976).

[11] *Grundfragen,* p. 265; E.T. *Basic Questions in Theology,* II, p. 81.

[12] Pp. 276f. (E.T. II, p. 95).

synthesis?[13] In reality the Greek-Hellenistic terms are simply vessels for reflection which serve as a container for a third thing, the gospel. Once these terms begin to rule instead of serving and claim kerygmatic significance (1 Corinthians 1:23f.), they are assigned to their proper limits. But when this happens Hellenism and Judaism are not seen in synthesis but in permanent antithesis.

The process of an instrumental use and not a syncretizing of Greek concepts is demonstrated (in Scholastic terms) in the discussion of the NT use of Logos by Jacques Maritain (*An Essay on Christian Philosophy* [New York, 1955]). Preparation was necessary to make it humanly possible to arrive at the essentially supra-philosophical idea of a "Logos consubstantial with the Father." This preparation consisted of the prolonged philosophical discussion of the idea of the Logos. This produced the idea and the term, which prepared the way materially for the revelation of the Son. But the transcendence of the revelation of the Son, which is completely new, shows that it was not the same idea of the Logos. At this point Maritain hints at the problem in every theological statement. It has to use existing terms. But this carries with it the virulent danger that the linguistic media will rebel and try to introduce their own ideological contents. From Paul onward there may thus be seen in the history of theology a permanent struggle to assign to adopted concepts their instrumental limits (cf. R. Röhricht, *Theologie als Hinweis und Entwurf* [1964], esp. pp. 15f.).

In spite of his individual criticisms of Hegel's construction of an evolutionary religious history which contradicts the empirical data, the speculative premise points to more than remnants of Hegel in Pannenberg. These come to expression especially in his concern to explain the unity of religious history by a single principle. This principle is not supposed to be imported into the history. It is not supposed to manifest itself in the core form at the beginning.[14] It finds expression as a conclusion and its reality is manifested in an intensifying trend toward integration. In the iteration of constant critical revision of each of its stages, religious history is the infinite way on which the infinite determination of man for the infinite God moves toward its appropriate realization and on which it is even manifested—as opposed to the self-consciousness of the religions.[15]

If in relation to primitive Christianity we had to ask whether the syncretistic integration of Pannenberg is correct, we must now ask whether this trend toward integration can in fact be read off from the history of religion. Beyerhaus ("Zur Theologie der Religionen . . . ," *op. cit.*, p. 97) has good reason to ask whether detailed analysis does not show that a process of division runs parallel to this process of intermingling and this splits all the higher religions as well as Christianity into a host of small sects. In encounter with Christianity polarization takes place instead of integration, so that, e.g., the messianism that is attained when we meet the gospel takes on a competing and anti-Christian character in the religions (and in political ideologies). The list of similar examples of disintegration can be extended at will.

For Pannenberg the *telos* of integration is connected with an interpretation of

---

[13]*Loc. cit.*
[14]Pp. 264f. (E.T. II, pp. 80f.).
[15]P. 288 (E.T. p. 109).

religious history which understands it as the history of the self-disclosures of an infinite God. An unending series of manifestations may thus be expected in the future.[16] In this God who may be seen within the contrast of the finite and the infinite, the world spirit of Hegel is clearly enough riding again.

Necessarily, then, Christianity is smoothed into religious history so that the question of its special position, its exclusiveness, its antithesis to the religious world, becomes irrelevant (though this does not have to mean a disallowing of its own religious title). This question can have no place in a construction which, as in Pannenberg, regards religious history as an objective process in which the divine mystery that is presupposed in the structure of human existence is manifested but is also at issue.[17] The connection between the divine mystery that comes and the human consciousness that is determined by the question of its basis can be demonstrated and hence does not require any dogmatic formulation. As though man's self-transcendence were objectifiable and without dogmatic presupposition! As though, even assuming objectifiability, the religions were so plainly phenomena in which man's infinite determination for the infinite God moves toward appropriate realization—with no supranatural principles, no reference to the Christian revelation, no interposition of the Christian standpoint.[18]

In contrast to this supposed demonstrability of a "logic" of religious history, which is unlike Hegel's in detail but analogous in schema, a theological expert in empirical religious history like N. Söderblom is incomparably more restrained. As he sees it, the history of religions leaves the question of a revelation open. One can tackle it from various angles. On the one hand a supranatural reality may be seen behind the phenomena of religion. But one can also adopt a questioning, uncertain, or even agnostic attitude. Indeed, one may be fully indifferent in relation to the question whether religion is "true."[19]

As the price of this objectifying phenomenology which Pannenberg later tried to establish epistemologically, the core problem of a theological discussion of religious history had to be abandoned or suppressed as insoluble. This is the question how revelation is to be understood when it cannot be integrated into the sphere of norms of the manifestations of the infinite God but transcends this sphere and becomes a criterion for it. In other words, the exclusiveness or uniqueness of the truth of the gospel can no longer be discussed here.

In contrast it is like a trick—though this is not to impugn its serious purpose—when Pannenberg, always anxiously rejecting any arguing from a standpoint of faith,[20] tries to regain the position of a Christian theologian with the help of the thesis that the idea of his God who is manifested in religious history could hardly arise without reference to the God of the Bible and his eschatological revelation in Jesus Christ.[21] For the God of whom Jesus spoke is the power that changes his earlier manifestations and thus stands in the background of the constant upward

---

[16]*Loc. cit.*
[17]P. 290 (E.T. II, p. 111).
[18]Pp. 293f. (E.T. II, pp. 115f.).
[19]N. Söderblom, *Der lebendige Gott . . .* , p. 372.
[20]Pannenberg, p. 290 (E.T. II, p. 112).
[21]*Loc. cit.*

trend which may be noted in religious history. In him the *telos* of this history may be seen, for as the power of the future, thought of in terms of its futurity and coming, he cannot be surpassed by any other future, by any new experience of God. In this eschatological power one may see that all new experiences of the divine mystery are to be understood only as new forms of manifestation of himself. They are to be seen, then, in the light of that *telos*.

To this extent the God of the coming divine kingdom whom Jesus proclaimed precedes all later epochs of the history of the church and of non-Christian religions. He is the anticipation of that toward which religious history presses as its *telos*. At this point one may ask whether this is not a secretly introduced dogmatic thesis, or at any rate a standpoint of faith.

Jesus himself becomes on this view a mere point of transition for the eschatological event. He is the revealer of the infinite God only insofar as he points away from his own person to the coming rule of God. He did not tie the infinite God to his own finite person but sacrificed his person in obedience to his mission.[22] As in Lessing's *Education of the Human Race*,[23] he was just a pacemaker in relation to other religions, but with no qualitative difference. The deficiency in the other religions as compared with Jesus is derived by Pannenberg from the objectifiable observation that they fall short of what they ought to be by constantly imposing finite limits on the concept and worship of God.[24] This is their demonstrable "brokenness" which the eschatological horizon of the proclamation of Jesus transcends.

We conclude, then, that hardly anything can be said here about looking at the history of religion theologically. The pacemaker Christ who is a kind of corrective on the margin of religious history cannot by a long way justify missionary work in the name of a quality which shows him to be in contrast with all natural knowledge of God, whether in the sense of Romans 1:18ff. or Acts 17:22ff. On this basis mission must be replaced by a dialogue with the religions in which—in the style of the early Apologists—Christians confront them with the question whether the truth that is fragmentary in them does not appear in fulness in the gospel. (It is not disputed that mission may involve dialogue of this or a similar kind, though not as its main point, and that it may pursue these questions and approaches to life instead of being content to proclaim a mere "God has said.")

At any rate the claim of the Johannine Christ that he is the way, the truth, and the life (John 14:6) is a check which this view does not and cannot cover.

The poet Hölderlin foundered on this question of the uniqueness of Jesus, who in a banal solution is here seen only in his reduced anticipatory significance as a pacemaker. In a late poem called "The Unique One" (1802) Hölderlin refers to the tension between exclusiveness and kinship which marks Christ's relation to the religions or the gods. He does so in a way which leaves no room for either speculation or a numinous feeling as a means of seeing Golgotha and Olympus together.

Hölderlin says first that Christ is of equal rank with his brother-gods under their

---

[22]P. 292 (E.T. II, p. 114).
[23]Cf. Thielicke, *Offenbarung . . .* , pp. 63ff.
[24]Pannenberg, p. 293 (E.T. II, p. 115).

common Father on high. But Christ refuses to be put in the circle of the gods. The poet with horror sees the conflict in himself. He cannot love Christ as freely as the other gods. He knows that Christ is the brother of Heracles and Dionysus but he cannot compare the Savior and these worldly men. What is clear to knowledge is rejected by piety. Hölderlin tries to convince himself that God is not just the Father of Christ but also sent the gods of antiquity. He mirrored himself in them and accepted union with men through their mediation. He did this in a series of emanations. But if he asks the ancient gods about Christ they hide him, and if he asks Christ about his brother-gods he refuses to be counted among them.

Hölderlin does not discuss the reason for this incompatibility (what we here call the exclusiveness of Christ). He offers no speculative reasons for or against it. He simply says that his inability to achieve reconciliation fills him with sadness. He fears that the heavenly beings will be angry with him because he cannot serve them all or put them together. He regards this as a fault. He confesses that his failure is due to his being caught up in worldly affairs. Even poets are worldly. Though their concern is for the Spirit they cannot escape worldly entanglement. What he means by this is not sensual bondage but the limitation of knowledge and vision which is part of being human.

In a later version of the same poem Hölderlin seems to overcome his helplessness to some extent. He even sounds notes which seem to be echoed in Pannenberg's ideas about the *telos*. It is here that he offers his vision of a "clover-leaf" of heroes. Christ has the free and loving manner of heaven whereas the others are more like mortal gods. Hölderlin does not abandon faith in the unity of the world. But is that which he longs for really faith? There are hints of insight into a world order in the background. Heracles is the hero who orders chaotic nature, Dionysus is the enthusiastically reconciling common spirit, while Christ brings the fulness of the earthly presence of the heavenly. He is the "end" who makes up the lack of the presence of the heavenly in the others.

Here again one might perhaps say that the fulness of the religions is anticipated in Christ and that the Father of Jesus Christ embraces the gospel and religion in his identity. But it is an open question where Hölderlin disclosed the greater and real truth for him, in his failure to bring Christ and the gods together as the one numen or in his concern to achieve the longed for unity of a cosmic background and to see in Christ the fulness of what the gods have only as fragments. (In interpreting the poem the author is indebted to W. Michel, *Das Leben F. Hölderlins* [1963], esp. pp. 435ff., for some essential clues.)

A. Evaluation of the Interpretation of the History of Religion and Attempt at a Legitimate Understanding of Exclusiveness

XXVI

On Understanding Religion and the Religions

1. STARTING POINT

We have seen on what presuppositions the question of the exclusiveness of the truth of Christian revelation not only cannot be answered but in some circumstances cannot even be raised because it would be absurd. When the latter situation arises some schema is always presupposed into which the gospel and the religions are set. The result of such a schema is (1) that both are brought under an all-comprehensive evolution (Hegel), or (2) that both are set in a steplike (e.g., moral) world-order (Lessing), or (3) that both are interpreted as projections of human existence (Feuerbach), or (4) that the two come into antithesis in an abstract polarity of time and eternity, of this world and the kingdom of God, of truth and falsehood (Barth), so that it is useless to put the question of absoluteness and exclusiveness to a world of religion which is seen pejoratively from the very outset and cannot engage in dialogue.

Alternatives (1) and (2) make it possible to give Christianity a top position[1] along the lines of Troeltsch, Harnack, Kittel, and others, but in principle there is no room for qualitative difference in the sense of exclusiveness, even though the author concerned may not see this.

Alternatives (3) and (4)—for very different reasons—make the question of a top position or of absoluteness a wholly pointless one.

If we for our part want to ask concerning the uniqueness of what Christian faith believes to be truth, we cannot do so without first developing in the light of this truth an understanding of the religions which confront the gospel. Only on this basis can the gospel and the religions be seen both in relationship and distinction. In doing this we have to guard against the various schemata either of coordinating integration or of disqualifying separation. To enable us to recognize the danger of

---

[1]In the parable of the rings in *Nathan* there is fundamental equality.

schematizing which will always prejudice the result we have already stated and discussed our typology of religious criticism. This was a preliminary exercise in locating sources of error.

We begin with some theses on the understanding of religion in which we shall take up and develop the insights won in our criticism.

2. THESES ON THE CONCEPT OF RELIGION

1. Religion is the transparency of what encounters us as final reality or what Tillich calls ultimate concern. In religion I experience and express a reference to the basis of reality. I see myself compelled to confess that this final reality has gripped me and that I must now pursue it with all that I am and do. Seizure and pursuit express themselves in the varied forms of adoration, worship, and practical life.[2]

What encounters us and becomes transparent in this way can be very diverse. It can be a historical event or a complex of events in which is manifested the blind power of *tychō* or moira, or a planned teleology, or the personal will of a judge. It can be nature in its fruitfulness or fearfulness. It can be magic, a secular thing which in the style of *mana* enables me to share the power of the gods.

The transparency of what encounters us can thus be experienced in the most varied ways, in the ecstasy of the experience of not being conditioned, or in the rationality of metaphysical reflection,[3] in receptivity to signs, as in the various forms of what are called nature-religions, or in the setting up of signs, of cultic ciphers, as in every form of developed liturgical ceremonial.

This variety makes it possible (and may induce us today) to seek the social conditioning and function of the religious in these forms of experience. Thus E. Durkheim finds in religion a socially available ensemble of normative and cognitive definitions of reality which function as common reference-points for social action. These go back to a collective and comprehensive experience of reality. In calling this religion he seems to have in mind a world-view (E. Durkheim, *Les formes de la vie religieuse* [Paris, 1960]; E.T. *The Elementary Forces of the Religious Life* [London, 1915]; also, with M. Mauss, *Primitive Classification* [Chicago, 1963]). Similarly T. Luckmann (*Das Problem der Religion in der modernen Gesellschaft* [1963], p. 36; E.T. *The Invisible Religion* [New York, 1967]) says that religion as the integrated meaning of the social order is something objective, namely, an expressible, intelligible, and communicable work to which the individual is oriented as a political being and from which he can read off the meaning of his individual existence. Seen functionally in this way religion is to be understood as transcendent meaning. The general and basic form of religion is originally nothing other than the meaningful structure of the social order, the inner form of the world-view of a society.

Finally, ultimate reality can be interpreted in many ways, as basis or abyss, as

---

[2]Ebeling is moving in the same direction when he defines religion as the historically conditioned and variegated veneration of a manifestation of the mysteries of reality ("Evangelium und Religion," p. 251).

[3]Cf. Spinoza.

power or value, or as a complex of final entities such as R. Otto analyzed in his concept of the numinous.

2. Man's ability to be aware of this transparency of what encounters him rests on his memory of an original contact, a previous fellowship with the final reality that meets him now in sign. Only because he comes from this original contact is he conscious of the presence of the final reality hidden in the sign.

If we use the term "memory" (*anamnēsis*) to interpret the phenomenon of religion theologically, it is primarily to indicate that we do not have in religion a creative activity of man that is related to poetry, nor an act of projection in Feuerbach's sense. Instead man is here the object of something that comes to him.[4] He experiences this as one who knows that he is at a distance from it. He is aware of this distance as something that is to be overcome, for he recognizes that he was originally in union with what encounters him.

The word "memory" as the epitome of this recognition bears witness to the authenticity of what encounters him—as opposed to illusionary projection and invention—and also to the history of a relationship with it.

3. To the phenomenology of religion belongs the observation that what encounters us continually loses its transparency and the sign itself comes to be taken for the final reality. What encounters us, the holy, is thus locked up in the finite instead of being attested by it. We can be assured of the assent of Roman Catholic theology if we say that in some forms of popular piety the veneration of images becomes the worship of images.

There are many ways in which the holy can be made finite.

(1) It happens when magic regards a thing, animal, tree, or person as charged with *mana*.

(2) It happens when myth, as existential hermeneutics has shown, presents an understanding of existence and the world in narrative form, especially as a story of the gods. Myth is meant to be a symbolical transparency and it demands interpretation. But instead of being taken as a means it can become an end in itself. This happens in two main forms. First, the mythical images and persons are treated historically as though we had here real (finite) events. Thus Dionysus and Apollo cease to represent dimensions of being and are taken for what they are in themselves.[5] Second, the myth is no longer understood as a mere form of expression for an underlying kerygma but itself becomes the kerygma. We have expressly dealt with this in Volume I.[6]

(3) The crassest way in which the holy is made finite is when it is ideologized, i.e., allotted a purely pragmatic function, whether it be that of offering the comfort of an afterlife and thus bringing about the antirevolutionary pacification of those who threaten to revolt against their social plight, or whether it be that of bringing about a politically desired unity and philosophical homogeneity.[7]

4. We have stated already that we have here something that needs to be understood

---

[4]In our debate with Feuerbach we expressed this by opposing a theomorphism of reality to his anthropomorphism.

[5]Cf. W. F. Otto, *Die Götter Griechenlands;* E.T. *The Homeric Gods* (London, 1954).

[6]EG, I, pp. 95ff., esp. p. 97; EF, I, pp. 84ff.

[7]On ideologizing cf. ThE, II, 2, §§154ff.; E.T. II, pp. 84ff. On the corresponding degeneration of Christianity cf. §§375ff., 418ff.; E.T. II, pp. 26ff., 62ff.

theologically and not psychologically. We thus return for yet another time to the classical passage in which Paul analyzes it (Romans 1:18ff.).[8] Along the lines of our present discussion one might say that this provides the reason why man shatters the transparency of the finite and tries to lock up God's eternity in it. This happens because the creature man has lost contact with him who wills to shine through here. The creature has not honored or thanked the Creator. He suppresses the truth of the Creator and will not recognize his creaturely dependence and obligation. Thus the process of creation is reversed and in the true sense perverted. Man no longer wants to be God's image. He makes God in his own image. He fashions him in such a way that he fits in smoothly and exerts no pressure. This God who is modelled on man himself no longer calls him in question but simply confirms him. We have in fact an expression of his pride when he thus seeks to validate his total self-determination by this manipulation of the concept of God.

Awareness of this perversion is what constantly leads the OT prophets to heap scorn on the impotence of the gods that are made by man, on their unreality—they are called "nothings"—on the inability of idols of wood and stone and even gold to hear, to answer, to intervene in human affairs. If they are still powers, this is not due to their ontic force—they are "nothings" in this regard—but to man's relationship and bondage to them. We dealt with this understanding of idols in Volume I (EG, I, pp. 108ff.; EF, I, pp. 96ff.) and shall content ourselves with this brief reference here.

In spite of the unreality of manufactured gods, in spite of the reversal of Creator and creature, and in spite of the functional dependence of the gods on the creature, the gods are still supreme. In the category of the dynamic, then, they have privileges. This is why the process of reversal cannot be described merely in terms of ontological thinking. For this enables us to speak only of their ontic power without being aware of the basis on which it rests. For Paul the true basis lies in the realm of personal categories. In face of his refusal of self-limitation as a creature, in face of his rejection of the obligation of obedience, and in face of his suppression of guilt and of the need of forgiveness, man protects himself by making gods that resemble himself.

Here and here alone we see the element which relatively justifies the intrinsically far too massive and wholesale theory of projection. It describes the making of the gods in the image of man.[9] The fact that man constantly finds himself forced into this process of projection, that the development of religion seems to be one of the characteristic marks of human nature, is not just to be explained as self-objectification, as in Feuerbach. The process is complex. It presupposes that God's self-disclosure has been imparted to man as an event, that God has made finite creation a transparency for his deity (*theiotēs,* Romans 1:20).[10] This is why religion is not simply man's action but his reaction to an experience, to a revelation, to the work of the Pneuma. Before he ever claimed to be subject by making God in his image man was first the object of an event. Religion does not just derive

---

[8]Cf. also Wisdom 13:1–9.

[9]In antiquity Aristophanes made fun of the humanity of Homer's gods.

[10]P. Althaus refers in this connection to primal revelation. We avoid this term, not because it is not appropriate, but because it suggests the "natural theology" with which it is linked in Althaus.

from man's creativity. It is a product of his reaction to an original pneumatic experience of the *theiotēs* of God which was imparted to him in a prior stage of commitment to the Word.

For Paul, then, the generative impulse in every religion is this memory (*anamnēsis*) of a preceding ultimate reality which does not leave itself without a witness. Only man's repudiation of his allotted role of being only man and not superman or "like God" (Genesis 3:22) leads to the depicted process of repression which perverts the memory of God's *theiotēs* into a projection of the image of man and gives primacy to man in his partnership with God. Man says with Nietzsche, "If there is a God, how can I bear not to be God?" and it thus comes about that the madman is finally left acting alone on the stage.[11]

In religion, then, we do not have the creative action of man in the sense that he made God, but in the name of man's self-protection and justification we have his reaction to something that encounters him and his perverting of the concept of God.

5. One of the places where man experiences this encounter is the frontier situation. As the term indicates, the question of final reality arises especially on the horizons of human existence, in suffering, disaster, death, extreme anxiety, and the confrontation with what seems to be meaningless—in short, in situations of trial which usually pose the question of theodicy. Situations of this kind are crucial points for religion because they have a special measure of transparency for the final reality in its significance as omnipotence, destiny, judgment, and eternity far transcending our finite existence.

We see from Revelation, one of whose themes is the eschatological structure of these situations, that even in these crisis "hours" of religion the transparency can be lost and the "home-seeking" element in it may not be perceived. We read constantly that "they did not repent" but refused the proffered message (Revelation 2:21; 9:20, 21; 16:9, 11).[12] The situations thus lose their significance as visitations, or, better, it is taken from them. They are integrated into self-resting finitude and lead either to defiance as a form of arrogance or, among moderns, to nihilism, i.e., the acceptance of blind fate (*tychē*).

Yet even when religious man remains open to the transparency of such situations and extols (and exploits homiletically) their religious fruitfulness, transparency is lost in another way as man removes the actuality of final reality from the center of life with its celebration and joy and love of life. Sermons play on the atom bomb and airplane crashes and earthquakes because only a reference to the *numen tremendum* seems to produce an effective shock and lead to a desire for repentance and a readiness for salvation. Here psychological calculation becomes a mode of human action which replaces that which comes upon us. It thus destroys transparency.[13]

---

[11]Cf. the section on Nietzsche in EG, I, pp. 354ff.; EF, I, pp. 249ff.

[12]Cf. the role of Pharaoh in Luther's *Bondage of the Will*.

[13]Possibly this lies behind Bonhoeffer's demand that we are to seek God at the center of life and not on the margins. But the perverted use of frontier situations causes him to throw out the baby with the bath water and discredit these situations as such, as we have seen.

3. MODEL: THE AREOPAGUS ADDRESS

When the first Christian witnesses arose with the message that we find in the NT, they spoke in a world which was full of religion. Naturally, to make themselves understood, the NT witnesses used the terms and concepts of this religious world and even addressed the feeling for life of those who were religious in this way. Thus the preacher on the Areopagus in Acts 17:22ff. says to the Athenians: ''I have wandered through your city, observed your forms of worship, and found an altar with the inscription: 'To the unknown God.' I now proclaim to you the one to whom without knowledge you bring your worship.'' When Paul says this, he is speaking to people whom we usually call polytheists, although they were this in a heavily secularized sense attenuated by philosophical enlightenment. Concerned lest they might have forgotten one of the gods, they had put up an altar to this unknown X. What Paul is in effect saying according to the account in Acts is that he will complete for them this garland of deities around the decisive figure whom they have indeed missed. He will tell them about the true Creator of heaven and earth and the Father of Jesus Christ.

What happens, then, is this. According to Luke, the preacher first integrates his message into the religious structure of polytheism. Naturally he does not think that the message about Christ can be fitted into general religious and Stoic categories. But he has a socratic purpose. If the Athenians—though only with the religious categories available to them—are at all ready to receive the message of Christ, if they will first receive him into the circle of their deities, then the authority of this Christ will burst open the initial schema from within. They will be set before the problem which we encountered in Hölderlin's poem ''The Unique One.'' Receiving Christ into the circle of the Olympian gods is impossible. To put it abstractly, integrating him into a religious formula destroys the formula.

The Hellenistic character of the address shows how far what we have here is a screen, a pseudonymous form of speech after the manner of Socrates or Kierkegaard. A scholar like M. Dibelius can say[14] that this is a Hellenistic speech with a Christian conclusion. With its rational character, which is assimilated to Stoicism, it leaves the NT pattern. It is alien to it. Dibelius, it seems to me, recognizes the intentional foray into the pagan world even though he does not put the fundamental theological problem which this entails.[15]

At any rate, the reaction of the hearers justifies the socratic intention. For the offense that develops at once shows that the Athenians identified Christians behind the front of their own tradition. They had a keener sense of what was happening than many later historians, who find here only a Christian address with a harmless Christian appendix, a degree of assimilation which is more like absorption by the pagan schema which is addressed.

The important thing is to recognize that what we have is a methodological problem that is not without significance for missionary approaches to other religions. The speaker uses the words of his religious background in such a measure and to such an extent that he makes allowance for a syncretistic interim, a phase in

---

[14]*Paulus auf dem Areopag* (1939), pp. 36ff., 56.

[15]He simply says (p. 56) that Luke had Paul preach in a leading Greek city as he thought people ought to preach to the Greeks in his own day, i.e., with philosophical proofs, a relative recognition of Greek polytheism, and an appeal to the wisdom expressed by the Greek poets.

his preaching which to those outside and to later historians looks like a fusion of the Christian message of salvation with the world around, i.e., like a Hellenistic address.

Similarly, even the Christian concept of the Savior (*sōtēr*) was common in Hellenism before and outside Christianity and was taken over from it. Ideas and concepts from the Gnostic redeemer-myth were pressed into service in order to describe the figure of Jesus Christ and the nature and work of his community.[16] Motifs from Stoic theology and ethics were used as schemata in which the Christian message found expression and to which it attached itself.

Whether one finds syncretism here or a kerygma which, being wholly other, is not tied to traditional forms of expression but uses them only instrumentally, depends on two factors.

First, it depends on whether we really have here only the instrumental use of these forms of thought and expression, whether there is only verbal accommodation to Hellenistic and other hearers, and not also a material assimilation to their religion—as there sometimes has been and still is. Accommodation relates only to the address on the letter, not to its contents.[17] If the contents are syncretistically assimilated and levelled down, then the holy is made finite, the form of expression is elevated above what is expressed, and the transparency which should let something else shine through is lost.

Second, discovery of that "wholly other" kerygma depends on the readers and hearers. Only those who are gripped by the kerygma will be able to recognize it under its alien cover and to relativize this cover. Those who are distant and uncommitted spectators will see only syncretistic conglomerates.

A good example of the way that Jesus himself used the concepts and ideas of the pagan and semi-pagan world around him, but still left them transparent for what is made clear by and with them, may be found in Mark's account of the woman with the flow of blood (Mark 5:25–34). This woman comes behind Jesus and seeks magical healing by touching his garment. For her—how pagan!—he is a redeemer-figure in a world of magic. Jesus accepts this notion and speaks in magical fashion of power leaving him at her touch. He does not correct her notion even though it is alien and indeed antithetical to the gospel. Instead, he turns to her and grants her healing and peace. He, too, claims for a moment what we have called the syncretistic interim. He can do this with the certainty that his personal address will make the alien magical notion transparent for his true and unique being. He met the woman where she was but did not stay there or confirm her magical world. Instead he led her out of that world to himself.

4. EPILOGUE: SURVEY OF APPARENT RELIGIONLESSNESS (EXAMPLE: GOTTFRIED BENN)

A fundamental problem to which we shall briefly turn might be formulated as follows in relation to the problem of accommodation.

What does it mean for the Christian message if it can no longer be directed, as in

---

[16]Cf. R. Bultmann, *Das Urchristentum im Rahmen der antiken Religion* (1949), p. 197; E.T. *Primitive Christianity in its Contemporary Setting* (New York, 1956), p. 198.
[17]Cf. Volume I, Index "Accommodation."

the Areopagus address, to a distinctly religious world, but has to be given to a world that to a large extent is—apparently—religionless, and if the nature of the presentation cannot remain unaffected by this supposed or real religionlessness? This question of a vocabulary that is divorced from religion arises—at least as a question—if we want to act today as the primitive Christian witnesses did in their way and situation.

The problem contains two further questions.

The first is whether the statement that there are religionless people can be the subject of statistical and analytical investigation. Is not the question really a theological one that we have discussed already, namely, whether religion as man's transcendental reference does not have an indelible character, just as the ontic relation of man to God has this character, no matter whether the religion or relation can be empirically proved or is noetically accepted? When Bonhoeffer overlooked this basic question and noted only the recognizable presence or absence of religion he reduced the theme of religion to questions of consciousness and related it only to particular epochs. It was in this sense that the present epoch seemed to him to be religionless.

Second, even granted that there are religionless or semi-religionless periods (from the phenomenological standpoint), and even granted that proclamation must accept this and offer a secular interpretation of the biblical message, will not the message which goes out and does not return empty reconstruct religious schemata? Will it not—I am bold to ask—create a religious style and produce cultic and liturgical forms which may be very different from the conventional ones? Will not religion reappear in this way?

In spite of the indelible character of religion it is (phenomenologically) a mark of the nihilism so prevalent among us[18] that the question of the meaning of life is secondary to that of ends. Thus the question of final reality, the religious question, is not just given a negative answer in many circles but it is not even put, perhaps because a negative answer is expected. An example of this silence may be found in the work of G. Benn.

If we ask why this work has such a fascination for secular intellectuals, it is too trivial simply to speak of its poetic rank, its basic images, and its staccato style ("lyrical rhapsodical eruptions," H. E. Holthusen). Its suggestive power of expression is a result rather than a cause of the fascination. It is the symptom of a deeply wounded existence which radiates magnetism as such. When man is hurt and under ultimate threat he seems to long for homoeopathic consolidations, for something similar to his own incurability. He hopes he will receive comfort by finding a poetic companion in pain. In a different way the saying in the passion hymn applies here too: Wounds must heal wounds. The objectifying of incurability in poetic statements offers freedom from the complex of a dull sense of hopelessness and serves as a kind of catharsis. Hence the fascination for Benn's person and work has tremendous significance as a sign of the times. (Naturally other signs of this type could also be used as examples.)

The humanity depicted here is perplexed and alien and alone in its world (in obvious kinship to the solipsism of Sartre). The trumpets of the night are heard in

---

[18]Cf. EG, I, pp. 355ff.; EF, I, pp. 249ff.

this world (cf. Kafka). Its horizon is surrounded by chaos and the Midgard serpent. It would be mere weakness to try to put meaning in it, to try to help out with the "as if" of Vaihinger, because we are too weak to accept resignation and futility. The only meaningful thing for Benn is the creative work of art which for a moment brings ordered form into the flood of chaos (cf. ThE, III, §3123).

The question naturally arises again whether the indelible character of religion may not be seen in the fact that in creative work the sphere of the unconditioned finds a place in a chaotic and futile world. For we see here the relation to the unconditioned even if it is not viewed as a religious relation by the author. Yet even if we do regard creative work as the sphere of a religious reference in this sense, it would be wrong to subsume this kind of religion under a common term which also embraces a cultic relation to the unconditioned. We have to make a distinction here between voluntary religion and the involuntary religion which will be perceived only by someone who understands an author like Benn better than he understands himself.

Luther in his exposition of the first commandment said that that on which our heart hangs and trusts is really our God. It is thus our religion too. This is true at least if what is being said is that I can never break away from my ontic relation to God and that positively or negatively I always live out this relation. But one has to ask whether it can be brought into agreement with general usage if I define as religion the relationship of the heart which plainly does not wish to be related to God (even though it is so ontically). If I do call it religion, and make a rule to this effect, then manifestly the concept of religionlessness at once becomes absurd.

If Benn in his famous address on the problem of older people and art (*Merkur*, No. 74 [1954]) can say in face of the threat of nothingness: "With their backs to the wall, in the pain of weariness, in the horror of emptiness they read Job and Jeremiah and endure," he obviously does not mean that Job and Jeremiah have any message of salvation in the theological sense. As he sees it, they are both people who live in a hurt and hopeless world and who hold on only with a Nevertheless—more like the soldiers of Pompeii in Spengler than OT men of God as the Bible depicts them. The comfort that Job and Jeremiah have to offer is just the same as what makes Benn himself a comforter to many. They do not find comfort in the divine promise that they receive—this is unattainable for Benn—but they comfort one another through the despairing existence to which they are abandoned on the human level and which enables them to find a foothold of solidarity according to Benn.

What will be the form of Christian proclamation in accommodation or address to those who regard themselves as religionless and confronted with nothingness? It will certainly express more than sympathy or solidarity in the pain of weariness and the horror of emptiness. If it were not more than that it would simply extol the creative provocation of sorrow and nothingness. God (if he can be spoken of at all) would be locked up in finitude. Suffering and nothingness would lose again their transparency for the *theiotēs* of God and its summons. They would be given the rank of final reality as ends in themselves.[19] There would have to be contact and restoration here too. Hebrews speaks of the sympathy of Christ our High Priest

---

[19]Cf. the Sisyphus myth in Albert Camus (EF, I and II, Index).

who is tempted as we are (4:15). According to the oldest account the last saying of Jesus on the cross speaks of his testing by dereliction (Mark 15:34). God accommodates himself in fellow-suffering to the man who is assaulted by nothingness and meaninglessness. His condescension to man's destiny is motivated by love. But being condescension it transcends this destiny just as the Pneuma transcends psychic emotions. The power of redemption is at work to free us from our destiny. The station on the cross which is that of despairing confrontation with nothingness is only a transitional one.[20] It remains transparent for the rule of the Lord of this situation, for the proclamation of his liberating address.

This affirmation is most important not only for preaching but also for pastoral care.[21] Group dynamics and psychologically structured exercises in dialogue follow a pattern in which the concern of the listener (or confessor) is to show the understanding and solidarity of a partner who reflects and repeats the problem that is entrusted to him and seeks to stimulate spontaneous self-disclosure in this way. In Christian counselling this solidarity can be no more than a first and transitional step. It will mark the place of contact where we cannot stay but from which attention must be directed to the efficacious Word, to forgiveness and pardon. The situation of need is left open as a transparency for him who sends the problem and wants his summons to be heard in it. The dark valleys as well as the mountains are to magnify his glory. It is to be feared that secular techniques of understanding not only aid Christian counselling—which is good—but can also thwart it, so that the idea of accommodation loses its Christian point and the winning back of those who regard themselves as religionless becomes self-deception. The place of meeting is not seen as a transitional station but is made into a definitive dwelling place. The proclamation of solidarity becomes a new form of secular religion.

---

[20]Cf. EG, II, pp. 475ff.; EF, II, pp. 385ff.
[21]Cf. C. Rogers.

XXVII

The Special Feature in the Truth of Revelation

1. DEAD ENDS IN SEEKING THE SPECIAL FEATURE

If we are not to have the decree of a dogmatic "God says it" but evidence of a truth of revelation to which the Spirit bears witness, this witness cannot be independent of those to whom it is given. We have shown to what extent revelation is bound up with accommodation. We have shown that the latter is validated by the condescension of God, by the incarnation of Jesus Christ, by his cross and passion. Outside the sphere of a rigid sectarian orthodoxy there has never been any proclamation, let alone missionary preaching, which has not in some way addressed the recipients.

We took the Areopagus address as an example. For the relation between the commands of God and the receiving conscience cf. ThE, I, §§1643-73; E.T. I, pp. 321-25; EG, I, pp. 177ff.; EF, I, pp. 138ff.

Kierkegaard has given us the most profound analysis of the relation of Christ to humanity in his *Concluding Unscientific Postscript* to the *Philosophical Fragments.* The human possibility of religion and the new relation to God mediated by revelation are set over against one another by Climacus as Religion A and Religion B. The first puts man in a process which carries him beyond the ethical but only in such a way that while he refers all the impulses and moments of his finite life to the absolute relation with God, he is also aware that he resists this relation and is unable to put it into effect. What he attains beyond the ethical is simply a deepening of his sense of guilt. He may worship, but his worship is constantly beset by offense at God, resistance, and fear.

In the new relation to God shaped by Christian faith and called Religion B by Climacus, all the elements in A are adopted. Thus the new thing in the Christian life is attached to the old. It builds on the old and uses it as a presupposition. But it is also a "wholly other" which does not complete the process but comes into it from another direction. For unlike Religion A the reconciliation received here does not come from human inwardness but is received from God as a pneumatic miracle by the new birth. Thus the sense of sin is radicalized but certainty of forgiveness is also received, an unconditional desire for purity of heart is kindled, and so, too, is a readiness to renounce any attempt at self-validation before God.

In a detailed dialectic of which only a sketch can be given here Kierkegaard explains how revelation addresses religious man and aims at his existing consciousness—using his antennae, as one might put it—but also transcends this and strips him of his own possibilities by the miracle of regeneration.

Revelation is never to be understood as an act in itself. As a message addressed to man it stands in correlation with its recipient and his prior understanding—even though it goes beyond this understanding and radically alters it.[1] This pre-understanding is essentially characterized by the fact that man is a being that transcends itself[2] and asks concerning destiny and meaning, being thus referred to a mystery which is above his finitude and forms the fulfilment of his existence. In saying this we point to a structure of being which in the light of our earlier discussion may be called religious in the ontological (not the noetic) sense.

This observation raises the question whether an anthropological structure of this kind does not offer itself as a criterion—even perhaps an objective criterion—for the truth-content of the religions and therefore for the special feature in the truth of Christian revelation. Might it not serve as criterion to the degree that it helps us to answer the question whether this or that religion does or does not do justice to the reference, grounded in the very structure of existence, to the basis, goal, and meaning, to the eternal, to that which transcends our finitude? Or does it perfectly fulfil this reference (as Christians assume that the biblical revelation does)?[3] Certainly this anthropological criterion would claim the whole of human existence and avoid one-sided restriction to moral or rational (the Enlightenment) or religious (Schleiermacher) criteria. But does this mean that we are on the right track?

Two difficulties block our path.

First, when we survey the anthropological pre-understanding—transcendence— as a point of contact both for religion and for revelation in the Christian sense, we make a remarkable discovery. In clarifying this we shall limit ourselves to the Christian sphere, for the history of theology places some striking examples at our disposal.

Wherever the anthropological pre-understanding is investigated theologically it is with the goal of discovering hermeneutical presuppositions for the understanding of revelation. The center of interest is the correlation between revelation and our consciousness, whether in the relating of the two as question and answer or in an attempt to show why the message of salvation concerns us unconditionally, why it reaches home to us. This attempt underlies, e.g., both the existential interpretation of Bultmann and Tillich's principle of correlation.[4]

Used in this way the criterion of consciousness is meant to establish the in-

---

[1] On Bultmann's concept of the pre-understanding, which we have rejected, cf. EF, I, Index.
[2] Cf. Anthrop, pp. 218, 393 *passim*.
[3] Kierkegaard hints at the inadequacy of this criterion when he says that the provisional Religion A can be the presupposition but not the norm of Religion B.
[4] Cf. EG, I, p. 39; EF, I, pp. 48f.

telligibility of the kerygma and thus to eliminate its distance from us as an authoritarian "God says it" or as a transcendent work of the Pneuma. But in fact it can block the coming of the kerygma to us. For surreptitiously this criterion threatens to become a normative court instead of a hermeneutical aid, filtering into the content of revelation and letting it reach us only in reduced form. The presuppositions of our consciousness become conditions that must be fulfilled if the content of revelation is to be acceptable to us. What does not apply unconditionally in terms of these presuppositions is irrelevant to us. Along these lines what ought to help open up our consciousness to the content of revelation enables this consciousness to exercise dictatorship over the content.

We are thus placed yet again before a fact already noted, namely, the use of a schema of encounter between revelation and consciousness which does not remain a mere framework but itself becomes the content. This process, which calls in question the anthropological criterion, has been expressly described in our debate with Bultmann.[5] But what proves to be questionable in defining the relation between revelation and consciousness can hardly be used to discover a criterion for the uniqueness or exclusiveness of the truth of Christian revelation. What we have here—although not in the same sense as in Troeltsch—is a schema which subjects both the gospel and the religions to the same existential investigation and levels them down in advance in the name of this schema.

Second, there is the difficulty that to make the basic anthropological structure the criterion for the truth-content of revelation and the religions is to build on a basic structure (especially self-transcendence) which is not an objective reality that can serve as a fixed standard.[6] Might there not be views of man in which it is treated as doubtful? It can apply only where the unconditionality of the individual, the "infinite value of the human soul" (Harnack), is upheld. This emphasis on unconditionality makes sense only where the individual sees himself related to the unconditional, to an ultimate reality. Hence an anthropology like that of Marxist Leninism, which merges the individual into a collective,[7] does not find any place for the relation to the unconditional even as a question, let alone as the content of an anthropological thesis.

In my conversation with the Japanese Zen-Master Hoseki, to which I referred earlier, the same problem arose on a different philosophical level. In talking about archery (cf. E. Herrigel, *Zen und die Kunst des Bogenschiessens* [1948]; E.T. *Zen and the Art of Archery* [New York, 1953]) and the mystery of meditative and not athletic accuracy, he said to me: "The archer is one with the bow, the arrow is one with the mark, and the bow is one with the arrow." On this mystical view of the primal contact of all elements of being, it is possible for the archer, arrow, and mark to become one because they already are one. The unparalleled skill of the mystically trained bowman is not the result, as in Western thought, of a struggle with the mark which he is trying to hit but of a union with it. It repeats and makes present an existing unity.

---

[5]EG, I, pp. 54ff.; EF, I, pp. 57ff.
[6]I have the impression that Pannenberg treats the basic anthropological structure as an axiomatic, indisputable, and universally valid reality.
[7]Anthrop, pp. 267ff.

There is thus needed a surrender of the self as an independent factor that stands in opposition to the mark. The I has to become a formless self. If it is objected that this rules out all encounter and communication between the I and the Thou, the answer is that we have here a total communication between the I and the totality of being in all its elements. In contrast, the Christian certainty that the I attains uniqueness by its reference to the unconditioned, to its alien dignity, means that on this view the self is lost in the totality of being (in the name of "one and all").

The basic difference between Christian anthropology and Zen anthropology is clarified by their different views of the Word and Spirit.

For Christians the Word is the basis of fellowship between God and man and also between man and man. But for Zen it has only a peripheral rank and even no rank at all. For in the Word speakers are given their own distinct profiles. (One is reminded of the polar significance of the Word in judgment and grace.) As the medium between a specific I and a specific Thou, the Word both binds and separates, accentuating otherness. When the two melt into one another and lose their identity the Word becomes superfluous and gives way to silence.

This is exactly what happens in Zen-Buddhism. It removes the distinction between I and Thou, enlightened man being aware that originally and mysteriously, with no cooperation on his part, he is related to all men and all creatures and melts into this original relationship (Herrigel, *Der Zen-Weg* [1958], pp. 123f.).

Pneumatologically the same difference may be seen. As we have seen (EG, I, pp. 244ff.; EF, I, pp. 181ff.), the Holy Spirit as the efficacious power of the Word brings man to himself and establishes his true identity. The reason for this is that man has his true being only in fellowship with God. In himself he is a "copy" of an alien entity, e.g., the spirit of the time, but the Spirit awakens the "original" in him and thus brings into being his distinctive individuality.

The significant thing for me, however, was that while the Zen-Master did not contest the transcendent character of the human I he took a wholly different view of it from that of the Western tradition which has been influenced by Christianity. More clearly here than in the case of Marxist collectivism I saw that the basic anthropological structure of which I spoke is not an axiomatic reality of objective stringency and cannot, therefore, be a "self-evident" criterion for the truth-content of the religions. It is a factor which already has something to do with faith.

Since we cannot adopt this way of using anthropological criteria to distinguish between the religions and to find the uniqueness of the truth of Christian revelation, another way toward the goal which might commend itself is that of typological comparison.

In a survey of the many offers and ideas of salvation certain fundamental structures emerge which as constant factors cut right across the different religions, including Christianity. They may be seen in much more delicate nuances than the coarser typologies of pantheism, polytheism, and monotheism. Thus the confessional dualism between Roman Catholicism and Protestantism occurs not only in Christianity but also, as a type, in India and Japan as well.[8]

In Indian Buddhism we find two schools which typologically are amazingly like

---

[8]Cf. R. Otto, *Vischnu Narayana. Texte zur indischen Gottesmystik* (1917), pp. 122ff.; H. Frick, *Vergleichende Religionswissenschaft* (1928), pp. 86ff.

the Christian confessions. The first (Southern) school takes the path of believing love, despising merits. Thus Krishna in the *Bhagavad Gita* invites us to renounce all legal righteousness and seek him alone as a place of refuge (18:66). But as James opposed a certain type of Paulinism, we find a ("Roman Catholic") countermovement in the other (Northern) school. This regards the reduction of piety to grace alone as an intolerable restriction. It thus teaches a certain activism of salvation whose chief representative is the yogi, the Indian monk.

As Frick points out (*Vergleichende . . .* , pp. 88ff.) we have here some exact parallels to the confessional debates of the 16th century.

The Northern school says that grace is merited and bought. If works and knowledge are not a direct way to salvation they cooperate in the achievement of saving *bhakti*.

In contrast the Southern ("Reformation") school says that grace is given freely, that it works freely and irresistibly, and that it has regard only for the readiness of the heart to receive it.

The difference is strikingly expressed in the description of the Southern school as the way of the cat and the Northern school as that of the ape, for whereas the cat carries its young in its mouth with no cooperation on their part the ape carries its young but they have to cling to it and thus cooperate to a slight extent.

We find the same structural difference between Zen-Buddhism and Amada-Buddhism in Japan. The former practices piety as a methodical discipline and seeks by meditative training to attain a mastery of spirit, soul, and body over external things. The latter argues against this "work-righteousness" that since man is lame and blind he cannot achieve salvation (Nirvana) on his own but must be carried to it by a ship (H. Haas, *Amida Buddha unsere Zuflucht* [1910], pp. 38f.).

The Jesuit father Franciscus Cabralis came across this analogy to the confessional differences in Europe as early as 1571 and with shock and astonishment he said that he had found the Lutheran heresy in Japan in the form of the Amidist doctrine of grace.

When we consider these typological parallels we are tempted to think that it is not a matter of deciding *between* the religions and *for* one religion (e.g., the message of the gospel) but rather that the alternatives are set before us by these ongoing types. Figuratively, then, we have to choose between the way of the ape and the way of the cat, the choice of the religion which follows this way being a matter of relative indifference. The dubious factor here is that in the necessarily generalizing tendency of such typologies it is possible to include in this structural relationships even antitheses such as Christianity and anti-Christianity.

Typical here is that M. Greiffenhagen in his *Hitler's Children* (London, 1977) can find a structural analogy between the terrorists U. Meinhoff and G. Ensslin and the pietistic or orthodox confessional tradition of their parents. With their global criticism of systems these women represented the antichrist model in political understanding but also the readiness for suffering resistance that they had found in the pious resoluteness of their family tradition (*Spiegel*, XLV [1977], p. 58). Structural analogies, then, can embrace antithetical contents, or, better, they are only formal schemas and are thus indifferent to antithetical contents.

The cloven hoof of these typological formalisms is that they are nonhistorical.

They are indifferent to the question what salvation or what savior is meant or whether they may be connected with totally antithetical contents. Work-righteousness and faith, merit and grace, become formal principles whose kerygmatic intention is not considered. Formalism always implies a tendency to generalize and this exposes the nonhistoricity of the outlook that is predominant here. For historical understanding—in contrast to natural science—individualizes (H. Rickert). It is idiographic rather than nomothetic.[9] Within the formal generalization there is no distinction between Nirvana and being in Christ, between the *bhakti-marga* that appeals to Krishna and the "faith alone" that lives by Christ. They are all forced into a typological identity that they do not really have.

Once again, then, we see the fate of schematism as we have observed it already. Schematism levels down distinctives. It is egalitarian. It robs history of its point by de-individualizing it. Aloof from history it forces on us the position of a spectator who is outside the area of decision and commitment.

M. Eliade offers an example of typological egalitarianism. Taking direction from C. G. Jung's doctrine of archetypes, he attempts to find in all religious history a single schema of hieraphonies which extend from the most elementary embodiments in sacred stones, in statues of Jupiter, or in the epiphanies of Yahweh, to the supreme incarnation of the Logos in Jesus Christ. Viewed from an absolute standpoint all these embodiments are equal or illusory (Eliade, *Die Religionen und das Heilige* [G.T. 1954], p. 51, cf. pp. 119ff.).

We face, then, a hard decision.

It is true that Christian truth stands in correspondence with our prior consciousness, whether in its existential contents as these are expressed in our questions, hopes, and anxieties and therefore in the religions, or in its rational structures, which bring typological categories into play and subsume Christian truth under the type of religions of salvation and redemption.

Yet for two reasons, as we have seen, this anthropological situation cannot serve as an objective criterion for the truth-content of the religions or the uniqueness or exclusiveness of the truth of revelation.

The first reason is that the presupposition of human consciousness, i.e., self-transcendence in terms of basis, goal, and meaning, is not objectifiable; the human is already the object of some faith. The second reason is that the rational structure of our consciousness leads to formal schemata which level things down and thus lead away from the area of decision.

That there are fundamental reasons why a criterion of this kind cannot be found means that neither in encounter with the religions, nor in the testing of their truth-content, nor, therefore, in the proclamation of the gospel as *the* truth, can we escape the testimony of the Holy Spirit and the decision of faith that this makes possible.

But does not this conclusion raise a new dilemma? For it seems as if any talk of the exclusiveness of the truth of Christian revelation rests merely on a subjective decision, on an inner process that cannot be investigated and cannot appeal to any

---

[9]Cf. H. Rickert, *Die Grenzen der naturwissenschaftlichen Begriffsbildung*, 5th ed. (1929), pp. 533f.; W. Windelband, *Präludien*, II, 9th ed. (1924), pp. 145ff.; Anthrop, pp. 400ff., 500, n. 17.

transsubjective court. Even the appeal to the assurance of the Spirit's testimony cannot dispel the impression of mere subjectivity that is given to those outside.

Now it need not be disputed that this subjective decision may have absolute rank in its own sphere, i.e., for the subject. But this is to deny it any general claim in the sense of universal validity.[10] Giordano Bruno, Jaspers thinks in this connection, championed a panentheism which was unconditionally certain to him but was riveted to his subjectivity and therefore had no objective cogency but was dependent on his testimony. Hence he accepted martyrdom for it. Galileo, however, championed an objective truth of science which would triumph apart from him and he could thus recant without doing any damage to this type of truth.

When we talk about the exclusiveness of the truth of Christian revelation we seem to be in a twilight zone. As the certainty of faith this seems to represent a type of unconditionality similar to the subjective conviction of Bruno. But when in the form of mission this truth is proclaimed to all the world with a claim to universal validity it seems to be claiming the privilege of Galileo's objective truth of science.[11]

If it were merely a matter of truth in the sense of abstract normativity there would no point in claiming exclusiveness for the truth of revelation in the sense of its being *the* truth, the only truth for all the world. In spheres that lie outside the competence of synthetic judgments *a priori* I can speak only of what is true for me and offer only my subjectivity as a guarantee. In some sense this limited understanding of truth applies to the interpretation of history, where subjective presuppositions and prejudices undoubtedly influence the judgment that this or that historical truth is the truth of history itself.[12]

2. THE ROAD AHEAD

In face of these difficulties we can advance only if—in distinction from the abstract normativity of objective truth or purely subjective conviction—we understand the character of truth as it is understood in the gospel. In this regard I shall build on the relevant discussion of this issue in EG, I, pp. 278ff.; EF, I, pp. 202ff.

It is characteristic that truth according to the gospel is related to the *person* of Christ, not just in the sense that he speaks the truth as a contribution to what is meant by truth but also in the sense that he *is* this truth in person.[13] Now the form of access to a person which gives insight into his or her rank is trust. A person cannot be subsumed under a concept of norms. A person has individuality.[14] No

---

[10]Cf. K. Jaspers, *Der philosophische Glaube* (1948), pp. 11ff.; E.T. *The Perennial Scope of Philosophy* (New York, 1949); in reply cf. EG, II, pp. 377ff.; EF, II, pp. 307ff.

[11]Truth on the Christian view is in fact identical with neither of these two understandings of truth (cf. EG, II, pp. 377ff., esp. p. 381; EF, II, pp. 307ff., esp. p. 310).

[12]It is a sign of illegitimate ideologizing that the historical materialism of Marx presents its view of universal history as *the* truth, or scientific truth (cf. ThE, II, 2, §§196ff.; E.T. II, pp. 38ff.).

[13]Cf. the "I am" sayings in the gospels (E. Stauffer, art. "Ego," TDNT, II, pp. 348ff.; TWNT, II, pp. 345ff.).

[14]We have discussed this before in connection with the norm of the good (EG, II, pp. 102ff.; EF, II, pp. 84ff.) and the uniqueness of the name (EG, II, pp. 130ff.; EF, II, pp. 107ff.).

criteria, then, can objectively display the character, spiritual rank, or claim of a person. The relation of trust does not arise out of the causative reasoning of a Therefore. It is in the venture of a Nevertheless that "I am continually with thee" (Psalm 73:23).

That Christ is *the* truth in this sense means that in person and attitude he is transparent (or, better, becomes transparent through the witness of the Spirit) for the final reality, God, and also for man.[15] It is precisely the latter reference (the anthropological reference in this sense) that the dialogue with the religions can take up, not in the sense of an objective criterion by which one may venture to show to the religious their own relativity and one's own absoluteness, but in the form of the address of proclamation. From what angles can this address be undertaken?

1. Everywhere in religious history one finds a concept of man in which he is not what he should be but is promised a goal that can be reached through religion. The defect in man can be seen in primitive forms of bondage from which there are magical methods of release or in more profound forms of inner and outer bondage for which there is redemption by methodical exercises, ethical action, or the application of grace. The gospel finds one of the normative defects of the human in the perversion of fellow-humanity which derives from a perverted relationship with God and which comes to expression in the lack of love for neighbors and the inability to love enemies. The transparency for the true view of man and his divine original is manifested in the person and attitude of Jesus inasmuch as Jesus breaks through the deadly circle of hate and counter-hate and shatters the curse of the echo principle with his message of love, which is not a reaction to something already there but a new and creative beginning. The address to other religions (and world-views in general) consists of the question whether the true concept of man is not manifested here. This question is set in relief by the uniqueness—the exclusiveness—of the picture of Jesus. The foil for this picture, expressed in the echo principle, is the universal symptom of alienated man.

2. The message of love carries another insight which has a part to play in address to the other religions. Love as the fulfilment of the law (Romans 13:8) frees us from domination by all forms of heteronomy. Law places me under an alien will which is not my own, even though it be God's will. Love, however, is a spontaneous act in which I am alone and identical with myself. Love, then, cannot be commanded. I can only be liberated for it by the assistance of the Spirit (Galatians 5:22; Ephesians 5:9). Only because I am myself accepted, as the gospel says, can I accept others, i.e., love them (Matthew 18:23ff.; Luke 7:42; 1 John 4:19). I am freed for this spontaneity by a prior address to myself. I thus address the religions and world-views with the question whether the longing of man for identity is not fulfilled here (no matter how it may be with other offered fulfilments, e.g., the dissolution of the self in a collective or in the "one and all").

3. The dialogue of this address can go further. While the truth in person which the gospel proclaims is subject to no criterion, it is itself a criterion for the understanding and criticism of the religions. Here again Romans 1 has paradigmatic significance.

---

[15]On this twofold transparency cf. EF, II, cc. XXVI and XXVII (pp. 84ff., 107ff.).

For here the question is put to the religions whether and how far they conform to man himself and thus entail a reversal of Creator and creature. Even epistemologically the question of their conformity to man can be put only from a place which transcends the human and sees it from outside. By definition this transcendent place is not demonstrable but it sets us before the question—this is why we speak of address—whether man does not recognize himself in this view of himself and his religion. There is no doubt that Paul's argument is shaped by the purpose of address.

4. Further, the gospel itself knows and explains the impossibility of investigating its message with the help of higher criteria. This may be seen negatively—we have discussed this expressly in our pneumatology—in its need for the testimony of the Holy Spirit if it is to be revealed as God's Word. Man does not reveal God but God reveals himself and enables man, as we have said, to have a share in his self-knowledge. To that extent Christian theology addresses the religions with the question whether, along the lines of 1 Corinthians 2:11 (cf. Matthew 11:27), a God can be thought of as God only if he is thought of as a self-revealing God.[16] The gift of this revelation and its disclosure by the Pneuma means that the spiritual man judges all things but is judged by nobody (1 Corinthians 2:15) because the revelation granted to him is itself the criterion and the Pneuma as God himself cannot be subjected to any other criterion. We have seen earlier that this witness of the Spirit cannot be understood as an element of subjectivity, as the spirit or religiosity of man. On the contrary, the spiritual man sees that he is caught up in a transsubjective saving event which causes him to *be* in the truth, which transcends his natural self, and which leads him to identity with God's image of him at creation.[17]

5. Finally, truth in person, in contrast to truth that is viewed as abstractly normative, carries with it the implication that it can be expressed and explained only in narrative form and not in that of argument. Christian truth has to be *told*. The God of history and the incarnate Logos present themselves in an event, in history and stories, in saving events and exemplary deeds. The Bible is full of these. Grammatically the verb predominates, not the noun. The style, whether in telling about the biblical events of salvation or telling one's own spiritual story, corresponds to the nonargumentative address which at root simply presents the message to others.[18]

The truth in person proclaimed by the gospel opens up a highly significant possibility of addressing the religions which is ruled out when truth is viewed as an abstract norm. For we do not have to be bound here by the principle of noncontradiction, by the alternative of truth or falsehood. We have seen that especially in the early Barth the underlying abstract antitheses of eternity and time, of God's kingdom and the world, made that kind of logic inevitable, so that the truth of the gospel had to be opposed to the lie of the religions. But truth in person, which enables us to understand this person as love, makes possible the mercy of understanding. Mercy here means that even in what is distorted and alienated we can see the distorted and alienated truth from which people come and for which they are

[16] Jüngel, *Gott als Geheimnis . . .* , p. 211.
[17] EG, I, pp. 198ff.; EF, I, pp. 152ff.
[18] Cf. Jüngel, *Gott als Geheimnis*, pp. 427ff.

looking. What is sought is not just the ground in which the pearl is hidden but the pearl which is hidden in the ground. This applies to world-views as well, even of the ideologized variety.

If this forbids an abstract and curt negation of the religions, it also means positively that we must differentiate between them as regards their relation to the gospel. People can be close to God's kingdom or far from it as well as inside or outside (Mark 12:34).

What this implies may be seen in the stories of the woman with the flow of blood (Mark 5:25ff.) and the Canaanite woman (Matthew 15:21ff.). Even a theologically uncontoured view of pity and a magical concept of the savior can be closer to the good news of God's mercy than a correct legal righteousness and a supposedly sure possession of truth in the true Christian sphere. Not for nothing, therefore, is the faith of pagans extolled and described as ''great.''

We may sum up the result of our deliberations in two affirmations.

First, in terms of a truth that is truth in person the claim to uniqueness and exclusiveness cannot mean the exclusion of all other truth. This truth is unique and exclusive inasmuch as it sees the original behind the perverted understanding of truth and embraces this in its original form. Even in the idol it finds the God who is left and sought.

Hence truth in person does not look upon itself as truth and everything else as falsehood. It is the authority which divides between truth and falsehood. It thus stands in criticism of the religions. Pursuing misappropriated truth with understanding, just as God pursues the man who holds down the truth in unrighteousness, keeping constantly on his track, it recognizes a closeness to God's kingdom and a farness from it. But since there is no abstract criterion of truth by which to assess closeness and farness, this cannot mean that it demands a hierarchical ranking of the religions according to the amount of truth in them. This would imply that the truth of revelation puts itself at the top of the hierarchy, viewing itself as the fulness of truth as distinct from the individual fragments found elsewhere. We have seen what opposes this view and what Hellenistic (the Apologists) or evolutionary (Hegel) ideas lie behind it. Truth in person is denied if it is integrated into a schema of this kind.

Second, exclusiveness means the inaccessibility of a truth which declares itself as *God's* truth only in the form of his self-disclosure, as presentation by the witness of the Spirit. The person who is thus addressed is the one who has already been addressed by God before and given a capacity for the Word. The religions bear witness to this. Their idols are not just of human manufacture. They are not just projections. Among them one may see the recollection of something that has been heard but forgotten, denied, and alienated.

XXVIII

The Question of Anonymous Christianity

1. THE BASIC THEOLOGICAL SCHEME

In its relation to other religions Roman Catholicism does not run into the same difficulties as Protestantism, which develops diametrically opposed positions and goes through a swing of the pendulum between radical rejection and dialogical synthesis. Within the Roman Catholic tradition the basic analogy of nature and grace (the analogy of being)[1] makes provision for relating the religions to Christian truth—at least as a fragmentary anticipation.

In connection with this concept of analogy Vatican I can say in chapter 2 ("On Revelation") that God, the basis and goal of all things, can through the light of natural human reason be known with certainty from created things.[2] Along the same lines Vatican II finds traces of this knowledge of God before revelation, e.g., in the concern for the divine mystery in Hinduism, the awareness of the radical inadequacy of the mutable world and the struggle for liberation and enlightenment in Buddhism, consistent monotheism in Islam. . . .[3]

Important inferences for missionary strategy are drawn from this in the decree "Ad gentes" (c. 23). Missionary encounter with the religions cannot take a purely negative form. We need to see more clearly how faith, using the philosophy and wisdom of the nations, can gain a better understanding and bring the various customs, views of life, and social orders into harmony with the ethos of divine revelation. Without yielding to syncretism we can in this way adjust the Christian life to the spirit and distinctiveness of every culture. The different traditions and gifts of the nations, illuminated by the gospel, can be brought into catholic unity.

Debate within Roman Catholicism itself shows that this analogy and the principle based upon it are not without problems. The Epistle of James follows that to the Romans with correctives and warnings. Thus Paul VI at the Bishops' Synod in

---

[1] Cf. ThE, III, Index.
[2] Denz., 3004; E.T. 1785.
[3] "Nostra aetate," pp. 2f.

Rome in 1974 draws attention to the correctness of pedagogical accommodation but also to the limits of theological accommodation. In obvious allusion to the missionary decree of Vatican II he stresses that the goal is to find a better expression of the faith in harmony with national, social, and cultural conditions but he also points out the danger of speaking of different theologies in different continents and cultures. The content of the faith will either be catholic or not. We have all received it by a constant tradition. Peter and Paul did not alter it to assimilate it to the Jewish, Greek, or Roman world.

Several Roman Catholic theologians living amid paganism echo these warnings. Thus William Mpuga of Uganda calls for liturgical and educational reforms but emphasizes the fact that eternal truths are independent of culture or nation. The Christian faith leads to a transvaluation of values and rejects accommodation and reduction ("Zum Problem der Adaption," *Theologie und Kirche in Afrika* (ed. H. Bürkle [1968], pp. 169ff.). Most critical of accommodation is the missionary expert L. Rütti (*Zur Theologie der Mission* [1972], pp. 320f.), who finds in accommodation a way to break the norms laid down by the Western church through limited and controlled concessions, so that it becomes a mechanism to suppress and domesticate issues, veiling the true state of affairs and acting as an alibi for a nonexistent openness.

In terms of our own position and vocabulary we might say that the danger here is that of detaching the Pneuma from the Word, so that the vestiges of the Holy Spirit in the religions are seen as preliminary forms of revelation. Quite apart from the attitude to tradition this can lead to a pluralism which in 1974 the African bishops did little to avert by trying to modify accommodation christologically and speaking of Christ's incarnation in every culture (*Katholische Missionen,* XCIV [1975], pp. 19f.).

That storm warnings were rightly hoisted may be seen from the most interesting but very dangerous inference drawn by the Indian Roman Catholic theologian R. Panikkar in his book *Christus der Unbekannte im Hinduismus* (Lucerne, 1965); E.T. *The Unknown Christ of Hinduism* (London, 1964). Panikkar goes far beyond the elements of truth in "Nostra aetate" and thinks that at root the religions aim at the same truth as Christian revelation and that the differences lie only in the different philosophical and cultural systems with which the religions have all allied themselves. If we pierce through these amalgamates we shall find the same core. His goal is thus to find the Christian truths hidden in Hinduism. Christ is already present here, but his full face is not seen nor is his mission complete. He still has to be crucified, dying to Hinduism as he did to the Jewish and Hellenistic religions and rising again as the same Christ, but as resurrected to Hinduism, to Christianity (p. 36; E.T. p. 17).

A subtle interpretation of some pertinent passages in the *Brahma-Sutra* leads to an equation of Brahma with Christ and the construction of an implicit Christology in terms of the *Advaita-Vedanta* (pp. 140ff.; E.T. pp. 126ff.). Panikkar even finds a direct analogy between the Mahma of Hinduism and the preexistent and cosmic Christ of the NT. Interest in this parallel causes him to submerge the historical nature of Christ in his suprahistorical significance. As a passing phenomenon of human history he is limited and sets limits. His true being is as the ground of all being. Ultimately he is not a historical person. Western debates about his nature and person belong to the misleading and divisive amalgamates. His person is the divine person which embraces all history (p. 87; E.T. p. 74).

Here the analogy comes close to identification. Christianity is less a gracious enhancement of Hinduism and more a Hinduism freed from its latent Christology. Hinduism is not confronted with revelation. It is itself manifested in crucifixion and resurrection. Epigrammatically one might say that when it meets Christianity Hinduism learns to see its own true point. In this sense the Hindu is an anonymous Christian.

2. THE IMPLICATION: LATENT CHRISTIANITY OUTSIDE CHRISTIANITY?

Even when the concept of analogy is not pushed to extremes as in Panikkar, the idea of the anonymous Christian—a term coined by Rahner and almost made into a slogan—will occur in some form, at least as a question.[4]

As Rahner puts it, up to the time when the gospel really comes into the historical situation of a particular person, that person's non-Christian religion contains not only elements of a natural knowledge of God mixed with sinful depravity, but also by grace some supernatural aspects as well, so that at different levels it can be recognized as a legitimate religion.[5] Hence Christianity does not encounter non-Christians as mere non-Christians but as people who might be called anonymous Christians.[6] Fundamentally encounter with the gospel achieves just one thing, that of making unconscious Christianity conscious and making the anonymous Christian a person who is aware of his Christianity in the depth of his being and also in a social confession, in the church.[7]

Rahner bases his right to speak of anonymous Christians on his view of analogy, which relates not only nature and grace but also revelation in the non-Christian sphere and revelation in the Christian sphere. For him the religions are not just self-interpretations of human nature but manifestations of revelation, emanations of supernature, even though this contradicts the noetic understanding of religious man or is not at least expressed in it. Only against this background can we understand Rahner's statement that all people are exposed to a supernatural divine grace which offers inner fellowship with God whether they accept it or not.[8] Rahner no longer seems to share the view of Thomas that nature is distinct from grace. For him there is only one human nature and this is permeated and filled by supernature existentially dwelling within it.

This challenges the principle of no salvation "outside the church," although Rahner's dialectic—on which we have commented already in our discussion of Scripture and tradition—can immediately bring back again that part of the tradition which seems to be slipping away. At any rate, he stands by his point when he

---

[4]R. Rothe had spoken already of "unconscious Christianity" (cf. M. Kähler, *Geschichte der protestantischen Dogmatik im 19. Jahrhundert* (Theologische Bücherei ed., No. 16 [1962], p. 109).
[5]Hampe, III, p. 570.
[6]P. 572.
[7]P. 572.
[8]*Schriften*, V, p. 145; E.T. *Theological Investigations*, V, p. 123.

endorses the view (and calls its rejection the Jansenist error) that grace is not just offered outside the Christian church but proves victorious in the free acceptance by men which it itself brings about.[9]

The axiom that salvation lies only in the church stands fast because the church is necessary to salvation and it claims absoluteness. It is not the exclusive fellowship of salvation but it is its mediatrix and visible form. It also offers a greater possibility of salvation than is given in the inarticulateness of anonymous Christianity.[10]

In an earlier essay on church membership after the encyclical of Pius XII, "Mystici corporis Christi" (*Schriften*, II [1962], pp. 7ff.; E.T. *Theological Investigations*, II, pp. 1ff.), Rahner had prepared the ground for the idea of anonymous Christianity though he did not refer to it specifically. As he put it, because God's Word has become man, humanity has already become ontologically the people or the children of God with the gracious sanctification of individuals. Consecrated humanity is thus a real unity. In the supranatural unity of the church as a social and legal organization there exists already a people of God which is as wide as the human race (p. 90; E.T. pp. 82f.). Here the question of "outside the church" is relatively (not totally) irrelevant because ontologically there is only a potential "in the church" (cf. pp. 91 and 94; E.T. pp. 84f. and 87f.).

We may sum up as follows.

1. Both theological and existential motifs lie behind the idea of the anonymous Christian. Among the former is a christologically deepened principle of analogy (the cosmic Christ) which virtually identifies nature and grace. Among the latter is the impact which is made by the great figures in non-Christian religions and which forbids us to see in them merely *tabulae rasae* ("empty slates") whom God has totally abandoned. The comprehensiveness of grace means for Rahner that we can think of no sphere that is not comprehended by it.

2. Thus understood, the correspondence between nature and grace leads to the (wrong) view that there are only damaged and no shattered elements in the non-Christian religions. This has three implications.

First, no place is left for the idea of a strict anti-Christianity nor for the revolt and human arrogance which Barth erroneously regarded as *the* mark of religion but which has to be kept in mind as at least a possible attitude or element in it.

Second, the elements of truth in the religions which are postulated and then asserted in the name of a christologically understood principle of analogy have to be hierarchically ordered and compared to the rungs of a ladder, the Christian truth of revelation being seen as the fulfilment of prior anticipation and containing quantitatively more truth.

Third (formulated as a question), does not the concept of contact and accommodation as Vatican II espoused it lead necessarily to a typological schema in which the gospel is simply the dot on the "i" or the top rung in the hierarchy of religions? By means of this underlying schema has not Rahner involuntarily exposed himself to the relativizing of Christian truth which we have noted in every type of schematization, although paradoxically it was meant here to promote a form of

---

[9]P. 146; E.T. p. 124.
[10]Fahlbusch in *Kerygma und Dogma*, II, pp. 69, 83.

absoluteness? Did not Panikkar unmask the implicit result when he came to identify Christian truth with the waiting truth in the non-Christian religions?

3. Our criticism of Rahner's idea of the anonymous Christian will move in the same direction as that of the early Christian apologists whose schema recurs in modified form in Rahner. The Christian missionary does not here enter the world of religions with the message of the transvaluation of all values (W. Mpuga) and the appeal for conversion. He can offer the other religions only the fulness of what they already have in fragmentary form as the *logos spermatikos*. H. R. Schlette perhaps gives to this position its most extreme formulation which is also its criticism. If the religions are ways of salvation in the general history of religion, then they are general ways of salvation, and if over against the general history of salvation the church stands as a special disposition on the side of the special history of salvation, then one can speak of the way of the religions as the ordinary way of salvation and that of the church as the extraordinary way.[11]

We can give a pneumatological accent to the basic problem of theological principle which is at issue here.

The traditional Roman Catholic concept that the Pneuma is not bound to the Word but also works in active tradition and causes a second source of revelation to well forth in the church's teaching office finds itself confirmed here on a different and broader level. The Pneuma gives revelation even outside the zone of the Christian proclamation of the Word, i.e., in the religions. It creates anonymous Christians. But since we have to do with the Spirit of God, who is the author of the Word, the missionary leading of non-Christians to the Word cannot properly be called conversion or the transvaluation of all values but can denote no more than the overcoming of a specific insight of faith by the fulness of truth. The Spirit is already leading along a path to the goal which agrees analogously with that of the Christian kerygma. The Spirit is thus understood as the reality in which Christian truth and non-Christian truth coincide.

The concept of the anonymous Christian has also been contested—with largely different arguments—within Roman Catholic theology itself, most sharply, perhaps, in H. U. von Balthasar and H. de Lubac in *Geheimnis, aus dem wir leben* (Einsiedeln, 1967) and *Cordula oder der Ernstfall* (Einsiedeln, 1966) (cf. HK, II [1976], p. 76). The only defect in Balthasar is that he attacks the concept of anonymous Christianity, which Rahner does not use, rather than that of the anonymous Christian. H. Schlier also criticizes Rahner's concept in *Das Ende der Zeit* (1971), pp. 234ff. H. Küng's objections are less against the theological basis of the concept than its tactical purpose. For him it offers only the poor consolation of a mere appearance. A society which wants more members cannot cure the situation by calling nonmembers members. Küng fears that this is to fail to take the representatives of other religions seriously and to do injury to the Christian cause by equating the church and Christianity with the world (*Christ sein* [1974], p. 90; E.T. *On Being a Christian* [Garden City, 1976], p. 98).

---

[11]H. R. Schlette, *Die Religionen als Thema der Theologie* (1964), p. 85; E.T. *Towards a Theology of Religions* (New York, 1966), pp. 80f.

XXIX

The Principle of Exclusiveness and the Question of Toleration

Bibliography: P. Althaus, "Toleranz und Intoleranz des Glaubens," *Theologische Aufsätze*, II (1935); M. S. Bates, *Religious Liberty* (New York, 1947); H. Bornkamm, art. "Toleranz," RGG³, VI, p. 933 (with D. Lerch); H. Fries, "Kirche, Toleranz und Religionsfreiheit," *Wir und die andern* (1966), pp. 103f.; A. Gilbert *et al.*, "Die Religionsfreiheit," *Concilium*, II (1966), pp. 567ff.; E.T. "Religious Freedom," *Concilium*, XVIII (New York, 1966), pp. 3ff.; J. Habermas, *Erkenntnis und Interesse* (1968); E.T. *Knowledge and Human Interests* (Boston, 1971); A. Hartmann, *Toleranz und christliche Glaube* (1965); H. Helbling, ed., *Religionsfreiheit im 20. Jahrhunderts* (1977); J. Locke, *A Letter Concerning Toleration* (New York, 1950); R. Niebuhr, *The Children of Light and the Children of Darkness* (1946), c. 4; Pius XII, An Address on Tolerance (12/6/1953) to the Fifth National Congress of Catholic Jurists, MD, I (1954), p. 7; R. Röhricht, "Theologische Aspekte des Toleranzproblems," LMH, XII (1969), pp. 604ff.; E. Ruppel, "Toleranz und Freiheit in pluralistischer Gesellschaft," LMH, IV (1965), pp. 168ff.; H. R. Schlette, art. "Toleranz," HThG, IV, pp. 245ff.; R. Schottlaender, "Der Gedanke der Toleranz und seine Geschichte," *Studium generale,* II (1949), pp. 307ff.; Vatican II, "Declaration on Religious Freedom" ("Dignitatis humanae"); E. Wolf, "Toleranz nach evangelischem Verständnis," ZEE (1957), pp. 97ff.

1. THE STATE AND TOLERATION

Except in religious and ideological spheres, both of which, even though with a difference of intention, raise a claim to absoluteness, the problem of toleration is fairly easily solved. With the modern, post-Enlightenment pluralism of values and norms, the democratic state obviously has to be tolerant. The secular state has no "message" of its own apart from a broad framework of basic rights. Hence it has to be neutral in relation to all the viewpoints and religions represented within it. This neutrality can go so far that in America even devil-worshippers and the celebrants of "black masses" can enjoy the protection of the Constitution so long as they have the legal status of a church. This toleration on the basis of impartiality is one of the outstanding features that separate a constitutional state from ideologically totalitarian regimes.

Only in two cases does this toleration run up against a barrier beyond which it is compelled to be intolerant.

The first case is when a group arises which makes extensive claims to absoluteness and thus shatters the pluralistic structure of society by a lack of forbearance. We see this acutely today among cadres of Marxist-Leninists and Maoists who are trying to replace pluralism by their mono-ideology and are thus forced into intolerance. In this case the constitutional state may find that for the sake of toleration it has itself to be intolerant and to pass anti-radical laws in its own defense.

The second case is when religious and philosophical groups begin to draw ethical conclusions, especially in politics, which impinge upon the state's own domain. Though inner convictions do not affect the state, their practical implications undoubtedly do.[1] Thus toleration reaches its limit when convictions lead to violations of human dignity, revolutionary movements, or ritual murders. When King Maximilian Joseph IV of Bavaria denied civil rights to a Munich evangelical in 1801, he stated precisely the distinction between religious motivation and the sphere of ethical action, and at the same time formulated the criterion by which to fix the radius of the state's readiness for toleration, by asking whether Protestants could obey the laws as good citizens if they were already worshipping at different altars.

2. THE CHURCH AND TOLERATION

The religious aspect of toleration is of more interest to us here than the political side. The question at issue is this. Does not the claim of Christian truth to unconditionality and exclusiveness rule out in advance any possibility of recognizing the legitimacy of diametrically opposing claims to truth and therefore of tolerating them?[2] Can an enlightened Christian readiness for toleration be anything other than an externally necessary requirement,[3] an unwillingly accepted compromise between the radical claim and the limiting demands of the pluralistic system within which one lives? Is it possible to exist in this tension between absolute truth and a relativizing system except half-heartedly and with a bad conscience? Does not this raise the self-critical question whether as Christians and the church we are not among the revolutionaries who would like to overturn the pluralistic system of our society and replace it by a homogeneous theocracy, as Franco's clerical supporters wanted to do in Spain?

For the Enlightenment which is the source of the modern understanding of toleration this polarity did not exist. In its view the positive religions were all ciphers for an underlying truth of the rational and the good. (We have only to think

---

[1]ThE, III, §§603-71.

[2]We have seen that this problem still arises for Roman Catholicism even though it finds some truths in the religions and rejects suppression. The only true religion is actualized in the catholic apostolic church which has received from Jesus the Lord the commission to extend it among all nations (cf. "Dignitatis humanae," 1 and 2 [*Vatican II Documents*, pp. 677-80]).

[3]Or, as Küng suggests, a stratagem.

of Lessing's *Nathan*.) These ciphers were merely relative, historically and geographically conditioned phenomena which could not present competing claims to truth. Once we see them in this way as purely symbolical expressions of the religious, they can live in peace with one another and toleration is no problem. The light of the one unconditional truth of reason in which they can all unite breaks up in them into the colors of the rainbow, into separate bursts of light, into subjective aspects. Goethe, in the famous letter to Jacobi (1813) which we have already quoted, draws attention to the fact that the religious claim to unconditionality is in this way reduced to a mere problem of perspective.[4]

As should be obvious from the theology of the Word and Spirit presented here, the Christian can find in this reduction of the truth of faith to a mere matter of perspective no more than a conjecture which does not do justice to the unconditional character of the truth that is here at issue and which ultimately represents indifference. In this respect H. M. Robinson was right when in his novel *The Cardinal* he said that much that passes for toleration is simply a lack of personal conviction. It is very easy for the indifferent to be tolerant.

But does not toleration lose its true force in such a case? At root the word "toleration" carries with it the idea of a readiness to "bear," to "forbear." Forbearing the convictions of others does not presuppose indifference but its very opposite, namely, the true commitment which does not find it self-evident to live alongside different convictions but demands a special act of self-conquest and clarification. But what does such an act mean when what we are dealing with is, as in faith, an unconditional form of the certainty of truth?

This form of unconditionality is constitutive for Christian faith. This is plain, as we have seen, in the NT. We need only recall the saying of the Johannine Christ: "I am the way, the truth, and the light; no one comes to the Father, but by me" (14:6). Cf. also Peter (Acts 13:47) and Paul (Galatians 1:7f.).

Luther already in his work *On Secular Authority* (1523)[5] rejects any attempt on the part of the state either to establish a monopoly with the help of this unconditional claim to truth or to give legal recognition to the institutional exclusiveness of Christianity or one of its confessions. Positively he pleads for religious freedom.[6] God neither can nor will let anyone rule over the soul except the soul itself. When secular powers venture to make laws for the soul, they violate God's rule and simply lead the soul astray and corrupt it. It is quite impossible to order or force anyone to believe. Faith is a free work which cannot be forced on anyone. It is a divine work in the Spirit and external powers should not try to enforce or create it.

In Luther's defense of freedom of conviction against regimentation by the state, the decisive argument is not political. His primary interest is not in the question of dealing with citizens of different confessions and keeping this micropluralism within the limits of effective government. (In addressing this question he recommended emigration and thus did not progress beyond the contemporary principle of *Cuius regio, eius religio*.) Much more serious was his theological insight that faith is violated in its inner substance if one tries to force it on people by law. It

---

[4] "As a poet and artist I am a polytheist, but a pantheist as a scientist," etc.

[5] Clemen, *Bonner Studentenausgabe*, II, pp. 360ff.

[6] *Ibid.*, pp. 377ff. and *passim*.

then becomes hypocritically external and under its mask we find lying, denying, and saying other than what is in the heart. Luther's point, then, is that in a (pseudo-)theocratic or ideological regime which does not allow religious freedom violence is done to faith itself. Positively, the faith that is bound to the unconditional has to want freedom of faith.

We shall now step back a pace to consider how far compulsion and intolerance—as the opposite of religious freedom—necessarily rob faith of its true nature. I will simply indicate the main points.

First, the truth of Christian faith views itself and will let itself be viewed only as a given truth which we do not and cannot attain to on our own initiative but which reveals itself to us. Our pneumatological deliberations have shown us that not only the truth itself but faith's access to it must be opened up. To demand the acknowledgment of this truth by others is necessarily to pervert it and to deny its mediation by the Spirit.

Second, the gospel initiates a process which through experience of God's love invokes the reaction of loving him in return (1 John 4:19) and then of loving the neighbor too. The law appeals to the will but the gospel produces a free spontaneity of love which is again mediated by the Spirit. This central intention of the gospel is changed into its opposite if it is commanded, that is, if Christians require that others be Christians and no longer allow the Pneuma to initiate the process.

Third, compulsory faith, or the nontoleration of unbelief or other beliefs, is in total antithesis to the point of real Christian faith. A human pseudo-Christian ideology replaces the divine address. As ideologies misuse the spiritual as a means to other ends[7] and set it in the service of other interests, so faith is pragmatically misapplied here. It is made to serve the inner homogeneity of the nation so that the people will be more easily ruled and an obligatory set of values will be placed at the disposal of the rulers within which subjects can be more easily manipulated than is possible where there is a pluralism of views and values. This ideologizing of Christianity—it is no less—is what arouses the suspicion of Marxists that religion is being used as an opium of the people and is serving the purpose of directing attention away from social distress and thus striking at the heart of revolutionary impulses which press for change.

Fourth, the danger of this type of falsification calls for the preventive of toleration and religious freedom. To this extent these are a postulate of faith itself. To put it paradoxically, tolerating other faiths and their understanding of values and norms is bound up with the claim of the Christian truth of revelation to exclusiveness. For this claim is exclusive inasmuch as this truth cannot be mastered, that it is a truth which is disclosed by the Pneuma, and that it is thus protected against any pragmatic attack. For the sake of its absoluteness in this sense it cannot be exposed to the relativity of a means of domination whether in the political or the clericalist sphere.[8]

Those who are seriously grasped by faith do not see the strongest threat to its

---

[7]Cf. ThE, II, 2, §§154ff.; E.T. II, pp. 26ff.

[8]For this reason, to take a concrete example, education ought not to be confessional. While this might seem to be desirable, it forces people into a schema they might repudiate. It can thus be a source of hypocrisy and legalism.

unconditional certainty in different beliefs that they reject but in the possibility that it might be robbed of its unconditionality and divine legitimation by the granting to it of an institutional monopoly, a political claim to exclusiveness, and its consequent subjection to political and pragmatic conditions. In this way their faith would be changed from a gift into an all too human trick. Hypocritical opportunism would be stirred up instead of a confident turning to God.

We are thus forced to the paradoxical conclusion that it is because of its so-called claim to absoluteness, not in spite of it, that Christian faith must demand freedom of faith and religion, or, more precisely, that it finds this in itself or else it fatefully misunderstands its own nature.

The toleration at issue here rests on the opposite of self-relativizing and the indifference that this entails. It rests on commitment to an unconditional truth. This kind of unconditionality will not tolerate any institutional privilege. It wants to be proclaimed amid the multiplicity of serious and questionable, consenting and opposing confessions. It relies on the proof of its own evidence. This proof lies outside the range of human competence. It lies within the competence of the Spirit's witness. Only here is there "demonstration of the Spirit and of power."

3. "DIALOGUE" AND MISSION

The proclamation of a truth which regards itself as *the* truth—truth represented in a person—will not stand merely in a dialogical relation to non-Christians. Underlying dialogue with them is neither the Socratic premise that the truth will be released maieutically in others as self-discovery nor the premise that it can be induced by arguments. Neither of these ways corresponds to the truth of revelation. We have seen how unsuitable they both are from many different angles.

As Kierkegaard sees it, Socrates, a virtuoso in making contact, cannot point the way to Christian truth because this is not a potential which is already waiting to be unleashed and which can be awakened by provocative irony. Socrates as a pagan did not see that human redemption demands more than mere superiority to the folly of the world, that it demands a crucified God. Socratic irony can result only in the disclosure of impossibilities, in infinite and absolute negation. It cannot make this sage of antiquity into anything more than an intellectual martyr (W. Rehm, *Kierkegaard und der Verführer* [1949], pp. 447ff., esp. p. 449).

Dialogue serves a Socratic type of releasing function in the missionary Christian himself. The conflict of mission and the spreading of Christianity are necessary for our own inner development, Troeltsch could say.[9] Or, as Masao Takenaka puts it, faith which expresses itself in dialogue with other religions (and is not monologic or solipsistic) faces the challenge of others and therefore the possibility of change and growth. To grow is not to borrow from these religions. It is not to make a more attractive religion in syncretistic fashion. Dialogue with other religions offers a chance to understand better and more clearly what lies in our own faith but is not yet plain to us.[10] The dialogue is not Socratic because it releases "natural" truth in those who are addressed but because in the mirror of other beliefs our own faith

---

[9]W. Koehler, *E. Troeltsch*, p. 115.

[10]"Christentum und nichtchristliche Religionen in Japan," *Areopag*, II (1963), pp. 143ff., esp. pp. 148f.

brings to light hitherto unknown dimensions and displays a fulness of truth which could not be seen with an introverted glance.

For this reason dialogue cannot be the goal, as some tendencies in relativism desire. It can only be prolegomena to mission. First it exposes faith to the attacks of other religions and puts its truth to the test. Confidence in this test is itself missionary witness. Then the stage of dialogue enables us to listen to the questions of others and not to do our missionary work without paying any attention to their presuppositions. To do this would be to wrap Christian truth in dogma and open ourselves to the charge that Christianity is a foreign import.[11] It would also leave unconquered some remnants of paganism which would never be exposed to Christian truth. As suppressed regions these would sooner or later show through the varnish of Christianity.

Thus a legalistically enforced monogamy in polygamous areas will only be "pasted on" externally so long as the connection between monogamy and Christian love is not brought out in a long process of growth (cf. ThE, III, §§2045ff.; E.T. *Ethics of Sex,* pp. 86ff. Some tribes in Africa have left Christianity and reverted to their ancestral cults. They adopted the Christian concept of God within the framework of their polytheistic schema and their belief in spirits. But they could not integrate it into this schema and as in biology the transplant was rejected. Missionaries had ignored the framework and failed to overcome it. In Japan missionary work that does not pay attention to the Japanese idea of the divinization of heroes can give rise to the grossest of misunderstandings when it proclaims the deity of Christ, since this is not understood as the descent of God but as the ascent of a hero (cf. what is said about Odagiri in EG, II, pp. 451ff.; EF, II, pp. 368ff.).

Even where dialogue is refused in principle or conceded only opportunistically in simulation of a readiness for communication there will still be (or ought to be) an openness on the Christian side to hear, to question oneself, and to be questioned. We find such a refusal of dialogic encounter in the case of Islam.

Troeltsch could see no point in even trying to approach Islam since he regarded the struggle with Islam as military rather than missionary. Some prominent attempts at understanding were made, as by the Greek Archbishop of Baalbek, Elias Zoghby, and the Franciscan orientalist Louis Massignon (b. 1883), who established a "house of peace" in Cairo (*Dar al Salam*). But these failed, and some were brought to a bloody end by fanatical Moslems. In a letter to the Vatican the apostolic vicar of the Latin Christians in Lebanon, Bishop Paul Bassim, suggests that the reason for this refusal of theological dialogue by Islam lies in the Koran (FAZ, CCLX [1977], p. 10). Theocratic equation of religion and politics can allow for no toleration in principle, the only alternatives being conformity or subjugation: Fight those who do not believe in Allah and the last day, who do not forbid what Allah and his prophet forbid, and who do not confess the truth, until, completely humiliated, they pay tribute (Koran 9:20).

The representative of Christian truth cannot react in kind to this rejection of dialogue. His investigation of the existential background of those of other faiths and his readiness to expose himself to their claims to truth are themselves an inalienable part of his witness.

---

[11]This may be seen not only in the translation of European hymns but also in the adoption of pseudo-gothic church architecture, etc.

Part Five

THE TRANSCENDING OF
PRESENTATION: ESCHATOLOGY

XXX

The State of the Discussion

1. THE DESTRUCTION OF ESCHATOLOGY IN THE NINETEENTH CENTURY

If eschatology comes at the end of our dogmatic journey, this does not mean that we grant to it only the function of an appendix. It is one of the implications of all the topics discussed thus far and receives emphasis in this way. For example, we referred to the significance of the Pneuma as a deposit (*arrabōn*) pointing to the future. In this final chapter, then, we shall simply be explicating what has gone before, not in the sense of drawing conclusions from it, but in that of referring what the Bible says about the last things to what has already been developed. Only when all dogmatics is permeated by an eschatological element, only when it is shaped by the relations of promise and fulfilment, faith and sight, already and not yet, does it remain faithful to its theme of salvation conferred and expected.

One of the marks of the false theological developments found in the 19th century is that they are suspiciously lacking in eschatology. "The eschatological office is for the most part closed" was the view of Troeltsch at the beginning of the present century when he thought of the theologians of his day. Some years ago this statement was reformulated by H. U. von Balthasar when he suggested that "the office is now working overtime."[1]

The age of overtime was undoubtedly ushered in with a great fanfare by Marxism, which oriented its historical understanding and action to the eschatological-utopian vision of a classless society and saw in this the goal of history. It discovered herewith the mobilizing force of utopian ends.[2] Its activist impulse arose out of the double character of the utopia—first, its ability to offer a discernible goal of history which leads to long-range planning and prevents resignation in face of tactical reverses, and second and supremely its intrinsic power to criticize the

---

[1]Cf. the discussion between H. G. Koch and W. Kasper on death, judgment, and the hereafter in HK, III (1977), p. 130.

[2]Cf. EG, I, pp. 572ff.; EF, I, pp. 389ff.

present. When present-day social relations are measured against the goal they fail the test with a blast of drums and trumpets. Criticism of the present unleashes a readiness to protest and a desire for revolutionary change. If the early Marx was motivated primarily by humanitarian concerns, this suggests that in part at least Christian theology adapted the utopia-motivated criticism of society and tried in this way to give a social form to *agapē*. Without mentioning the Marxist background M. Kohnstamm has expressed the point of this concern in what has become the famous slogan "love in structures."[3]

The theological reception of the utopian motif and the related reawakening of eschatology can take either a highly intellectual form[4] or a popular form which opportunistically exploits the human urge for hope, happiness, and utopia.[5]

The theological adoption of Marxist views usually produces a very fragile and twisted parallel to the NT kerygma in its relation to the OT. As the NT integrated Jesus into the OT schema of promised salvation and in so doing shattered the schema, so an effort is often made to fit Christianity into the schema of Marxist expectation and in this way to harness and collect scattered religious energies (Ratzinger, *Eschatologie* [1977], p. 19), though this usually means the ideological absorption of the kerygma. Cf. R. Frieling, "Die lateinamerikanische Theologie der Befreiung," MD, II (1972), pp. 26ff.; T. Rendtorff and H. E. Tödt, *Theologie der Revolution* (1968), pp. 117ff.; "H. Marcuse und die prophetische Tradition (Interview)," in H. E. Bahr, *Weltfrieden und Revolution* (1968), pp. 291ff.; G. Greshake and G. Lohfink, *Naherwartung, Auferstehung, Unsterblichkeit*, pp. 30ff.

At any rate it is a symptom of the present age that the future and hope have again become themes which can count on sympathy and expect a ready hearing. Nor can there be any doubt that openness to the future is an integral part of the Christian message. But the question at once arises: What future? No matter what our answer to this question may be, two things should be made clear in advance.

First, faith has always resisted a one-sided commitment to eschatological expectation, as among enthusiasts who forgot the present for the future or those who at the Lord's Supper so overlooked present needs as to leave their neighbors hungry (1 Corinthians 11:20ff.). Second, it has never been contested that hope for a final future, for God's definitive victory, does not rest on the assumption that human activity will usher in this future but on faith that God will accomplish it in face of what are often our arrogant efforts. As understood in this way the future does not correspond to human deeds but to man himself, to his person which is visited in it. Fundamental, then, to any eschatological discussion is Bonhoeffer's distinction between the ultimate and the penultimate.[6] Human actions and planning deal only with penultimate goals, and the certainty that the ultimate is beyond our compe-

---

[3]In an address to the Hamburg faculty of theology in 1974.

[4]As an example cf. Shaull's theology of revolution or Moltmann's theology of hope, which in Barth's view (*Letters* [1981], No. 172) baptizes Bloch's philosophy of hope.

[5]Cf. the grotesque book of the Jesuit Luigi Majocco, *L'Umanesimo celeste* (Turin, 1968), in which eternal life is depicted, if not as an amusement park, at least as a perpetual vacation, an unceasing festival, a never-ending weekend (592 pp.!).

[6]*Widerstand und Ergebung*, pp. 113, 123, 180; E.T. *Letters and Papers from Prison*, pp. 86 (157), 94 (168), 141 (281).

tence helps us to be relaxed in our immediate steps. The distinction between the relative and the absolute future is at the heart of all eschatology.

In the theological and secular revival of eschatological interest, in the overtime worked by the eschatological office, there may be seen a need to make up for the unquestionable deficiency of the preceding epoch. This deficiency derived not least of all from theological omissions from the time of Schleiermacher, no matter whether these be regarded as causes or symptoms.

A typical low point in eschatological concern is reached in Schleiermacher's *Christian Faith*. Here the last things occur only as an appendix which functions only as a model to which we should approximate[7] and which seeks to portray the state after death.[8] Eschatology, then, cannot have the same rank as the other topics treated.[9] Schleiermacher, the virtuoso of religion, handled all the dogmatic themes, including the attributes of God,[10] only in their relevance for the human consciousness. Hence they are all tied to the recognizable subject existing here and now. Since this bond is broken in eschatology, no real statements are possible. There thus arises what E. Brunner rather tartly called the "eschatological gap" in Schleiermacher's theology.

Another low point in eschatological thinking (or nonthinking) may be found in the extremely influential Ritschlian school. Following Kant, for whom the eschaton was the organization of the human race according to the laws of virtue, Ritschl saw in the kingdom of God an immanent goal of history, a religious and moral end which would mean the spiritual government of the world. The impulse of love set in train action which is directed toward the moral organization of humanity.[11] What we called the penultimate of the relative future is here made the content of eschatology and in a notoriously noneschatological dogmatics it can be only an appendix which has nothing, or at least nothing new, to say.

To those who found peace in immanence the theses of J. Weiss[12] and A. Schweitzer[13] came as a terrible shock as they reread the NT. The radical eschatology that these two writers saw in the NT, its imminent expectation of the end of history, brought a sense of alienation from this world and seemed to set the familiar figure of Jesus at a remote distance. As Schweitzer said, the Jesus of Nazareth who came forward as the Messiah, proclaimed the morality of the kingdom of God, established the kingdom of heaven on earth, and died to consecrate his work, never existed. He was a figure suggested by rationalism, given life by liberalism, and clothed with historical learning by modern theology.[14] In the new eschatological light it is impossible to impose on Jesus modern ideas such as that of the evolution of the kingdom of God and then to take them back from him

---

[7]*The Christian Faith*, §157.

[8]§158.

[9]§159.

[10]§50; cf. Ebeling, *Wort und Glaube*, II (1969), p. 305.

[11]*Die christliche Lehre von der Rechtfertigung und Versöhnung*, 3rd ed. (1889), p. 14.

[12]*Die Predigt Jesu vom Reiche Gottes* (1892); E.T. *Jesus' Proclamation of the Kingdom of God* (Philadelphia, 1971).

[13]*Geschichte der Leben-Jesu-Forschung* (1901, 1906); E.T. *Quest of the Historical Jesus* (1910); *Geschichte der paulinischen Forschung* (1911).

[14]*Leben-Jesu-Forschung*, 1st ed., p. 396; E.T. p. 396.

through NT theology as Ritschl so naively did.[15] This eschatology bears no relation to the modern ethics which is ruled by the idea of autonomous morality and an ultimate deveiopment to perfection. It is now outdated. The expected end did not come. The wheel of history moves on and hanging on it are the scraps of the body of the uniquely and incalculably great man who was strong enough to think of himself as the spiritual ruler of humanity.[16]

The bankruptcy of this eschatology leads in Schweitzer to a dialectical reversal. The last cry of the crucified with its despairing renunciation of the eschatological future is his affirmation of the world. The ''Son of man'' is buried in the ruins of the collapsing eschatological world. Only Jesus the man lives on.[17] When the eschatological husk has been completely stripped off and proved to be unacceptable, we are left only with the example of a man who could sacrifice himself even though it was an illusion for which he gave his life.

In a highly dialectical way Schweitzer thus returns to the liberal view of Jesus which he set out to attack. He shattered what the Ritschlian school had erroneously imported into history only to set up Jesus as a moral example again when the ground had been cleared.

2. EXAMPLES OF A NEW CONCEPTION (BARTH, DODD, BULTMANN)

The shock caused by Schweitzer's picture of a historically remote eschatology helped to shift the emphasis in eschatology from a spectral future to the present. This shift of accent is unmistakable in the early Barth. When in his *Romans* he says that a Christianity which is not wholly and utterly eschatological has nothing whatever to do with Christ,[18] he is not referring to a crude and brutal and theatrical spectacle but to the eschatological quality of the ''moment.'' At issue is the unconditionality of the ''now'' when we hear his voice (Psalm 95:7f.). People talk about the delay in the Parousia without seeing that what we have here is not a temporal event, the fabled end of the world, but the real end, so much the end that nine hundred years make no difference, that Abraham saw this day and was glad. What is missing is not the Parousia but our expectation of it (p. 484; E.T. p. 500).

Later Barth modified this one-sidedly present eschatology by differentiating the event. The event is eschatological throughout. It is the last time which is the time of the world, the history of all of us whose end was fixed with the death of Jesus. Easter shows us that the time that is left to us can only be the end-time, the time that is hastening to its set end. Easter is thus the first and original eschatological event. Distinct from it is a third act, the goal of the end-time when it will reach its end as this is set already by Christ's death and manifested already in his resurrection. Since this third and last stage will mean the end of temporality, it may be called the nontemporal end. The saying of the earlier Barth that what is at issue is not a final spectacle, a theatrical event in history, is thus given a sublimer sense here (KD,

---

[15]P. 248; E.T. p. 250.
[16]P. 367; E.T. p. 369.
[17]P. 282; E.T. p. 284.
[18]*Römerbrief,* 5th ed. (1929), p. 298; E.T. p. 314.

IV,3, §69,4; CD, IV,3, p. 274; cf. also II,1, pp. 698–722; CD, II,1, pp. 608ff.) and *Letters, 1961–1968,* No. 172). I mention this later modification so as not to tie Barth to his early stage. It was this stage, however, that initiated the phase of what is called realized or present eschatology.

C. H. Dodd[19] and R. Bultmann found a NT basis for this new eschatology and Dodd gave it the name of "realized eschatology."[20] On this view Christ exists eschatologically here and now. The term has no future sense. It "simply" means that those who are addressed by the kerygma and respond to it with an act of decision are taken out of the subject-object schema of their secular existence. So long as we are in this schema we are riveted to what is before us and cannot attain to our individuality. We press toward this through an act of decision which is made possible by encounter with the kerygma and the summons of Christ. Because Christ frees us from the subject-object correlation and determines us by something that transcends it, i.e., his kerygma, we have here an eschatological event. It is eschatological because it ends for us the time of this world and brings the last day here and now as the moment of our decision.[21]

With this existentially based "desecularization" Bultmann avoided any conflict with scholarship and could scorn all apologetic manipulations. Theology is no longer invaded by theories of history or evolution which attack its visions of the eschatological end of the world, for that type of end is no longer at issue. Nor is there any need for the attempts of positive or liberal theology to prove the historicity of Jesus of Nazareth or the gospel stories. The subject of historical research lies in the material world and the subject-object correlation which have now been transcended. If through the kerygma I press on to my own individuality this event of salvation moves on a level which is above the correlation and therefore can no longer be contested by it.

It is fairly obvious that theological developments associated with realized eschatology would have little contribution to make to orientation to the present world. This weakness came out strikingly when a new generation found itself faced with the tasks of shaping the world and thought that it had been abandoned by theology, or at least by this theology. Once again there had to be a correction in eschatological direction in an attempt to fill the vacuum, not merely by a return to the biblical understanding of a salvation history related to world history,[22] but especially by borrowing from Marx and by a theology of hope (Moltmann) whose Marxist connections by way of E. Bloch are unmistakable. There has thus arisen a new epoch in theological history in which the eschatological office has indeed been working overtime.

It has often been pointed out that it was Bultmann who with his desecularizing and consequent detachment of theology from the world caused the pendulum to

---

[19]*The Apostolic Preaching and Its Developments* (New York, 1962), esp. pp. 63ff.; *The Parables of the Kingdom,* 17th ed. (1965), pp. 35ff., 54, 81.
[20]On Bultmann cf. EG, I, esp. pp. 50ff.; EF, I, pp. 55ff.
[21]Bultmann found this figure of the last day too romantic. It is needed only to illustrate the eschatological character of the event.
[22]Cf. in this regard O. Cullmann, *Christus und die Zeit* (1946); E.T. *Christ and Time* (Philadelphia, 1950) and *Heil als Geschichte* (1965); E.T. *Salvation in History* (London, 1967).

swing back to the opposite extreme of a new eschatological boom and subjected philosophical markets to a plundering of their thisworldly stocks. Theologically the weakness in Bultmann was given emphasis by H. Jonas in his memorial address "Im Kampf um die Möglichkeit des Glaubens" (FAZ, 11/19/76), in which he said that religion cannot be content with the inwardness of the Word in existence but must keep before it, and ascribe to God's causality, its original public appearance in the world as the self-revelation of the will of God through human words. The most colorful diagnosis is that of E. Bloch, who speaks of Bultmann's religious chamber. Here is the "cut-off straw" of the individualism which is all that is left for remaining Christians of this kind, everything physical, social, or cosmic being set aside as secular (*Der Atheismus im Christentum* [1968], pp. 69ff.; E.T. *Atheism in Christianity* [New York, 1972], pp. 38ff.). For Barth's criticism of Bultmann cf. his work "R. Bultmann. Ein Versuch, ihn zu verstehen," *Theologische Studien*, No. 34 (1952) and Barth-Bultmann, *Letters, 1922–66* (1971), pp. 287ff.

A. Individual Eschatology

XXXI

On the Understanding of Death

Bibliography (apart from works of dogmatics and OT and NT theologies): A. Ahlbrecht, *Tod und Unsterblichkeit in der evangelischen Theologie der Gegenwart* (1964); P. Althaus, *Die letzten Dinge,* 3rd ed. (1926); also "Retraktationen zur Eschatologie," ThLZ, LXXV (1950), pp. 253ff.; J. Amery, *Über das Altern,* 2nd ed. (1969); P. Arles, *Studien zur Geschichte des Todes im Abendland* (1976); C. Barth, *Die Errettung vom Tode in den individuellen Klage- und Dankliedern des AT* (1947); L. Boros, *Mysterium mortis,* 5th ed. (1960); E.T. *The Mystery of Death* (New York, 1975); E. Brunner, *Das Ewige als Zukunft und Gegenwart* (1953); E.T. *Eternal Hope* (Philadelphia, 1954); H. Bürkle, "Der Tod in der afrikanischen Gemeinschaften," *Leben angesichts des Todes* (1968) (quoted as *Leben*), pp. 243ff.; J. Choton, *Der Tod im abendländischen Denken* (1970); O. Cullmann, "Unsterblichkeit der Seele und Auferstehung der Toten," *Theologische Zeitschrift* (Basel), II (1956), pp. 126ff.; G. Fohrer, "Das Geschick des Menschen nach dem Tode im AT," *Kerygma und Dogma,* IV (1968), p. 249 (Bibliography); S. Freud, *Das Ich und das Es* (1923); E.T. *The Ego and the Id, Major Works,* pp. 697-717 (cf. M. Schur, S. Freud, *Sein Leben und Sterben* [1973], pp. 436ff.; E.T. S. Freud, *Living and Dying* [New York, 1972]); G. Greshake, *Auferstehung der Toten* (1969); also with G. Lohfink, *Naherwartung, Auferstehung, Unsterblichkeit,* 2nd ed. (1976); H. E. Hengstenberg, *Tod und Vollendung* (1938); M. L. Henry, " 'Tod' und 'Leben,' Unheil und Heil als Funktionen des richtenden und rettenden Gottes im AT," *Leben,* pp. 1ff.; B. Hildebrandt, "Die theologische Bedeutung des Todes," *Theologische Versuche,* VI ([East] Berlin, 1975), pp. 193ff.; P. Hoffmann, *Die Toten in Christus* (1966); C.-H. Hunzinger, "Die Hoffnung angesichts des Todes im Wandel der paulinischen Aussage," *Leben,* pp. 69ff.; F. Husemann, *Vom Sinn und Bild des Todes,* 2nd ed. (1954); E. Jüngel, *Tod,* 3rd ed. (1973); E.T. *Death* (Philadelphia, 1974); U. Kellermann, "Überwindung des Todesgeschicks in der alttestamentlichen Frömmigkeit," ZThK, III (1976), pp. 259ff.; K. Koch, "Der Schatz im Himmel," *Leben,* pp. 47ff.; H. J. Kraus, "Vom Leben und Tod in den Psalmen," *Leben,* pp. 27ff.; E. Kübler-Ross, *Interviews mit Sterbendenden* (1971); E.T. *On Death and Dying* (New York, 1969); R. Leuenberger, *Der Tod. Schicksal und Aufgabe,* 3rd ed. (1973); W. Lohff, "Theologische Erwägungen zum Problem des Todes," *Leben,* pp. 157ff.; B. Lohse, "Gesetz, Tod und Sünde in Luthers Auslegung des 90. Psalmes," *Leben,* pp. 138ff.; H. R. Müller-Schwefe, "Tod und Leben in der modernen Dichtung," *Leben,* p. 223; S. Neill, "Die Macht und die Bewältigung des Todes im Hinduismus und Buddhismus," *Leben,* pp. 283ff.; G. von Rad and R. Bultmann, TWNT, II, pp. 844ff.; E.T. TDNT, II, pp. 843ff.; K. Rahner, *Zur Theologie des Todes* (1958); E.T. *On the Theology of Death* (New York, 1961); also *Grundkurs des Glaubens* (1976), pp. 417ff.; E.T. *Foundations,* pp. 435ff.; J. Ratzinger, *Eschatologie—Tod und ewiges Leben* (1977); R. Reiner, *Ars moriendi* (1957); H. P. Schmidt, "Todeserfahrung und Lebenserwartung," *Leben,* pp. 191ff.; C. Stange, *Das Ende aller Dinge* (1930); H. Thielicke, *Tod und Leben* (1943); E.T. *Death and Life* (Philadelphia, 1971); also Anthrop, pp. 381ff.; W. Trillhaas, *Religionsphilosophie* (1972), pp. 159ff.; H. Volk, *Der Tod in der Sicht des christlichen Glaubens* (1958).

1. THE IDEA OF IMMORTALITY AS A SUPPRESSING OF THE FACT OF DEATH

In our attempt to get at the Christian understanding of death we shall keep to the main points and use the form of theses.[1]

1. Not only in the modern (clinical) evasion of death but also in concealing burial practices death is almost always an object of repression.

2. The intellectual form of such repression may be found in the various doctrines of immortality. For all their differences these have a basic theme in common. Man is divided into a perishable part and an imperishable part. The perishable part in all cases is the physical body which is given a limited span and then crumbles into dust. The imperishable part is interpreted in different ways. It can be an immortal soul which is detached from perishable corporeality. The classical form of this is found in Plato's *Phaedo.* The soul does not come into being but is preexistent. Nor does it die, for as an identical substance it lies behind all closed and dissolving and therefore changing relations to the body. The body as a sensory phenomenon represents the flight and decay of phenomena. The soul is the epitome of that which endures.

The two acts of binding and loosing are not limited to the two moments when they are most manifest to us, namely, birth and death. They determine life between these boundaries. They do so quantitatively by beginning and ending it but also qualitatively by constituting its content. This content depends on our attitude to our own death. The degree to which a life presses on to true knowledge and therefore to the ground of being depends on this attitude.[2] The following consideration shows that the ineluctability of death directs attention to this ground of being as the thing which really counts.

In Platonic thinking the immortality of the soul is closely connected with the relation of the soul to the *ousia* (essence) of things. In its own being the soul corresponds to this *ousia* while the body is referred only to the phenomena of the *ousia* as an adequate observer. Body and soul are referred to the spheres of being from which they come, the soul to the eternal sphere, the body to the corruptible sphere as it appears to the senses.

---

[1]The reason for this is that immediately after the completion of this volume I intend to write a completely revised edition of my monograph *Tod und Leben.* (This is now available with the title *Leben mit dem Tod* [1980] and an E.T. is being prepared.) Cf. on the theme the bibliography to Anthrop.

[2]Cf. Cicero's statement that the whole life of philosophers is a commentary on death.

One may thus conclude—here Plato's Socrates reduces childish fear of death to the absurd[3]—that the soul is as little exposed to dissolution and death as is the sphere of being from which it comes. Metaphysical entities (e.g., concepts like sphere and cylinder) do not decay but are always the same even though their concrete manifestations perish. The invisible endures, the visible changes.

This demonstrates the immortality of the soul. In *Phaedo* (cc. 54f.) the soul is the principle or essence of life, its invisible *ousia*. By definition it cannot die. It is, then, the opposite of mortal, i.e., immortal (*athanatos*). As snow cannot be warm nor fire cold, so the soul which gives life cannot be dead.[4]

The content of the separation in death of the mortal body from the enduring and immortal soul is that the soul goes to what is akin to it. But we have to differentiate here between different attitudes and qualities of soul. There is the "philosophical" soul which even in life is detached from the body and senses and is oriented to the *ousia*. For it what is akin is the divinity and eternal felicity to which it goes after death. But the soul which is subject to the corruptible, to the body, and which is thus a kind of nonsoul, will also be subject to what is akin to it. It must wander around until it is again united with a body, which according to its previous disposition may be that of a donkey, hawk, wolf, bee, or ant.

Man is immortal to the extent that only something in him is mortal and subject to time and change—only his bodily existence. His true being, the soul, is of an indestructible quality.

This brief sketch of the Platonic doctrine of immortality, which has often been taken up into the Christian tradition,[5] poses a question which we shall have to deal with later, namely, whether its dividing of man can be harmonized with the understanding of man as a totality in biblical anthropology, and how the immortality of the soul stands in relation to the resurrection of the flesh. For the moment we simply note the problem.

We note, too, that man has a double quality as both an individual and also the bearer of supraindividual powers. Not just in Germanic religion[6] but in Homer too[7] death is hardly portrayed as an individual event. Man the individual is less prominent than man the representative of a transsubjective entity which engulfs him and in which he is absorbed: the welfare and honor of the clan among the Germans; *moira,* which embraces both gods and men, in Homer. The particularity of dying is missing because there is no personal understanding to serve as a basis of particularity.

The lack of personal individuality is not just related to an archaic or primitive stage when the sense of it has not yet awakened. It is found in later reflection too. Among many possible examples we may refer to Hegel, for whom the individual is simply an interim transitional point in the supraindividual process of the development of the spirit.[8] We again ask how this unimportance of the death of the

---

[3] "It is the child in us that fears death" (*Phaedo,* c. 24).
[4] c. 55.
[5] E.g., at the Fifth Lateran Council (Denz., 1440; E.T. 738).
[6] W. Grönbech, *Kultur und Religion der Germanen* (1937).
[7] W. F. Otto, *Die Götter Griechenlands,* esp. p. 176 and pp. 340ff.
[8] Cf. on this ThE, II, 1, §§75ff.; also EF, I and II, Index.

individual can be reconciled with the biblically understood unconditionality of the person who is called by name and is unique before God, so that individual death necessarily becomes a problem.

Hegel's understanding of individuality and individual death recurs in the collectivism of Marxist anthropology and has been spread by Marxist propaganda. Certain statements of Hegel have only to be modified by substituting class for species and we have a Marxist variant (cf. Hegel, *Enzyklopädie* [Meiner], §370, pp. 327, 331, etc.). Along these lines Marx can say that death is a harsh victory of the species over the individual which seems to contradict the unity of the species, but the individual is only one of a species and as such mortal ("Nationalökonomie und Philosophie," *Frühschriften,* ed. Landshut, p. 239). On the Marxist view of death as a whole cf. H. Rolfes, *Der Sinn des Lebens im marxistischen Denken* (1971).

In the depreciation of the individual in favor of such supernatural forces as the welfare and honor of the clan, the world spirit, and the Marxist collective, these entities take the place of Plato's soul. They alone are immortal, while the original unsuitability of the individual for universality is its original sickness and the native seed of death.[9] In Plato, however, the immortal soul is the core of the personal self and, as we would put it today, constitutes its identity. But here the immortality of the general and supraindividual lays stress on its nonidentity with the person. Because of this, death is of no concern to the individual person. This person can have no name which endures in eternity and is written in the book of life. At this point we are as far away as possible from the biblical understanding of the person.

With these examples that point to a different spiritual background from that of the Bible we must be content.

2. THE BIBLICAL UNDERSTANDING OF THE END OF LIFE. DEATH AS A PERSONAL EVENT

a. Knowledge of Death

Doctrines of immortality can be regarded as a suppression of the knowledge of death, as a refusal to accept it. When the Psalmist asks God to "teach us to number our days that we may get a heart of wisdom" (Psalm 90:12; 39:5; cf. Job 14:5), this presupposes a knowledge of death but also its suppression. Man's spirit is from the very outset one that holds down the truth in unrighteousness (Romans 1:18ff.). The Pneuma has to take away its blindness, which it cannot itself overcome.

The Psalmist's prayer for a disclosure of the suppressed knowledge of death can be helpful to us only if we see to what knowledge it relates and see also that suppression of the fact of death by reinterpretation or denial is a fault.

It would be wrong to think that man's natural knowledge of death is no more than thinking about his last hour. If this were so, the knowledge might be reserved for old people who are close to this hour. But in fact we are always thinking about death even though this may often be only in symbolical form. We hurry to finish

---

[9]Hegel, *Enzyklopädie,* p. 331.

our life's work because we know that our span is limited. The knowledge of death is present here in a code. The young are subject to it as well. They know that they are young only once and they must make the most of it. Football players and athletes realize that their day will soon be over and their physical constitution will deteriorate. It is thus true: "That we shall die, we know; 'tis but the time, And drawing days out, that men stand upon."[10]

This knowledge of death is related to a specific view of time. Time is not seen as something that constantly revolves or renews itself, as the Greeks believed and as the clock might suggest. The knowledge of death presupposes that time is a direct line which like a road leads by way of the present from the past to the future. We are traversing a long corridor with many doors that have handles on the other side.

The constant feature in this irreversible movement is the faithfulness of God in whose hands time lies (Psalm 31:15). The prayer that God will give us a clear knowledge of time is also the prayer that my temporality may be present to me—its character as the finitude within which I have to decide between flesh and spirit—but also the fact that it is held in the hands of the one in whom I trust.[11]

Death is not feared, then, merely because it is the physical moment when life ends. This may be far away and it may come upon me with no terrors, either deceiving or erasing my consciousness. Death is feared because it lies like a shadow over the whole of life, characterizing it as a "being for death." The finitude of life which death proclaims is what I suppress. This mystery of suppression is what lies behind the saying of Pascal that death, if we do not think of it, is easier to bear than the idea of death when we are not in danger and the moment of our physical end seems to be remote.[12]

That the knowledge of death expresses itself in a specific view of life, namely, that it is "being for death," distinguishes man from animals. Animals live for the moment with no future in view. They are aware of death only when they are in acute danger. Man looks ahead to the future. This future is present to him in his anxiety (Heidegger). What causes him anxiety is that he must grasp his destiny in this time of his.[13]

Hölderlin in his ode "Man" views death as a power that overshadows life and depicts the birds, which have no awareness of death, as breathing more freely and living as it were in an eternal present. In the same way the child, not knowing death, can be called immortal. This would not be possible were death simply a final point, for Hölderlin knows well enough that the child will cease to be a child and grow old and come under the law of mortality. He can speak in this way because for him the nature of death is that through knowledge of it it influences the whole of our lives. Only in this sense is the child still exempt from it.

The Psalmist's prayer: "Teach us to number our days . . . ," stands against the background of this knowledge of finitude which is imposed on us but which we suppress. The question raised by death is whether the world or God is the binding force in our lives.

---

[10]Shakespeare, *Julius Caesar,* Act III, Scene 1.
[11]On the Greek view of time in distinction from the idea of history cf. Anthrop, pp. 35ff., 327ff.
[12]*Penseés,* 83 (*Great Books of the Western World,* Vol. 83, p. 203).
[13]Anthrop, pp. 218, 393 and *passim.*

As I see my finitude I find myself forced to decide what my attitude to the world should be. If the world is for me a self-resting finitude, then I can enjoy what it offers according to my wishes. If, as Paul says, the dead are not raised, if I am finally to be snuffed out, then the obvious course is to eat, drink, and be merry, for tomorrow we shall die (1 Corinthians 15:32; cf. Isaiah 22:13).

If, on the other hand, I know that someone has called me by name, and that I am bound to him in life and in death (Romans 14:8), then I know an infinite worth which transcends my finitude and which is given to me by the fact that I am bought at a price (1 Corinthians 6:20; 7:23; 8:11). Hence, knowing my end, I can no longer live uninterruptedly by "things." Death undoubtedly ends my relation to things, to what is before me in my finitude. It thus raises the question what I am apart from all this, or whether I am anything at all apart from it.

By "things" the Bible means for the most part mammon. This is the chief representative of the powers with whose help I try to find security and buy time. But it is said of the one who relies on mammon that "when he dies he will carry nothing away; his glory will not go down after him" (Psalm 49:17). "For we brought nothing into the world, and we cannot take anything out of the world" (1 Timothy 6:7). Our life does not consist of such goods or such artificial fulfilments. They will not last. They perish in death. Discovering this is the tragedy of the rich farmer of Luke 12:16ff.; he is summoned away from his full barns in which he had found security and apparent peace. Who is he now without this false basis on which he relied? As who does he stand before whom?

As those who live before God and by faith in him we have a self which exists beyond things—barns, mammon, the collective—and which can be detached from them. To use for a moment the dubious subject-object schema, we are the subject of faith. Faith, however, is not a human product or work. It is awakened by the Pneuma. Hence this self of ours is also the object of a history which God has begun with us and which even death cannot arrest or end. We, of course, can be brought to an end by death. We are. We are not immortal. We must die. We have no more than "a house not made with hands, eternal in the heavens." We must go through death. But God keeps this heavenly house ready for us (2 Corinthians 5:1f.). He keeps it ready in spite of all-embracing death.

b. Death as Judgment

As death determines life as "being for death" and thus raises the question of the self, and especially the question whether we live by things which abandon us or are held secure with time in other hands, a quality is assigned to death which transcends its significance as a biological event.[14] This metabiological understanding of death is not restricted to the biblical understanding and the related decision. It has constantly played a role in philosophy too. This was inevitable, for the knowledge of death and finitude, with its suppression, will always have, either in the form of care and anxiety or in that of an eudaemonistic confession, consequences which go beyond the sphere of the biological.

This extra element comes out most clearly in the experience and the poetic and

---

[14]Cf. ThE, II, 1, §§1195ff.; Anthrop, pp. 106ff.

philosophical treatment of the incomprehensibility of death, which contrasts sharply with its biological comprehensibility. Thus the psychiatrist E. Hoche calls it an intolerable thought that the huge subjective world within us should be wiped out while others go on boastfully as if nothing had happened. The strength of this feeling defies all logic (*Jahresringe* [1936]). The biological logic of death is shattered existentially by the feeling of absurdity. Guy de Maupassant in his novel *Bel Ami* has the same thought that it is unimaginable that I should perish while others live on. The sight of a corpse does not trigger this feeling of incomprehensibility because here death is objectified and does not touch those who are still alive. In *Narziss und Goldmund* H. Hesse, on the basis of his central theme of love and death, derives death's incomprehensibility from the relation of life to others, to the countryside, to animals, and to much else—a relation which is broken by death. (Cf. Tolstoy's "Death of Ivan Ilych" in *Master and Servant* [E.T. New York, 1973] and Heidegger's interpretation of this in *Being and Time* [New York, 1962], p. 495, n. xii).

R. M. Rilke made the sharpest break between the biological view of death and the existential view when he distinguished between "little death," which is related to sickness and involves a mere exit, and "big death," which ripens in us and is part of our lives (*Malte*, V, p. 13; cf. also *Weisse Fürstin*, I, p. 384 and *Stundenbuch*, II, p. 273).

This existential view determines the biblical interpretation of death when it makes it a sign of our finitude and of the judgment that falls on us. The biological aspect is not denied. On countless occasions human life is connected with conception, birth, and explainable decay. But the mystery of death is not, in modern terms, exhausted by a zero reading on an electrocardiogram or encephalogram. In the medium of biological processes a very different reality comes to light. Psalm 139 (vv. 13ff.) expresses the fact that the beginning and end of life have two dimensions. It refers to the embryo developing in the womb but in such a way that the development is more than a process of becoming and cannot be explained merely as such. The essential point is that it is God who is at work in the medium of the natural process and who designs the developing child: "Thy eyes beheld my unformed substance; in thy book were written, every one of them, the days that were formed for me, when as yet there was none of them" (v. 16).

Our present question is how the Bible views this metabiological side of dying.[15] We shall try to consider especially how we are to understand from this standpoint such prominent sayings as that of Psalm 90:7: "For we are consumed by thy anger," or the dictum of Paul in Romans 6:23: "The wages of sin is death." In neither statement is death a natural necessity that comes upon us or a law in face of which I am a mere object. In both it is an event which I myself have caused, over against which I am subject, and which I have freely brought about as a responsible person. In my relation to death I am not just a representative of *bios* but a person. The wrath of God which comes to expression in death is in this sense God's reaction to our personal action. Which action?

The answer may be given in two theses.

---

[15]It arises in many different ways in both the OT and the NT. We shall deal here only with the meaning of death as judgment.

First, death represents a limit, the fact that life has a goal and we have to leave it.

Second, man in contradiction, i.e., man who has broken away from God, represents the basic violation of this limit.

The second thesis needs elucidation. Biblically sin is always described as the violation of a limit. In it man tries to be as God (Genesis 3:5). Adam threatens to become as one of us (Genesis 3:22). As in the building of the tower of Babel, he tries to lift himself up into God's sphere (Genesis 11:1ff.). Sin, separation, is not just a negative thing. It is not just a withdrawal. The withdrawal is accompanied by a usurpation of God's throne and a titan-like invasion of heaven. Man wants to be superman.[16] If there is a God, how can I bear not to be God?

As we have seen, in Paul idolatry is the chief manifestation of this attempt to shape ultimate reality in man's image and to make this the measure of all things and values. The same naturally applies to the impersonal but unchanged tendency of idolatry which is expressed in the worship of ideas (ideology) or the worship of pleasure or the worship of mammon. The difference is based only on the difference in the human types which make God in their own image, no matter whether the word "God" is used or not.

If we contrast the two theses—death as a limit and man as notoriously without limits—we see the personal character of death in and over against the biological aspect. It comes on man the day that he eats the forbidden fruit which lies beyond the limit. The barrier of finitude is lowered against the one who wants to be without limits.

The first limit, i.e., the boundary between God and man, which it was left to man's freedom of obedience to respect, was wickedly violated by man in this freedom. Hence a second limit was set which he could not overcome and which entailed a radical division between corruptible man and the eternal God. This limit is death. It is an uncontrollable event which happens *to* him and to which he is subject. The titanic pride which grasped at God's eternity will also attack this decree of temporality and try to make death a fulfilment of sovereign human freedom.

Nietzsche is an example of this. Man as self-creator must freely destroy himself too (8, 144f.). He must turn the stupid physiological fact into a moral necessity (16, 315). Natural death is death under contemptible conditions. It is not free. We should will death freely and consciously, with no room for contingency or accident (8, 144). We should stop eating when our taste is at its best and die victoriously surrounded by those who hope and praise (6, 105). This protest against death, with its postulate of free death, was taken up, radicalized, and given a Marxist point by J. Amery (*Hand an sich legen* [1976]).

Even without the extreme thinking which makes suicide a human virtue and a sign of promethean sovereignty, hybrid defiance of the judgment of death can manifest itself in scorn of death. Luther interpreted it in this way and denounced it

---

[16]E. Benz, "Das Bild des Übermenschen in der europäischen Geistesgeschichte" and L. Müller, "Das Bild des Übermenschen in der Philosophie Solovjevs," in E. Benz, ed., *Der Übermensch* (1961), pp. 19ff., 163ff.

as contempt of God and blasphemy (cf. Commentary on the Psalms [WA, 40/III, 485, 13ff.; 520, 10ff.; 537, 18ff.; LW, 13, 76.98.107]).

We can trace the course between creation and the fall as follows.

The divine likeness means being allowed to live with God and hence to be free from death. The last enemy (1 Corinthians 15:26) has no function here. But the attempt at equality with God, which is not content to live with God and wants autonomy instead of relationship, leads to death. Indeed, it is death. "The wages of sin is death."

In this personal character of death Luther sees the difference between human death and that of animals. Man was created to be like God, not to die but to live in and with God. Death was brought in by his refusal to accept his limits. For man, then, death means infinite and eternal wrath as a punishment for sin. If Adam had not eaten the forbidden fruit, he would have been immortal. Death is thus a contradiction of the purpose of the Creator for man, who was created to dwell in God (WA, 40/III, 513, 18ff.; LW, 13, 94).

The terror of death is not, then, that it is the quantitive end and limit of life but that in death a limit is set to those who want to be without limits. Or, more sharply, God who alone is eternal contradicts finite man in his attempt to be without limits. Death is interpreted here as a phenomenon in our history with God. A dimension of meaning may thus be seen which is hidden when it is considered only biologically. It is viewed here as a fact of "history" and not of "nature."

This does not mean that we can historically (*historisch*) explain human death by the fall. Many orthodox theologians fell victim to this misunderstanding in the 17th and 18th centuries with the very logical result that a different physiology was ascribed to Adam and Eve before the fall. (On the epistemological and hermeneutical reasons for this misunderstanding cf. ThE, II, 1, §§1207ff.). The relating of the fall and sin is not an alternative to a scientific interpretation of death. It arises on a different level where judgment is seen *in* the medium of natural processes (not *instead* of them).

Death is not characterized merely by the *fact* that it is a limit but also by *him who* is limited, namely, limitless man who wants equality with God and not just likeness. Death is characterized, too, by *him who* imposes the limit, namely, the Holy One who will tolerate no other gods and who therefore humbles the superman. Biblically, death is not the death of man as a mammal but the death of man as one who wants to be God and hence has to learn that he is only man.

Since man is at the same time both mammal and a personal representative of pride, death has also a biological side. But this is not the true reality, just as man's true reality is not that he is a mammal. This is only the physical basis of the true reality. Man's true reality is to be a person.[17] The true reality of death through the biological medium is, then, the contradiction of his person, i.e., limitlessness.[18]

The double aspect of man as *bios* and person may be seen also in the curse of

---

[17]For the concept of "person" cf. Anthrop, Index.

[18]A similar absorbing of the biological medium into personal processes is shown in sexuality, which also involves an I-Thou encounter (ThE, II, 1, §1198; III, §§1902ff.; E.T. *Ethics of Sex*, pp. 44ff.). Only from this angle can one see the relation between *erōs* and *agapē* in theological ethics.

Genesis 3:19 which imposes the sentence of death. Man must now eat his bread by the sweat of his brow and endure this until he returns to the dust from which he was made: "You are dust, and to dust you shall return."

"You are dust." You belong to the earth. You are subject to the God above whom you have exalted yourself and in your series of revolts will try to do so again by building the tower of Babel. "To dust you shall return." By being brought back to dust you will be reminded that you have been thrust back behind the frontier you crossed. Your death is thus a warning that you belong to earth and that the eternity which you assume to yourself is not yours. Sin as the background of that assumption gives death a claim over you. It is the basis of death: "The wages of sin is death."

We see, of course, how the biological and personal factors intertwine. Returning to dust is not just being pushed back into the zone of limitation. It is also perishing physically. That which determines living man, his twofold character as *bios* and person,[19] also determines his end.[20]

The element of judgment cannot be objectified or demonstrated. Its certainty is accessible only to faith which lives by the turning of the eternal God to finite and—for good reason—hiding man (Genesis 3:8). We cannot reach this certainty by speculation. It is not within the reach of reason. According to the texts, especially those of Paul, it is based on God's self-disclosure by his Spirit.

One attempt to objectivize the relation between death and judgment is that of historicizing it and deriving physical death from the divine sentence. The stories of creation and the fall, however, are not meant to be history (*Historie*). (The history [*Historie*] of the human race can only portray its history [*Geschichte*] between the fall and the last judgment, i.e., a history under the shadow of death, so that the proton and the eschaton lie outside the epistemological presuppositions of such historicizing.) The original estate of man and the fall are not to be viewed as a chronology of the earliest epochs. They describe our own here and now and expound the belief that God created us. We are at issue, not the world. We have to see *ourselves* as those who have come from God's creative hands and cannot give ourselves back to them as we came. We have to see in ourselves those who (as illustrated by the *exemplar*, Adam[21]) break loose from life as God created it and throw off our subjection to him.

Creation and the fall are as it were the horizon of our lives and aim at *us* from all sides. If we want a graphic description of the intention of the early stories, we should not see them as the portrayal of a span of time prior to our own but as a

---

[19]Dilthey illustrated this twofoldness by the Sphinx with its human face and animal body (Anthrop, pp. 139ff.).

[20]Cf. M. Schmaus, *Katholische Dogmatik*, III (1941), p. 493: "In the domain of physiological laws something takes place that no experiment or experience can verify but faith alone can affirm: the idea of a divine judgment."

[21]Luther likes the word *exemplar*, especially in relation to Christ, whose righteousness and humanity are ours (cf. his sermon on Matthew 11:25ff.). All that is Christ's can be said to be of those who believe in him (WA, 2, 531, 10; LW, 27, 282). We have to rely on what he did and suffered as if we ourselves did it (WA, 2, 140, 7; 40/I, 278, 6; LW, 42, 12). Cf. also the Hebrews Lectures (G.T. E. Vogelsang [1939], p. 40). Adam is an *exemplar* too, his creatureliness being ours, his fall and sin our fall and sin (1 Corinthians 15:45ff.). Cf. theological identity with Adam in my book *Geschichte und Existenz*, pp. 239ff.

circle lying around us and enclosing our own personal world. They have rightly been called a backward-looking prophecy which lights up my existential standing before God in the light of a "then" and tells my own story in terms of this "then." Resorting to this prophetic category draws attention to the witness of the Spirit which alone enables us to see things in this way.[22]

c. The Psyche and the Totality of the Person

In order to develop the idea of personal totality in contrast to the division which we found in the concept of immortality we shall give a brief sketch of the terminology of the NT, especially Paul. The main terms are body (*sōma*), flesh (*sarx*), soul (*psyche*), and spirit (*pneuma*). In this outline I am following the penetrating analyses of R. Bultmann in RGG[2] and *Theologie des NT* (1953), pp. 188ff.; E.T. *NT Theology*, I, pp. 191ff.

In Paul, unlike Plato, these terms do not denote separate spheres arranged hierarchically with *sarx* at the bottom and *psyche* and *pneuma* higher up. They all express the total person and simply emphasize specific relations of this person.

Thus *sōma* is not just man's external form. It is man himself, so that one can say, not that man has a *sōma*, but that he is *sōma* (*Theologie des NT*, p. 191; E.T. *NT Theology*, p. 194). Thus *sōma* can often be translated I (1 Corinthians 13:3; 9:27; 7:4, etc.) or you (1 Corinthians 6:15; 12:27). The whole person is described by the term but in a particular relation. Man is *sōma* insofar as he can make himself the object of an action or experience himself as the subject of an event . . . insofar as he has a relation to himself (p. 192; E.T. p. 195). The synonymous nature of *sōma* and I comes out especially in Pauline eschatology when the natural body (*sōma psychikon*) of the first Adam is contrasted with the spiritual body (*sōma pneumatikon*) of the second Adam (1 Corinthians 15:44ff.). Body here is a state that lies beyond our present corruptibility (15:42f.) and is not to be equated with any conceivable corporeality of our present world of experience. Paul does not speak in this way because he is anti-spiritual but because *sōma* describes our I-ness and is thus indispensable to denote our identity in this life and the resurrection life.

As regards *sarx*, apart from occasional overlapping with *sōma*, the particular point is that it represents a force which makes man carnal, i.e., which subjects him to the present corruptible order. Often the phrase "according to" (*kata*) precedes it (Romans 8:13; cf. 7:14ff.). It denotes the whole person insofar as this person belongs to the perishable world that is hostile to God. "Insofar as" expresses a relation of the person.

In regard to the problem of death our main interest is in *psyche* because the totality of the person denoted by it stands in total antithesis to the dividing of the I in the Platonic doctrine of immortality.

As the use of *sōma* has suggested, the *psyche* in Paul is not separated dualistically from the body. It does not represent the center of man, as in Plato, nor does it have the quality of immortality. On the basis of the OT term *nephesh*, which is translated *psyche* in the LXX, it again denotes the whole person insofar as there is

---

[22]We cannot discuss here the relation between human death and death in the nonhuman cosmos (Genesis 6:7; Romans 8:19, 22). Cf. in *Death and Life* the chapters "Death in the Cosmos" and "The Biological and Personal Dimension of Sickness" (pp. 207ff.) (E.T. of *Tod und Leben*).

reference to its living character. The most striking difference from Plato may be found, not in Paul, but in the parable of the rich farmer (Luke 12:20). True reality is at issue here but it is not described by the word *psyche*. True reality is in fact described negatively by what it is not. It is not having or possessing a carnal relation to things. If we think it is, we lose everything in death, including ourselves. We come under a rule of subtraction and are reduced to nothing. True reality is being rich toward God (12:21). Unlike provisional wealth this cannot be consumed by moths and will not perish in death. In this parable the term *psyche* denotes only life. You are a fool—you who have put your trust in earthly things. When this night you lose your *psyche,* your life, then what will you have left of your crowded barns?

The word *psyche* emphatically does not express here the true reality in man but denotes the physical basis of natural life on the basis of which I may find or miss the true reality (riches in God) in the time allotted to me. *Psyche* is used in a similar way in the saying in Luke 12:23 that "life (*psyche*) is more than food, and the body more than clothing."

In Paul, too, the term *psyche* means man's person or I in relation to his life. When he says that he would "gladly spend and be spent for your souls" he means "for you" (2 Corinthians 12:15; cf. Bultmann, p. 200f.; E.T. p. 204). In view of this, Paul, in contrasting Adam and Christ, can say that Adam "was" (not "had") a *soma psychikon* and he can differentiate him as a *psyche zosa* ("living being") from the life-giving spirit of the last Adam (1 Corinthians 15:44f.).

Yet the participle "living" being denotes a deeper or human dimension of the psyche which does not allow us to use *psyche* for the life of animals. The participle (*zosa*) comes from *zen,* or the noun *zoe.* This does not merely differ from natural life (*bios*) but is opposed to it. In Gnosticism *zoe* is the transcendent divine power or the *aphtharsia* based on it (TWNT, II, p. 841; TDNT, II, p. 841), which is not found in earthly life. The situation is much the same in the NT but without Gnostic dualism. Occasionally we can read of a *zen en sarki* (Galatians 2:20; Philippians 1:22). But this is not strict usage. True *zoe* is God's. Without it man with only psychic life can be called dead (*nekros*) (Matthew 8:22; Luke 15:32; Colossians 2:13). This true *zoe* is promised to us as future (*mellousa*) (1 Timothy 4:8). It can thus be called eternal life (*zoe aionos*), e.g., in Mark 10:17; Romans 6:22f.; Galatians 6:8. It can also be equated with the state of salvation (*soteria*) (Romans 5:10). It is the resurrection life which is given to us and is outside human control (cf. TWNT, II, p. 864; TDNT, II, p. 863).

When Paul links the participle of *zen* to Adamic life this helps us greatly to see how he is using *psyche.* Adam's life (*psyche*) differs from that of animals because in it is the seed of *zoe,* his determination for speech. We do not read in too much if we see here a background reference to the two forms of Adam. The second Adam, Christ, is the Spirit who gives *zoe* (*pneuma zoiopoioun*) while the first Adam is the creature that receives *zoe* (A. Schlatter, *Paulus . . .* [1956], p. 437). But what else can this receiving mean in Paul than Adam's receiving of the firstfruits of the Spirit (Romans 8:23) which lead him toward the promised future *zoe*?

His *psyche,* however, is again his I, this time with the special nuance that his living I is the vessel that contains his determination and receives the first installment of his future *zoe.* Thus Bultmann is probably right when he rejects the false view that in Paul the *psyche* is to be interpreted as the general principle of animal life (p. 201). It belongs instead to Adam and denotes specifically his human life with its projected determination. This specific human factor is that man, unlike animals, is faced with the decision whether he will accept his determination or sabotage it. Purely psychic man, who has no more than natural life, is one who does not have the *pneuma* (1 Corinthians 2:14).

We thus maintain that in distinction from the division of the I in Plato, which grants immortality only to the *psyche,* the anthropological terms used in the NT—especially *psyche* but also *sarx* and *soma*—refer to the whole person in a specific relation. This anthropological schema leaves no place for a Platonic or Hegelian concept of immortality. The conquest of death according to the NT message must be sought elsewhere. We shall now take up this search as we take a look at eternal life and the resurrection of the dead.

XXXII

Life after Death

1. THE QUESTION OF ETERNAL LIFE

We shall unfold the meaning of eternal life as a Christian answer to the question posed by the idea of immortality, i.e., in the context of what is traditionally called individual eschatology. No apologetic purpose underlies the juxtaposition of immortality and eternal life but rather the conviction that the concept of immortality can exercise a fruitful heuristic function as we seek the sharp contours of the concept of eternal life.

Although death can be called the last enemy (1 Corinthians 15:26, 55; cf. Revelation 20:14; 21:4), it is not an independent theme in the NT. We do not stare at it as a rabbit does at a snake. The impression that this is so lies behind the idea that a motive of suppression lies behind resurrection myths and leads to wish projections in the sense of Feuerbach. In the NT death is simply the dark foil for the figure of him who conquers it. Only in faith in the risen Lord and in union with him do we see—as it were in retrospect—the darkness of existence in the world which is overshadowed by guilt and death. Only in the light of the fulfilment can we see fully what it meant to be unredeemed. Only when the gospel grants us closeness to God can we appreciate what distance from him is.

We relapse into legalism if we expect or desire that the way be prepared for openness to the liberating news of the gospel by exercises which enable us to measure the full darkness of guilt, pain, and death. In preaching, as many preachers should note, there is no need to play on nuclear weapons, drugs, or other apocalyptic terrors to make people receptive to the heavenly Jerusalem. We first learn the thick darkness of the world of death when we are saved from it. We see the darkness plainly only in contrast with the light that we have received.

Hence death cannot be an independent theme in the field of the gospel. Whatever may be the attitude of believers to the end of this age and the apocalyptic finale of the cosmos, they should not walk in darkness but with uplifted head because their redemption draws near (Luke 21:28); this is true also of the end of their own lives.

Paul's theology climaxes in the chapter on the resurrection in 1 Corinthians (c. 15). Only in the certainty of Christ's resurrection and in its connection with the resurrection of the dead (15:12ff.) may we meditate on how comfortless and futile would be our imprisonment in a finitude which granted us no prospect of eternal life.[1]

When the question of eternal life arises in the dialogues of Jesus (Matthew 19:16; Luke 10:25) the reference is primarily to that which endures and is of unconditional validity in contrast to the emptiness of the corruptible world that grants no fulfilment and does not quench our thirst (John 4:13). Implicit in this question is the further question of what endures and is valid beyond death.

The story of Nicodemus is an example (John 3:1ff.). Though we are not told what the question of Nicodemus was but move on at once to the answer (vv. 2f.) we may reconstruct the question from the dialogue. Like the scribe and the rich young ruler he was almost certainly asking about eternal life. Instead of speaking about eternal life Jesus in his first answer speaks about seeing the kingdom of God (v. 3) and says that there is no access to it unless a person is born again from above (cf. 1 Peter 1:23; James 1:18). This reply shocks Nicodemus (v. 9). As a son of Abraham and a scribe he was seeking the rule of God, the kingdom of God, or eternal life—the expressions all denote the same reality which cannot be expressed in our categories—by taking the path of obedience to the law. Jesus, however, intimates that there must be a totally new beginning. We have to be refashioned and regenerated by the water of baptism and the transforming Spirit of God. What happens to us must precede what we do.

At the start of the way that leads to eternal life there thus stands our transformation by the Spirit. This makes us adequate and sets us in conformity with what the natural man cannot see or receive (1 Corinthians 2:14). The Spirit of God is active here (in the sense discussed earlier) as the power of presentation. Presentation has here the special nuance of *our* being made present, open, and receptive to the Holy Spirit, so that the way to God's kingdom is opened to us. This kingdom, eternal life, discloses itself as experience of the love of God that comes to us in the giving of his Son (John 3:16).

Eternal life is thus the power of renewal by the Spirit as this comes to us *now* as regeneration. Eternal life dawns in this life. It is depicted to us as the living water (John 4:10) which replaces the "broken cisterns" (Jeremiah 2:13) that in the service of corruptible being cannot satisfy our thirst. What we now experience of eternal life necessarily raises the question whether this living water will cease to flow after death, whether the love of God that is granted to us lasts only for this finite span of ours, whether the eternity of eternal life does not even in time burst through the limits of our temporality. As in the OT the certainty of victory over death grows with the image of God, so here it develops with the christologically filled out image of him who represents the love and condescension of his father, with the resurrection life of the victor over death.

---

[1] Cf. Jean Paul's "Sermon of the Dead Christ from the Edifice of the World on the Theme That There Is No God" (EG, I, pp. 331-37; EF, I, pp. 236-39).

2. PREPARATION FOR FAITH IN ETERNAL LIFE IN THE OLD TESTAMENT

Our last statements show that the question of eternal life presupposes a process in which it is raised and another process in which the answer develops. The question and answer were not always there, nor did they just arise later "in some way." They both develop the implications of God's turning to us and the form of this turning in Jesus Christ. This may be seen already in the lengthy processes in which certainty of victory over death developed during the time of the old covenant.[2]

In the earliest period death seems to pose no problem and is accepted as part of life. The urge to think about individual immortality is not active, as we have seen, where there is no awareness of individual personality. As the ancient Germans merged into the welfare and honor of the clan, so the early Israelites were so hidden and absorbed into the tribe that personal existence had no contours of its own. Furthermore, nomadic people like pre-historic Israel cannot think about death because they have no family graves in the midst of them to promote thoughts about death. Thus Abraham and the other patriarchs die "in a good old age . . . and full of years" (Genesis 25:8). Death is no problem. They are buried "as a shock of grain comes up to the threshing floor in its season" (Job 5:26). Death is so normal a part of the curve of life that the same expression can be used for it as for sexual intercourse, namely, "the way of all the earth" (Genesis 19:31; 1 Kings 2:2, etc.).[3]

Later the position changes. Death is an imperious limit that God himself has set to life's relationships (Isaiah 38:10ff.; Psalm 88:5, 10). To overlook this and trust that things will go on as usual is folly. This explains the petition in Psalm 90 that God will "teach us to number our days that we may get a heart of wisdom" (v. 12). An element of despondency also finds expression in the comparison of death to "water spilt on the ground which cannot be gathered up again" (2 Samuel 14:14) or to a scorching wind which withers up plants (Psalm 90:6; 103:16).[4]

A first consolation in face of death is that in Israel the individual is seen in the context of the family and tribe. These entities which surround and support individual life maintain a name after death and in them the individual under the promise returns as it were (Sirach 44:10ff.). This immortality by preservation in memory serves at least as an intermediary stage.

A further step is the thought that not only does the memory of the clan survive death but the promises of Yahweh are still in force after it. Thus the dying patriarch Jacob in his parting address to Joseph becomes a witness to the promise of Yahweh which will survive him who has lived under it: "Behold, I am about to die, but God will be with you, and will bring you again to the land of your fathers" (Genesis 48:21). Here the dying man knows that he is lifted up in the ongoing blessing of Yahweh.

If I am right, this is a decisive breakthrough which shatters original similarities

---

[2]On this cf. U. Kellermann, ZThK, III, pp. 259ff.; C. Barth; G. von Rad, *Theologie des AT*, I (1957), pp. 274ff., 385ff., 402ff.; E.T. I, pp. 275ff., 387ff., 404ff.; W. Eichrodt, *Theologie des AT*, III (1939), §24; E.T. II, c. 24.
[3]Kellermann, p. 259.
[4]Eichrodt, p. 152; E.T. II, p. 502. For further examples cf. Kellermann, p. 263.

between the understanding of death in Israel and its understanding in the ancient Near East.[5] For here the conquest of death is based neither on an immortal I-substance of the soul (Plato's *psychē*) nor on the supraindividual clan, but on something outside man, namely, the memory of Yahweh who knows our names and thinks of them eternally, having written them in the book of life.[6] Here are some first intimations of what I have called man's alien dignity (in distinction from his own worth). Our identity does not have its ground in any immanent personal core but in God's remembrance. The parable of the prodigal son takes this view of identity (Luke 15:11ff.). The previous being of the prodigal is unrecognizable. No demonstrable continuum establishes identity between the early stay-at-home, the one who goes further and further into the far country, and the one who comes back. The only continuum of his identity is the image that his father has and keeps of him. Divine likeness is in this sense the image that God has of us.

This thought that relationship with God survives death because God's memory does not let slip those who go down to the grave gradually established itself and became a prelude to the NT belief in the resurrection. But it involved wrestling with Sheol, with the world of the dead and the shades.

In this regard we hear two antiphonal voices in the Psalms, Job, Isaiah, and especially the Wisdom literature.

The first voice speaks of Sheol as the land of no return, which means exclusion from God's saving dealings with his community. Since salvation is history—in God's mighty acts and in worship—exclusion from history is particularly painful. It involves the contradiction that on the one side life is ordained for God's honor and praise and on the other side it is lost in the land of no return.[7] "Is thy steadfast love declared in the grave, or thy faithfulness in the abyss?" (Psalm 88:11); "for Sheol cannot thank thee, death cannot praise thee" (Isaiah 38:18); "save my life . . . for in death there is no remembrance of thee; in Sheol who can give thee praise?" (Psalm 6:4ff.).[8] In Job, too, death is in this sense an enemy because it breaks the union with God. When it threatens Job, it robs him of any possibility of reaching certainty about God and thrusts him into utter hopelessness. Human death is far more comfortless than natural death. Plants spring up again but man cannot be fetched back from the realm of the dead (Job 14:7-20).[9]

The second voice, that of hope, confronts this voice of resignation. The same image of God gives rise to it. For if God gives both life and death, and if he is not dualistically related to life alone, then the realm of the dead is also in his sphere of power. As the devout of the old covenant in innumerable thanksgivings trace their deliverance from misfortune, sickness, and persecution to God, they bear witness to God's power over these heralds of the world of death. "From here it is only a step over the biological frontier of death."[10] Thus the realm of the dead is brought into Yahweh's sphere of lordship (Job 18:6, 14; Psalm 22:29; 88:6). It is so in such

---

[5]Kellermann, pp. 261, 270, n. 63.

[6]Isaiah 4:3; Ezekiel 13:9; Daniel 12:1; cf. in the NT Philippians 4:3 and repeated references in Revelation.

[7]Eichrodt, p. 152; E.T. II, p. 502.

[8]Cf. also Psalm 28:1; 30:9; 115:17; Isaiah 38:11.

[9]Eichrodt, p. 162; E.T. II, p. 503.

[10]Kellermann, p. 273.

a way that both poles of God's activity, his judgment *and* his grace, may be seen in relation to the dead in Sheol: "Though they [the wicked] dig into Sheol, from there shall my hand take them; though they climb up to heaven, from there will I bring them down" (Amos 9:2; cf. Psalm 139:8). God's judgment reaches beyond the frontier of death.

The same applies to his grace. Death cannot exclude from this, as the voice of resignation says. Psalm 49 asks concerning Yahweh's grace of life for individuals and reaches the answer that the arrogant wealthy will remain in death: "No man can ransom himself, or give to God the price of his life" (49:7). But the righteous can say: "God will ransom my soul from the power of Sheol, for he will receive me" (v. 15).[11] The poetic form of the Psalm, von Rad thinks,[12] should not mislead us into thinking that the theological problem is not pressed to the limit. For how is this related to the blessing and help of God for those who are faithful to him if these are both obscure to the point of death and the righteous can find themselves only "envious of" those who are rich and proud (Psalm 73:3ff.)?

It is here that the certainty of unlimited fellowship with Yahweh plays its part. This is indestructible. It cannot be broken by death. The main elements in this confidence are: "You are my portion," and: "I am always with you."[13] To the extent that this certainty is achieved Sheol ceases to be a foreign land outside Yahweh's domain. It is now subject to his sovereignty.[14]

Looking back from the NT one gets the impression that an idea is widespread which the Johannine Christ expresses: He will prepare a place for his people in the many dwellings in his Father's house so that they may be where he is (John 14:1–3). Here death cannot break fellowship once it is concluded. According to John this is said by Jesus while he is still on earth. It is all that can be indicated prior to the resurrection about the inability of death to overthrow the certainty of the "You are and will always be my portion." But how frail the certainty is at this stage is plain from Peter's denial (John 18:25ff.).[15] The event of the resurrection may be prepared for by the promise of enduring fellowship after death but not in such a way that it is only a step away and becomes a mere dot on the "i." Otherwise the third day would not have caused such shock and misapprehension. It is a long way from certainty about God's faithfulness after death to the hope of the resurrection. This way was taken prototypically in the OT, or at least its first stages were traversed.

It is in the OT a kind of detour on which the thought arises that Yahweh, doing the impossible, will raise up or reawaken his people (Isaiah 26:13ff.; Ezekiel 37:1ff.; Hosea 6:1ff.) and will finally swallow up death forever and wipe away the tears from all faces (Isaiah 25:8).

The apocalyptic message of Daniel brings the first breakthrough to actual belief

---

[11]Cf. on this H. J. Kraus, *Psalmen,* I (1960), pp. 367ff.

[12]G. von Rad, I, p. 404; E.T. I, p. 406.

[13]P. 405; E.T. I, p. 407.

[14]In the Wisdom literature Kellermann finds some astonishing parallels between Greek (Euripides) and Israelite ideas on the conquest of death through immortality (Sirach 40:11; Kellermann, pp. 278, 281).

[15]Among the many striking Synoptic examples cf. Peter's role after the confession at Caesarea Philippi (Matthew 16:22 and par.).

in the resurrection. This speaks about the final eschatological drama of history, for which there is already a model in the tradition. This last act affects the whole world and for this reason it affects the individual too. It is thus related to the coming resurrection of the dead (Daniel 12:1–3).

We have seen that the Bible has no uniform message about death and victory over it. We find instead a chorus of many voices within which the definitiveness of death and resignation to it are heard but also triumphant voices singing Yaweh's dominion over Sheol and even the first hints of a belief in the resurrection which will be completed in the NT.

Yet the figure of a chorus is not very exact because in the main the voices do not sing together but in succession. We have here a historical process in which certainty of victory over death gradually develops in the direction of the NT, though without bridging the cleft between the old covenant and the new which the Easter event denotes.

It should be observed, however, that this historical process is not an evolution brought about by immanent forces. Its point is understood only when we see clearly that what we have here is a history with and under God, a *dialogical* history. Israel goes through a long historical process of learning in which it gradually comes to know what it means to be a partner in covenant with Yahweh. In this process the certainty gradually strengthens that what is called the covenant faithfulness of Yahweh has no temporal limits and therefore cannot cease when death calls us out of temporality.

Hence the growing certainty of victory over death is not an autonomous evolution but the gradual discovery of a mystery which is posited from the very first in partnership with the covenant God and which can come to consciousness only through the witness of the Spirit. It is as it were released from the stage of incubation and becomes virulent.

3. ETERNAL LIFE IN THE LIGHT OF THE NEW COVENANT

a. On the Statements in the New Testament[16]

The NT statements about eternal life are based on the fact of the resurrection of Jesus Christ, no matter whether they point forward to it (the gospels) or backward to it (e.g., Paul). The resurrection is the incisive new factor in the new covenant in distinction from the old covenant and from the OT lines which intimate belief in the resurrection.[17]

This new factor, which accepts and transcends the OT (Matthew 5:27–48), is prepared for by the prophetic life of Jesus himself, especially by the indirect sayings about himself which we gathered together under the heading of implied Christology.[18] Only this preparation helps us to see why the changed figure of the risen Lord awakens recollection of the earthly Jesus and effects equation with him.

---

[16]On the descent into hell cf. EG, II, pp. 513ff.; EF, II, pp. 415ff.

[17]Cf. the chapter on "Promise and Fulfilment" in Volume II.

[18]EG, II, pp. 436ff., 561ff.; EF, II, pp. 355ff., 453ff. Cf. the chapter on "Continuity and Discontinuity between the Earthly Jesus and the Risen Christ" (p. 554; E.T. p. 447).

On the road to Emmaus the disciples, after the Lord met them, said: "Did not our hearts burn within us?" (Luke 24:32).[19] Their hearts acted here like Geiger counters which moved because early and hardly conscious associations with Jesus of Nazareth began to form when he met them.

Doubting Thomas recognized the risen Lord by his nailprints and then confessed: "My Lord and my God" (John 20:27f.). This confession testifies to what the other manifestations intimate, namely, that he is also "wholly other," that in this new form he does not fit into their horizon of expectation, and that for this reason their eyes must first be opened by the miracle of the Spirit. Recognition does not just occur. It is possible only as the risen Lord discloses himself. Mary Magdalene does not know him at first. She thinks he is the gardener at the grave. Only the word of the transfigured Lord calling her by name takes the blindness from her eyes (John 20:15f.).[20]

The way in which the earthly Jesus prepares for the resurrection of the dead—not just his own resurrection but the act of God which will not abandon his people to death—shows how he stands on the soil of OT traditions and accepts the total context of the salvation event. One may see this in his debate with the Sadducees in Mark 12:18-27. In the Pentateuch, the normative canon, the Sadducees find no reference to a resurrection of the dead and they treat the error ironically by pointing to its grotesque implications. (Seven brothers successively marry the same woman; whose will she be in the resurrection?) Jesus meets them on the basis of the same canon. After dismissing their question and showing how absurd it is, he takes them to the Pentateuch, specifically to the story of the burning bush (Exodus 3:2-6), and shows them what resurrection means. When God says: "I am the God of Abraham, Isaac, and Jacob,"[21] he confesses that the dead patriarchs are also his. He wills to be a God of the living and not the dead (Mark 12:27). Death can never break off fellowship with him. This enduring relation, this faithfulness of God, is the real issue in the resurrection. "You are quite wrong."

In the light of this understanding of God the resurrection from the dead is filled out christologically in Paul. The front of death is broken by the resurrection of the Kyrios. He is the "firstfruits (aparchē) of those who have fallen asleep" (1 Corinthians 15:20). Certainty of this is not given merely by the attested fact (vv. 1-8) but also by the preparatory and encircling belief that there will be a resurrection—even though the event on the third day bears the stamp of uniqueness and particularity (v. 13).[22] Certainty of the resurrection of the dead—our resurrection and victory over death—finds its basic support in Christ's breakthrough. Our hope in Christ, in a perpetual relation to him, cannot relate only to our present life; if it did, we would be deceived deceivers, we would still be in our sins, and our faith would be futile (v. 17); the dead, too, would be without hope (vv. 18f.). But no: "As in Adam all die, so also in Christ shall all be made alive" (v. 22). We have certainty of eternal life beyond death because Christ lets us continue to be his,

---

[19]Cf. the exposition of this story in EG, II, p. 558; EF, II, p. 450.

[20]A weakness of the vision hypotheses is that they refer to direct recollection and identification (cf. the debate with Bultmann [EG, II, pp. 544f.; EF, II, pp. 440f.]).

[21]Cf. the famous saying of Pascal.

[22]Cf. the chapter on the resurrection in EG, II, pp. 522-60; EF, II, pp. 423-52.

and no one and nothing, not even death, can snatch us out of his hands (Romans 8:38).

Many hymns refer to the certainty of this unbreakable bond. The head takes his members with him. Clinging to him as our head, we are Christ's companions through sin and death and hell (P. Gerhardt).

In Romans 6:3ff. this same bond that endures through death means that—specifically by baptism—we die and rise again with Christ. To be sure, rising again here means in the first instance (but only in the first instance) being awakened and empowered to live a new life (*kainotēs zōēs*, 6:4). But as this new life comes from Christ and is life with him, his resurrection means that death no longer has dominion over us. As Christ will never die again after his resurrection, so we shall live with him (6:8f.). Because by dying with him we are dead to sin (6:3; Galatians 3:27), we are taken out of the spheres of that which imposed death on us and which set it in motion as a "sting" (1 Corinthians 15:55f.). The relation between sin and death is broken. Recollection of the fall can no longer frighten us. Those who have given themselves to Christ as obedient servants, who have put themselves under him (*hypakoē*, Romans 6:16), can no longer be those who, as they try to be without limits and strive after equality with God, find the barrier of temporality crashing down in front of them.

Thus death is robbed of its point (6:23). We shall live even though we die (John 11:25f.). Whether we die or live we are the Lord's (Romans 14:8; cf. 1 Thessalonians 5:10).

Similarly in Johannine theology those who are linked with Christ in faith, and who are nourished by the bread of life, will be transported through death with the relationship unbroken. The limit of death will be removed for them. Christ *is* the resurrection and the life. The key saying in the story of Lazareth is this: "Whoever lives and believes in me shall never die" (John 11:25f.). To be related to him is to be placed already in the resurrection life.

Here again there are echoes of the connection between sin and death. To share the life for which death is no longer a limit is not to come into judgment. Not to have access by faith to this resurrection life is to be judged already here and now (3:18; 5:24). The presence or absence of judgment and death is acutely relevant now: "He who hears my word and believes him who sent me, has eternal life; he does not come into judgment, but has passed from death to life" (5:24).

According to the Fourth Gospel eternal life is not present as a mere invasion of our temporality. It transcends this temporality by going beyond it and finding eschatological actualization at the last day as resurrection from the dead (6:39f., 44, 54; 11:24; 12:48). One may say that expectation of the last day is expectation of the confirmation of what is given us here and now, enabling us to escape both death and judgment.

Bultmann naturally seizes on John's unmistakable emphasis on the "now" of eternal life in order to justify his own realized eschatology and to support his existential interpretation. Eschatology finds its truth in what takes place *now* (*Johannes Kommentar* [1941], pp. 111f.; E.T. *Commentary on John* [Oxford, 1971]). He rejects the idea that judgment is a dramatic cosmic event; it takes place in one's attitude toward the word of Jesus (*Theologie des NT* [1953], p. 385; E.T. *Theology of the NT,* II, p. 38). If there are some sayings in which the hour of resurrection is put in the future, these are, he thinks, later redactions which distort what John is saying. As examples of such "corrections" Bultmann adduces especially John 6:39f., 44, 51b–58 and 5:28. Here we have a good example of a hermeneutical principle—existential interpretation—becoming a dominant and normative principle which is brought into the text and which regulates it (cf. EG, I, pp. 50ff.; EF, I, pp. 55ff.). On the dubious nature of Bultmann's conjuring away of futurist eschatology (E. Schweizer, J. Blank), cf. H. Conzelmann, *Theologie des NT* (1967), §48; E.T. *An Outline of the Theology of the NT* (New York, 1969), c. 48. Systematic theology has also rightly objected that to eliminate futurist eschatology in the Fourth Gospel is to weaken its realized eschatology. If transition to the christological sphere is not entry into a definitive life which survives death, it is no real transition but simply a turn in the unconquerable hopelessness of one's own sphere which confirms rather than negates its futility (J. Ratzinger, *Eschatologie*, p. 103).

b. The Question of the "How" of Eternal Life

When the NT speaks about the resurrection of the dead at the end of the ages it has in mind the resurrection of the body. As we have seen in our discussion of *sōma* the term "body" denotes the identity of personal being. This makes possible even a paradox like the "pneumatic body" that Paul refers to in 1 Corinthians 15:35–49. But the reference is *not* to this resurrection of the body when we are told about the transition of the dying from temporality to eternal life. Neither when we read about the poor man whom the angels took to Abraham's bosom nor when Jesus says to the thief: "Today you will be with me in Paradise," is there any reference to a resurrection body that will be given to us after death. Paul does speak with some anxiety—which he overcomes—about the bodily nakedness to which those who die before the end, before the Parousia, will be subject. But fear of this nakedness is taken away the moment the apostle remembers the "guarantee" of the Spirit (2 Corinthians 5:5) which, even as we are distant from the Lord, gives us a foretaste of what it will be to be with the Lord even in this prior interim period in which the dead can only look forward to the end. In this regard it makes no difference whether the intermediate state is described as sleeping (1 Thessalonians 4:13ff.) or as being under the altar (Revelation 6:9).[23]

Apart from the reference to being with Christ statements about the nature of eternal life after death are very restrained and discreet. No state is described. Many expressions suggest total otherness. We now live weak and destructible lives in the natural body; the resurrection will bring strong and indestructible lives in the pneumatic body (1 Corinthians 15:42ff.). Because of this flesh and blood cannot inherit the kingdom of God (15:50).

Legend tells us of two medieval monks who talked constantly about death and the future state. They hit upon the idea that whoever died first would appear to the other the next night. In answer to the question *qualiter?* (How is it?) he would answer either *taliter* (as we thought) or *aliter* (other than we thought). When one

---

[23]Cf. O. Cullmann, *Vorträge und Aufsätze* (1966), p. 403.

did in fact die, he came back for a moment the next night and being asked with eager expectation *qualiter?*, he answered *totaliter-aliter*.

Totaliter-aliter does not denote an abstract antithesis or contradiction such as that between the provisional and the definitive or between misery and glory, at least if these are free concepts detached from a christological interpretation. The truth is that as the resurrection body is spiritual, so the state of eternal life is spiritual. There is thus a continuity between the now and the then which overcomes the *totaliter-aliter*. For if we are weak now and cannot comprehend the change into what is totally different, we are still earthen vessels in which the power of God is at work (2 Corinthians 4:7) and we can be content with the grace of God because this power is strong precisely in the weak (12:9f.; Philippians 4:13). It is the dying of the Lord Jesus that we carry about in our bodies (2 Corinthians 4:10). In his fellowship our suffering becomes dying with him. For this very reason we share in his resurrection life (4:10f.).

The *totaliter-aliter* relates to the inconceivability of what we wait for, the cutting across all the lines that our postulates draw between the here and the hereafter, the now and the then. But the difference is transcended and sustained by an analogy between walking in the here and now and being with the Lord of the dead on whom light perpetual shines. What we now have as a deposit of the Spirit we shall then know in its fulness. What we now see in a mirror and an obscure word we shall then see face to face (1 Corinthians 13:12). What is now by faith will then be by sight (2 Corinthians 5:7; 1 John 3:2). The one who has now led us by his spirit will then beyond the grave be manifest in his identity. We shall recognize him who after the resurrection still carried the nailprints and yet was quite different. Coming out of the shadows of the world of death we shall enter into his ineffable light. The voice of the good news which reached us in the dark valleys of blindness, deafness, lameness, and death (Matthew 11:4–6) will still be familiar to us in the very different landscape of light. The Spirit, the Word, and the Lord will still be the same.[24]

Because we believe in this identity which embraces the *totaliter-aliter* we can rejoice already at the thought of being with the Lord (2 Corinthians 5:2, 8; Philippians 1:23). An abstract antithesis of time and eternity detached from this christological foundation would only make the idea sound strange. If the inconceivability of the hereafter were all that we could discern, crossing the frontier of death would be like a step into nothingness.

As Paul puts the counterquestion: Supposing there were no resurrection?, and as Jean Paul does the same in relation to the existence of God: Supposing there were no God?, so we may ask: What would survival after death mean if there were no continuation of our fellowship with the Kyrios? We might take Christopher Marlowe as an example here. After twenty-four years of his pact with the devil, Marlowe's Faust fears the hereafter. He asks the hills to fall on him, the earth to swallow him up, and the cosmos to be dissolved in him. He takes the wings of the morning to flee from himself (Psalm 139:9). Immortality without the grace of God is a dreadful thing. To have to go on when the eternal foundation has been lost and

---

[24]I cannot wholly follow Ebeling in the far-reaching inferences he draws in his concern for an eschatology of glory (*Wort und Glaube*, III, pp. 439ff.).

nothingness encircles us, is hell. Hence Faust longs to be swallowed up in Nirvana just as the Buddhist wants to break out of Samsara, the eternal cycle, and drive toward ever new existence. At this level it is hard to conceive of the joy to which we referred. In Marlowe fear replaces it.

If, then, Christology is the true key to everything that is said about the eternal life that overcomes the world of death, one might say that this life is "ec-centrically" determined. We thus see profound diastasis in relation to an immortality which is projected from its own center, a quality of the psyche. Luther describes the "ec-centric" character of this life most precisely in his famous saying about the changed understanding of immortality which necessarily arises in the light of this "eternal life": Wherever God speaks or with whom, whether in wrath or in grace, that person is immortal. The person of God who speaks and the Word show that we are the kind of creatures with whom God wills to speak immortally and to all eternity.[25]

According to this saying what causes us to live on is not a quality of the soul that survives death unscathed. It is rather that God has entered into a history with us and that this history will not cease throughout eternity. Thus the power that prevents death from laying its hand imperiously on us and plunging us into nothingness is *God's faithfulness*. This is signified by the resurrection of his Son by which he is the Lord of the dead and the living (Romans 14:9), as is declared to us in the first instalment of the gifts of the Spirit.

The certainty that God's faithfulness does not end, and that the end of death is meaningless for it, does not derive from experience of death or the shock of corruptibility. These would destroy our confidence and, as in the case of immortality, would make us think that it was all wishful thinking. In fact God's faithfulness has been experienced over a long span in innumerable living encounters from the days of the patriarchs, in which the God of Abraham, Isaac, and Jacob demonstrated it, to our own time. A cloud of witnesses, of patriarchs, prophets, and men and women of God, right up to "today when we hear his voice" (Psalm 95:7f.), stands about us (Hebrews 12:1). They all confess that this God freed them from chains, liberated them from anxiety, and pardoned their guilt, opening up for them a wholly new beginning of life.

Those who are sure of this—but only those—will then ask: But what about death? What can it do when this other hand is laid upon me? And painful and difficult though our end may be through cancer or multiple sclerosis or earthquakes or air crashes, even these most bitter things can be only a visitation, a taking home. We are expected.

Because the faithfulness of God is paradigmatically presented in his confession of his Son, one might say that the history with us that Luther stressed is fulfilled first and typically in the death and resurrection of Jesus Christ and therefore the certainty of life after death is christologically fulfilled. Just the one saying of the Johannine Christ: "Where I am, there shall my servant be also" (John 12:26), helps me to understand the merriment in Christ and the defiance of death which ring out in Johann Franck's "Jesus My Joy" and echo from the frail walls of our decaying world: "Though sin and hell terrify me, Jesus will shelter me." The

---

[25]*Lectures on Genesis* (WA, 43, 481, 32; LW, 5, 76).

hymns about eternity can give us some impression of how triumphant is this sense of victory and how persuasive is this certainty of the life everlasting.

From this angle we may understand why the Bible is so very reserved and discreet in its references to the so-called hereafter. This hereafter, on which all Christian thinking is focused according to many atheists and other depressed groups, is in a deeper sense uninteresting. Instead the commitment of disciples is wholly and utterly to union with their Lord who leads them from faith to sight, from the obscure mirror to face-to-face. When this is so, the "how" of the final state and the scenery of the hereafter are suddenly of no concern.

In the parable of Dives and Lazarus (Luke 16:19–31) it is plain that the message of eternal life does not fix our gaze upon the world to come but forces us to look at this world. Eternal life covers both dimensions.

At a first glance it might seem that we are given some scenes from the next life. There is a reference to Abraham's bosom on which the poor man can rest from his sufferings. There is also a reference to the fire of hell in which the rich man is parched with heat, experiencing in his own body some of the torment which when alive he failed to see in the other. The theme of the next world seems to be raised and not a few theologians have deduced from the parable a kind of topography of it.

They are guilty of poor hermeneutics. For the point of the parable lies elsewhere. The real message is that it is only in hell and torment that the rich man experiences for the first time the love that cares. He then remembers that he has five brothers who have no more considered than he himself did whether their lives have a foundation which will stand after death, and who are just as pitiless toward the poor men at their gates as he was—he who is now suffering the consequences of his wasted life. Now, when it is too late, he begins to tremble for his five brothers and he asks father Abraham to send to them a reporter from the hereafter who can tell them convincingly about the vital decision that is at issue for them. But Abraham replies: "No eyewitness will be sent. Your five brothers, poor rich man, have Moses and the prophets." This Word of God, we might add by way of interpretation, is a continuum which binds together this world and the next, the world of the living and the world of the dead. It is the basis of the history which God has initiated with us, whether in wrath or in grace. "If they will not hear Moses and the prophets," Abraham says, "it will be no help to them if a reporter is sent from the next world." As they suppress God's Word and keep it at a distance, so they will find arguments for talking down any report from the world to come, no matter how vivid.

The fate of the five brothers, who still live this side of death and who threaten to forfeit their eternal destiny here in the present life, is the real point of the parable. This does not mean that a nontranscendent this-worldliness is the theme and that our history is only a history *before* death. On the contrary, it means that the eternal life which finds its consummation in "Abraham's bosom" is already actualized here and now and embraces both the present world and the world to come.

This is plain from the other continuum which alongside Moses and the prophets unites being *before* death to being *after* death. This second continuum is the love which Dives and his brothers did not have. Love is shown here and now in this world. But the uniting of love of God and love of neighbor shows that it is not exhausted here and now. In our neighbor we love him who first loved us (1 John 4:19). We thus enter the sphere of the history into which God has entered with us and which does not cease to all eternity. Nor does love cease—even though prophecies and tongues and knowledge do (1 Corinthians 13:8).

In a deeper sense, then, it is "foolish" to follow the wise of this world (and secularized theologians) in playing off this world against the next and denouncing the next as a world of dreams. It is "reactionary" to go back behind the break which was made by Christ and by which death has had to give up its function as a boundary and can no longer part us from a love which in the light of the resurrection embraces both the living and the dead. This equalizing forbids us either to flee this world because of a fixation on the next or to become secular because of a fixation on this world.

How much the christological filling out of eternal life robs the question of the state and setting of its relevance may be seen plainly from the account of the death of the father of A. Schlatter. On his deathbed devout brethren gathered round and tried to comfort him by saying that he would soon be in the golden palaces of Zion and would see the crystal sea. But he raised himself and said: "Do not trouble me with all that slush. I only want to cling to my Father's neck." He desired only the one image, that of the way the Father received the prodigal son and kept faith with him. He had seized on the essential point. He did not want information about the geography of heaven, not even about the streets of Zion. He was concerned only to follow God's history to the end and to find peace at the place which the Lord had prepared (John 14:2).

This is how we should interpret the saying to the penitent thief: "Today you will be with me in Paradise" (Luke 23:43). The "today" signifies that the history that God had begun with the thief would be neither stopped not interrupted. "Paradise" is not meant to link up with the traditional imagery and evoke association with glorious forms of enjoyment. It is itself interpreted by the "with me" (*met' emou*). Paradise is abiding fellowship with the crucified one who has overcome death. It is clinging to the Father's neck.

I do not believe in the future life because of some dream of the hereafter. I believe in it because I am already the companion of him who has begun a history with me and will never let me fall away from his faithfulness. With him I go confidently into the darkness and inconceivability and total otherness of the future world. For he, who is one and the same, will never be alien or other to me. I shall always recognize him whose voice has always been as familiar to me as the shepherd's voice is to his sheep. In his person the dialectic between continuity and discontinuity which has permeated all reflection on existence before and after the resurrection is finally stilled.

The question of eternal life ceases to be a mere question of the hereafter. Eternal life embraces both this world and the next. It thus shines into life's present hour and becomes our portion (Psalm 16:5; 73:26; 142:5). We have the star to look at, the rock to stand on. We have the bread of life to feed us. Having eternal life, we know what this present life can be. This world is transformed by it. We see our fellows in a new light. They are no longer important because of their functions but as people with whom God has begun his never-ending history and who are furnished with the "alien dignity" which sets them under his patronage (Romans

14:15; 1 Corinthians 8:11). Suffering also takes on another sense. It shares the relativity of the world of death. It becomes a new means of salvation which purifies us (Psalm 66:10-12). In the light of the new covenant it makes us pay heed to the thoughts of life that are thought about us. In the reflected light of eternal life we acquire new criteria. There is a transvaluation of all values. Much that was important apart from eternal life loses its dominant rank and dissipates. Other things that we previously overlooked take higher rank. The question of the meaning of life—beyond every goal—is one of these. So is our new view of communication with others, and not least of all the understanding of guilt and forgiveness.[26]

c. Epilogue: The Intermediate Time between Death and Resurrection

In the history of theology the concept of time has always raised problems when applied to eschatological statements, e.g., to eternal life and the post-resurrection state. It has no real object here and contradictions appear in which post-Kantian metaphysics is entangled and which Kant deals with in his antinomies. The most disruptive contradiction seems to be the one between (a) the enduring life which rests on God's history with us and (b) the resurrection on the last day. Time—in this case the intermediate time between death and the end of all things—produces tension in statements about eternal life.

Fundamentally this is the same problem as one finds in universal eschatology. There it takes the form of the delay in the Parousia, of the time between the resurrection of Christ and his return and the final resurrection. It has led to different conclusions, some saying that the final resurrection has already taken place (2 Timothy 2:18), others that the second coming is imminent, and others still that there must first be the great apostasy and the working out of the full potential of wickedness (2 Thessalonians 2).

The two intermediate forms differ inasmuch as individual survival after death involves a state transcending temporality whereas expectation of the Parousia presupposes life in temporality and an attitude to continuing time and history.

As regards eternal life after death Luther describes this posttemporal state as "soul-sleep" (Stange, *Das Ende aller Dinge*, pp. 180ff.; Althaus, *Die letzten Dinge*, pp. 271ff.): "They sleep a painless sleep . . . they rest in peace and are tormented by no more suffering" (in a sermon on Matthew 9:1ff. [WA, 37, 174ff.]). Luther meant two things by this soul-sleep.

First we can have no ideas as to the "how" of this state. The dead are at peace. Negatively the main point of this is that the current theory of purgatory is set aside (Stange, p. 181). More interesting theologically, however, is that the metaphor of sleep suggests that the dead have left the world of temporality, so that the intermediate period between their present state and the resurrection on the last day does not pose any problem of time. Those who are awakened out of sleep think that they have hardly slept an hour or two when in fact the whole night has passed (Stange, p. 183). The final resurrection is the awakening out of this sleep. The problem of the intermediate time is a problem only for the living, not for the dead.

---

[26]Cf. the verse in M. Schmalenbach's chorale: "Eternity lit up time so that the small became small to us and the great great."

Those who know how important corporeality is in Luther's theology—we met with it in the doctrine of the Lord's Supper—will perceive that the idea of soul-sleep brings him into a certain conflict with his own understanding, for it means the separation of the soul from the body. In his "Table Talks" (WA Tischreden, 5, 219, 11 [LW, 54], No. 5534) he can sometimes pour scorn on such a separation. Speaking of Abraham he says that he lives, for God is the God of the living. But this does not mean that his soul alone lives. One cannot tear out a part of Abraham and say that this lives. This is the way the philosophers talk. Only a silly soul would be in heaven without a body. All Abraham, the whole man, lives. Yet the whole man, body and soul, will be awakened only at the last day. It is thus impossible that there should be a being with the Lord without some concept of the soul. (When Martin Schalling in the final chorale of Bach's *St. John's Passion* speaks of the angels taking our souls to Abraham's bosom, this is a good evangelical statement and we must protect it against the desire of purists to see it erased.) The question is not *whether* we must speak of the soul but *how* we are to define it and what possibilities there are of distinguishing it from the immortal *psychē* of Platonism.

Luther himself speaks of the incorruptible soul (Commentary on Romans [LW, 25, 11] and Tischreden, 3, 696) but we must always be aware that it is eccentrically determined as well as incorruptible. He interprets it in terms of the first commandment and sees his eschatology as well as his doctrine of justification in the light of the statement: "I am the Lord your God" (cf. Althaus, *Theologische Aufsätze*, II [1953], pp. 1-10). Similar statements may be found in his exposition of Psalm 90 and Psalm 118 (WA, 31/I, 154; cf. LW, 14, 87).

Soul is man as he is addressed by God's Word. It is the epitome of the relation to God, of incorporation into his history with us. This means that Luther sees the state of the souls of those who sleep in faith within the framework of this relation: The soul or spirit has no place to stay except God's Word until we see God clearly on the last day. As regards the negative form of this view in relation to the wicked greater difficulties arise. Here, it seems to me, Luther resorts to the Platonic view that souls that have attained to no vision find no rest. He speaks of a nonbodily hell where the ungodly find themselves after death. This consists of a "bad conscience" which is without faith and the Word of God. It is to be distinguished from the real hell, which will begin on the last day (sermon on Luke 16:19-31 [WA, 10/III, 191f.]).

One can hardly escape the impression that Luther is on the edge of a slippery slope here. The one firm point is that the concept of the soul cannot be abandoned when we have to speak of bodily death, and yet we may also say that the history that has begun with God cannot be ended by death. Soul is thus a term for partnership in this history. It denotes the I in fellowship with God's Thou. It thus remains relational.

If Luther gets into trouble when he tries to describe the state after death ontically, this warns us to be content with the confession that we are and will always be the Lord's (Romans 14:8). It is beyond our competence to say how believers or unbelievers, atheists, and agnostics are the Lord's. By being content with the confession we show faith and trust. The living commend the dead into the Lord's hands, scoffers as well as believers. There are points at which theological statements cannot be expressed as dicta but only as prayers. If we try to go beyond this in a search for material security the threat arises that preoccupation with the scenery of Paradise will replace communication with the Thou of God. We recall that in the saying to the penitent thief the term "Paradise" finds its meaning in the words "with me."

The Roman Catholic tradition runs into similar difficulties with its teaching that the soul is immortal as the form of the body (Vienna 1312 [Denz., 902; E.T. 481]; Lateran V [Denz., 1440; E.T. 738]). The problem resulted from the adoption of the Aristotelian unity of body and *psychē* in which the latter is form and the former matter. For there was also a need to avoid Aristotle's view that as this form the *psychē* is brought into constitutive connection with the corporeal matter. If the *psychē* is form, then it belongs to the bodily world and to death (Ratzinger, *Eschatologie*, p. 125). Hence the soul has to be taken in another sense as the spirit that constitutes the person. Only after a long process did this modification take place in Thomas. Ratzinger describes the consequent following of Aristotle and divergence from him as follows. The soul belongs to the body as form but what is the form of the body is spirit and makes man a person, thus opening up immortality for him. This view is a new product of the Christian faith and its claims on thought. It has as little to do with antiquity as the concept of resurrection (p. 126). (The author admits that it is not clear to him what "spirit" means here. It is obviously not the *Pneuma,* but what then?)

The ontological schema that permeates the Roman Catholic tradition (ThE, I, §§1084ff.; E.T. I, pp. 222ff.) obviously makes it unavoidable that the concept of the soul should come to resemble that of Plato. This is unintentional, however, and Aristotelian terms are used only to express something which must have looked like a "metaphysical impossibility" to the Aristotelian tradition (A. Pegis, quoted in Ratzinger, p. 126).

It is hard to see how this concept of the soul, which reinterprets it as a nonindividual and nonpersonal spirit (p. 125), can be harmonized with Denz., 902 (E.T. 481) and especially 1140 (E.T. 738). These refer specifically to the individuality of the rational soul, which is not the same in all of us but can be multiple in accordance with the multiplicity of the bodies into which it is infused (Denz., 1140; E.T. 738). But this is not our present concern.

The essential point is that there is an obvious intention to break away from the ontological schema and to arrive at a dialogical immortality (p. 132) which is to be understood in terms of a relation to God or an ability to relate to him (p. 130). Nevertheless, the question arises whether this intended view of immortality does not mean something different in principle from that of Luther, who found its basis in God's initiation of a dialogue that can never cease to all eternity.

Luther had problems with his personalist schema. Platonic elements could sometimes break into it, as we have seen. This is linked with a basic problem of theological language, namely, that it has to use existing thought-forms but must not let them control it. We have already seen how John's Gospel uses the term Logos but sets aside its Stoic origin and the related ideologies.

Along these lines it seems unmistakable to me that Roman Catholic theology is wrestling with its Aristotelian schema (cf. especially the debate of Pius XII with the French existentialists in his encyclical "Humani generis") and trying to relativize it as an instrument. The question of the suitability of instruments of thought and speech certainly arises and the answer probably lies in a consideration of which carry the greater liabilities and which have the greater adequacy. But both positively and negatively only comparative distinctions can be made.

Language, including theological language, is the verbal medium of sinners. Being justified, sinners aim at goals that transcend the medium. Ultimately they are assessed and judged, not by what they are, but by that to which they look. In this case both Roman Catholic and Reformed Christians look away from the ontic quality of the soul toward the relation, the dialogue between the I and God's Thou, which is not linked to finitude and death no matter whether it be determined by God's wrath or by his grace (as Luther would say).

Controversial theology, as we have learned from this chapter on the intermediate state, can be conducted only with an awareness of the inadequacy but also the unavoidability of the forms of thought at our disposal. On both sides today an effort to make the current form transparent and to relativize it is obviously (and happily) discernible. Often, then, the lines meet at the goal of what is being said. This seems to take place in what Ratzinger has in mind when he refers to ''dialogical immortality.'' It is along these lines that we should carry on the discussion.

B. Universal Eschatology

Bibliography (apart from the books listed in c. XXXI): K. Barth, *Die Auferstehung der Toten,* 2nd ed. (1926); E.T. *The Resurrection of the Dead* (New York, 1933); J. Bautz, *Die Hölle* (1905); O. Cullmann, *Christus und die Zeit* (1956); E.T. *Christ and Time* (1951); and *Heil als Geschichte* (1965); E.T. *Salvation in History* (1967); G. Ebeling, "Erwägungen zu Eschatologie," *Wort und Glaube,* III (1975), pp. 428ff.; L. Goppelt, *Theologie des NT,* I (1975), §§7, 16; E.T. *Theology of the New Testament,* I (Grand Rapids, 1981); II (1976), §44; also "Apokalyptik und Typologie bei Paulus," *Christologie und Ethik* (1968), pp. 234ff.; K. Heim, *Jesus der Weltvollender* (1937), pp. 175ff.; E.T. *Jesus the World's Perfecter* (Philadelphia, 1961); W. Joest, *Ontologie der Person bei Luther* (1967), pp. 331ff.; E. Jüngel, "Abstand des Glaubens von der Politik," DAS, I (1975); M. Kähler, "Die Bedeutung, welche den 'letzten Dingen' für Theologie und Kirche zukommt," *Dogmatische Zeitfragen,* I (1898), p. 242; W. Kamlah, *Christentum und Geschichtlichkeit. Untersuchungen zur Entstehung des Christentums und zur Augustins "Bürgerschaft Gottes,"* 2nd ed. (1951); E. Käsemann, "Zum Thema der urchristlichen Apokalyptik," *Exegetische Versuche und Besinnungen,* II (1964), pp. 105ff.; E.T. *NT Questions of Today;* W. Kasper, "Interview über Tod, Gericht, Jenseits," HK, III (1977), pp. 130ff.; G. Kretschmar, "Auferstehung des Fleisches," *Leben angesichts des Todes* (1968), pp. 101–37; W. von Loewenich, *Augustin und das christliche Geschichtsdenken* (1947) (cf. *Augustin und Luther* [1959], pp. 44ff.); K. Löwith, *Weltgeschichte und Heilsgeschehen* (1953); E.T. *Meaning in History* (Chicago, 1949); W. D. Marsch, *Zukunft* (1969); G. Noller, "Trinitarische Eschatologie," *Festschrift für H. Diem* (1965), pp. 77ff.; W. Pannenberg, "Eschatologie und Sinnerfahrung," *Kerygma und Dogma,* I (1973), pp. 39ff.; W. Schenk, "Naherwartung und Parusieverzögerung. Die urchristliche Eschatologie als Problem der Forschung," *Theologische Versuche,* IV ([East] Berlin, 1972), pp. 47ff.; P. Stuhlmacher, "Erwägungen zum Problem von Gegenwart und Zukunft in der paulinischen Eschatologie," ZThK, IV (1967), pp. 433ff.; also "Das Bekenntnis zur Auferweckung Jesu von den Toten und die biblische Theologie," ZThK, IV (1973), pp. 365ff.; H. Thielicke, *Geschichte und Existenz,* 2nd ed. (1964); P. Tillich, *Systematic Theology,* III (1976), pp. 297–423.

XXXIII

The Basis of Hope

1. PRESENT AND FUTURE

Why is there a doctrine of the last things? Why is there hope of the coming again of Christ and the definitive institution of the kingdom of God? Why does the NT protest against the teaching of the enthusiasts that the resurrection has already taken place, that the present already conceals fulfilment within itself (2 Timothy 2:18; cf. 1 Timothy 6:20)?[1] Should we not stop at the eschatological implications that have met us in all the previous chapters, especially in pneumatological contexts? Do we not learn from the treatment of the final eschatological chapters as a mere epilogue or appendix in some theologies (Schleiermacher) that any explication will either be along the lines of immanent evolution (A. Ritschl) or, as an unfolding of transcendent events, will run into insuperable epistemological difficulties and attempt to express the inexpressible in metaphysical speculations?

Historical objections also arise. When futurist eschatology occurs in the NT, is it not determined by late Jewish apocalyptic and Gnostic redeemer myths, so that it is a foreign body within the real kerygma?

This question has become an acute one with the existential interpretation of the NT. For Bultmann the word "eschatological" does not denote a final goal of God's saving work which has still to be reached in time but the definitive event of salvation here and now.[2] What is stated in terms of a temporal future merely symbolizes the present moment.

The impulse to take this line has always been present. Apart from traces of it in the NT itself research into Luther has raised the question whether the Reformer did not champion a present eschatology. Thus W. von Loewenich believes that the later Luther found the reference point of faith, not in an invisible future, but in the present where we receive forgiveness and salvation, so that he speaks almost

---

[1] Another form of fixation on the present may be found in the sacramental realism of the enthusiasts which sees perfect redemption in the mediation of a heavenly spirit-body at baptism and the degrading of the earthly body to an inessential and corruptible shell (Käsemann, p. 121).

[2] Cf. W. Schmithals, *Die Theologie R. Bultmanns* (1966), pp. 306ff.; E.T. *Theology of Bultmann* (London, 1968), pp. 301ff.

exclusively of a present possession of salvation (*Theologia crusis* 4th ed. [1964], pp. 105ff.); cf. Ebeling ("Die Anfänge von Luthers Hermeneutik," ZThK, XLVIII [1951], pp. 226f.). In my view W. Joest has convincingly refuted this interpretation (*Ontologie,* pp. 335ff.), but since this is simply an example of the debate between future and present eschatology we need not pursue the matter further in this context.

This tendency to regard the future merely as an apocalyptic-mythological description of the present, and thus to change a future eschatology into a present one, has the following basis.

Although the future of the last things transcends our time, it has a fundamental impact on our present. What is to come throws light on what is. We shall give some illustrations.

1. When Kierkegaard says that most people take an absolute view of the relative and a relative view of the absolute, so that their values are confused, a correction of orientation comes when the final and definitive victory of God's kingdom is perceived. We can no longer assign eternal value to what is temporal and transitory. We see such things at a distance "as though we had them not" (1 Corinthians 7:29–31), "for the form (*schēma*) of this world is passing away." Augustine points in this direction at the beginning of his work *On Christian Doctrine:* Present things are for use (*uti*); only God can be enjoyed (*frui*). God can never be an object of mere use. Kierkegaard's dictum seems to be anticipated here.

2. Luther was continually pointing out that eschatological pictures of heaven and hell are symbols of states of conscience and thus express something present. Thus in Thesis 16 on indulgences[3] hell, purgatory, and heaven represent despair, near despair, and assurance.

3. Expectation of final victory resists the anxiety which threatens to rule us now. Those who come to their last hour need not fear any more the next minute.

4. Trust in God's coming reign is a spur to activity in the interim. To wait in the biblical sense is not just to sit around. It is to go to meet what is coming. It is an active vigilance. "With their gaze confidently set on the supraterrestrial fulfilment the first believers went forth to win the world."[4] Where enthusiastic impatience is held in check by watchful soberness (1 Thessalonians 5:6; 1 Peter 5:8) this activity will always take the form of an encouragement to take small steps. The modesty of small steps is possible because there is no illusion that we ourselves can bring God's kingdom but there is the assurance that it will come. Thus Barth can say in his *Final Testimonies:* "I cannot look without hope, then, on a world where small steps can be taken with the prospect that one day everything, literally everything, will be made new. When we view the whole we can view the parts too without despair or agitation" (p. 26).

For all the differences in other respects, we find a similar impact of the future on the present in the case of utopias. The Marxist goal of a future classless society may be cited as an example. Utopias affect the present because they criticize it and offer a program for the future (cf. EG, I, pp. 572ff.; EF, I, pp. 389ff.; Anthrop, pp. 371ff.; Kähler, p. 242).

---

[3]WA, 1, 234, 7; LW, 31, 27 (Thesis 16).
[4]M. Kähler, *Dogmatische Zeitfragen,* I, p. 243.

5. Finally, and negatively, apocalyptic of various kinds has discredited visions of the future because of its eschatological constructions, its extravagant concepts of the end, and its attempts to provide various depictions of the world to come. In post-Kantian thought speculations about a hereafter in time are epistemologically suspect. Kähler adeptly parried the threatened apocalyptic disappearance of futurist eschatology by refusing to speak of the last things and speaking instead of the last person who can be this only because he is also the first (Revelation 1:17; 2:8; 22:13; Colossians 1:15f.).[5] Not the mansions in the Father's house but the Father himself, not the golden city of the heavenly Jerusalem but the king with the sickle and the crown is the eschatological goal. He who is Alpha and Omega, the First and the Last, orients to himself what lies between and gives time its goal.

Käsemann in his work on apocalyptic shows how Paul fills out his adopted apocalyptic christologically. For Paul the resurrection is not primarily a reawakening of the dead. It is oriented to the reign of Christ. Since Christ will be the eschatological ruler, he cannot hand over his people to death, which is the last enemy in this aeon. Conversely, since his people have already committed themselves to Christ in their being in this world, they bear witness here and now to his rule as the cosmokrator and thus symbolically anticipate the final future of resurrection and Christ's unrestricted sway (pp. 129f.).

The elementary impact of the goal of eschatological hope on the present has, materially, an anthropological basis.[6] The goal finds an echo in man's impulse toward self-transcendence. We need only some acquaintance with Ernst Bloch and his anthropology of the "not yet" to realize that this self-transcendence lies especially in our openness to the future. As noted in the chapter on death, we know our finitude and so we have to think both of the limit to our future and then of the future itself. We anticipate this future in anxiety. But above all we have to take hold of ourselves, being projected toward a future destiny. We are thus oriented to hope. The relation to the future, and to time in general, which is manifested in hope, is an existential one which distinguishes us from animals and their fixation on the moment. As we receive our determination from the Word and Spirit, the "infinite passion of our inwardness" awakens (to use a Kierkegaardian phrase) and it brings us this determination as a burden and promise.

If we receive the firstfruits of the Spirit in this way, we receive the living water and shall never thirst again (John 4:13f.). But when the forces of the passing world, which can never give us peace or satisfaction, are done away, there comes another hunger and thirst which stands under the patronage of the promise and blessing, namely, the hunger and thirst after greater and fuller righteousness (Matthew 5:6), after the greater nearness and fuller presence of God, after the perfecting of discipleship, which is always threatened by unfaithfulness, after the final overcoming of that which still stands between God and us and which can be penetrated only by the nevertheless of faith.

---

[5]P. 245.

[6]The question of the finitude of our future (not here in the sense of hope) has a cosmological dimension in science because of the law of entropy (cf. Klaus Müller and W. Pannenberg, *Erwägungen zu einer Theologie der Natur* [1970], p. 48).

2. EXISTENCE AND HISTORY

a. The I and the Fallen World. The Eschatology of the Sermon on the Mount

We have already found the first traces of that which kindles hope. We have found them in the human constitution in general—we are beings that transcend themselves—and in Christian existence in particular. We shall now seek such traces in the sphere of faith.

(1) Almost all religions live by the awareness that man and the world are in contradiction to what they ought to be and need redemption from bondage to their being. Secular ethics expresses this in the antithesis of what is and what should be. In the form of postulates, as in Kant, it can arrive at ideas of an eschaton in which there will be liberation from this enslavement.[7]

To Christians this contradiction is known as a contradiction of God when in faith they commit themselves to the event of salvation that comes to them. Although we have eternal life here and now, we only have its commencement, the firstfruits of the Spirit. Although we are justified here and now and are right with God, we still live as both saints *and* sinners. Although we are certain of the God of salvation, his government of the world and life is hidden from us and contradicts appearances. We now see through a mirror "dimly," but then face to face. We now know in part but then we shall know as we are known (1 Corinthians 13:12; 2 Corinthians 5:7).

Rudolf Hermann (*Luthers These "Gerecht und Sünder zugleich"* [1930], pp. 285f.) points out that hope springs from this *simul*. We pray that our present righteousness may be perfected. Luther in his Romans calls hope the perfecting of righteousness (Ficker ed., II, 96, 19f.) in which the active power of disruption must finally yield to the power of righteousness. The *simul* causes what we now have "only" with the certainty of faith to move into experience. We are confident, then, that one day we shall live with Christ. . . . "We do not know that we live, nor do we have experience of being justified, but we believe and hope" (on Romans 6:8; cf. LW, 25, 52).

We have discussed already the eschatological aspects of baptism and the Lord's Supper. By way of recollection and summary we may refer to the statement of Käsemann that as those who share Christ's cross we also share his resurrection and enthronement, being liberated from the old aeon of death and the powers and set in the new one of Christ's kingdom (p. 120).

(2) What gives us hope beyond this world is contained in the implications of the Sermon on the Mount. The radicalizing of the Mosaic law (Matthew 5:27-48) results from its eschatological perspective. It commands us as though we *still* lived before the fall and as though the new aeon of the fulfilled lordship of God had *already* come. It commands us—this is why it is so radical—without regard for the structural factors of this aeon which force us into competition and egotistic self-assertion. It knows no compromise with these factors. It treats us as we came from God's hands at creation or as we shall be when what is perfect (*teleion*, 1 Corinthians 13:10) is imparted to us.

From this eschatological standpoint the Sermon on the Mount brings to light our

---

[7]Cf. my book *Das Verhältnis zwischen dem Ethischen und dem Ästhetischen* (1932), pp. 208ff.

aeonic existence, our being in secularity. The radical nature of its demands would be absurd if they left us with the excuse (Bert Brecht) that "this is not the way things are," if we could appeal to the supposedly superior power of the structural laws of the present aeon. To the objection that the Sermon on the Mount is remote from the world and life because it cannot be fulfilled as things now are, the reply is that on the contrary the world is far from the kingdom of God—this is why all our attempts at fulfilling it fail.

If the structures of this aeon cannot be interpreted as a higher power working outside us, the only alternative is that they must be put to our account (*imputari*) and regarded as a power in us. This is the logic of the Sermon on the Mount. Its eschatological view unites anthropology and cosmology and shows that this world with its structures is *our* world. It does not regard us as isolated individuals and entelechies but sets in relief our being in secularity. The fallen world which is meant here is our world. It is the world of the first Adam who is its representative in creation and the fall. Its structural egoism simply reflects ours. The questionability of its orders (the laws of repression and self-assertion) are simply an institutionalization of our own questionability. Francis Thompson expressed this correlation of the I and the world with classic precision in his verse: "Our towns are copied fragments from our breast, / And all man's Babylons strive but to impart / The grandeurs of his Babylonian heart."

One might express this identification of man with his aeonic existence in the statement: "I am my history."[8] Only if this be true can we say that the radical demands of the Sermon on the Mount are not just rhetorical declamations that provoke the excuse of higher power but a serious indictment of man in his secularity.

This indictment and our reaction that "we should but cannot" make it clear that God's kingdom has not yet reached its full presence in this aeon although it has drawn near and is among us in the figure of Jesus (Matthew 3:2; 4:17; Luke 17:21). These first instalments of the kingdom in our alien aeon give us cause to hope for its definitive coming and the fulness of its presence.

They also enable us to hear and accept the questioning of our world and ourselves by the Sermon on the Mount. This questioning judgment comes to us as those who stand in the shadow of the coming redemption. Already saved, we can now stand at a distance and see our plight in the light of our salvation. The repeated "Blessed . . ." serves as a prelude to the stern absoluteness of the demands. Before the claim of the radical requirement reaches us, we are addressed as those who have already crossed over the saving boundary (Matthew 5:3ff.) and gained the shelter where nothing can separate us from the love of God (Romans 8:39). This instalment of final salvation which is granted to us with the "Blessed . . ." calls forth hope for its completion. And the radical elements that follow take on a new and surprising meaning. Seen in this light, their core is not to be found in their paralyzing rigor, as might appear to secular ethics, but in the direction of our gaze more yearningly and passionately and confidently away from the far country to home, away from the first instalment to the final fulfilment. Only thus can one see the true eschatological perspective of the Sermon on the Mount.

---

[8]This is the central theme of my book *Geschichte und Existenz;* cf. Anthrop, pp. 86ff.

b. The Antithesis to the Eschatology of Historical Immanence and the Idea of Progress

All this implies that in the light of eschatology there exists a specific view of our historical being and history as a process. Negatively this means that the kingdom of God transcends this aeon as a *totaliter-aliter*. The history of this aeon cannot lead to the eschaton of the kingdom of God. This eschaton encounters it from outside itself.

Theologically this means that Ritschl's attempt to view the kingdom immanently and ethically was a mistake which was closer to Enlightenment ideas (e.g., Lessing's *Education of the Human Race*) than to the NT. As he saw it, salvation is present as in the obedience of faith dominion over the world is given us and the value of the personal spirit is upheld and confirmed over against the obstructions of nature or the natural operations of human society (*Theologie und Metaphysik* [1881], p. 7). The kingdom is a goal which can be achieved. Members of the community help to set it up by right conduct (*Unterricht in die christliche Religion* [1895], §6). It is the totality of subjects united by right conduct (§7). If Kant defined the kingdom as a union of men through the laws of virtue, Ritschl simply gave these laws of virtue a Christian coloring and could follow the same eschatological line as that of Kant. Assuming that the kingdom of God was the moral goal of the religious society founded by Jesus, Ritschl supplied this Christian coloring by defining the kingdom as the organizing of humanity by conduct based on love (*Rechtfertigung und Versöhnung,* III, 3rd ed. [1889], pp. 11f.; E.T. *The Christian Doctrine of Justification and Reconciliation* [1900], p. 12). This kingdom can be called supernatural insofar as it surpasses the moral forms of society and is thus above this world (i.e., the nexus of naturally determined and imparted being). Nevertheless it is a goal that is immanent in history and can be attained by Christian action. It was Ritschl's own son-in-law Johannes Weiss who, followed by A. Schweitzer, opposed to this historical immanence the supraterrestrial and transcendent character of the kingdom of God, which has no place in the present world order (J. Weiss, *Die Predigt Jesu vom Reiche Gottes,* 2nd ed. [1900], p. 73; E.T. *Jesus' Proclamation of the Kingdom of God* [Philadelphia, 1971]).

Eschatology in the NT sense carries with it a criticism of every kind of belief in progress which views the kingdom of God as a utopia. If our interpretation of the Sermon on the Mount is right, at every stage of possible development we are tied to our identity with the history of this aeon. Any progress will be marked by profound ambivalence. Man subdues the earth (Genesis 1:28) and thus fulfils the Creator's command but he does so with the methods of the fallen world: tyranny, force, competition, and self-interest,[9] so that as the light of creation increases its shadow also increases. It is in this context, perhaps, that the NT never portrays the process of history as a straight-line development to the kingdom. With the approach of the kingdom—as in the case of demons when Jesus approaches—the forces of the abyss and antichrist achieve supreme escalation (cf. Revelation 12 and 13). We can never go beyond ourselves but always take ourselves with us and

---

[9]Cf. the environmental problems caused by modern technology.

develop within this identity, i.e., within our determinative polarity as both creatures and sinners.[10]

This status of ours does not change even when we change as individuals. The basic structures of the aeon remain unaffected and unaltered. A legal analogy might help. Even if a criminal changes personally and accepts his guilt he will still have to pay for what he has done. The payment in our case is the order of the present aeon.

Yet to accept the permanence of historical structures is no reason for resignation. It cannot mean that we must believe in fate and mark time. It cannot mean that every effort to change the perverted conditions of the world is a hopeless initiative. (We have already pointed out what impulses derive and will always derive from eschatology.) What it does mean is that modesty is enjoined. It tells us that attempts to change things can produce only gradual improvements. We can undertake partial modifications. We can make the world a little more just and prosperous and free. We can try to replace dictatorships by slightly less bad democracies. We live within the limit of comparatives. We will be proof against utopian superlatives. Along these lines eschatology can achieve great historical power, for it offers protection against illusionary radicalism and enthusiastic absolutizing and requires of us only little steps instead.[11]

To sum up, the history of this aeon is the way between the fall and judgment. In it both creation and the coming kingdom of God are obscured. Its structures are objectifications of both. Hence it can neither produce nor prepare a place for the kingdom of God in which God will be "all in all" (1 Corinthians 15:28). Nevertheless God's kingdom is among us through the coming of Jesus. Since his incarnation God has not just been outside the world. He has come into our aeon and made his salvation present in the person of Jesus. Along the lines of the Chalcedonian Definition one might say that in Jesus Christ God acts as God, immediately divine, and God acts as man, in historical mediacy.[12]

c. The Antithesis to a Normativity of Secular Laws. Eschatology and Politics

The historical power of this eschatological initiative may be seen from another angle. For it confronts us with the question whether we can change the necessity of aeonic history—its being *only* the way from the fall to judgment—into a virtue, or whether we see how dubious it is under the judgment of the eschatological kingship of God and acknowledge it to be such. My concern is to make this investigation as concrete as possible. What does it mean to make a virtue out of the necessity of history?

A certain this-worldly realism might lead to the programmatic conclusion that if it is the law of this world that there be egotistic self-assertion and competitive self-interest, then a thing can be effectively done only if I make this law of the world the norm of my action. If the wood is full of wolves then we must howl with the wolves.

---

[10]Cf. the discussion of the belief in progress in Anthrop, pp. 361ff.; also Teilhard de Chardin, pp. 473ff.

[11]Insofar as visionary pictures and ideals can serve a heuristic purpose, they are not to be rejected out of hand (cf. EG, I, pp. 590ff.; EF, I, pp. 401ff.).

[12]Ratzinger, *Eschatologie*, p. 161; cf. J. Daniélou, "Christologie et eschatologie," *Mit ihm und in ihm. Christologische Forschungen und Perspektiven* (A. Grillmeier) (1975).

Hitler is an example of this attitude. His cynical power politics rested on the thesis that in the world might is above right and those will be most successful who have most power and who use it most unscrupulously and consistently, i.e., who accept and use the laws of this world and translate "I must" into "I will." Attempts to oppose this law of force, to set the principle of right against it, to restrain its unscrupulous use, will be like tilting at windmills and will simply reduce one's own power. On the other hand, acceptance without reserve of the law of historical dynamism (and proceeding along the lines of Machiavelli's politics) will produce the best results. It will not reduce power by fruitless opposition to the law of history but increase it by willing what history wills and making the dynamic thrust of history the agent of one's own will. In this sense the necessity of history—that might is stronger than right—is made into a virtue and assimilation to the laws of the world leads to the greatest success. It should also be noted, of course, that this formula of conformity to the world [Romans 12:2] does not in fact work out, as Hitler shows. The final reason for the disaster of World War II was that Hitler's power principle, being bound by no values, produced an incalculable force which made treaties impossible. Hitler did not regard treaties as binding but simply as the temporary expressions of political interests which could be cynically discarded when convenient. The Western powers found themselves forced into a declaration of war the moment Hitler finally set aside the role of a possible treaty-partner and proved to be a "non-serious firm" with whom normal business relations could no longer be established.

When, however, we do not make the laws of our world, especially the law of force, into a normative principle for our own conduct, and do not make a virtue of the world's necessity, then creative restraints arise. These restraints see to it that what a statesman may have to do in the name of political egoism will be accompanied by horror at the necessity. They lead to the experience that while we cannot govern according to the Sermon on the Mount (by declaring it to be the constitutional law of this world), this is not because the Sermon on the Mount is remote from this world but because this world is alien to the kingdom of God. Acting in the name of the structures of this aeon does not make a thing right. Killing and violence are not justified by invocation of the principle: "C'est la guerre." They need forgiveness.

By calling this world in question, e.g., through the demands of the Sermon on the Mount, Christian eschatology engenders these restraints, resists the conversion of the world's necessity into its virtue, and thereby manifests its power. Where its message is accepted, it is bound to have a profound influence on political programs. It is bound to do so even where it works only indirectly in the secular world through Christian tradition and the "common sense" which this produces. Along these lines E. Fridell can speak of the enormous advantage of the post-Christian and secularized age over that of antiquity. People have not changed. They still live sensually, look out for themselves, use force, deceit, and wrong. But they no longer do it easily and confidently (making a virtue out of necessity). They do it wanly, secretly, and anxiously. They no longer have the good humor of the beast of prey. This is perhaps the one success of Christianity thus far. It is the result of its eschatology.[13]

---

[13]Egon Fridell, *Kulturgeschichte der Neuzeit* (1927), p. 317.

It is beyond question that the so-called moderation of Bismarck was directly due to the impact of the Sermon on the Mount (cf. the analysis in ThE, II, 2, §§534ff.; E.T. II, pp. 92ff.). Frederick the Great shows that Christian eschatology can also have an indirect influence in secularized spheres. In the introduction to his *Denkwürdigkeiten* (1742), which were written for his successors, he shows how difficult it is "to keep one's character pure and honorable" when one is sucked into European politics. Constantly a terrible choice has to be made between "sacrificing one's people and breaking one's word." Power conflicts with moral norms. Politics often contradicts private morality. Princes by tacit consent do what advantage dictates. We must hope that "a more enlightened age will yield to honor the place which is its due." Frederick, then, does not defend statecraft; he simply takes stock of the actual situation (L. Reiners, *Friedrich* [1952], pp. !06f.).

In contrast to Machiavelli, Frederick with his belief in progress, i.e., the hope of a more enlightened and upright age, expresses the questionability of compliance with the laws of this world. Though it is unlikely that this restraint arose under the influence of the Sermon on the Mount, it could be an indirect consequence by the detour of the Christian West. Frederick was one of the statesmen who could not do what he did without concern. He was in a field of force from which Hitler "the lawless one" (2 Thessalonians 2:8) flagrantly emancipated himself.

d. The Antithesis to a Chiliastic World Consummation. The Millennium

The eschatological radicalness of the Sermon on the Mount challenges the structures of our aeon. By its "still" and "already" it characterizes the aeon as the interim of a fallen world. Yet at the same time it reveals a final dimension of Christian hope. The eternal life which is given us here and now with the dawn of God's reign is more than the eternal life of the individual. Assurance is given that this world with its aeonic structures will be redeemed and that Christ as pantokrator will assume dominion over the whole cosmos.[14] The meaning of this hope is that he who is at the beginning and the end embraces the cosmos and will lead even the intervening interim to definitive victory.

If the structures of our aeonic world can neither produce the kingdom of God nor, without being shattered, receive it; if the kingdom of God and world history are totally different from one another, then the eschatological kingship of God is not a conceivable consummation of this history. This means that the apocalyptic idea of a millennium has to be put in the field of mythology.

The idea occurs only once in the NT in Revelation 20 (it is contested in 1 Corinthians 15). Here Satan is bound for a thousand years (20:2f.). In this period Christ and his elect rule the world (vv. 4ff.). Christ resides in the city of God on Mt. Zion (v. 9). His kingdom is ushered in with a resurrection of the dead (v. 5) which as the first resurrection is expressly distinguished from the second and last resurrection. It embraces only a minority of people, namely, those who have not worshipped the beast (v. 4). This happy first phase of fulfilment is simply a prelude to the final conflict which is started by the adversary himself.

The Reformers did not use the same argument as we have done for not taking

---

[14]For the concept of pantokrator cf. Revelation 1:8; 4:8, 11:17, etc.; also O. A. Dilschneider, *Pantokrator* (1962), esp. pp. 107ff.

this apocalyptic vision literally. They saw in a literal interpretation a return of the OT idea of a messianic kingdom in history and therefore a "Jewish view."[15] In the background, however, they sensed the incompatibility of this aeon with the perfected lordship of God.[16] Above all it is worth noting that they rejected millennialist teaching in spite of their loyalty to the Bible. The historical occasion of their opposition is certainly to be found in the drastic adoption of the concept of the millennium by the Anabaptists and radicals.[17]

Ideas of growth are not, of course, alien to the NT. There ought to be growth in the community in every way (1 Corinthians 1:5; Ephesians 4:15). We should all grow to maturity in Christ (Ephesians 4:13). Acts and the epistles often speak with joy of intensive and extensive growth. The missionary commission embraces "all nations," "every creature" (Matthew 28:19 par.). But this growth, unlike the progress of rational belief, does not take the form of a crescendo. It is not uniform nor apparent. The spiritual life is hidden (Colossians 3:3). Furthermore the growth of the new involves the constant destruction of the old. Tares are sown with the wheat (Matthew 13:15ff.). In this regard the NT itself stands opposed to chiliasm.

Yet the question arises—as a material and not just a literary question—how this apocalyptic element came into the NT and whether it is or is not an alien element. The millennium is undoubtedly not a utopia in the sense of a final state introduced by men. It has nothing whatever to do with a kingdom of peace which is the result of moral striving for human unity on the basis of love (Ritschl). Not man but an angel defeats the dragon and ushers in a period of eschatological peace. This kingdom is one that "comes," not one that is achieved by us. The real problem is the different one: How can there be history in the dragon's absence? How can there be a perfect culture without a Cainite background?[18] How can we live at peace in history without the "challenge" and "response" of Toynbee? The kingdom of peace as such is not the problem in this vision. The problem is that it does not transcend history, as the kingdom of God does, but is set in history itself as the precursor of the kingdom.

But why? The simple answer that we have "judaizing" here, that this-worldly messianic concepts are illegitimately revived, is too easy. For it provokes the further question why this revival took place.

Figuratively one might perhaps say that we have here a historically formed mirage of eschatological hope of the kingdom, or the visionary form of an argument. This argument—an argument of faith—is operating with the thought that the kingdom of God must not be regarded as belonging only to the world to come and that a simple reference to the "among us" is not enough to remove the distance of other-worldliness. Christ as pantokrator does not just take control of hearts. He is also Lord of history and can set up his kingdom in this aeon as he already manifests it from time to time in his mighty eschatological acts.

Possibly we have here a reversal of the projection of Feuerbach. This world is not now projected into the next world but the next world is projected into this

---

[15]CA, article 17; cf. Second Helvetic Confession, c. 11.
[16]For Luther this would be an implication of his doctrine of the two kingdoms (cf. ThE, I, §§1783ff.; E.T. I, pp. 359ff.).
[17]W. Nigg, *Das ewige Reich*, 2nd ed. (1954).
[18]Cf. the author's book *Wie die Welt begann* (1960), pp. 246ff.; E.T. *How the World Began* (Philadelphia, 1961), pp. 228ff.

world.[19] This projection suggests the idea of a mirage. It points both to the reality of the background (the eschaton of God's kingdom) and to the unreality of the figure.

Another reason in addition to the pantokrator argument might have contributed to the inclination to take the mirage literally and to go out into the desert after it, namely, the longing for a goal of human activity such as one finds in the creation of utopias from Thomas More by way of J. V. Andreae[20] to Karl Marx. There is obviously a primal human need to hunt for the unconditioned in order to reach an optimum within the conditioned, to want the absolute in order to win the relatively highest. Plainly the absolute needs a visionary form to be effective as an ethical force.

It would be cheap to condemn enthusiasts simply because they are enthusiastic. Perhaps one should say with Kierkegaard that their purity is that of desiring only one thing. Yet we do need to awaken enthusiasts out of their ethically creative dream. The father lets his son play with building blocks. In play the son thinks that what he has put together is a real house in which he can live a human life. But in the evening the time comes when his father tells him to pull it all down and pack it away. He then sees that it was all play and the painful act of pulling down helps him to take a step toward reality. In the same way enthusiasts may build peacefully by day but they have to come to the evening hour. Then it makes some sense that they have built only what must be pulled down again. For it can help them to work toward a historical goal. It can help them to write down ways and goals with chalk on a blackboard where they will be rubbed out. For this reason Barth made a felicitous statement, which reminds us of the relativity of all chiliastic ideas, when he once said that without chiliasm, even if only a dash of it, there can be no ethics, any more than there can be without the idea of a moral personality.[21] For Barth the idea of a moral personality is elsewhere a despised Romantic bubble. But in a heuristic interim, as it were, it can and must take on a temporary function in the moral concept.

Thus the Reformers were right to reject chiliasm[22] even though their theological argument was concealed by contemporary polemics and they did not investigate the mistaken reason for the teaching.

For the rest, one might say that the history of chiliasm is also its refutation. Some elite communities have tried to anticipate the millennium but they have all failed, at the latest in the second generation. Cf. E. Brunner, *Die denkwürdige Geschichte der Mayflower Pilgerväter* (1920); Richard Niebuhr, *The Kingdom of God in America* (1937).

Fundamentally similar are the objections that must be brought against the ideological context of certain liberation movements, especially when they are supported by theological notions of an uncontrolled historical goal for which

---

[19]One senses this in the pleading of L. Ragaz for the millennium in his *Der Kampf um das Reich Gottes in Blumhardt, Vater und Sohn . . .* (1922), p. 47.

[20]*Rei publicae Christianopolitanae descriptio* (1619).

[21]*Das Wort Gottes und die Theologie* (1929), p. 140; E.T. *The Word of God and the Word of Man* (Boston, 1928), p. 158.

[22]Cf. in Roman Catholic theology the decree of 7/19/1944 (Denz., 3839; E.T. 2298).

chiliastic visions are the model. Thus authors like Harvey Cox and R. Shaull (*Theology of Revolution*) all draw upon Bloch's idea of hope. For criticism of the ideology of liberation cf. L. Bossle, "Der neue Mensch in einer neuen Gesellschaft—Eschatologie oder anthropologischer Irrationalismus," *Utopie der Befreiung*, ed. F. Hengsbach and A. L. Trujillo (1976), pp. 86ff.

Some more cautious and guarded echoes of an immanent eschatology along the lines of chiliasm seem to me to occur occasionally in Rahner (*Schriften zur Theologie*, VIII, pp. 598–609) and E. Schillebeeckx, "Einige hermeneutische Überlegungen zur Eschatologie," *Concilium*, I (1969), pp. 19ff.; E.T. *Concilium*, XLI (New York, 1969), pp. 42ff., but we cannot go into this here.

XXXIV

The Crisis of Hope (Delay of the Parousia)

That the primitive community understood the kingdom of God, not as the *telos* of aeonic history, but as a transcendent event, is shown very simply by the christological foundation of its hope. On the basis of Daniel (7:13; cf. Revelation 1:13) it expected Jesus as the coming Son of Man who does not come out of history but comes to it. It regarded this expectation of the Parousia as having been introduced by the manifestations of the risen Lord—another event which transcends the aeonic history that stands under the lordship of death, and therefore an "eschatological" event in the strict sense. Primitive Christian eschatology is not grounded, then, in apocalypses of the future. What will happen in the future, the Lord's Parousia, has its ground in what already has taken place with the event of the resurrection. The community of Christ already has the eschatological event behind it; it comes *from* it. What it awaits as still to take place is the end of this aeon and the coming of the perfect rule of God. This is imminent expectation. The decisive thing has already happened and it presses on toward what has still to happen. The great concluding chord is already quivering in the air.

That the dawn of the eschaton is already an event—even before the resurrection—finds testimony in the synoptic apocalypse when Jesus, in reply to the question of the Pharisees when the kingdom of God will come, says that it is already "among them" (Luke 17:20f.). What is still to come is also close at hand: "Truly, I say to you, there are some standing here who will not taste death before they see the kingdom of God come with power" (Mark 9:1; 13:30). In a saying to the disciples which alludes to their uncompleted mission in Palestine Jesus says: "You will not have gone through all the towns of Israel, before the Son of man comes" (Matthew 10:23). In the light of the resurrection of Jesus we can see the reason for the direct nearness of the coming consummation (1 Corinthians 15:51; 1 Thessalonians 4:15, 17). Death has already been swallowed up in victory (1 Corinthians 15:55, 57). We stand before the imminent end of this age (7:29). Hence we cannot fit ourselves in it. We can only stand aloof so as not to be carried to destruction with it. We can "have only as if we had not" (7:29ff.).

This imminent expectation was not met. The last chord never sounded. From a human standpoint this would seem to compromise primitive Christian eschatology and to bring on a crisis of the first order. That there was no crisis, and the disappointed expectation persisted, can hardly be explained psychologically. We have here a theological problem which is posed already by the relation between promise and fulfilment in the OT.[1] The promise is not understood there as a direct prediction which is marked on the calendar so that we can get a handle on the known future by means of it. The events which follow the promise—even though they seem to be strange and even contradictory as fulfilments—are regarded as a new experience of faith. In the light of them, even when they point in a different direction from that expected, a new understanding of the promise is sought. The understanding of the promise is corrected by the course of events. The future is not explained by the promise but the experienced future explains the promise. Human, all too human thoughts and expectations are no match for the "higher thoughts" (Isaiah 55:8f.) that were hidden in the promise. God interprets his promises by the way he fulfils them. Even the prophesying of Jesus is subject to interpretation in the light of what happens (John 13:7).

In the Lucan writings, then, the unexpected extension of the time between the resurrection and the Parousia becomes a phase of new experiences of faith by which the understanding of the earlier eschatological prophetic event is broadened. For this intervening time becomes the time for the works of the Holy Spirit in the primitive community and as such the time for a new presence of the Lord. As people experienced constantly surprising forms of fulfilment, previously concealed contents of the promise came to light. The promise-event which *has already* taken place eschatologically takes precedence over all expectations of what is still to come. There may be disappointments as what is expected either does not happen or happens in a different way. But there is still expectation of that which is to come as that which will contain the key to the true meaning of the promise-event.

So little was the promise questioned that even at a time when it was clear that the coming of the bridegroom was delayed (Matthew 25:5) the community could still transmit accurately what Jesus said about his imminent Parousia and not suppress it as a false prediction. Through the impact of the works of the Spirit in the primitive community the prolonged interval took on its own significance.

The pause, the unexpected extension of time up to the last day, also caused it to look in other directions and to learn the laws of God's kingdom. Three answers in particular were suggested.

1. 2 Thessalonians finds the reason for the delay in the ungodly power which still holds up the salvation event (*katechein*, 2:3–7). The world that stands under this power is not yet ripe for the fulfilment. From the very first God's plan does not take the form of a mechanism in which it is "cause" and history is "effect." The time between the resurrection and the return does not just run on but is exposed to incidents which arise through human traffic with what is wicked and ungodly. Thus salvation does not simply unfold in this aeon. It also provokes its opposite and the conflict between Christ and antichrist undergoes extreme escalation. Thus

---

[1]Cf. c. XI and Anthrop, pp. 342ff.

a longer process of struggle is needed before God's "victory day" can be declared.

2. That we have received the firstfruits or pledge (*arrabōn*) of the Spirit means that this gift is to be authenticated "away from the Lord" in the "tent" of the body and that this time of authentication, which is also a time of expectation, still proceeds (2 Corinthians 5:4–10).

3. Death and resurrection with Christ is to be worked out in discipleship (Romans 6:8; 14:8; Galatians 2:19; Colossians 3:3). Since the time that is allotted and that remains to us in this aeon is the time of this discipleship and incorporation into Christ's body, it becomes very important. It is not just a time for winding up things. It is not time that is emptied by the end that is coming. It takes on the quality of the *kairos* (2 Corinthians 6:2).

We have to ask, then, whether nonfulfilment of imminent expectation means nonfulfilment of the promise or whether we have here a postponement which conceals a fulfilment that has yet to be discovered and that will manifest itself as a new time of salvation.

Related to this fulfilment is the fact that delay in the Parousia did not cause the crisis of hope one might have expected. The context of the other Parousia sayings of Jesus strengthens this view: "Of that day or that hour [that of the end and his coming again] no one knows . . . not even the Son" (Mark 13:32). In the light of this statement that only the Father knows the time, the chronology cannot be the point of the promises of Jesus but imminent expectation as such. According to the schema of promise and fulfilment the meaning of "imminent" had to be shown by what the one who gave the promise did in the time that followed. Hence those who received the promise had to wait for the fulfilment. Waiting here is not just a psychological state of phlegmatic patience that helps us through the interim period. It is also a questioning attitude, expectation of something whose "how" and "why" could not be known at the time of the promise and that will thus come as a surprise. Thus the question that is put to the future is: How am I to understand the promise in terms of what is fulfilled later? What did it really say to me? Along these lines, in the light of what happened, the primitive community found two answers to the question what Jesus' sayings about imminent expectation meant for them.

First, they noted the suddenness of the Lord's Parousia, its unannounced and incalculable nature in spite of all the signs. We are already surrounded by his coming and do not know from what direction he himself will come. Hence waiting means extreme vigilance: "Watch and pray" (Matthew 13:33). The nearness of the Lord gives to each moment an unconditioned accent and confirms from this side, too, that the coming end does not empty our time but fills it. We cannot postpone discipleship till later or claim this day as our own (Luke 14:18–20). If the day of the Lord comes like a thief in the night (1 Thessalonians 5:2; 2 Peter 3:10), then the appeal in its various forms is valid: "Today, when you hear his voice, do not harden your hearts" (Hebrews 3:7f.), or: "Watch therefore, for you do not know on what day your Lord is coming" (Matthew 24:42). The steward who knows his master's calendar and can be sure that he will not come unexpectedly can do as he likes, saying, "My master is delayed in coming," beginning to beat the menservants and maidservants, and eating and drinking and getting drunk

(Luke 12:45). But if he knows that his master is at hand and may arrive suddenly he will behave soberly and watch with loins girded and lamps burning (12:35).[2] Similarly, imminent expectation divides people into "wise" and "foolish" virgins (Matthew 25:1-13).

If in a way that differs inconceivably from the statement of Jesus the course of this world continues as though nothing had happened and he had not been there, and if the primitive community looks at what follows to find the meaning of the promise that it originally understood differently, then the conclusion it reaches is that the core of the statement about the imminence of the Parousia could not be chronological. The indifferent steward and the foolish virgins were interested in chronology. This interest is a sign of noncommitment. We, however, realize that each day in continuing time is qualified by the nearness of the Lord and the unforeseeability of his coming. We no longer ask: *When* is his future? We ask: What does it *mean* for us? It means: Watch. But watching is a form of soberness which demands extreme realism. To be realistic here is not to confuse the transitory with the eternal, the little with the big, the useful with the "one thing needful" (Luke 10:42). It is not to treat the relative absolutely. Watching means being ready to effect a transvaluation of all values.

In this way the history of God can be understood only in connection with my own history, God's coming only in connection with my watching.

As we learn from the doctrine of the two natures of Christ, history is neither an exclusively human nor an exclusively divine dimension. Since the incarnation of the Word the two dimensions have been linked together. Thus the history of the final future, the Parousia of the Lord, is also my own history, the history of my watching, my soberness, and my transvaluations.

Second, the question what the promised nearness of the return and its delay can mean in the light of what takes place later receives a further answer.

The certainty that the kingdom of God has drawn near rests primarily on the fact that in the person of the risen Lord the world of death has been decisively broken and the end has been anticipated. To use a metaphor of Luther's, the serpent's head has been broken. All that the time of this world can now bring is the writhing of its body. Or, to use another of Luther's metaphors, its poisonous teeth have been broken. In the form of sin and death it can only snap at us without doing any harm. Remaining history, measured by the weight of this event, has no specific weight of its own. (This corresponds dialectically to an earlier statement in which we spoke of the unconditional nature of the *kairos*.)[3] The direct relation between the resurrection and God's final triumph, the anticipation of the end that has already taken place, makes the intervening time transparent, so that he who is to come may be seen already. The prophets bring the end close with a telescope, looking "over" the time between. It seems to be a law of prophetic vision[4] that it marks clearly the lines that point to the end but draws them together in such a way that one can speak of a "prophetic shortening of the perspective."

---

[2]This applies on the individual level, too, for we need to be ready to be summoned out of this temporal life and set before the Lord. Cf. the hymns on death, e.g., the verse of Juliane von Schwarzburg-Rudolstadt: "Who knows how near my end is."

[3]In this regard 1 Corinthians 7 has been described as Paul's interim ethics.

[4]Cf. X, 4.

We trivialize this process if we try to psychologize it and say that the prophets have migrated out of the present, have left the waiting-room of the future, and in their imagination have already sat down at the messianic banquet (Cox). No, there is a *material* reason for the shortening of perspective. It is closely related to an understanding of history which has experienced it as salvation history. In the sequence of salvation events the decisive thing has already happened. The end has been anticipated. The interim prior to the definitive end does not signify a delay. The end is imminent, God's kingdom has drawn near. How else could it be when it has already been "among us" (Luke 17:21).

This explains the remarkable historical fact to which we have alluded already, namely, that the disappointment of imminent expectation caused no profound disturbance and that believers continued to hope even when the time fixed for the Parousia passed and nothing happened. They gathered at evening to await with prayers and hymns the coming of the Son of man on the clouds of heaven and when it did not take place they returned home as though nothing had happened. Even a sober Bible theologian like J. A. Bengel could give June 18, 1836, as the date of the beginning of the millennium. That these attempts at dating, which all proved wrong, did not undermine faith or discredit the claimed prophetic office must appear to be an insoluble riddle to those outside. This riddle can be solved only if we remember the priority that the anticipatory salvation event—the resurrection—has for faith. In this light all datings are relativized. Just because the point of eschatology does not lie in them, hope can spring up again the very morning after the disappointment (cf. Ebeling, *Wort und Glaube,* III, pp. 434f.).

O. Cullmann found an instructive analogy in the secular sphere for this shortening of perspective. When the decisive battle of Stalingrad had been fought in the Second World War, the rest of the war was a mere epilogue. Stalingrad was the real V-day. This led some serious and knowledgeable commentators (e.g., C. F. Goerdeler, who was to have been chancellor after the planned overthrow of Hitler) to miscalculate very badly the date of capitulation. They expected the war to end quickly, at the latest within three months. Yet they were not taken aback when the war continued past the expected date. The essential point in their prognoses was not the dating but the accurate tracing of the historical line that would lead to the final end. Nothing basically new was about to happen, only increasing military, economic, and physical exhaustion. Thus the V-day that had already come brought with it a kind of prophetic shortening of perspective. The error in chronology was simply a by-product. Indeed, in a sense it validated the correct diagnosis and prognosis. Its accuracy lay in recognition of the real V-day (cf. O. Cullmann, *Christus und die Zeit,* pp. 73, 124; E.T. *Christ and Time,* pp. 84, 141).

This understanding of the future is a paradigm of the biblical understanding of history.

The difference and even, phenomenologically, the contradiction between the promise and the transition to a new quality in its fulfilment has given the impression, outside the sphere of faith, that the promise has not been fulfilled. But faith, which trusts the God who says: "I am who I am" (Exodus 3:14; cf. Revelation 1:4, 8), finds the way from promise to fulfilment guaranteed by him—yet in such a manner that this way is left to his "thoughts," that he is master of it, and that only in his superabundant fulfilments will there be revealed the meaning of what human thoughts cannot yet recognize in the promise.

Only on this presupposition is there no substance in the human perception of a contradiction between promise and fulfilment. The basis of prophetic statements is that God is understood as the one who is Lord of his word, his deed, and his direction of history. This is hidden to those who engage merely in phenomenological history.

Even a deistic view of history can go astray here. If God is viewed as a clockmaker who has set the clock and then left it to tick away, we shall be convinced that we understand the course of the world once we grasp its causality. Since the principle of causality does not fit in hermeneutically with the correlation of promise and fulfilment, there is seen only a painful difference between the two. The prophets are compromised. This is the reason for the contradiction between the "timeless truth of reason" and the "accidental truth of history" which caused Lessing among others so much trouble.

Deism offers a good illustration of the difference between the two views of history. Its theory of the divine clockmaker leads to the conclusion that we can work back from causality to the first cause, the divine Inaugurator. On the biblical view, however, God is concealed in that which our eyes cannot see in its interrelationship. Only the Inaugurator himself is certain. Only faith in him produces the belief that history is his work even though the "how" of his presence in it cannot be seen and faith can respond to appearances only with a Nevertheless. In this belief history is his "likeness" even though appearances cannot equate events and their Inaugurator. We wait for the one who is thus unknown to reveal himself. We ourselves do not know the interrelation, not even between promise and fulfilment. But we trust him who designs it. We do not move from history to God (as all natural theology does); we move from God to history. This is the crucial difference.

XXXV

The Content of Hope

1. SIGNS OF THE END

How can that which does not come from our time but comes into it from outside, as do the Parousia and the beginning of God's definitive reign, still have signs *in* time? Although the end comes with unexpected suddenness and no one knows the day or the hour, the NT refers everywhere to signs of the second advent. When the disciples ask: "What will be the sign of your coming and of the close of the age?" (Matthew 24:3) Jesus gives an apocalyptic depiction of the end-time: the coming of false prophets and pseudo-christs (v. 5), wars and rumors of wars and chaos among the nations (vv. 6f.), the rise of unbelief and the persecution of the saints which will cause the love of many to grow cold (vv. 9–12), and finally cosmic disasters, the sun and moon ceasing to shine, the stars falling from heaven, and the powers of heaven being shaken (vv. 29ff.). First Thessalonians speaks of the threat of false security when the shadows of the end-time begin to fall on humanity (5:2–5). Revelation is full of visions of the woes of history and the revolts of ungodly power, though even these things cannot frighten people out of their security: They did not repent (9:20f.; 16:9, 11).

All these pictures of the end, being taken from this aeon, are inadequate. They simply show us that the time of this world is not circular, as the Greeks thought, but is a finite span. The apocalyptic events which are similitudes of the end are not perceived as such. People eat and drink and marry and are given in marriage as they did in the days of Noah when he went into the ark (Matthew 24:38). This is part of the hardening which intensifies as parables are given (Matthew 13:13). What increases the hardening is that people live with categories and concepts of this aeon, that they are too accustomed to the schema of its ongoing time to be open to the "wholly other" of God's coming kingdom, to have, in popular terms, an antenna for this "wholly other."

The kingdom of God can no more be the final point of an evolution of apocalyptic disasters than it can be the product of an immanent evolution in history. It is neither progress nor is it terror in the forms of this world. The signs are not the first act in a drama which will develop eschatologically in the same style. They are the signals of something dreadful which goes far beyond the symbols used for it.

This is why we have to ask how the transcendent lordship of God can have prefigurations in historical immanence. We can again give a christological answer along the lines of the two natures; Christ comes out of eternity into time and unites the two. In accordance with the Son of Man tradition Christ is the final fulfiller of God's will in judgment and salvation (Daniel 7:13ff.) as well as man among men. He thus represents God to men and men before God.[1] He himself in his cross and resurrection is the sign of his second coming. He already wears the crown on the cross.

Within this christological bracket every visitation is a prefiguration of final judgment and the last assize. In transitory judgments, such as the plague of locusts in Joel (1:4), the last judgment is present. This linking of the penultimate and the ultimate may be seen again and again in history according to the OT. One visitation—we do not know which—is the last before the end. The attack of the kings of the east precedes the devastation of Sodom and Gomorrah by fire and brimstone (Genesis 14:1ff.; 19:24f.). The attack of Antiochus, who for a time halted the worship of God in the temple, precedes the final destruction of Jerusalem in A.D. 70 and 135. If one judgment is penultimate, another is ultimate. We see this not only in the destruction of Jerusalem but also in the disasters which overtook Christianity in Asia and Africa (cf. H. Frey, *Das Buch der Kirche in der Weltenwende. Die kleinen nachexilischen Propheten* [1941], p. 240).

Here the penultimate and the ultimate are related within the historical nexus. Hence the comparison is a weak and imperfect one. The world and the kingdom of God are separated by the discontinuity of the wholly other.

Another comparison which tries to use the relation between the penultimate and the ultimate, or the provisional and the definitive, suffers from the same liability. Here the visitations and woes of history are viewed as the big hand on a clock which constantly comes to the critical point of 12 but then moves on. Unnoticed, however, the insignificant little hand is moving too until it reaches the definitive 12. We should point out—although it is a mistake to explain parables—that most people keep their eyes fixed on the big hand but Noah noticed the little one before he went into the ark.

That Christians can focus too much on the big hand is movingly expressed in the literary remains of Jochen Klepper from the period just before he committed suicide with his wife and stepdaughter. When Hitler's persecution of the Jews was reaching a peak and the net was being cast ever wider, along with the terrors of battles and bombings, he wrote that although he rejected ideas of the end of the world, he still had to say that the situation had for them something of the terror of the end-time, Christ's return being intimated earlier for them than for others (Rita Thalmann, *J. Klepper* [1977], p. 324). A life with so little future had to lead to eschatology (p. 326). Reference was made to 1 Peter 4:7: "the end of all things is at hand" (p. 343). The aversion to apocalyptic expresses the christological aspect of this expectation, the element of faith in the approaching end. Only in the name of faith in him who stands at the end with judgment and forgiveness, and who, as

---

[1]P. Stuhlmacher, "Das Bekenntnis . . .," ZThK, IV (1963), pp. 394f.

we read in the "Kyrie," does not let us come into judgment, can the Christian Klepper die by his own hand, committing himself into the hand of this last one. Unlike others, even other Christians, he saw the little hand.

The christological link between the signs and what they signify shows that speculative concern with the signs is unspiritual and means surrender to apocalyptic imaginings. Instead of relativizing the eschatological calendar it can give it the rank of an independent theme. Certain sectarian practices illustrate this. In contrast the christological background of the signs reminds us that not just our time (Psalm 31:15) but the end of time is beyond our control or calculation and known only to the Father (Matthew 24:36). Not the slide rule, then, but folded hands (Revelation 22:20b) express trust in the Lord of time and eternity. The signs are dumb if we do not look to him who gives us signs. God interprets his acts and Christ is the hermeneutical "principle" for an understanding of what this God is. Without fellowship with him, i.e., without the testimony of the Holy Spirit, the sign either loses its transparency and becomes an ordinary aeonic event[2] or it becomes an occasion of eschatological speculation that bypasses Christ.

Hence Christ, his being among us (Matthew 18:20), is the decisive sign from which all the others receive their light. All proclamation of the Word, all administration of baptism and the Lord's Supper, all forgiveness of sins, all proffered comfort is a sign and anticipation of the end and will be accompanied by the firstfruits of the Spirit, who points forward to the definitive rule of God and already manifests its power in the here and now.

One can (and must) put it paradoxically. The eschaton is a transcending of presentation by the Spirit. The event of the Word and Spirit, however, is already an anticipation of this transcending. Already here and now it is an eschatological event. The presence of God by the Spirit not only brings the event of salvation out of the past, and not only brings the mighty acts of God out of the past into the present, but also makes the coming fulfilment present as well.

2. THE PAROUSIA AND THE LAST JUDGMENT

a. The Parousia

The signs of the end are not just personal (oppression by demonic forces, the approach of death, etc.). They are also cosmic symbols denoting world-catastrophe (Matthew 24:29ff.).[3] Our references to the structures of the fallen cosmos, which we have interpreted as man's objectified secularity, have pointed us not only to the individual dimension of death and eternal life but also to the

---

[2]Cf. those who at the end do not repent, or those who had been miraculously fed but of whom the Johannine Christ says: "You seek me, not because you saw signs, but because you ate your fill of the loaves" (John 6:26). Instead of glorifying God they saw only a normal event.

[3]In the individualistic theologies of the 19th century and their successors this element is absent. Thus W. Herrmann deals only with individual hope in a brief epilogue (*Dogmatik* [1925], p. 53; M. Beintker, *Die Gottesfrage in der Theologie W. Herrmanns* [1976], pp. 27ff.). E. Hirsch calls the cosmic aspects "mythological productions." The advocacy of patience regarding the liturgical use of these productions (because they have been vessels of the hope of eternal life for countless generations of Christians) has a hypocritical sound (*Leitfaden zur christlichen Lehre* [1938], pp. 113 and 174).

cosmic dimension of the end of the world and the coming of the kingdom of God.

Paul sees both dimensions together. Individually death means a change of form. We have to die; "in the midst of life we are in death." But for those who are united by faith with Christ's death on the cross, death is no longer the wages of sin (Romans 6:23). For through the Spirit they acquire a share in eternal life, no longer snatching at this life in order to be like God. Thus death ceases to be judgment, the closed barrier of finitude. The broader cosmic aspects are worked out in Romans 8:18–23. With man all nature is subject to the law of threat and anxiety and death. In solidarity with man it yearns for redemption. But the sorrow of creation does not disclose its secret in terms of natural laws, i.e., as fate or *moira*. Paul regards this suffering of nature as part of man's history with God in rebellion and grace. Animals do not fall (that would be real mythology). Man, the goal of creation and in some sense its representative, falls. His breach with God has a universal dimension. If it is not a dogmatic truth it is also no romantic anthropomorphizing to say that one has only to look one's dog in the eye to get an impression of its longing for redemption. When Goethe once came upon a puppy just being born he took it by the ear, noted with astonishment how it was straining toward the light, and suggested that this was what St. Paul meant when he spoke about the sighing of the creature (cf. K. Heim, *Weltschöpfung und Weltende* [1952], p. 166).

The Spirit who helps our weakness as a pledge of future glory (8:23, 26), and gives us certainty regarding the future, enables us to face the background of a world of death and against all appearances still hope for an all-embracing redemption. The certainty that he gives is mediated by the love which is poured by him into our hearts (5:5). This love responds for its part to God's preceding love which has come to us in Christ's death for the wicked (5:6) and which remains faithful to us through the vicissitudes of history and nature right up to the final victory of the lordship of God.

The question whether the final end is just a time-bound mythologoumenon (as Hirsch thought) is one which we face today with much less rationalistic skepticism because the physical possibilities of an end of the world (atomic death, poisoning of the atmosphere, etc.) are plain to see. We can illustrate what is meant by the term "objectified secularity" by pointing out that much of the sighing of creation is in fact caused by man and is not just a transhuman fate which makes man an uninvolved and innocent victim. The ambivalence of the progress of science and technology[4] brings to light the ambivalence of man himself. On the one hand man can subject the world to himself by technology but on the other he is like the sorcerer's apprentice of Goethe's poem who cannot control the forces that he unleashes and thus becomes subject to them.

At this point, of course, we must be on guard against speculations which with the help of a variation of natural theology can produce a natural eschatology and lead to an indirect proof of God. The homiletical use of fear of the atom bomb as a means of softening people up for the consolation of the gospel reminds us painfully of such possibilities. The phenomenology of technological development no more enables us to understand and demonstrate the biblical eschatology of the end of the world than the fuller analysis of death enables us to disclose its secret as judgment.

---

[4]Cf. the possibility of genetic manipulation among many other things.

Certainty as to the end of the world as it is foreseen in Christian eschatology arises only when the cosmos is seen in its relation to God and when this relation reveals itself to be one of contradiction. From this standpoint it is unthinkable in the strict sense that the ontic being of a world in contradiction should be perpetuated forever or that God should forever be controlled by the law of reaction to man. Christian certainty in face of the course of this world leads to the very opposite conclusion. God will carry through his original purpose for creation. He will finally end the whole episode of man's history of revolt. Indeed, he controls this episode and makes it serve his own purpose, "riding the lame horse and chopping the rotten wood," as Luther says in his *Bondage of the Will*.

It is because of this contradiction that the pledge or first instalment of the Spirit comes as the miracle of an act of God that is still at work within the contradiction and that causes the light to shine in the darkness (John 1:5) and sparks of this light to shine forth in mighty deeds and signs (*terata kai sēmeia*). The shining of this light and the deposit of the Spirit are promises of what is to come and also a judgment on what is.

That both these things are true shows from this angle too that the end of history and the coming of the final victory are not a climax of history. On the contrary, the presence of light in the darkness means that the darkness not only does not comprehend it (John 1:5) but grows thicker and darker. As in the gospel exorcisms the unclean spirits become more active when Jesus appears, rattling their chains (e.g., Mark 5:7) and scenting their enemy, so the gospel message provokes contradiction, the Spirit awakens the virulence of the demonic spirit, and Christ stirs up the opposition of what is anti-Christian or even of antichrist in person (2 Thessalonians 2:3ff.; 1 John 2:18ff.; Revelation 13:1-18). The polar opposites of history intensify and their enhanced opposition to God, the inner decay of history, their incapacity for the divine, their revolt, is the very thing which paradoxically points to the Yes of God[5] and raises expectation of his final victory as this is intimated already in his eschatological acts in history.

It is from this angle that we are to view not only the Parousia as the final shining of the light but also the expectation of final judgment.

We cannot affirm more than the fact of this second advent. As the coming of the new aeon of God's lordship it is outside our time. It transcends our history insofar as this is the way from the fall to judgment and is bounded by death. The forms and categories which we have to describe it are all shaped by our being in this world. The signs are the final encounter of this history-transcending factor with history and they are given only in the light of this transcending factor. The epistemological limits to what we can say are indicated indirectly by Paul when he tells us that our knowledge is now partial (*ek merous*) and that we only have the promise of a knowledge that matches our being known (1 Corinthians 13:12). What is able to cross the limits of what we can say is neither knowledge nor even faith, which will be lost in sight, but only love (1 Corinthians 13:8). This is the continuum which unites my here and now with the first and second comings of the Lord.

The fact with which we must be content when we speak of the Parousia contains a final certainty that is analogous to the certainty experienced when we consider our finitude and death. As death does not just end life but forms a bridge to *eternal*

---

[5]Ratzinger, *Eschatologie*, p. 163.

life, so the second advent makes a positive out of the negative of the end of the world. All fear of a destruction of the world of some sort is forced to yield to expectation of an inconceivable future. The wholly otherness which is the basis of the inconceivability and inexpressibility[6] is overcome. It becomes nearness as we think of him whose voice is familiar, whose Spirit has touched us, and by faith in whom we live. The waiting and watching which the nearness of the last day demands is not a waiting in panic as the door closes. It does not involve a suppressing of the end which leads to the false security of eating and drinking, of marrying and giving in marriage. Faith does not lead to fear or foreboding of what is coming on the earth, nor does it cause us to hide, but it makes us lift up our heads because redemption is near and the Son of man is coming in great power and glory (Luke 21:26ff.). The signs are a reason for joyful anticipation. Paul's confession: "I have a desire to depart and be with Christ" (Philippians 1:23), which does not darken joy in life but lights up the darkness of death, applies to expectation of the end of the world as well. It does not make the present moment of life less important but it takes away from both our own end and that of the world the fear of sinking into nothingness. It causes every moment, however partial or fragmentary in the sense of 1 Corinthians 13, to await that moment which is fulness and which brings perfection with it.

To speak theologically about the Parousia is fundamentally to do no more than interpret "rejoicing in the Lord" (Philippians 4:4) and to find its basis in the Lord's nearness (4:5) both as his own nearness and the nearness of his coming.

No more need be said. We cannot describe the "how" of the Parousia in quasi-historical acts. If the NT offers us illustrations in the imagery of the present world, it is simply using a stylistic device, adopting OT proclamation of the day of Yahweh, which is now interpreted as the day of Christ, and using liturgical phrases in which we also find Near Eastern formulae from the emperor-cult—the emperor as cosmokrator. Its statements, then, are highly symbolical, and even if the symbols use the form of "our" time they do not relate to actual events in time. Hence the representation of the "how" of the Parousia in terms of historical events, as in Revelation, will at once become mythology if we overlook its symbolical character. In this case Bultmann's concept of myth comes into play, namely, that we think mythologically when we project the next world into this one.

b. The Last Judgment

(1) Earthly Judgment and the Last Judgment[7]
The Apostles' Creed unites the prospect of the last judgment to confession of Christ's exaltation: "who shall come again to judge the quick and the dead."

If the fallen world waits for its redemption, the appearance of the perfect after the partial cannot be conceived of unless the structural unrighteousness of this aeon (that might precedes right, that the strong triumph over the weak, that exploitation takes place) is also covered by this redemption. We must go further: The narrow limits of deliberately planned justice, as in the state, are painfully familiar to us.[8]

---

[6]Tongues also cease when the inexpressible comes (1 Corinthians 13:8).
[7]On guilt and judgment in history—world history as world judgment—cf. ThE, II, 1, §§2084-2331.
[8]Cf. the theology of law in ThE, III, §§995-1597.

(1) Earthly law goes by appearances, by what is seen, not by the heart as the personal center of motivation (1 Samuel 16:7; cf. Proverbs 17:3; Romans 8:27; 1 Thessalonians 2:4).[9]

(2) Earthly law is administered by finite men of limited judgment who themselves stand with criminals under God's final judgment.[10]

(3) Because of the above limitations many instances of self-sacrifice and loyalty go hidden and unthanked while secret crimes are not punished and the innocent are threatened by miscarriages of justice and even judicial murder.

(4) Individuals involved in supraindividual guilt which earthly law cannot deal with are not legally accountable. Thus the Stuttgart Declaration of Guilt after the Second World War, which caused much debate about collective guilt and collective responsibility,[11] cannot be the subject of judicial action. In biblical thinking, however, this transsubjective dimension of guilt is of fundamental importance. In the OT Israel and the nations are placed under judgment and grace as suprapersonal entities that include individuals. Jesus follows the same line of thought when he announces judgment on Bethsaida, Chorazin, Jerusalem, and Capernaum in their totality (Matthew 11:20ff.; 23:37ff.; Luke 13:34ff.; 19:41ff.). Here the individual shares the total responsibility that cannot be individualized, for the individual exists only with others and as part of the suprapersonal whole.

If the promise that all things will be made new (Revelation 21:5) is given to man in what we call his secularity, his structural involvement in this aeon, then this promise carries with it a final judgment in which unrighteousness is brought to light and the partial righteousness of earthly justice undergoes revolutionary correction. The "thoughts of the heart" are now the criterion, for these, unseen by us but known to God, qualify our acts.[12] The motive of murder underlies the vilifying of others (Matthew 5:21), desire underlies unfulfilled adultery (5:27), and the dominion of untruth underlies swearing (5:33). Furthermore, in God's eyes the latent principle of revenge lies behind the facade of a just balance of action and reaction in the "eye for an eye" and "tooth for a tooth."

It is no accident that the eschatological radicalizing of the Mosaic law in the Sermon on the Mount puts the emphasis on these criteria of the last judgment. In this light we can also understand the apostle's warning not to judge anything before the time, but to wait until "the Lord comes, who will bring to light the things now hidden in darkness [concealed from us] and will disclose the purposes of the heart [which we do not see]. Then every man will receive his commendation from God [which is not ours to give any more than censure is]" (1 Corinthians 4:5).

In poetry, especially when it is under Christian influence, there is constant reference to the thoughts of the heart in an effort to pierce the external facade and anticipate the view of the eternal Judge. Thus Goethe can speak of the terrible discovery of an inclination in the heart which might have made one a monster apart from the restraining hand of God (*Wilhelm Meisters Lehrjahre,* VI, Cotta ed.,

---

[9]ThE, III, §1174.

[10]In token of this many courts contain scenes from the last judgment.

[11]T. Heuss called it "collective shame."

[12]As Luther says, the work does not make the person but the person does the work (WA, 39/I, 283, 9; cf. LW, 25, 256).

p. 454). A. Stifter in his story *Zuversicht* refers similarly to a tigerish disposition which, because it is not awakened, we believe is not present. The most moving expression of this anticipation of the last judgment and its criteria is in Dostoevsky's *Brothers Karamazov,* in which Dimitri wants to be punished as if he had killed his father even though he has not. He accepts a trial and life imprisonment although with a normal defense he could easily have escaped. This drives his brother Ivan mad. He argues angrily that it is absurd to wind up the case in this way. For according to the standards used everyone in the court is as guilty as Dimitri, including the judge. Each has wanted his father's death, so why fix on Dimitri, who has done no more than that. But Dimitri is certain that the wish made him just as guilty as the act. S. Freud has drawn attention to the important parallel that Dostoevsky's own father died by an unknown hand (*Gesammelte Werke,* XIV, pp. 399ff.; cf. also Karl Menninger, *Selbstzerstörung* [1974], pp. 69ff.; G.T.).

Along the lines of these mere anticipations God or Christ[13] will judge with a knowledge of the heart and will bring what is hidden to light. This final judgment can also be committed to the saints, who undertake it at God's behest: "Do you not know that the saints will judge the world . . . how much more matters pertaining to this life!"[14] This judicial function of the saints at the final reckoning, when even angels will be cited before this forum (1 Corinthians 6:3), is certainly a sign of dignity which makes it clear to what rank and to what nearness to God faith exalts us. But it is not a Pharisaic or triumphal change of roles which makes those who were once lowly and afflicted into judges and avengers instead of defendants. For the saints are pronounced righteous by grace and will not want to play the role of the wicked servant of Matthew 18:28ff. In their present position a glance at their former guilt will provide an impulse to humility. They are not to go to law before pagan judges (1 Corinthians 6:1, 4, 6). It is more in keeping with their position at the last judgment to suffer wrong than it is to go to law (6:7).

John's Gospel deepens the concept of the last judgment christologically by linking together present and future judgment. At a first glance this combination of aspects seems to be contradictory. It is rewarding, however, not to stop at appearances nor to try to explain them away by redactional manipulation but to look for the real meaning.

Judgment seems first to be an eschatological event in the here and now. It takes place already when, faced with a choice between faith and unbelief, people opt for unbelief and thus miss the saving power of Christ (John 3:18; 9:39; 12:47). On the other hand, when they hear his word and believe in him who sent him, they already have everlasting life and have passed from death into life (5:24).

The forward look to the final judgment and the last day, which also occurs in John, can be explained only if we elucidate the contradictory role which Christ seems to play in these processes of judgment. The impression of a contradiction is removed only if we see that there are two series of statements.

---

[13]God in Matthew 6:4, 6, 15, 18; 10:28; Romans 2:3ff.; 3:6; 14:10; 1 Corinthians 5:13; 1 Thessalonians 1:5; Christ in Matthew 25:31ff.; 7:22f.; 13:36ff.; Luke 13:25ff.; 1 Corinthians 4:4f.; 11:32; 2 Corinthians 5:10; 1 Thessalonians 4:6.
[14]1 Corinthians 6:2f.; cf. Daniel 7:22; Revelation 3:21; Matthew 19:28.

The *first* is to the effect that God has not sent his Son into the world "to condemn the world, but that the world might be saved through him" (3:17; cf. Luke 9:56). The same point can be made in the "I" form: "I judge no one" (John 8:15; 12:47). But then the *second* is that the Father judges no one but has "given all judgment to the Son" (5:22), who executes it in the Father's name (5:30; 9:39).

The solution to the riddle of apparent contradiction lies in the christological deepening of the thought of judgment in the Fourth Gospel. Christ does not actually judge anyone. He brings salvation. But the Word that he speaks will judge on the last day (12:48). He himself makes no judicial decision but a decision does take place. Those who despise him and do not accept his Word (12:48a) have rejected the proffered salvation and therefore judged themselves. Though Christ pronounces no word of judgment but simply wants to be the way on which we can pass from death to life (5:24), those who scorn this way build a blockade which keeps them in *this* life. Precisely because Christ is only the Savior those who despise his saving Word will find that this Word condemns them at the last judgment.

This last judgment simply makes manifest what has already taken place here and now. Building a bridge to judgment in Matthew's Gospel, one might say figuratively that Christ as the Lord of the last judgment does not pass judgment but simply brings to light the self-judgment which people have passed by not knowing him, and repulsing him, in the hungry and naked and imprisoned (Matthew 25:41ff.). The word spoken to them in the last judgment is not one of condemnation; it is the statement: "I do not know you" (25:12; cf. 7:23). Perhaps, without being sentimental, one might imagine that it is spoken sorrowfully because those who have been sought have not let themselves be found.

(2) Judgment by Works[15]

The last judgment rewards and punishes. This raises a host of problems which threaten to call in question the biblical understanding of God, faith, and grace. Only as we discuss these problems can we hope to see what is meant here by reward and punishment.

To begin with the concept of reward, which is found everywhere in the gospels, this immediately raises the question of a visible correlation of achievement and reward which would seem hard to reconcile with a righteousness of faith that frees us from bondage to the law and from the implied principle of merit. The difficulty raised by the concept of reward is both dogmatic and philosophical. Dogmatically it threatens the "faith alone" and "grace alone" of the Pauline and Reformation tradition. Philosophically, as Kant's ethics has shown convincingly and definitively, it compromises the ethical claim because it involves an eudaemonistic motive. To live and act with the idea of standing in the judgment, of winning heaven and escaping hell, reduces the thesis of justification by grace to absurdity.

A brief survey of the relevant passages will be helpful.

The reward of those who are persecuted for their confession is "great in

---

[15]H. Graffmann, "Das Gericht nach den Werken im Matthäus-Evangelium," *Barth Festschrift* (1936), pp. 124ff.; G. Bornkamm, "Der Lohngedanke im NT," *Studien zu Antike und Urchristentum* (1959), pp. 69ff.; ThE, III.

heaven'' (Matthew 5:11f.; 10:32f.; 10:41f.). The practice of secret almsgiving or fasting or praying which cannot be seen by men will be rewarded by the Father who sees what is hidden (Matthew 6:4, 6, 18). Following Jesus gives treasure in heaven (Matthew 19:21). We should lay up treasures in heaven, a kind of heavenly balance which will be paid out at the last day (6:20). Those who follow Jesus and bear his cross now will sit on twelve thrones and judge the tribes of Israel at his coming again. Those who leave houses, brothers, sisters, fathers, mothers, wives, children, or possessions for Jesus' sake will receive them back a hundredfold (19:18–30). This answer was given to Peter when he asked expressly what would be given to those who left everything for Jesus (19:27).

We can even establish a graduated system of recompense. Rewards and punishments correspond to three things: the amount of knowledge given (Matthew 21:32), the amount of money entrusted (25:14ff.), and the person toward whom guilt is incurred (11:22, 24; 12:31, 33ff., 41f.).

The correlation is qualitative as well as quantitative. Those who do not forgive will not find forgiveness (Matthew 6:15; 18:35). Those who judge will be judged (7:1f.). Those who deny the Lord will be denied by him (10:33).

An astonishing fact is that Paul, whose theology is definitely oriented to ''faith alone'' (Romans 3:28) and to the rejection of a correlation of achievement and reward and guilt and retribution, can still speak of an eschatological judgment by works. Thus in Romans 2:5b–10 he refers to a righteous judgment of God in which he rewards us all according to our works. Again he says that we shall all come before the judgment seat of Christ and receive rewards in accordance with what we have done in the body (2 Corinthians 5:10; cf. Romans 14:10).

How are we to understand this constant correlation of guilt and punishment and achievement and reward? If what is meant is something similar to our own judicial system, and the principle of ''an eye for an eye'' and ''a tooth for a tooth'' is being reestablished, it seems that the privileges of the ''higher thoughts'' and God's own criteria are being set aside or that confident trust is being replaced by aloof calculation and the eudaemonism that Kant denounced (Luke 18:9ff., esp. v. 11).

We shall try to find an answer step by step.

1. The exegetical findings show incontestably that reward is never the motive of conduct but is an incidental and unmerited result.

It is worth noting that indirectly and on another basis the idea of reward does play a part even in Kant's categorical principle of duty. Since our striving for happiness, which is oriented to reward, is directed to a good which belongs constitutively to our existence (and hence cannot be eliminated), and since this good does not come into play as an ethical motive, the uniting of duty and reward, of obligation and happiness, is brought about by God in the hereafter as an eschatological supreme good (*Critique of Practical Reason*, p. 131). One cannot will this supreme good directly, i.e., one cannot make it the goal or motive of action. It is given later without disturbing the purity of ethical motivation. It is not a possible motive of ethical conduct but a necessary postulate based on ethical conduct. As in Descartes, God, who gives it, is the postulated bracket around contradictions which cannot be reconciled here. In Kant the contradictions are duty and inclination, which are both basic elements of human nature. In Descartes they are the thinking I and the objective world.

At any rate, in at least formal similarity to Kant, one may say of the NT verses that the concept of reward is not a motive in them. For man is portrayed in them as a slave who belongs to a master and can claim no reward. Even when we have been obedient and done our duty we can say only that we are unprofitable servants and have simply done what we were under obligation to do (Luke 17:10; cf. Matthew 18:23ff.; 25:14ff.; Luke 16:1ff.).

Again, love of enemies (Luke 6:35 par.) is set in antithesis to the calculating love which hopes for repayment. "If you love those who love you, what credit is that to you? For even sinners love those who love them" (Luke 6:32). Our love is genuine only when it is not calculating and hopes for no repayment. Only then do we act in a way that is analogous to our Father's merciful dealing with us (6:36).

Finally, the parable of the workers in the vineyard offers a normative interpretation of the NT concept of reward (Matthew 20:1–16). This shatters the carefully described suggested system of earthly justice, whose basic relation of achievement and reward is designed here to show that before God it is useless to speculate about rewards. They are not refused, but the goodness of God (not his caprice) grants and increases them according to its own standard and not according to our criteria. Thus the concept of reward is never regarded as a possible motive of action on the basis of faith.

2. The exegetical findings also show that the concept of reward (which is not a motive) does not come independently *between* God and us. If it did, God would be a kind of faceless official who distributes rewards and is concealed behind the autonomy of the process. In the NT, however, the reward is simply a cipher for God's own attitude. It expresses God's good pleasure, just as punishment represents his displeasure (Matthew 25:21, 23, 28ff.). God's pleasure or displeasure at what we have done has an authentic place in a theology of grace. To this extent the last judgment also has a place in this theology. Thus Paul can ask (Romans 6:1ff., 15ff.) whether we can continue to sin in the name of the unconditional grace which is stronger than sin. He answers that forgiveness does not set us in the freedom of doing what we like but that we stand under a new bondage (*douleia*). Grace demands specific action. The indicative of the divine promise carries with it the imperative of a claim.[16] Hence this action arouses either the pleasure or the displeasure of the gracious God. In this sense it is symbolically evaluated in the concept of reward (James 2:14–17, 26).

3. Material things are used in the NT to portray reward (houses, land, treasure, etc.), but it is plain that as figures of the "wholly other" kingdom of God they are dematerialized: "Flesh and blood cannot inherit the kingdom of God" (1 Corinthians 15:20). This applies even to the figure of wife and children, for there is no marrying in God's kingdom (Luke 20:34f.). One may thus state that the kingdom does not consist of what we acquire but of what we come to be.

This "being" is not characterized by a material something which is increased by a reward. It consists of seeing what we have believed (1 Corinthians 13:12; 2 Corinthians 5:7). We shall be delivered from mediacy to God, from indirect access by way of the dark mirror, and we shall be set in immediacy to him. We shall have as our reward, not something, but God himself. If we want a separate reward,

---

[16]ThE, I, §§315ff.; E.T. I, pp. 83ff.

something that is given by God and is thus distinct from him,[17] we shall be disappointed, for the reward is identical with God and with the fellowship that binds us to him. If the latter is the reward we want—an imperfect metaphor and limping symbol—then reward will no longer be a motive, for goal and orientation will be one and the same. The normal concept of reward does not consider orientation but focuses on what will accrue to us, and in the long run it matters little who gives it. If God is himself the reward, and if in fellowship with him we come to ourselves and find our true identity, then every concept of reward is transcended.

The NT, then, knows nothing of the eudaemonism that Kant attacks. Eudaemonism says: I do what is right, not for its own sake, but for what it brings. If, however, heaven is not something that I get as a result of my conduct ("make me good that I might go to heaven"), but if it simply represents promised fellowship with God, Abraham's bosom (Luke 16:22), then it is the good itself. Hence I do good for its own sake if I do it for the sake of heaven.

Everything depends on what I mean by heaven. I might misunderstand it as a something. Bad though they are, spatial portrayals of Paradise are less bad than this. Far worse is the euphoric expectation of a state when earthly existence will be fantastically idealized and moral effort will be well rewarded by sweet scents, teeth that do not fall out, enhanced enjoyment of sex, etc. (Luigi Majocco, L'Umanesimo celeste). This is admittedly an extreme position but a caricature can show where some popular conceptions tend. What heaven is in the Christian sense is well expressed by Kierkegaard's burial inscription which describes it as a form of being in which I "talk forever with Jesus." It is the dimension of immediacy to God in which we encounter the unbroken sway of his will (cf. Matthew 6:10).

4. Finally, judgment by works at the last assize tells us that the gospel, that pardon on the last day, is a miracle that we cannot postulate. To denote this miracle there is needed the background of the law which condemns us but from whose fetters we are released as those who are justified. Grace would be "cheap grace" in Bonhoeffer's sense if it were self-evident and if I could understand it and count on it as a law of divine reaction.

This would make God the "dear Lord" whose job it is to forgive (Heine) and it would make grace a suprapolar principle of indifference (in Abelard's sense) instead of a miracle that overtakes me. That it does overtake me as a miracle, breaking the law of sin and retribution as God's own act, is clear to me only if I keep in view the valid correlation of achievement and reward and guilt and punishment. There is thus expressed in the tension between reward and grace no other than the dialectic of law and gospel.[18] This dialectic is reflected again even in the last judgment.

---

[17]This idea is fostered by the ontological schema which finds in grace not just an attitude of God (his favor) but also a gift that is different from him though not unrelated. One has only to think of the idea of infused grace and the system of graces to get the impression of grace which is distinct from God as a gift (cf. ThE, I, §§1140f.; E.T. I, pp. 238f.). The more Roman Catholic theology since Vatican II has seen the relativity of this schema the more it has stopped the misunderstanding of grace. Only on this level can we engage in relevant debate, which will often bring to light an astonishing closeness.

[18]ThE, I, §§554ff.; E.T. I, pp. 94ff.; EG, II, §14, pp. 219ff.; EF, II, c. XIV, pp. 184ff.

(3) Punishment. On the Understanding of Hell and Damnation[19]

If the last judgment has to do with reward and punishment along the lines suggested, the theme of eternal rejection or hell (the opposite of eternal life) becomes an acute one. Plastic apocalyptic depictions of an eternal lake of fire—from the great Dante to the lesser Bautz—have to a large extent removed hell from the sphere of serious discussion and discredited it even more than Paradise with its scenes of light. Because of the law of comic contrast humor and wit have been devoted to it rather than metaphysical interest.[20] The actuality of hell persists as a symbol for states of terror here on earth (the hell of air raids) or for the dubious background of human existence.[21] Luther, as we have already pointed out, continually related hell to this world, seeing it in the torment of conscience and temptation. (But he did not abandon its eschatological significance.) Quite apart from the fact that in an age dominated by sociological categories the terms guilt and punishment have lost much of their plausibility and could hardly command a consensus, the idea of irreversible punishment which is associated with hell causes particular aversion and provokes the snobbery of a rationalistic sense of superiority to the world of mythology.

Biblical, patristic, and historical usage, however, forces us to analyze the term more closely. It also lessens the shock caused by the pre-judgment that the word necessarily indicates something "out there." What could that be?

We have already discussed the theme of hell and Sheol so that what is now required is a systematic conclusion. I may refer especially to the chapter on the descent into hell in EG, II, pp. 513ff.; EF, II, pp. 415ff. We have also considered OT ideas of Sheol and God's power over this form of being or nonbeing in the chapter on death in the present volume.

To the NT data we may add that hell is used here as a cipher for final and radical separation from God; this is shown particularly impressively in the parable of Dives and Lazarus (Luke 16:19ff., esp. vv. 23, 25f.). It should be recalled that here the separation is that of man, the rich man. In no way does it interrupt or deny the later Sheol-tradition of the OT that God's arm rules over hell and can reach across the "great gulf" (Luke 16:26).

Nothing tangible is said about the duration of punishment in hell. Some passages speak of eternal punishment or destruction (Matthew 18:8; 25:14, 46; Revelation 14:11; 2 Thessalonians 1:9). But eternal here might not mean unending. Like similar terms (omnipotence, foreordination, etc.) it remains subject to God's will and purpose (B. Reicke, RGG[3], III, p. 405). Later we shall examine passages which seem to hint at an overcoming of this state and a final universal reconciliation (1 Corinthians 15:24ff.; 1 Peter 4:6).

No matter how we twist and turn (and we hope we have not done so), it is impossible to avoid the conclusion that the alternative of eternal life and eternal separation from God stands with monumental and terrifying clarity at the limit of our field of vision. It is important that we have to speak about this *field of vision* and that a sense of perspective can protect us against false absolutizing.

---

[19]The next section (c) will offer further insights on hell.

[20]Cf. the author's book *Das Lachen der Heiligen und Narren*, Herder Taschenbuch, p. 491.

[21]Cf. J.-P. Sartre's play *Bei verschlossenen Türen*.

Two theological intentions may be perceived in this eschatological dualism.

First, it gives the present moment of decision the eschatological weight of the unconditional. The parable of Dives and Lazarus is again instructive in this regard. The condemned man for whom it is now too late and who has missed his chance reminds Abraham that he has five brothers who are still alive and still have time (Luke 16:27f.). Abraham, however, refuses (and is unable) to inform them about the twofold destiny. He simply says that they have Moses and the prophets and should listen to them (16:29). Here and now God's will is presented to these brothers by the Word and Spirit. Hence the moment is given an absolute accent. In it the decision is made whether the word of Moses and the prophets will be for them a message of salvation or perdition, whether it will lead to life or death. In themselves Moses and the prophets are in the line of God's purpose to save. Whether their intention will be realized or its opposite depends on what attitude the five brothers take to them. The eternal destiny of the brothers is implicated in this decision.

Eternity hangs on a moment in time. Hence this moment takes on an eschatological quality. The field of vision that opens up from it contains the prospect of the twofold outcome of the lives of the five brothers: heaven or hell. This sheds theological light on Abraham's refusal to send back to the five brothers someone who could give them a report on the next life. It is trivial simply to point to the technical difficulty that there are no bridges between this world and the next. The real reason for the refusal is deeper. If Abraham had sent the brothers someone to give a report on hell there would have been a kind of metaphysical shock therapy which would certainly have made clear to them the unconditional accent of the moment but would have done this in a legalistic way through the threat of punishment and the enticement of reward, thus releasing eudaemonistic impulses (in Kant's terminology). Certainty about the unconditional nature of the moment ought to be reached in a different way, i.e., as the Word, being presented by the Spirit, makes the present unconditional, so that *this* unconditionality creates the field of vision at whose limit may be seen the twofold possibility of one's eternal destiny.

Second, any attempt to solve this dualism of eternal life and its opposite intellectually, e.g., by arguing that eternal perdition is intolerably cruel or incompatible with the God of love, ends with a problem that is no less severe. For it must either use a dialectic of which Hegel's "cunning of the idea" is representative—the negative of guilt, punishment, and death is simply a transition which in the automatic process leads to a higher synthesis and is thus transcended—or it must make the love of God a monistic principle which embraces polar opposites. This, too, is Hegelian—an alternative within the same schema: The eternal spirit is identical with himself even in his negation. God is thus reconciled with himself even in his antithesis. God's love is a principle of indifference which is intrinsically superior to the opposition that is brought against this love by man.

This principle of indifference is expressed profoundly in André Gide's story *The Parable of the Prodigal Son* in which the returned prodigal sends an imagined younger brother into the far country in order that he, too, might share the same productive experience and come to maturity as a result. The returning son can now no longer greet his father with the words of the original parable: "Father, I have sinned against heaven and before thee and am no more worthy to be called thy son'' (Luke 15:18f.), but will have to say instead: ''Father, I have matured in the far country; I have profited by the exercise; I am now qualified for reconciliation with thee (for synthesis).'' There is also a christologically based monism which strips evil of its power and changes it into nothingness.[22] In both cases God is placed under a principle so that theologically his personality is weakened and anthropologically the moment is emptied of its unconditionality.

c. The Question of the Demonic and of the Personal Power of Evil. The Problem of the Devil

Bibliography: G. Bernanos, *Die Sonne Satans* (1927); F. Zündel, *J. C. Blumhardt,* 1st ed. (1880); W. Foerster in TWNT (TDNT): *diabolos,* II, pp. 69ff. (II, pp. 72ff.); *satanas,* VII, pp. 151ff. (VII, pp. 151ff.); *daimōn,* II, pp. 1ff. (II, pp. 1ff.); H. Haag, *Teufelsglaube* (1974); E. Kästner, *Aufstand der Dinge* (1973); pp. 241ff., esp. pp. 247f.; L. Kolakowski, *Leben trotz Geschichte* (1977), esp. pp. 187ff., 202ff.; also Interview in HK, X (1977), pp. 501ff.; T. Mann, *Dr. Faustus,* 1st ed. (1948), c. XXV; H. Obendiek, *Der Teufel bei Luther* (1931); H. Thielicke, ''Über die Wirklichkeit des Dämonischen,'' *Fragen des Christentums an die moderne Welt,* 4th ed. (1947), pp. 170ff.; E.T. ''The Reality of the Demonic,'' *Man in God's World* (New York, 1963); also ''Exorzismus,'' XL (1974); Vatican, ''Christlicher Glaube und Dämonenlehre'' (also Paul VI), HK, VIII (1975), pp. 379ff.; cf. III (1973), pp. 126f., 129.

The problem of hell cannot be treated without discussing the devil. Yet satanology has so many layers and takes so many forms not merely in the history of religion but also in the biblical materials and theology that we should have to refer to almost every head of doctrine to deal with it thoroughly. We can thus focus only on a few important points whose selection is determined particularly by the standpoint that we have here a problem of dualism, i.e., of polarity between the personal God[23] and a personally defined power of evil.

It is odd that while the Enlightenment and modern rationalism reduce hell and its punishments to a mere symbol or laugh them out of court as indisputable superstition, many of its illustrious representatives do not try to contest the idea of a demonic counterpower (the devil) even though they are unable to overcome a certain shame in recognizing it. Apart from Goethe's Mephistopheles it is perhaps symbolic that in our own century such different people as Thomas Mann and Leszek Kolakowski have developed an express satanology which mocks at rationalistic arrogance and—as in Kolakowski—protests against the lack of satanology and the illusion of progress in Christian theology.

In ''The Devil's Press Conference'' in *Leben trotz Geschichte* (pp. 203ff.) reference is made to the terrible idol of modernity which makes people afraid of being thought superstitious and out of date. Unbelief undoubtedly begins with this ideological slavery to the age and rejection of all thought of the devil. ''Unbelief

---

[22]In ThE, I, I have tried to show how close Barth comes to this. Cf. also W. Krötke, *Sünde und Nichtigkeit bei Karl Barth* (1971).

[23]EG, II, §7; EF, II, c. VII.

begins with me," says the devil. And T. Mann has the devil say that there can be no theological existence without him, religion being his specialty and not bourgeois culture (p. 387).

In spite of such pleas for the existence of the devil both inside and outside Christianity, many theologians find the theme embarrassing. Kolakowski speaks ironically of their throwing a cover over the devil, and Haag says that they resolutely turn their backs on him.

An attempt to diagnose this aversion leads directly to satanology itself. There are three reasons for it.

The first is the fear of being thought out of date and thus becoming a figure of fun. Behind this fear stands bondage to a spirit of the age for which conformity means progressiveness. In terms of Satan's activity this bondage to the spirit of the age is already a demonic form of slavery, a form of encirclement by an alien spirit—we shall avoid the term possession here—which *blinds* us to realities in the name of an enlightened realism.

A second and deeper reason for not recognizing the power of the demonic is that it cannot be objectified and put in object-related terms. Shakespeare can help us here. Lady Macbeth tempts her husband to commit murder. When he yields and murders the king he comes under the power not only of his wife but also of a force which grips her too and is more and other than she is, she being merely its executive instrument. But Macbeth sees only the temptress and not the actual tempter who uses her. This is not just because the demonic power is not an empirical object as Lady Macbeth is but even more so because the demonic power, evil, makes itself invisible, getting behind those who are tempted and directing their gaze without itself coming within its range. This is plain in the biblical story of the fall where the serpent does not play the role of tempter but disguises himself as the initiator of a discussion about God: "Did God say . . . ?" Evil is not a tangible partner in possible communication, as Lady Macbeth is. It lies outside the language which is our means of communication. Hence demonic power cannot be brought to verbal account. It lies below the limit of language in a soundproof cellar.[24] To speak of the devil is linguistically difficult. The difficulty lies also and primarily in the matter itself, not just in conformity to the rationalistic spirit of the age.

The third reason is also pertinent to the issue. Untruth remains undiscovered because, as Paul says, the truth is held down and suppressed in unrighteousness. Being in untruth conceals untruth. The same applies to evil. It is of the essence of wickedness that it cannot see itself. The spell under which it comes leads in the first place to blindness to itself. In this it resembles stupidity. Stupidity cannot see itself because some unattainable intelligence is needed to see it, to confess knowledge of one's ignorance. That wickedness cannot see itself but must be opened by the Pneuma to do so finds striking expression in its constant justification, exculpation, and validation of itself. In its own eyes it is not wickedness. A related fact is that the demonic power behind wickedness shares this fate of invisiblity, or, better, initiates it. It is a power in the background and not in the objectifiable foreground. People never see the devil even when he has them by the throat.

---

[24] T. Mann, *Dr. Faustus*, p. 389.

Everything depends on our understanding at the root the incomprehensibility or, more accurately, inexplicability of evil. Evil is inexplicable in principle. It cannot be explained either from the causal standpoint of possible derivation (e.g., from the devil!) or from the teleological standpoint of having a meaningful part in the historical process, as in Goethe, whose Mephistopheles always wills evil and does good, or in Teilhard de Chardin, who finally resolves all polar opposites at the Omega Point.[25]

In attempts at causal derivation evil is weakened by the changing of guilt into fate. In our dubious features we view ourselves as the mere effect of an external cause (background, historical pressures, the devil). As victims of circumstances we are excused; fate determined things. The teleological explanation of evil weakens it in the same way. It becomes a power of contradiction and opposition to God in the Hegelian sense of a mere transition which antithetically serves a positive telos.

Being nonderivable, evil resembles the dimension of the personal, which is also nonderivable. We are thus confronted with the question of personal evil, the devil.[26]

That the personal is no more causally explicable than evil finds expression in Dilthey's profound distinction between perceiving and understanding. Perceiving relates to objectifiable objects whose causes and conditions can be investigated. It can thus be a subject of partial psychological study. But the totality of personal life cannot be grasped by it. This totality is open only to understanding. Understanding alone can capture another and analogous personal life with the help of divinatory sympathy. Cf. "Ideen über eine beschreibende und zergliedernde Psychologie" (1894), *Gesammelte Schriften,* V (1961), pp. 139ff.; "Die Entstehung der Hermeneutik," *ibid.,* pp. 317ff., esp. pp. 326, 329, 331; and "Studien zur Grundlegung der Geisteswissenschaften," *ibid.,* VII, pp. 205ff.

The idea that evil is personal helps us to understand why in biblical thinking the devil is never regarded as the cause of evil and those who have dealings with him are not excused as mere victims of "our ancient foe." We cannot hide behind demons (as Barth fears will happen when theologians use the category of the demonic). Apart from the fact that demonic powers cannot be derived from anything else,[27] it is impossible to derive personal life from another personal life and to see the two as bound together in a causal nexus. One person can give stimuli to another and therefore be a temptation for another, but even if this has a very important impact no relation of dependence arises which is ethically indifferent and removes responsibility.[28] If we speak decidedly *only* of a power of the demonic without emphasizing its *personal* character, the question necessarily remains an open one whether we are not innocent victims of usurpation who have been robbed of their own personality.

Although it seems to make sense to introduce the category of the personal and to

---

[25] Anthrop, pp. 473ff.

[26] On the terms *daimōn, diabolos,* and *satanas* cf. Foerster.

[27] We are not told that God placed the serpent in Paradise. What matters is not his origin but the fact of his function relative to man.

[28] On the social and legal relevance of this question cf. ThE, III, §§95ff., 1416ff.

think of "the evil one" rather than "evil," it should not be overlooked that the concept of person is simply a halting figure of speech here and if for different reasons it faces similar limits to those we encountered when discussing the personal God in Volume II. The concept of person never denotes a self-enclosed entelechy or monad (Leibniz) but is always a being oriented to the Thou and thus tied to communication. But this aspect of the personal does not arise in satanology. The devil does not open himself up to a Thou in any form, nor is he a Thou whom one can address (except in the perversion of black masses). Proper objections also arise against allowing one's conviction about the existence of the devil to be described as a belief "in" the devil. We must be content with symbols at this point.[29] Even the term "person" is only a symbol. We do not define the devil in terms of it. We use the term for the devil only in a partial sense. Hence we must note the point at which it applies.

In dealings with demonic power there is no personal communication. This is where the concept of the personal reaches its limit. On the contrary, what takes place is "possession" by an alien force and an attack on human personality. Thus exorcism in the name of God is the only form of a Thou-encounter with demonic power and the dominion to which it aspires.[30]

We see the personality of demonic power only indirectly and not directly. Hence it cannot be an independent subject of theological statements.

The analogy to the problem of the personality of God can be elucidated christologically. Melanchthon in his 1521 *Loci* rejected speculation about Christ's person and proposed instead that we may know him simply by his acts toward us and his history with us. To know Christ is to know his benefits. With tongue in cheek one might say the same about the person of demonic power. In an adaptation of Melanchthon's thesis one might say that to know the devil is to know his attacks.

To complete a trinitarian approach one might also explain demonic power in terms of pneumatological analogies. As there is the Spirit of God who "takes possession" of us, so there is a demonic spirit that "possesses" us. The difference between "taking possession" and "possessing" shows that the analogy is restricted to a single point, that of being "seized and filled by. . . ." Apart from that we have a radical difference instead of an analogy. The Spirit of God brings man to his true identity and opens him up to divine-human fellowship. In contrast the demonic spirit leads him into alienation and attacks his identity. It also robs him of speech and the Thou. An alien spirit sounds forth from him.

This attack on personality finds illustration in ideological dictatorships (but not in those alone). Ideologies are insinuated into the consciousness by psychostrategical measures so that alien voices are heard from those affected even though they think they are their own. When the domination ends, as with the collapse of National Socialism, they deny that these were their own words and acts. They do not always do this in self-protection. Some people really do not recognize themselves in what they did when under ideological control. Here they say: "I cannot

---

[29]T. Mann, *Dr. Faustus*, p. 389.
[30]Superstitions regarding exorcism should not cause us to dismiss the *fact*. The exorcising of Gottliebin Dittus by Blumhardt in Bad Boll was very sober and full of biblical realism. On possession cf. F. Wolfinger, "Die Kirche und die Macht des Bösen," HK, VII (1978), pp. 364ff.

have been like that.'' There takes place here a division (similar to exorcism) between true identity and the alien spirit. One can thus say with Oscar Wilde that to influence someone is to give him an alien soul. He no longer thinks his own thoughts and is no longer torn by his own passions. His virtues are no longer his and even his vices are only borrowed.

Exorcism as liberation from possession by something alien has from this standpoint both a positive and a negative side. Positively it means filling with the Spirit of God which drives the demonic spirit out of the vacant I, restores threatened identity, and brings to light the original person. Negatively exorcism shows that power is here mobilized against power and person against person and that argument is a blunt weapon against possession and domination. The sound-proof cellar resists speech as a mode of communication. It is the place where there is no fellowship, no Thou at all. Illuminating words are of no avail against demons. Words can even come under their power in the form of the spirit of the age. What avails against demons is only the word of command, the authority (*exousia*) which is ascribed to Christ when he drives out demons.

Rather beyond the limits staked out for us we should make some effort to find the real point in some of the mythical conceptions in satanology. By way of example we might take the idea that the devil is the fallen angel Lucifer. Traces of this may be found in the NT (2 Peter 2:4; Jude 6). It also occurs in 1 Enoch. Kolakowski links with it some profound reflections on evil as an ''integral and constitutive element of being.''

The fall of the demonic angel seems to reflect a basic principle of God's kingdom, namely, that everything demonic and ungodly points to original greatness. This applies to men and ideas too.

As regards men, animals could not have fallen in the same way as those who were designed for divine likeness. Great seducers of the race all show evidence of an inner rank which they had or for which they were destined. In the system of coordinates in God's kingdom the negative fall corresponds to the positive rank. The higher the rank, the greater the fall; the greater the loan, the worse the possible loss. Only men and not animals can come under demon possession. Nothing is so corrosive as ruined greatness. The worst of human rascals always had it in them to be the best examples. Man's misery is that of a great lord, a dethroned king (Pascal). It is that of perverted divine likeness and not of a return to a brutish state, as simple people imagine.

The same is true of ideas. The greatest ideas, which may well be of divine origin, change in a moment into their opposite when they break free from their origin. Freedom becomes license, equality the basis of claim, and brotherliness sentimentality.

The devil, then, is a personified symbol of the deepest fall. Lucifer, the fallen angel, represents a fall from original closeness to God. In this connection we find related ideas, e.g., that the devil is closely involved in the strategy of the kingdom of God and works against it accordingly. He can appear as an angel of light (2 Corinthians 11:14) because he knows the angels so well. He has all the passion and knowledge of a renegade. This is why he can do miracles as Christ does (2 Thessalonians 2:9; Revelation 13:11-13). Nor are his blasphemies mere anti-Christian tirades; they show a concern to act religiously and to speak as God does

(Revelation 13:5). In all that he does he apes God (Luther). The possibility of playing this role rests on recollection of lost greatness.

Satanology cannot be put in any categories of thought. Dualism, whether it be understood in the Gnostic or the Neoplatonic sense, is unsuitable. God and the devil are not polar or complementary principles that express a meaningful antithesis and are rooted in the unity of the same world-basis. Terms like personality are also inadequate. They are necessary protheses which help us in part to say what otherwise could not be said. Speech itself fails, for the reality at issue is absolutely beyond communication.

One might say that in its nonobjectifiability satanic power shares in the mysteries of God which also cannot be objectified and therefore cannot be demonstrated. But this, too, is only a necessary statement which immediately displays its inadequacy, for the mysteries of God are revealed whereas those of demonic power remain closed, or are opened up by *another* revelation. Of God's self-disclosure we read: "In thy light we shall see light" (Psalm 36:9). Of the closure of demonic power we should have to say: "In God's light—and only in this light—we see its darkness." Only in this way is its mystery revealed. Night is manifested only by day. To deny night is to be unaware of light, just as to deny law is not to be able to understand the gospel. Hence Kolakowski is right when he boldly says that unbelief begins with denial of the devil.

d. Borderline Questions: Apokatastasis and Purgatory. Universal Reconciliation and Restoration

In our discussion of hell we pointed out that the "principle" of love contains indifference to good and evil, guilt and punishment, and is thus outside the limits assigned to us. Nevertheless, Christian piety and theology have never ceased to cross the horizon of our field of vision. They have tried to do this with a view to avoiding the threatened indifference and constriction of dialectical automatisms (such as Hegel's idea of "transition").

What drives faith toward this kind of larger hope of universal reconciliation and salvation is reflection on the saving event, on the style, if one will, of the divine action. Have not judgments always had a positive and saving purpose?[31]

The prophetic preaching of judgment aims at the salvation that God offers the people by showing them in judgment their true situation. Thus in Jeremiah's words of judgment restoration is the real theme. Salvation is the goal both as a *hope* that the people will hear and turn from their evil ways and then as a *promise* that God will repent of the threatened judgment (Jeremiah 26:3).[32]

That judgment aims at salvation finds expression in the *patience* of God. He does not judge evil at once but through gradual explication gives us a chance to see it. In judgment, then, he offers an opportunity for conversion. The NT sayings

---

[31]Cf. Zephaniah 3:1-3, 9, 13, where the purifying of the nations and the renewal of Israel are the goal of judgment and visitation, or Romans 9-11, where the present judgment on Israel will be lifted in a final return. Only by way of exception is the way back from judgment blocked; cf. those for whom Jeremiah will not pray because God has judged them definitively (Jeremiah 7:16; 11:14; 14:11).

[32]The Hebrew suggests that the one simply follows the other, but a final sense seems to be implied.

about patience (*anochē*) are to be interpreted along these lines. God has "over-looked" the time of (culpable, Romans 1:18f.) ignorance; he has waited (Acts 17:30). He has left the Gentiles at peace in the far country, letting them go their own ways (Acts 14:16) without bringing down catastrophic judgment upon them. He has patiently let sin remain (Romans 3:25) and not punished it in spontaneous wrath. This rule of divine patience forces us to see that the goal of the explication of judgment is not just a giving up[33] or cursing but rather the blessing that in the explication God gives us time for repentance.

This final orientation of judgment as bringing home and also as the limit of the time of patience occurs in all the sayings adduced, as when we read that "now God commands all men everywhere to repent . . ." (Acts 17:30), the time of patient waiting being at an end, or when Paul says that through the mercy-seat of Jesus Christ we must accept the offer of the righteousness that avails before God (Romans 3:25), for this is why the patience of God has preserved us.

There is no need, then, of monistic thinking but simply of consideration for this style of God's work in judgment and salvation to raise the question whether the last judgment will not open up a way to universal salvation, whether this judgment will not be in truth a penultimate rather than an ultimate word, whether eschatological dualism will not finally be transcended in the all-embracing love of God.

Behind such a postulate of general reconciliation or apokatastasis stand many different motives of thanksgiving and faith and not just monistic principles which work with structural autonomy. A biblically based theological intention stands behind it. Not to see this difference is to lose the criterion for measured judgment.

The biblical basis, in intention at least, may be seen also in the appeal to texts that seem to hint at universal reconciliation. Paul in relation to the first and second Adams (1 Corinthians 15:45) says that "as one man's trespass led to condemnation (*katakrima*) for all men, so one man's act of righteousness leads to acquittal and life for all men" (Romans 5:18). Here already the question arises what it means that righteousness is for all. It is available for all. Will it be accepted by all? The question also arises whether God's new covenant will be ratified by all and can thus come into force for all. And if not? Does "all" have a double reference?

We may also refer to 1 Corinthians 15:22-28 which says that God's final triumph will make him "all in all." Here again we must ask whether this can be detached from the preceding text which it summarizes. For this says that God will subject all authority and power (*exousia kai dynamis*, 15:24) to himself, will rob death, the last enemy, of its might, and will thus set aside all the disruptive forces released at the fall. Does this mean that there will be universal conversion and that all will bow the knee to him? Is this still open? Might this beginning of God's unbroken rule mean that the opposing forces, instead of falling to their knees, will be forced to their knees? In this case will not the "all in all" go *along with* eschatological dualism? Similar questions may be put in relation to Colossians 1:20.

The two basic motives of expectation of apokatastasis to which we have referred alternate in church history. We cannot go into that now but might give one or two

---

[33]In the sense of the *paredōken* of Romans 1.

illustrations. Apokatastasis is suggested to the Christian Gnostics by the Stoic doctrine of world epochs and the Platonic doctrine of souls. It is thus determined in this instance by motives that are close to those that we described under monistic thinking. This is especially true of the main champion of the doctrine, Origen. More recent representatives such as Bengel, Oetinger, and Jung-Stilling are more or less biblically oriented, though this is not wholly true in the case of Schleiermacher or Lavater.

An obstacle to a definite acceptance of the apokatastasis of all things might be that Paul, who sometimes seems to move in this direction, teaches elsewhere a double end of history and refers to the lost (*apollymenoi,* 1 Corinthians 1:18; cf. Philippians 1:28; Romans 9:22). He does not try to harmonize the two sets of sayings.

In spite of all the exegetical and dogmatic objections to universal reconciliation it would be easy to affirm it. In so doing one would not just be in poor monistic company but also among respectable biblical theologians. But *how* can it be affirmed and *how* can one refrain from calling it an ''error'' (however unwillingly) according to the venerable judgment of theological history?

Certainly the doctrine of apokatastasis can never become a dogma. If we call it this, then in view of its monistic basis we can hardly avoid the result of annulling the unconditionality of the present hour of decision and letting things take their course in the name of the expected eschatological ''happy ending.'' In this case the ironical question of Paul: ''Are we to continue in sin that grace may abound?'' could no longer be answered by a ''By no means'' (Romans 6:1, 15). It would describe a serious possibility of conduct.

It says much for the spiritual instinct (if there is such a thing) of J. A. Bengel that while he personally inclined to a doctrine of universal reconciliation, he did not preach it publicly. This was because he realized that not everybody was ready for it. If it came into the hands of the wrong person—the person who would construe it legalistically—it would have a devastating effect. This effect would be much the same as that of untimely preaching of predestination. Improperly understood, this too could be taken fatalistically: Some are ordained to life and others to death and God's decision has left no room for ours. This is why Luther in his Preface to Romans (1522) points out that predestination can be understood only by those who have first grasped justification by faith. High-flying people who interpret it absolutely and therefore unseasonably yield either to despair or license, i.e., they necessarily become fatalists. We should not drink wine while we are still babies. Every doctrine has its measure, time, and age.[34] The same applies, perhaps, to the doctrine of apokatastasis.

But a final question remains: Is it enough to say that universal reconciliation is not a binding dogma but may be a private belief? Is it really only regard for the weaker brother that forces us to handle this mystery esoterically? We surely have to consider what theological rank a private belief can have. What right does it have when it cannot be propagated like God's Word or be put in the catechism? Does it have *any* validity? With such questions we are seriously trying to uphold the

---

[34]Munich ed., VI, pp. 105f.; LW, 35, 378.

communion of saints in the context of a teaching which many contest but some hold in high esteem.[35]

At this point (even in a systematic theology) I can only express a personal conviction. In my view there are some theological truths and circumstances—in this case the position of the lost—which cannot be the theme of theological statements but only of prayer. Nothing prevents people from praying that those who have rejected Christ will not themselves be rejected, that their history with God may continue in eternity, and that the boundlessness of eternal love will not stop at them. In this case we cannot enter into the speculative question of the "how," whether with the descent into hell or in some other way. Any attempt to formulate a dogmatic statement will only carry with it a series of additional hypothetical theses, so that the next minute we shall find ourselves in a world of fantasy manipulating the scenery of heaven and hell. Prayer for the lost can leave the validity of the object and the way of reaching it in the hands of him to whom the prayer is made. For this prayer, like all others, will be made within the circle of the general clause: "Thy will be done." This clause is a confession of confidence.

e. Purgatory

Bibliography: H. U. von Balthasar, "Pneuma und Institution," *Skizzen zur Theologie,* IV (1974), pp. 410–55; B. Bartmann, *Das Fegfeuer,* 2nd ed. (1930); R. Guardini, *Das Fegfeuer* (1940); J. Ratzinger, *Eschatologie,* pp. 179ff.; M. Schmaus, *Von den letzten Dingen* (1948) (with bibliography).

It is not primarily for polemical reasons that we take this brief look at purgatory but because our discussions of the intermediate state and apokatastasis (the saving ways of God in the next world) seem to have led us to some "geometrical places" which at least point in the direction of the problem of purgatory.

In this regard it is not our task to deal with the exegetical basis of the teaching. This has a cramping effect and plays a less prominent part in modern Roman Catholic theology. Nor are we interested in the historical development of the doctrine. Our concern is simply with the attempt of Vatican II to restate previous definitions in a simpler and more precise way (Ratzinger, *Eschatologie,* p. 180). Trent had said that there is a purgatory and that souls in it are helped by the intercession of believers and especially by the sacrifice of the altar, which is pleasing to God (Denz., 1820; E.T. 983). The protest of the Reformation took the form of warnings against indulgences, against covetousness, against the treatment of hair-splitting questions, and against sermons to simple people that do not foster edification or increase piety.

Whereas Luther at first still said that purgatory was most certain (WA, 1, 155), the later Reformers unanimously rejected it. Calvin called it a "fiction of Satan" (Inst., III, 5, 6) and the Smalkaldic Articles call it a "mask of the devil" (LBK, p. 420, No. 12; Jacobs, pp. 314ff., no. 12).

---

[35]The author confesses that reputable and highly respected men of God, from whose circles he would not want to exclude himself, have met him as representatives of that doctrine.

This sharp rejection of the abuse of purgatory was caused by the commercial aspect and the horrors of the trade in indulgences (cf. Luther's 95 Theses). The deeper reason, however, was that the penances laid on poor souls in purgatory dishonor Christ's justifying work and contradict the all-sufficiency of grace. Purgatory leads to an erroneous theory of merits in the afterlife and charges the dead with a satisfaction that was long ago made by Christ (CAApol, XII; LBK, p. 255, No. 13; Jacob, pp. 314f., no. 13; Calvin, Inst., III, 5f.).

Although purgatory has no biblical support, some systematic considerations might suggest ways to give it a certain justification and to take from it the divisive quality that the Reformers found in it. This is possible, however, only on the one decisive condition that there be dissociated from purgatory the theory of penitential satisfaction which has always clung to it, especially in popular piety.[36] Here the christological and soteriological objections of the Reformers were right. The only valid sense in the idea of purgatory consists of the hope that the event of salvation does not end at death. What we have called judgment by works suggests the eschatological relevance of the incongruity between being a sinner in fact and yet being justified. In terms of "purgatory" we may hope that this incongruity will be overcome by ways and means which we are unable and will always be unable to imagine. This hope would be related exclusively to a "that": that Christ's work will come to completion in this regard too and change the brokenness of "at once sinners and righteous" into an ontologically unequivocal "made righteous."

The rank of such a doctrine would be appropriately limited as in the case of apokatastasis. It could not be a dogma (as in Roman Catholic teaching). It could be only a concern for the dead which is committed to God in prayer. (We are thus faced by the same problem as in the doctrine of apokatastasis.) If such a concern relates to the completion of Christ's saving work, it will affect not only the baptized and believers, as in purgatory, but all people: Christians, the religious in a general sense, and also atheists and agnostics of every type, all the people who are in mind in the confessional affirmation of the descent into hell.

The question is, of course, an open one—if we may now declare our polemical interest—whether this does not completely shift the scope of the Roman Catholic doctrine of purgatory and change it into something totally different. Concern that our deliberations will not build any bridges of theological approximation is heightened by the observation that indulgences are by no means dead in modern Roman Catholicism[37] and that living references may still be found to satisfaction as the original and true point of purgatory.

On the other hand, in Roman Catholic *theology* there are signs of rethinking. Thus Ratzinger with his christocentric interpretation of purgatory comes close to what we have called the real intention of the statements. He does not see purgatory as the site of acts of satisfaction which the deceased must perform to attain to the

---

[36]Trent is more careful here but does not deny the element of satisfaction.

[37]There seems to be a gap here between official (not just popular) practice and theological reflection. This applies to the doctrine of purgatory in general. The word "indulgence" does not occur in the indexes to some Roman Catholic eschatologies. Nor is it mentioned, so far as I can see, in the brief remarks of Vatican II on purgatory ("Lumen gentium," 49, 51 [*Vatican II Documents*, pp. 80f., 83ff.]).

maturity of Paradise. He views it christologically by calling Christ himself the purifying fire which changes us and makes us conformable to his glorified body (Romans 8:29; Philippians 3:21). He finds a real christianizing of the early Jewish idea of purgatory in the insight that purification does not take place through a thing but through the transforming power of the Lord who burns open and melts our closed hearts so that they are fit to be living organisms of his body.[38] Along these lines he attacks Tertullian's conception of purgatory as a kind of concentration camp in which we must suffer penalties. Purgatory is instead a necessary process of change in which grace is not replaced by works (as the Reformers charged) but there is attained for the first time the full triumph of grace.[39]

Roman Catholic theology seems here to be on a path which stresses the primacy of grace over human action and thus exploits theological possibilities that are potentially present already in the Tridentine doctrine of grace. It may be asked which direction of thought will win out in this complex of opposites. There is ecumenical hope in interpretations—I deliberately do not call them reinterpretations though this objection will probably be raised—such as that of Ratzinger.

3. The Resurrection of the Dead

The Parousia of Christ includes the resurrection of the dead which is confessed in the third article of the creed. This is presupposed in what we said about the last judgment. By running up against the problem of the intermediate state our discussions of eternal life drew attention to the fact that the resurrection of the dead as an eschatological act has in view a specific happening which cannot be subsumed under "eternal life" or "being with the Lord" but expresses something extra. The resurrection of the dead is not to be regarded as the completion of eternal life but as the awaited victory of God in which he goes beyond every mere beginning, pledge, hiddenness, mirror, or obscure word to reach his definitive goal and to destroy death as the last enemy.

The term "happening," however, is a problematical one. We consider that we can think of happenings only in the framework of our temporality. A statement about the resurrection of the dead, however, transcends the form of our aeonic time. Does this mean that we must be content merely to speak negatively in nontemporal terms?

The problem is complicated by a further consideration.

As corporeal beings we participate in *physical* time. But this does not express the whole of our relationship to time. We constantly experience how different are the forms of time that coincide in us. We can ask one moment to tarry because it is so beautiful, but such moments of happiness and fulfilment continually slip away from us at once. Then in situations of extreme peril seconds can creep on and stretch out to hours. We participate not only in inner time[40] but also in *biological*

---

[38]Ratzinger, *Eschatologie,* p. 187.

[39]*Ibid.,* p. 188.

[40]Alexis Carrel, *Der Mensch, das unbekannte Wesen,* pp. 163ff.; E.T. *Man, the Unknown* (New York, 1938), pp. 159ff.

time, and both differ from the physical time denoted by the sun and the clock. The time of a tree with its rings has its own rhythm and movement which is distinct from the neutrally quantitative passage of clock-time. *Historical* time with its directed line differs also from the cyclic time of natural processes, although even in these entropy introduces another quality of time that is closer to linear historical time.

The creed, adopting ancient traditions,[41] speaks of *bodily* resurrection and originally, at any rate in the Roman and Egyptian traditions, of "the resurrection of the flesh."[42] Can this mean that when we go into the hereafter beyond death we take with us both our body and its time (but if so, which form of this time?)? That would be absurd if we were right when we spoke earlier of discontinuity between time and eternity, of things being "wholly other." Flesh and blood, our flesh and blood, cannot inherit the kingdom of God (1 Corinthians 15:50). Hence the time of this aeon as that of flesh and blood cannot accommodate the kingdom of God. This is for us the decisive argument against chiliasm.

Yet we cannot abandon the symbol of an event when we think about the resurrection of the dead and the last judgment—at any rate if we are not to accept a monistically understood continuum of time and eternity and let ourselves be dominated by a concept of timelessness which replaces God's action by the repose of a logical relation and an eternity of mere "now." It is essential, of course, that we be aware that we are using a symbol and that the *goal* of our statement differs from the temporal *means* that are used to reach it.[43] If we can conceive of an act of God like the resurrection of the dead or the Parousia as simply an act in time, we have to think of a new and wholly different form of time, perhaps in much the same way that Paul distinguishes between a pneumatic and an earthly body. The analogy to the different forms of time that we encounter already in this aeon may supply us with a rather lame comparison.

Some years ago the work of the young theologian H. W. Schmidt entitled *Zeit und Ewigkeit. Die letzten Voraussetzungen der dialektischen Theologie* (1927) aroused considerable attention. In their approach at least the theses that Schmidt advanced are close to the arguments used above. He says that the understanding of time must never be formally absolutized but must always be relative to the content which fills time. Thus the eschatological consummation contains the moment which gives meaning and ordains for time the giving of an appropriate form (p. 301). This is already made plain by the incarnation, the entry of the eternal into time. For in what takes place with the incarnation of the Logos we do not see the abolition of time in favor of a timeless idea of Christ (Abelard) but an entry into the form of being of history and its time. By God's immanence in time we learn his supremacy over time (p. 303). Thus Schmidt replaces eternity as timeless event with the idea of the fulness of time (p. 306). This is the consummation which remains itself, not reaching beyond itself yet not freezing into dead immobility (p.

---

[41]Kretschmar, *Leben angesichts des Todes,* pp. 101ff.

[42]*Ibid.,* p. 103.

[43]A symbol always points beyond itself. Thus a flag is simply a bit of cloth but it signifies something else.

307). The beginnings of this view of things may be found in Schmidt's teacher at Greifswald, W. Koepp (*Einführung in die evangelische Dogmatik* [1934], pp. 58f.).

In both cases there is an infinite qualitative difference between the time of this aeon and time in the eschaton. Hence there can be no time-continuum and the eschaton is not just the apocalyptic continuation of history, as in millenarian teaching. Whether theological novelties result from this view of time may be doubted, because fundamentally it simply represents a variation of the relation of the identity of salvation to its radically different forms. What is important is the theological interest kindled by the discussion. With the help of the concept of the incarnation it guards against an error in early dialectical theology, namely, that of an abstract distinction between time and eternity which makes eternity no more than a modified timelessness.

We may conclude that if the symbolical character of statements about eschatological acts is not borne in mind we may end up unexpectedly with apocalyptic speculation or sectarianism in which everything that is said about eschatology is taken literally and a chronology of events can be drawn up as though we were dealing in calendar time. *How* we express ourselves in this sphere of "dancing concepts," whether in terms of what is beyond our temporality or in terms of the changing of time into its fulness, can hardly be theologically relevant.

To get back to the question of bodily resurrection, what kind of bodiliness can be meant after all these qualifications? We are tackling the question with which Paul introduced his proclamation of the resurrection of the dead in 1 Corinthians 15:35.

Originally, as we have pointed out, the term "resurrection of the flesh" was used. The question what was meant and not meant by this had already confused and divided people in the 2nd century. (On what follows cf. Kretschmar, *Leben,* pp. 121ff.). Thus in the Valentinian Gospel of Philip we are told that some fear they will rise up naked (without a body). Hence they want to rise in the flesh. They do not realize that those who bear the flesh are really naked and those who put off the flesh are not naked but clothed. In the debates a subtle difference arises between those who speak of the resurrection *of* the flesh and those who speak of resurrection *in* the flesh. Tertullian calls the latter formulation a refined way of misleading orthodox Christians because it teaches that we experience the eschaton "in this flesh" during our lifetime. The resurrection of the flesh, on the other hand, refers to the fact of the last day which has not yet come and for which we wait.

The term "flesh" (*sarx*) undergoes a change of sense in relation to the eschaton. It no longer denotes earthly corporeality. On the basis of the eucharistic sayings of Jesus about eating his flesh and drinking his blood (John 6:53) it is understood as the flesh of the exalted Christ which now clothes him and does not leave him naked any longer.

As regards the abstruse and hypermythological Valentinian text, the idea behind it is not without theological profundity. For it is accompanied by the comment (p. 123) that in this world those who wear clothes are more important than their clothes (Matthew 6:26) but in the kingdom of God the clothes are more important than those who put them on. With many allusions to biblical statements this text has a soteriological intention, so that the ontic quality *sarx* has no real force of its own but is a transparency for what is really meant.

First, as Kretschmar points out, it takes up what Paul says about putting on Christ (Romans 13:14; Galatians 3:27) along with the promise that the corruptible will put on incorruption and the mortal immortality (1 Corinthians 15:54). Second, the parable of the royal wedding (Matthew 22:2ff.) and the wedding garment (Matthew 22:11) have undoubtedly influenced the use of the metaphor of "putting on," especially when it is christologically interpreted. We are reminded of the hymn: "Jesus, thy blood and righteousness, / My beauty are, my glorious dress; / Midst flaming worlds, in these arrayed, / With joy shall I lift up my head." Here—in an ironical and different use of the proverb—clothes really do make the man and it is no longer true that (biological) life is more than clothing. The wedding garment, the new resurrection life, is life in and with Christ and is not understood as the ontologically determined quality of life enjoyed by the resurrected. Life in the kingdom of heaven is being and living with Christ. It consists of the relation which is granted to me even here on earth by the Word and Spirit. As my righteousness in both cases is not my own being righteous but an alien righteousness that is mine by clinging to Christ, so my resurrection life is not my own as a quality of immortality but an alien life in which I participate by being a member of Christ's body.

Thus the Valentinian metaphor that on the last day the resurrected do not bear their own flesh but Christ's flesh as their clothing expresses a christological truth that stands at the heart of Paul's doctrine of justification.

Whereas the term *sarx* is here essentially a symbol with christological significance, in Justin the question what Paul meant when he said that flesh and blood cannot inherit the kingdom of God leads to a different result (p. 129). Death, Justin thinks, corresponds to flesh. Death cannot inherit anything, least of all God's kingdom. This is not an object of inheritance but always an active and creative subject. Being life, it shares this life with the body and makes itself an inheritance for the flesh. In terms of the creative event of the kingdom of God, death is thus swallowed up in life and the mortal body is transfigured. No wonder that the renewal of our corporeality has on this view an affinity to chiliastic expectation of the renewal of the world (as in Irenaeus [p. 129]). The chiliastic implication is the decisive argument against the continuity between earthly and eschatological corporeality that is championed here.

If we have used some historical illustrations to help us to understand from early Christian debates what the bodily resurrection can and obviously cannot mean from a soteriological standpoint, we must now ask what is Paul's concern in hanging on to the concept of *sōma* when he also teaches a radical discontinuity between the earthly and the pneumatic body (1 Corinthians 15:35ff.). Is he abandoning corporeal identity? What is meant by a pneumatic body? Does not the concept of a body which is not in time or space and is not limited by time and space involve the same kind of self-contradiction as wooden iron or a square circle? Why does he put up with such a strange concept of the body?

To make headway I may refer again to our earlier discussion of the anthropological terms *sōma*, *sarx*, and *psychē*. We argued that these terms do not denote partial—higher or lower—spheres of humanity but always denote the whole person even though with a specific reference. In this sense the body (*sōma*) denotes the I as it now is. As it now is, the I is a communicative being. It stands at the center of many relations: to the "thou," to things, to institutions, tasks, the spirit of the age, and much else. It takes part bodily in all these relations by presence or absence, by the senses, by the physical (corporeal) presuppositions of mind or spirit, by being young or old or man or woman.[44]

The relation to Christ can (and must) be expressed by the concept of the *sōma* since it is in the *sōma* that the Logos comes into our world of time and space, into history, that he takes upon himself the plight of our corporeality in life, suffering, and death, and that he is present to heal and save our sick bodies. Man in his secularity and corporeality is meant when Paul can say that "the body is for the Lord and the Lord for the body" (1 Corinthians 6:13). There is a similar allusion to corporeality when in comparing and contrasting Adam and Christ in 1 Corinthians 15 he says that "as we have borne the image of the man of earth, we shall also bear the image of the man of heaven" (15:49).

The indelible character of the term *sōma* obviously contains a reference to the fact that our individuation and power of communication, which are given by the body, do not cease at the resurrection of the dead but continue in eschatological union with Christ. Changing the Valentinian text, we may thus say that the resurrection does not leave us naked, i.e., does not divest us of the self or depersonalize us. The stress on corporeality, whether earthly or pneumatic, means that for all the discontinuity of modes of being before and after the resurrection there is still a continuum: We shall be kept in our identity. This identity is not an identical core of the I nor an enduring substance of the soul but the given identity which is ours because God has begun a history or conversation (Luther) with us. Our identity is kept in the eschaton of the resurrection of the dead as we are called by name. As we said before, we are the image which God has of us. Alien dignity makes me still myself even at the last day. Hence transfigured corporeality denotes the totality and uniqueness of our person which is summoned up from death.

Here is the direct opposite of what mystical pantheism or panentheism says about the elimination of individuation when, as in Zen Buddhism, personal individuality is compared to a stream that along with other streams empties into the ocean and is lost. Goethe's saying that when the individual finds himself in infinity he will gladly disappear and enjoy giving himself up finds a complete antithesis in the resurrection of the dead as Christians understand it.

Since we are dealing here with contents that transcend our form of time and express what is incommensurable, we shall immediately fall into error if we overlook the symbolical nature of what we say and inquire into the "how" of transfigured corporeality. Here again we must not confess or consider anything beyond God's faithful history with us. We know only that the new being before

---

[44]Käsemann seems to agree when he objects to Bultmann's thesis that the body expresses only man's relation to himself. As he sees it, the body cannot be viewed or interpreted apart from the individual. It is for the apostle man in his secularity, in his ability to communicate (*Exegetische Versuche ... ,* II, p. 129). But I do not understand why Käsemann can tie this in with a rejection of the body as a symbol of individuation, since this is the presupposition of every form of communication.

God to which the resurrection summons us is a part of the same saving event which is granted to us now and that the voice of the same shepherd who called us to life will also summon us from death. What spans the continuum of now and then is the familiarity of this voice. It is also the Spirit whose first instalments have been given us and who will be granted to us in his fulness as the Giver of life (1 Corinthians 15:45): "If the Spirit of him who raised Jesus from the dead dwells in you, he who raised Christ Jesus from the dead will give life to your mortal bodies also through his Spirit which [even now] dwells in you" (Romans 8:11). Looking back from the last day—this is Christian certainty—I shall recognize that the Spirit who was once for me the power of presentation is the same as he who is now mighty in the eschatological transcending of all presentation.

Because of the incommensurability of what is said here it is a mistake—which will mislead us into ontological thinking—to imagine and if possible describe a substratum to which God's thought of us can relate as an ontic subject and in which our identity can present itself. Once we take this course, we are compelled to reflect theologically on the pneumatic body in its eschatological form of being. Here again we cannot go beyond the "that" of the relation, the abiding relation, unless we are to end up once more with a topography of Jerusalem.

H. F. Kohlbrügge in a profound figure of speech has shown that we reach the limit of all theological statement at this point:[45] "Hence when I die—but die no more—and someone finds my skull, this will still preach to him: I have no eyes but I see him; I have no brain or understanding but I comprehend him; I have no lips but I kiss him; I have no tongue but I praise him with all you who call upon his name. I am a hard skull but I am fully softened and melted in his love; I lie here outside in the churchyard but I am inside in Paradise. All suffering is forgotten. His great love has done this for us, for he bore his cross and went to Golgotha for us."

This monologue of the hard skull speaks only negatively about itself (no lips, brain, etc.). It speaks only about a relation (praising and comprehending him). Yet what "follows" is that I am there to praise. Rather boldly, yet instructively, one might change Descartes here and say: "I shall see and praise him, therefore I shall be" (though nothing is or can be said about the form of being).

The absence of ontological statements about the form of being reminds us of analogous discussions of the nature of angels. C. Westermann says that God's messengers are known only by their commission and according to the oldest records (they are older than the gods) exist in changing form as the bearers of messages or as a symbolical form of the divine encounter. We cannot apply to them our own substance or concept of time and thus there is in the strict sense no "doctrine" of angels. Barth thinks similarly that the transcendent character of angelic being shows particularly impressively that "the whole history of the Bible . . . cannot be verified by the ordinary analogies of world history" (CD, III,3, p. 375; KD, III,3, pp. 433f.) and that it thus demands the genres of saga and legend. So far as I can see, Augustine was the one who in the early church most decisively rejected this question of ontic nature in eschatological contexts, especially in relation to angels; he understood angels solely in terms of their office and

---

[45]H. Klugkist-Hesse, *Hermann Friedrich Kohlbrügge* (1935), pp. 403f.

acts, refusing to say what they are and focusing on what they do: "Angel is the name of an office, not a nature ... the angel is by what he does" (Exposition of Psalm 103:1, 15; M. J. Rouet de Journel, *Enchiridion patristicum* [1937], No. 1484). Angels are to be understood in terms of their relation to the pure love of God which also governs their reason (*De Genesi ad litteram,* IV, xxxii, 49). Once we go beyond this relation or ministry of angels to questions of their corporeality we fall into daring speculation, like Augustine's pupil Fulgentius, bishop of Ruspe, who assigned to good angels an ethereal body and to bad (or demonic) angels an aery body (*De trinitate,* 9). Cf. also the apocryphal traditions of later Judaism which made their way into the NT and in which the heavenly beings are indefinable *dynameis* (Romans 8:38; 1 Corinthians 15:24; Ephesians 1:21) or *archai* (Romans 8:38; Colossians 1:16) or *exousiai* or *kyriotētes.* (See further C. Westermann, *Gottes Engel brauchen keine Flügel* [1978]; E.T. *God's Angels Need No Wings* [Philadelphia, 1979]; K. Barth, CD, III,3, §51; G. von Rad, G. Kittel, TDNT, I, pp. 74ff.; TWNT, I, pp. 75ff.; K. Kindt, "Versuch über die Engel," *Geisteskampf um Christus* [1938], pp. 243ff.)

In his *Disputatione de homine* of 1536 Luther says[46] that in this life we are simply God's material for the life to come, just as the creature is God's material for its future glorious form even though it is now subject to futility. As earth and heaven at the beginning were related to the form completed in six days, i.e., as the material for this, so man in this life is related to his future form up to the time when God's image is restored and perfected. Meanwhile man lives in sins and day by day is increasingly justified or corrupted.

In its Aristotelian terminology, which the contents transcend, this statement sums up all the questions raised by the chapter on eschatology.

The man of the first creation is nothing in himself and has no permanence. He is God's outline which will be brought to completion through the crises of the fallen world.

The image of God contained in this sketch will be brought to its full identity only in the future form. It is "brought" to this in the strict sense. It does not complete itself as an entelechy which as an impressed form engages in living self-development. As the grain must be put in the earth and die if it is to bear fruit (John 12:24), so man must perish if he is to be opened up to the new creation. For it is God's nature to make something out of nothing, so that God can make nothing out of him who is not yet nothing.[47]

Man's being, then, is his relation to him who planned him, who remains faithful to him as his justifier, and who on the last day will complete what he began, calling him from faith to sight.

In this change of our dimension of being the only constant thing is the address of

---

[46]WA, 39/I, 177, 3ff.; LW, 34, 139f. The author has already quoted this passage at the end of a previous book but does not hesitate to use it again because it formulates so well the link between justification and eschatology, between sinners in deed and the righteous in hope, between pilgrims and the resurrected.

[47]The Seven Penitential Psalms (WA, 1, 183, 39ff.).

God, who makes himself present to us by his Word and Spirit, reveals himself to us in fellowship, causes us to grow, and finally calls us out of the first instalments of the Spirit, his presentations in the dark, to abiding and living presence in the light.

All life's decisions are made in relation to this history of God. In it our life becomes an eschatological event. It is the crossroads which offers us the choice between being justified and corrupted, winning eternal life or missing it, completing God's outline or marring it.

In this way the eschaton affects the here and now. The future makes its impress on the present. We learn to distinguish between great and small, the many needs and the one thing needful. We become the five brothers of the rich man. Entering into the opened history with God and certain of its goal, we can no longer absolutize the relative or relativize the absolute. We can only use this world and not become its subjects.[48] We will maintain a final reserve or distance because we know what is truly ultimate and view the penultimate in the light of it.

Thus eschatology opens up the horizon of Christian ethics. The "one day" gives us standards for "today."

---

[48]We recall Augustine's dictum at the beginning of his *On Christian Doctrine* that things are for use and not enjoyment.

Indexes

1. NAMES

2. SUBJECTS

3. SCRIPTURE REFERENCES